Collector's Edition

CARDCAPTOR SAKURA

Staff

Satsuki Igarashi

Nanase Ohkawa

Tsubaki Nekoi

Mokona

Planning

and presented by

CLAMP

I FEAR I MIGHT MAKE THINGS DIFFICULT FOR YOU SOON, YOUNG SAKURA...

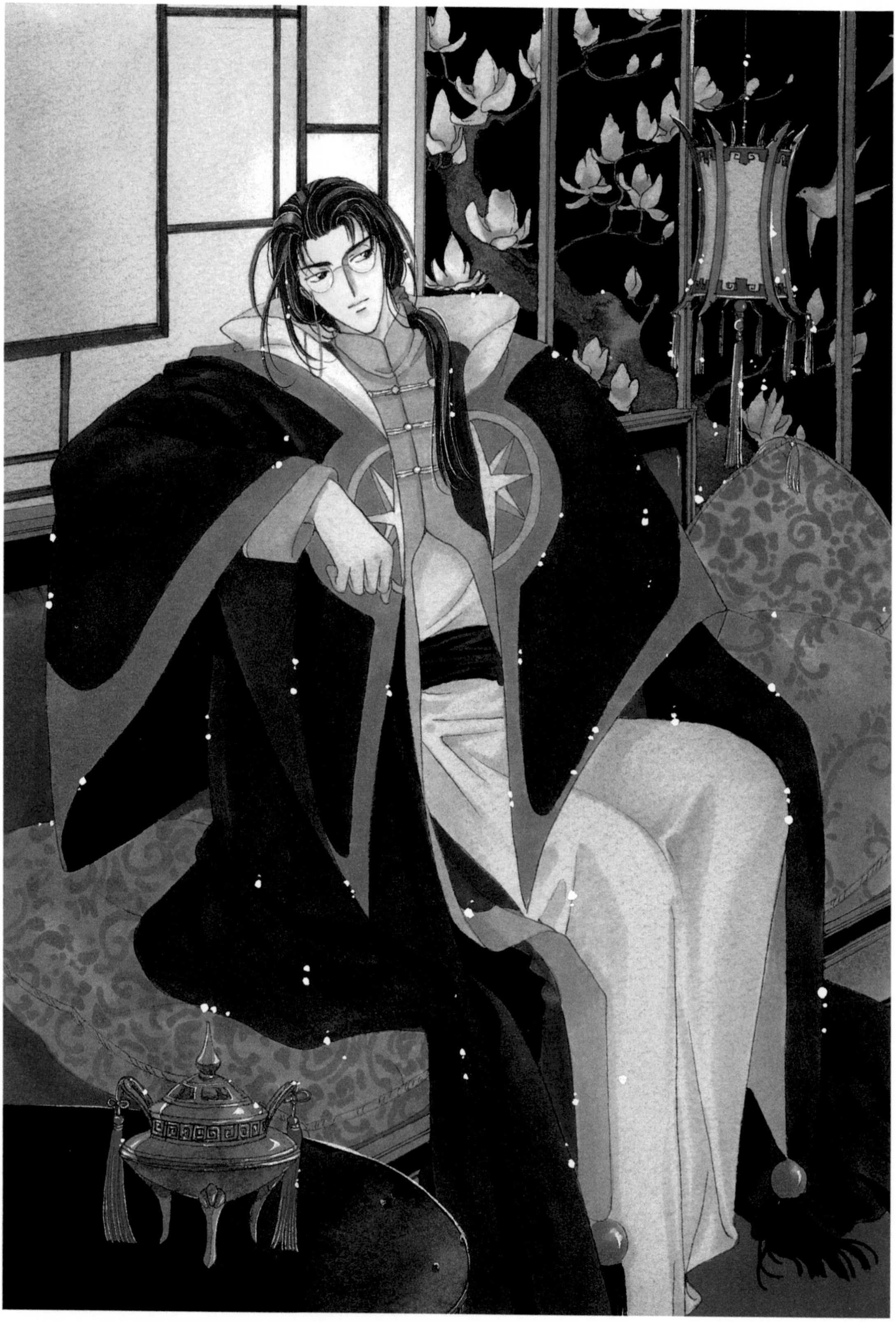

BUT AS YOU SAID YOURSELF, I'M SURE YOU'LL BE ALL RIGHT.

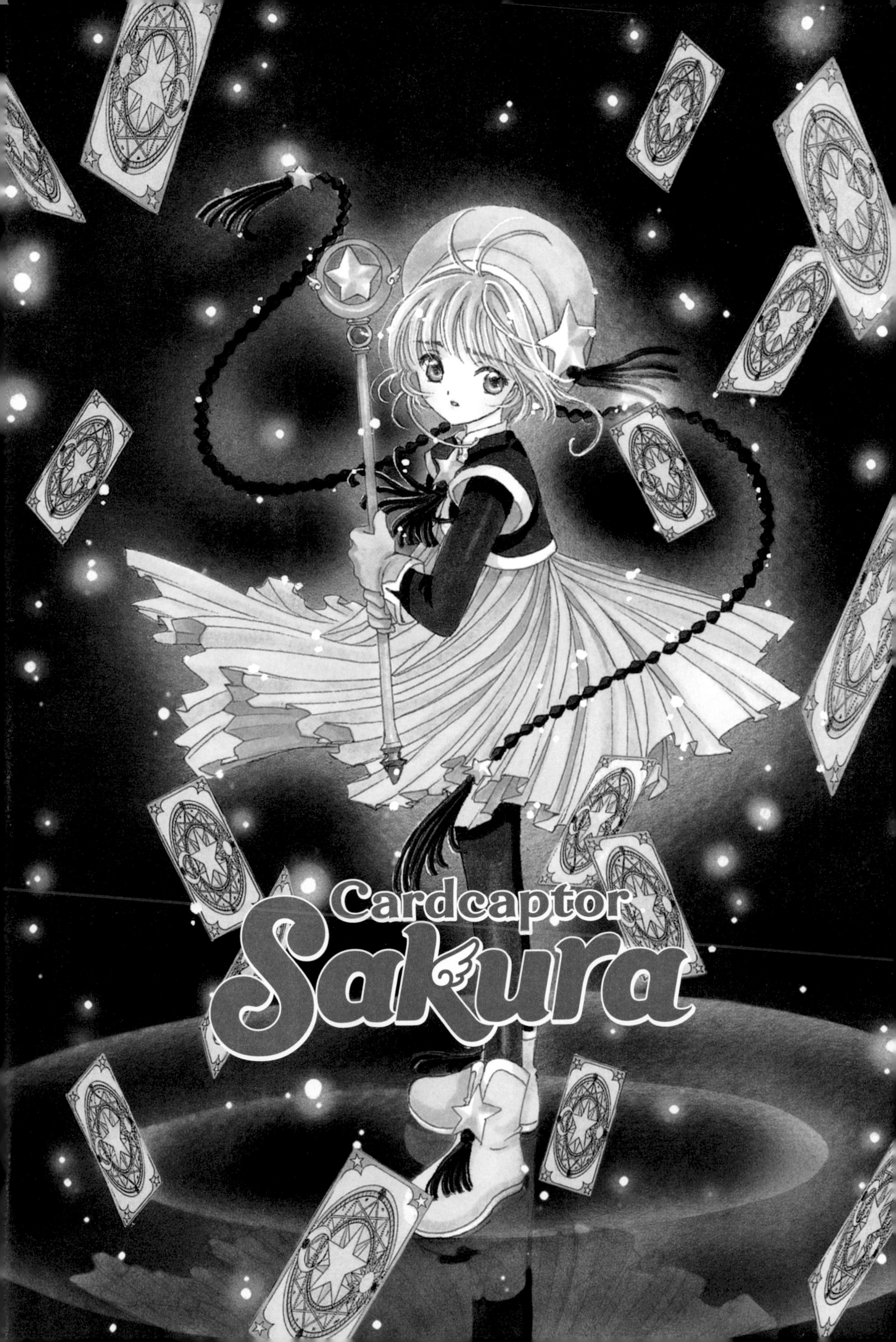
Cardcaptor
Sakura

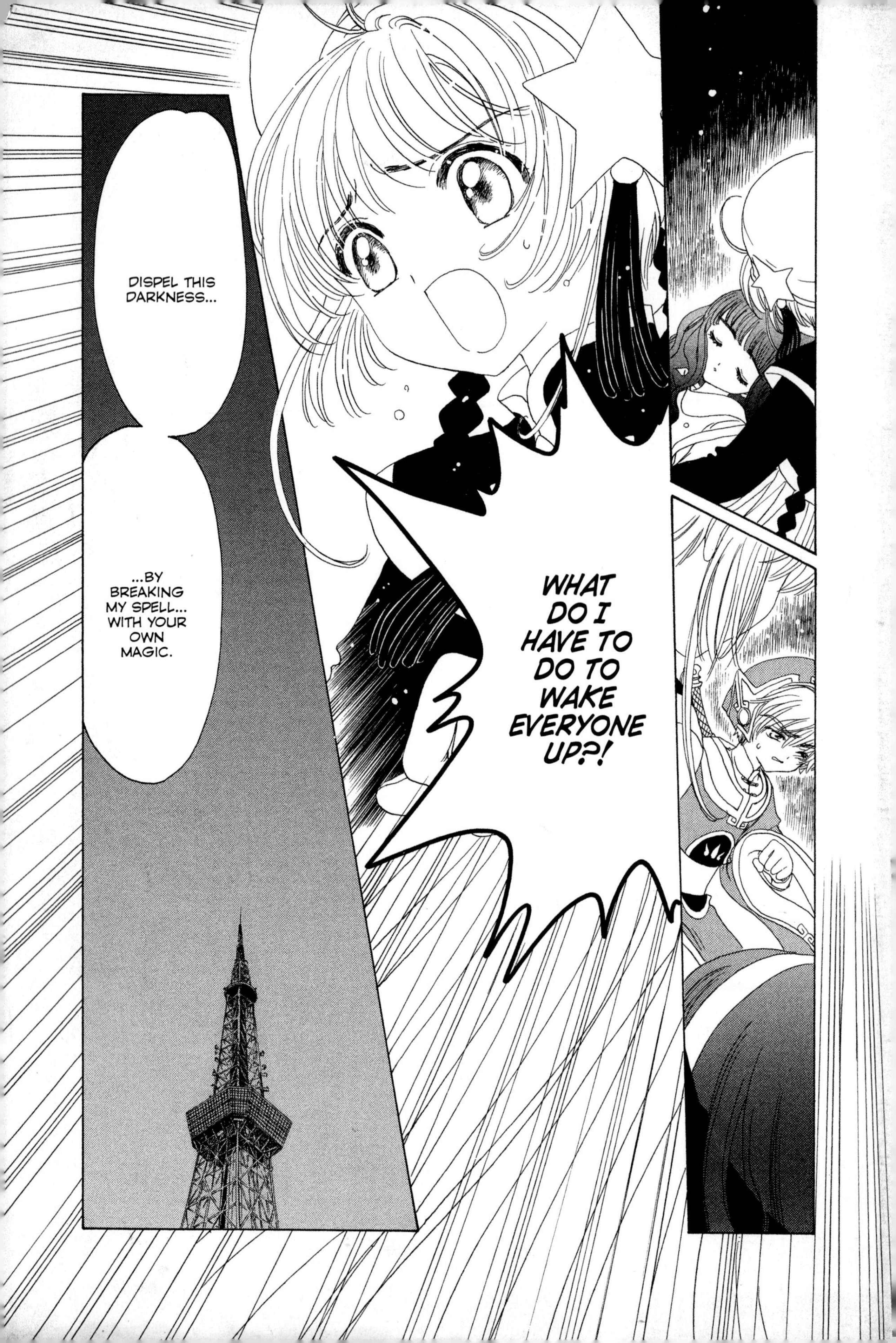
WHAT DO I HAVE TO DO TO WAKE EVERYONE UP?!
DISPEL THIS DARKNESS...
...BY BREAKING MY SPELL... WITH YOUR OWN MAGIC.

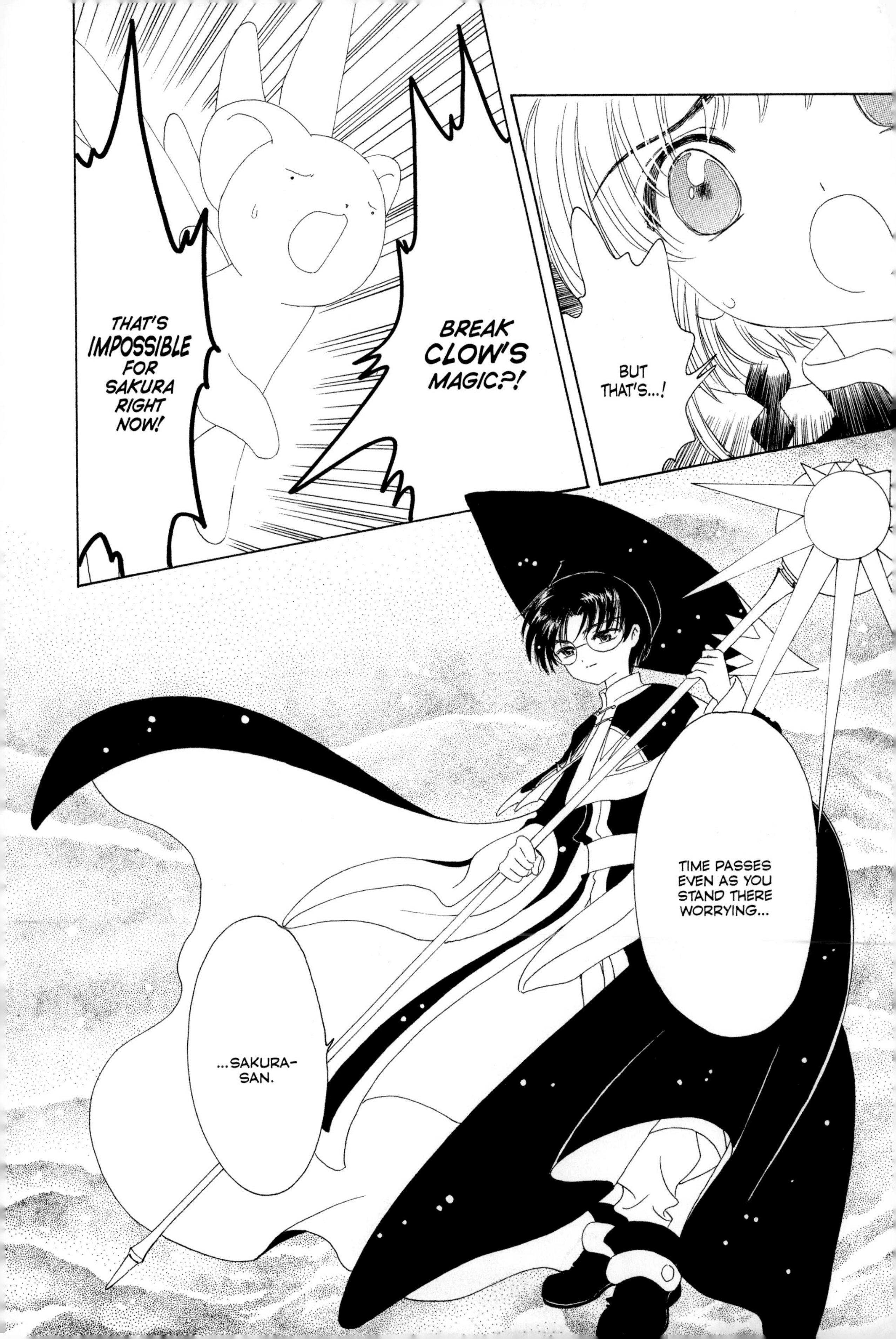
BUT THAT'S...!
BREAK CLOW'S MAGIC?!
THAT'S IMPOSSIBLE FOR SAKURA RIGHT NOW!
TIME PASSES EVEN AS YOU STAND THERE WORRYING...
...SAKURA-SAN.

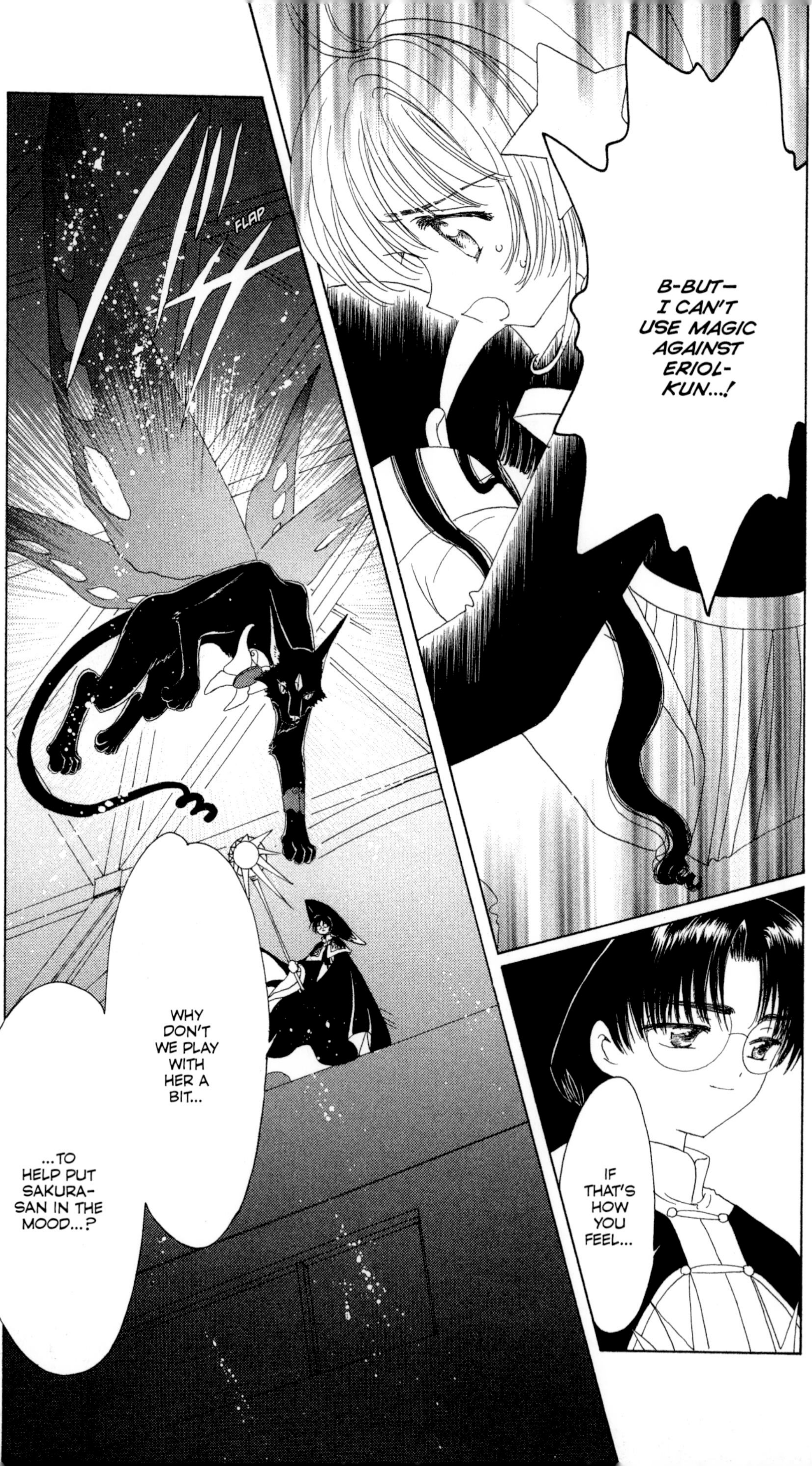
B-BUT— I CAN'T USE MAGIC AGAINST ERIOL-KUN...!
IF THAT'S HOW YOU FEEL...
FLAP
WHY DON'T WE PLAY WITH HER A BIT...
...TO HELP PUT SAKURA-SAN IN THE MOOD...?

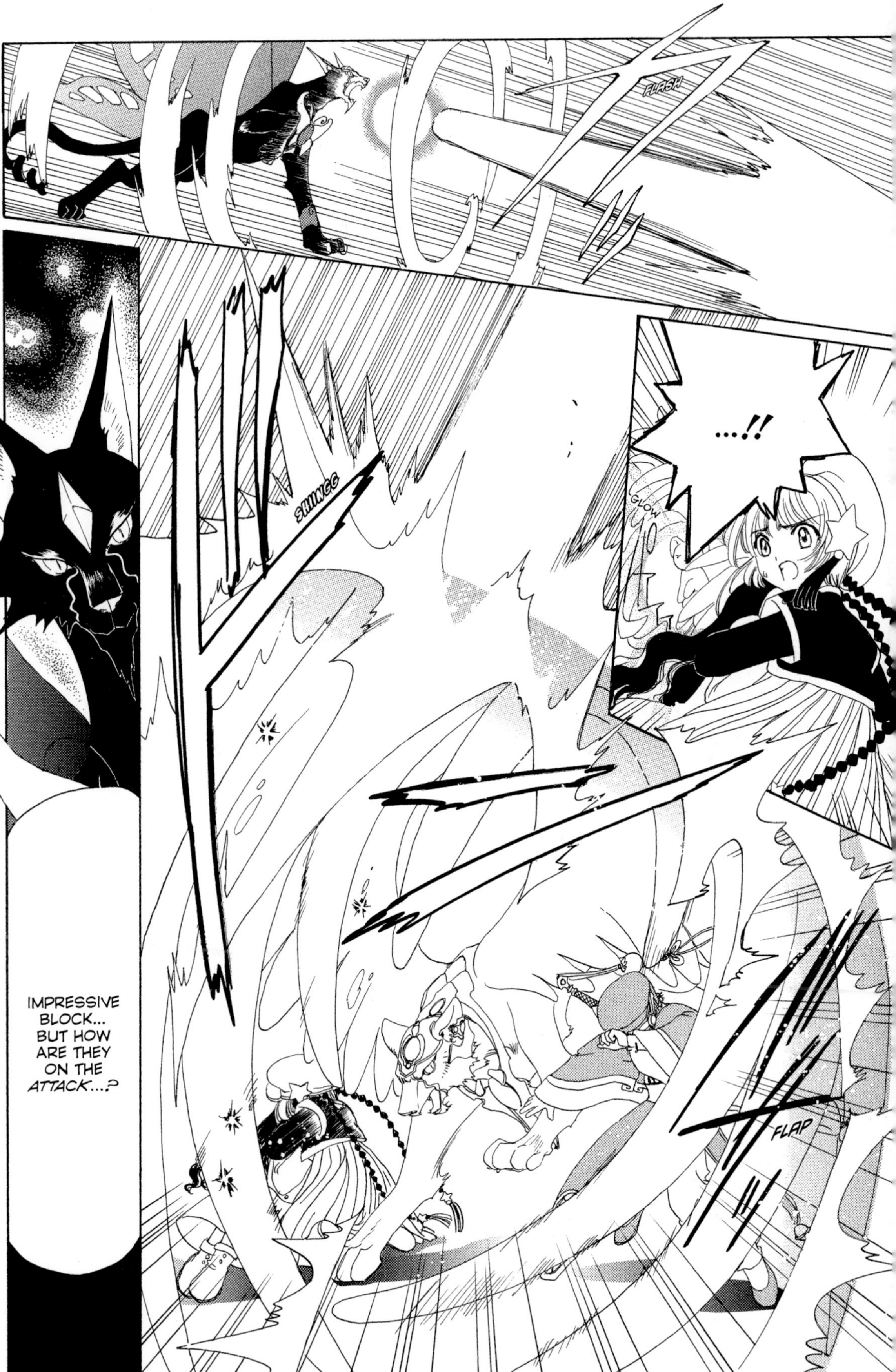
FLASH
...!!
GLOW
SHIINGG
FLAP
IMPRESSIVE BLOCK... BUT HOW ARE THEY ON THE *ATTACK*...?

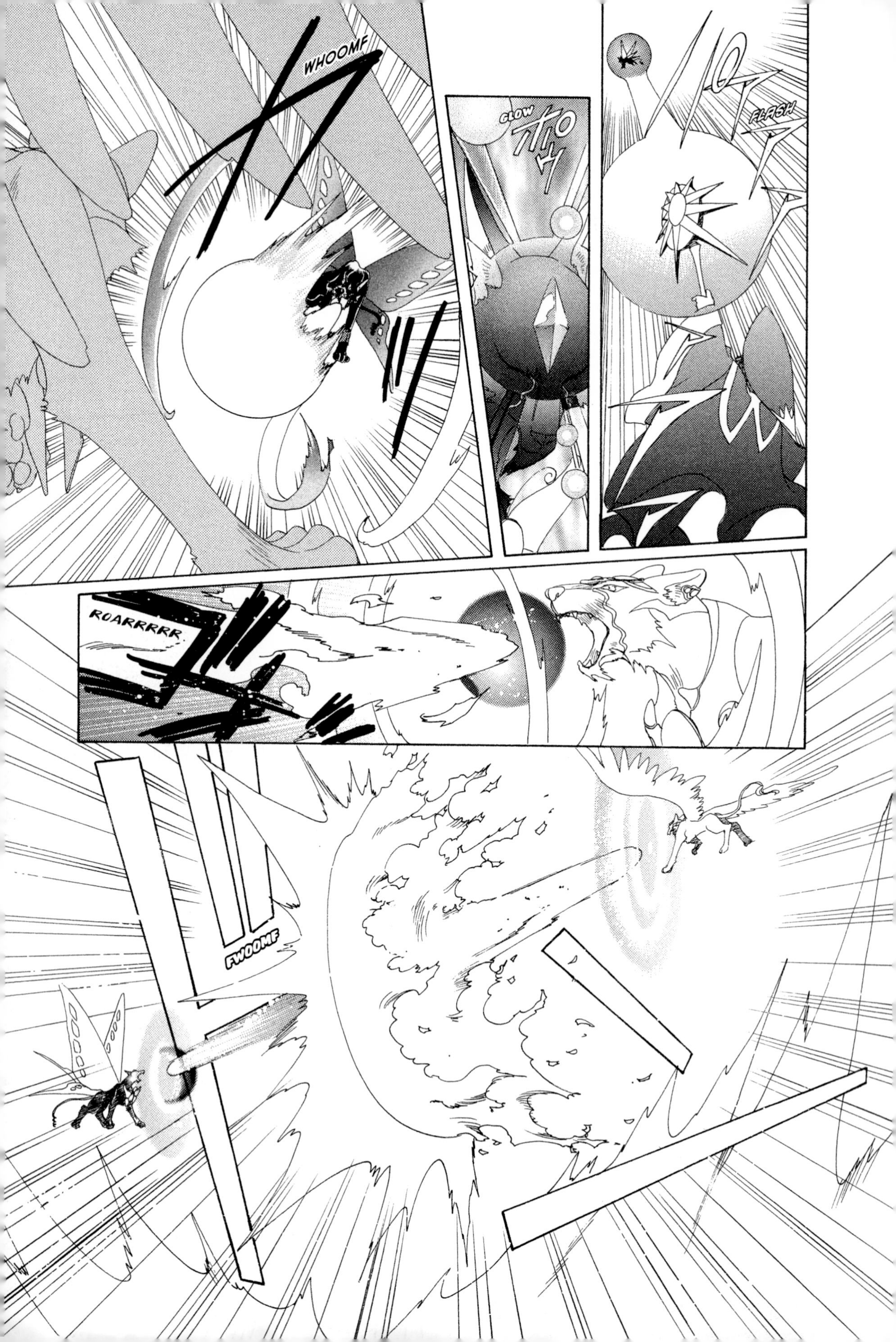
FLASH
GLOW
WHOOMF
ROARRRRR
FWOOMF

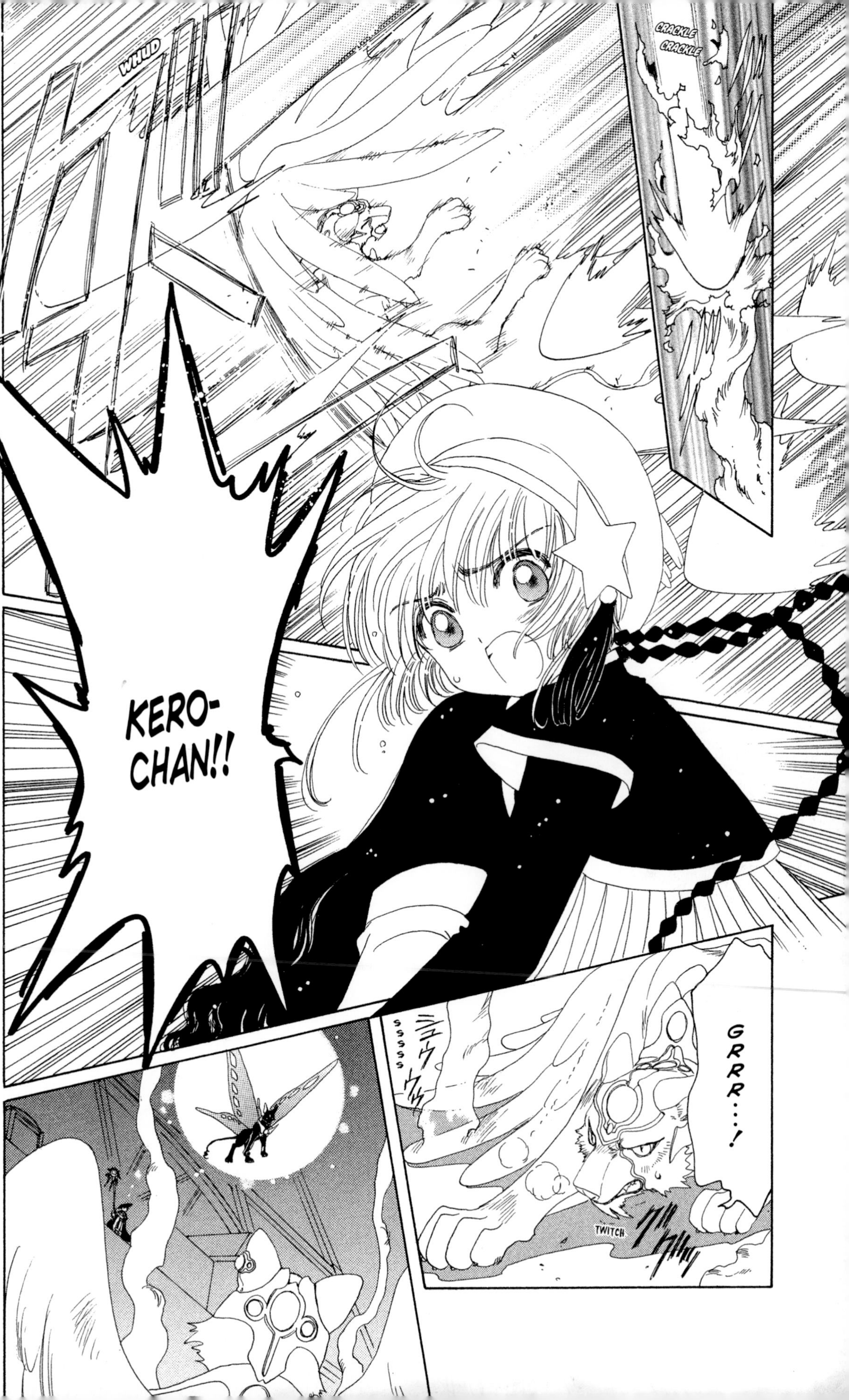
CRACKLE
CRACKLE
WHUD
KERO-CHAN!!
SSSSS
GRRR...!
TWITCH

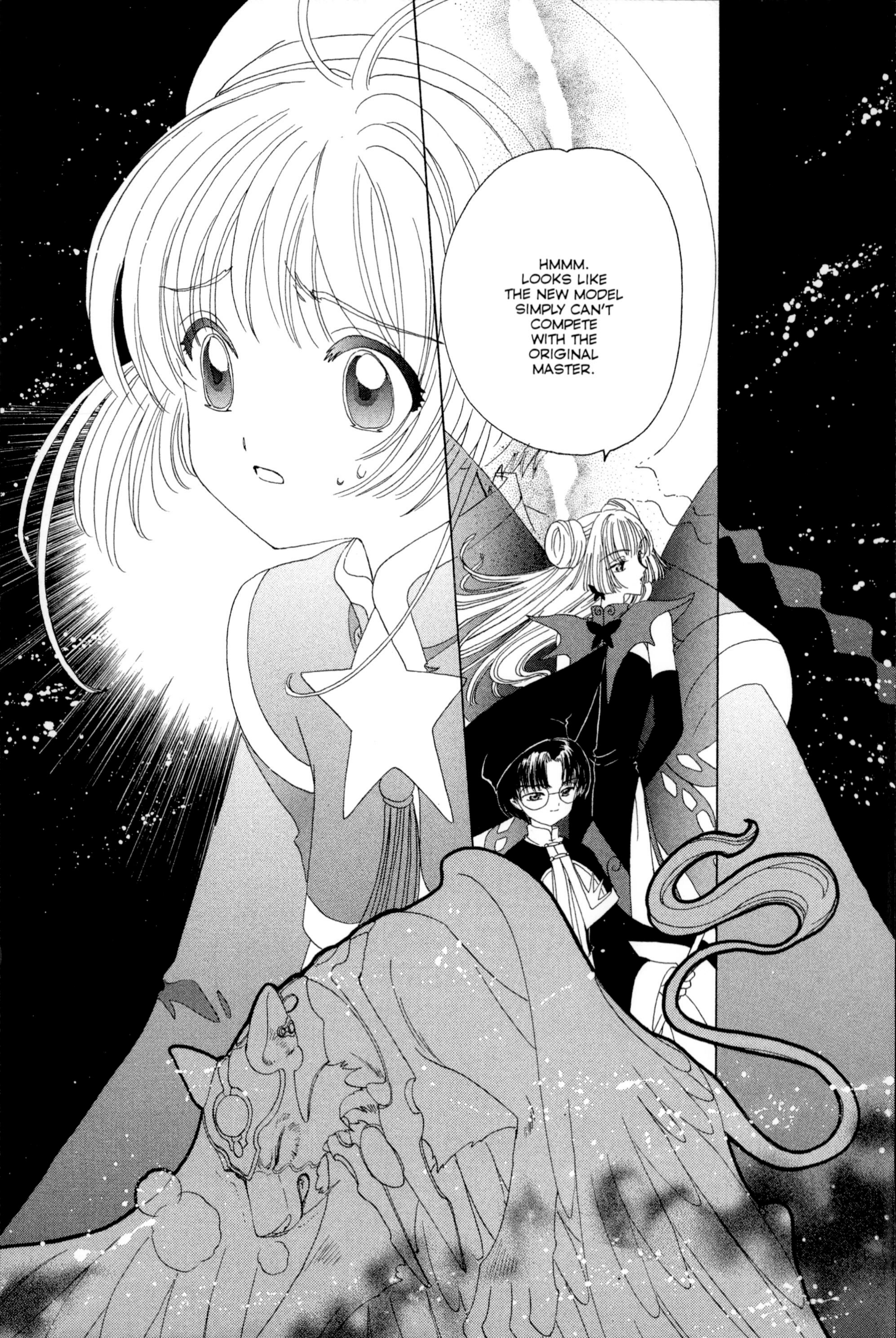
HMMM. LOOKS LIKE THE NEW MODEL SIMPLY CAN'T COMPETE WITH THE ORIGINAL MASTER.

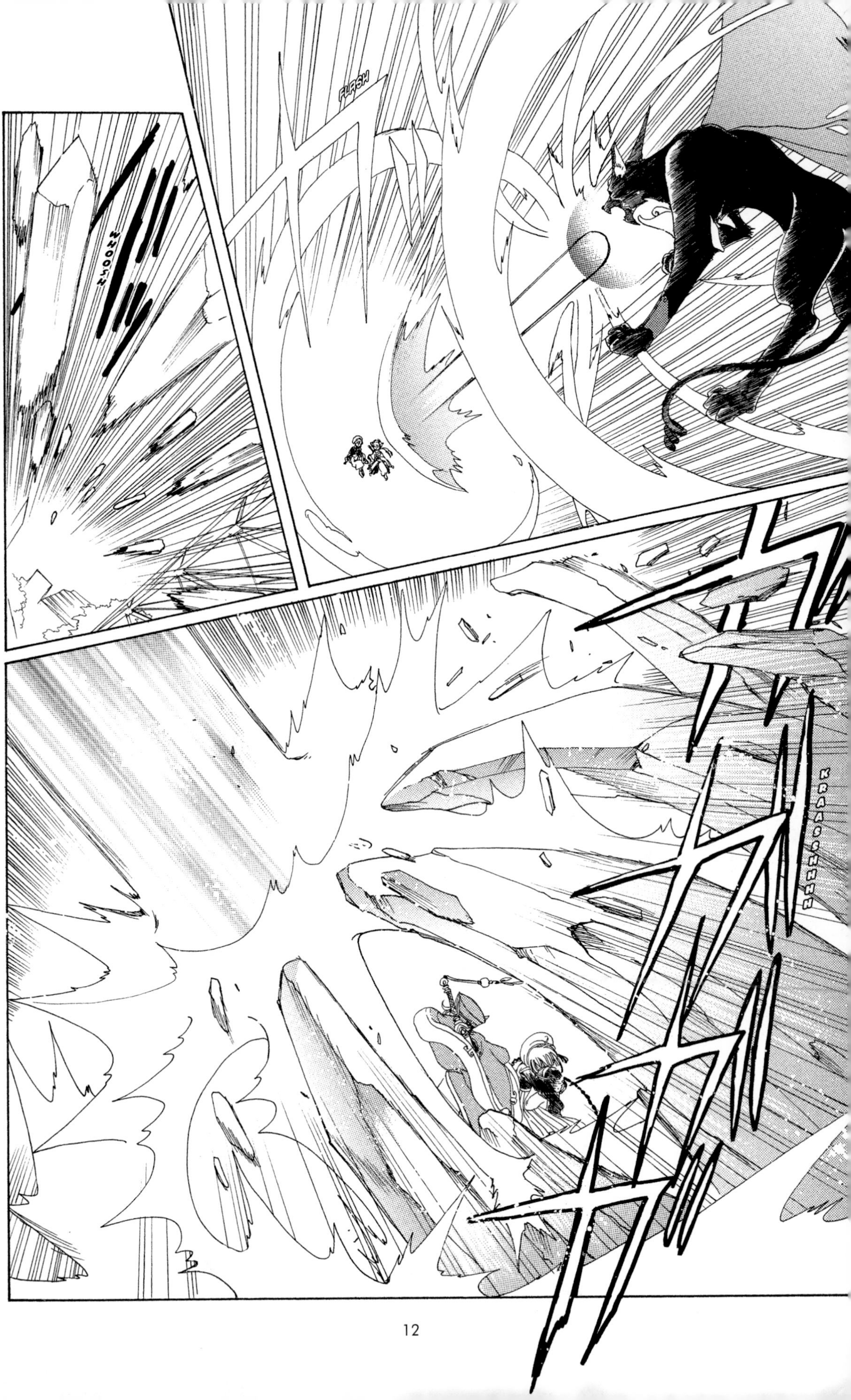
FLASH
WHOOSH
KRAASSHHHH

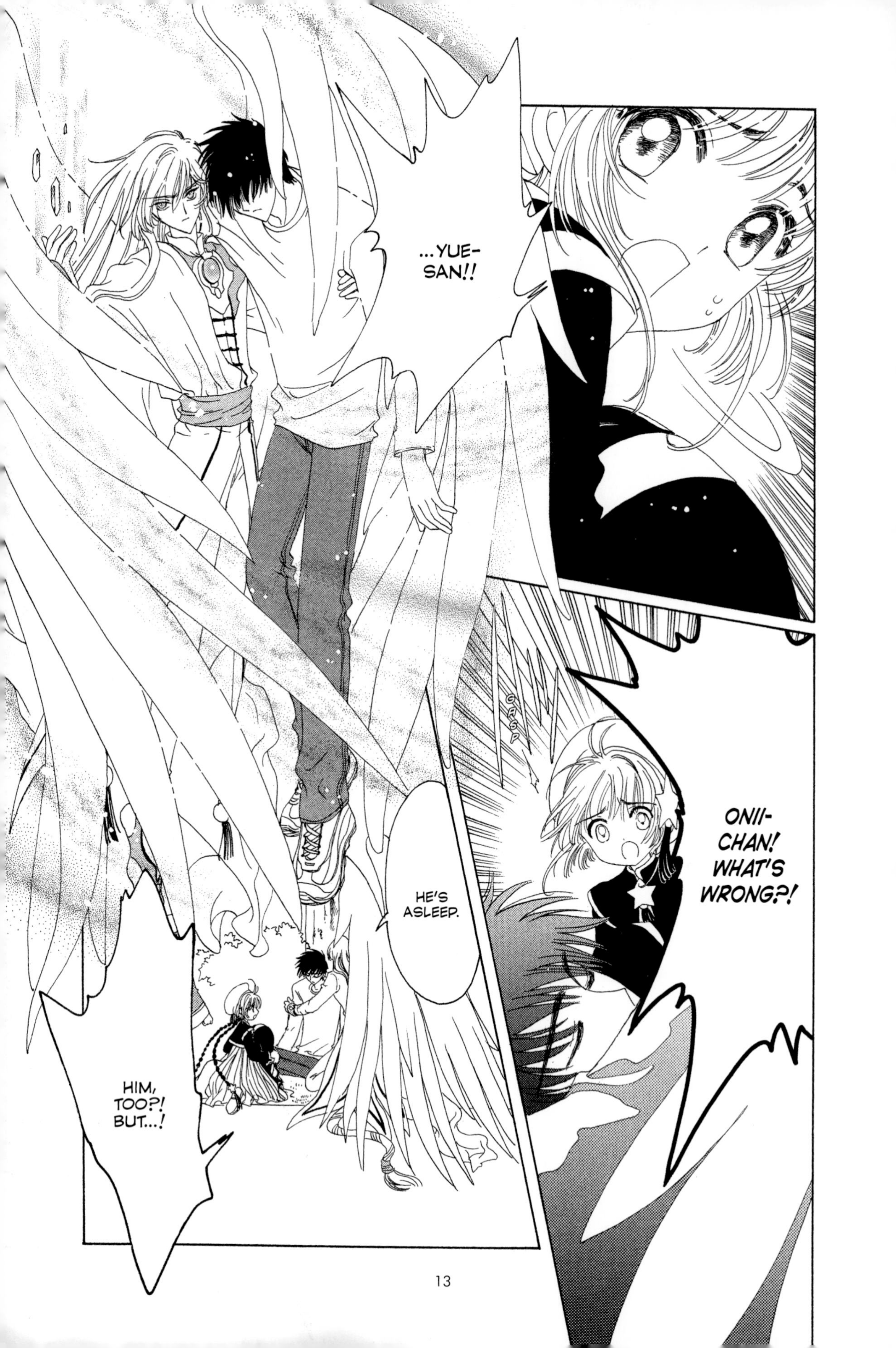
GASP
ONII-CHAN! WHAT'S WRONG?!
...YUE-SAN!!
HE'S ASLEEP.
HIM, TOO?! BUT...!

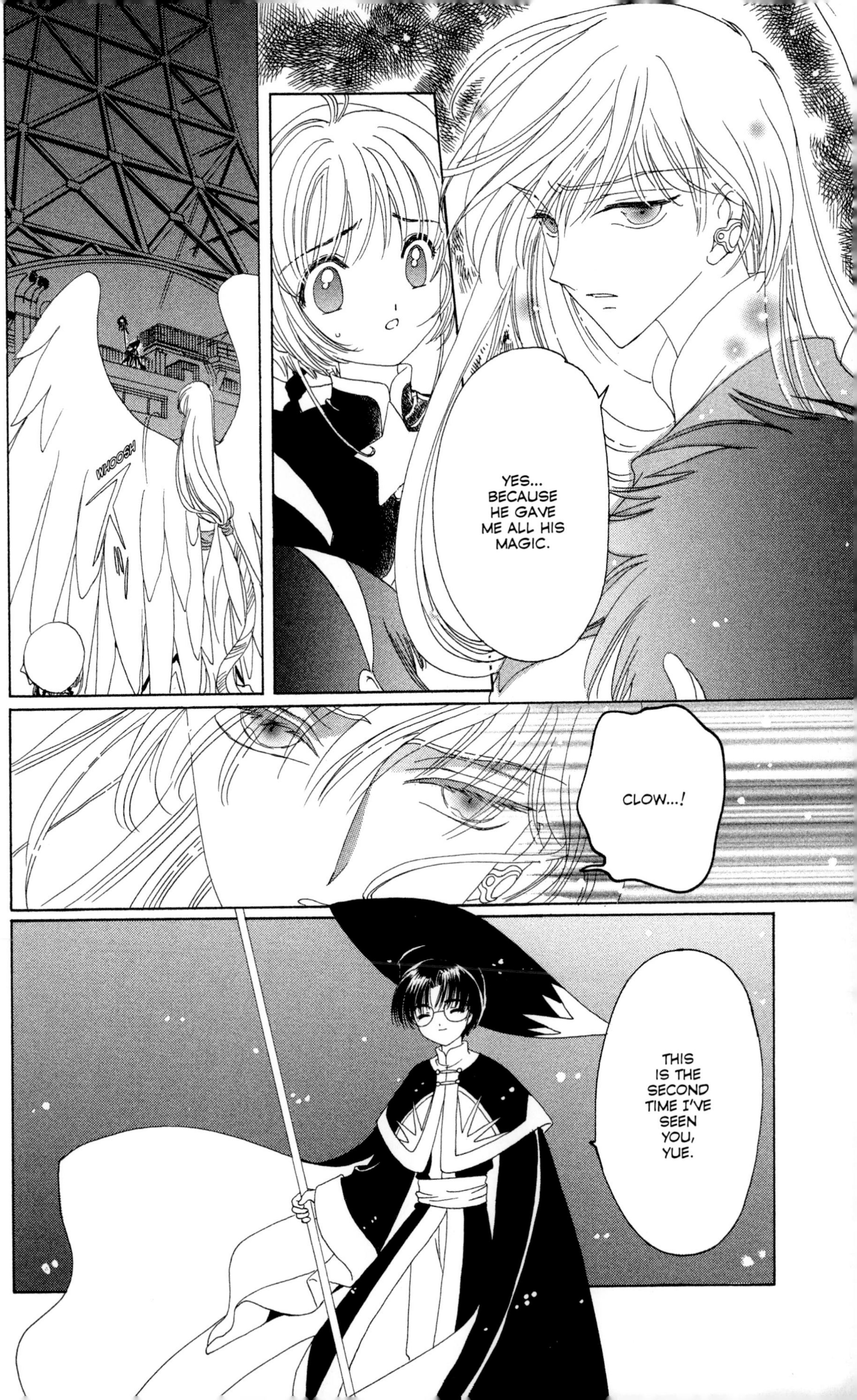
YES... BECAUSE HE GAVE ME ALL HIS MAGIC.
WHOOSH
CLOW...!
THIS IS THE SECOND TIME I'VE SEEN YOU, YUE.

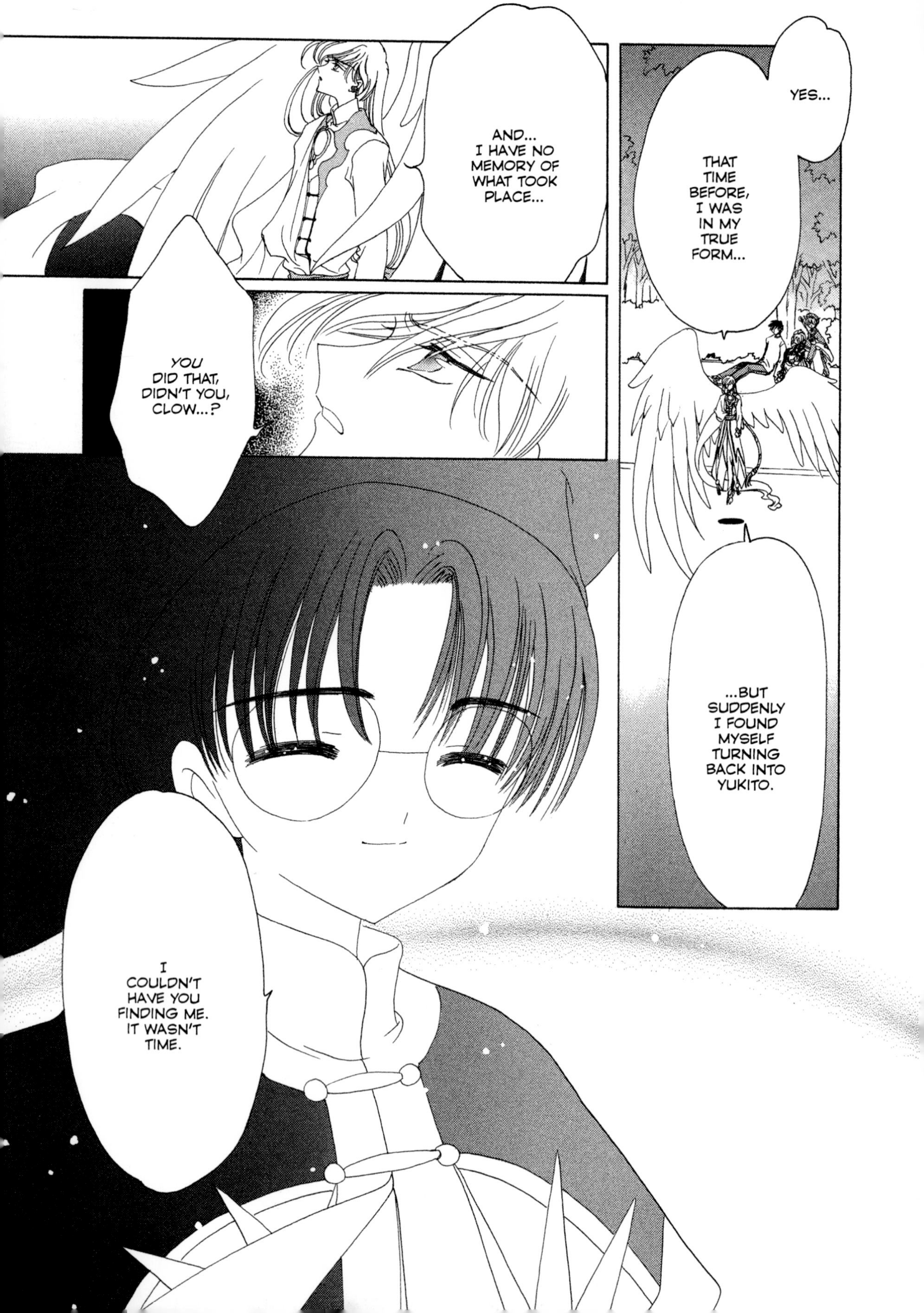
YES...
THAT TIME BEFORE, I WAS IN MY TRUE FORM...
...BUT SUDDENLY I FOUND MYSELF TURNING BACK INTO YUKITO.
AND... I HAVE NO MEMORY OF WHAT TOOK PLACE...
YOU DID THAT, DIDN'T YOU, CLOW...?
I COULDN'T HAVE YOU FINDING ME. IT WASN'T TIME.

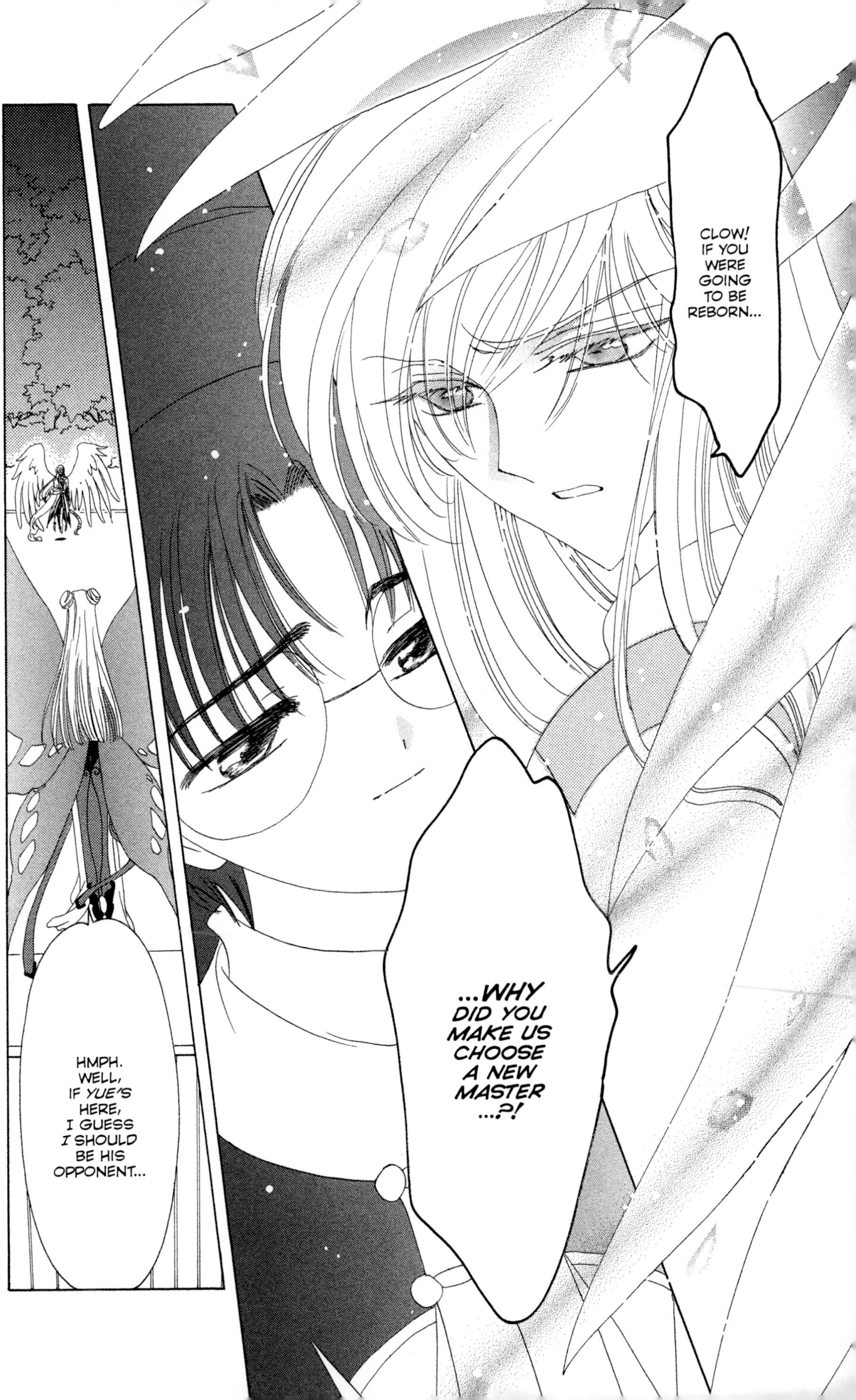
CLOW! IF YOU WERE GOING TO BE REBORN...
...WHY DID YOU MAKE US CHOOSE A NEW MASTER ...?!
HMPH. WELL, IF YUE'S HERE, I GUESS I SHOULD BE HIS OPPONENT...

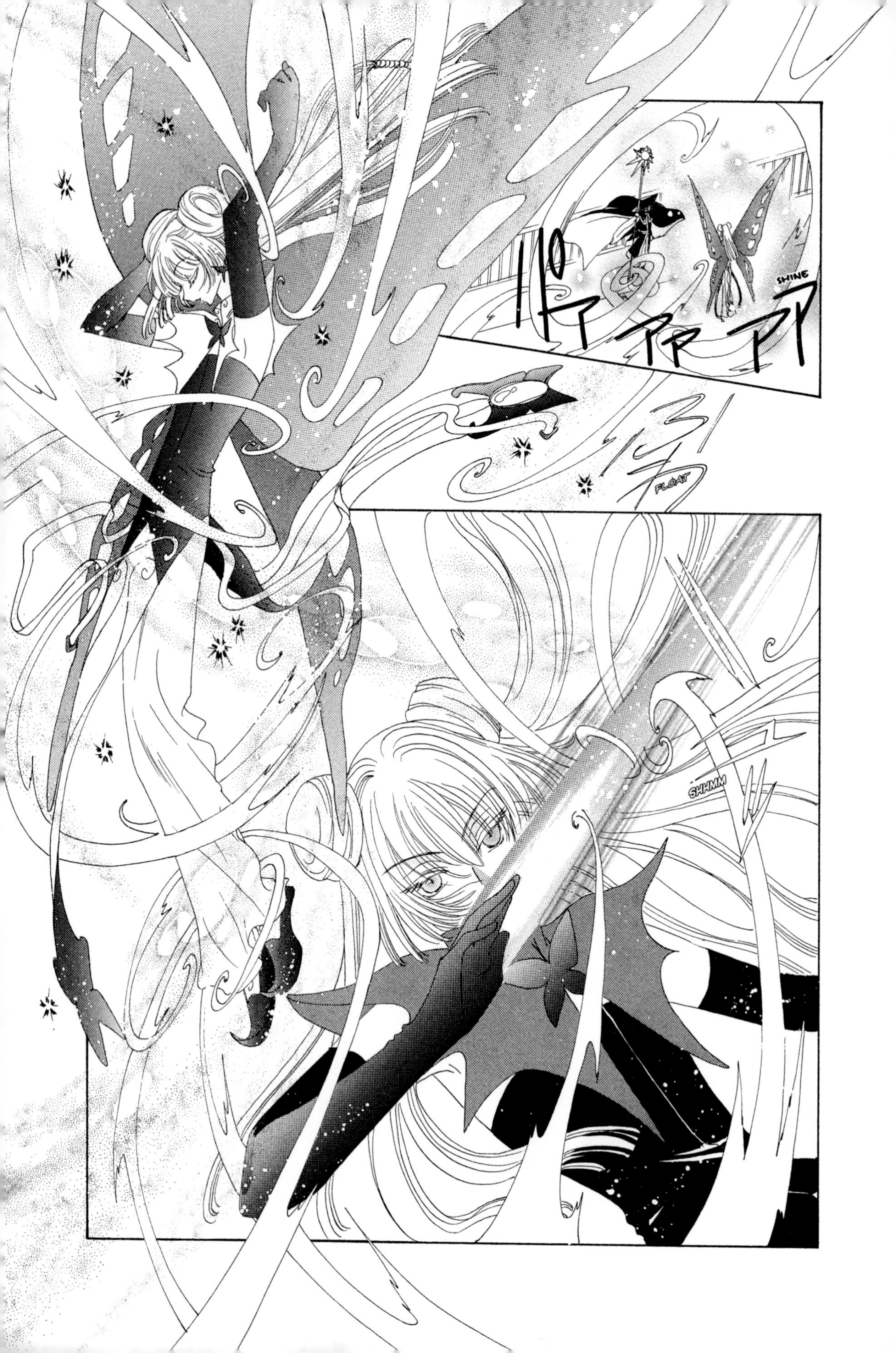
SHINE
FLOAT
SHHMM

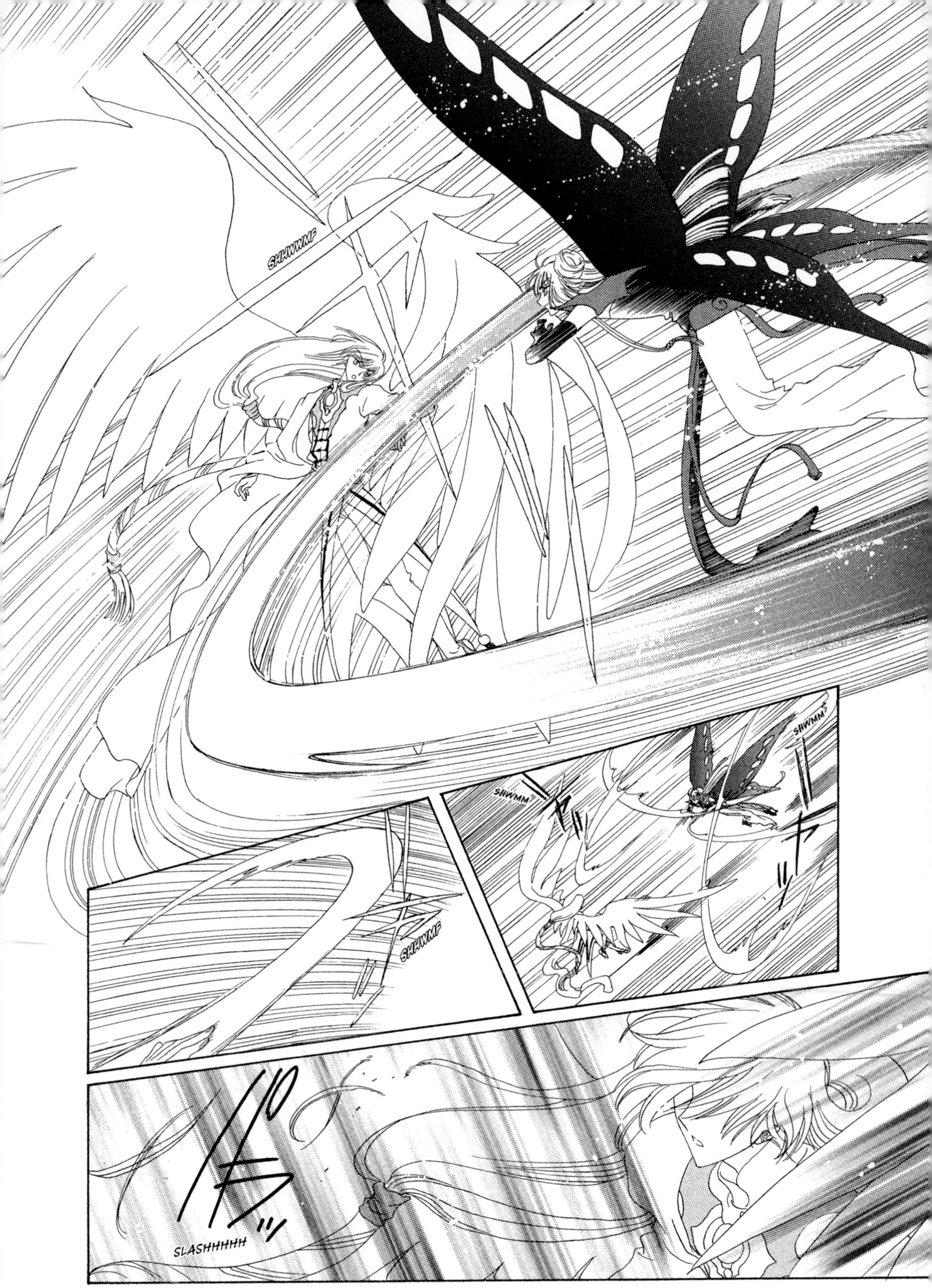
SHWWMF
SHWMM
SHWMM
SHWWMF
SLASHHHHH

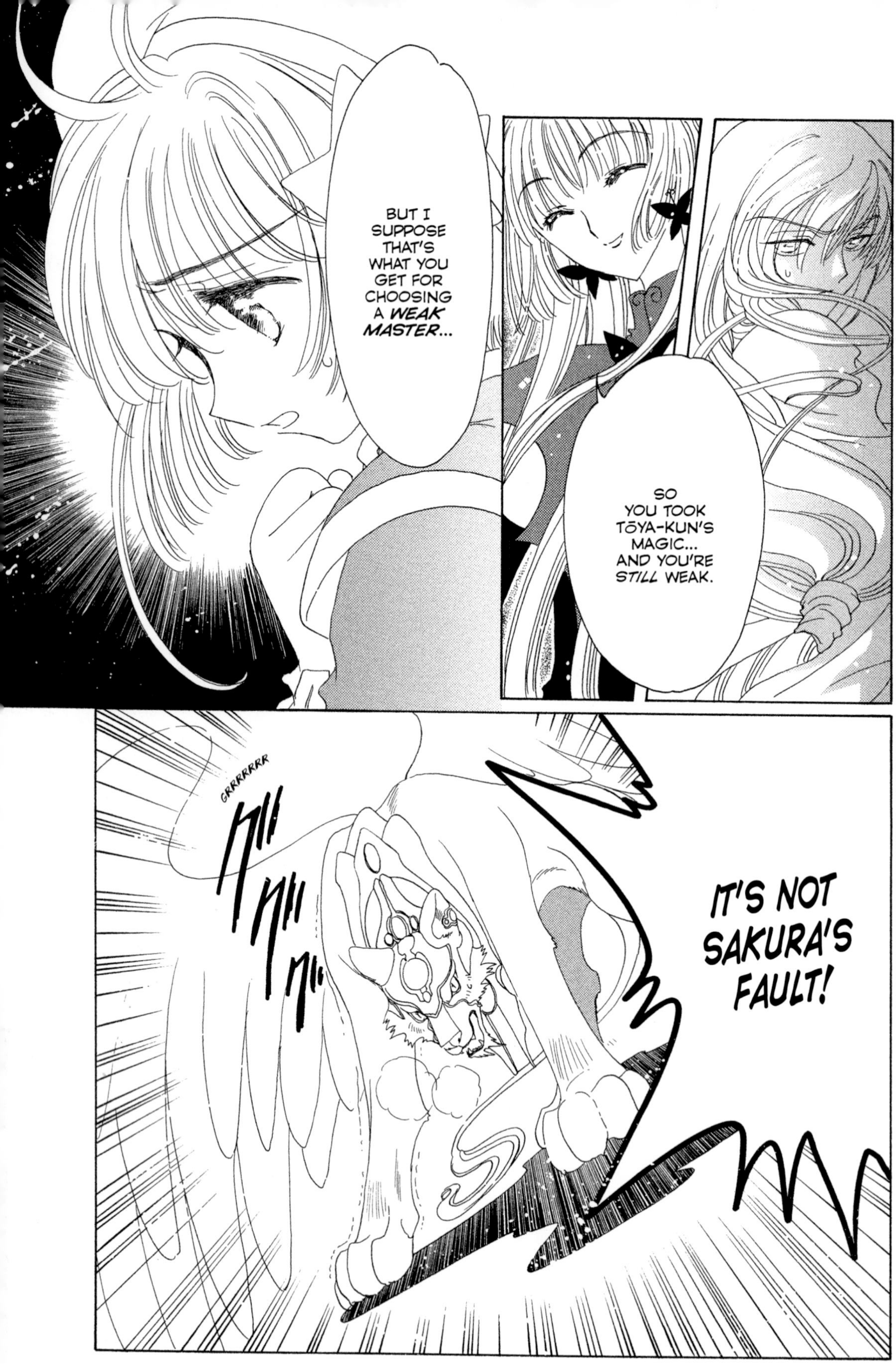
SO YOU TOOK TŌYA-KUN'S MAGIC... AND YOU'RE *STILL* WEAK.
BUT I SUPPOSE THAT'S WHAT YOU GET FOR CHOOSING A ***WEAK MASTER***...
IT'S NOT SAKURA'S FAULT!
GRRRRRRR

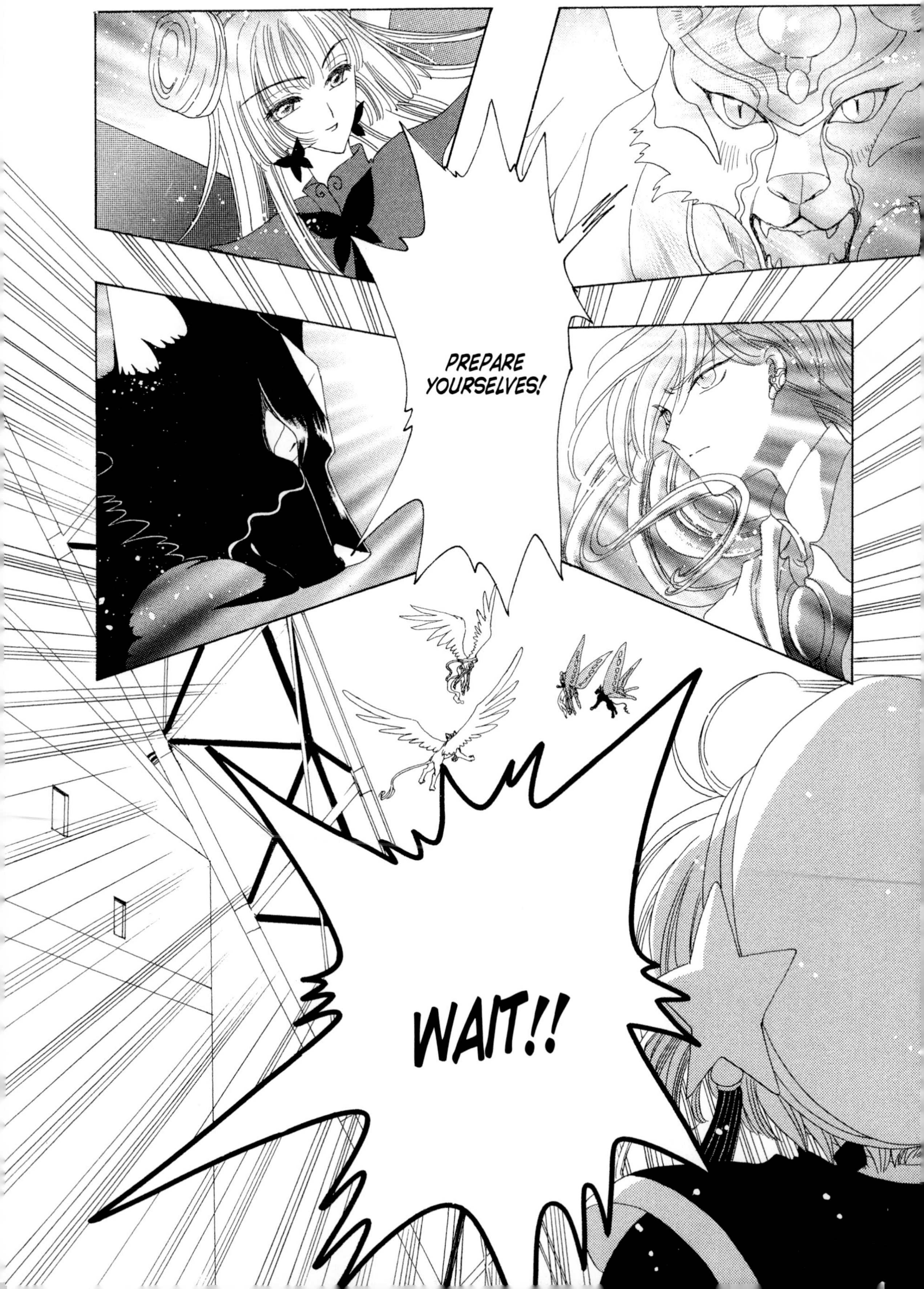
PREPARE YOURSELVES!
WAIT!!

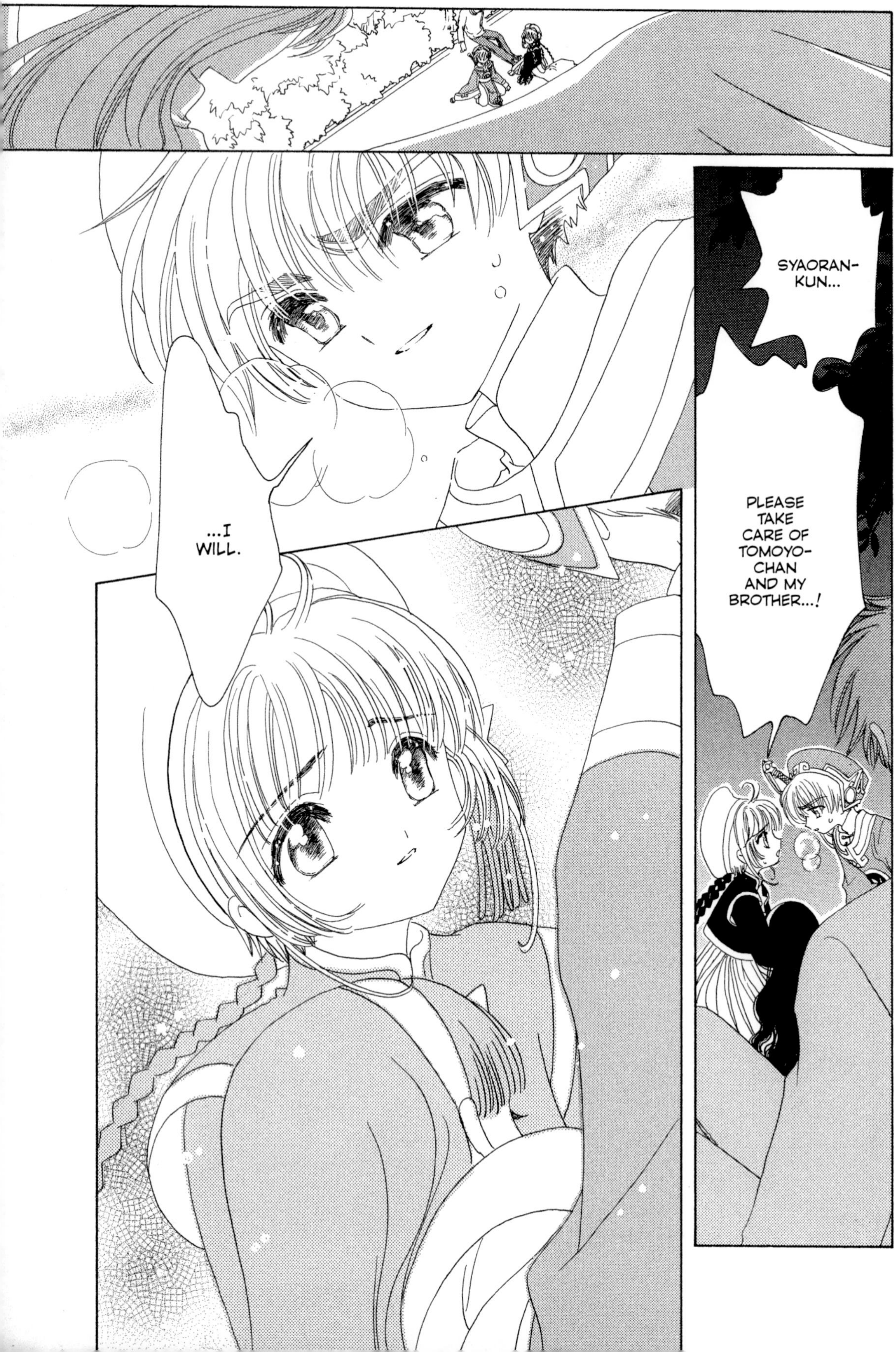
SYAORAN-KUN...
PLEASE TAKE CARE OF TOMOYO-CHAN AND MY BROTHER...!
...I WILL.

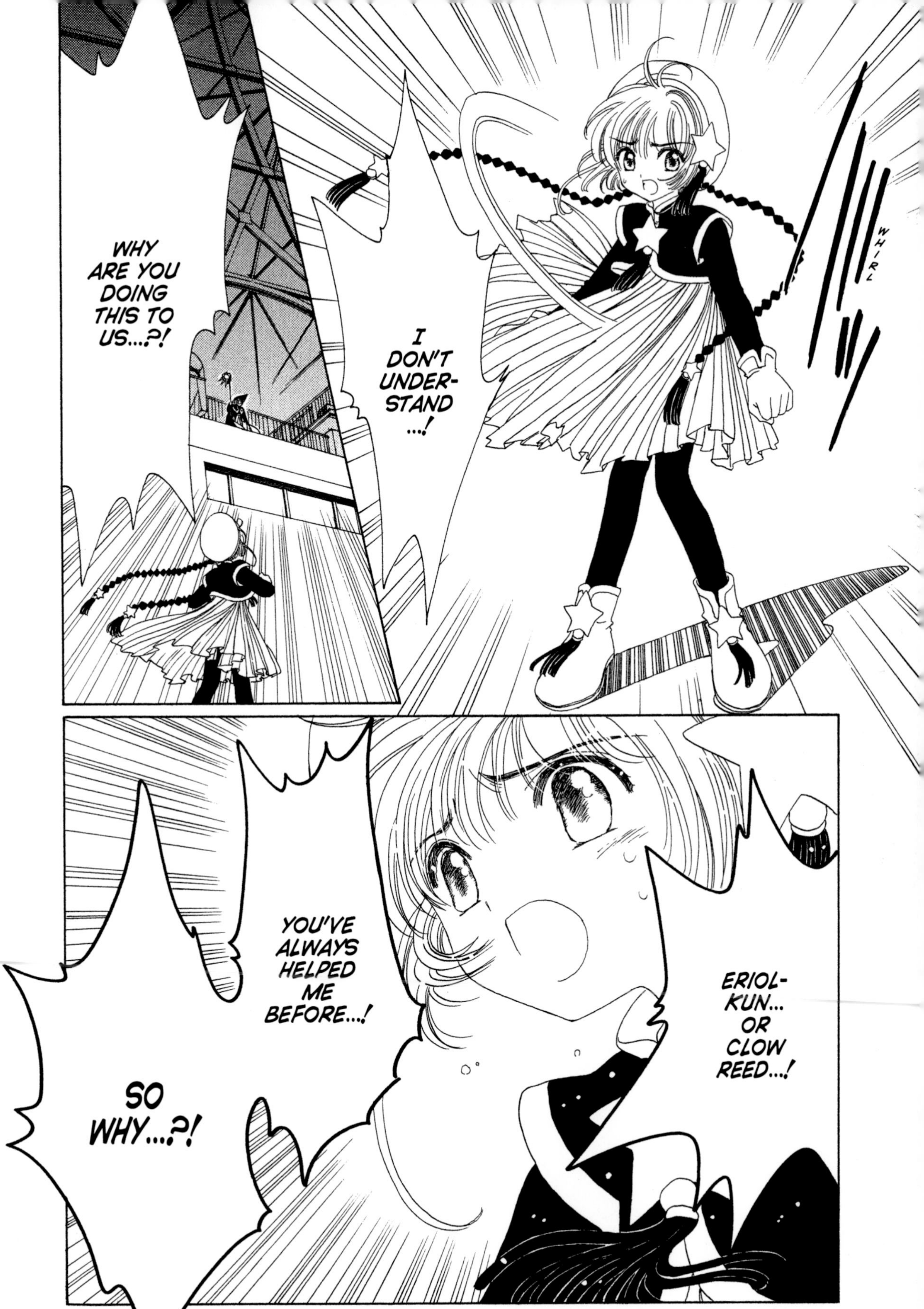
WHIRL
I DON'T UNDER-STAND ...!
WHY ARE YOU DOING THIS TO US...?!
ERIOL-KUN... OR CLOW REED...!
YOU'VE ALWAYS HELPED ME BEFORE...!
SO WHY...?!

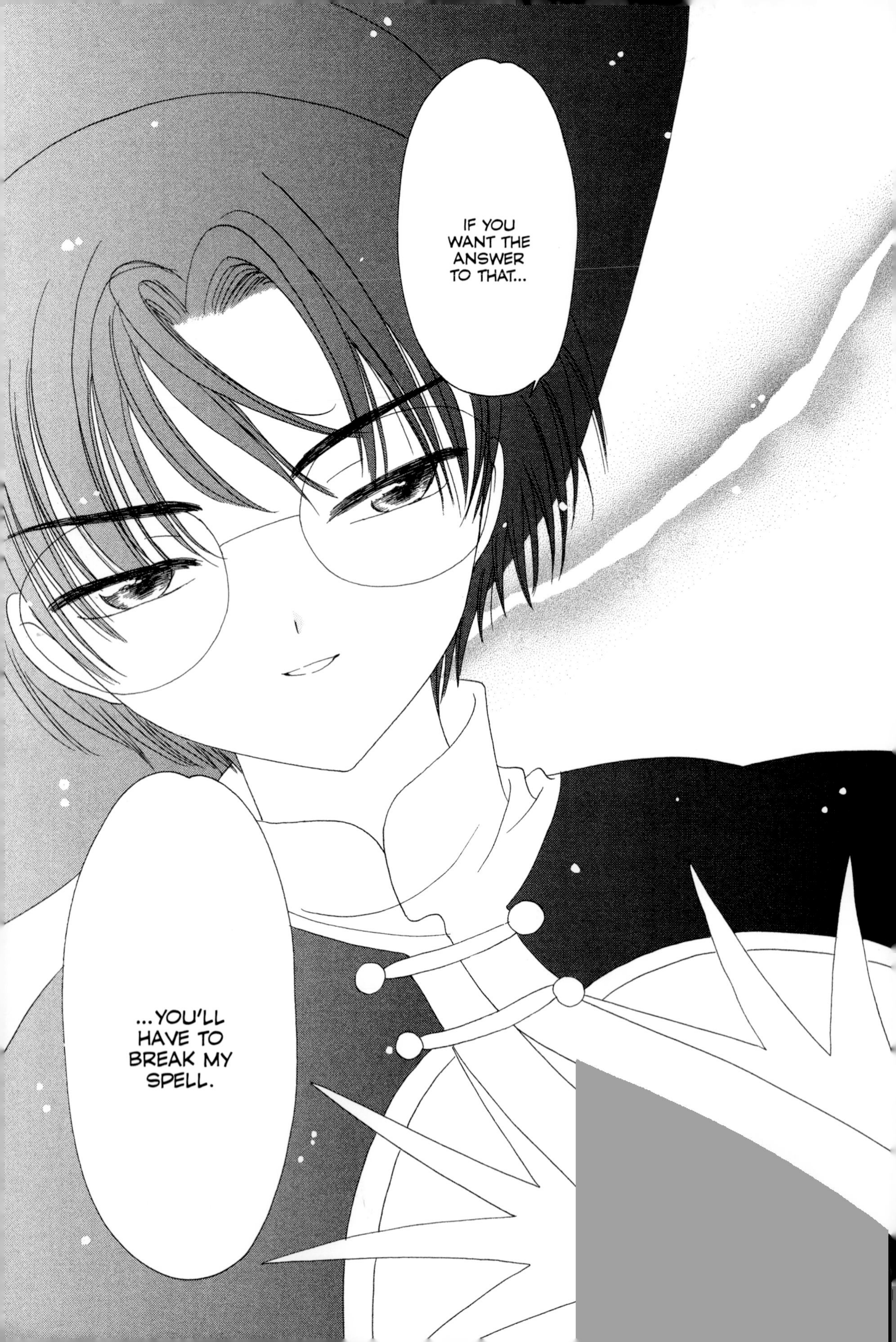
IF YOU WANT THE ANSWER TO THAT...
...YOU'LL HAVE TO BREAK MY SPELL.

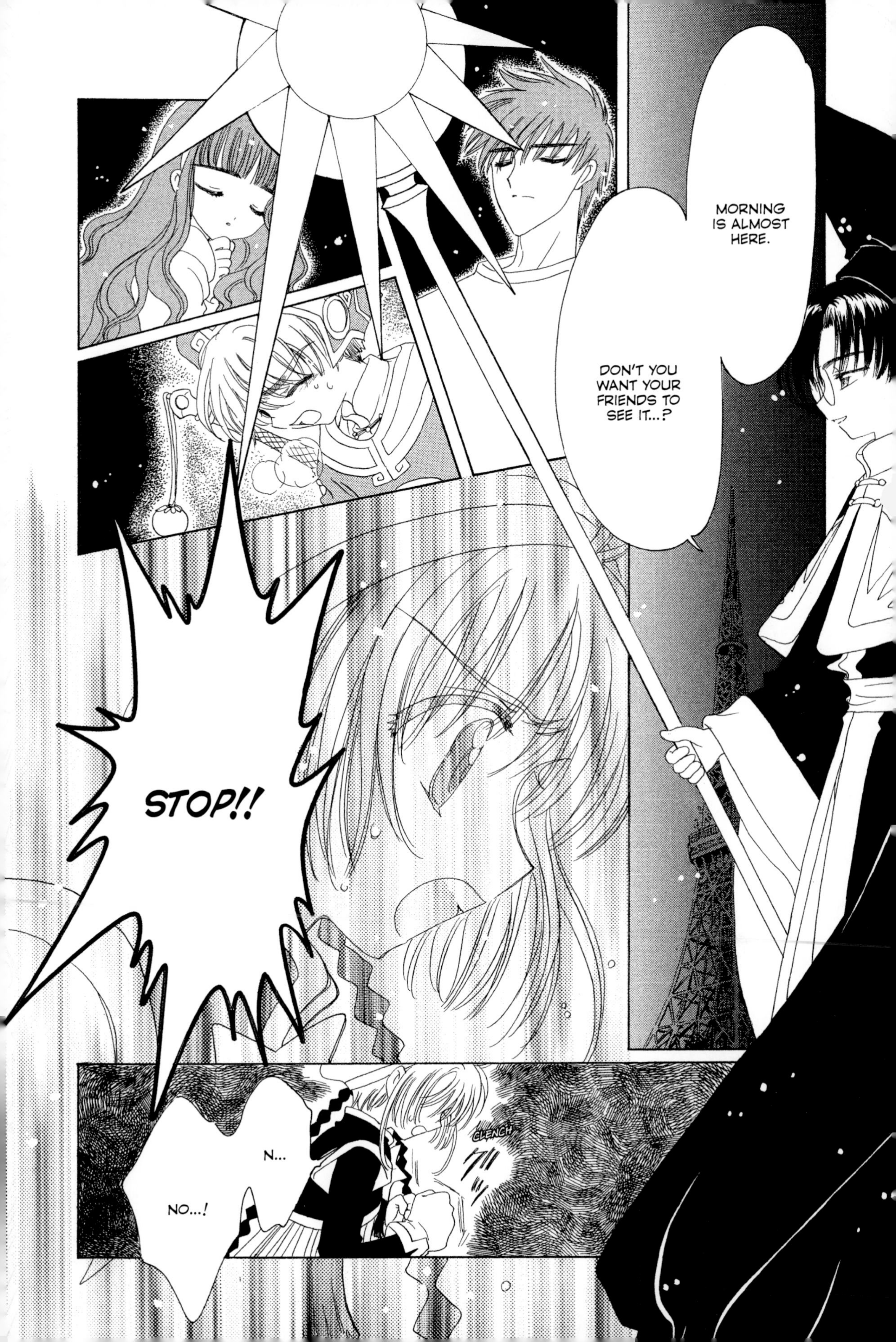
MORNING IS ALMOST HERE.
DON'T YOU WANT YOUR FRIENDS TO SEE IT...?
STOP!!
CLENCH
N...
NO...!

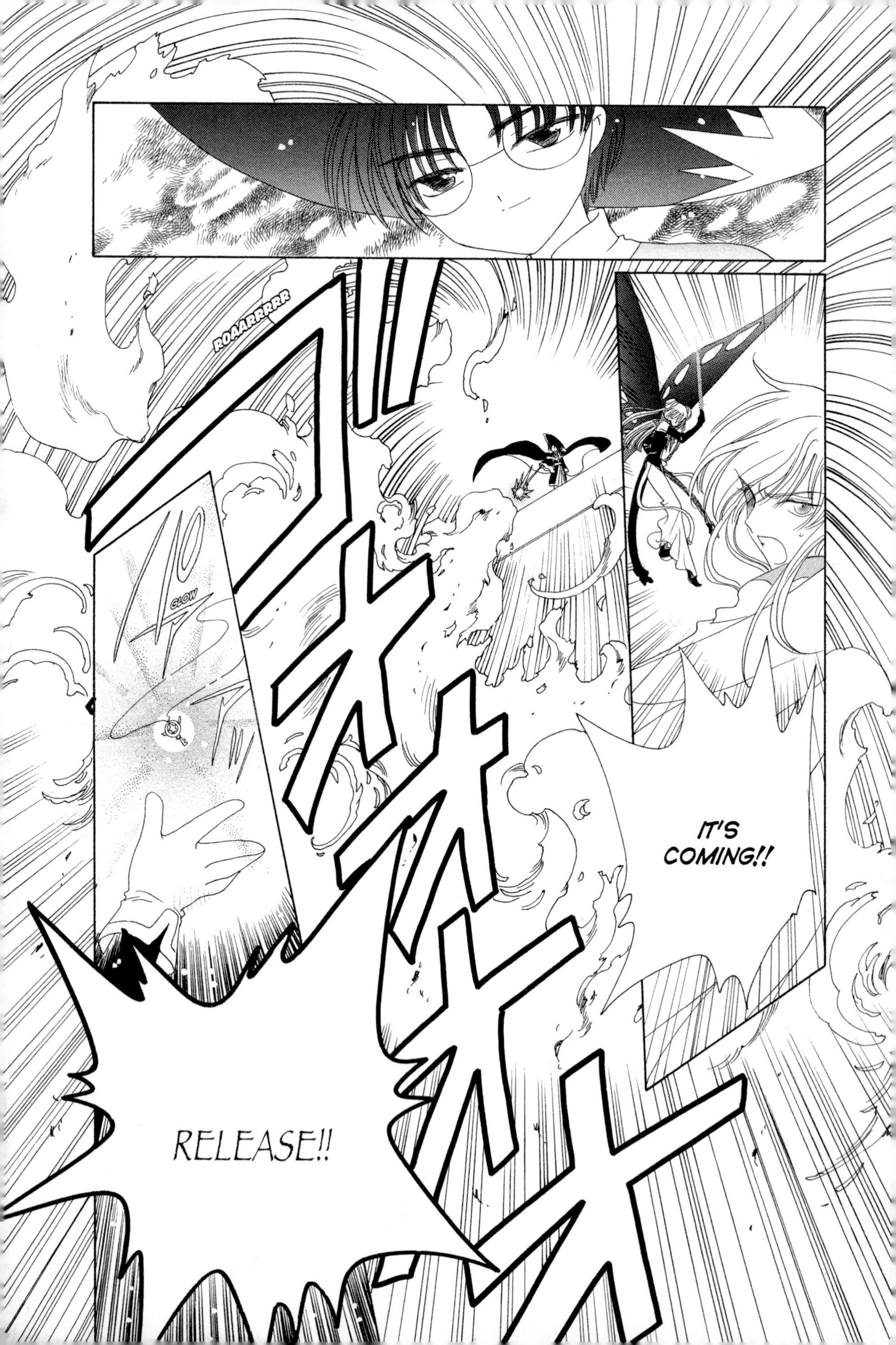
IT'S COMING!!
ROAARRRRR
CLOW
RELEASE!!

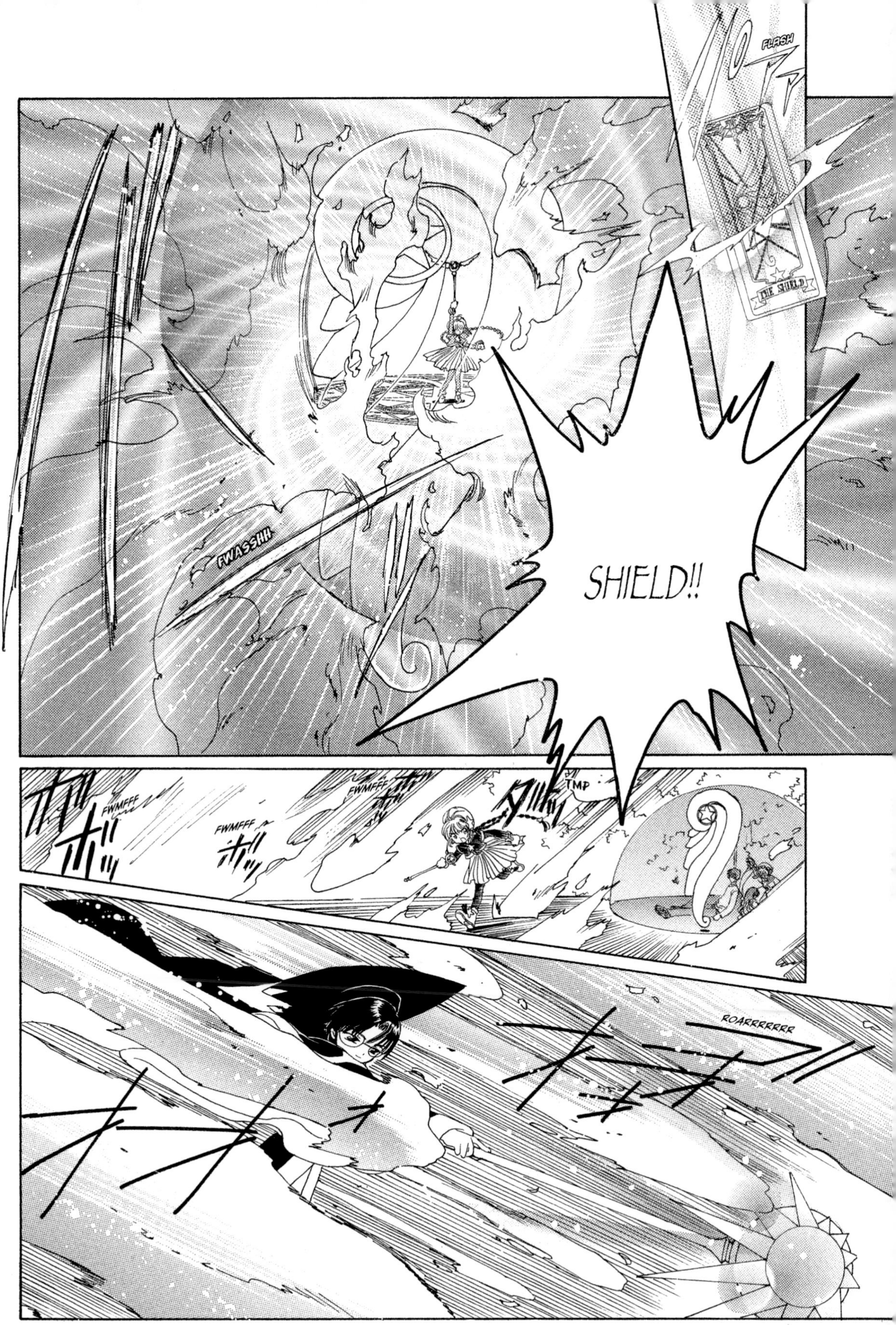
FLASH
THE SHIELD
SHIELD!!
FWASSHH
TMP
FWMFFF
FWMFFF
FWMFFF
ROARRRRRRR

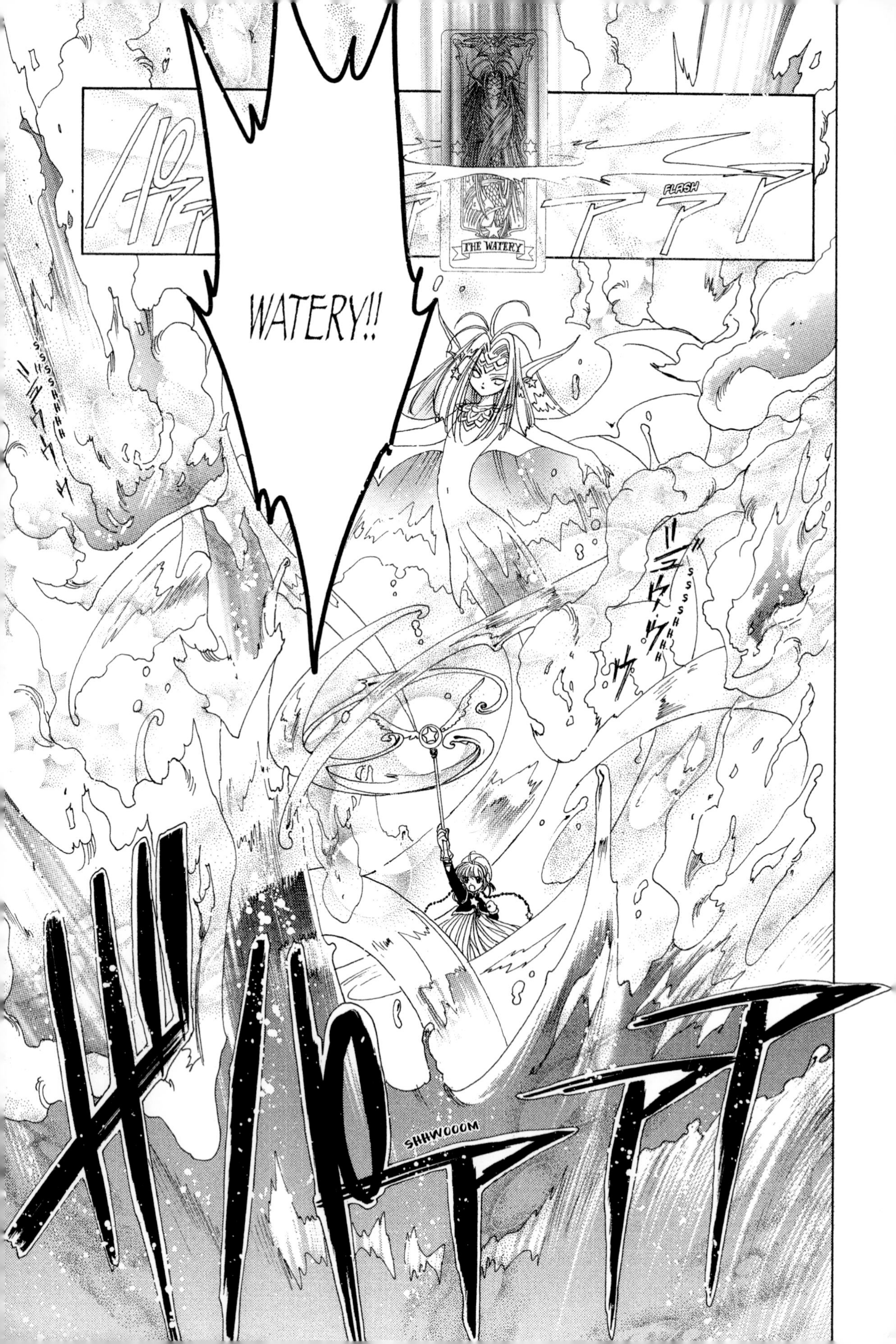
FLASH
THE WATERY
WATERY!!
SSSSHHHH
SSSSHHHH
SHHWOOOM

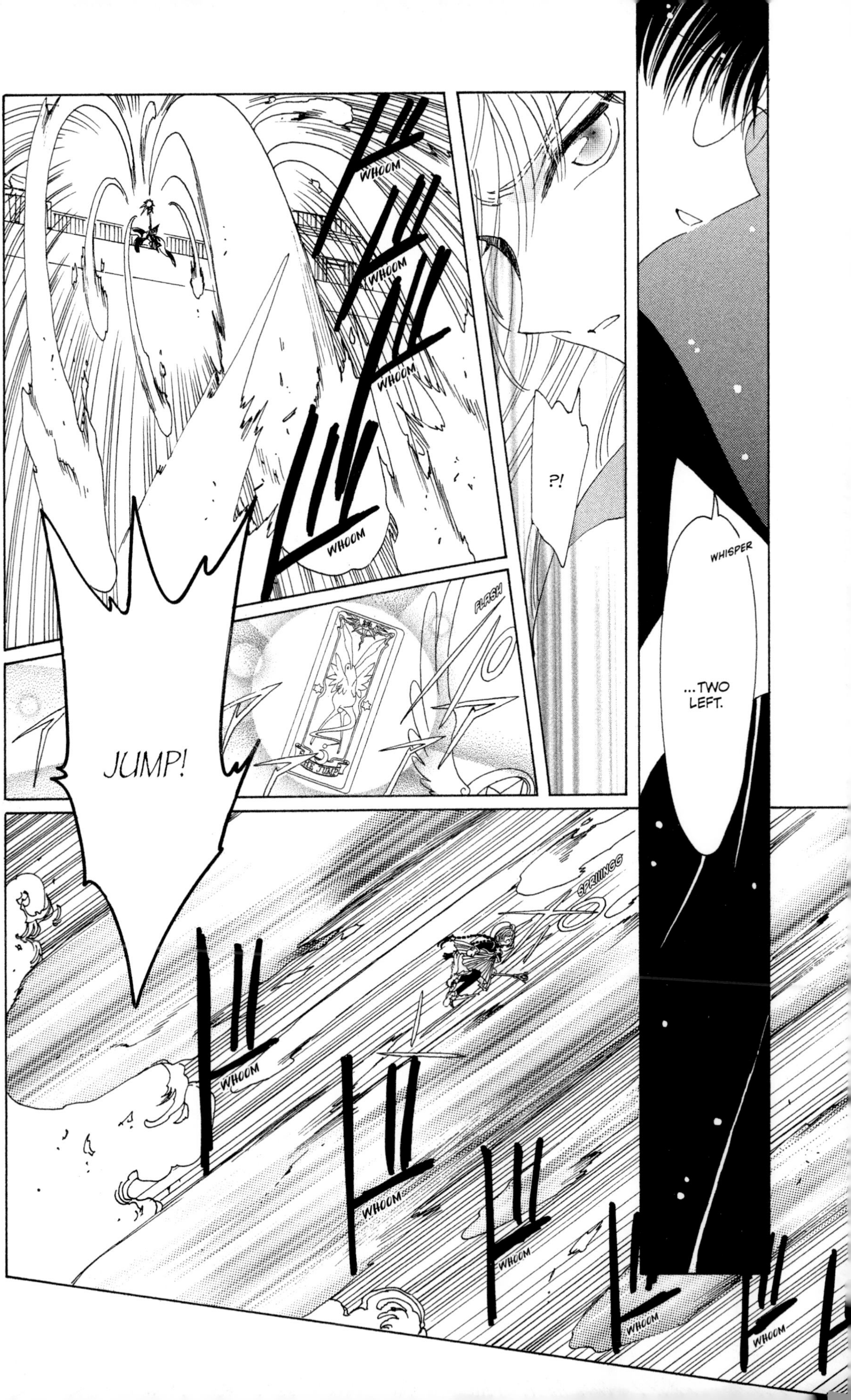
WHISPER
...TWO LEFT.
?!
WHOOM
WHOOM
WHOOM
WHOOM
FLASH
JUMP!
SPRIIINGG
WHOOM
WHOOM
WHOOM
WHOOM
WHOOM

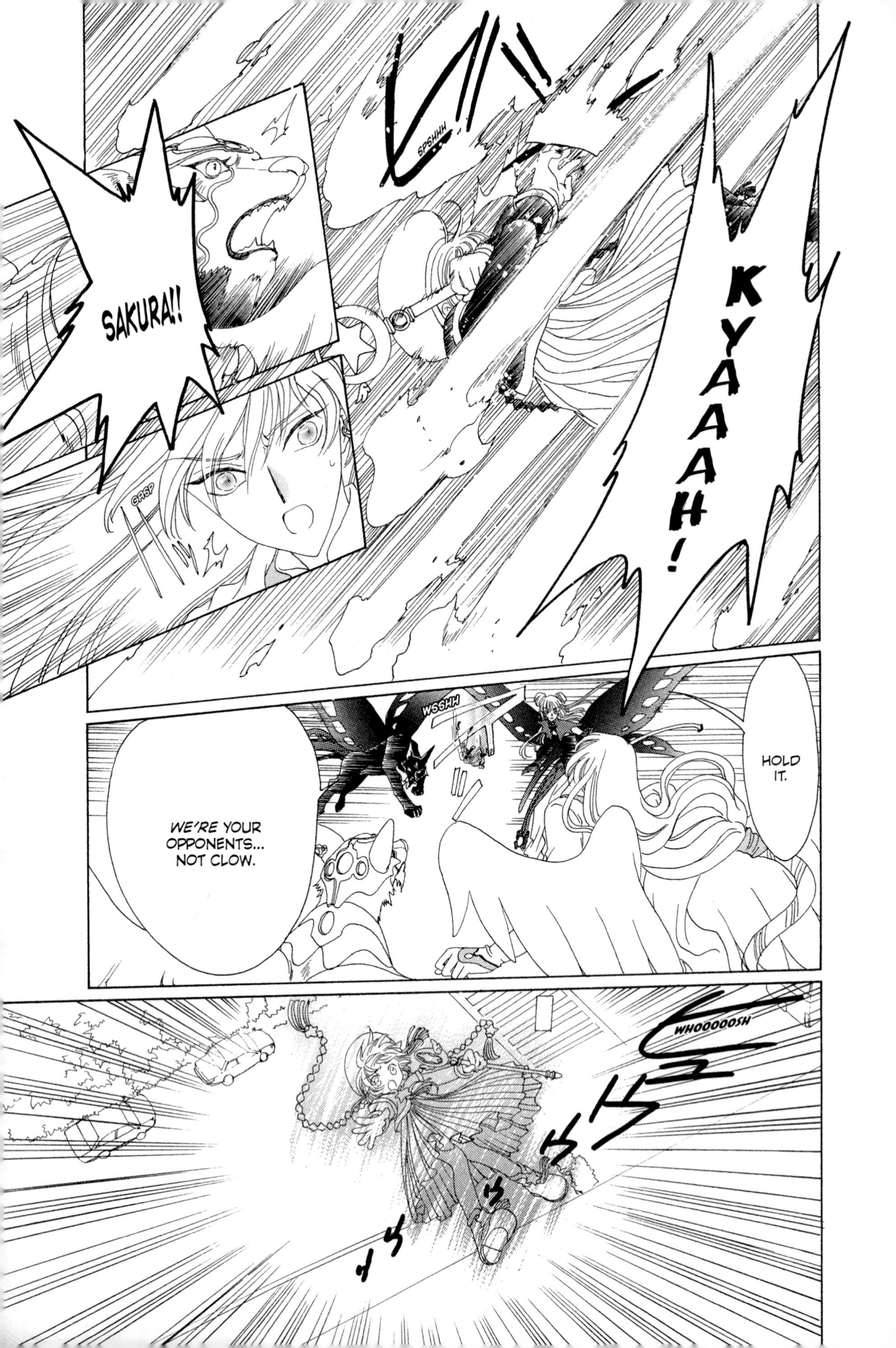

KYAAAH!
SPSHHH
SAKURA!!
GASP
HOLD IT.
WSSHH
WE'RE YOUR OPPONENTS... NOT CLOW.
WHOOOOOSH

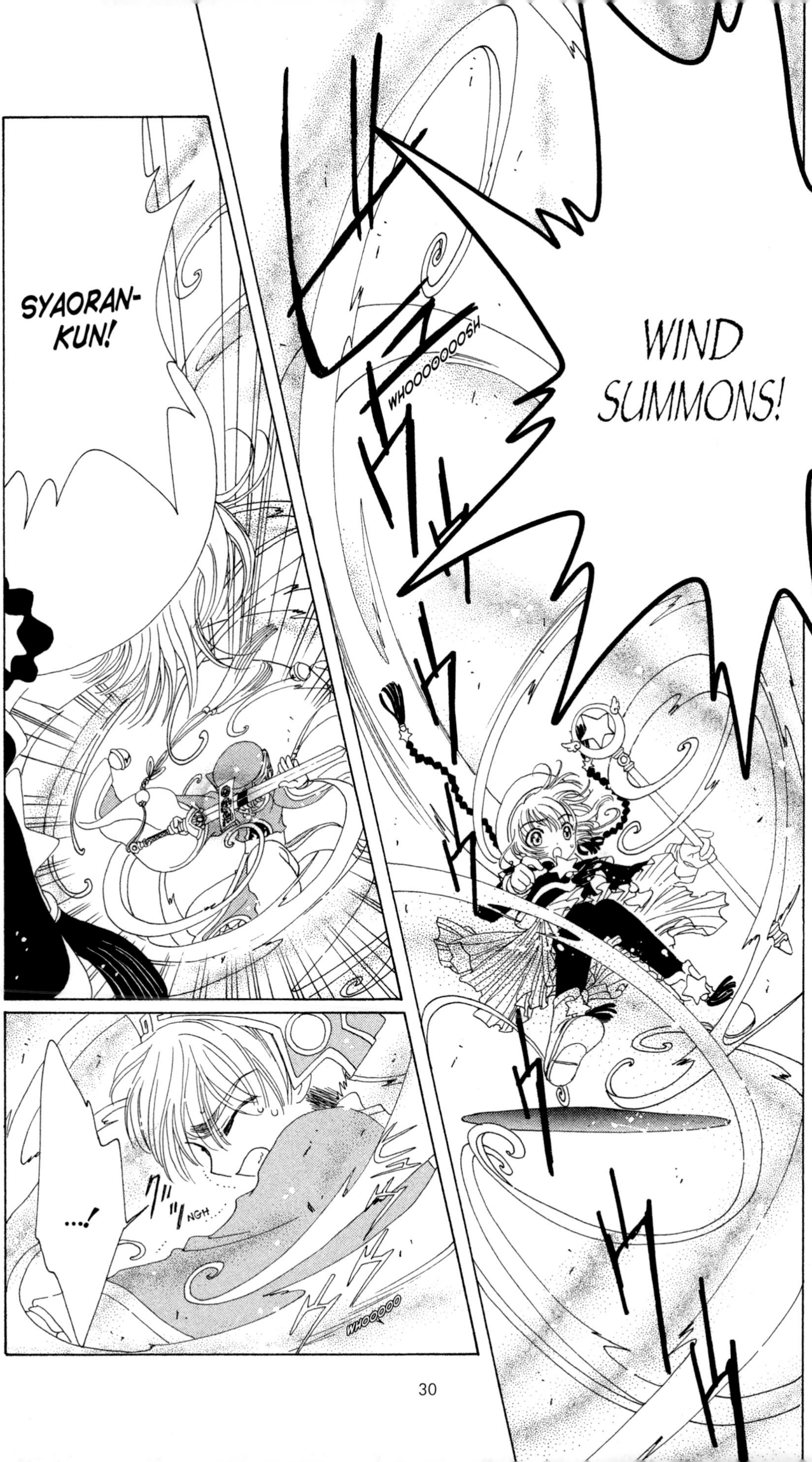
WIND SUMMONS!
WHOOOOOOOSH
SYAORAN-KUN!
...!
NGH
WHOOOOOO

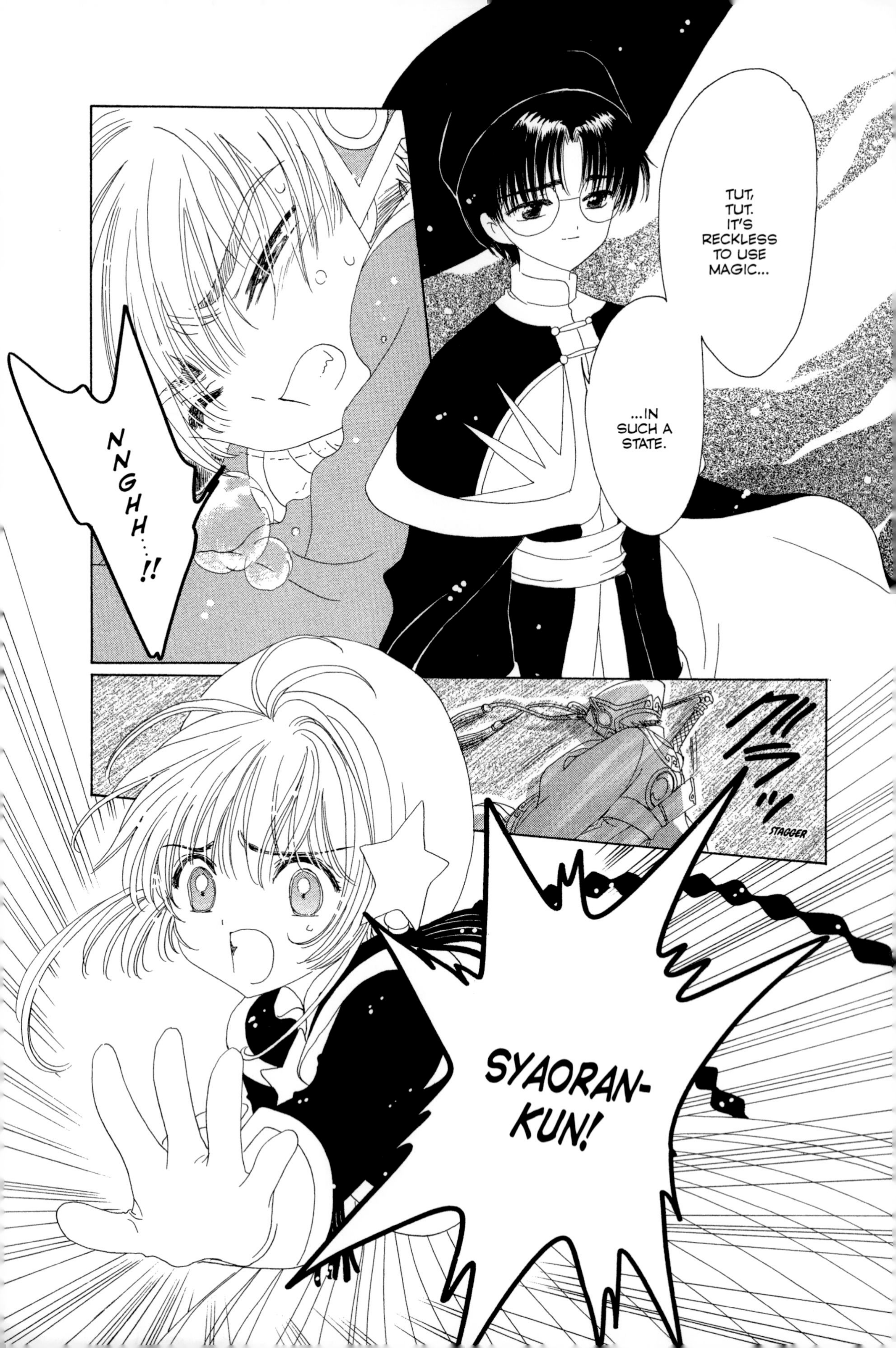
TUT, TUT. IT'S RECKLESS TO USE MAGIC...
...IN SUCH A STATE.
NNGHH...!!
STAGGER
SYAORAN-KUN!

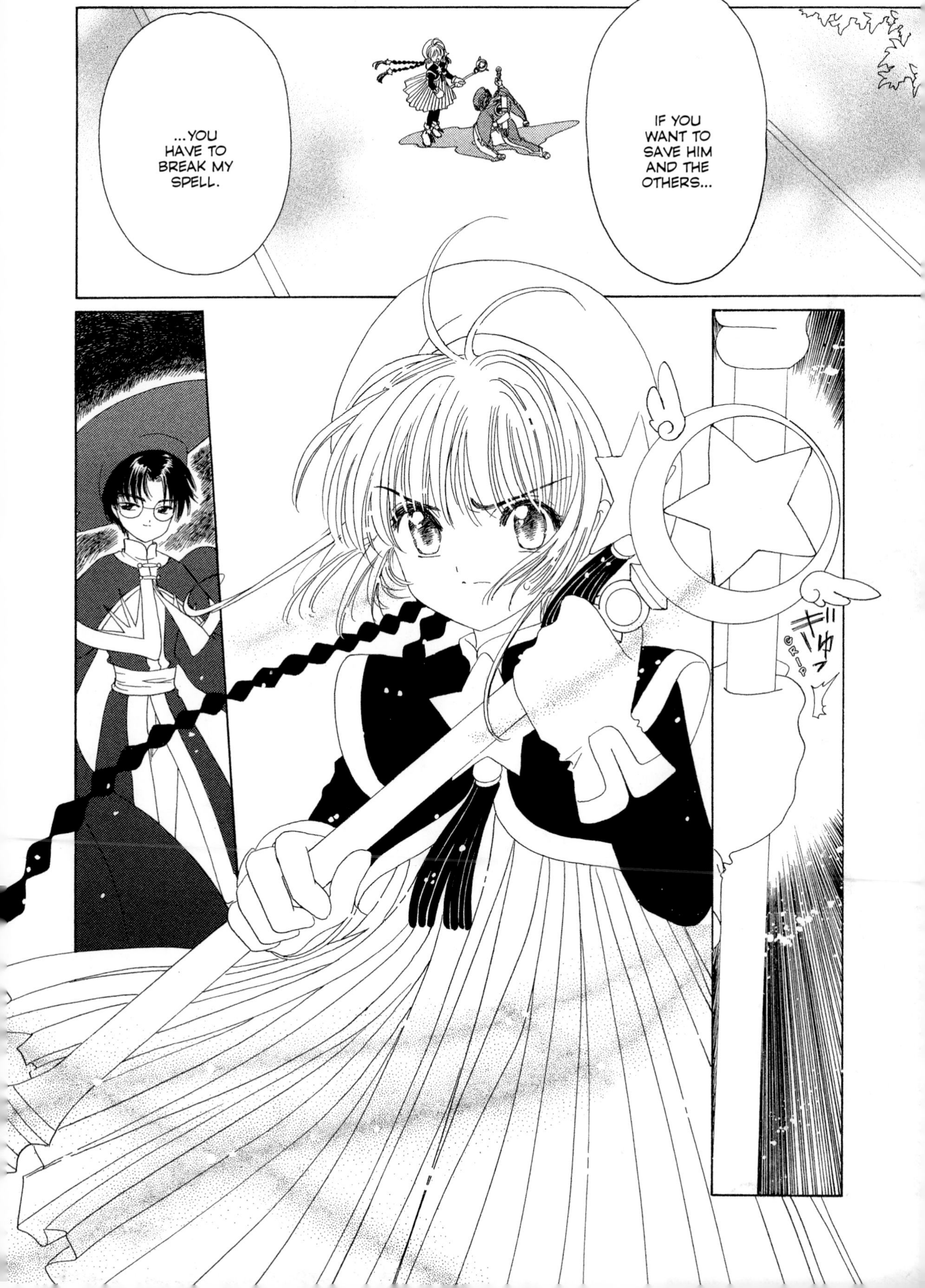
IF YOU WANT TO SAVE HIM AND THE OTHERS...
...YOU HAVE TO BREAK MY SPELL.
GRIP

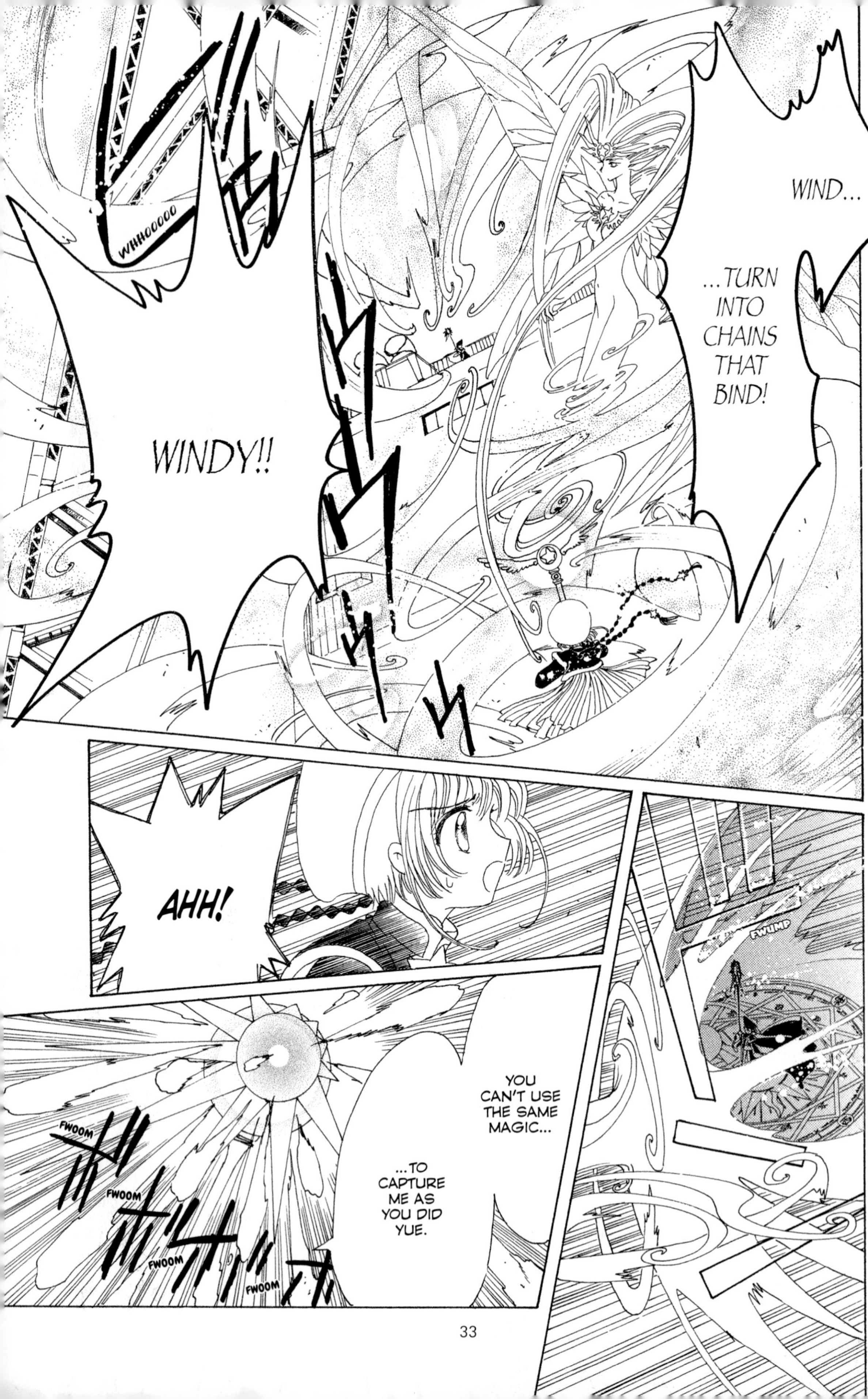
WIND...
...TURN INTO CHAINS THAT BIND!
WINDY!!
WHHOOOOO
FWUMP
AHH!
YOU CAN'T USE THE SAME MAGIC...
...TO CAPTURE ME AS YOU DID YUE.
FWOOM
FWOOM
FWOOM
FWOOM

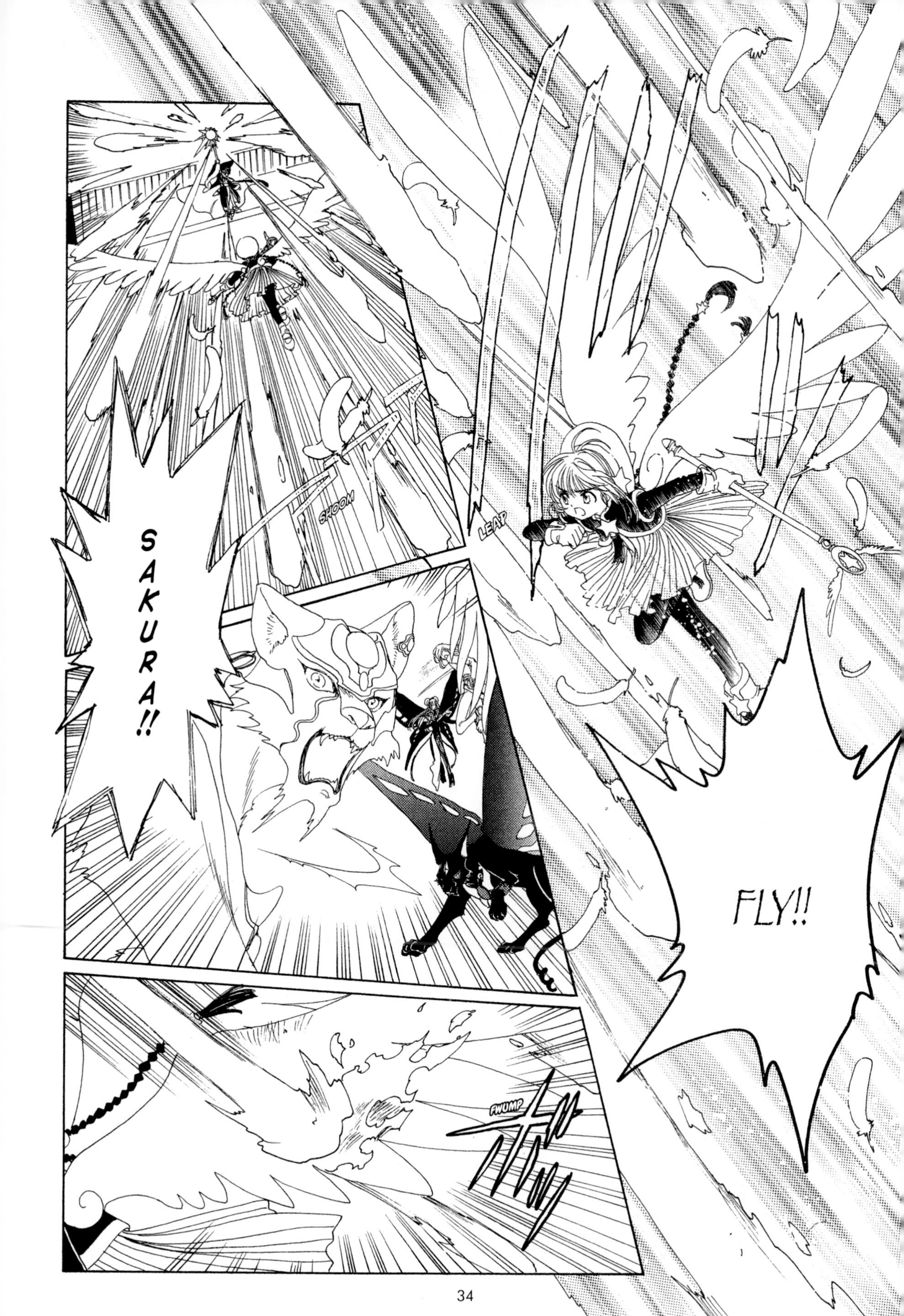
LEAP
FLY!!
SHOOM
SAKURA!!
FWUMP

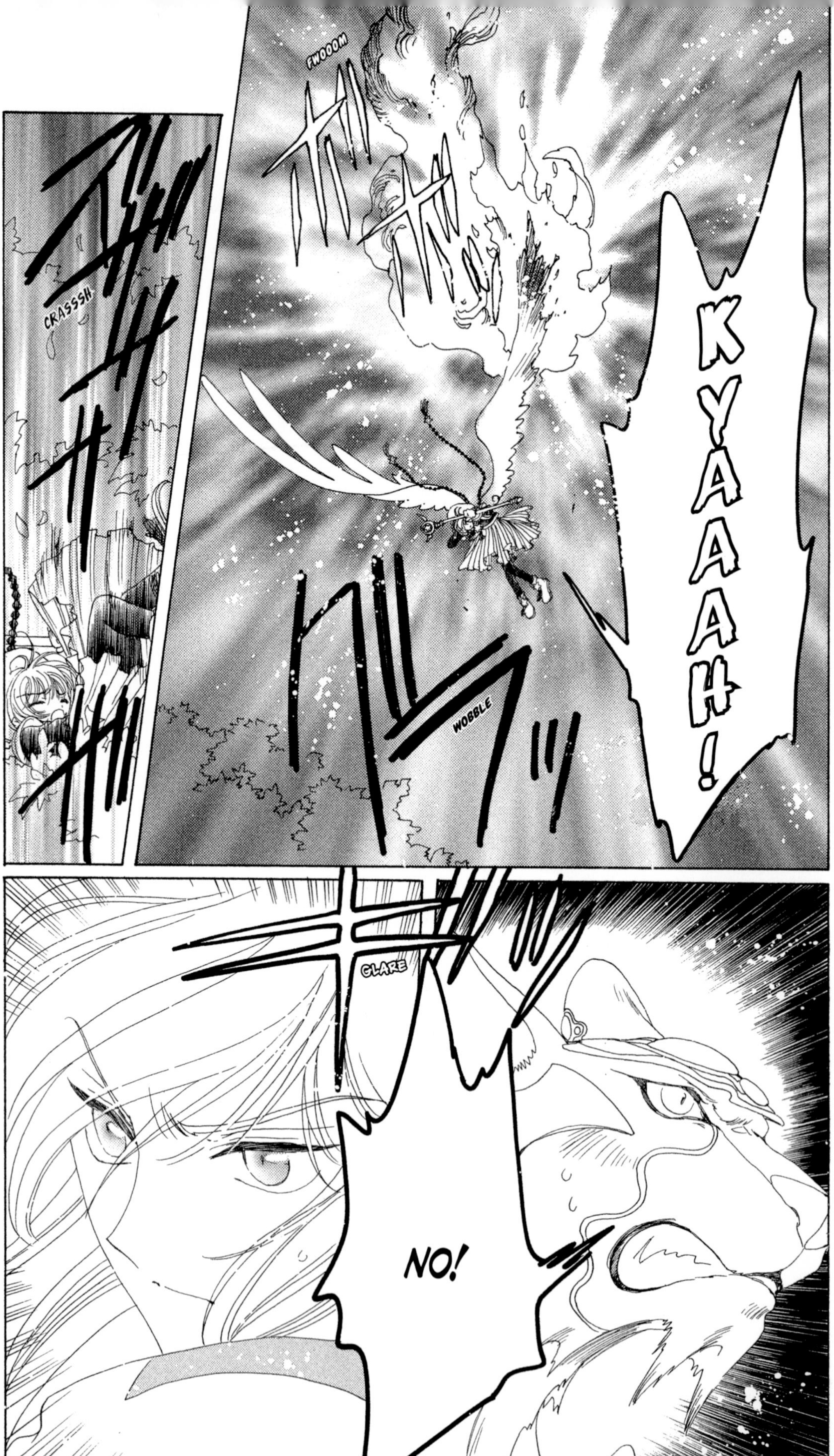
FWOOOM
KYAAAH!
WOBBLE
CRASSSH
GLARE
NO!

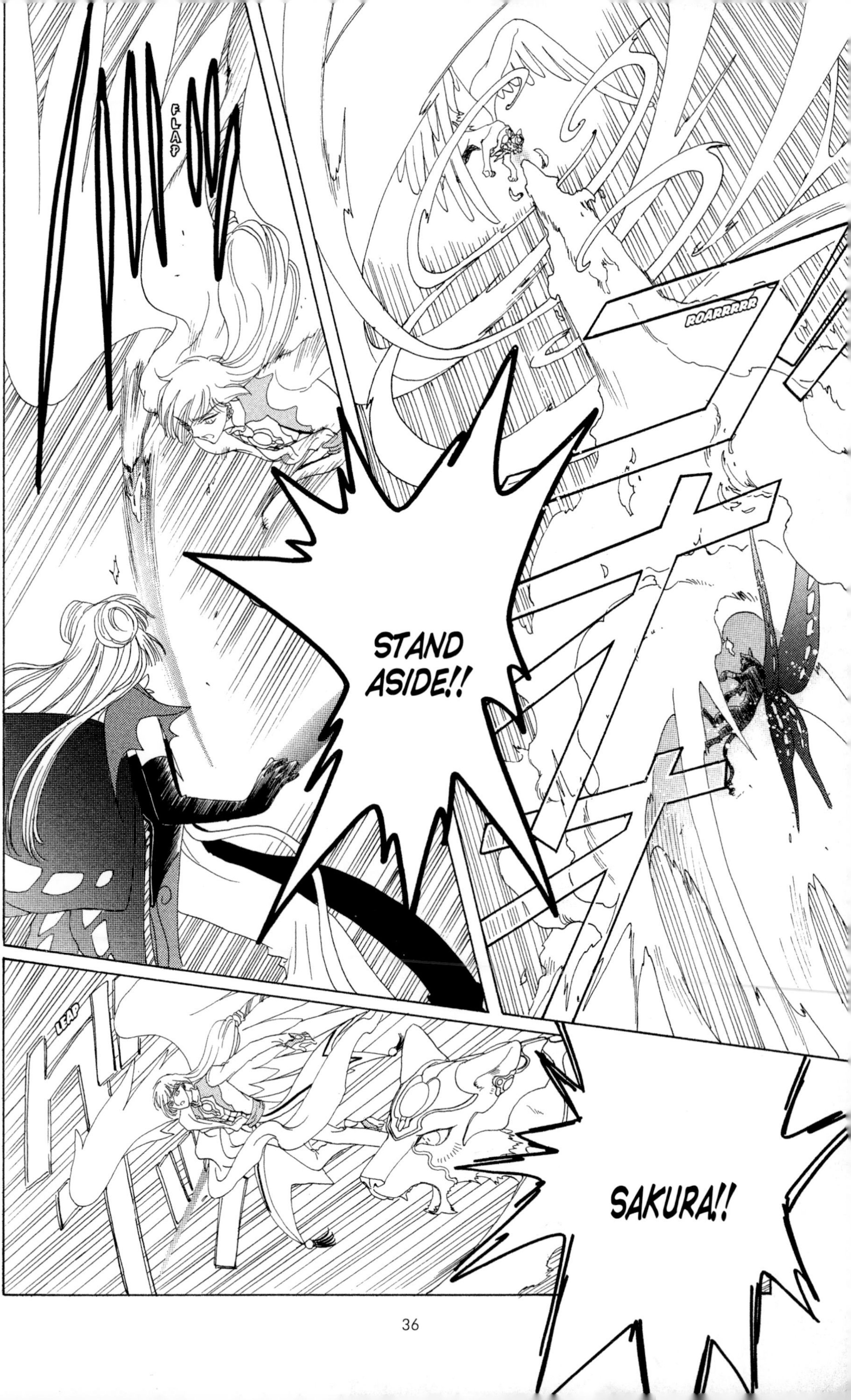
ROARRRRR
FLAP
STAND ASIDE!!
SAKURA!!
LEAP

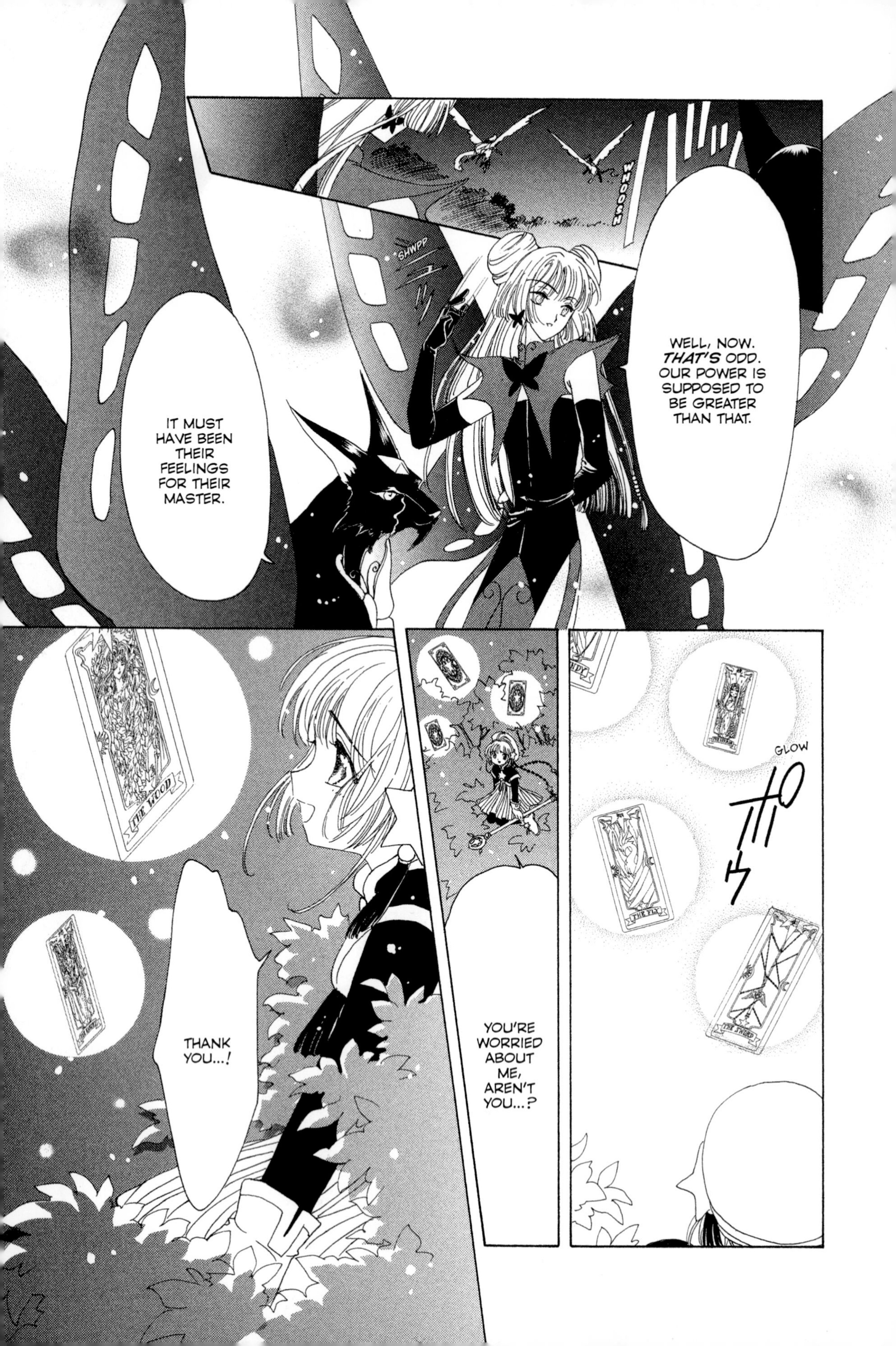
WHOOSH
SHWPP
WELL, NOW. ***THAT'S*** ODD. OUR POWER IS SUPPOSED TO BE GREATER THAN THAT.
IT MUST HAVE BEEN THEIR FEELINGS FOR THEIR MASTER.
GLOW
YOU'RE WORRIED ABOUT ME, AREN'T YOU...?
THANK YOU...!

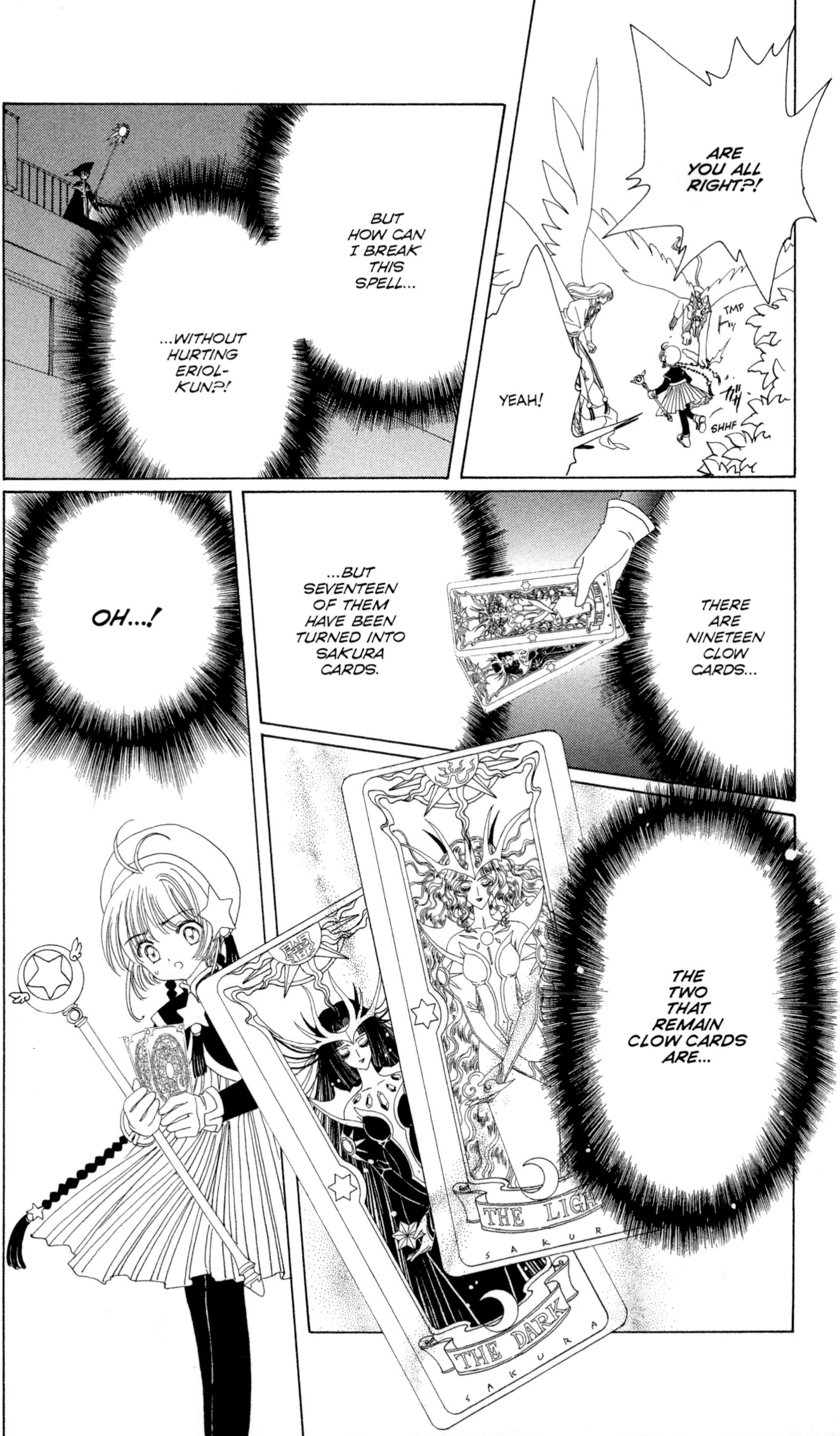
ARE YOU ALL RIGHT?!
TMP
SHHF
YEAH!
BUT HOW CAN I BREAK THIS SPELL...
...WITHOUT HURTING ERIOL-KUN?!
THERE ARE NINETEEN CLOW CARDS...
...BUT SEVENTEEN OF THEM HAVE BEEN TURNED INTO SAKURA CARDS.
THE TWO THAT REMAIN CLOW CARDS ARE...
THE DARK
SAKURA
OH...!

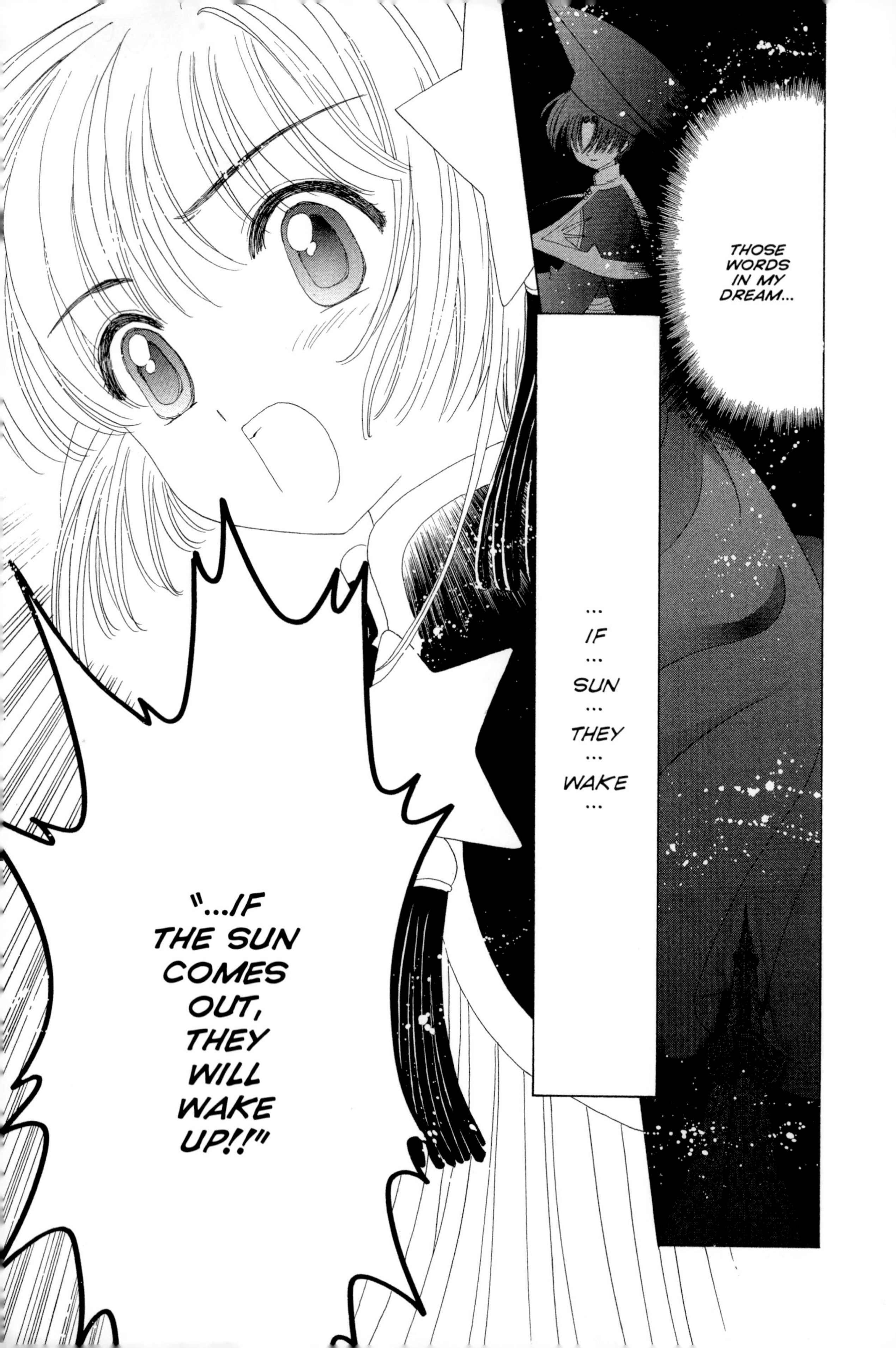
THOSE WORDS IN MY DREAM...
... IF ... SUN ... THEY ... WAKE ...
"...IF THE SUN COMES OUT, THEY WILL WAKE UP!!"

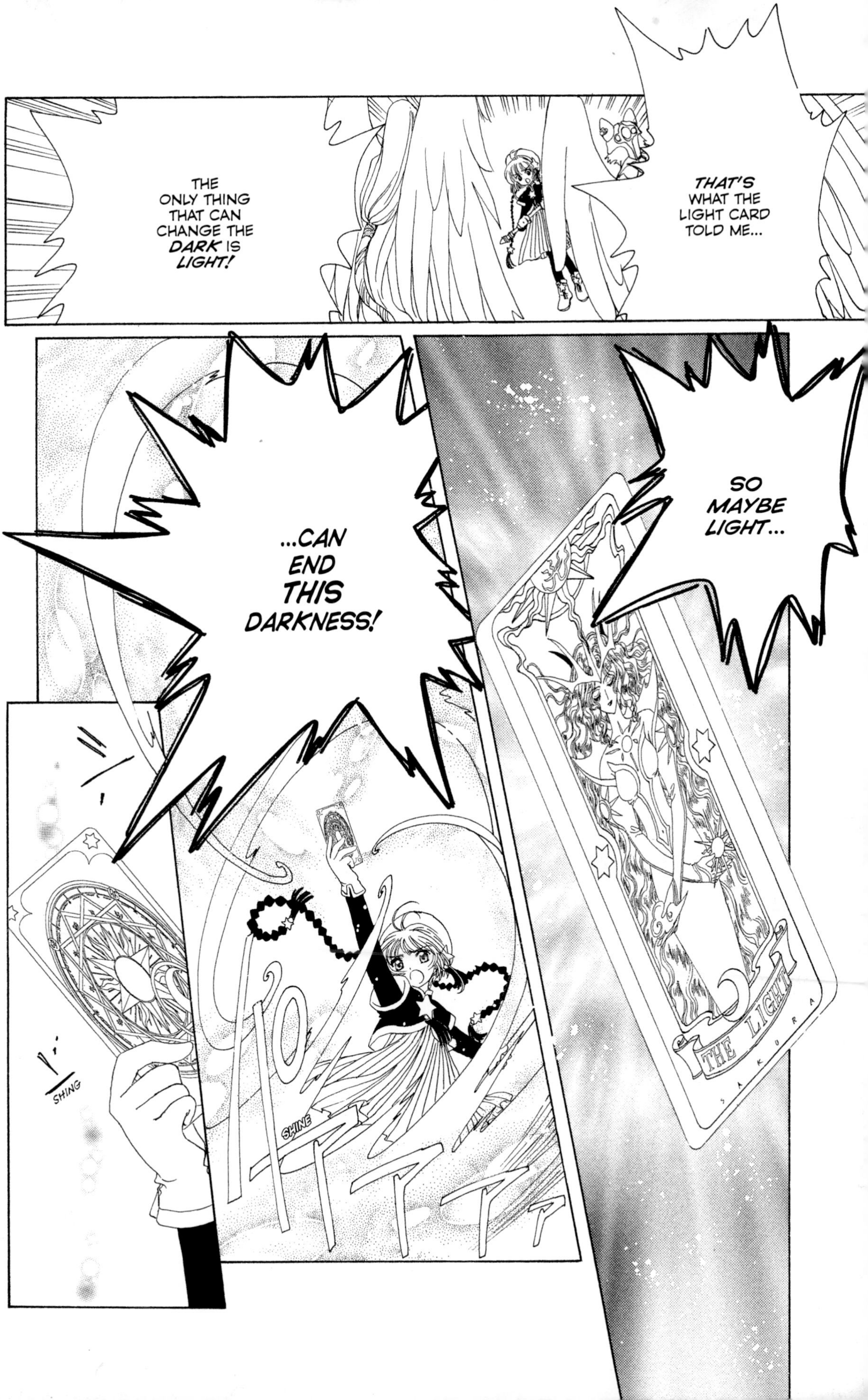
THAT'S WHAT THE LIGHT CARD TOLD ME...
THE ONLY THING THAT CAN CHANGE THE DARK IS LIGHT!
SO MAYBE LIGHT...
...CAN END THIS DARKNESS!
THE LIGHT
SAKURA
SHINE
SHING

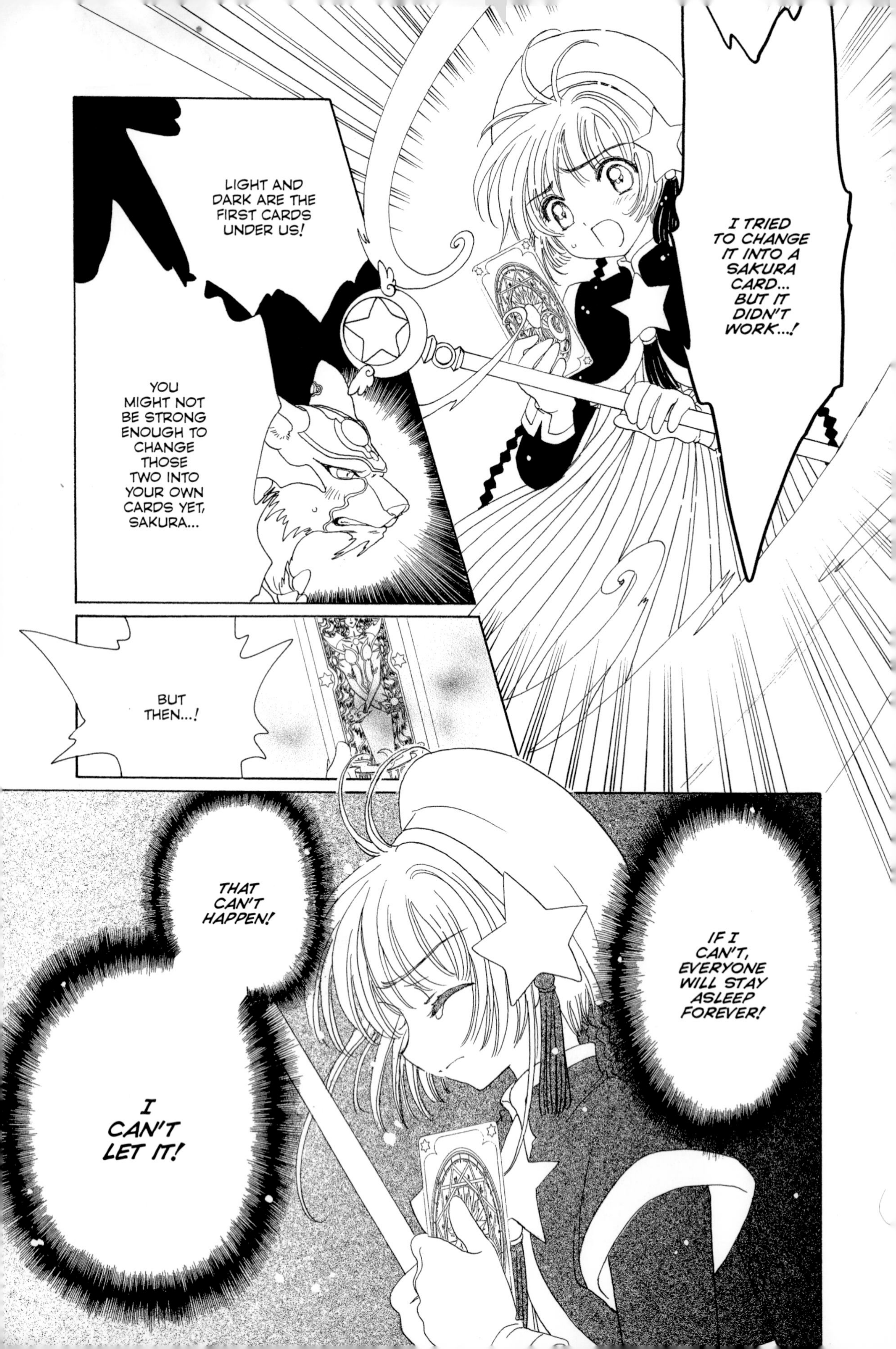
I TRIED TO CHANGE IT INTO A SAKURA CARD... BUT IT DIDN'T WORK...!
LIGHT AND DARK ARE THE FIRST CARDS UNDER US!
YOU MIGHT NOT BE STRONG ENOUGH TO CHANGE THOSE TWO INTO YOUR OWN CARDS YET, SAKURA...
BUT THEN...!
IF I CAN'T, EVERYONE WILL STAY ASLEEP FOREVER!
THAT CAN'T HAPPEN!
I CAN'T LET IT!

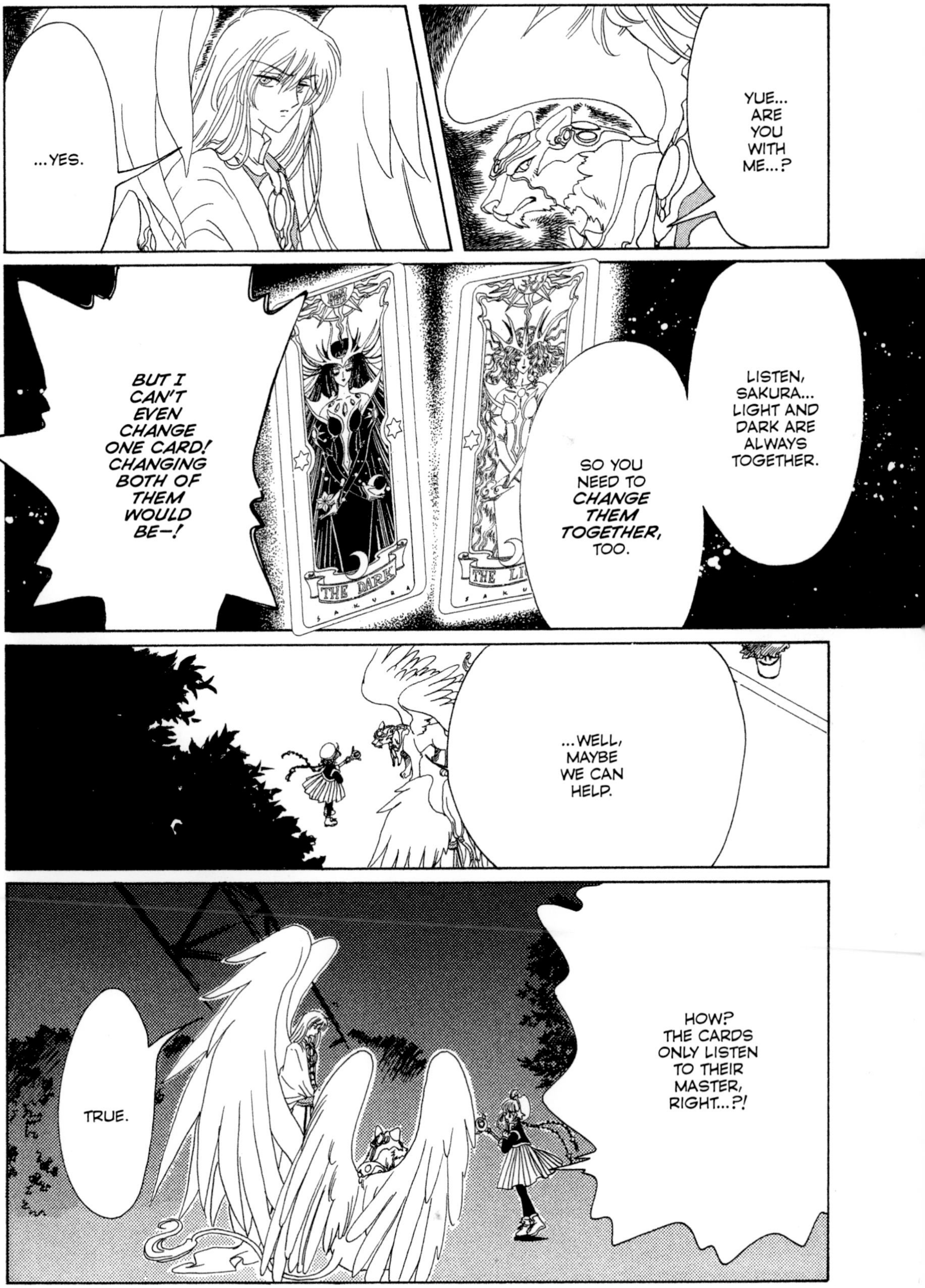
YUE... ARE YOU WITH ME...?
...YES.
LISTEN, SAKURA... LIGHT AND DARK ARE ALWAYS TOGETHER.
SO YOU NEED TO *CHANGE THEM TOGETHER,* TOO.
BUT I CAN'T EVEN CHANGE ONE CARD! CHANGING BOTH OF THEM WOULD BE—!
THE DARK
...WELL, MAYBE WE CAN HELP.
HOW? THE CARDS ONLY LISTEN TO THEIR MASTER, RIGHT...?!
TRUE.

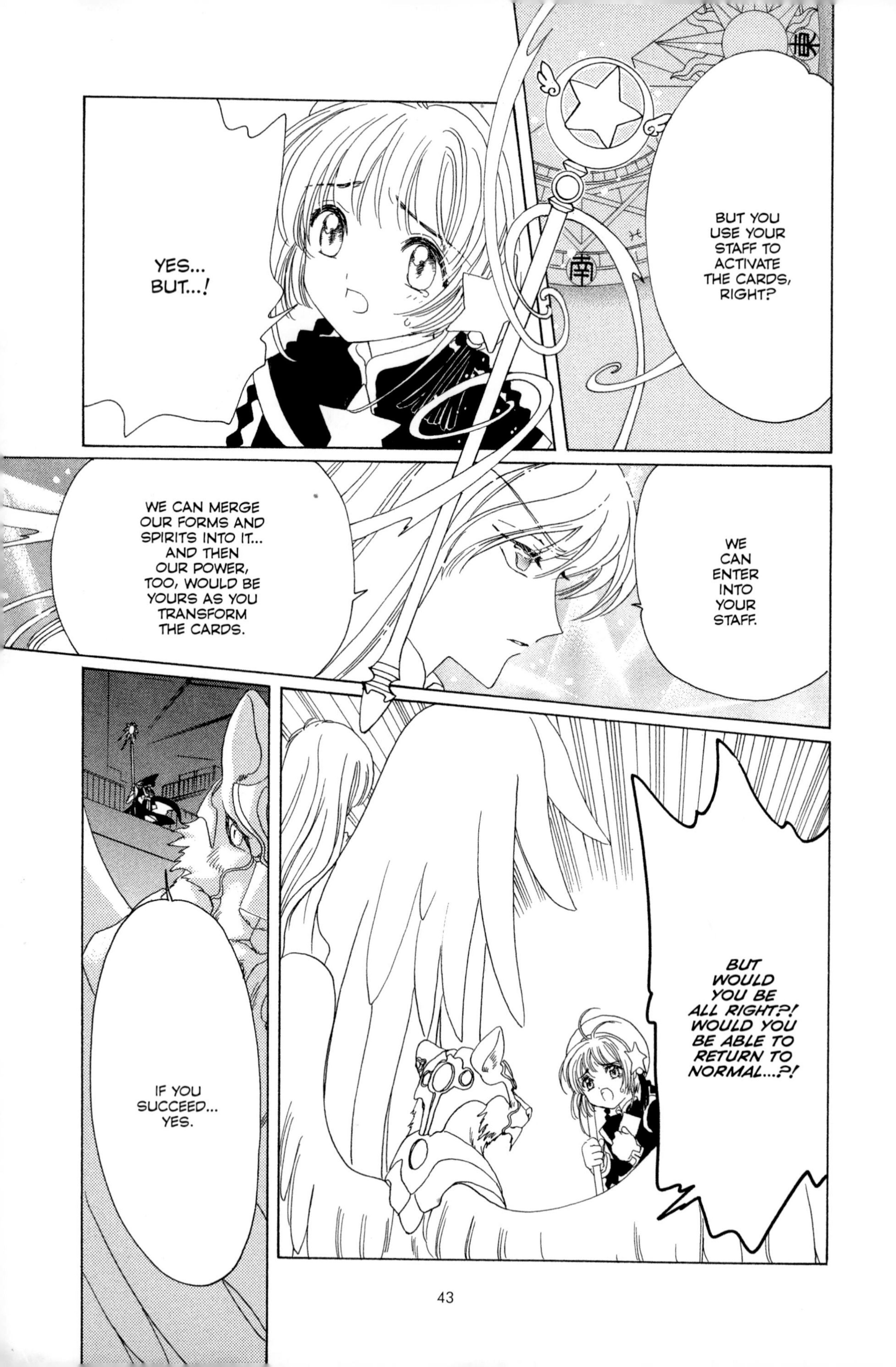
BUT YOU USE YOUR STAFF TO ACTIVATE THE CARDS, RIGHT?
YES... BUT...!
WE CAN ENTER INTO YOUR STAFF.
WE CAN MERGE OUR FORMS AND SPIRITS INTO IT... AND THEN OUR POWER, TOO, WOULD BE YOURS AS YOU TRANSFORM THE CARDS.
BUT WOULD YOU BE ALL RIGHT?! WOULD YOU BE ABLE TO RETURN TO NORMAL...?!
IF YOU SUCCEED... YES.

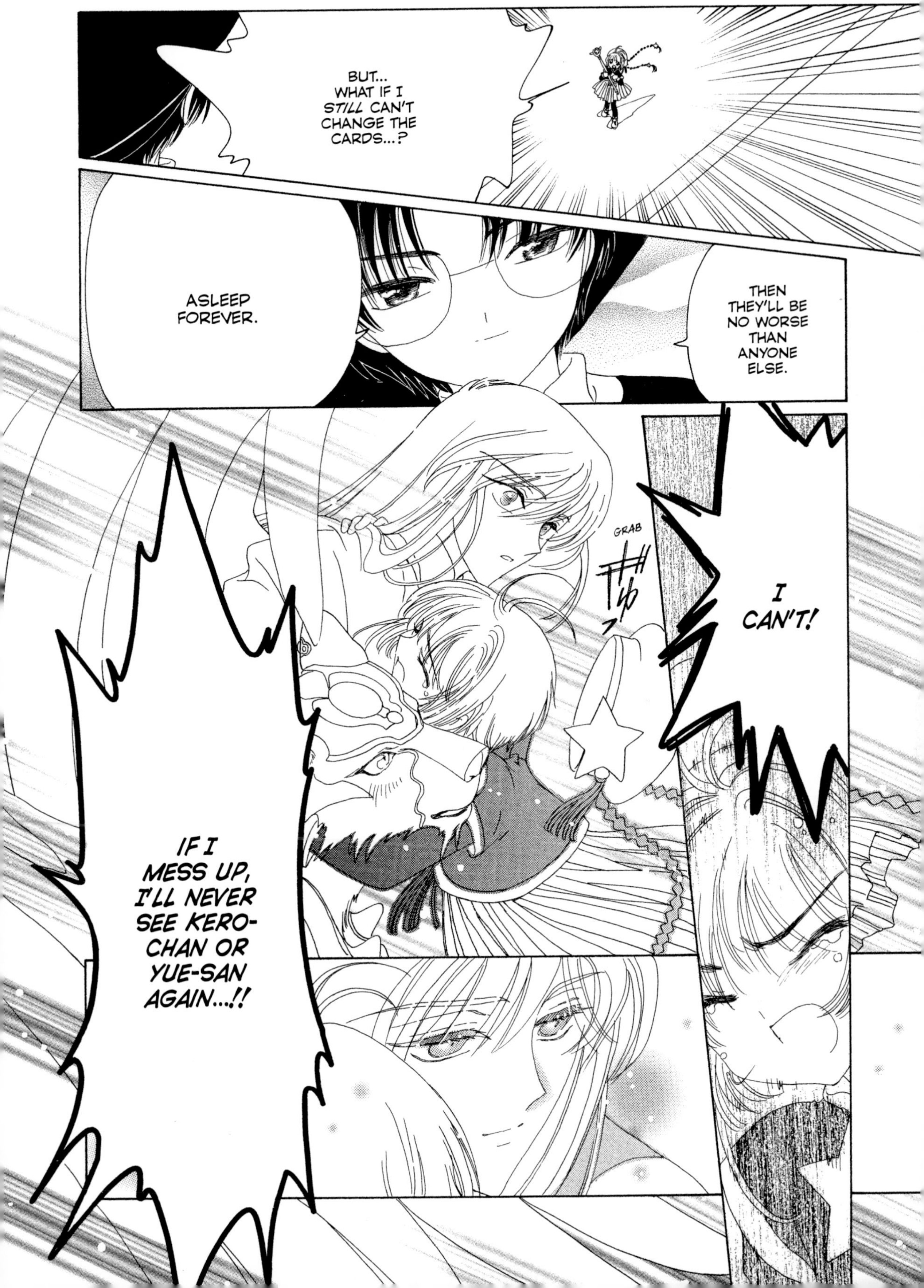
BUT... WHAT IF I STILL CAN'T CHANGE THE CARDS...?
THEN THEY'LL BE NO WORSE THAN ANYONE ELSE.
ASLEEP FOREVER.
I CAN'T!
GRAB
IF I MESS UP, I'LL NEVER SEE KERO-CHAN OR YUE-SAN AGAIN...!!

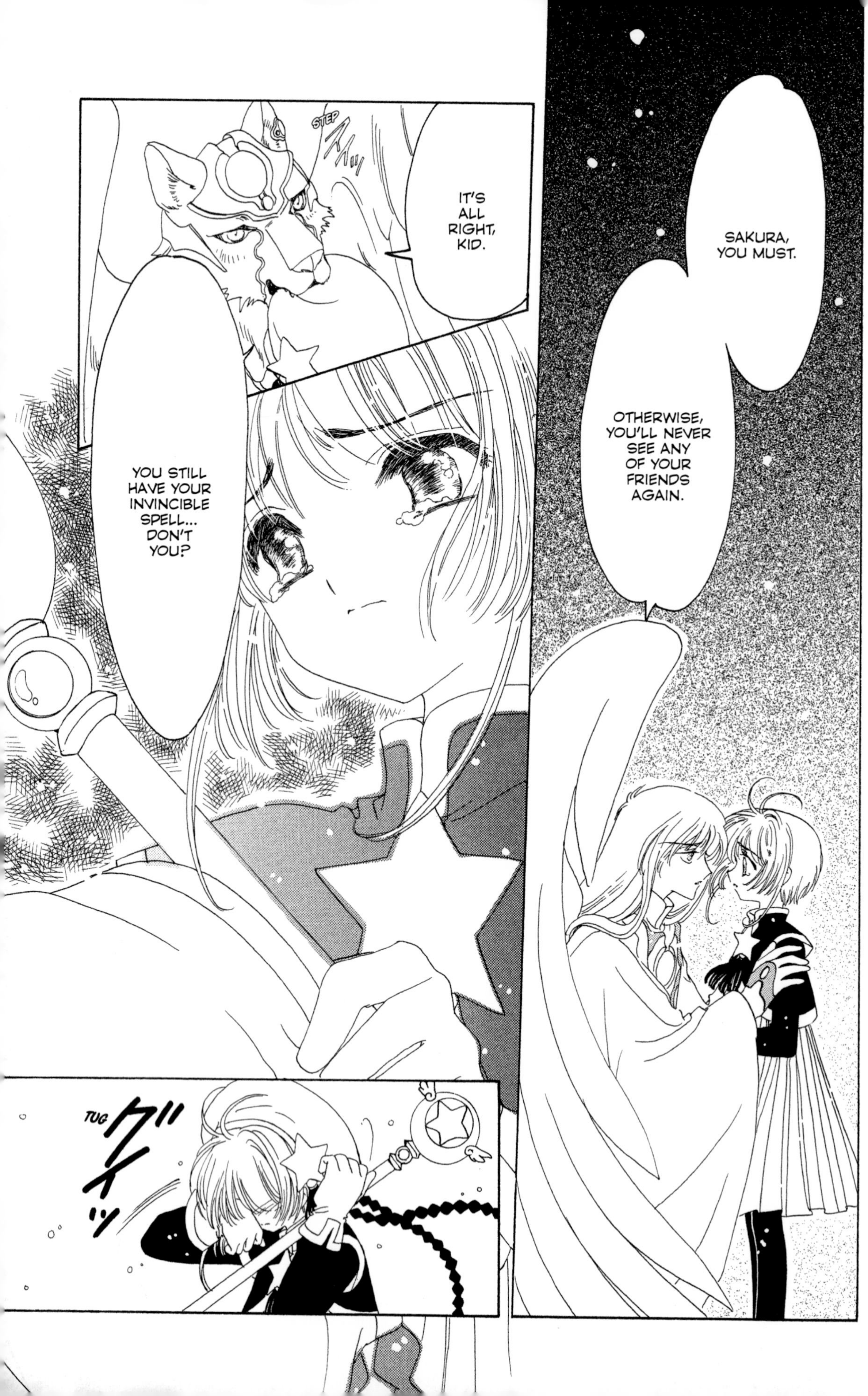
SAKURA, YOU MUST.
OTHERWISE, YOU'LL NEVER SEE ANY OF YOUR FRIENDS AGAIN.
STEP
IT'S ALL RIGHT, KID.
YOU STILL HAVE YOUR INVINCIBLE SPELL... DON'T YOU?
TUG

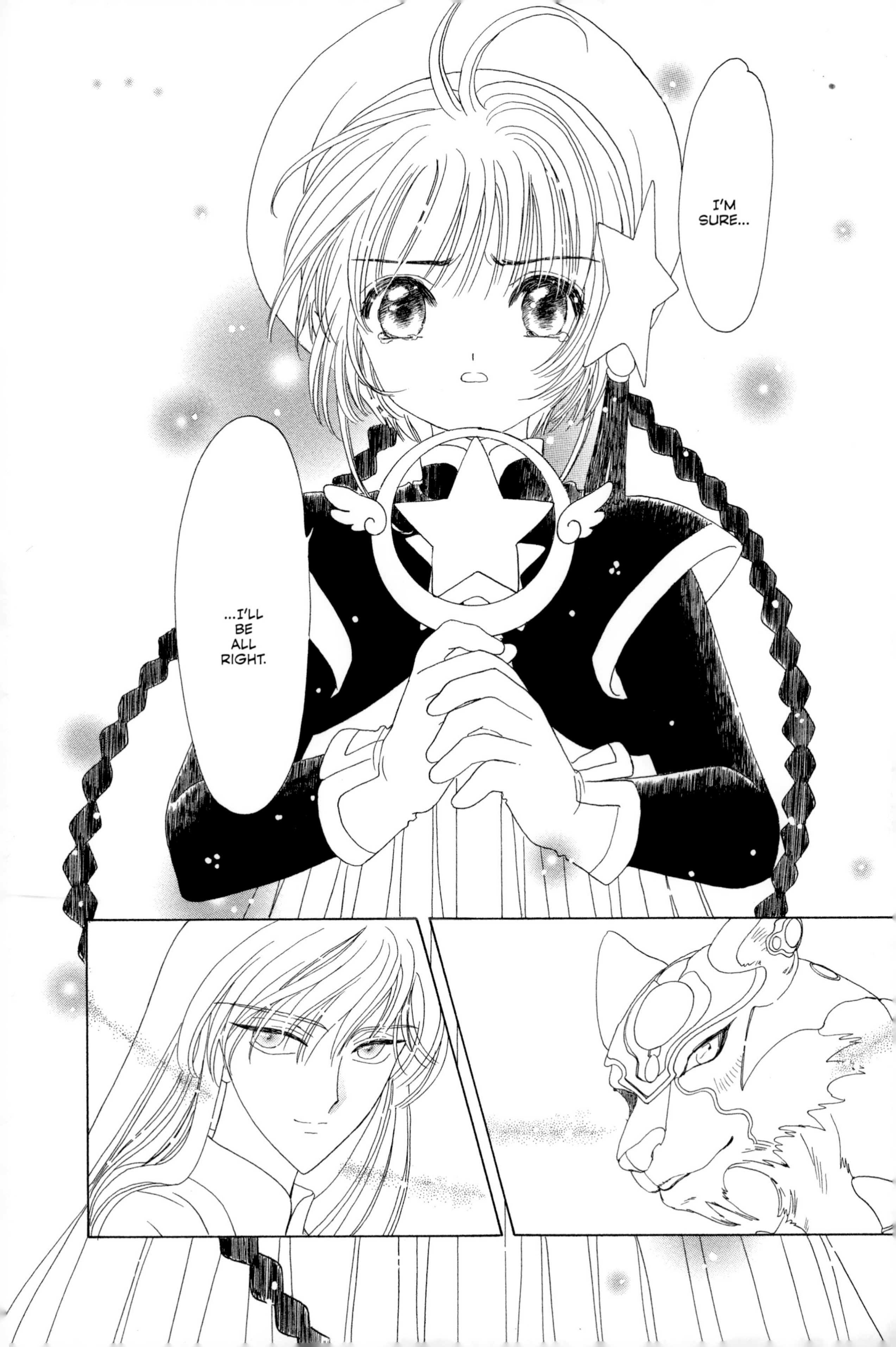
I'M SURE...
...I'LL BE ALL RIGHT.

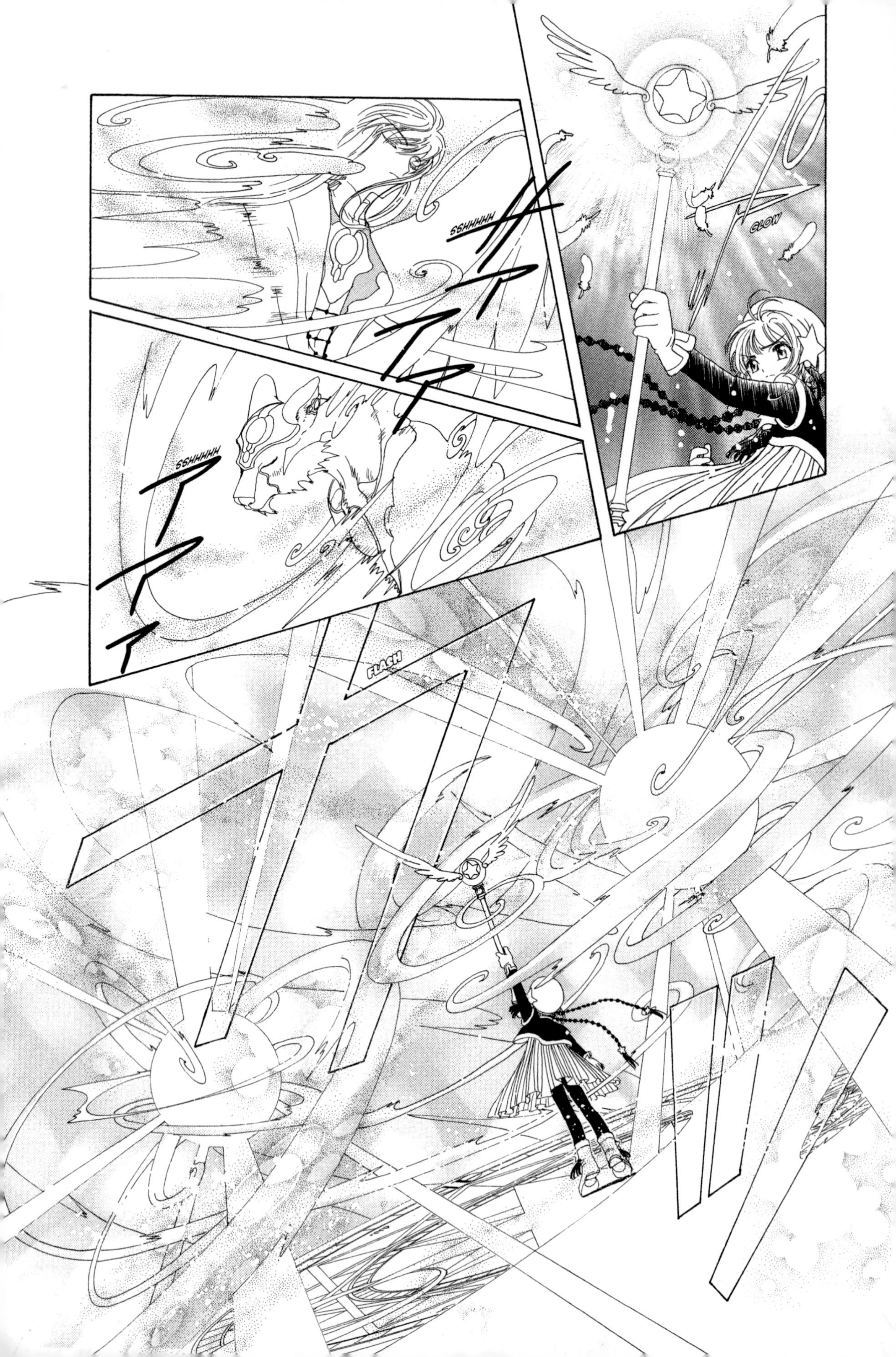
GLOW
SSHHHHH
SSHHHHH
FLASH

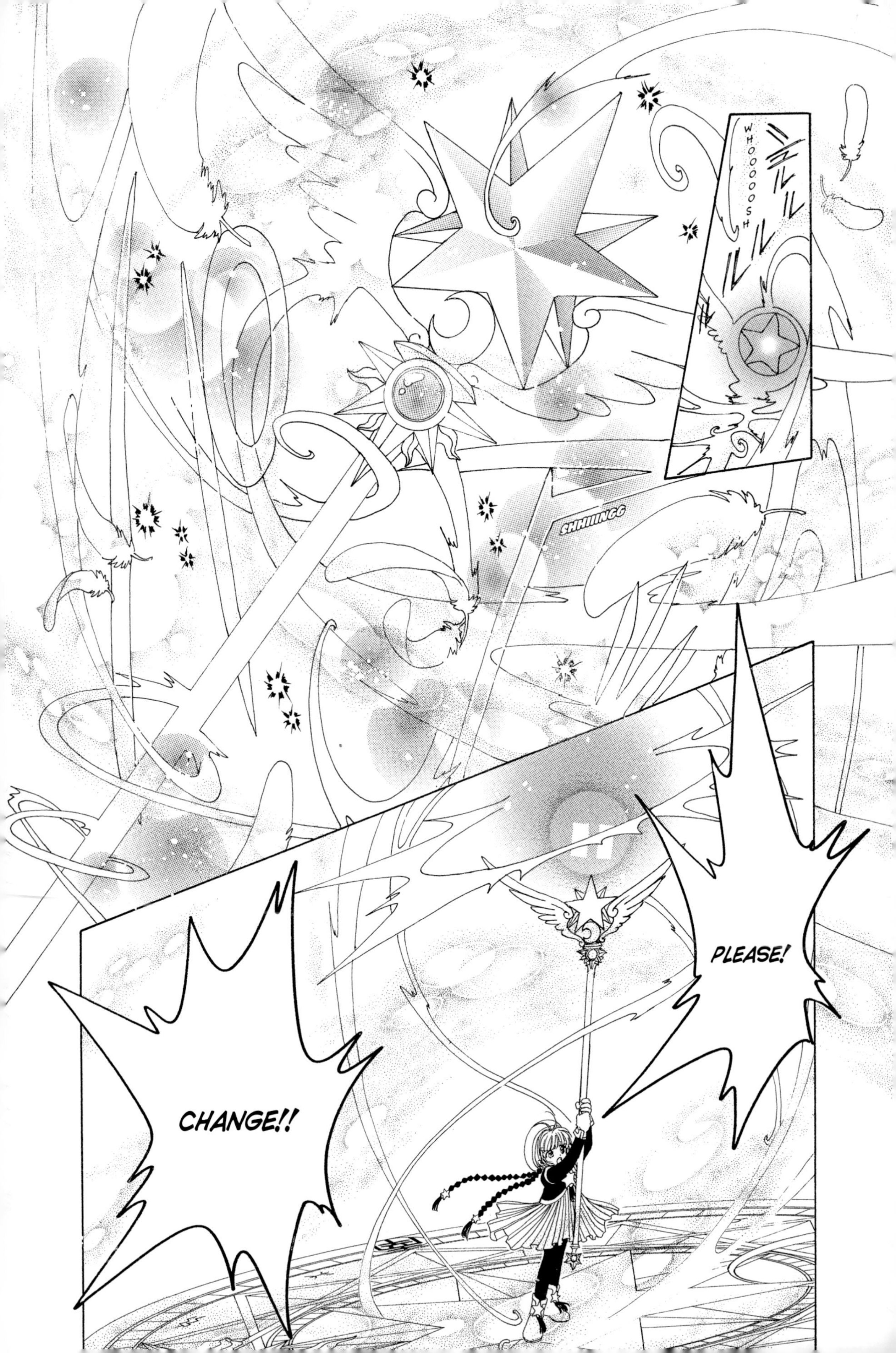
シュルルルル
WHOOOOOOSH
SHHIIINGG
PLEASE!
CHANGE!!

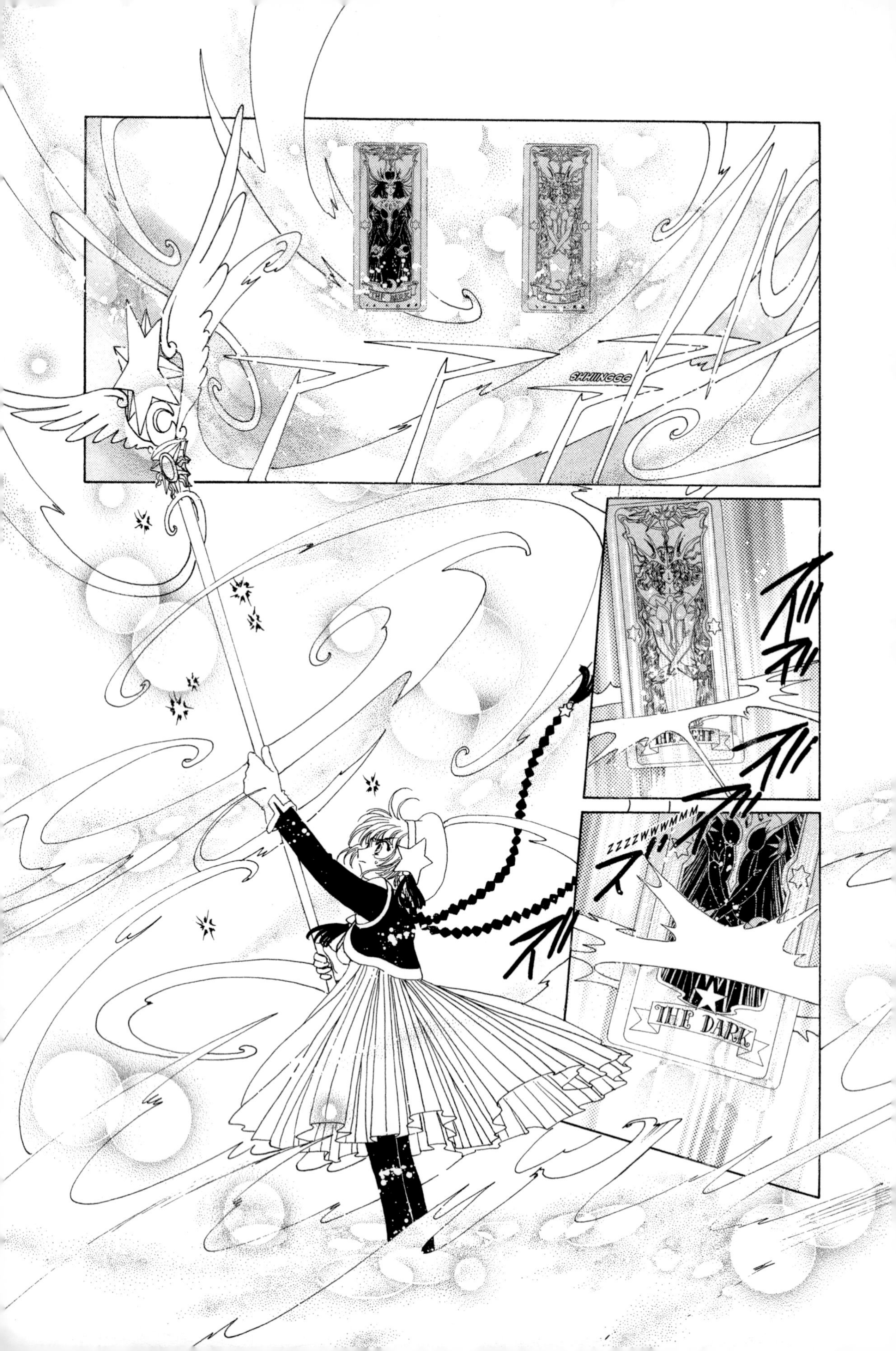
SHHIINGGG
ZZZZWWWMMMM
THE DARK

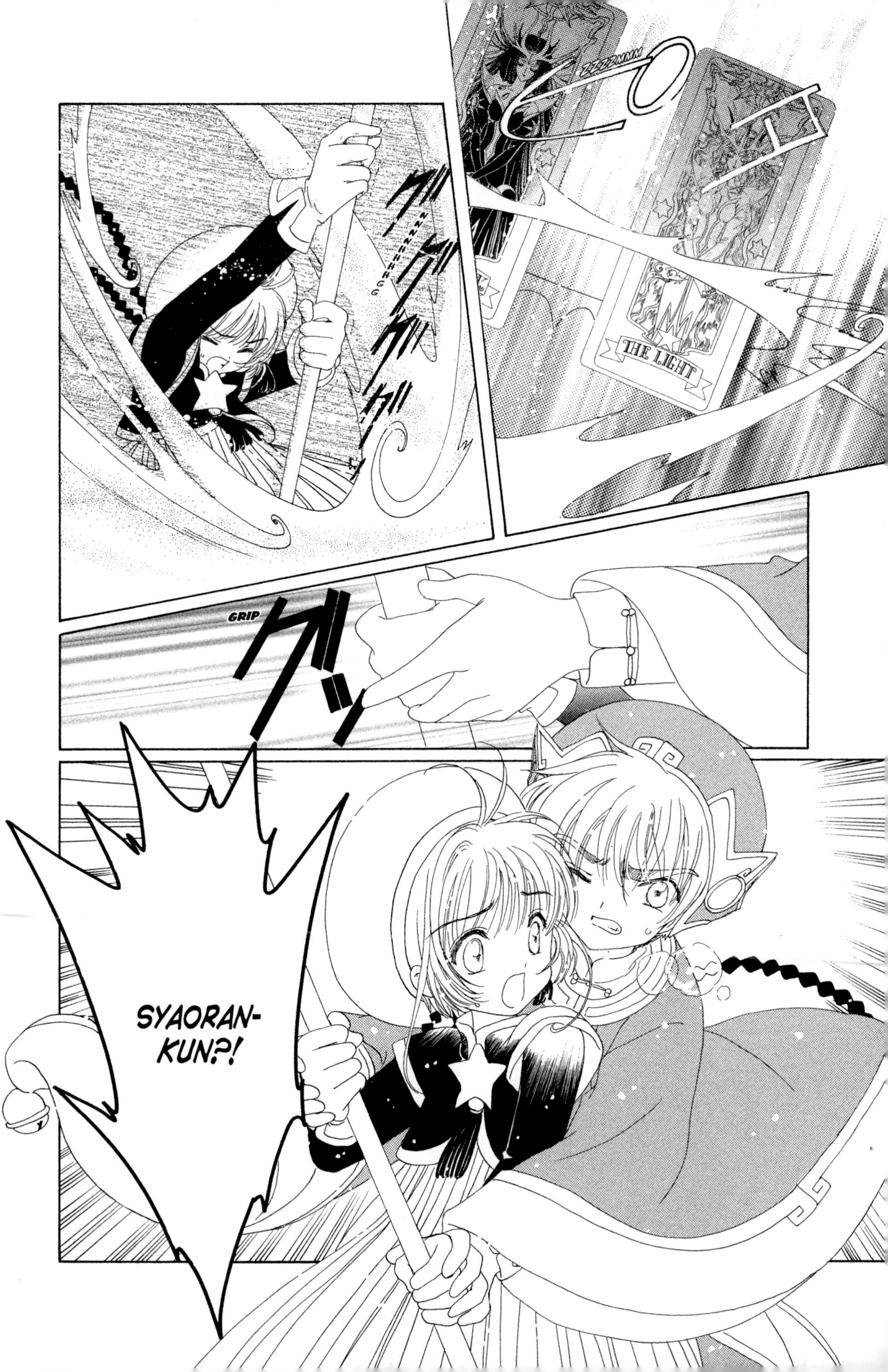
ZZZZZMMM
THE LIGHT
NNNNNHHHHHGG
GRIP
SYAORAN-KUN?!

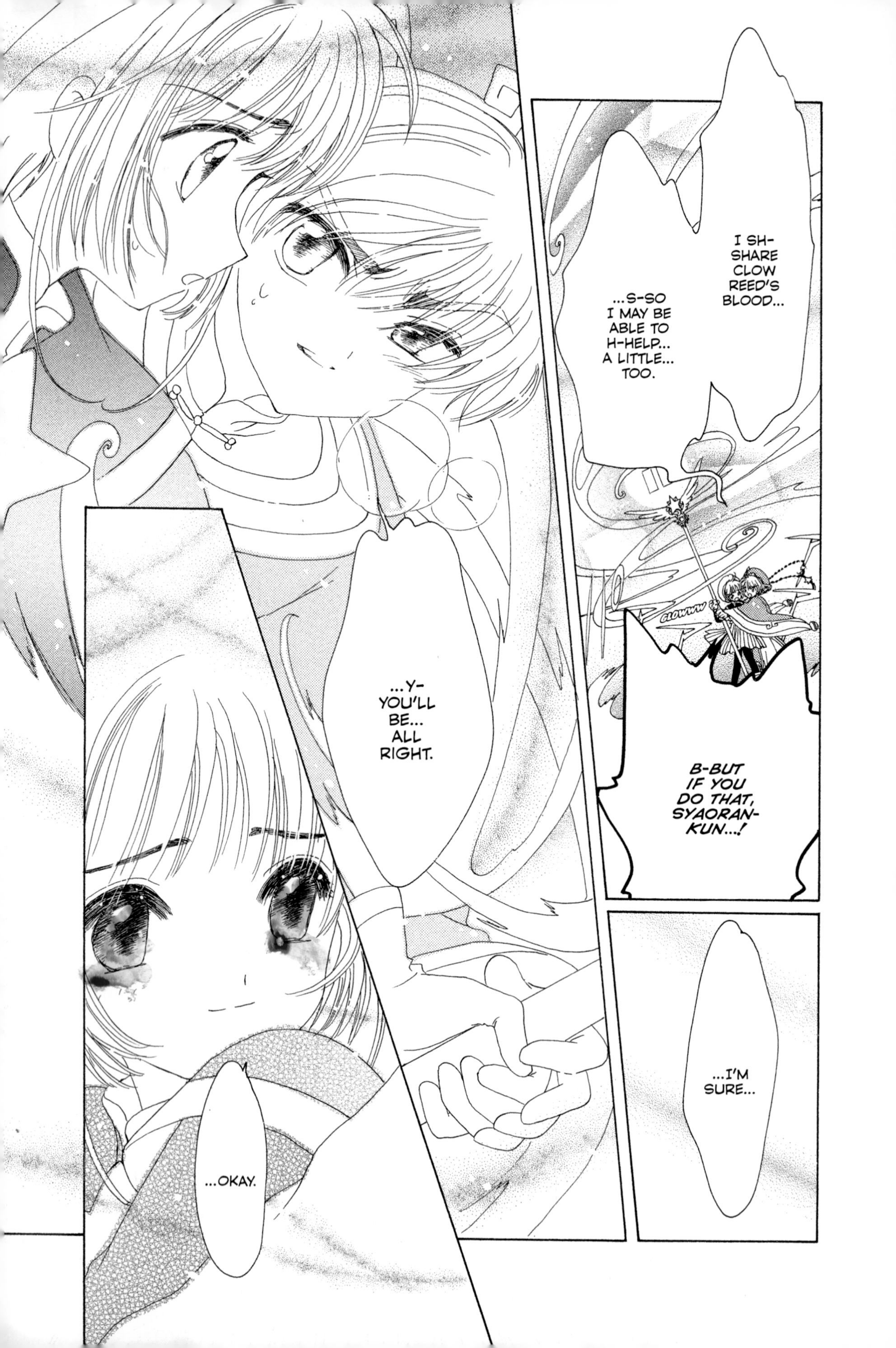
I SH-SHARE CLOW REED'S BLOOD...
...S-SO I MAY BE ABLE TO H-HELP... A LITTLE... TOO.
CLOWWW
B-BUT IF YOU DO THAT, SYAORAN-KUN...!
...I'M SURE...
...Y-YOU'LL BE... ALL RIGHT.
...OKAY.

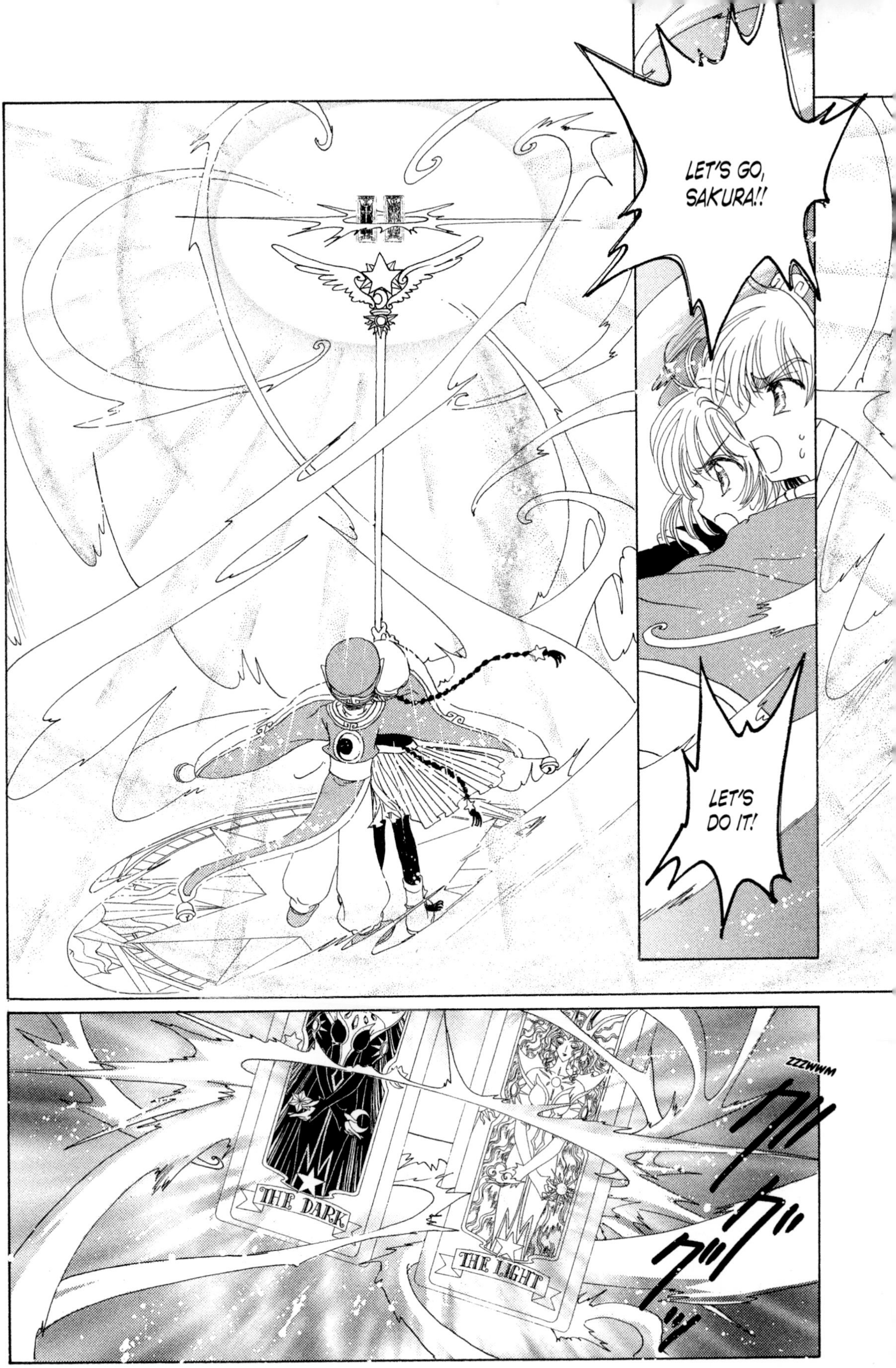
LET'S GO, SAKURA!!
LET'S DO IT!
ZZZWWM
THE DARK
THE LIGHT

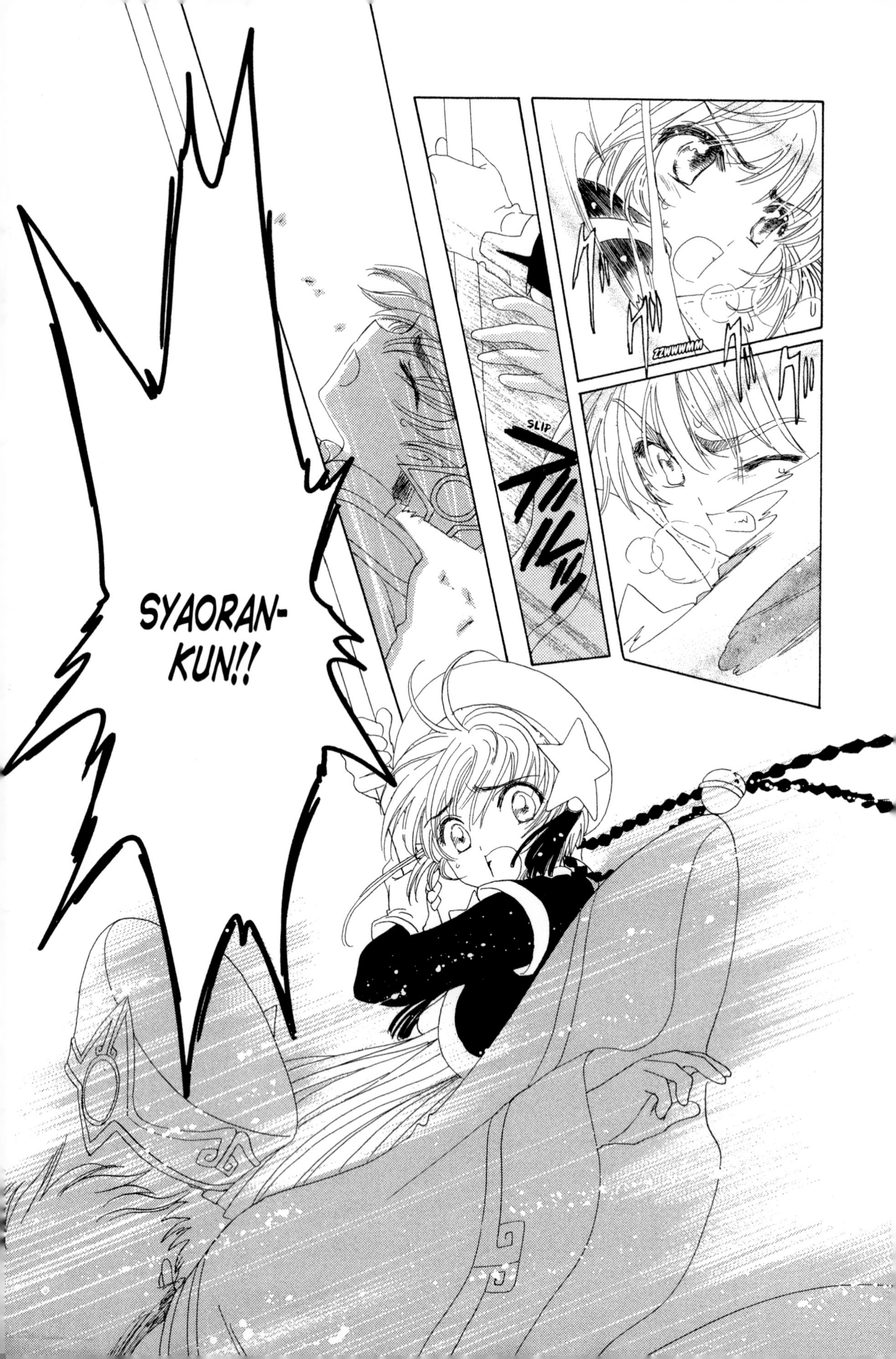
ZZWWWWMM
SLIP
SYAORAN-KUN!!

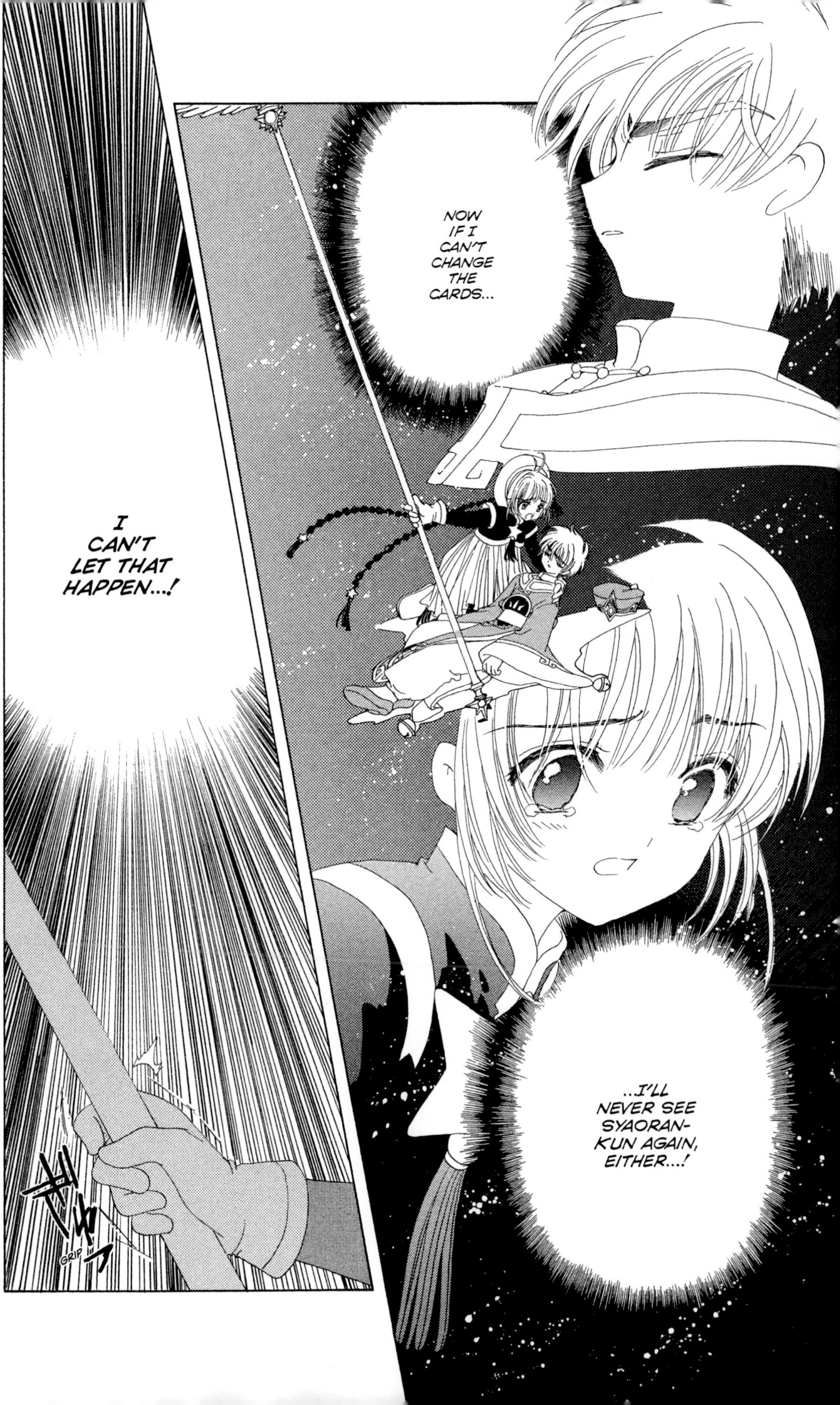
NOW IF I CAN'T CHANGE THE CARDS...
...I'LL NEVER SEE SYAORAN-KUN AGAIN, EITHER...!
I CAN'T LET THAT HAPPEN...!
GRIP

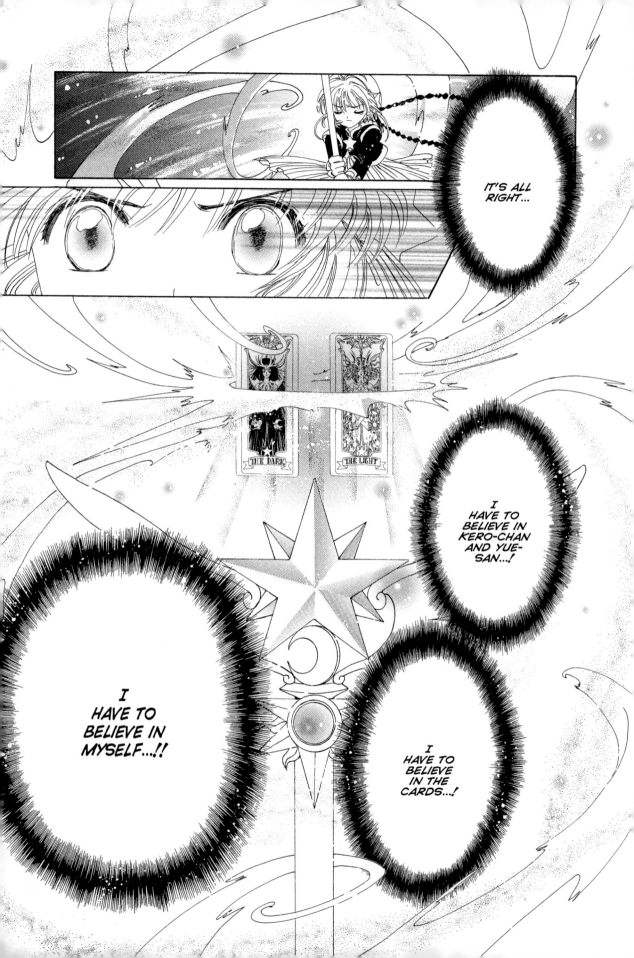

IT'S ALL RIGHT...

I HAVE TO BELIEVE IN KERO-CHAN AND YUE-SAN...!

I HAVE TO BELIEVE IN MYSELF...!!

I HAVE TO BELIEVE IN THE CARDS...!

THE DARK

THE LIGHT

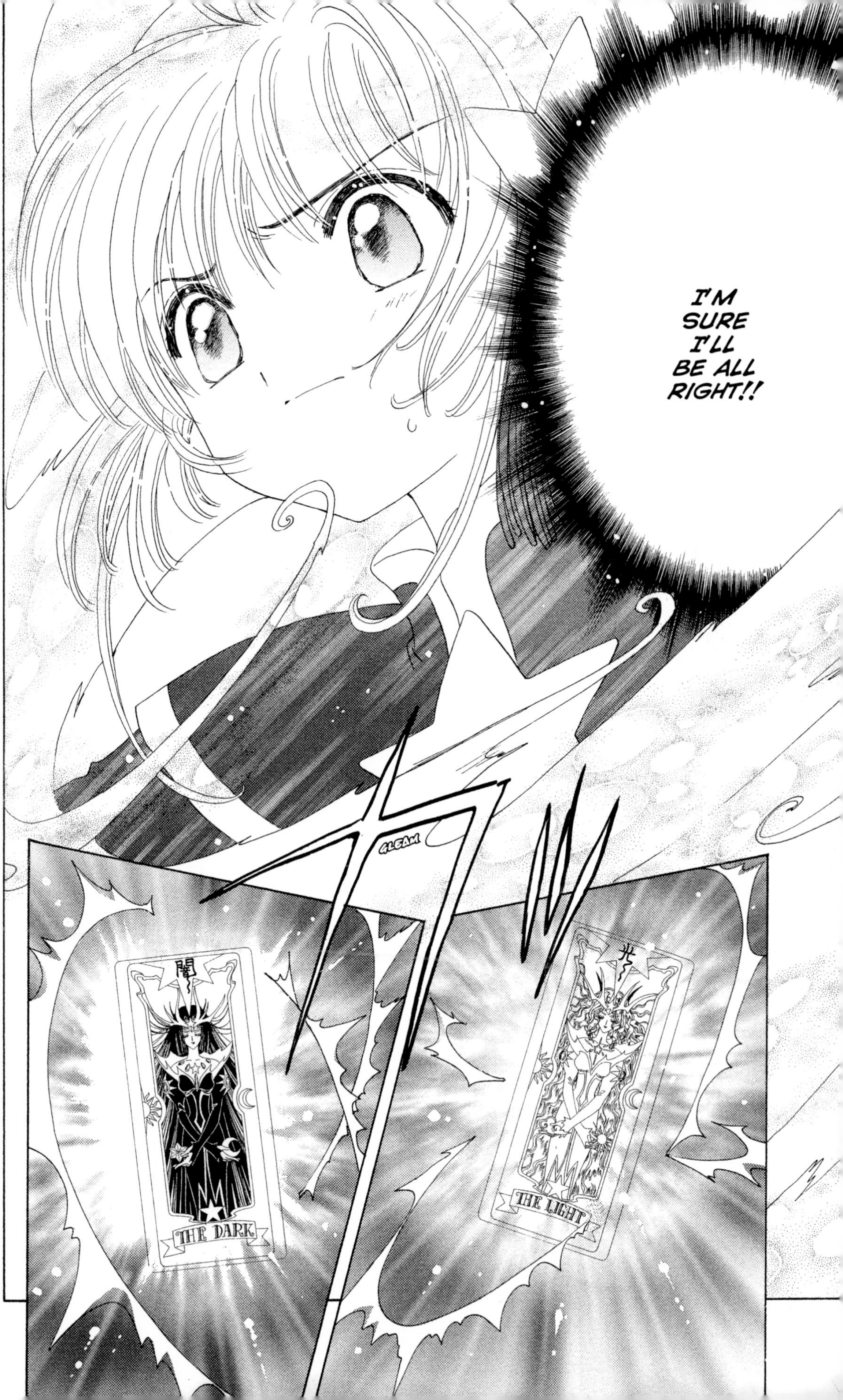
I'M SURE I'LL BE ALL RIGHT!!
GLEAM
闇
THE DARK
光
THE LIGHT

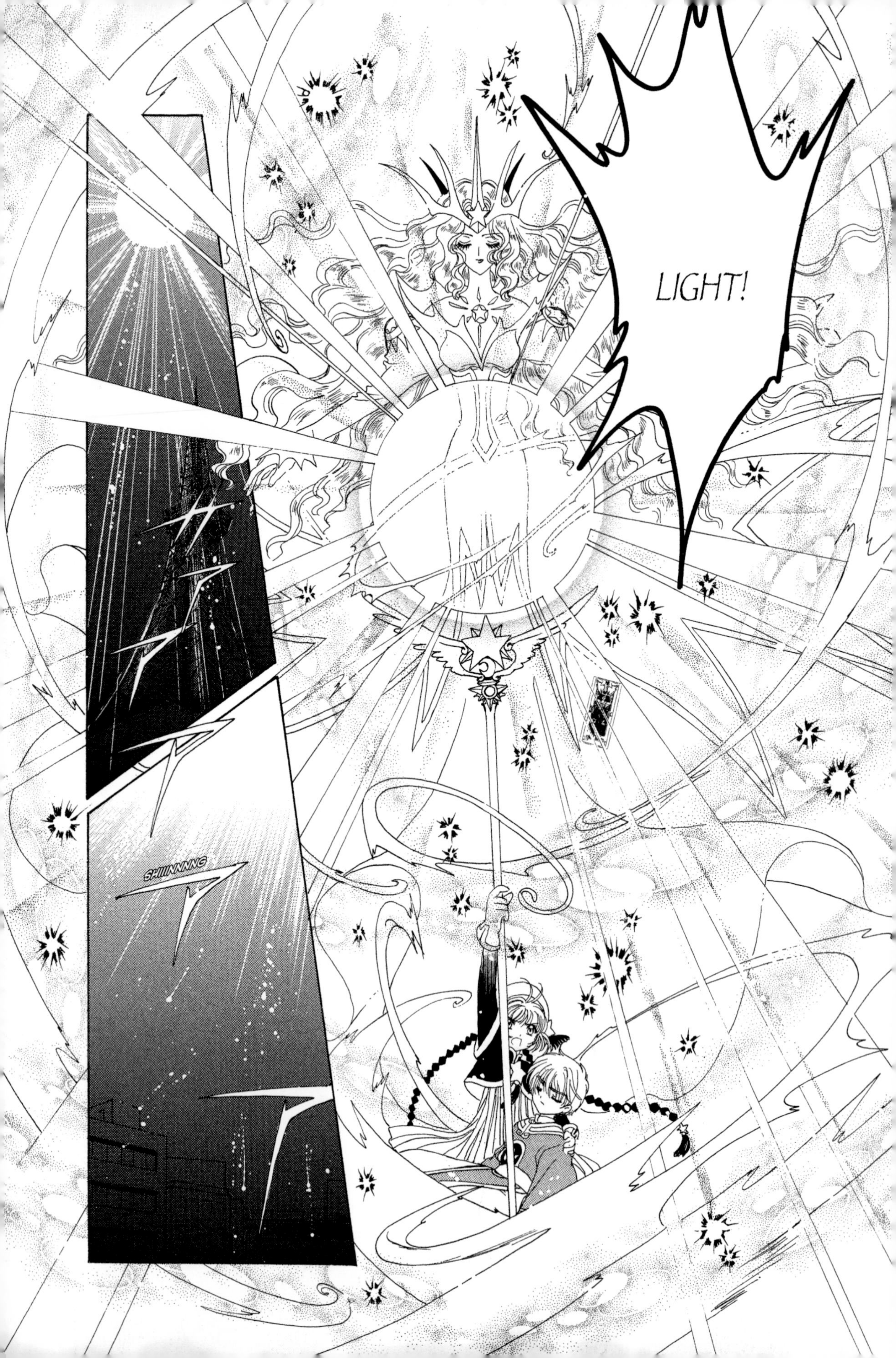
LIGHT!
SHIIINNNNG

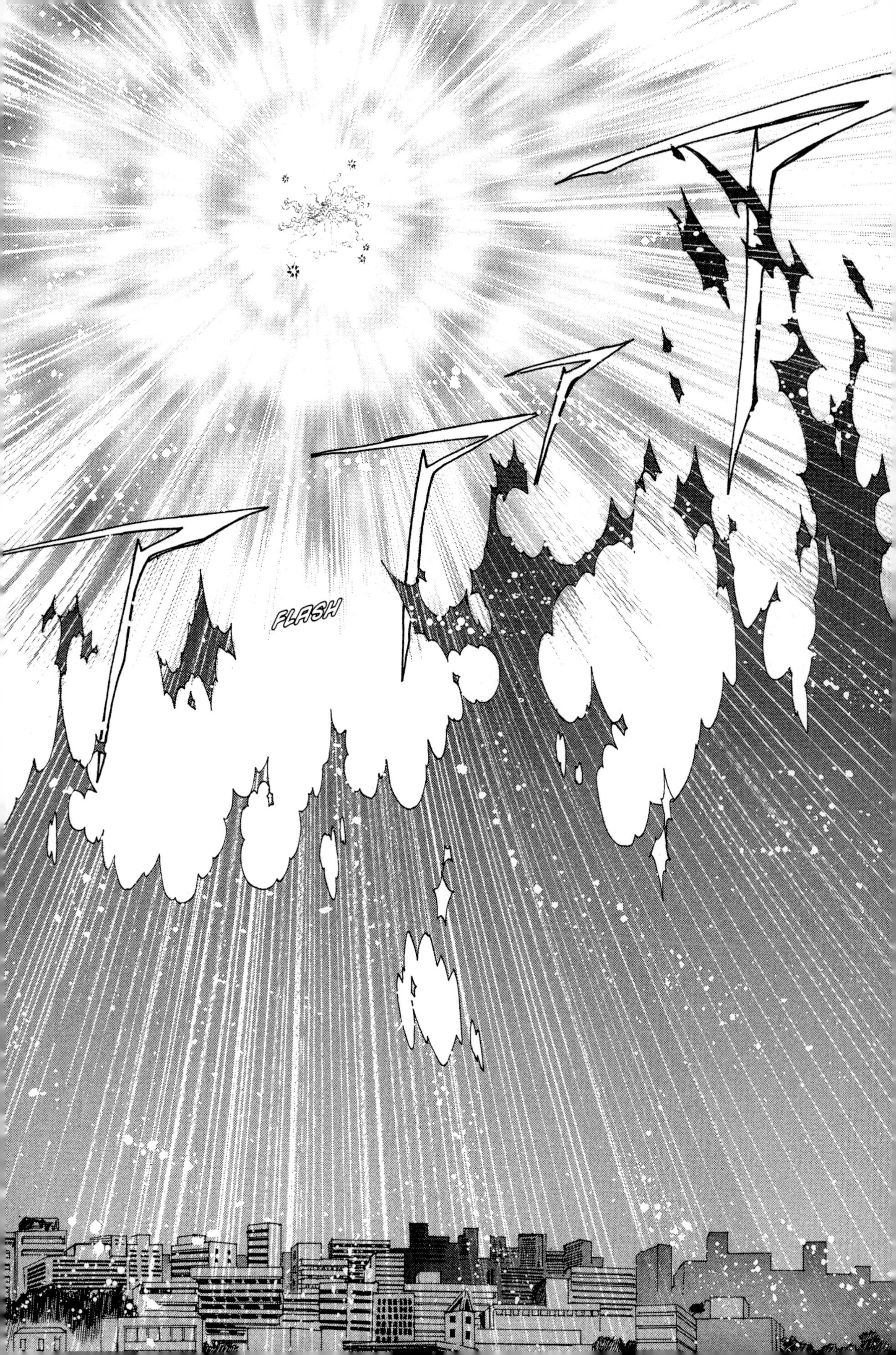
FLASH

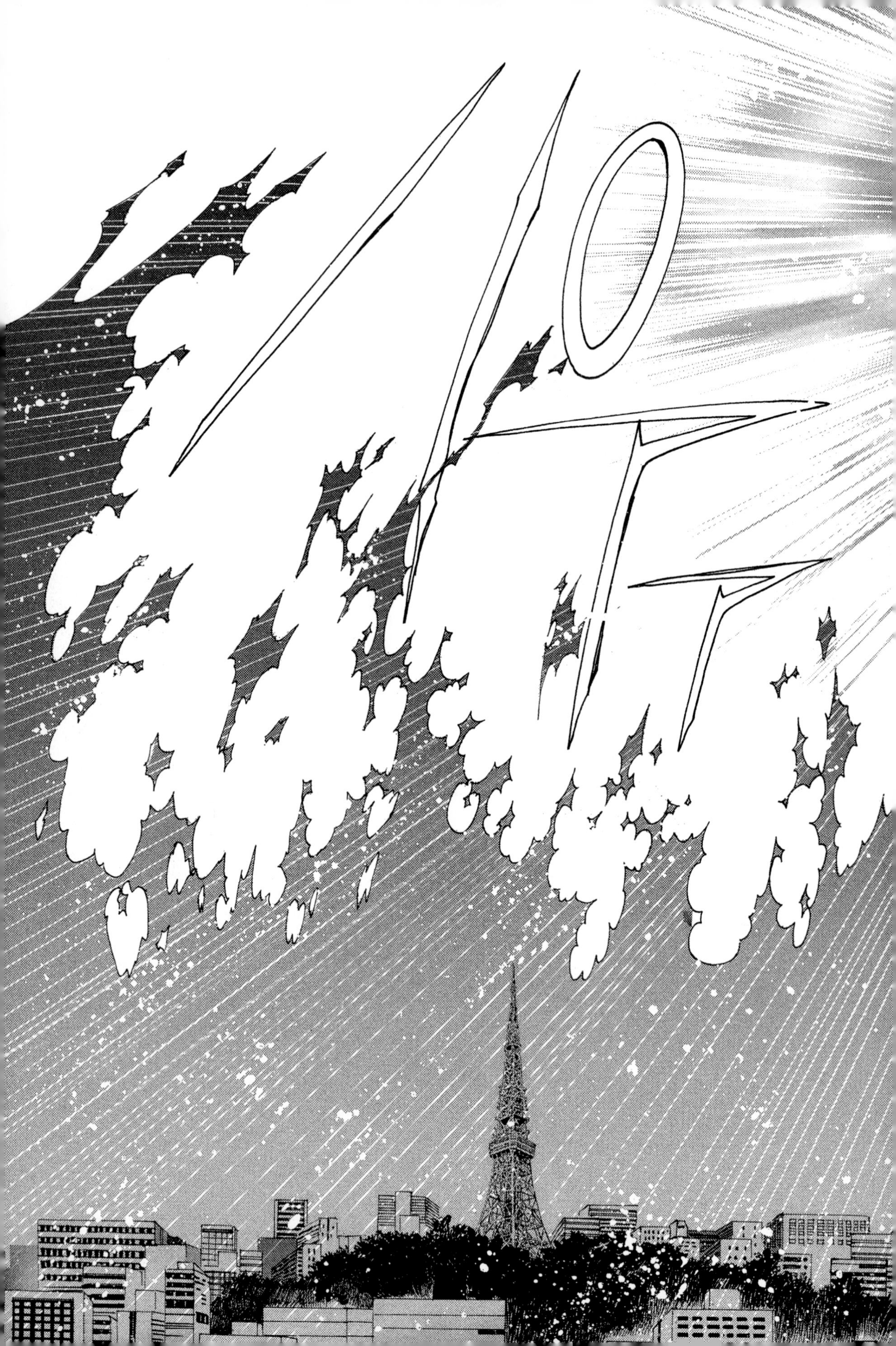

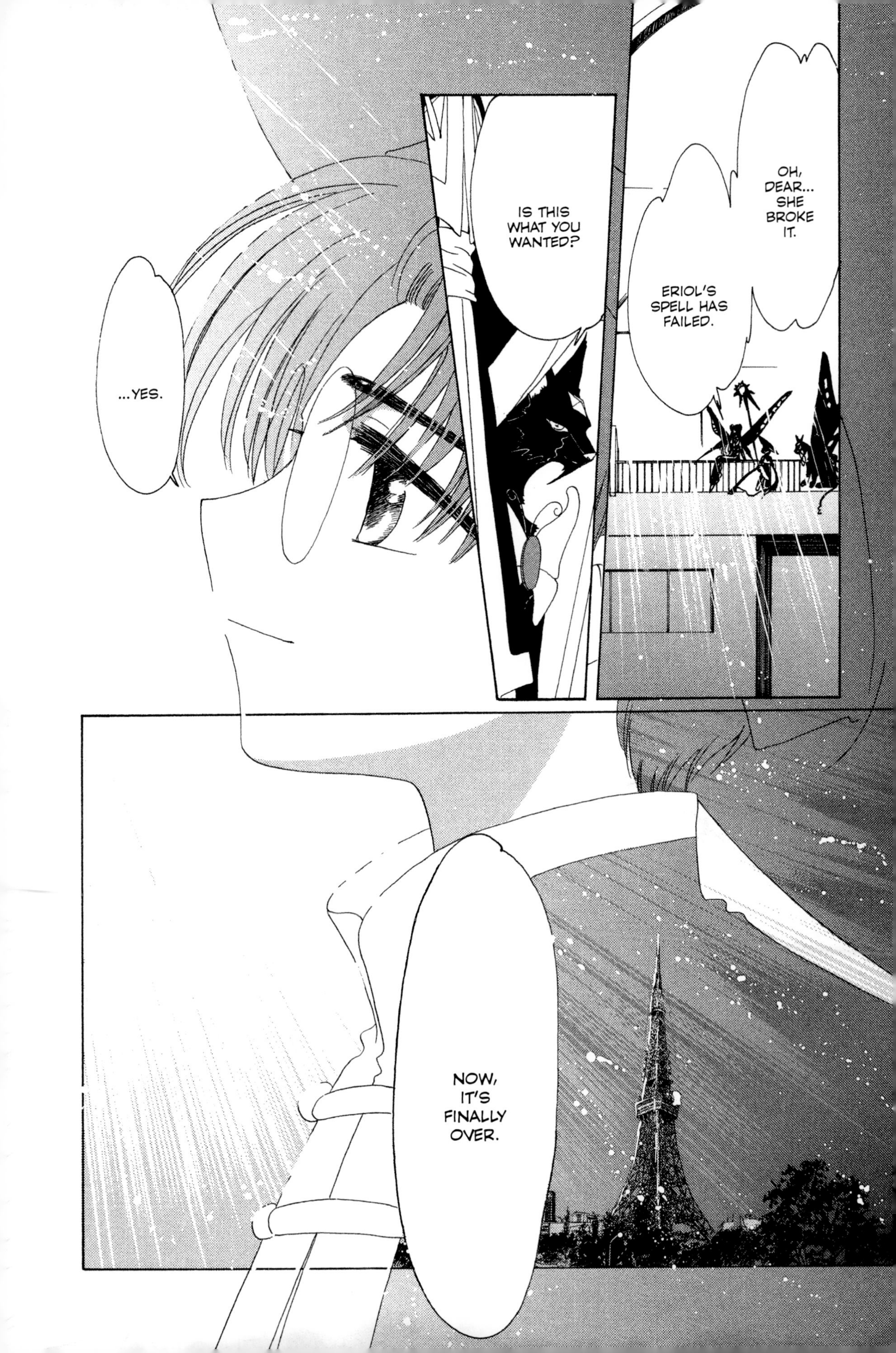
OH, DEAR... SHE BROKE IT.
ERIOL'S SPELL HAS FAILED.
IS THIS WHAT YOU WANTED?
...YES.
NOW, IT'S FINALLY OVER.

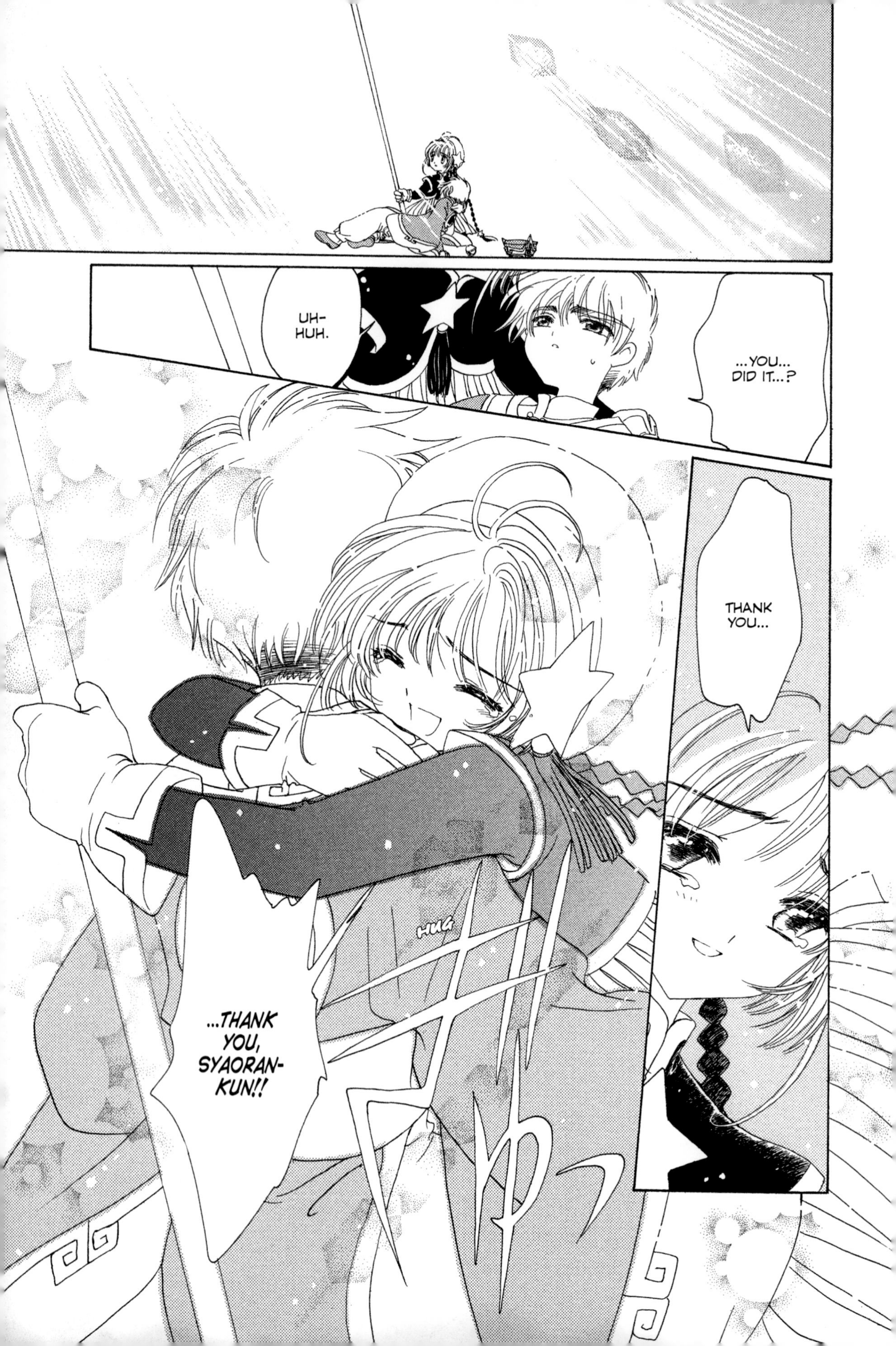
...YOU... DID IT...?
UH-HUH.
THANK YOU...
HUG
...THANK YOU, SYAORAN-KUN!!

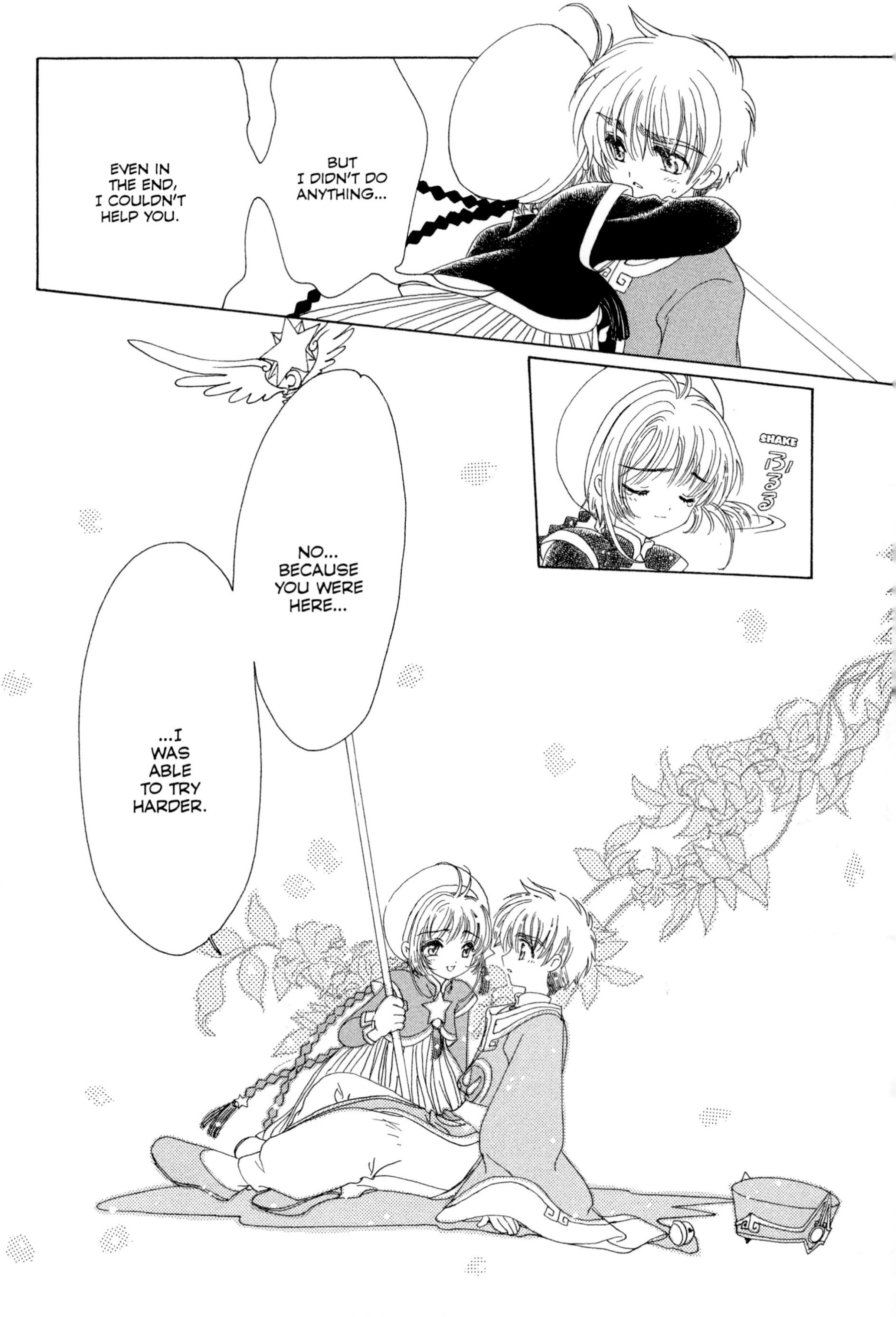
BUT I DIDN'T DO ANYTHING...
EVEN IN THE END, I COULDN'T HELP YOU.
SHAKE
ふるる
NO... BECAUSE YOU WERE HERE...
...I WAS ABLE TO TRY HARDER.

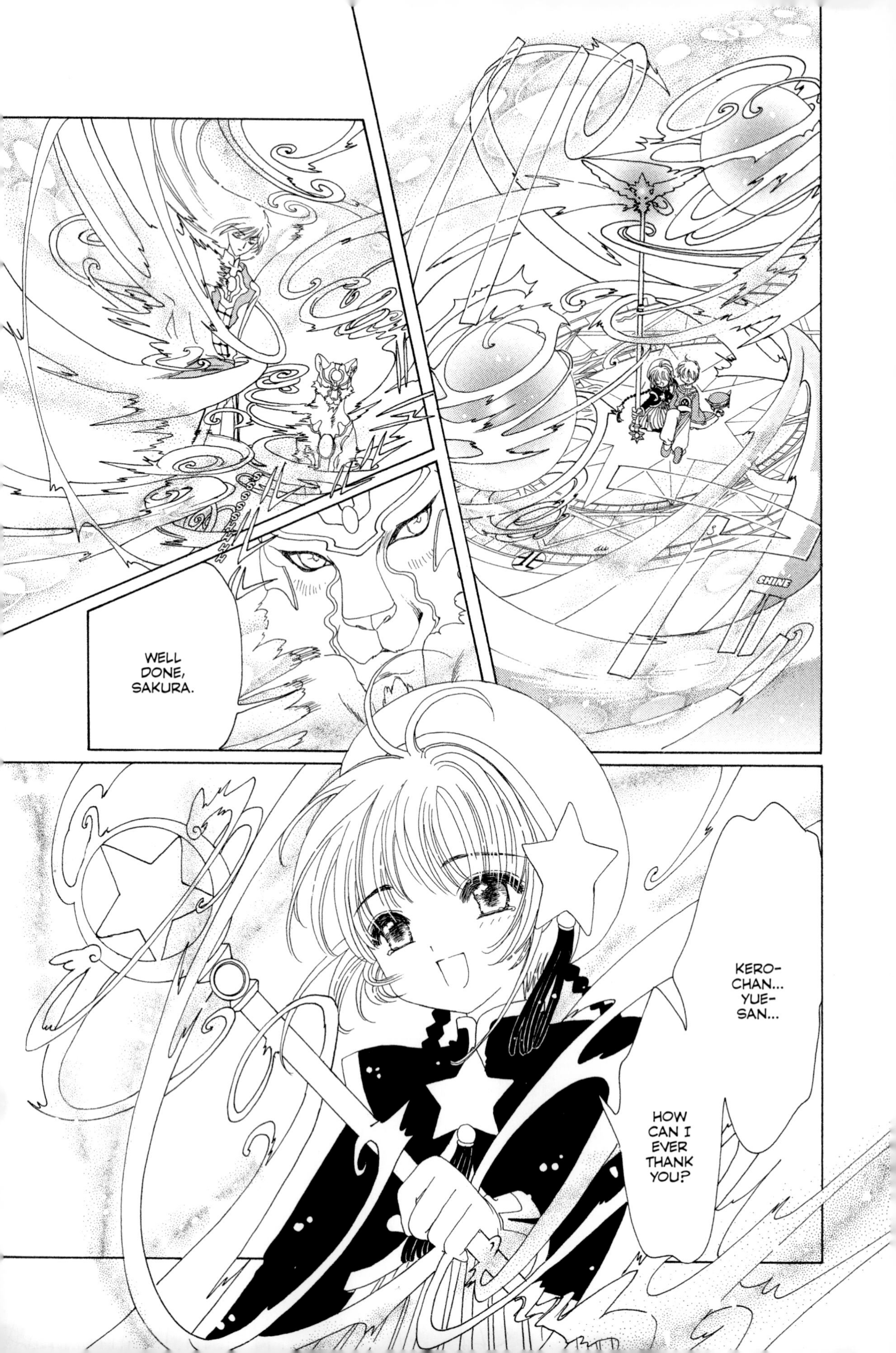
SHINE
WELL DONE, SAKURA.
KERO-CHAN... YUE-SAN...
HOW CAN I EVER THANK YOU?

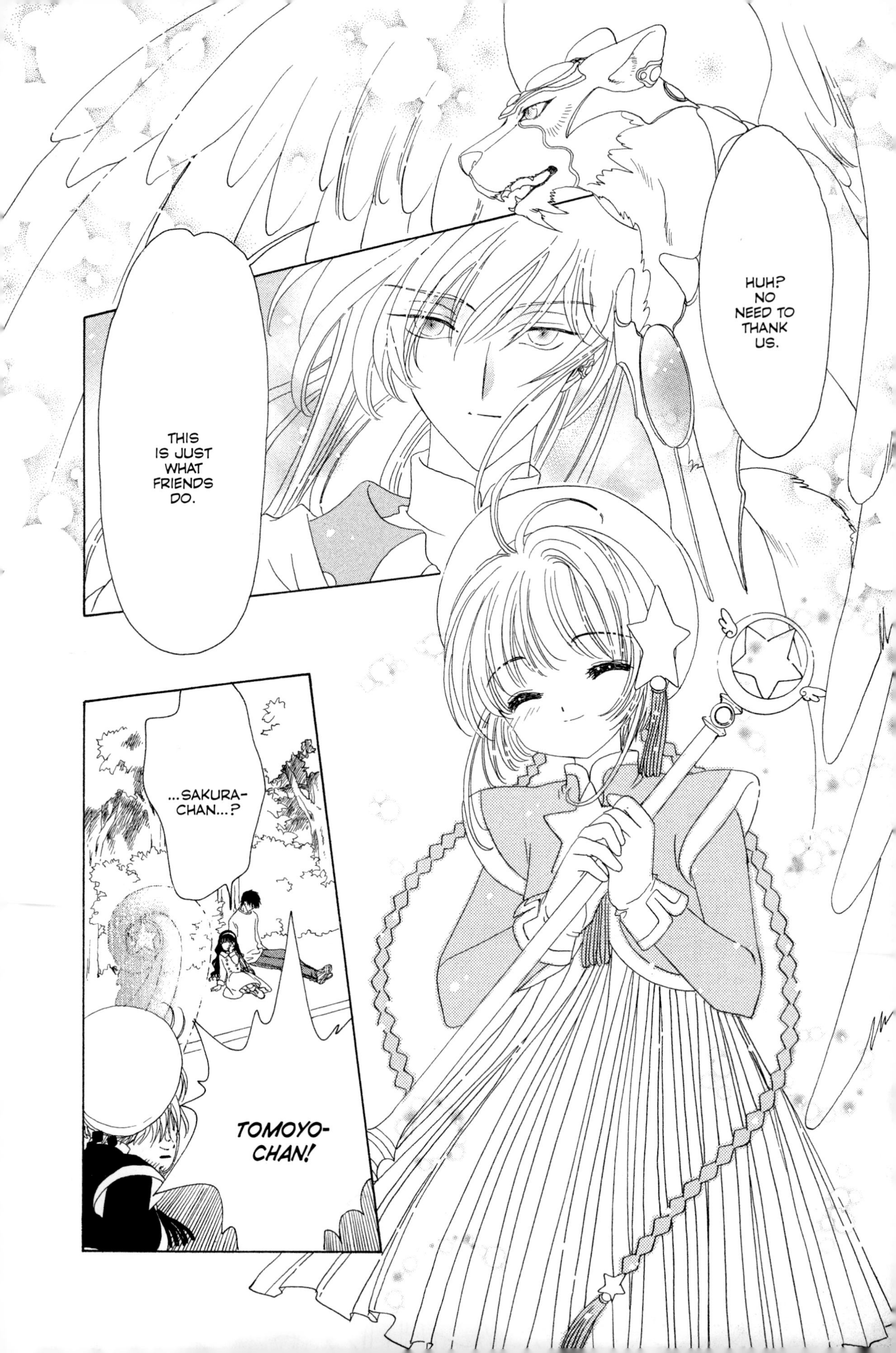
HUH? NO NEED TO THANK US.
THIS IS JUST WHAT FRIENDS DO.
...SAKURA-CHAN...?
TOMOYO-CHAN!

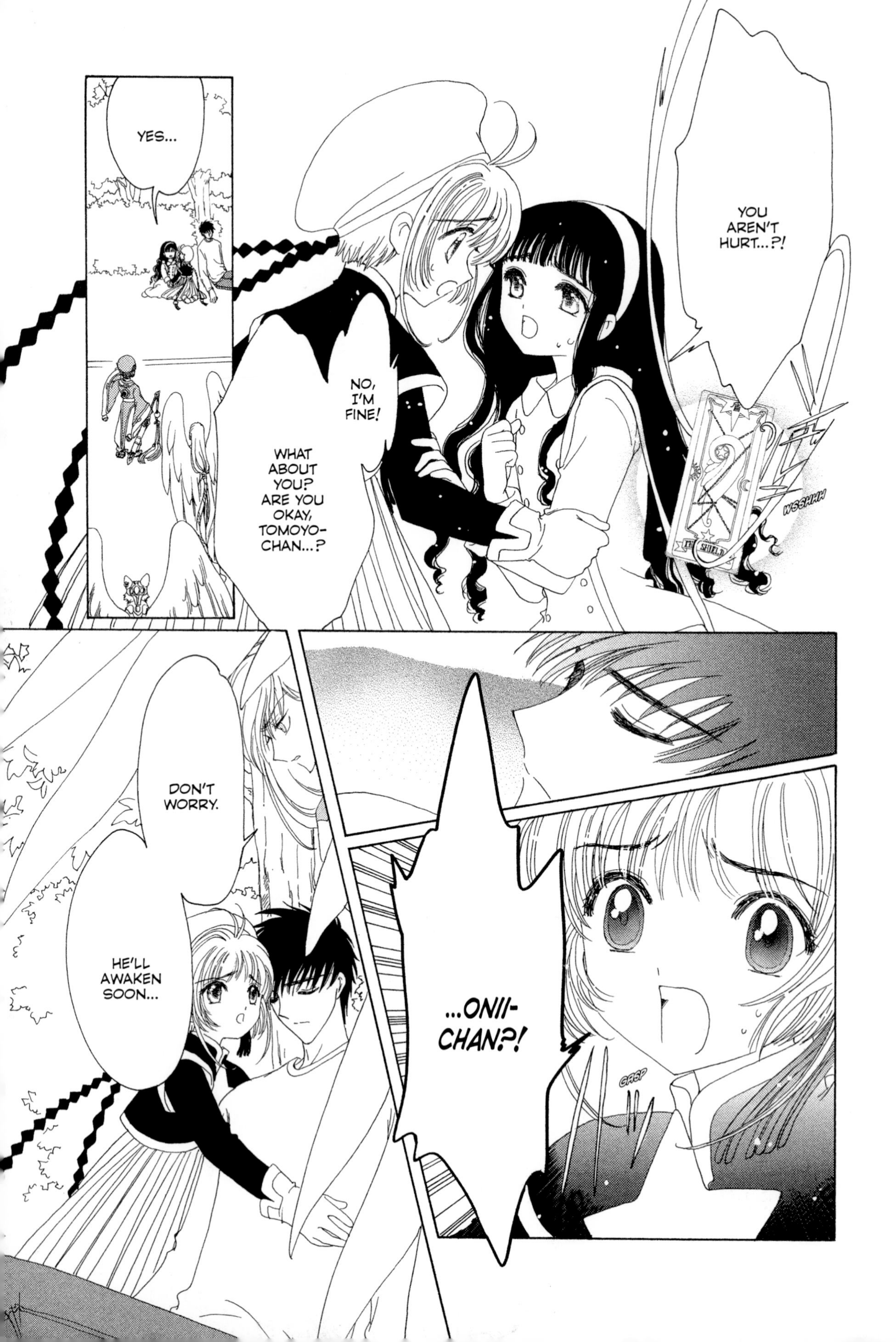
YOU AREN'T HURT...?!
NO, I'M FINE!
WHAT ABOUT YOU? ARE YOU OKAY, TOMOYO-CHAN...?
WSSHHH
YES...
...ONII-CHAN?!
GASP
DON'T WORRY.
HE'LL AWAKEN SOON...

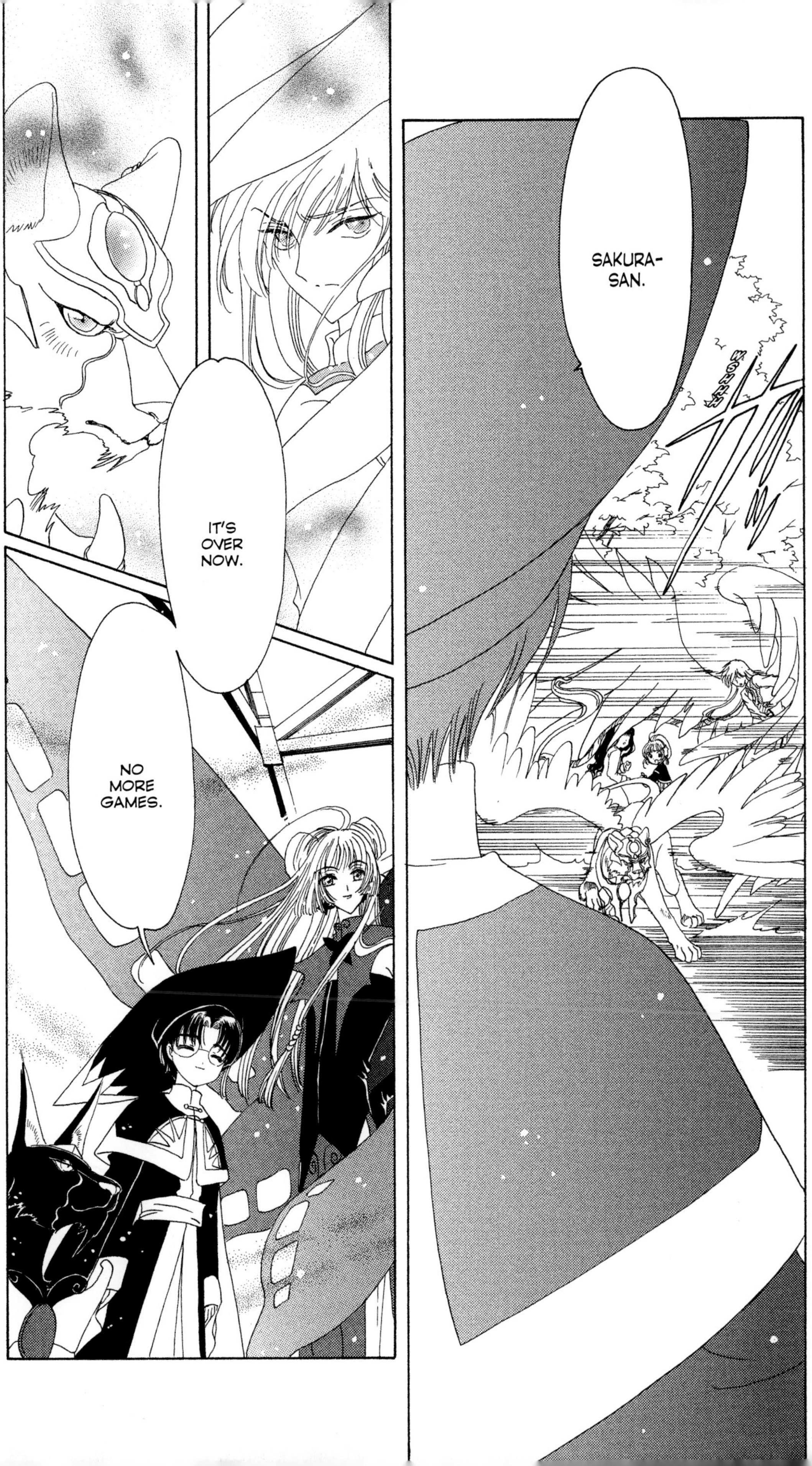
SAKURA-SAN.
WSHHH
IT'S OVER NOW.
NO MORE GAMES.

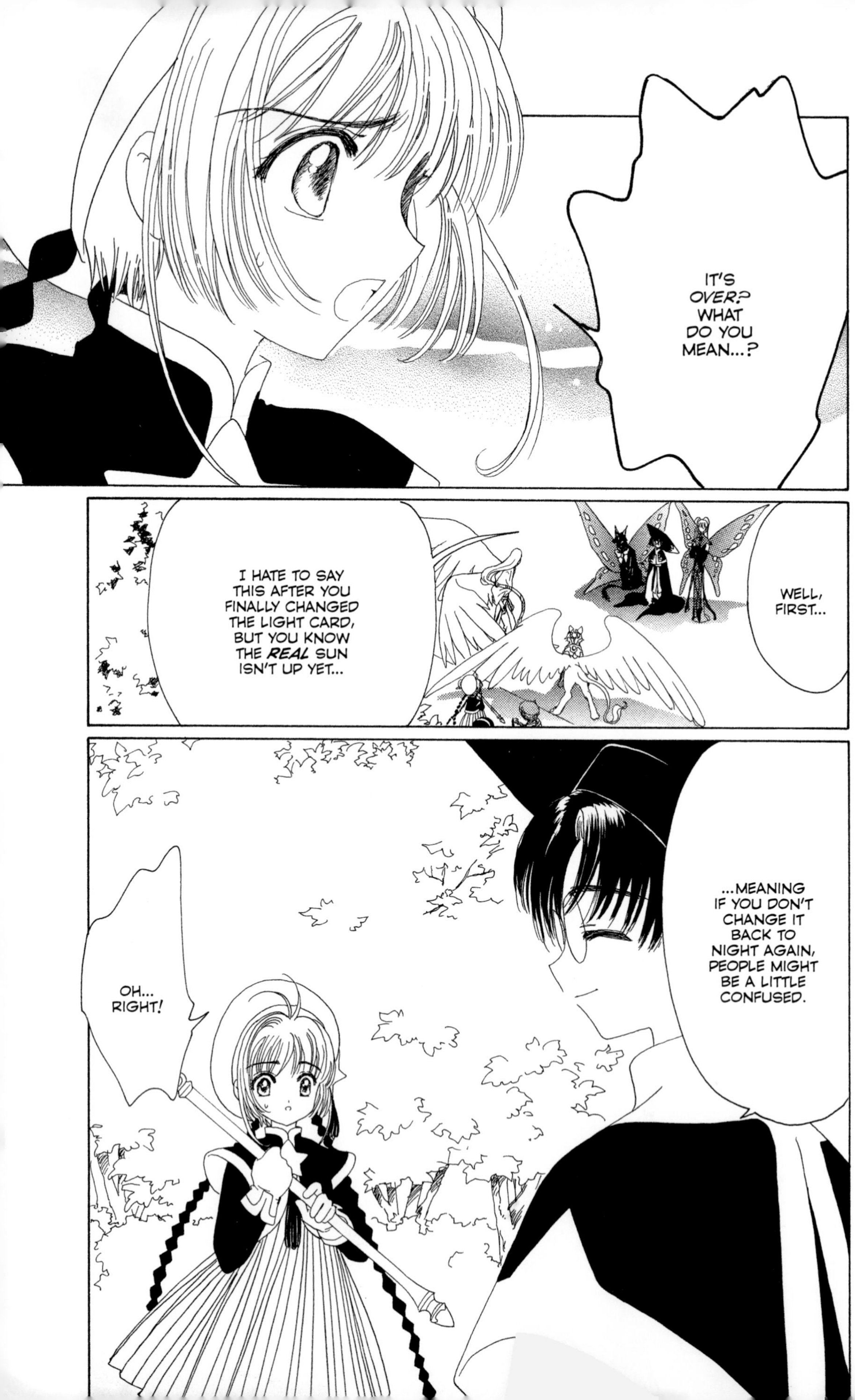
IT'S *OVER?* WHAT DO YOU MEAN...?
WELL, FIRST...
I HATE TO SAY THIS AFTER YOU FINALLY CHANGED THE LIGHT CARD, BUT YOU KNOW THE ***REAL*** SUN ISN'T UP YET...
...MEANING IF YOU DON'T CHANGE IT BACK TO NIGHT AGAIN, PEOPLE MIGHT BE A LITTLE CONFUSED.
OH... RIGHT!

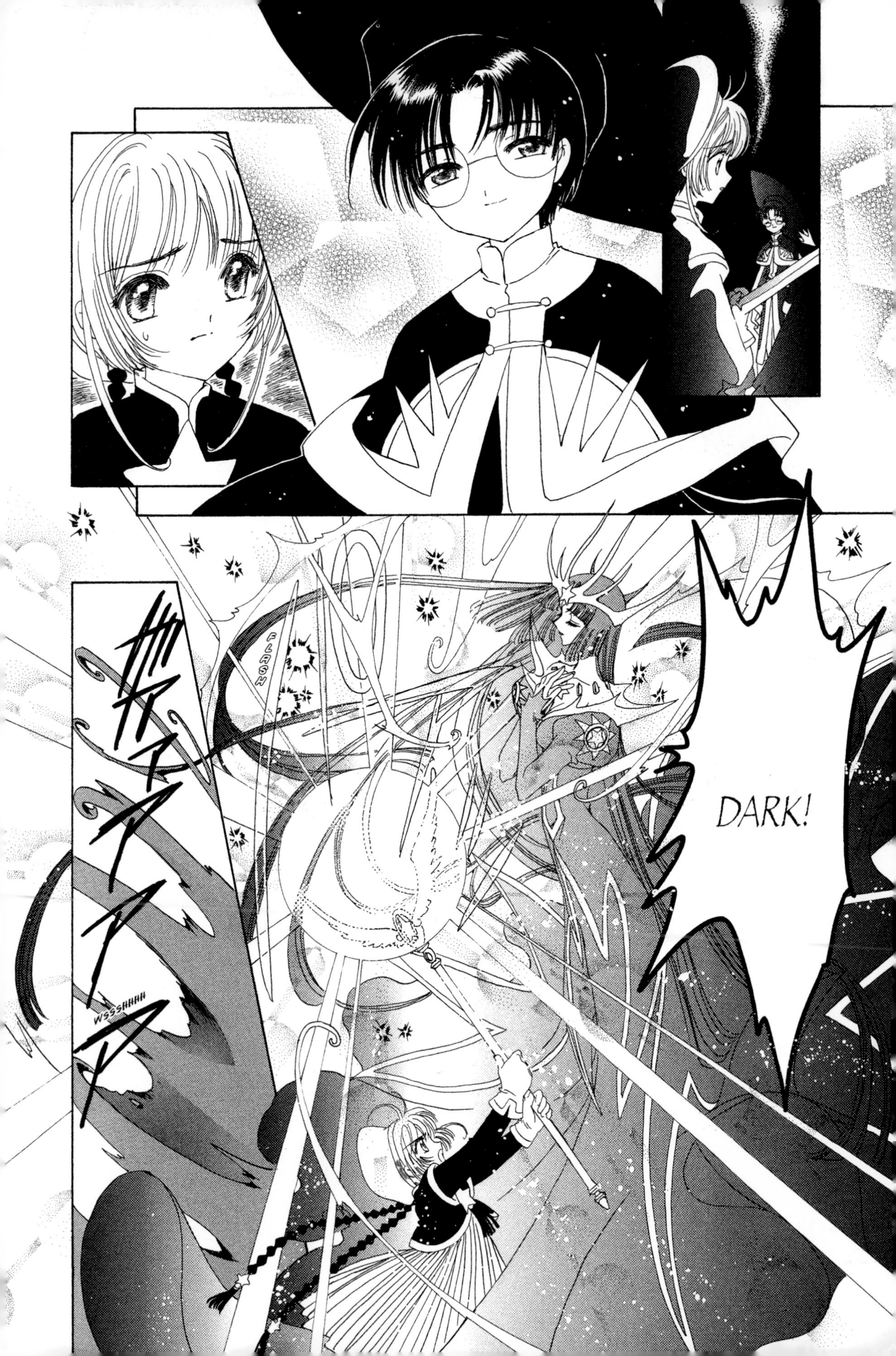
DARK!
FLASH
WSSSHHHH

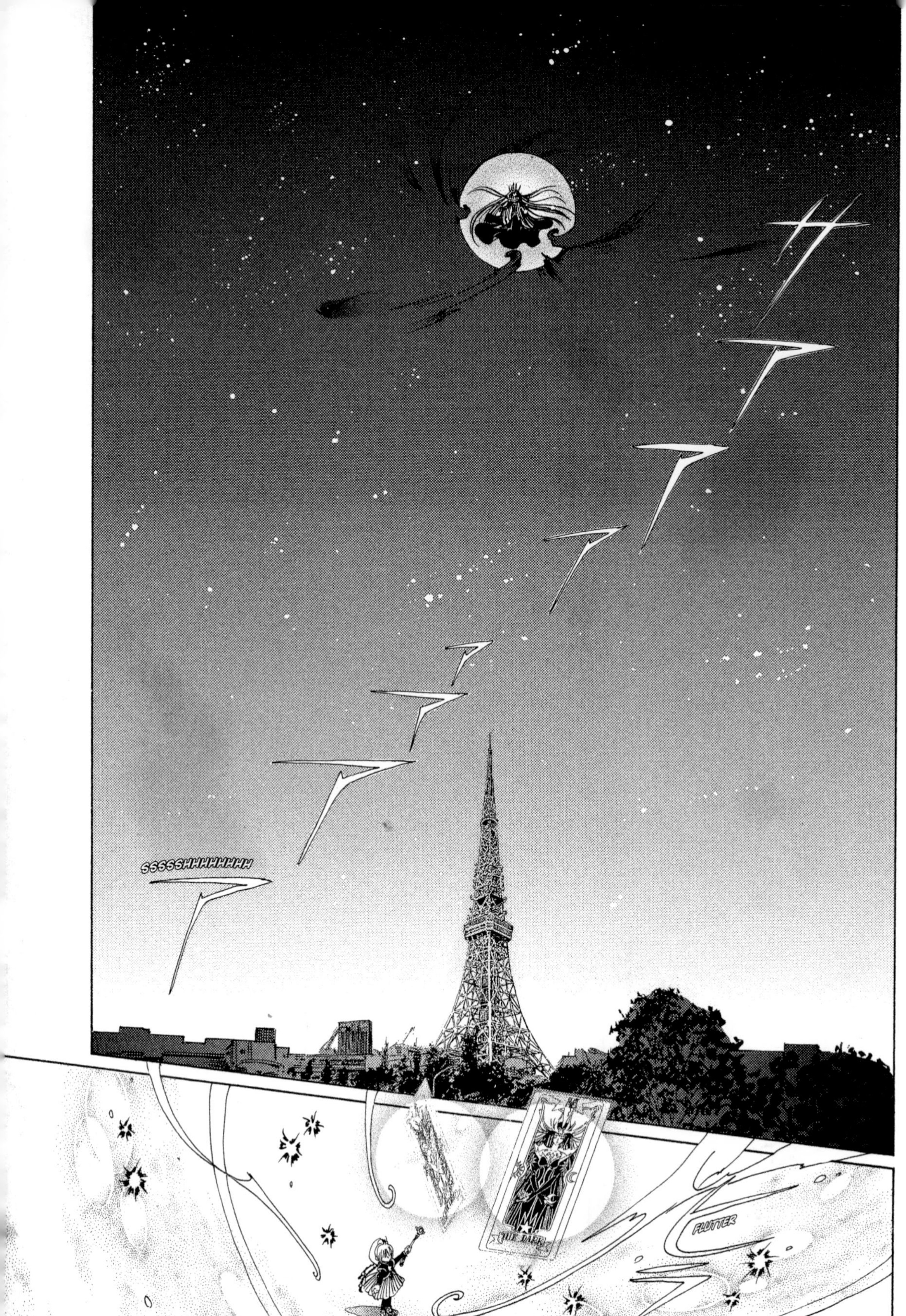
SSSSSHHHHHHHH
FLUTTER

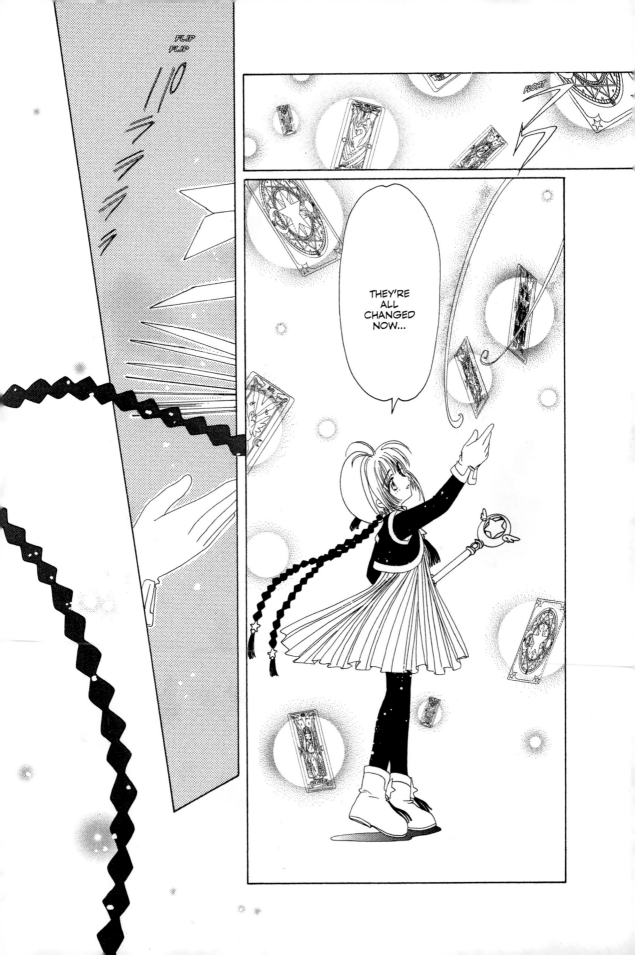

FLIP
FLIP

FLOAT

THEY'RE
ALL
CHANGED
NOW...

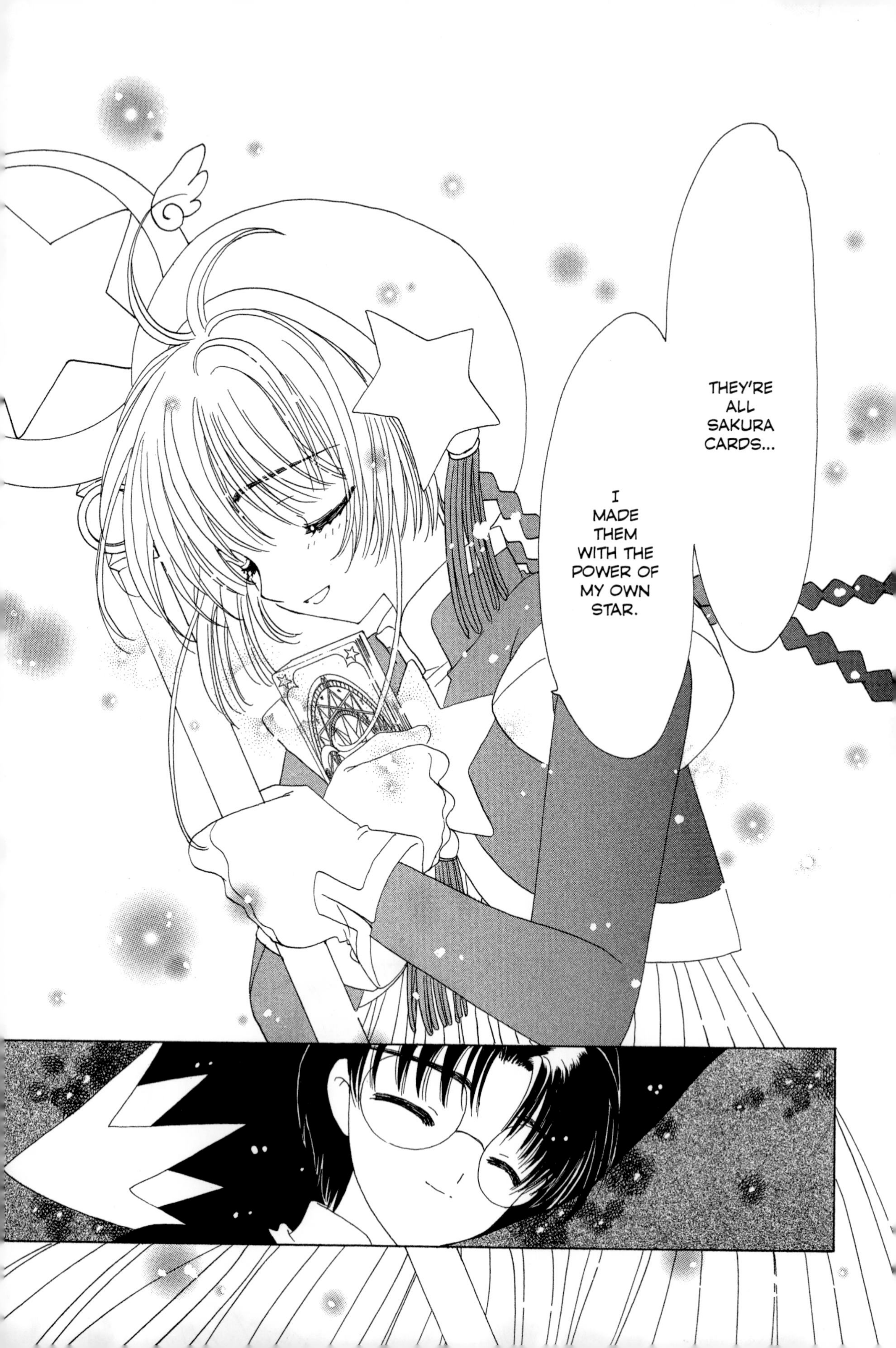
THEY'RE ALL SAKURA CARDS...
I MADE THEM WITH THE POWER OF MY OWN STAR.

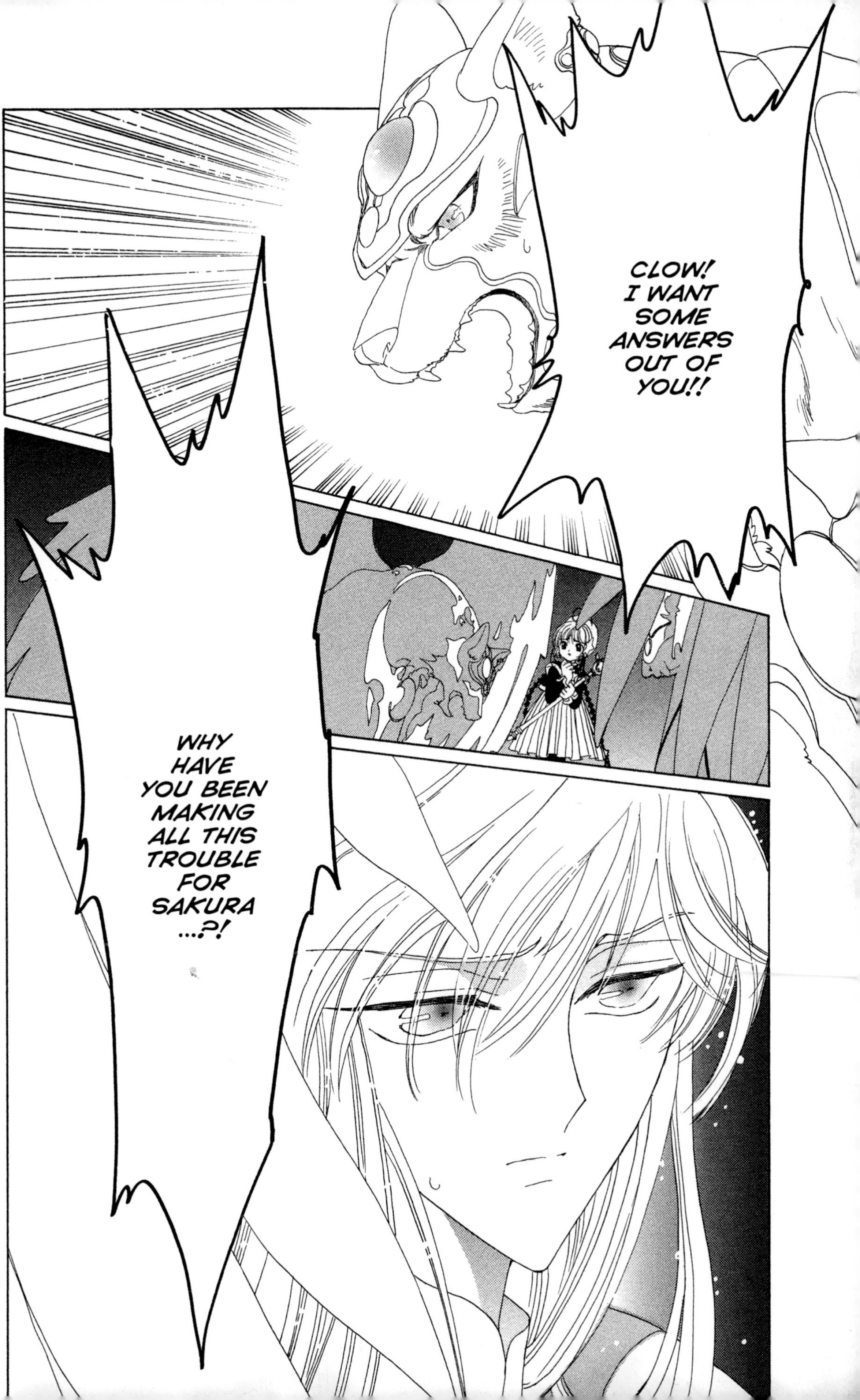
CLOW! I WANT SOME ANSWERS OUT OF YOU!!
WHY HAVE YOU BEEN MAKING ALL THIS TROUBLE FOR SAKURA ...?!

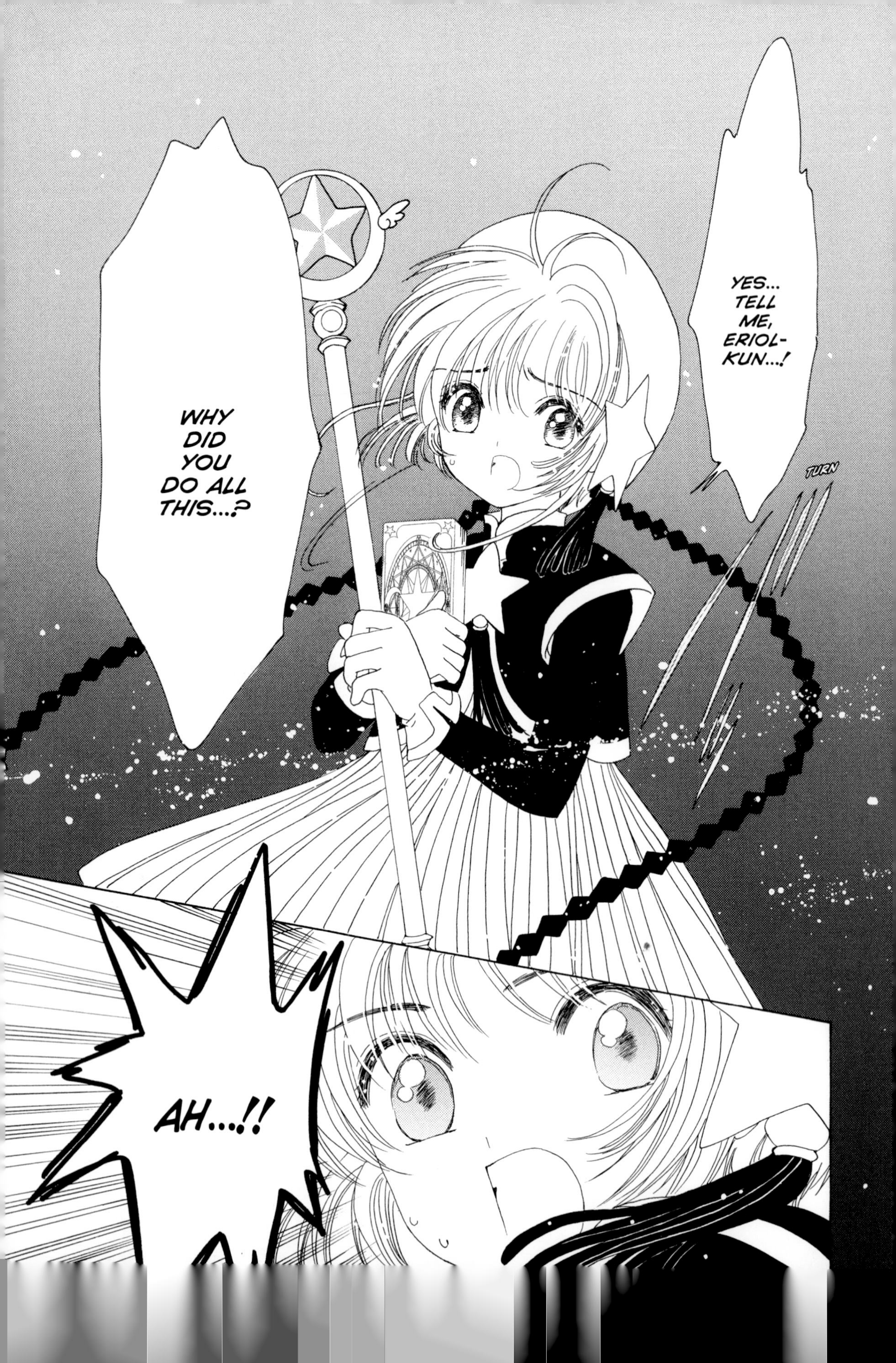
YES... TELL ME, ERIOL-KUN...!
TURN
WHY DID YOU DO ALL THIS...?
AH...!!

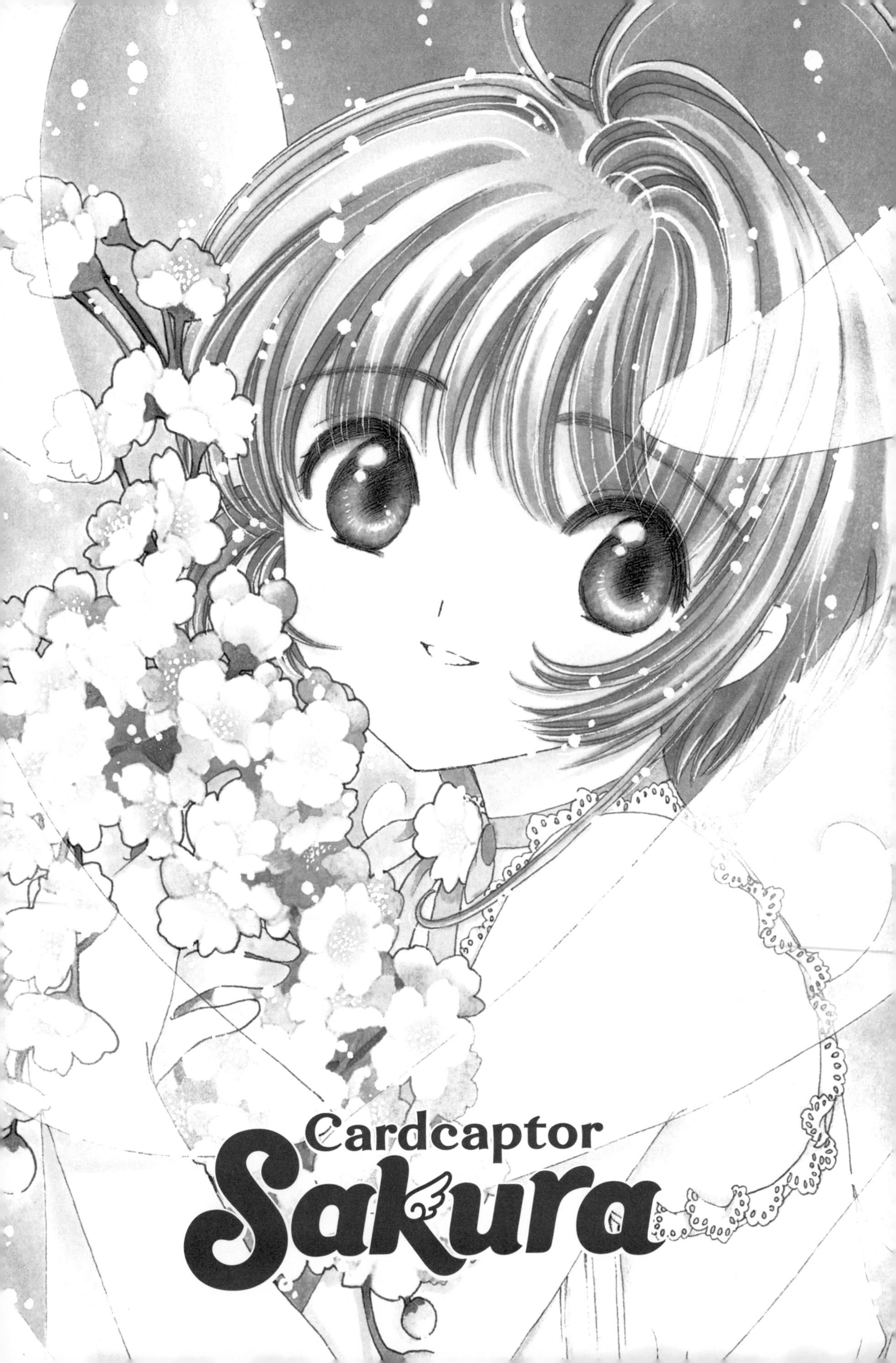
Cardcaptor
Sakura

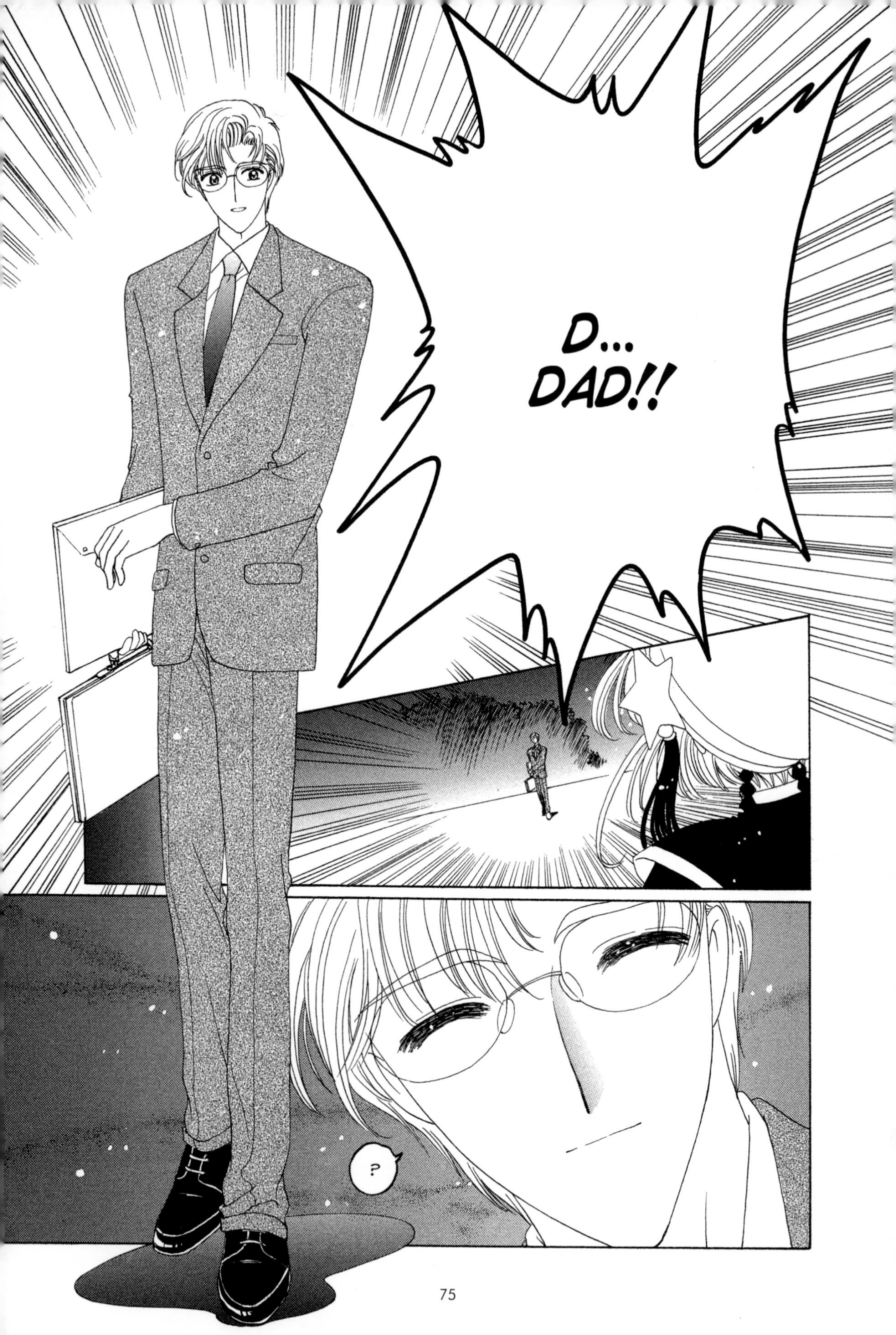
D... DAD!!
?

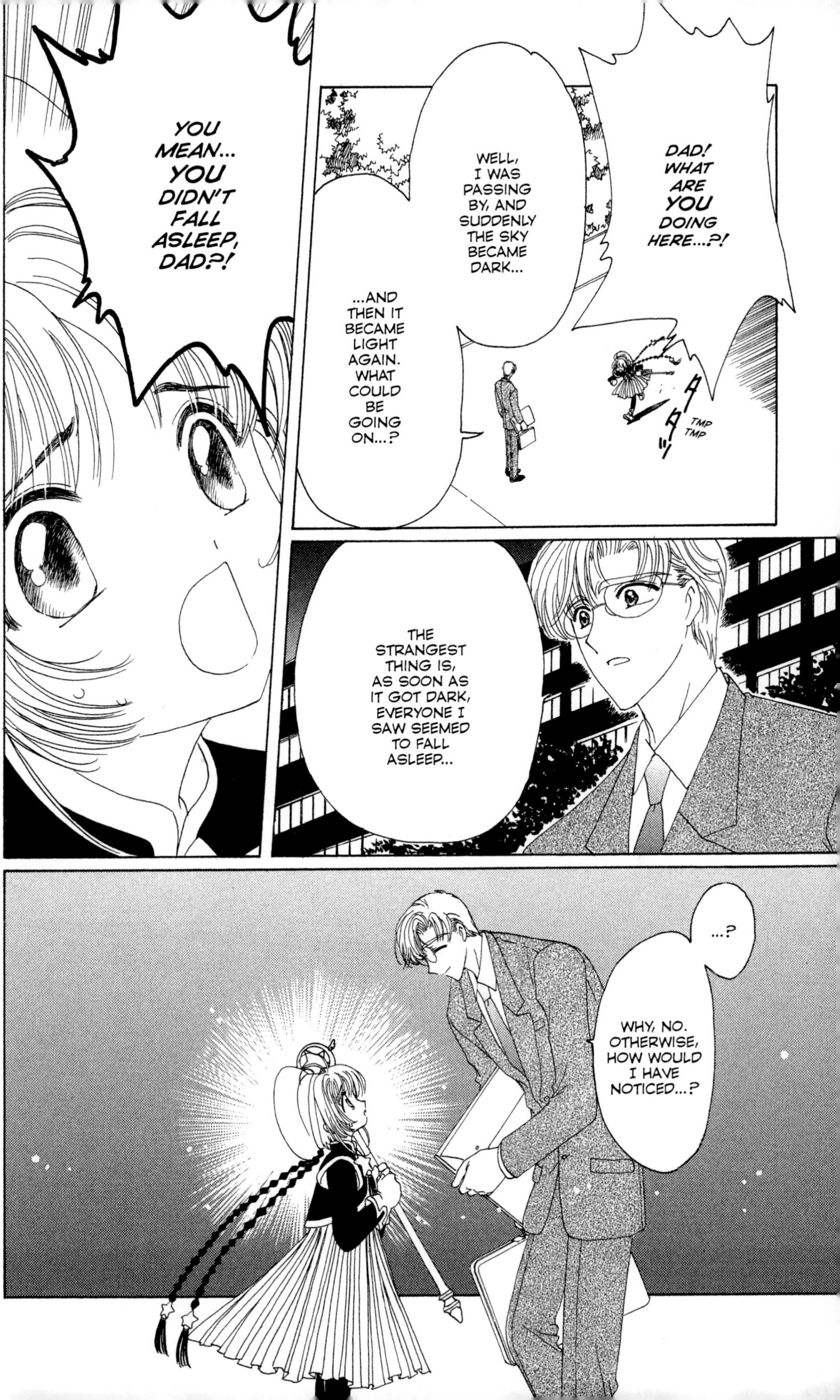
DAD! WHAT ARE YOU DOING HERE...?!
TMP TMP
WELL, I WAS PASSING BY, AND SUDDENLY THE SKY BECAME DARK...
...AND THEN IT BECAME LIGHT AGAIN. WHAT COULD BE GOING ON...?
THE STRANGEST THING IS, AS SOON AS IT GOT DARK, EVERYONE I SAW SEEMED TO FALL ASLEEP...
YOU MEAN... YOU DIDN'T FALL ASLEEP, DAD?!
...?
WHY, NO. OTHERWISE, HOW WOULD I HAVE NOTICED...?

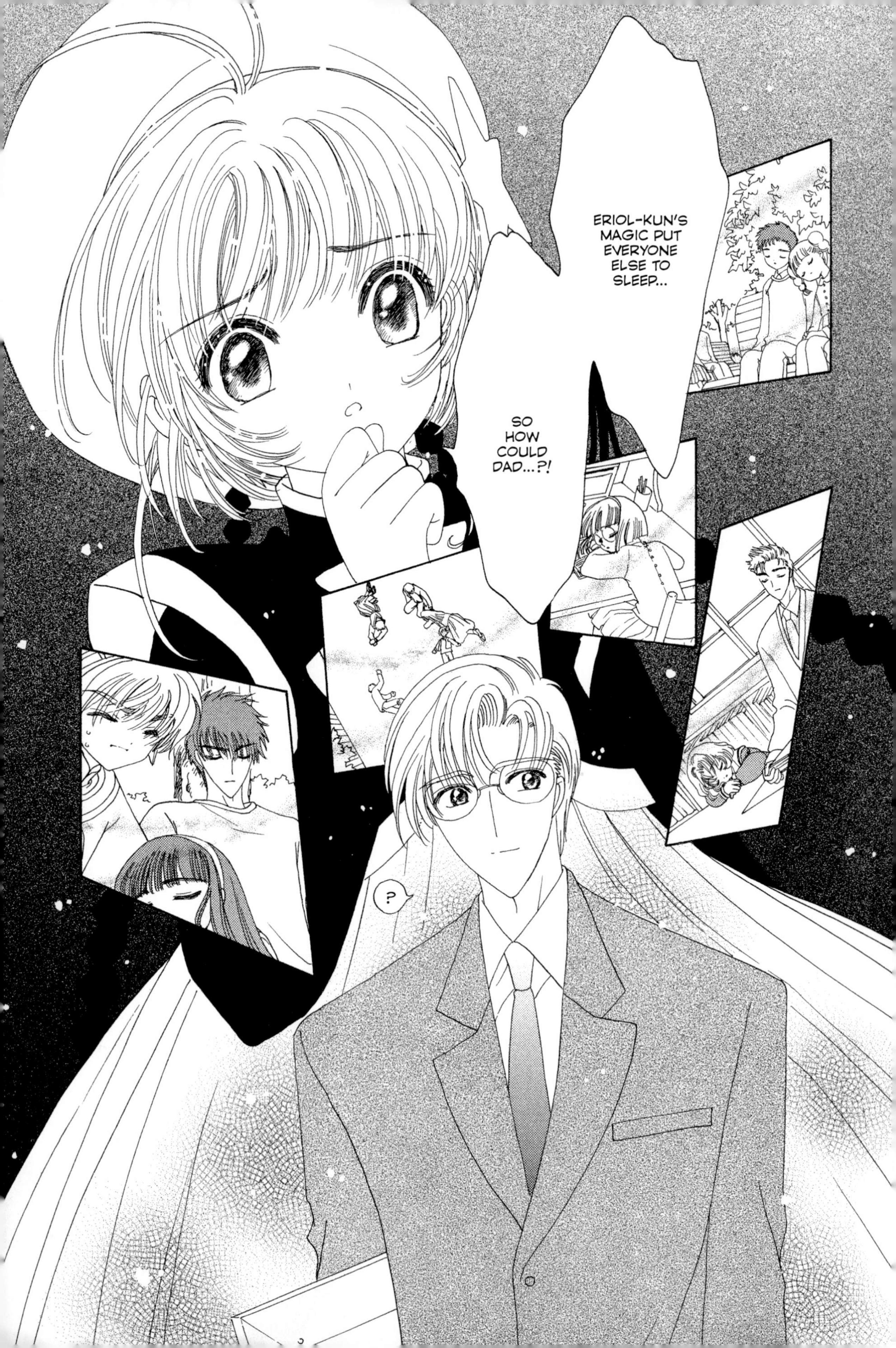
ERIOL-KUN'S MAGIC PUT EVERYONE ELSE TO SLEEP...
SO HOW COULD DAD...?!
?

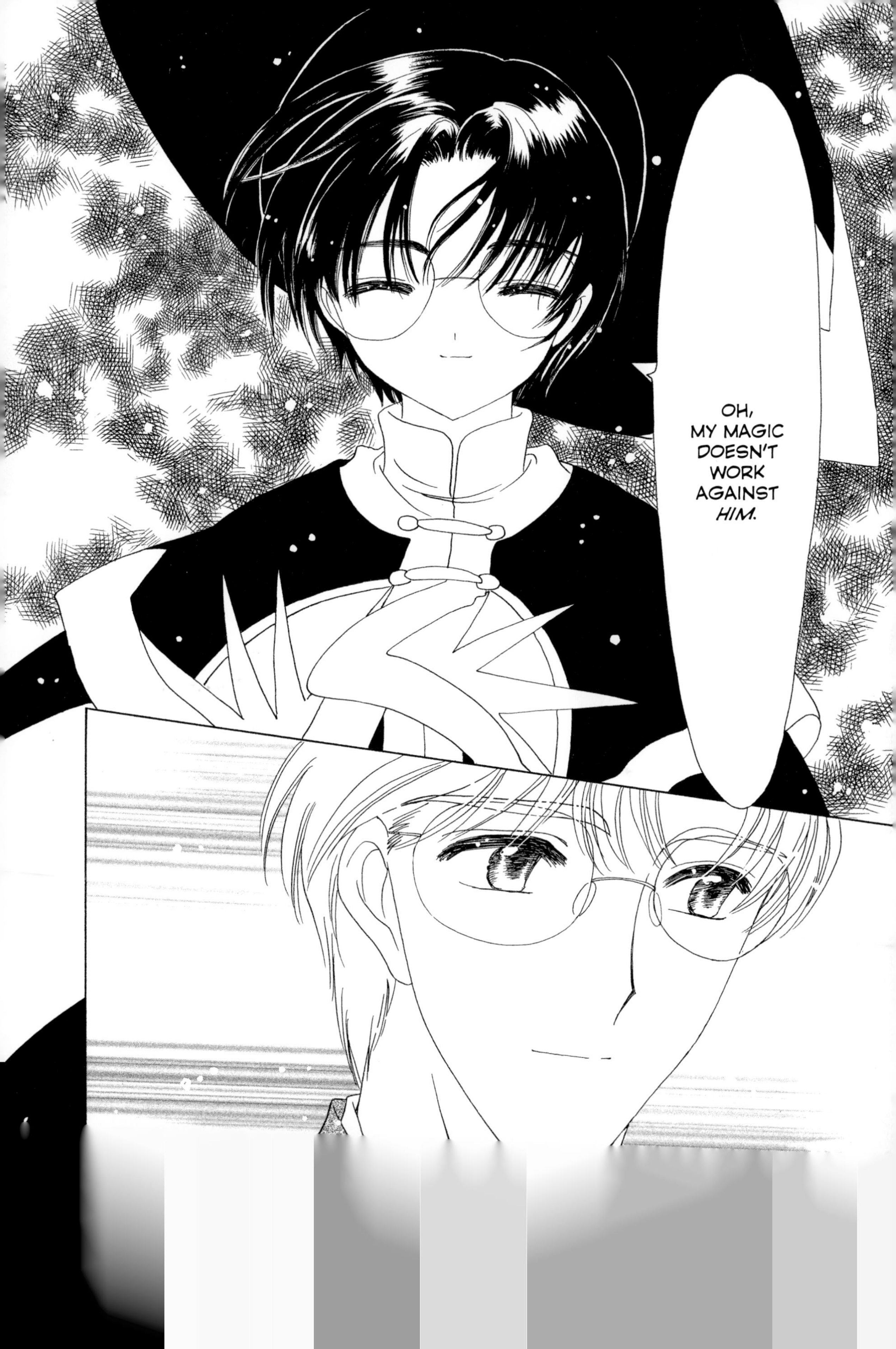
OH, MY MAGIC DOESN'T WORK AGAINST *HIM*.

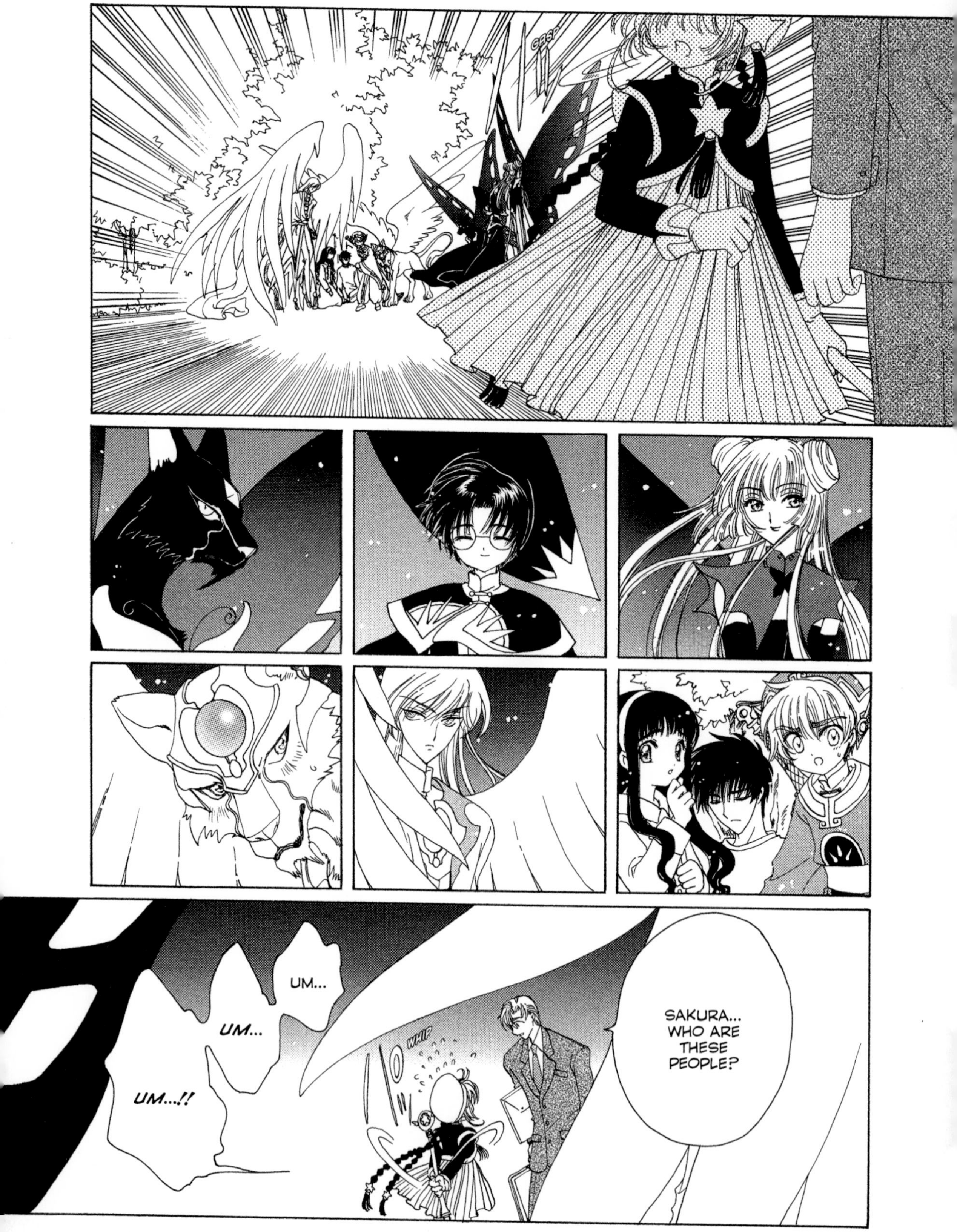
GASP
SAKURA... WHO ARE THESE PEOPLE?
WHIP
UM...
UM...
UM...!!

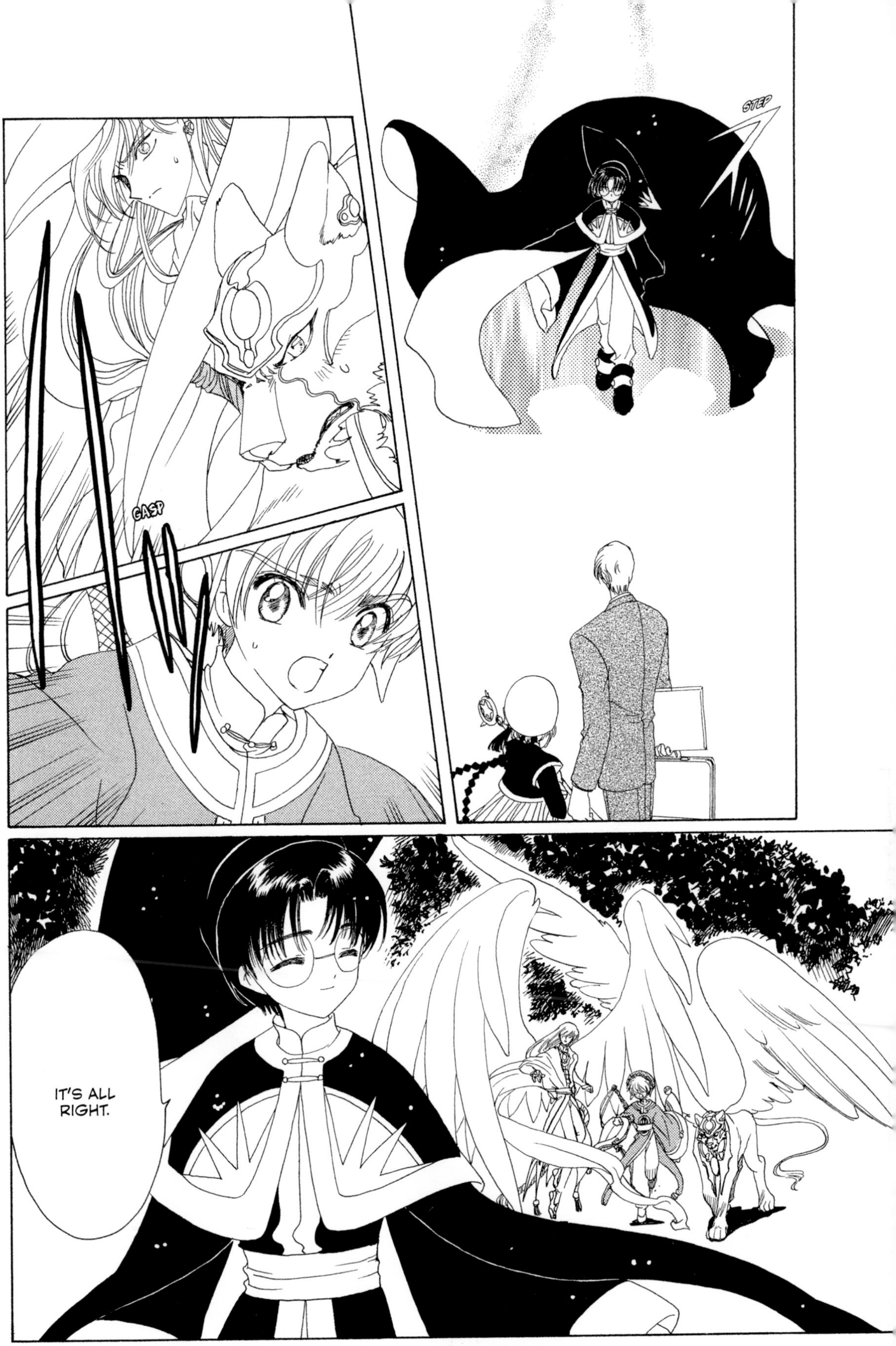
STEP
GASP
IT'S ALL RIGHT.

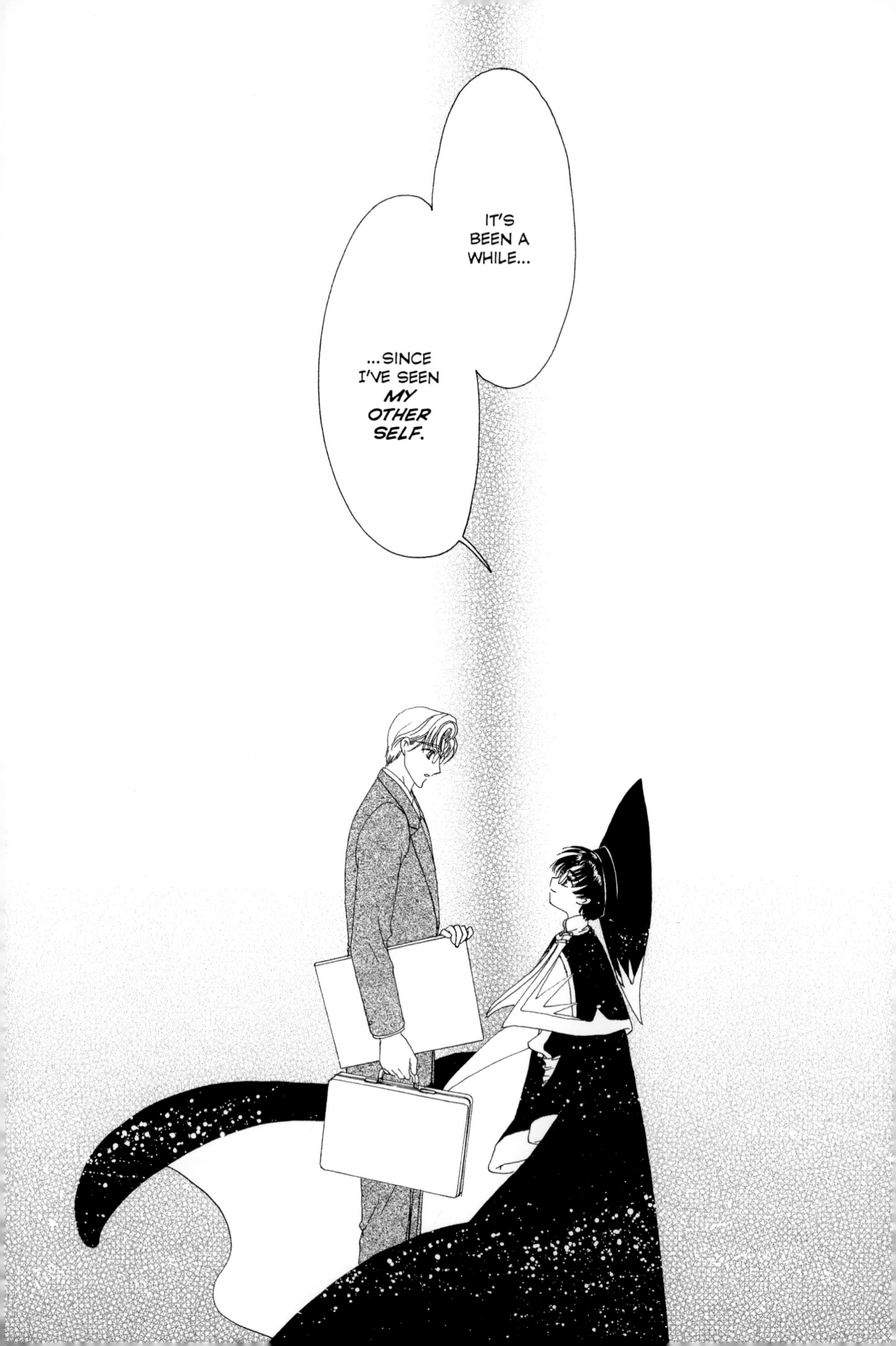
IT'S BEEN A WHILE...
...SINCE I'VE SEEN *MY OTHER SELF*.

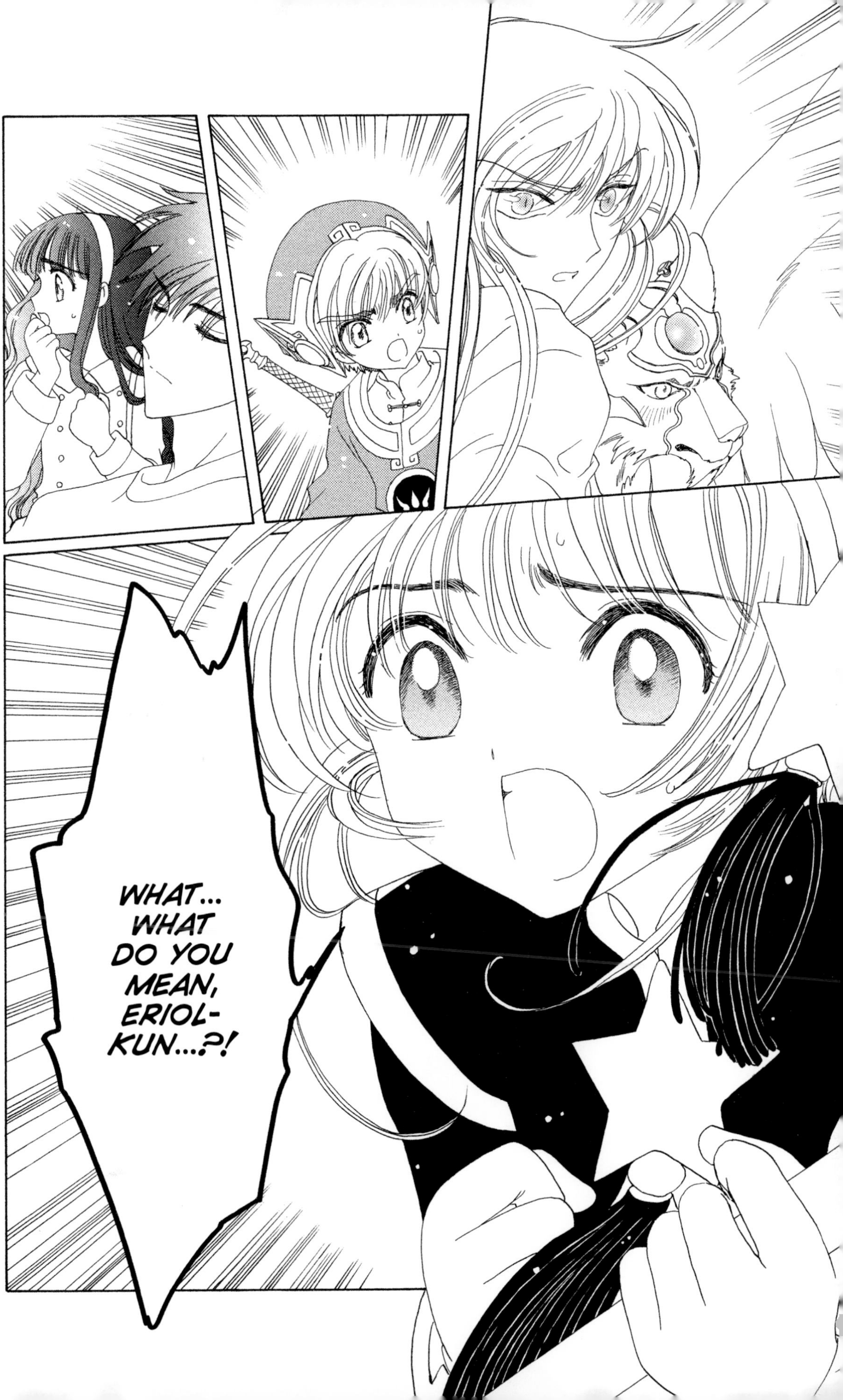
WHAT... WHAT DO YOU MEAN, ERIOL-KUN...?!

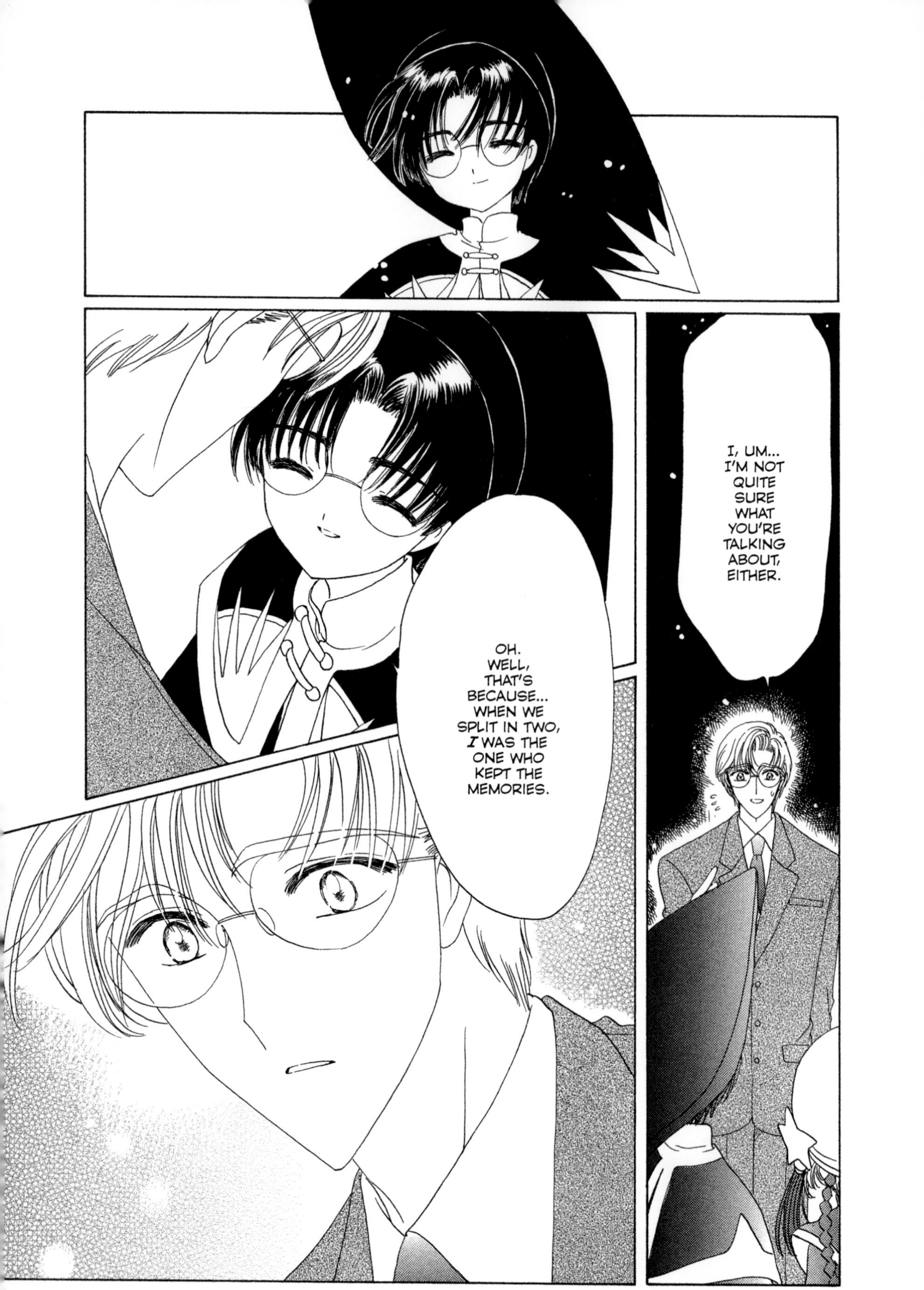
I, UM... I'M NOT QUITE SURE WHAT YOU'RE TALKING ABOUT, EITHER.
OH. WELL, THAT'S BECAUSE... WHEN WE SPLIT IN TWO, *I* WAS THE ONE WHO KEPT THE MEMORIES.

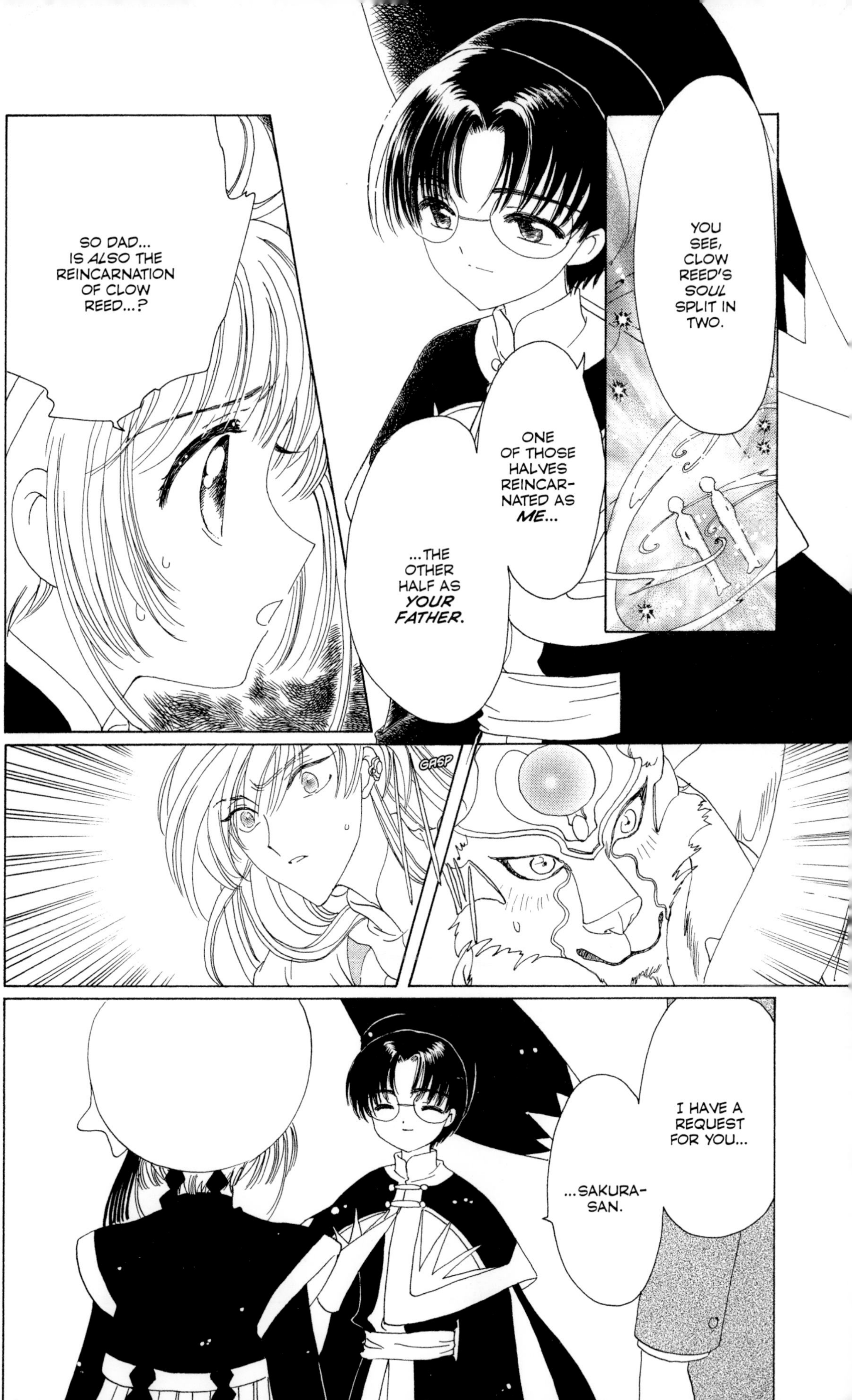
YOU SEE, CLOW REED'S SOUL SPLIT IN TWO.
ONE OF THOSE HALVES REINCARNATED AS ME...
...THE OTHER HALF AS YOUR FATHER.
SO DAD... IS ALSO THE REINCARNATION OF CLOW REED...?
GASP
I HAVE A REQUEST FOR YOU...
...SAKURA-SAN.

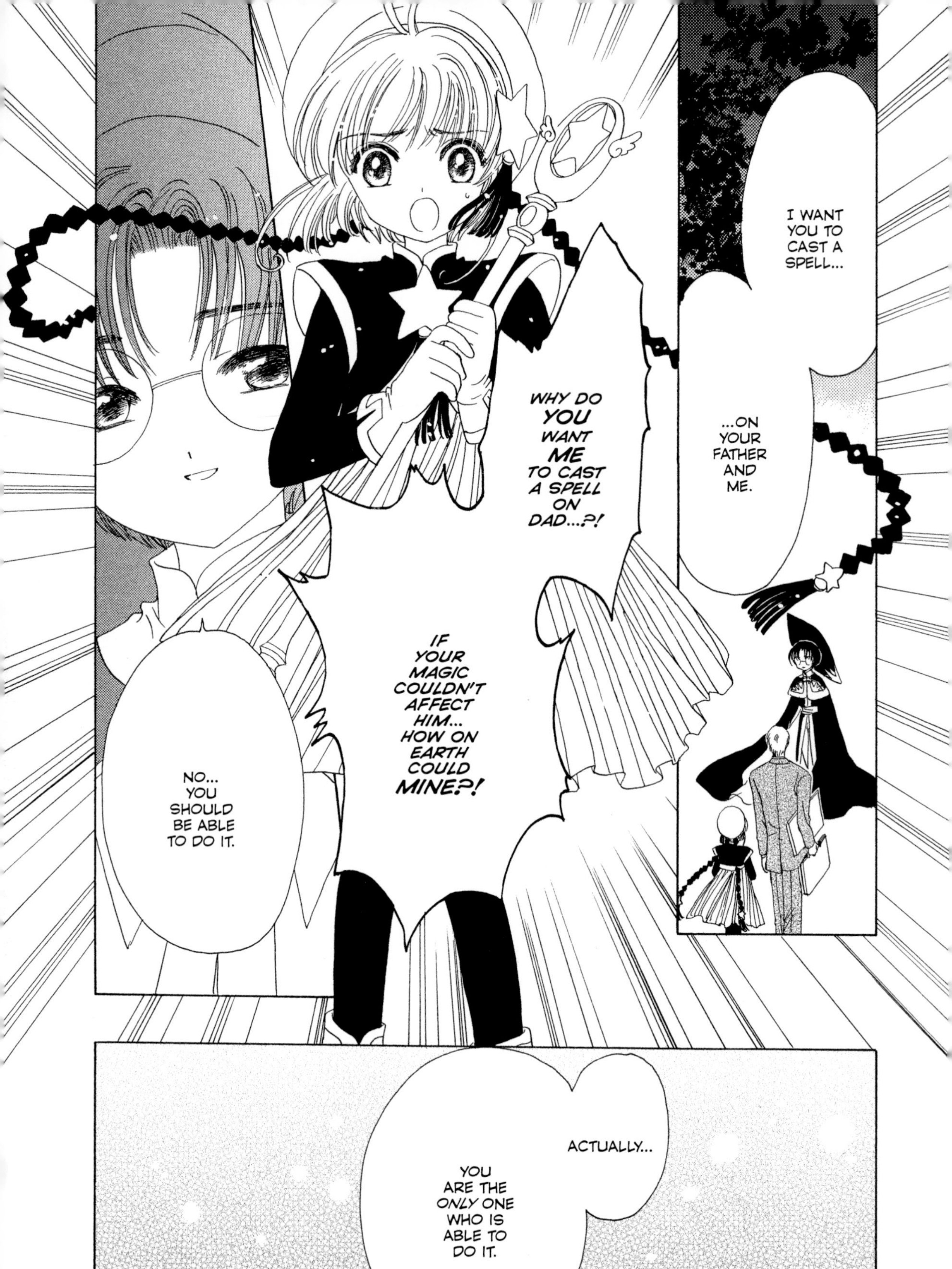
I WANT YOU TO CAST A SPELL...
...ON YOUR FATHER AND ME.
WHY DO ***YOU*** WANT ***ME*** TO CAST A SPELL ON DAD...?!
IF YOUR MAGIC COULDN'T AFFECT HIM... HOW ON EARTH COULD ***MINE?!***
NO... YOU SHOULD BE ABLE TO DO IT.
ACTUALLY...
YOU ARE THE *ONLY* ONE WHO IS ABLE TO DO IT.

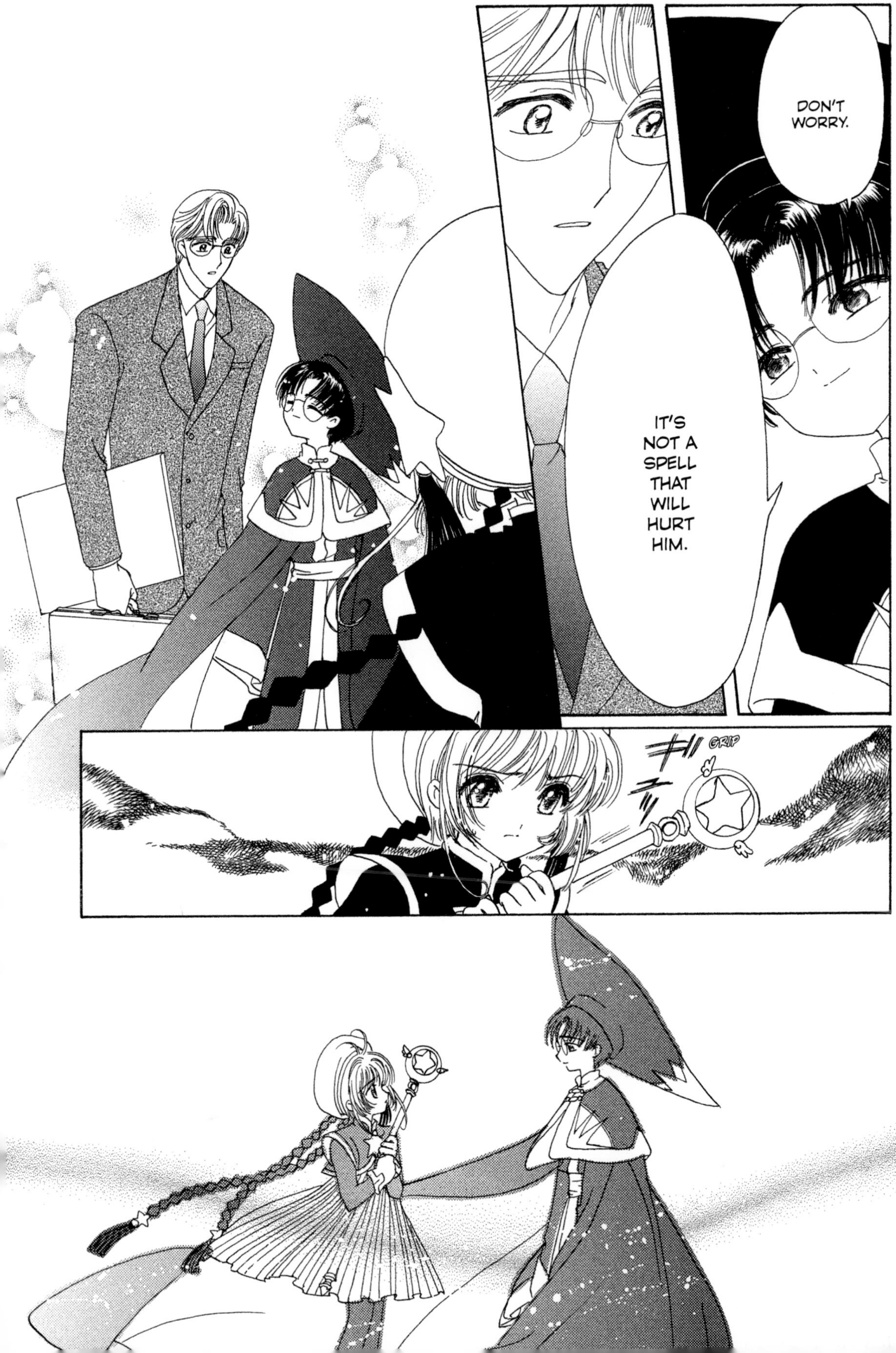
DON'T WORRY.
IT'S NOT A SPELL THAT WILL HURT HIM.
GRIP

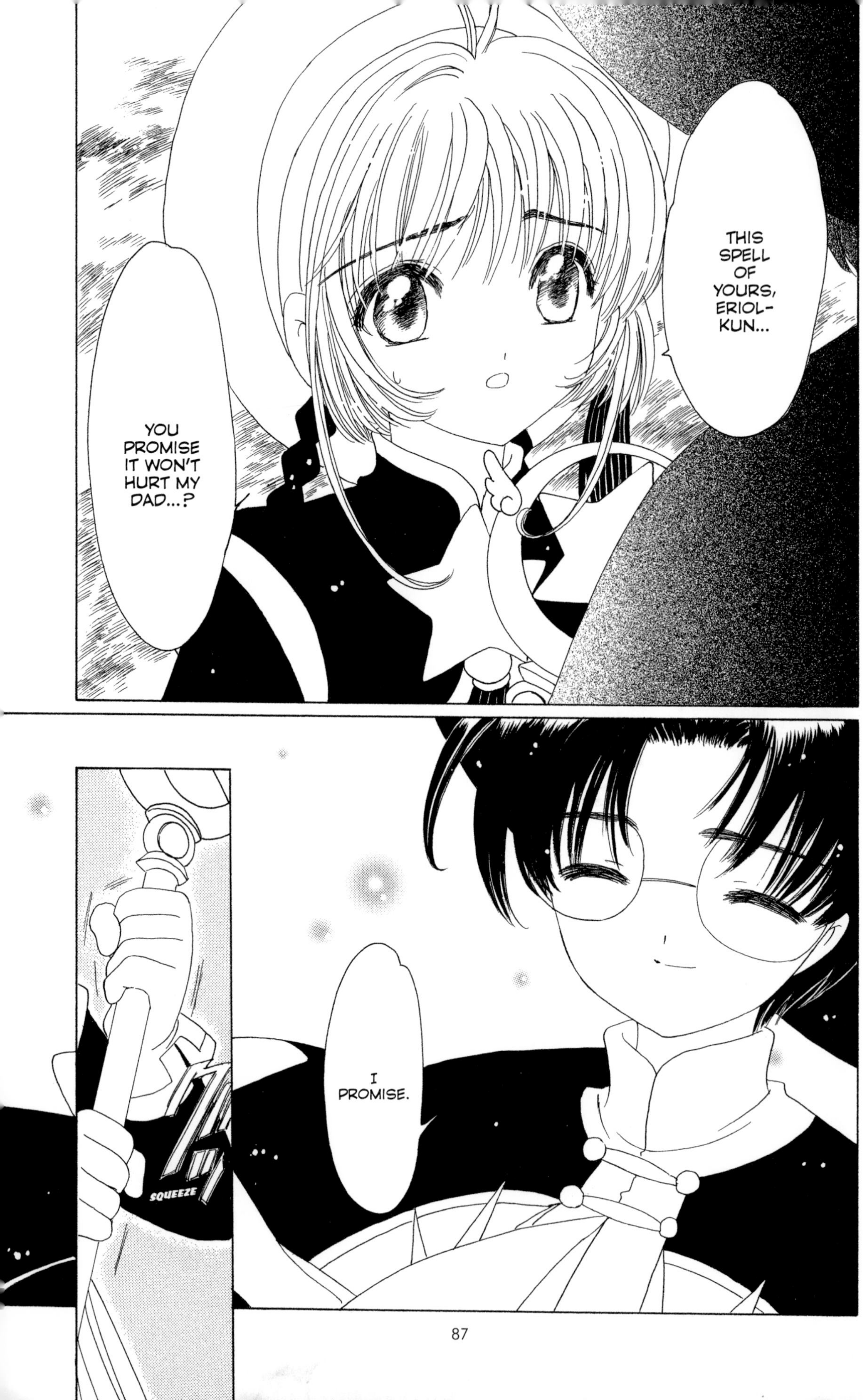
THIS SPELL OF YOURS, ERIOL-KUN...
YOU PROMISE IT WON'T HURT MY DAD...?
I PROMISE.
SQUEEZE

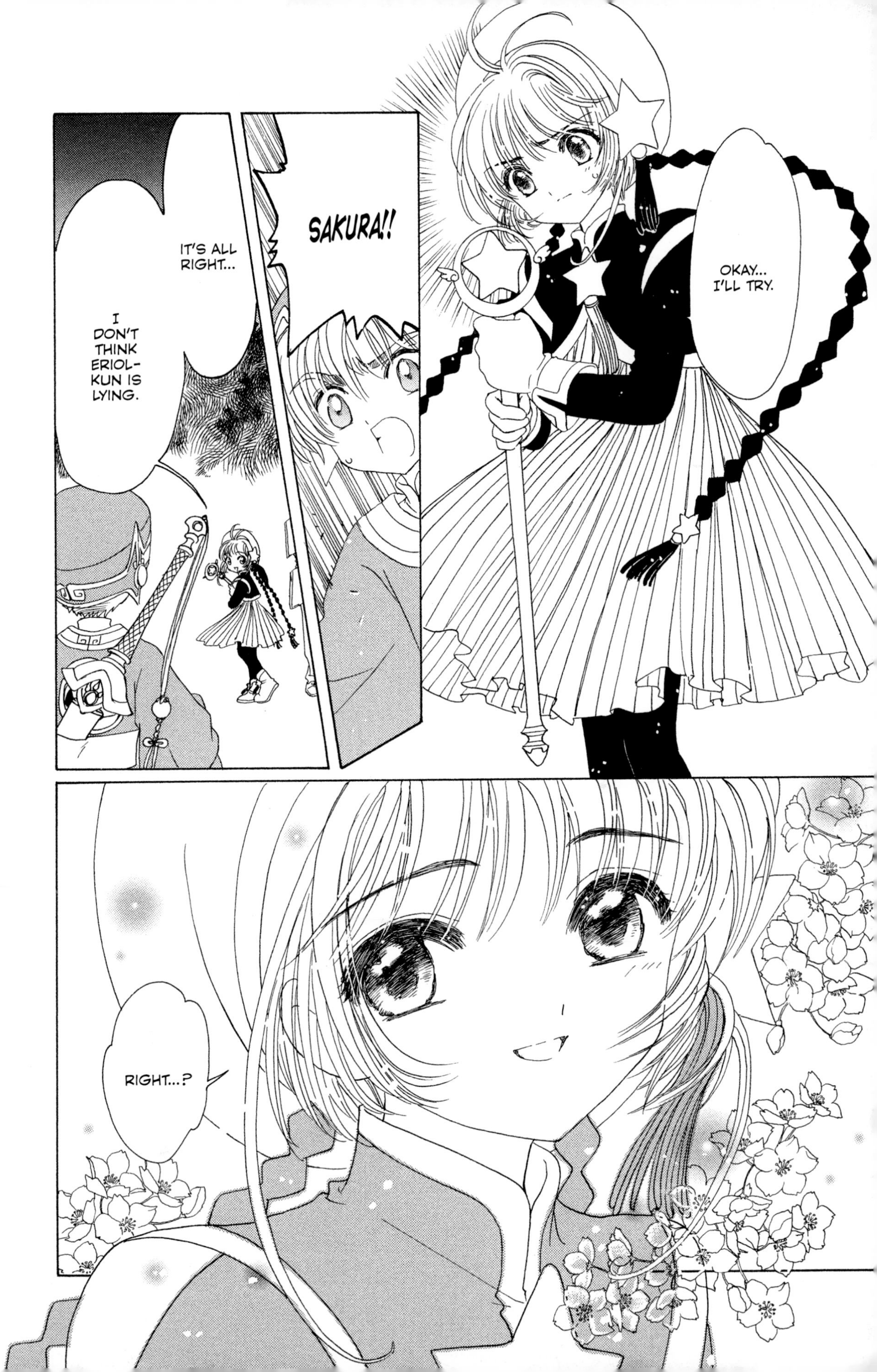
OKAY... I'LL TRY.
SAKURA!!
IT'S ALL RIGHT...
I DON'T THINK ERIOL-KUN IS LYING.
RIGHT...?

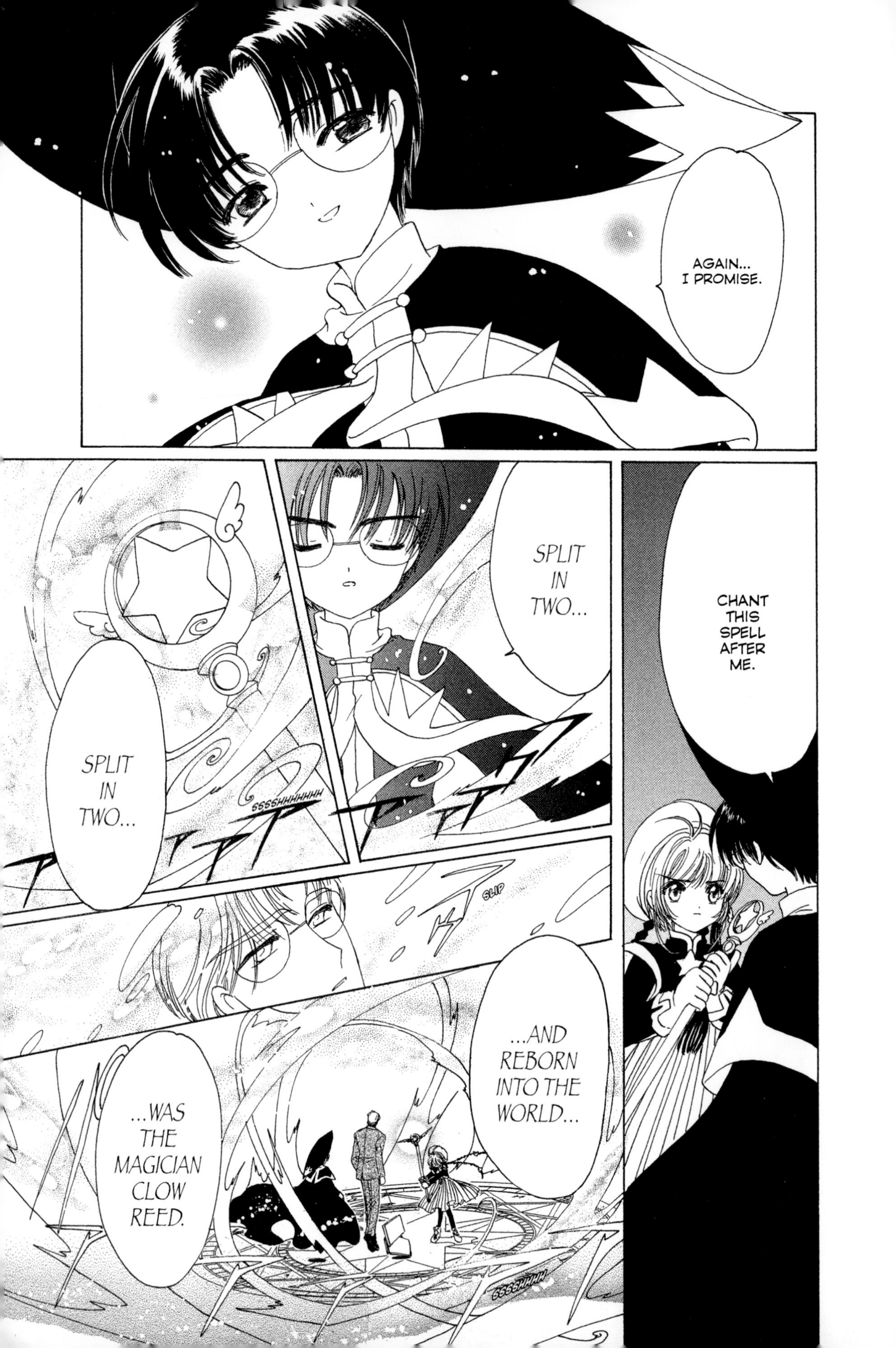
AGAIN... I PROMISE.
CHANT THIS SPELL AFTER ME.
SPLIT IN TWO...
SPLIT IN TWO...
SSSSHHHHHH
SLIP
...AND REBORN INTO THE WORLD...
...WAS THE MAGICIAN CLOW REED.
SSSSHHHH

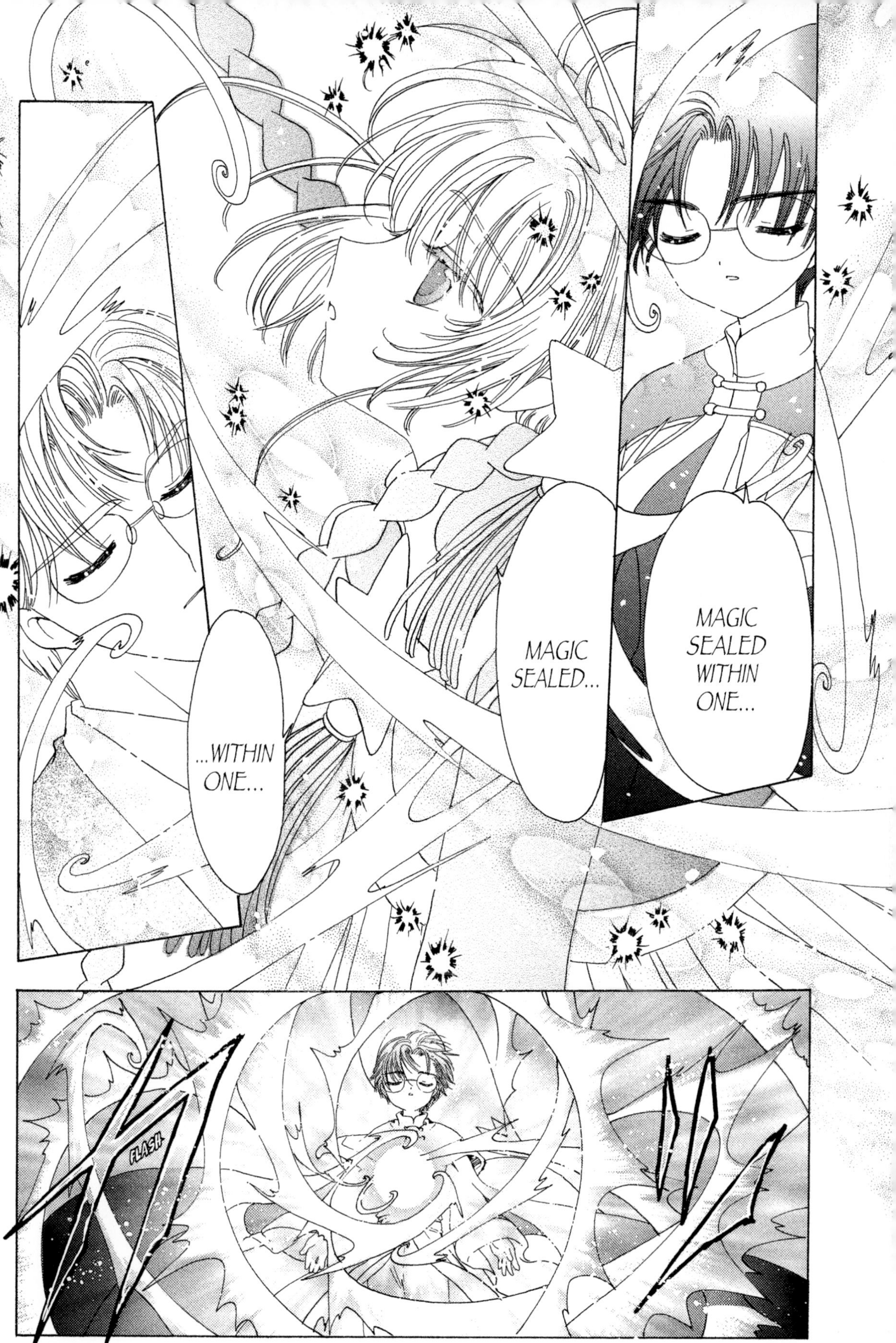
MAGIC SEALED WITHIN ONE...
MAGIC SEALED...
...WITHIN ONE...
FLASH

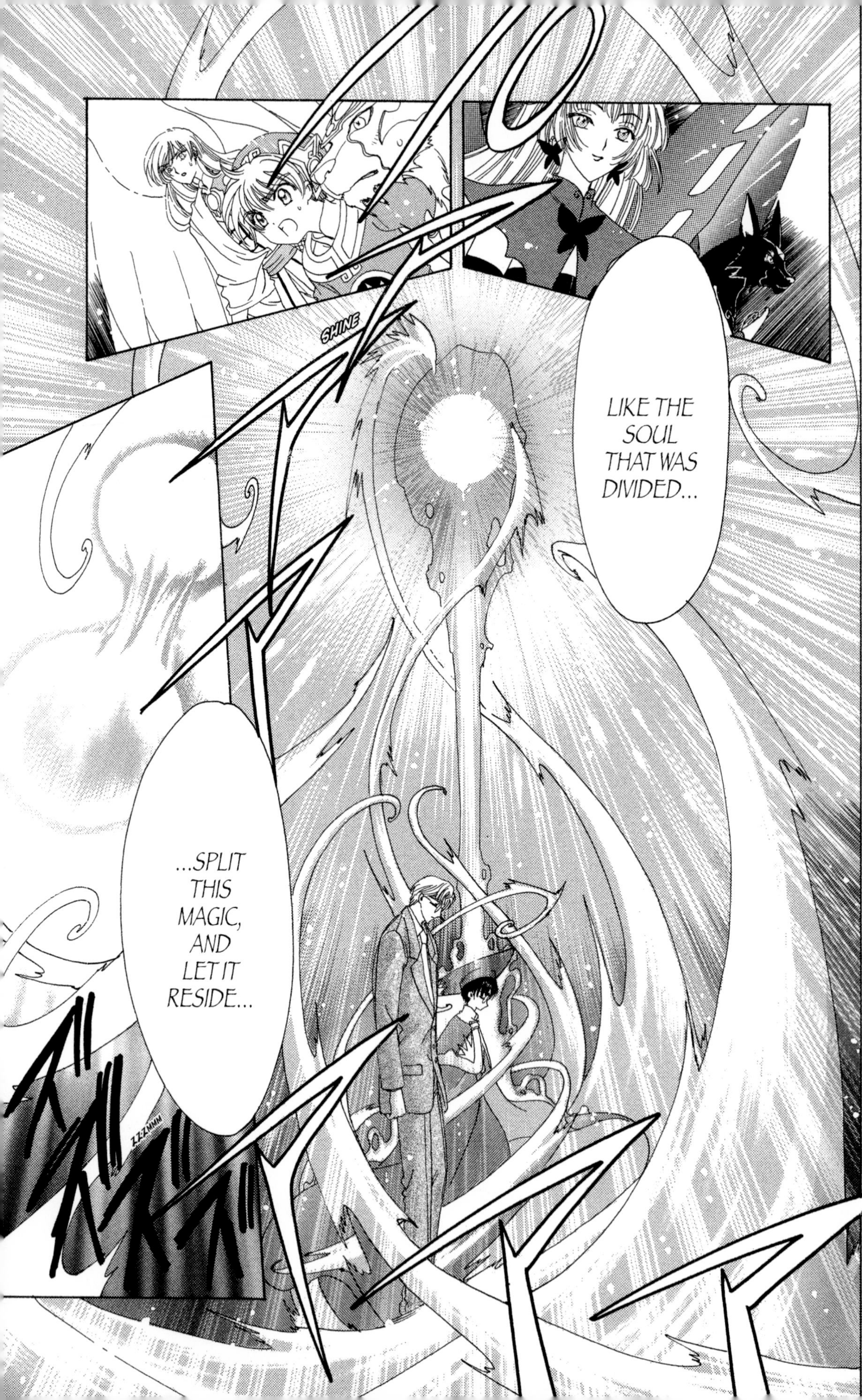
SHINE
LIKE THE SOUL THAT WAS DIVIDED...
...SPLIT THIS MAGIC, AND LET IT RESIDE...
ZZZMMM

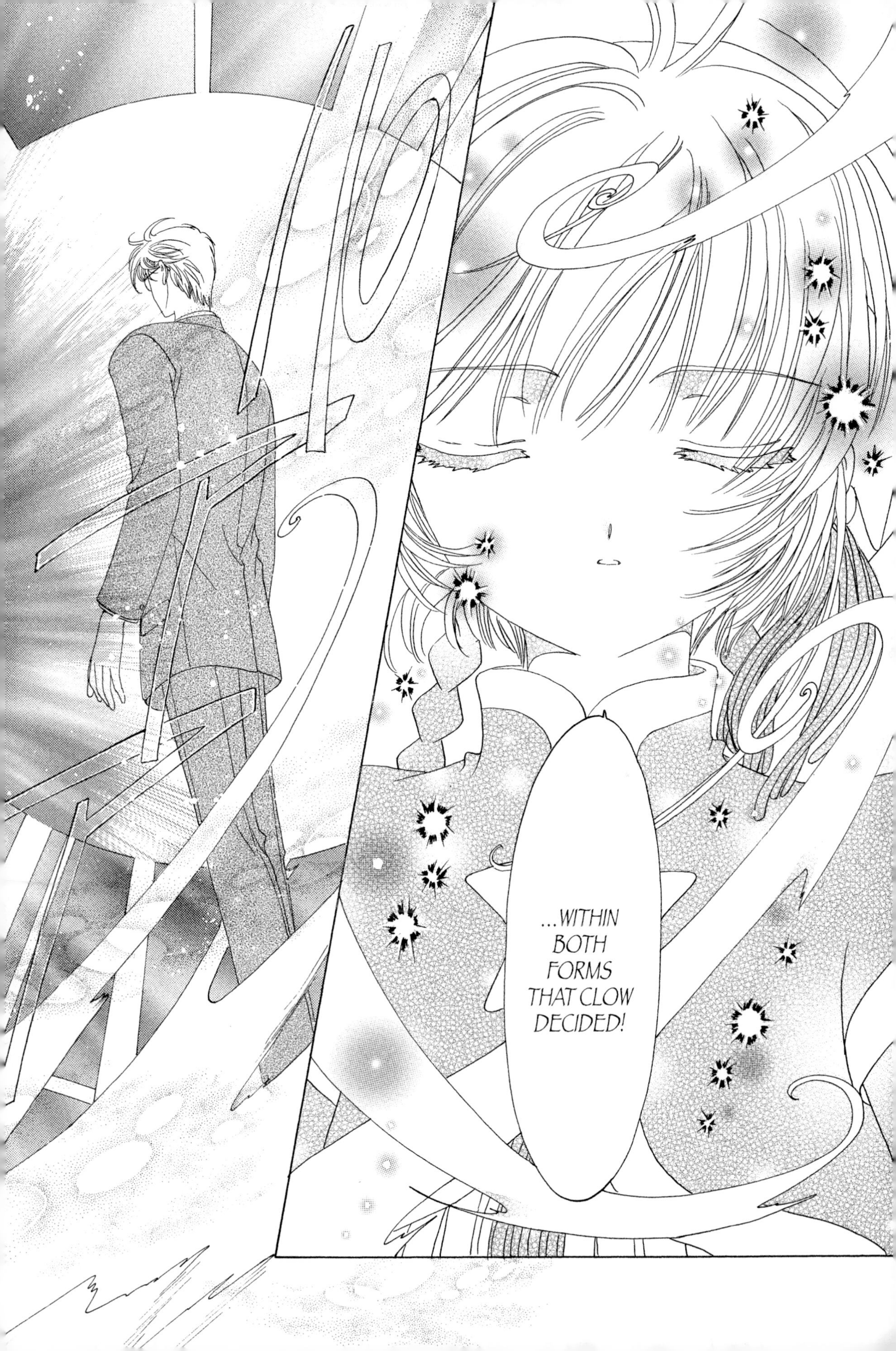
...WITHIN BOTH FORMS THAT CLOW DECIDED!

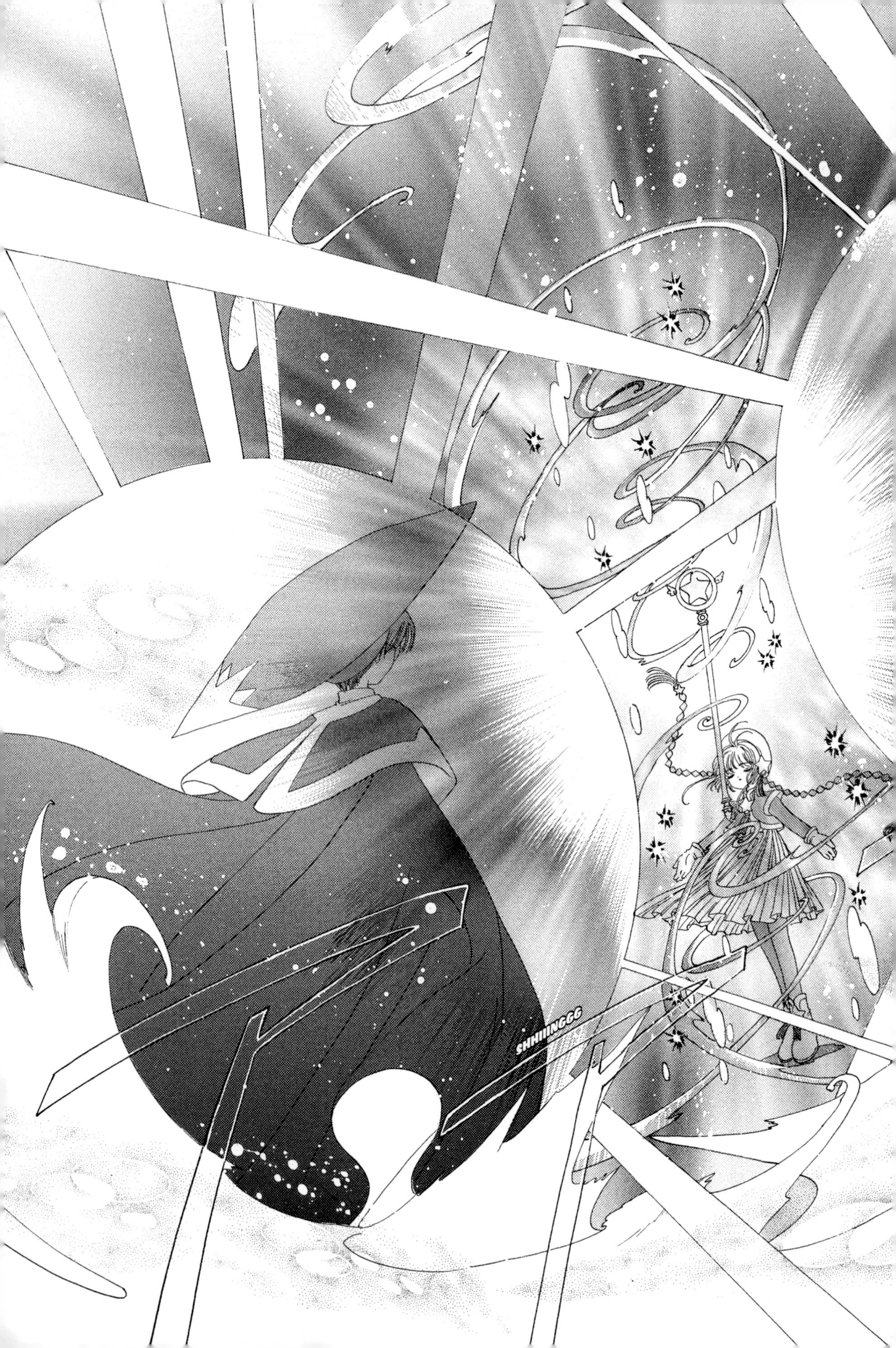
SHHIIINGGG

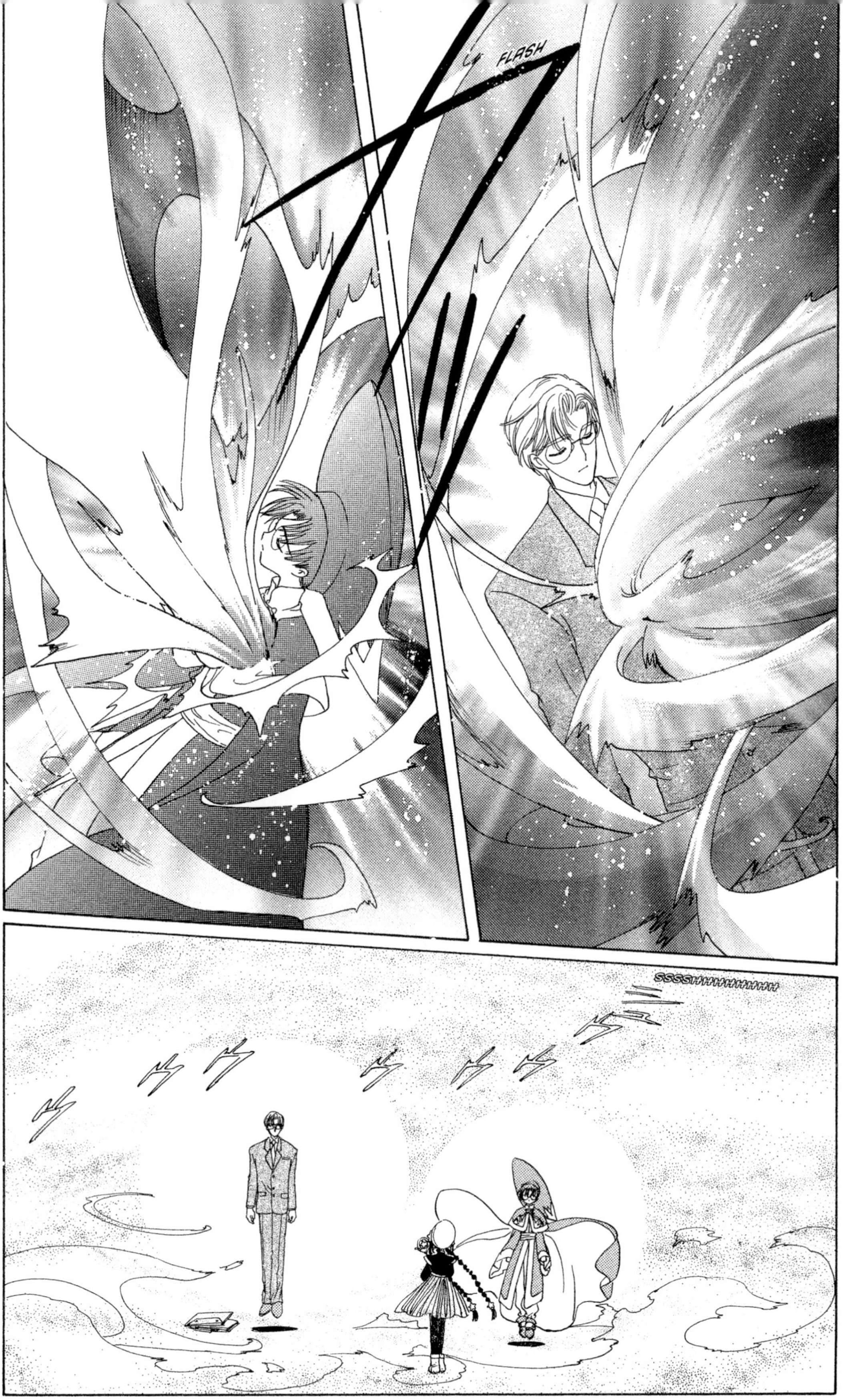
FLASH
SSSSHHHHHHHHHH

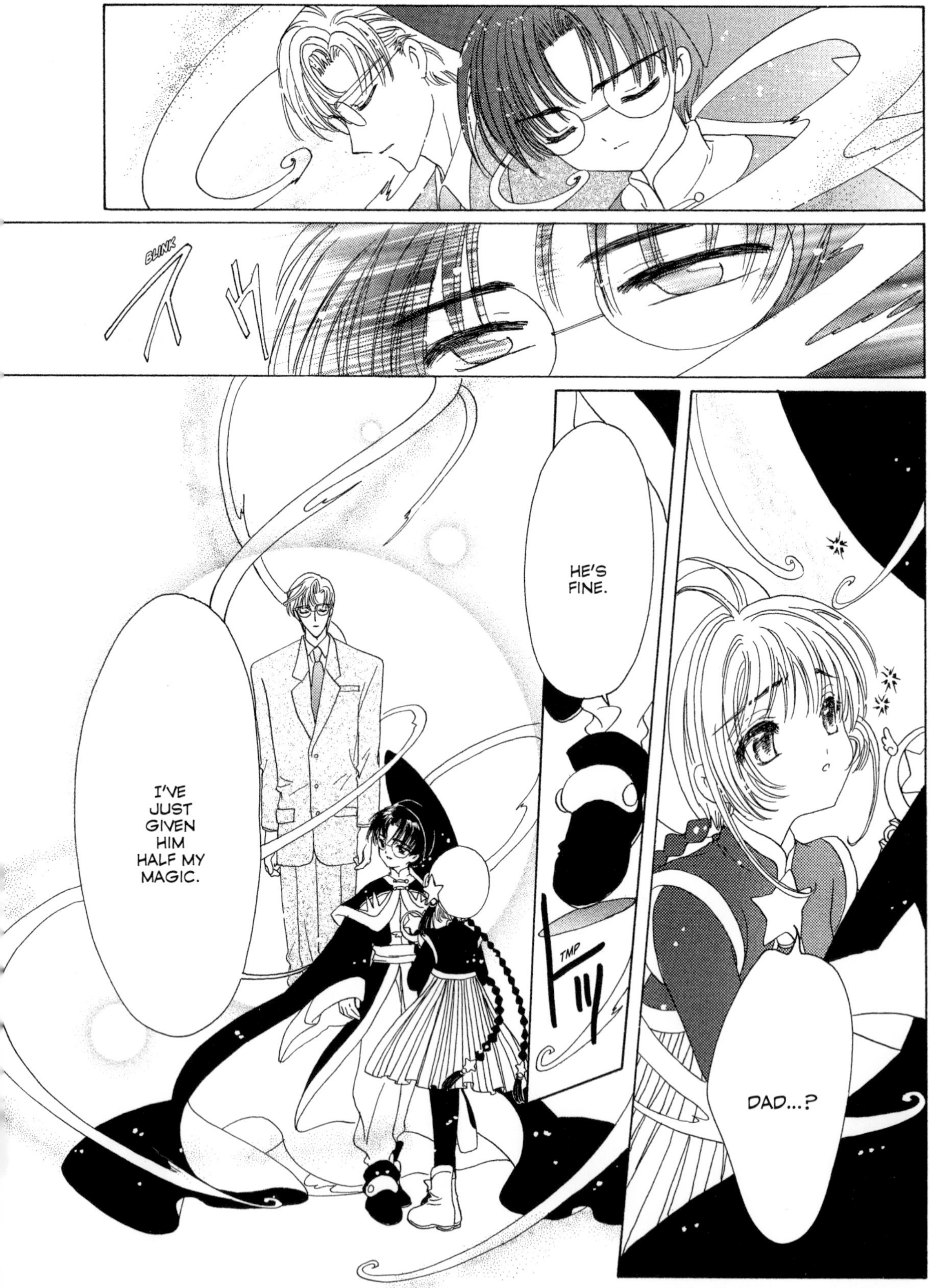
BLINK
DAD...?
HE'S FINE.
TMP
I'VE JUST GIVEN HIM HALF MY MAGIC.

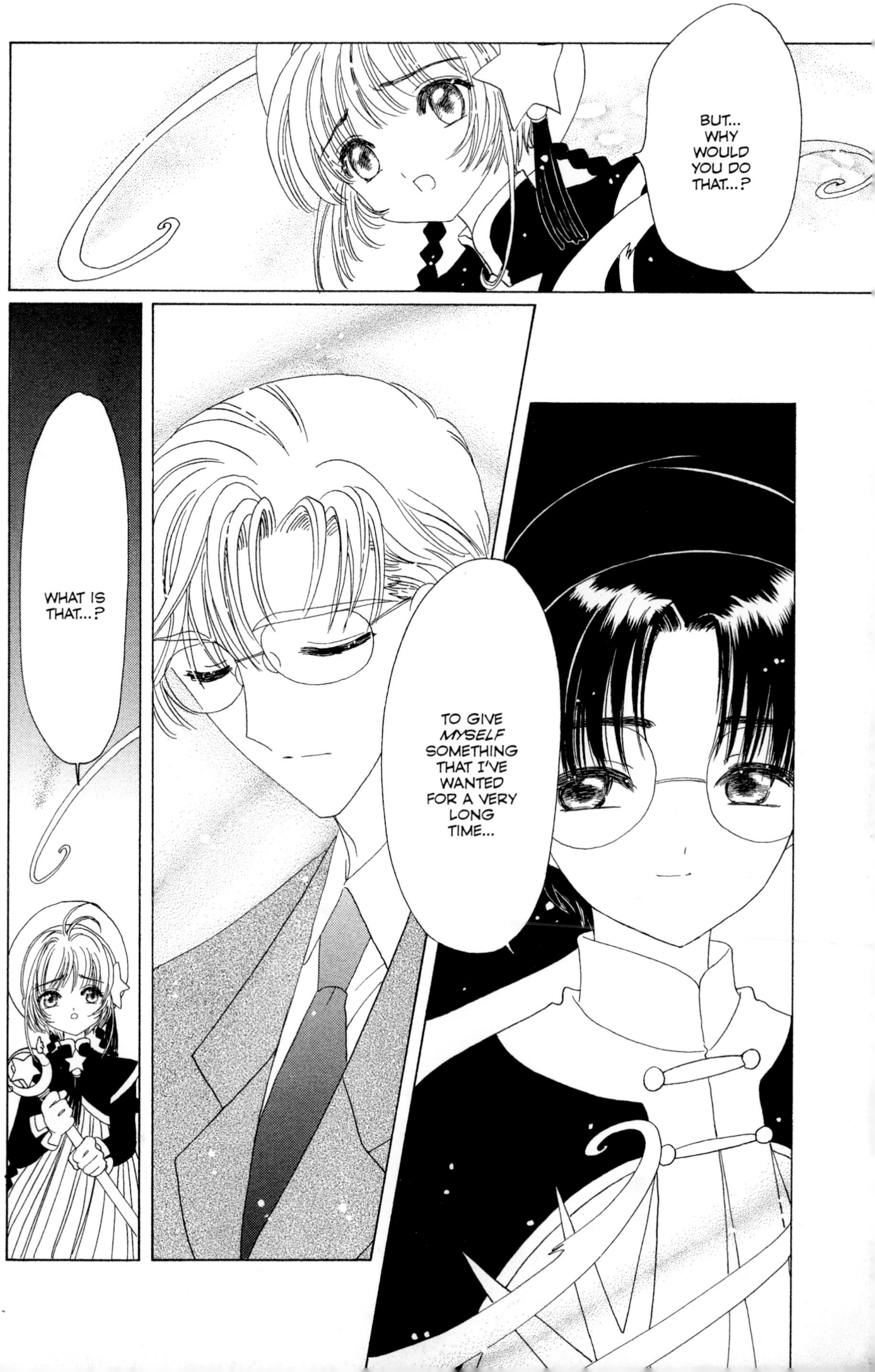
BUT... WHY WOULD YOU DO THAT...?
TO GIVE *MYSELF* SOMETHING THAT I'VE WANTED FOR A VERY LONG TIME...
WHAT IS THAT...?

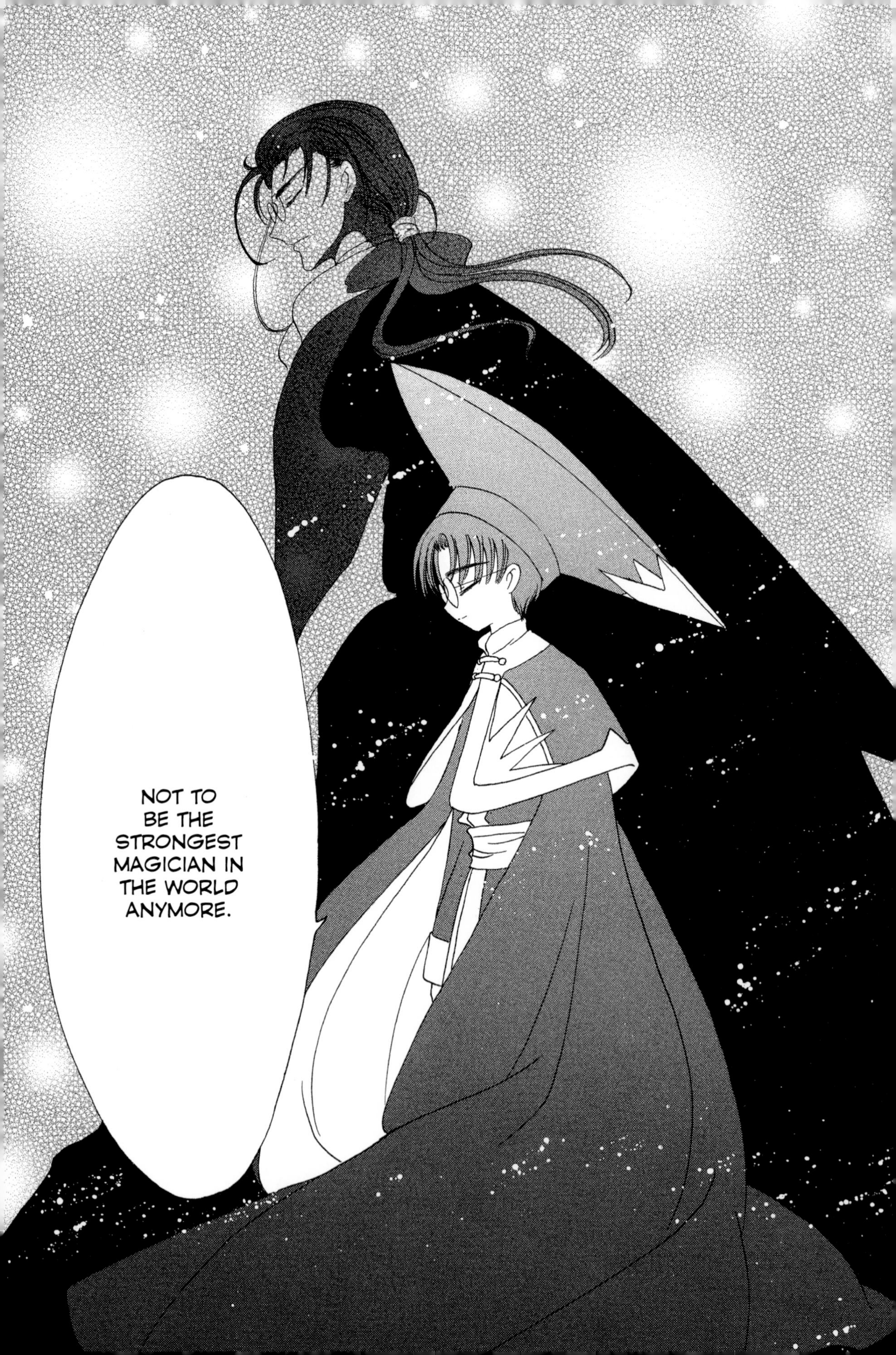
NOT TO BE THE STRONGEST MAGICIAN IN THE WORLD ANYMORE.

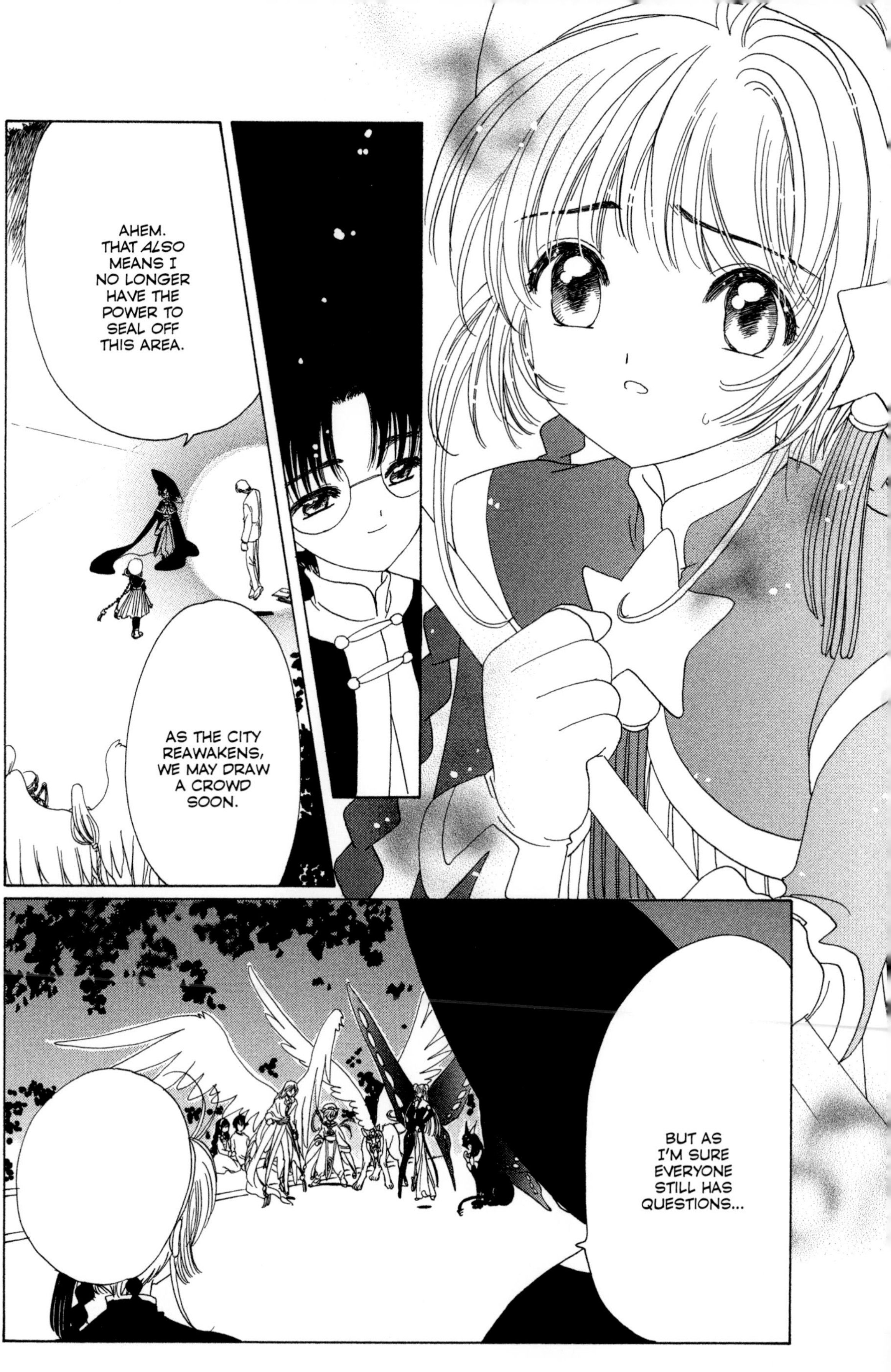
AHEM. THAT ALSO MEANS I NO LONGER HAVE THE POWER TO SEAL OFF THIS AREA.
AS THE CITY REAWAKENS, WE MAY DRAW A CROWD SOON.
BUT AS I'M SURE EVERYONE STILL HAS QUESTIONS...

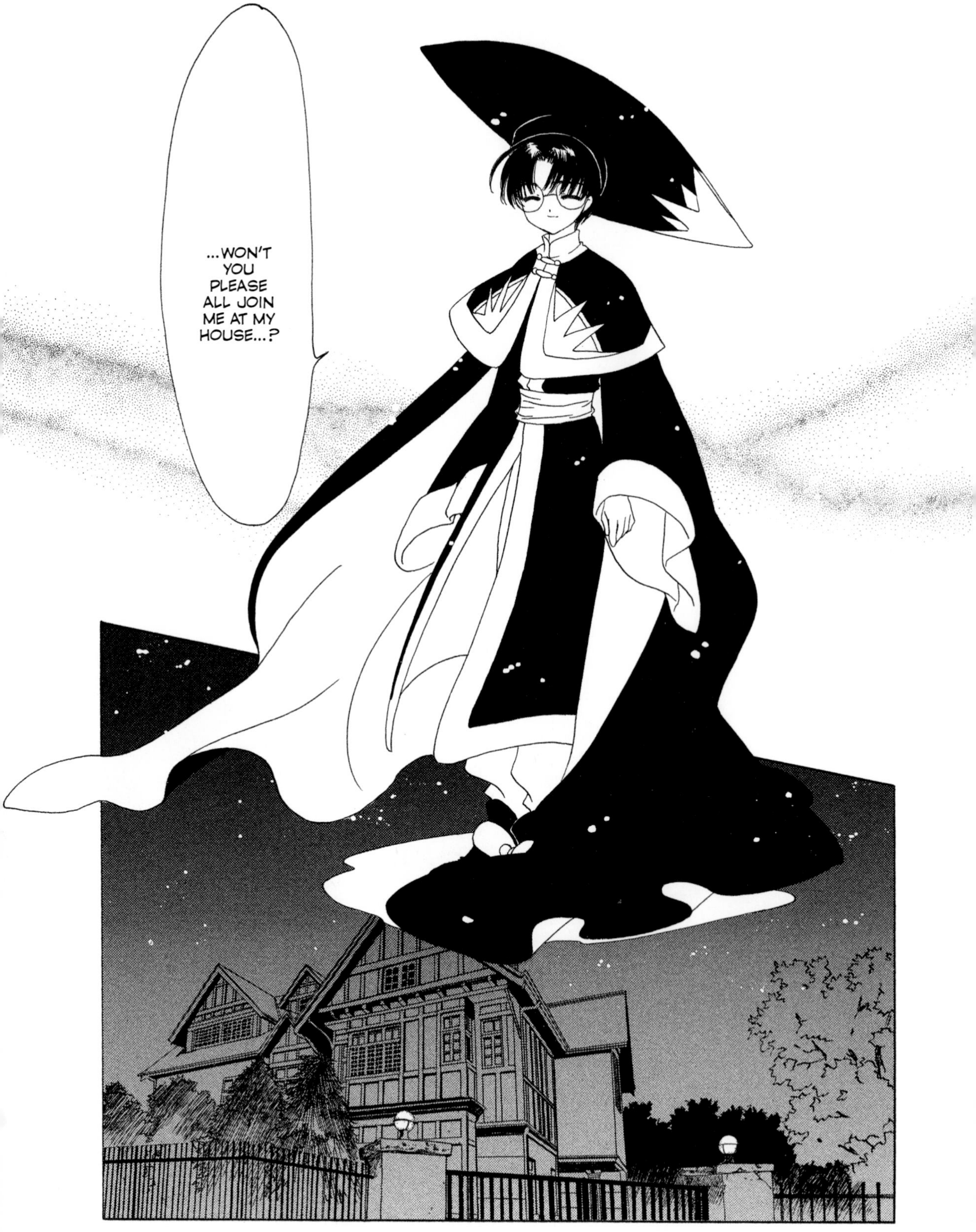
...WON'T YOU PLEASE ALL JOIN ME AT MY HOUSE...?

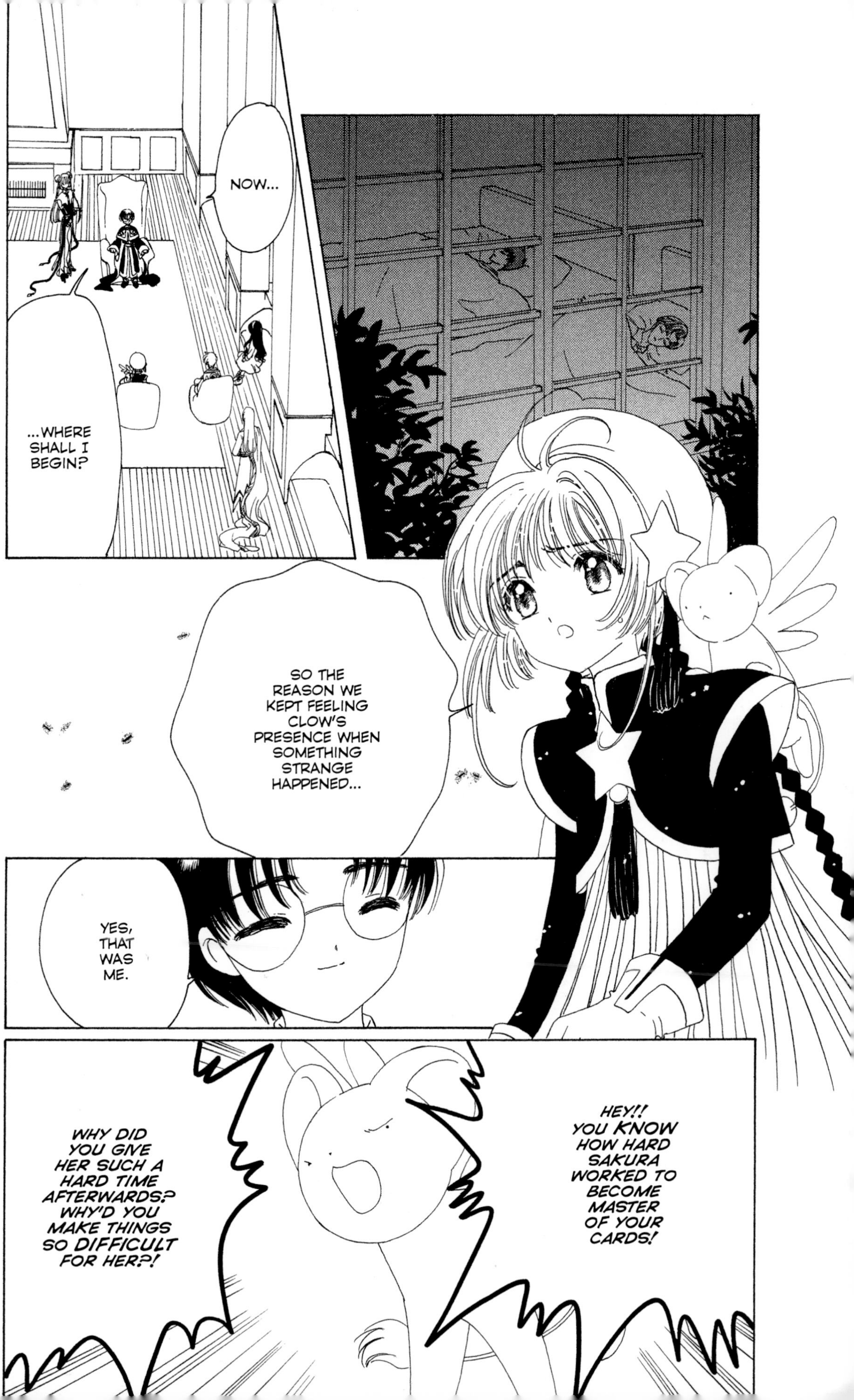
NOW...
...WHERE SHALL I BEGIN?
SO THE REASON WE KEPT FEELING CLOW'S PRESENCE WHEN SOMETHING STRANGE HAPPENED...
YES, THAT WAS ME.
HEY!! YOU KNOW HOW HARD SAKURA WORKED TO BECOME MASTER OF YOUR CARDS!
WHY DID YOU GIVE HER SUCH A HARD TIME AFTERWARDS? WHY'D YOU MAKE THINGS SO DIFFICULT FOR HER?!

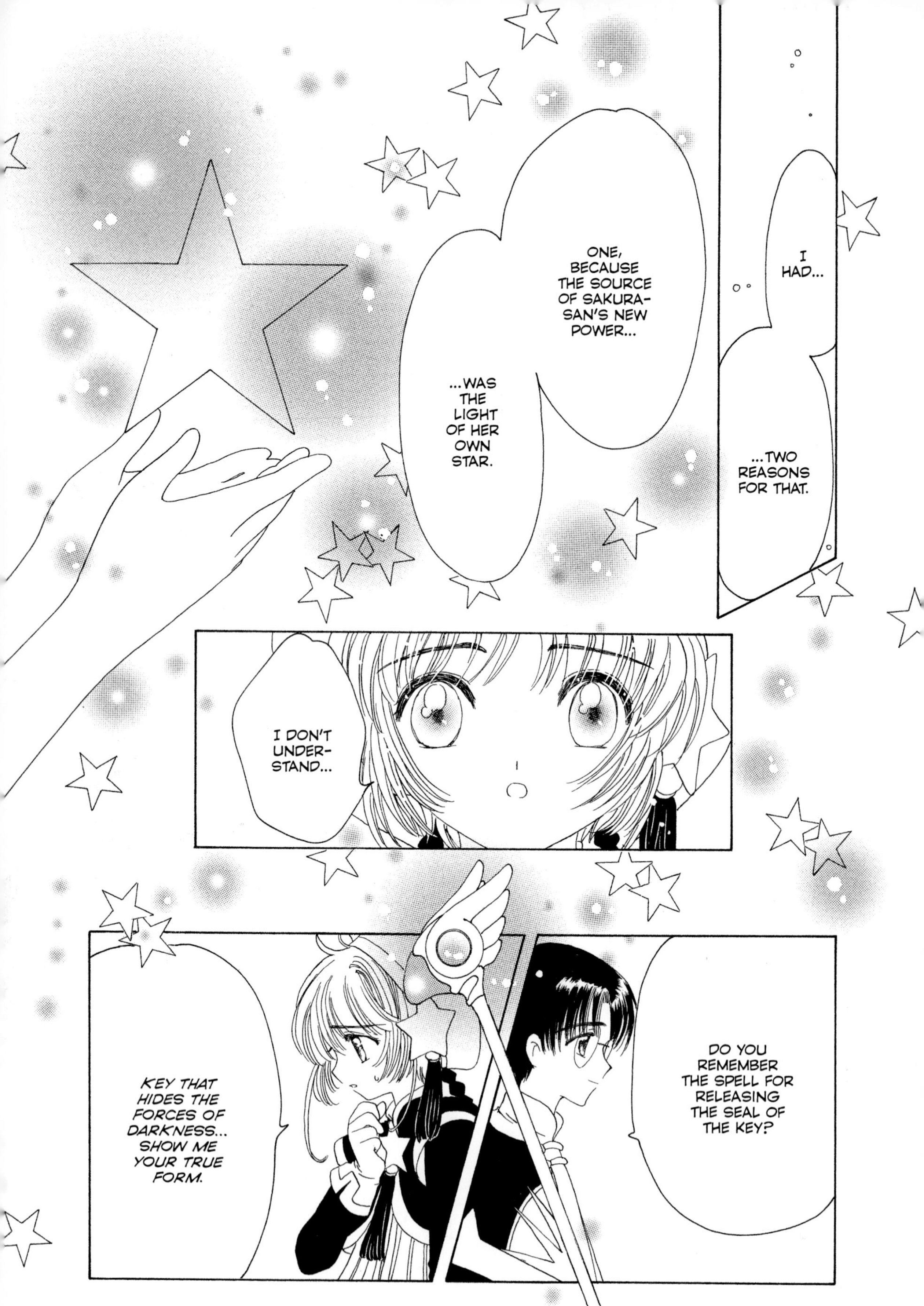
I HAD...
...TWO REASONS FOR THAT.
ONE, BECAUSE THE SOURCE OF SAKURA-SAN'S NEW POWER...
...WAS THE LIGHT OF HER OWN STAR.
I DON'T UNDER-STAND...
DO YOU REMEMBER THE SPELL FOR RELEASING THE SEAL OF THE KEY?
KEY THAT HIDES THE FORCES OF DARKNESS... SHOW ME YOUR TRUE FORM.

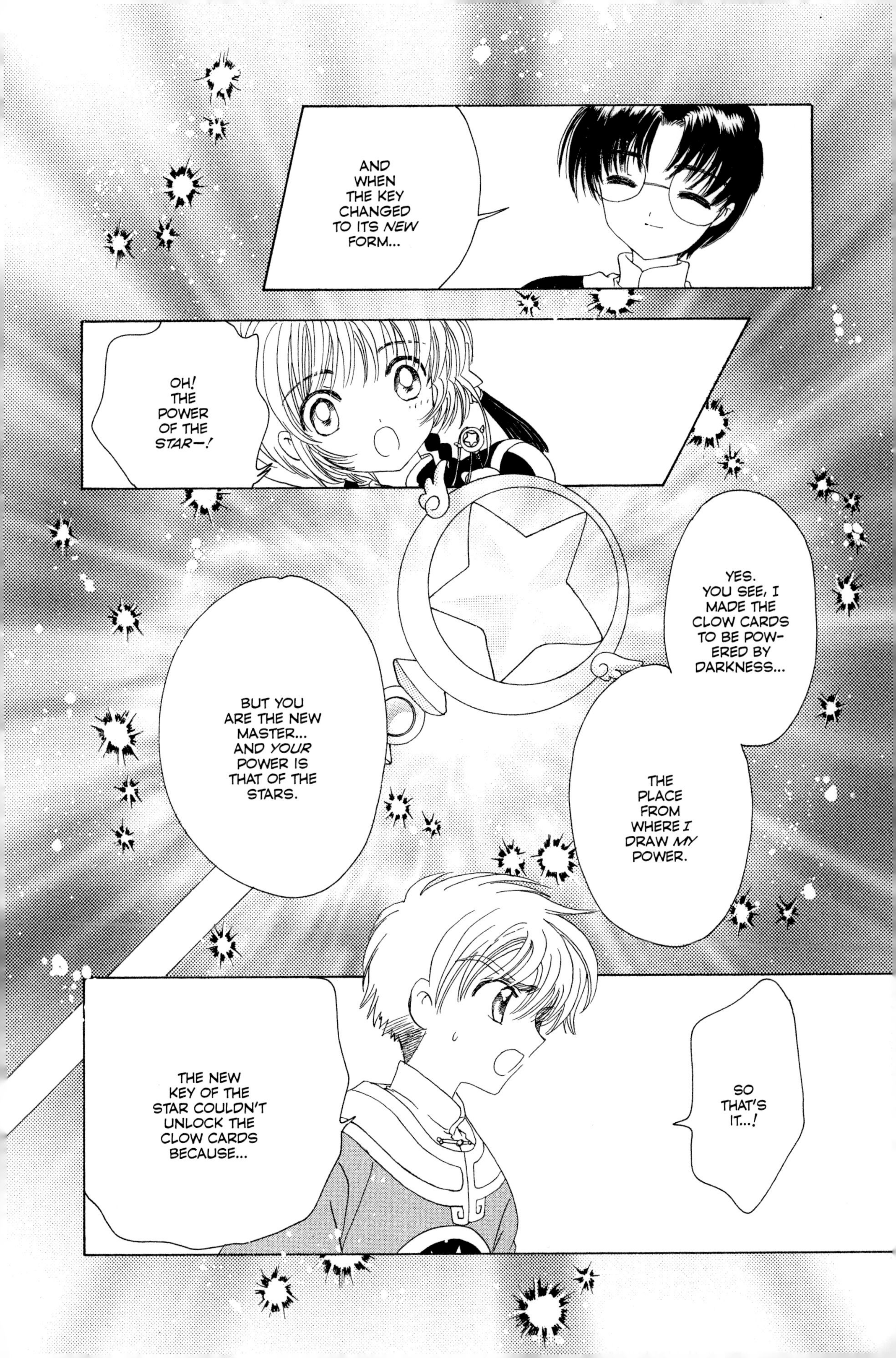
AND WHEN THE KEY CHANGED TO ITS *NEW* FORM...
OH! THE POWER OF THE *STAR*—!
YES. YOU SEE, I MADE THE CLOW CARDS TO BE POWERED BY DARKNESS...
THE PLACE FROM WHERE *I* DRAW *MY* POWER.
BUT YOU ARE THE NEW MASTER... AND *YOUR* POWER IS THAT OF THE STARS.
SO THAT'S IT...!
THE NEW KEY OF THE STAR COULDN'T UNLOCK THE CLOW CARDS BECAUSE...

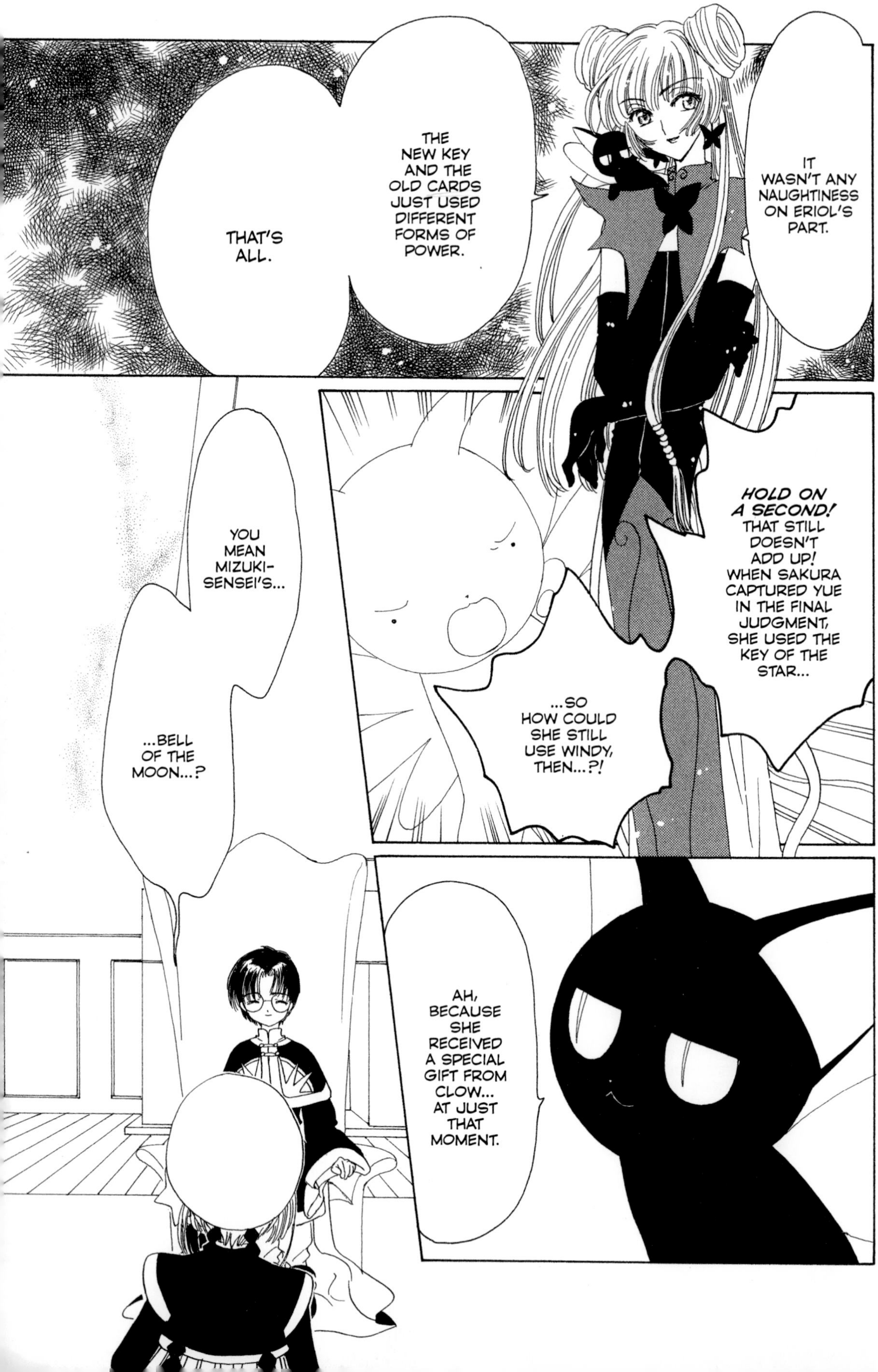
IT WASN'T ANY NAUGHTINESS ON ERIOL'S PART.
THE NEW KEY AND THE OLD CARDS JUST USED DIFFERENT FORMS OF POWER.
THAT'S ALL.
HOLD ON A SECOND! THAT STILL DOESN'T ADD UP! WHEN SAKURA CAPTURED YUE IN THE FINAL JUDGMENT, SHE USED THE KEY OF THE STAR...
...SO HOW COULD SHE STILL USE WINDY, THEN...?!
AH, BECAUSE SHE RECEIVED A SPECIAL GIFT FROM CLOW... AT JUST THAT MOMENT.
YOU MEAN MIZUKI-SENSEI'S...
...BELL OF THE MOON...?

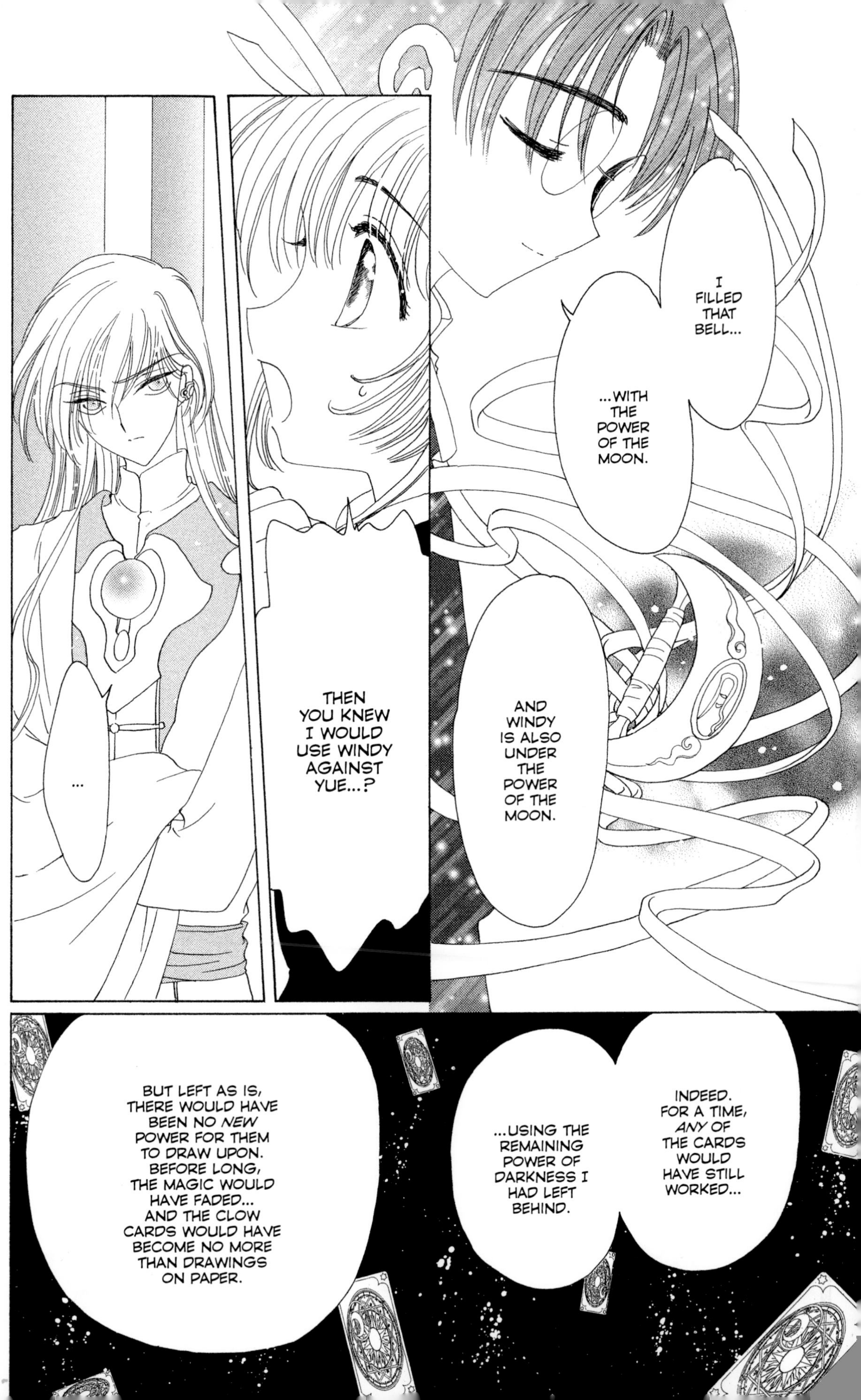
I FILLED THAT BELL...
...WITH THE POWER OF THE MOON.
AND WINDY IS ALSO UNDER THE POWER OF THE MOON.
THEN YOU KNEW I WOULD USE WINDY AGAINST YUE...?
...
INDEED. FOR A TIME, *ANY* OF THE CARDS WOULD HAVE STILL WORKED...
...USING THE REMAINING POWER OF DARKNESS I HAD LEFT BEHIND.
BUT LEFT AS IS, THERE WOULD HAVE BEEN NO *NEW* POWER FOR THEM TO DRAW UPON. BEFORE LONG, THE MAGIC WOULD HAVE FADED... AND THE CLOW CARDS WOULD HAVE BECOME NO MORE THAN DRAWINGS ON PAPER.

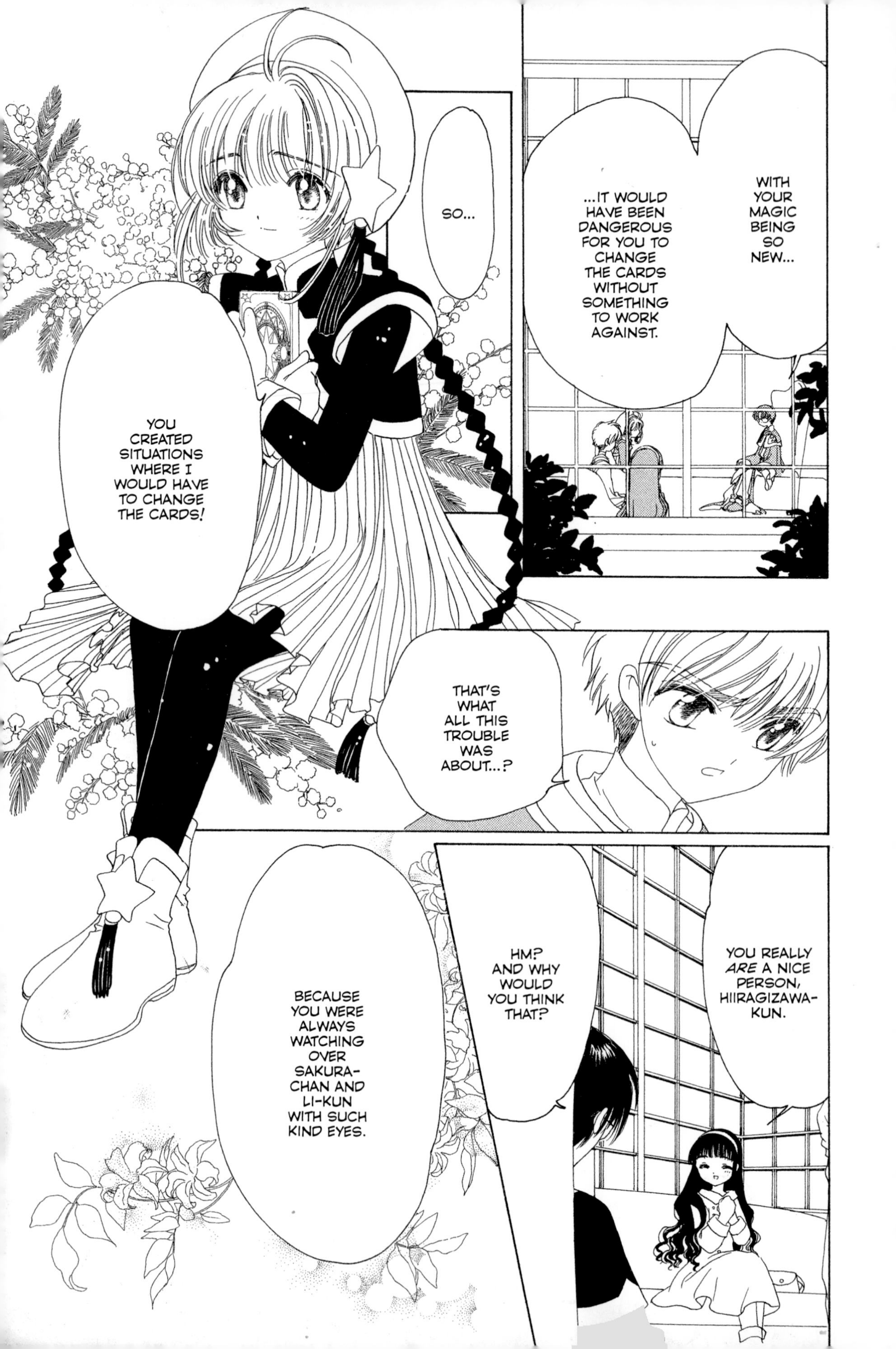
WITH YOUR MAGIC BEING SO NEW...
...IT WOULD HAVE BEEN DANGEROUS FOR YOU TO CHANGE THE CARDS WITHOUT SOMETHING TO WORK AGAINST.
SO...
YOU CREATED SITUATIONS WHERE I WOULD HAVE TO CHANGE THE CARDS!
THAT'S WHAT ALL THIS TROUBLE WAS ABOUT...?
YOU REALLY *ARE* A NICE PERSON, HIIRAGIZAWA-KUN.
HM? AND WHY WOULD YOU THINK THAT?
BECAUSE YOU WERE ALWAYS WATCHING OVER SAKURA-CHAN AND LI-KUN WITH SUCH KIND EYES.

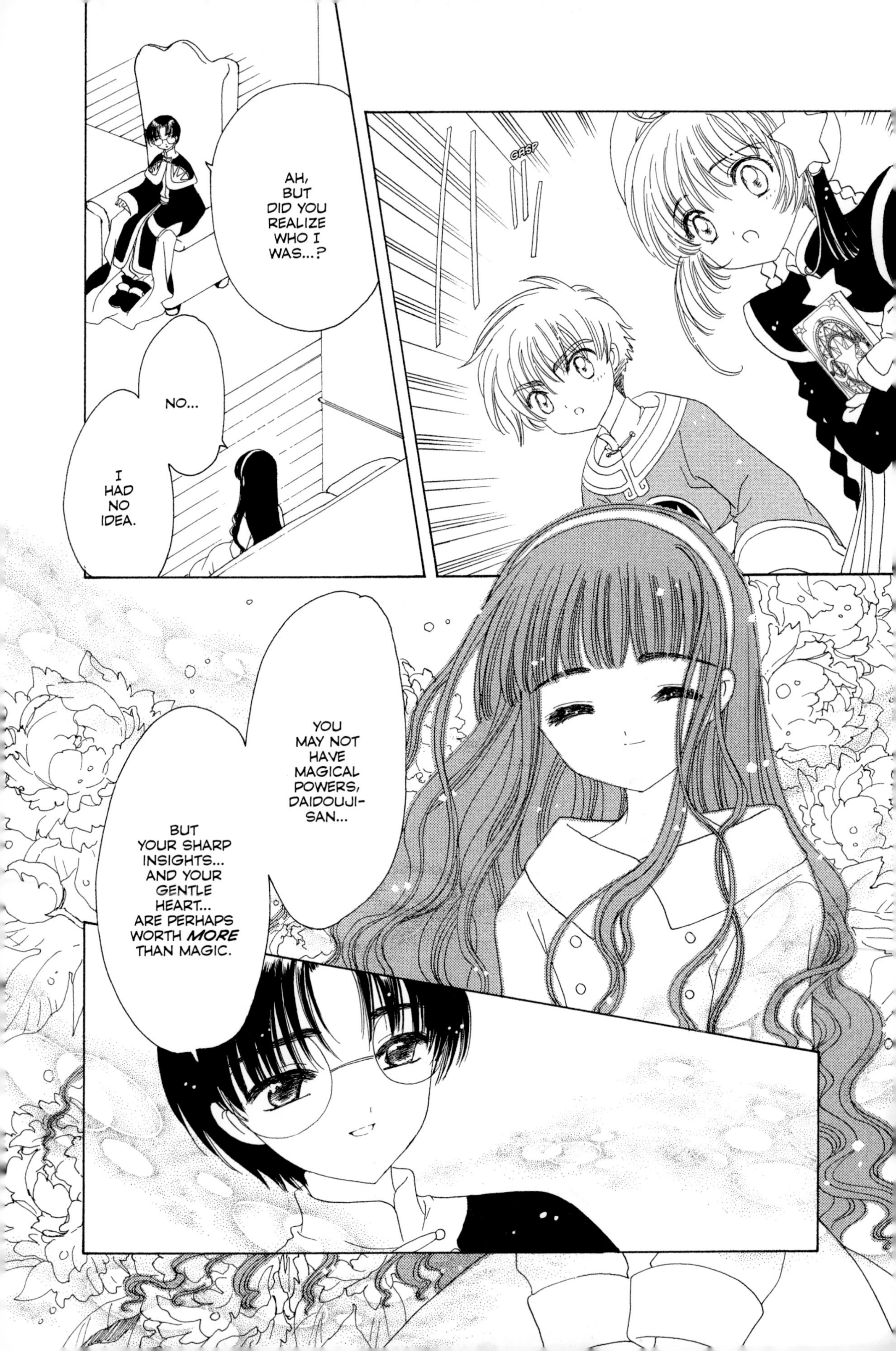
GASP
AH, BUT DID YOU REALIZE WHO I WAS...?
NO...
I HAD NO IDEA.
YOU MAY NOT HAVE MAGICAL POWERS, DAIDOUJI-SAN...
BUT YOUR SHARP INSIGHTS... AND YOUR GENTLE HEART... ARE PERHAPS WORTH *MORE* THAN MAGIC.

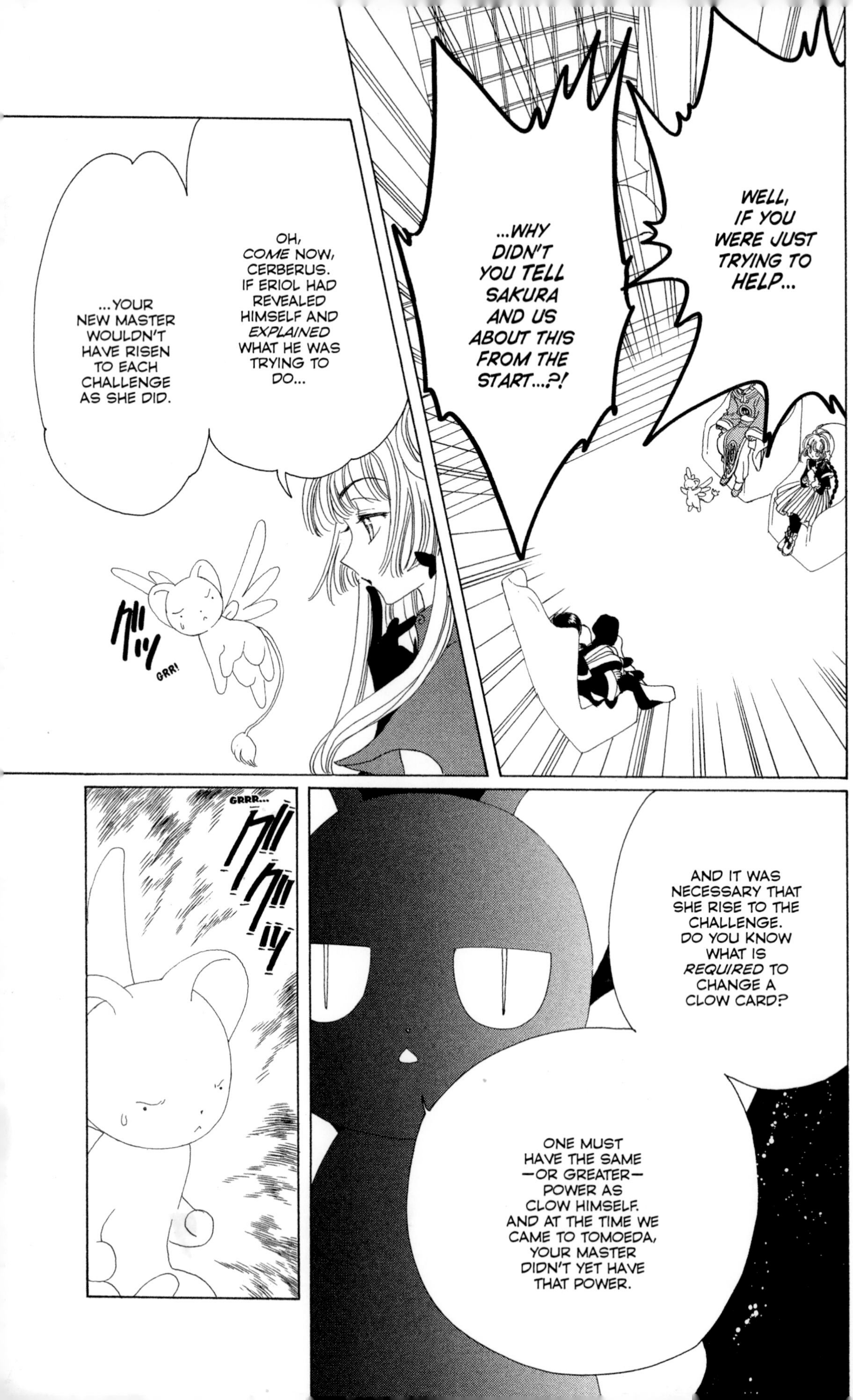
WELL, IF YOU WERE JUST TRYING TO HELP...
...WHY DIDN'T YOU TELL SAKURA AND US ABOUT THIS FROM THE START...?!
OH, COME NOW, CERBERUS. IF ERIOL HAD REVEALED HIMSELF AND EXPLAINED WHAT HE WAS TRYING TO DO...
...YOUR NEW MASTER WOULDN'T HAVE RISEN TO EACH CHALLENGE AS SHE DID.
GRR!
AND IT WAS NECESSARY THAT SHE RISE TO THE CHALLENGE. DO YOU KNOW WHAT IS REQUIRED TO CHANGE A CLOW CARD?
ONE MUST HAVE THE SAME —OR GREATER— POWER AS CLOW HIMSELF. AND AT THE TIME WE CAME TO TOMOEDA, YOUR MASTER DIDN'T YET HAVE THAT POWER.
GRRR...

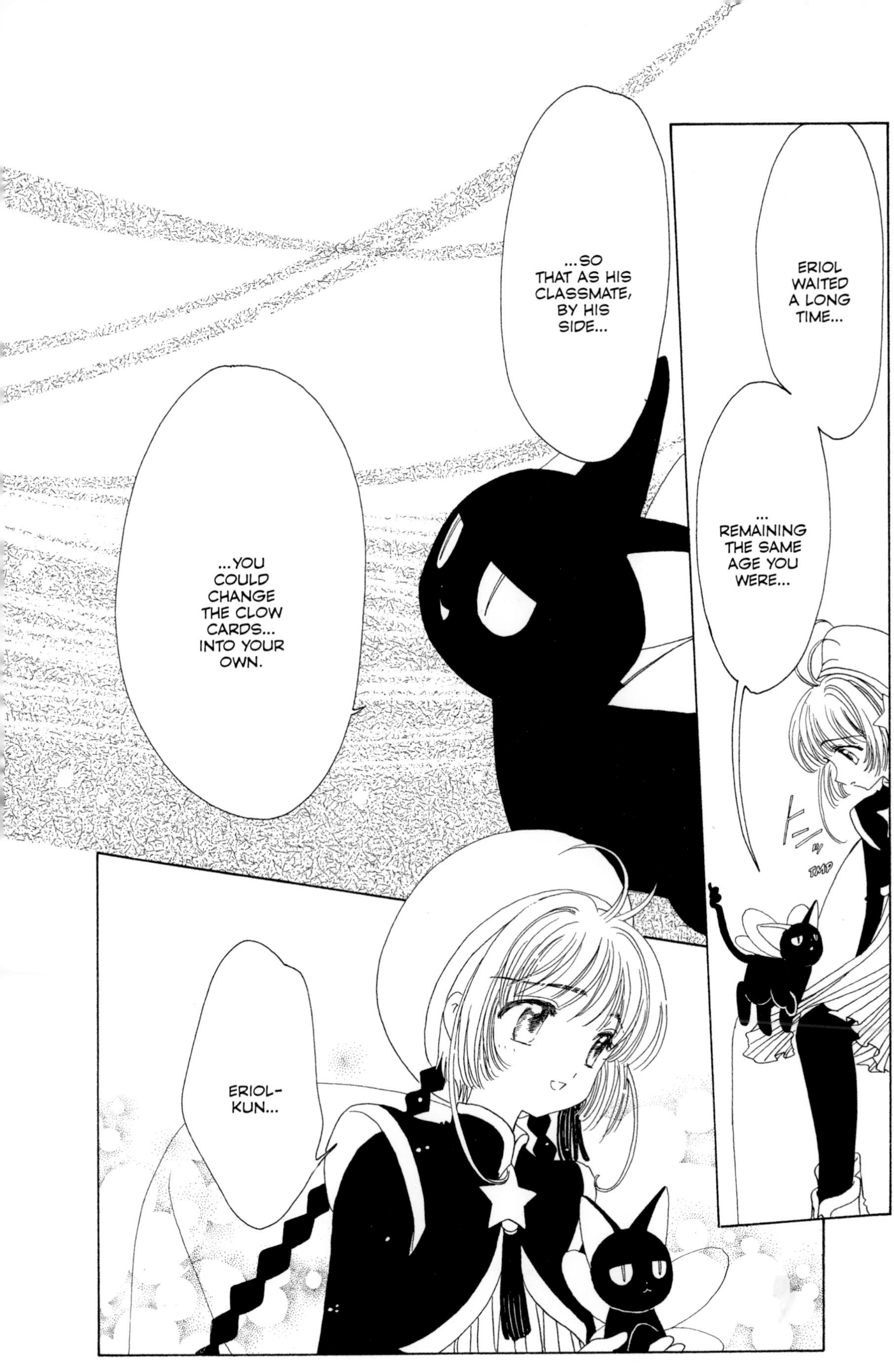
ERIOL WAITED A LONG TIME...
...REMAINING THE SAME AGE YOU WERE...
TMP
...SO THAT AS HIS CLASSMATE, BY HIS SIDE...
...YOU COULD CHANGE THE CLOW CARDS... INTO YOUR OWN.
ERIOL-KUN...

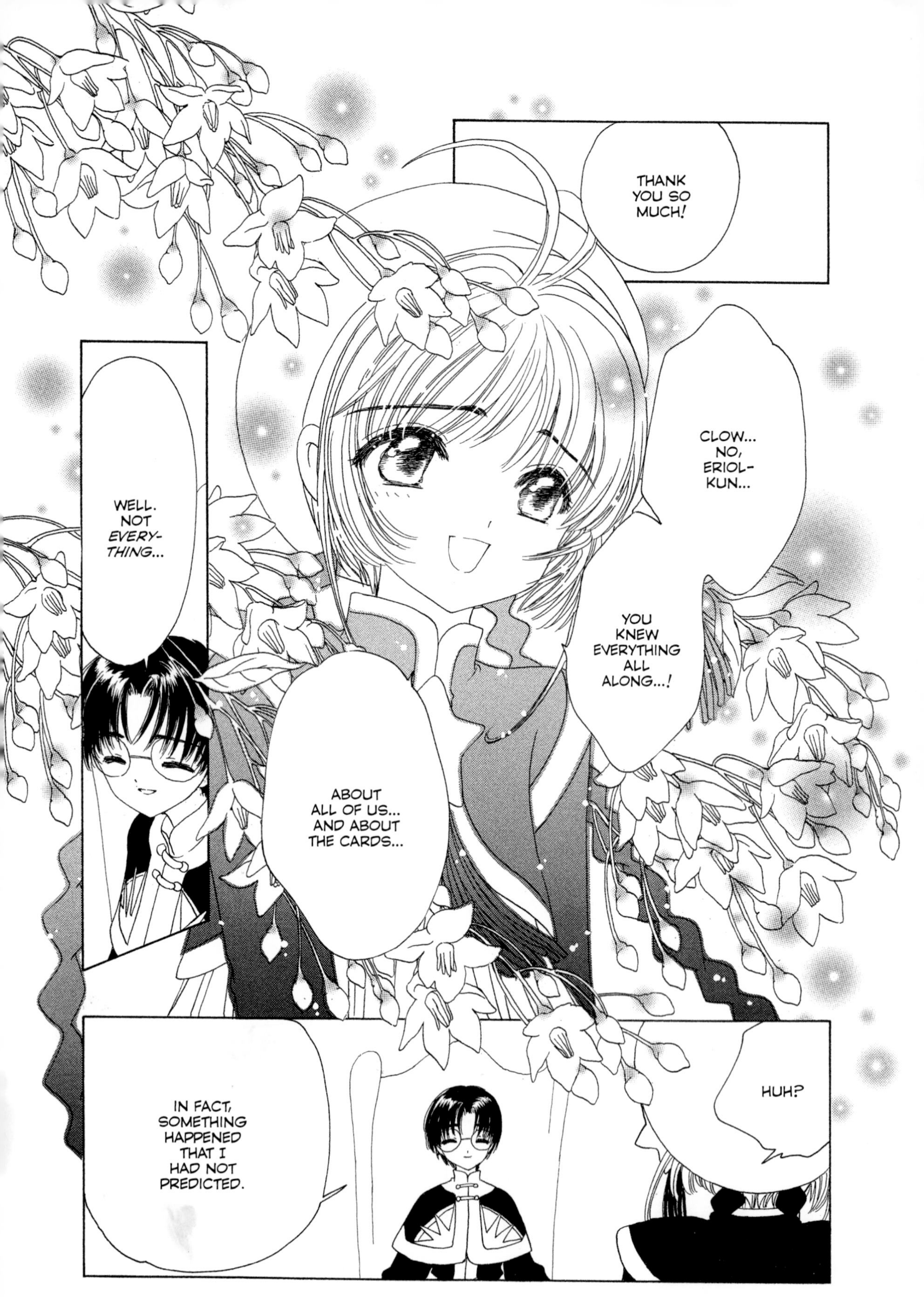
THANK YOU SO MUCH!
CLOW... NO, ERIOL-KUN...
YOU KNEW EVERYTHING ALL ALONG...!
ABOUT ALL OF US... AND ABOUT THE CARDS...
WELL. NOT *EVERYTHING*...
HUH?
IN FACT, SOMETHING HAPPENED THAT I HAD NOT PREDICTED.

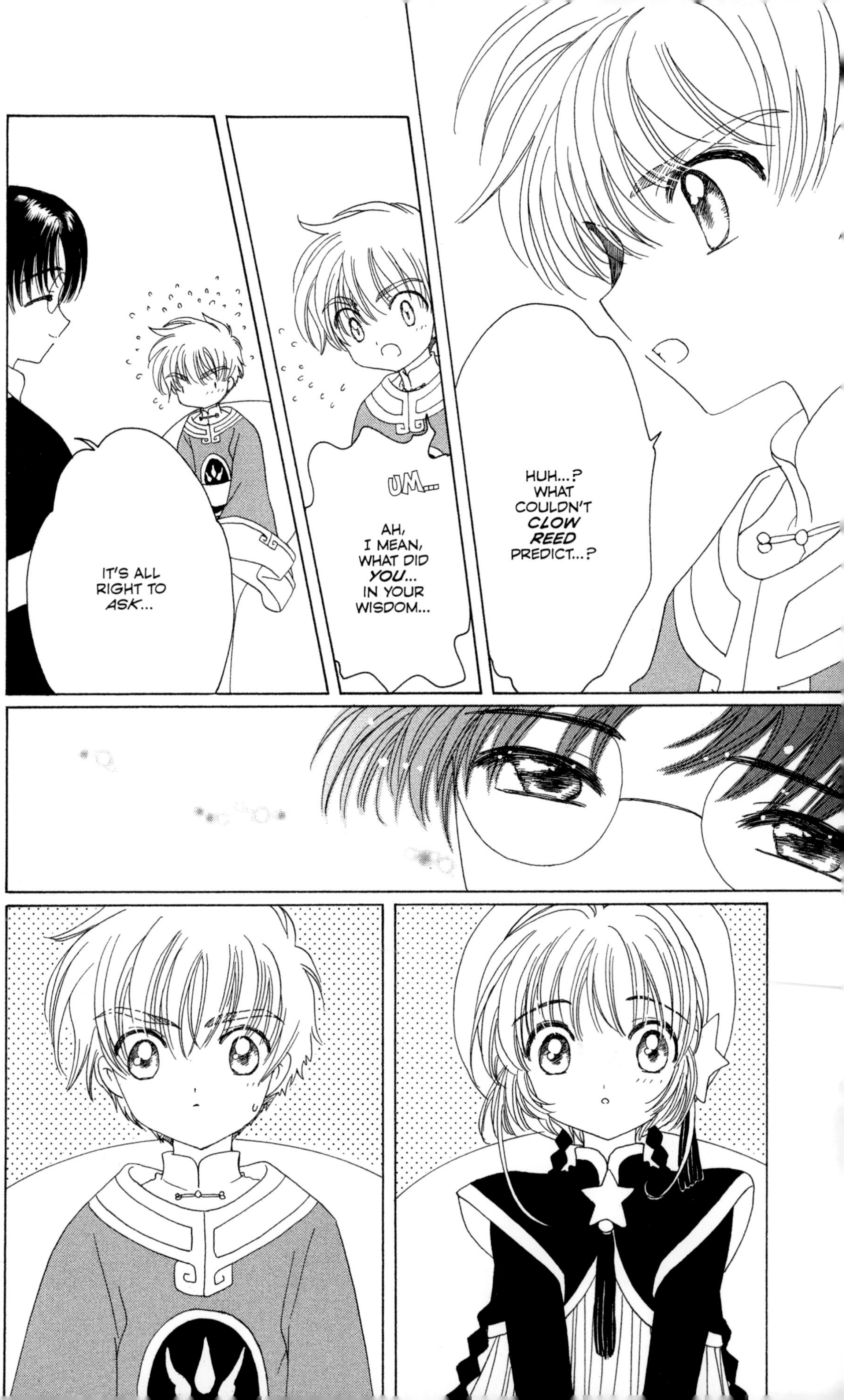
HUH...? WHAT COULDN'T *CLOW REED* PREDICT...?
UM...
AH, I MEAN, WHAT DID *YOU*... IN YOUR WISDOM...
IT'S ALL RIGHT TO *ASK*...

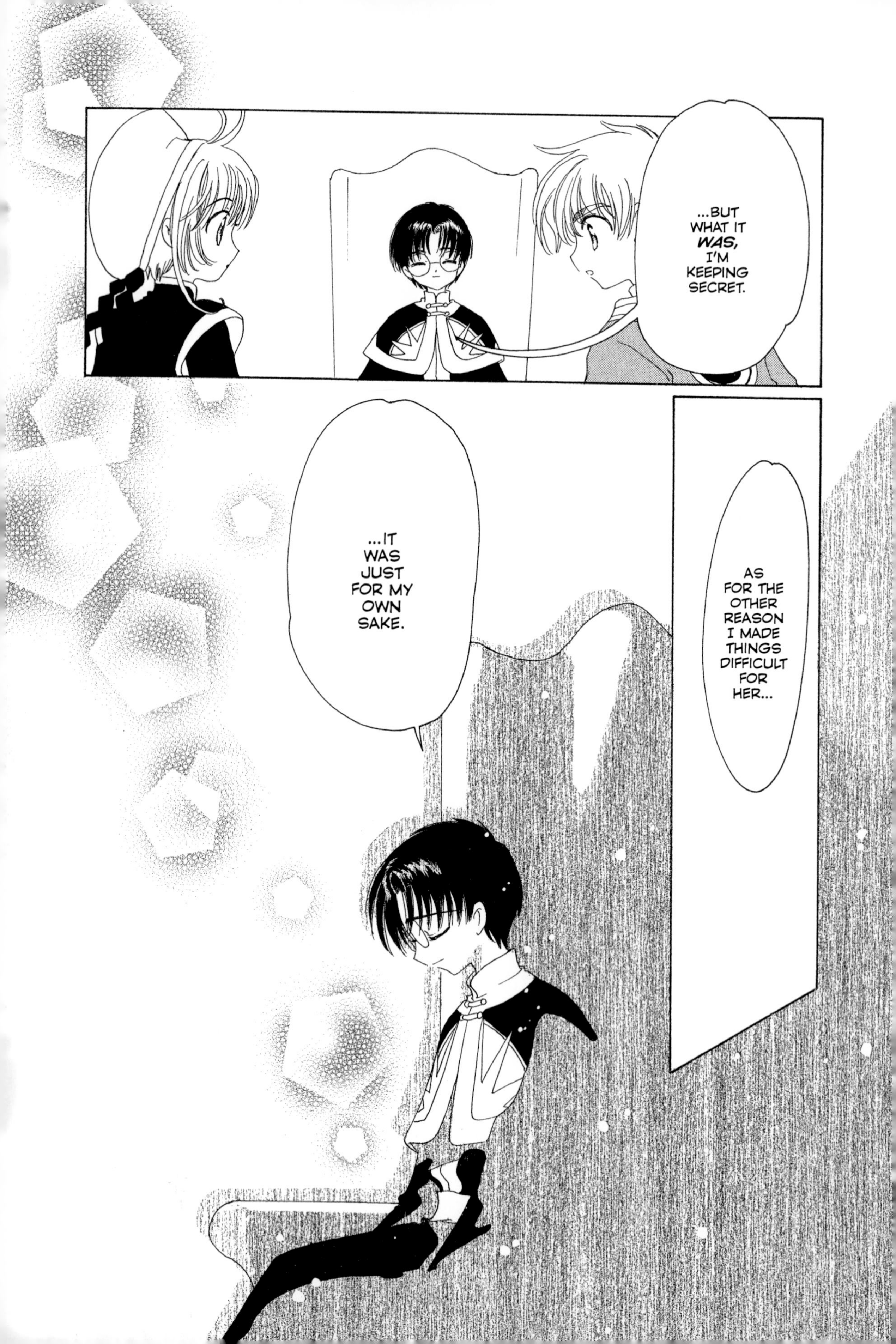
...BUT WHAT IT *WAS,* I'M KEEPING SECRET.
AS FOR THE OTHER REASON I MADE THINGS DIFFICULT FOR HER...
...IT WAS JUST FOR MY OWN SAKE.

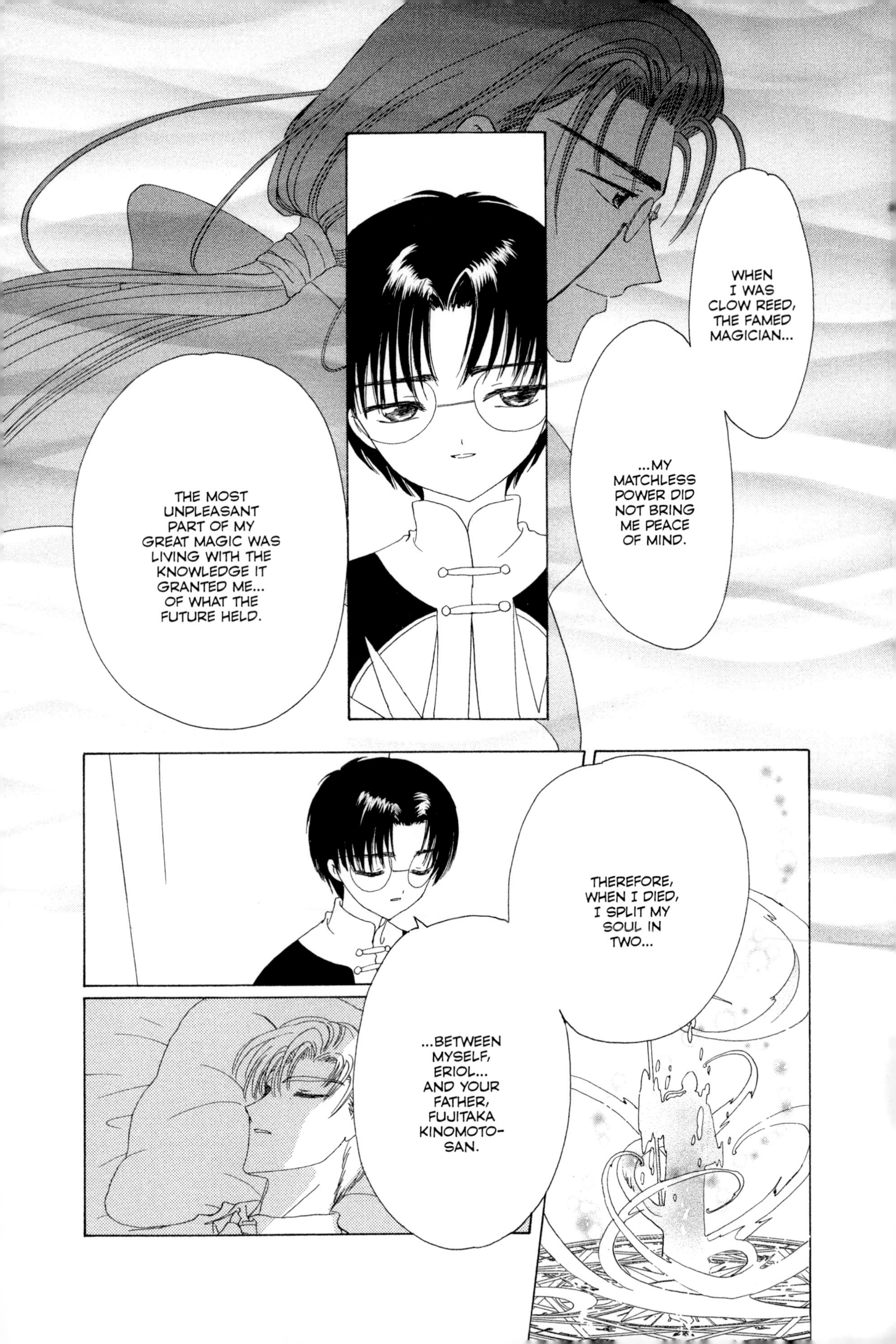
WHEN I WAS CLOW REED, THE FAMED MAGICIAN...
...MY MATCHLESS POWER DID NOT BRING ME PEACE OF MIND.
THE MOST UNPLEASANT PART OF MY GREAT MAGIC WAS LIVING WITH THE KNOWLEDGE IT GRANTED ME... OF WHAT THE FUTURE HELD.
THEREFORE, WHEN I DIED, I SPLIT MY SOUL IN TWO...
...BETWEEN MYSELF, ERIOL... AND YOUR FATHER, FUJITAKA KINOMOTO-SAN.

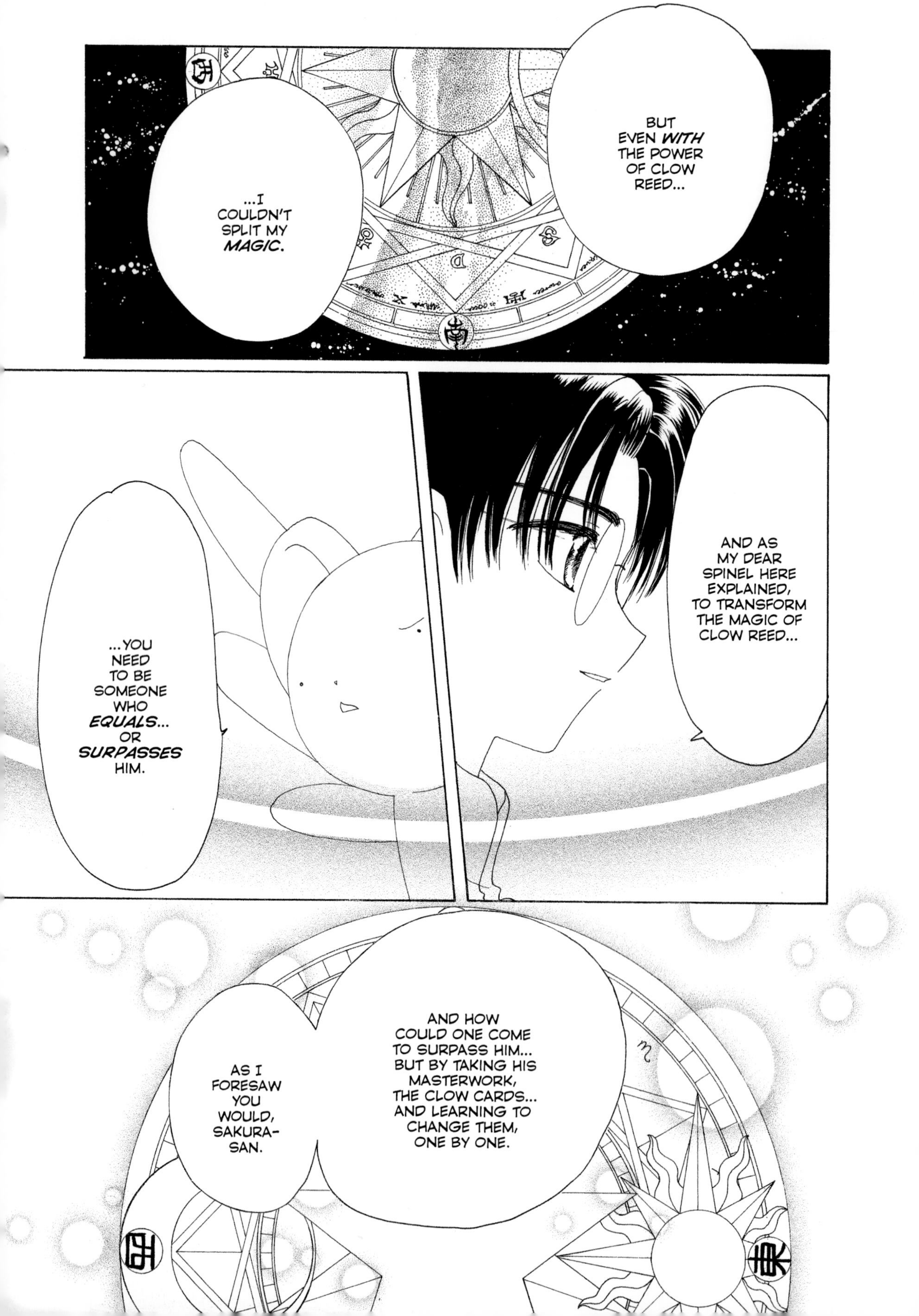
BUT EVEN *WITH* THE POWER OF CLOW REED...
...I COULDN'T SPLIT MY *MAGIC*.
AND AS MY DEAR SPINEL HERE EXPLAINED, TO TRANSFORM THE MAGIC OF CLOW REED...
...YOU NEED TO BE SOMEONE WHO *EQUALS*... OR *SURPASSES* HIM.
AND HOW COULD ONE COME TO SURPASS HIM... BUT BY TAKING HIS MASTERWORK, THE CLOW CARDS... AND LEARNING TO CHANGE THEM, ONE BY ONE.
AS I FORESAW YOU WOULD, SAKURA-SAN.

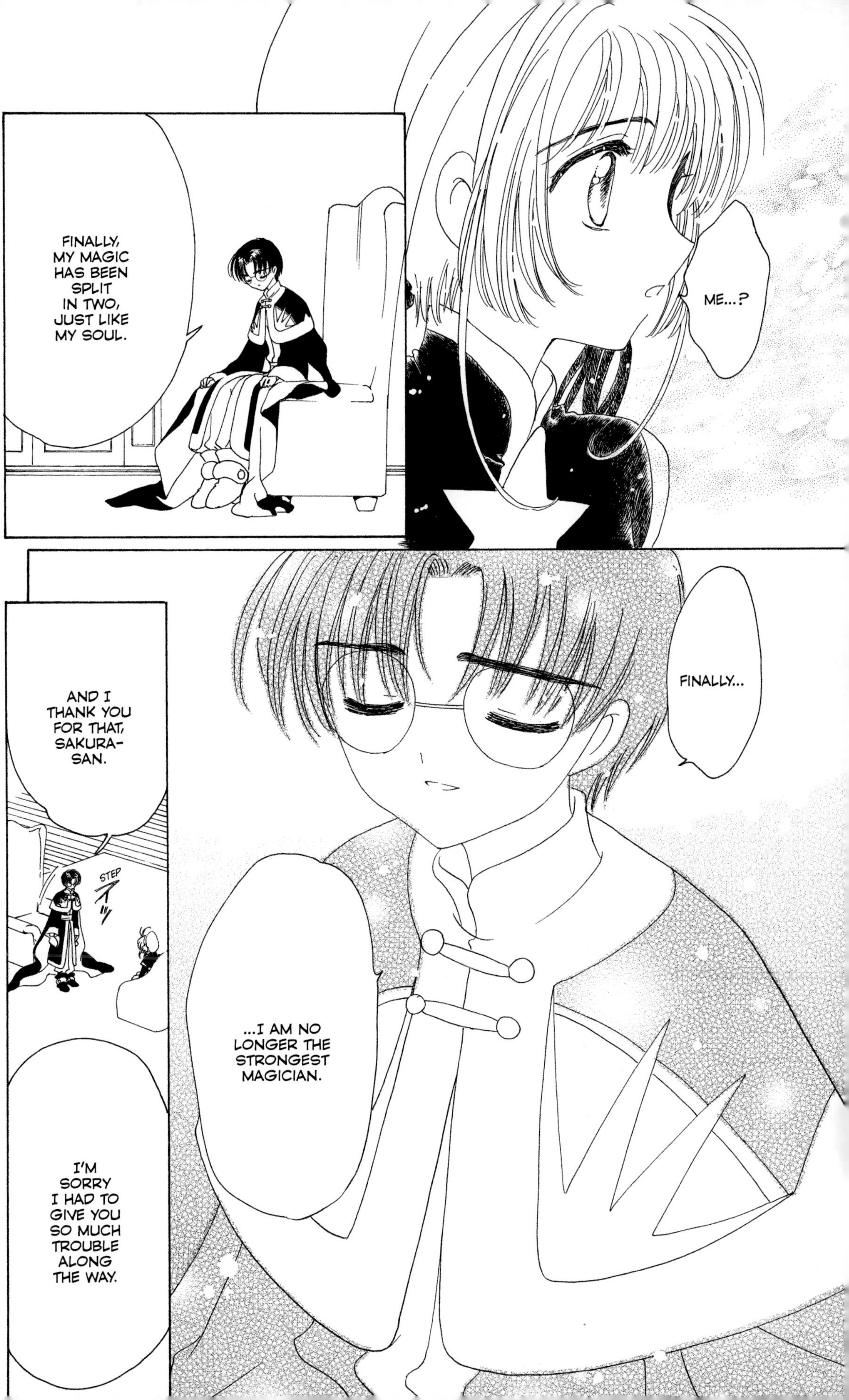
ME...?
FINALLY, MY MAGIC HAS BEEN SPLIT IN TWO, JUST LIKE MY SOUL.
FINALLY...
...I AM NO LONGER THE STRONGEST MAGICIAN.
AND I THANK YOU FOR THAT, SAKURA-SAN.
STEP
I'M SORRY I HAD TO GIVE YOU SO MUCH TROUBLE ALONG THE WAY.

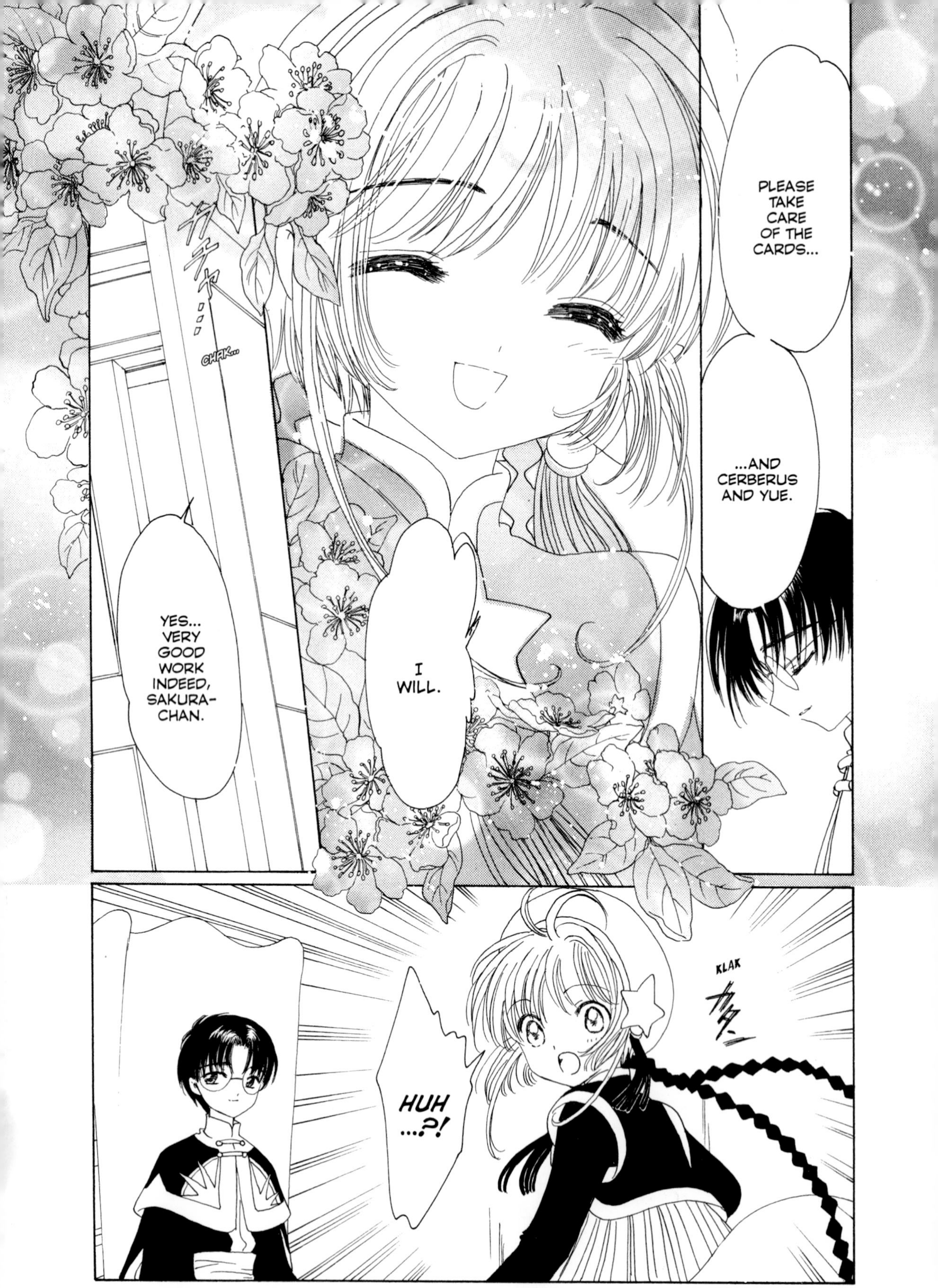
PLEASE TAKE CARE OF THE CARDS...
...AND CERBERUS AND YUE.
I WILL.
YES... VERY GOOD WORK INDEED, SAKURA-CHAN.
CHAK...
KLAK
HUH ...?!

< TO BE CONTINUED >

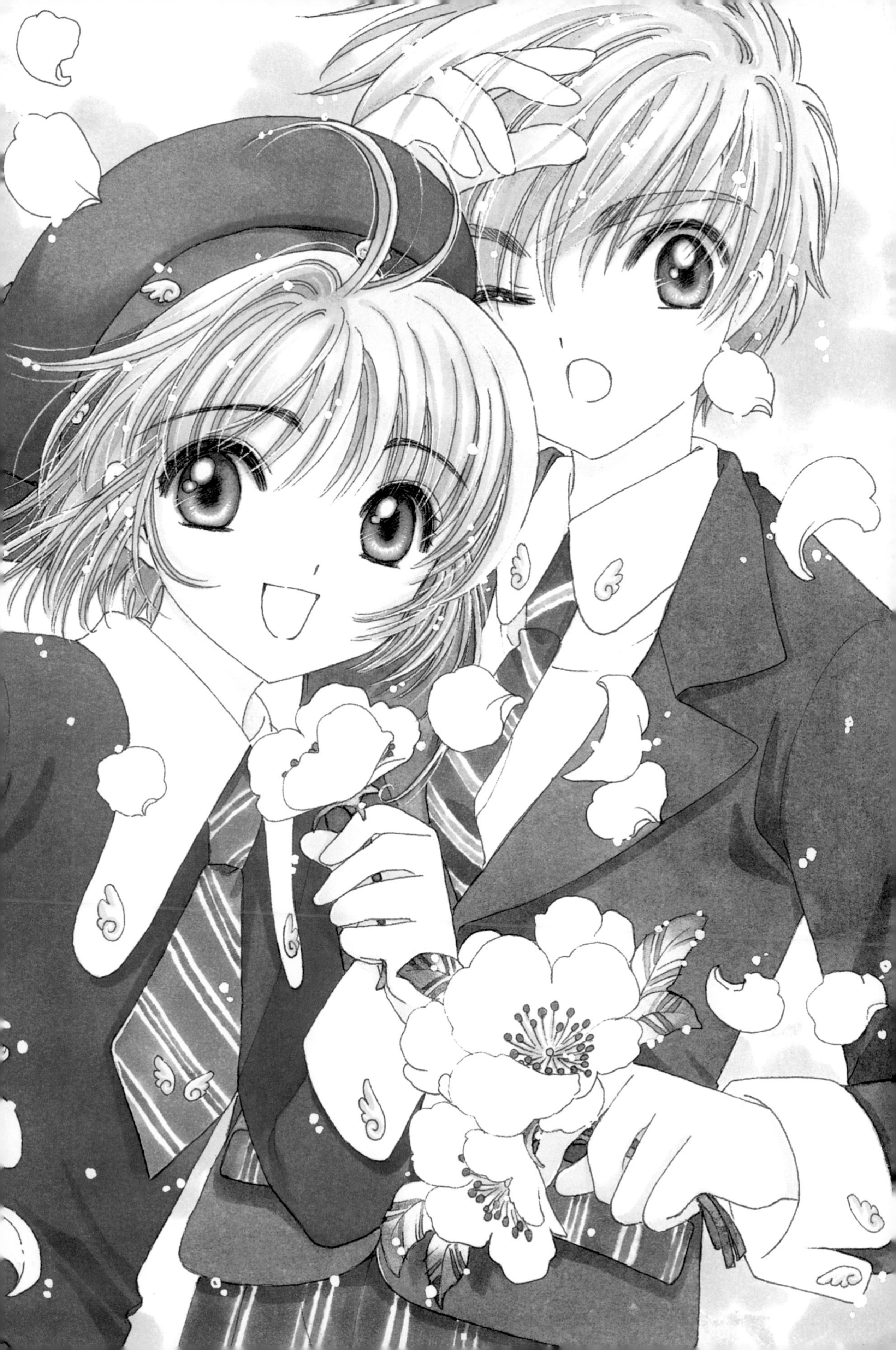

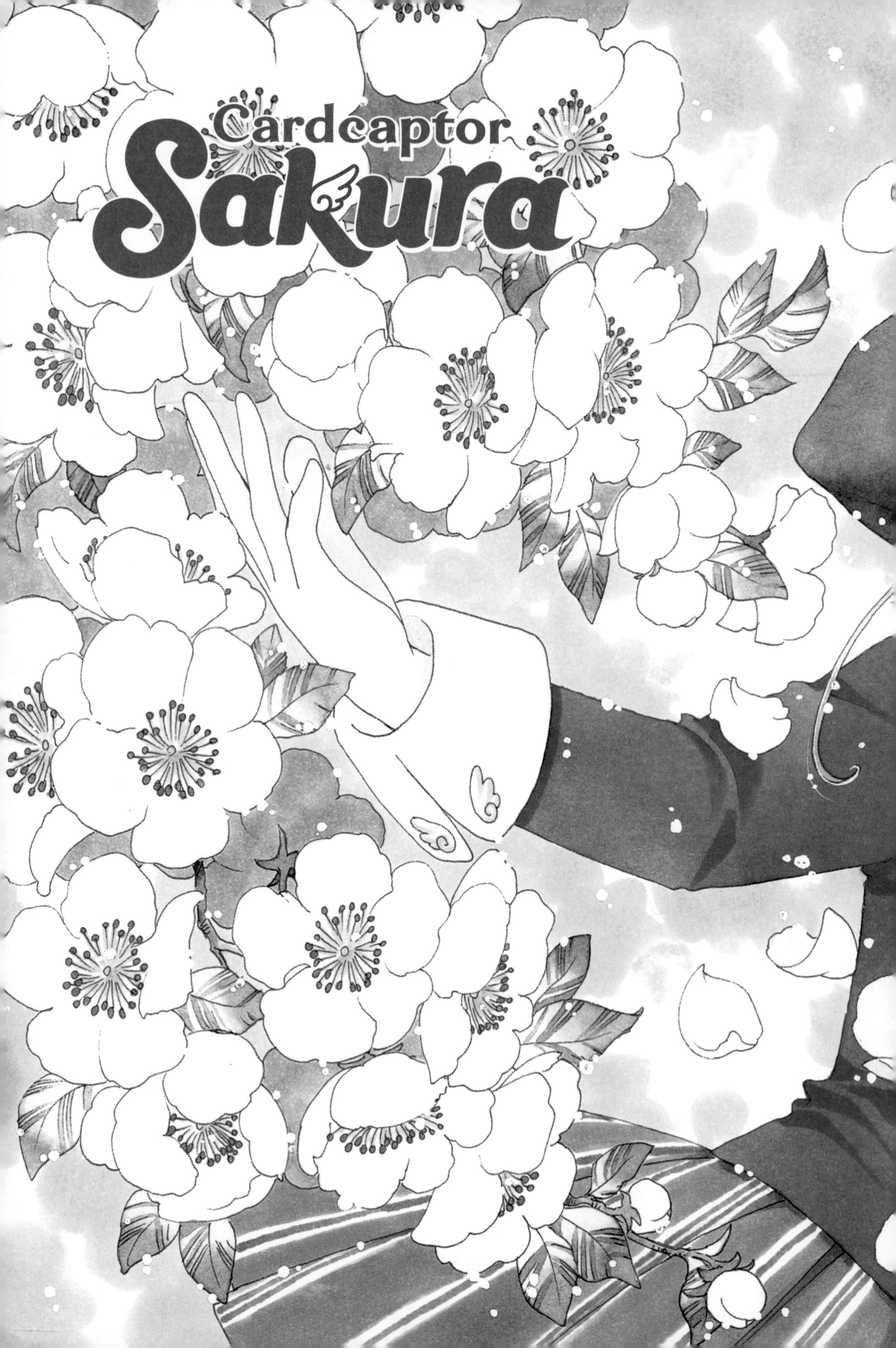
Cardcaptor
Sakura

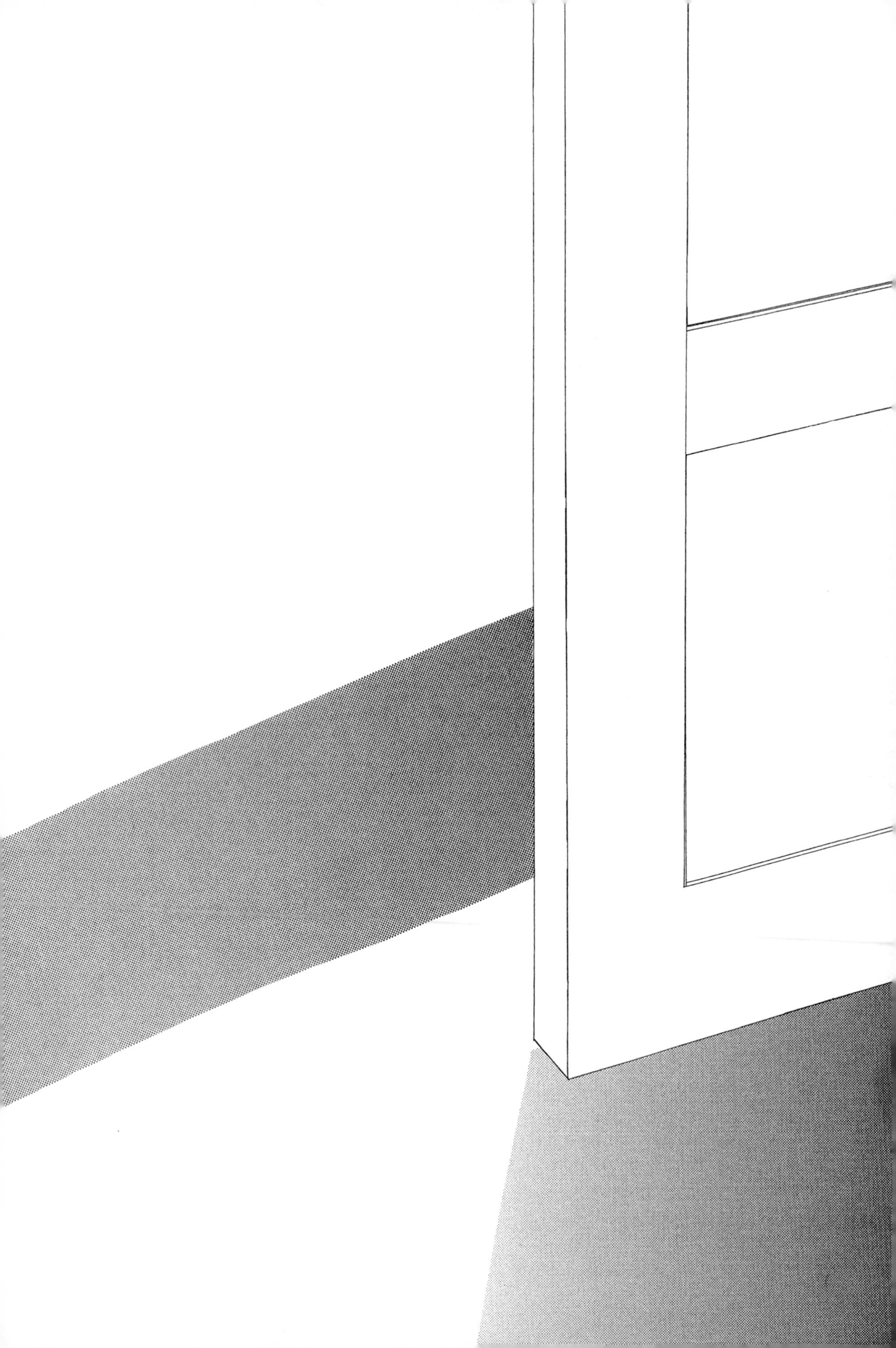

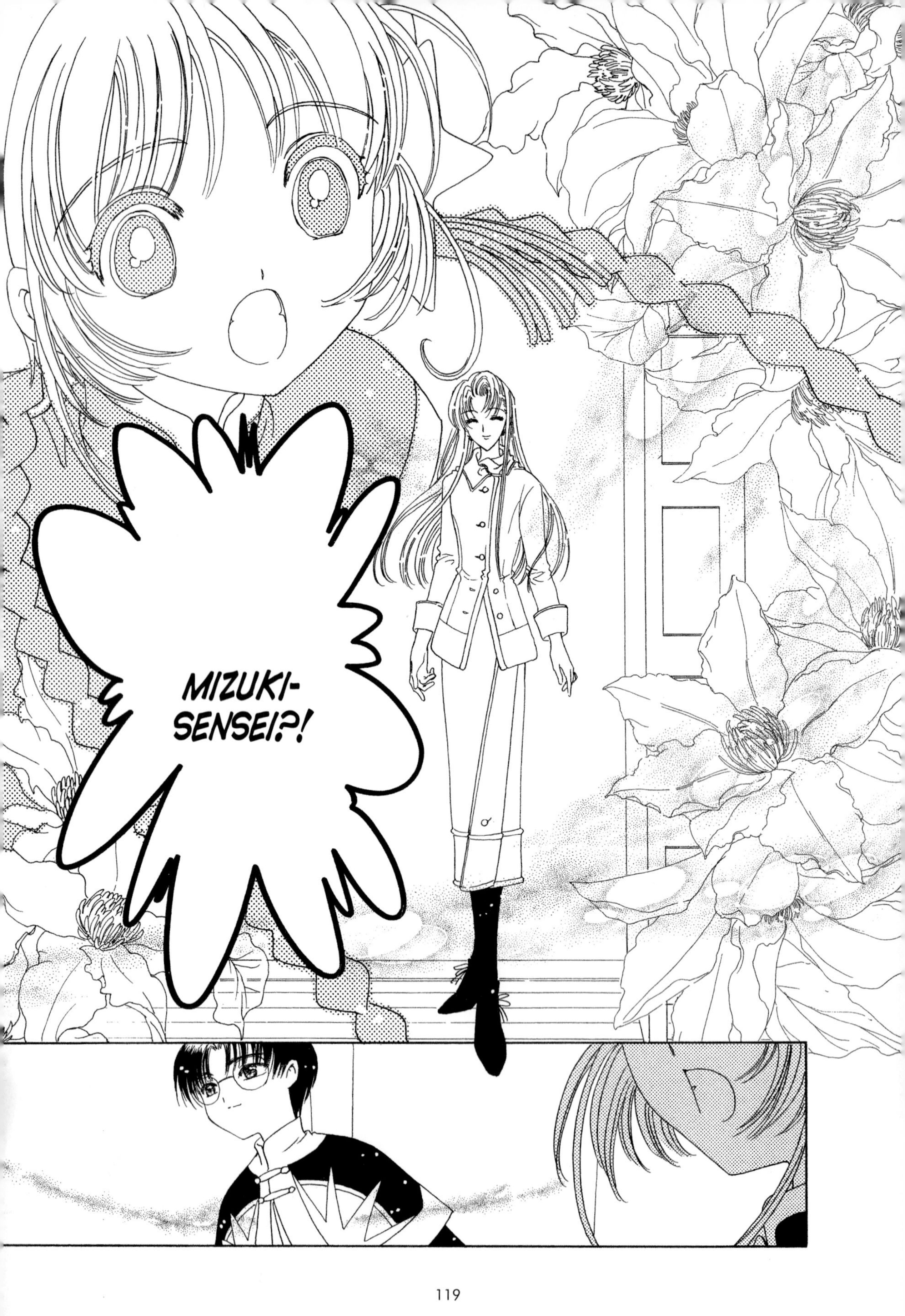
MIZUKI-
SENSEI?!

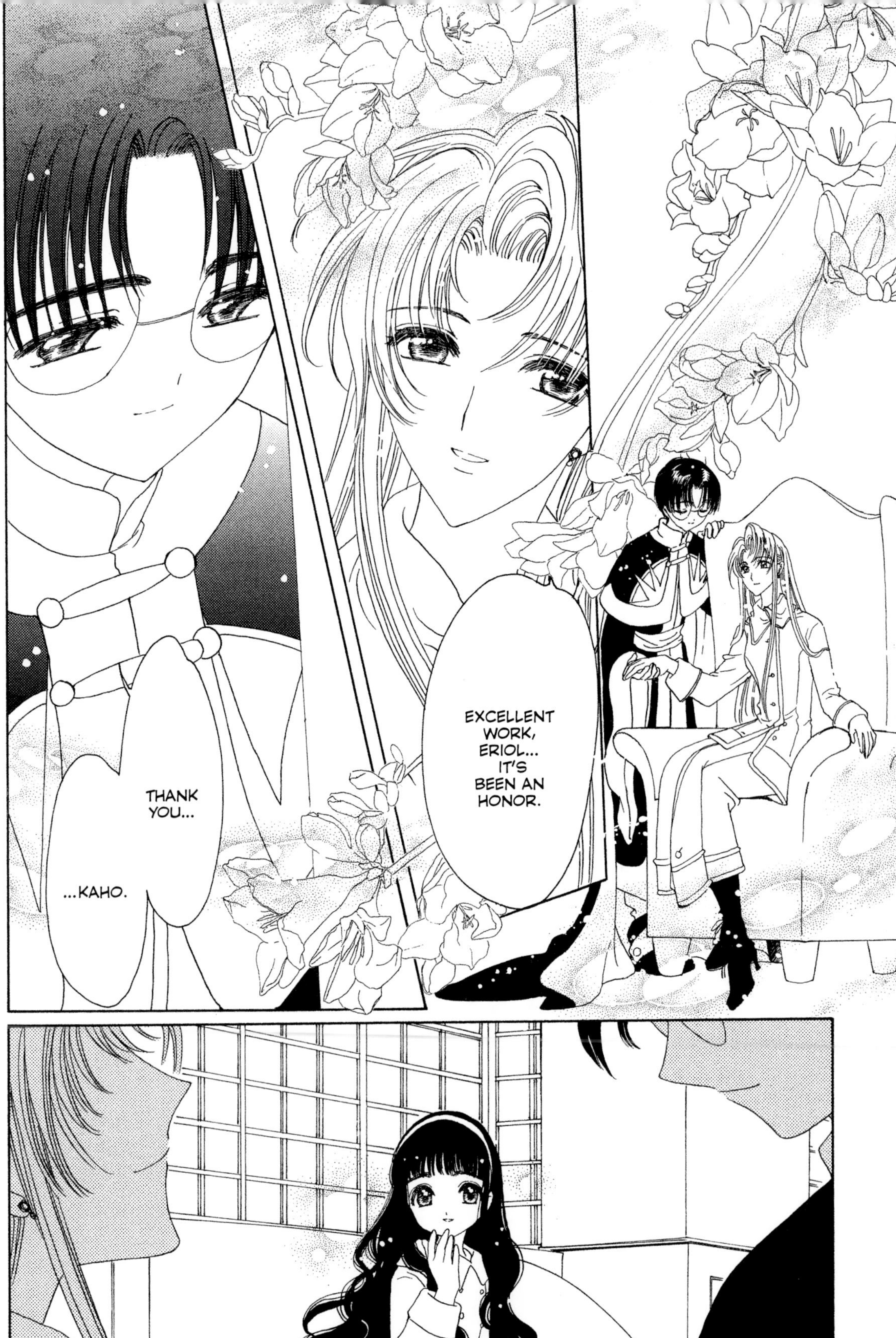
EXCELLENT WORK, ERIOL... IT'S BEEN AN HONOR.
THANK YOU...
...KAHO.

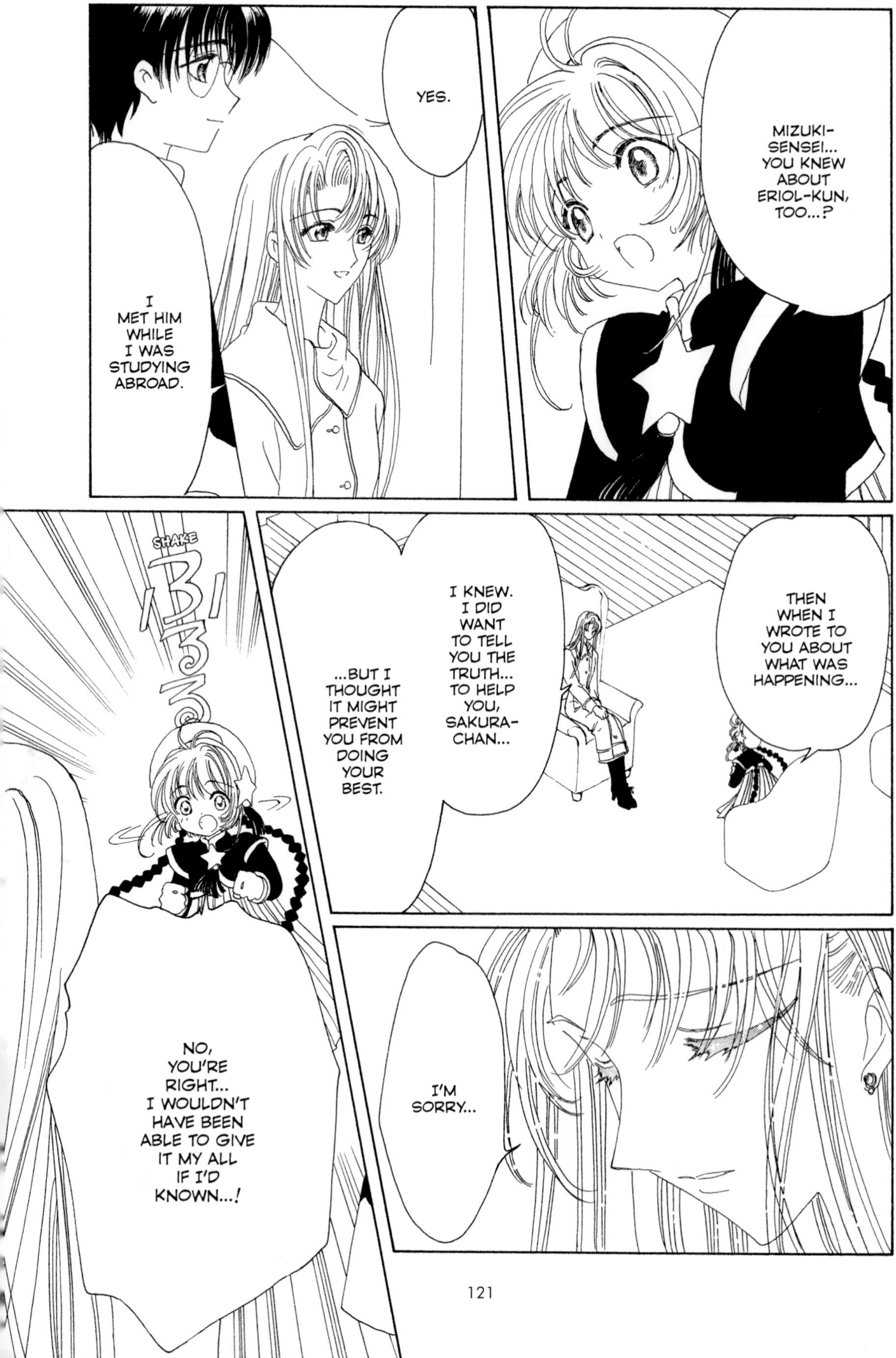
MIZUKI-SENSEI... YOU KNEW ABOUT ERIOL-KUN, TOO...?
YES.
I MET HIM WHILE I WAS STUDYING ABROAD.
THEN WHEN I WROTE TO YOU ABOUT WHAT WAS HAPPENING...
I KNEW. I DID WANT TO TELL YOU THE TRUTH... TO HELP YOU, SAKURA-CHAN...
...BUT I THOUGHT IT MIGHT PREVENT YOU FROM DOING YOUR BEST.
I'M SORRY...
SHAKE
NO, YOU'RE RIGHT... I WOULDN'T HAVE BEEN ABLE TO GIVE IT MY ALL IF I'D KNOWN...!

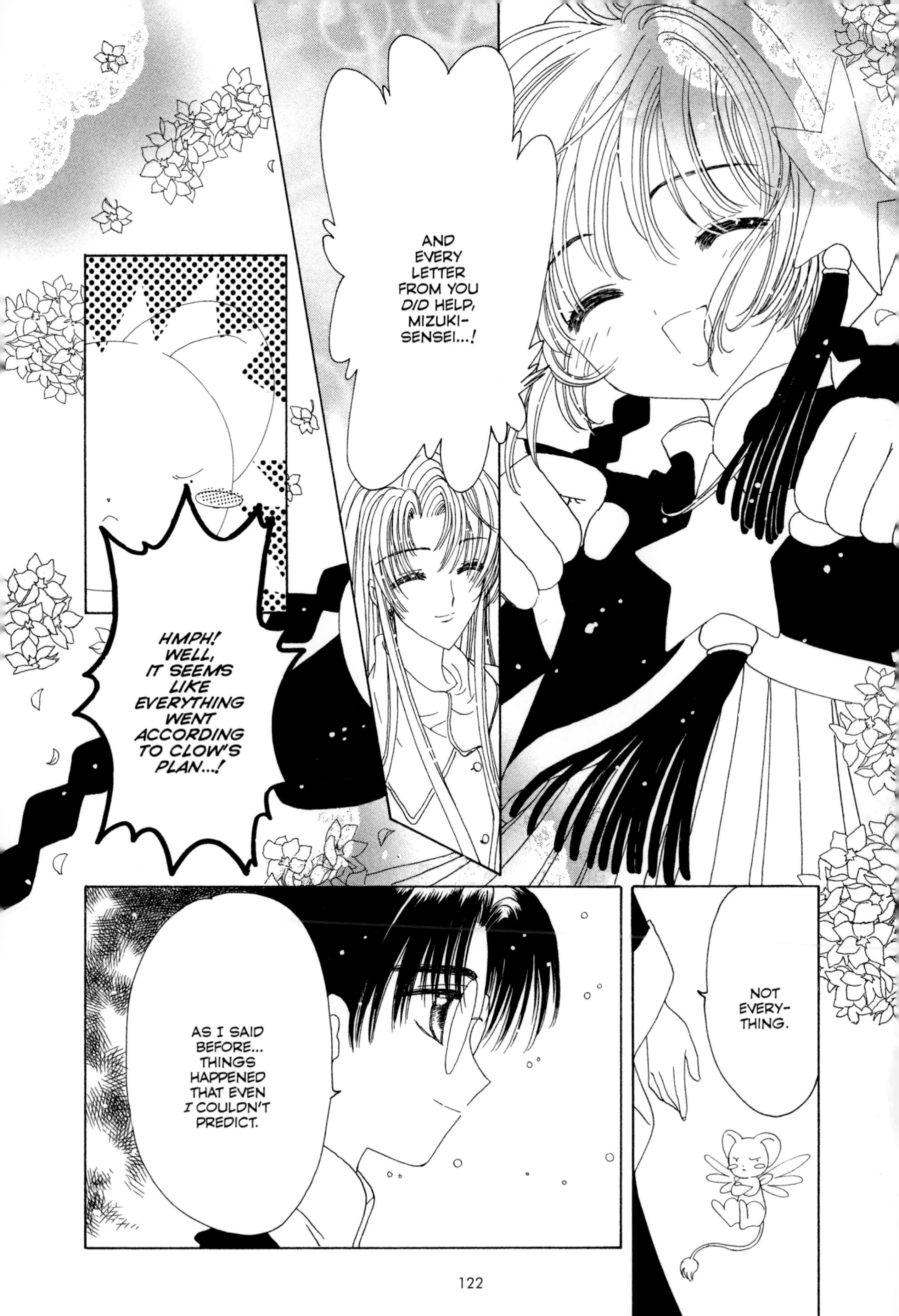
AND EVERY LETTER FROM YOU *DID* HELP, MIZUKI-SENSEI...!
HMPH! WELL, IT SEEMS LIKE EVERYTHING WENT ACCORDING TO CLOW'S PLAN...!
NOT EVERY-THING.
AS I SAID BEFORE... THINGS HAPPENED THAT EVEN *I* COULDN'T PREDICT.

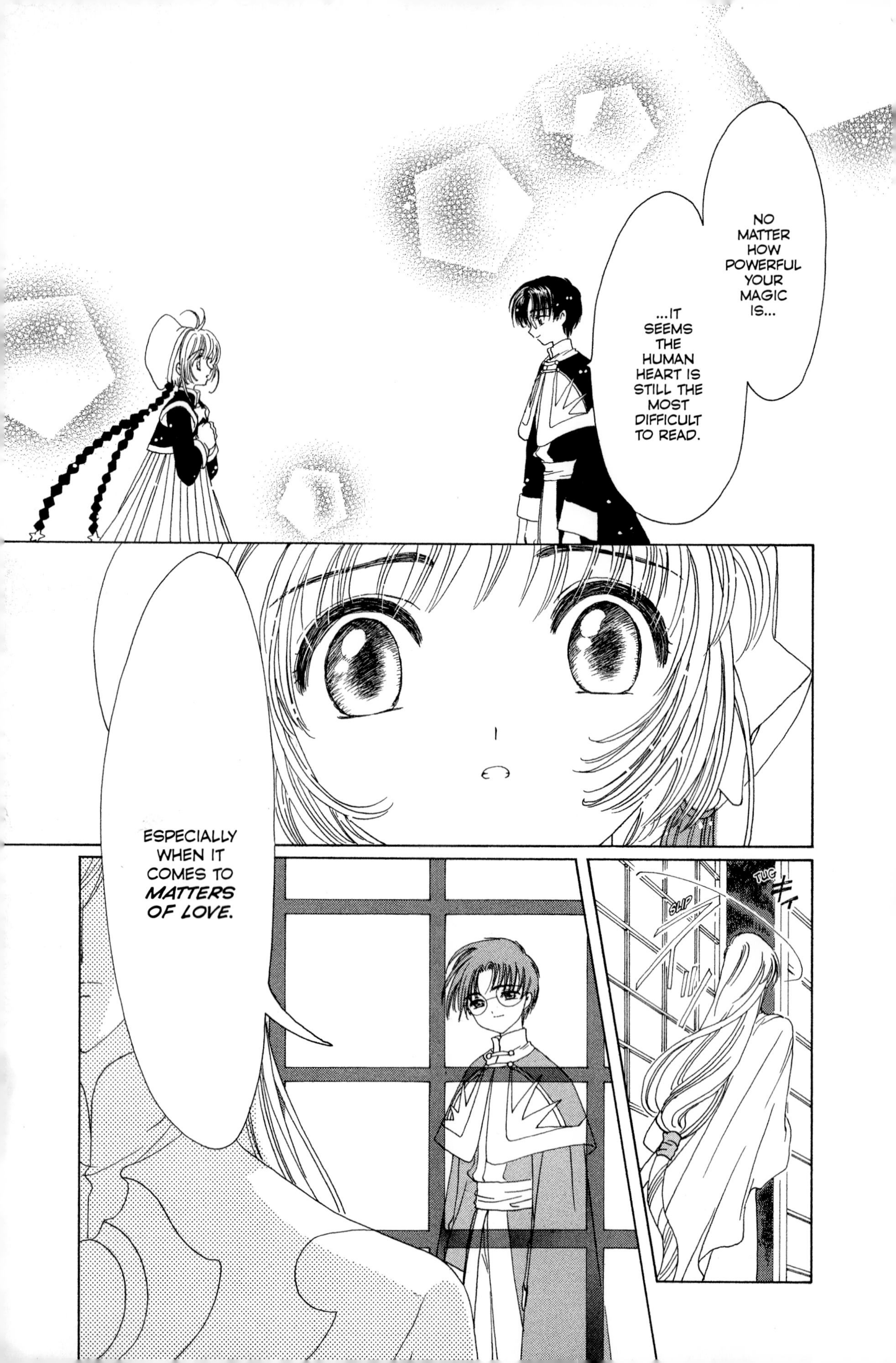

NO MATTER HOW POWERFUL YOUR MAGIC IS...
...IT SEEMS THE HUMAN HEART IS STILL THE MOST DIFFICULT TO READ.
ESPECIALLY WHEN IT COMES TO *MATTERS OF LOVE.*
TUG
SLIP

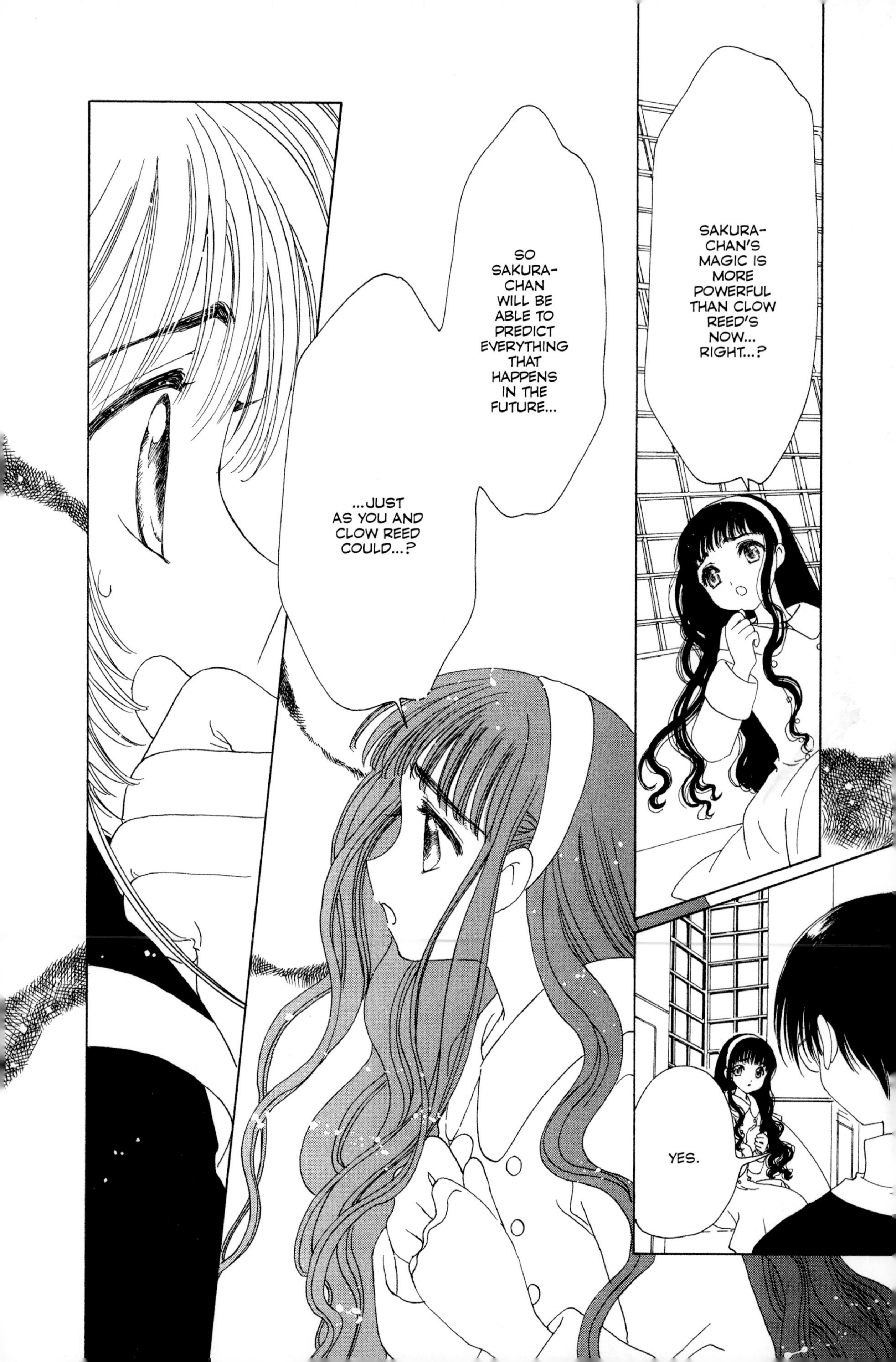
SAKURA-CHAN'S MAGIC IS MORE POWERFUL THAN CLOW REED'S NOW... RIGHT...?
YES.
SO SAKURA-CHAN WILL BE ABLE TO PREDICT EVERYTHING THAT HAPPENS IN THE FUTURE...
...JUST AS YOU AND CLOW REED COULD...?

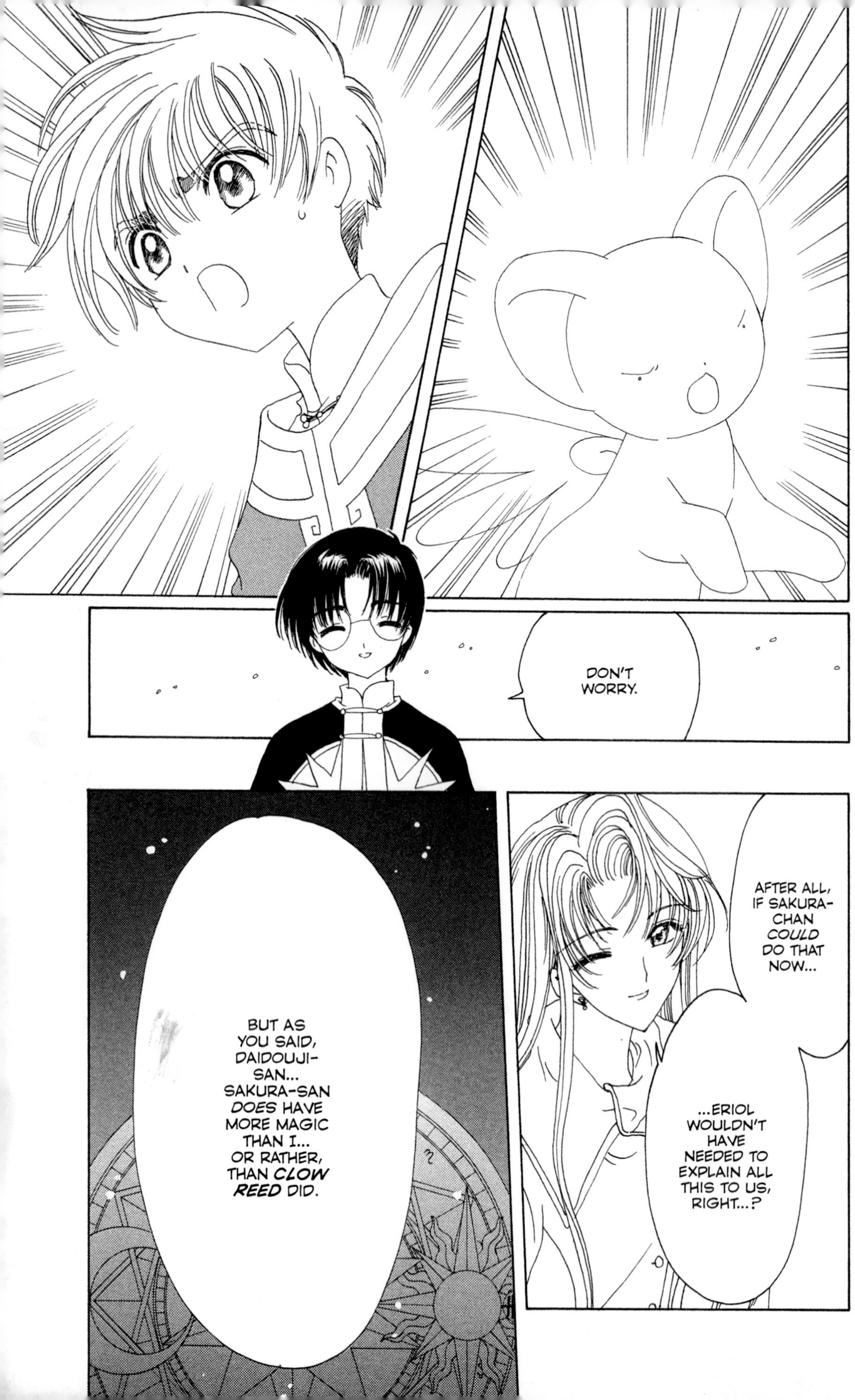
DON'T WORRY.
AFTER ALL, IF SAKURA-CHAN *COULD* DO THAT NOW...
...ERIOL WOULDN'T HAVE NEEDED TO EXPLAIN ALL THIS TO US, RIGHT...?
BUT AS YOU SAID, DAIDOUJI-SAN... SAKURA-SAN *DOES* HAVE MORE MAGIC THAN I... OR RATHER, THAN ***CLOW REED*** DID.

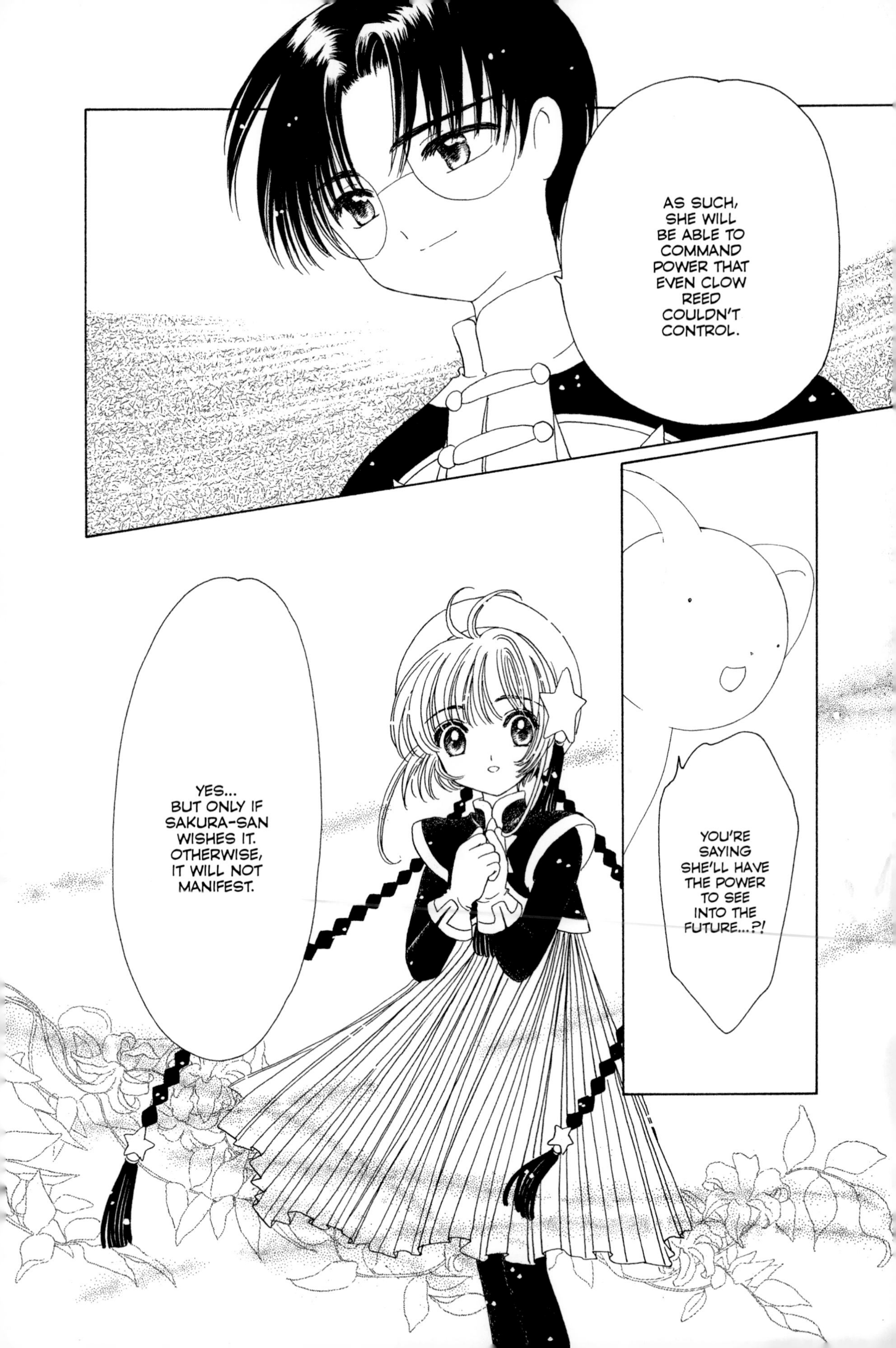
AS SUCH, SHE WILL BE ABLE TO COMMAND POWER THAT EVEN CLOW REED COULDN'T CONTROL.
YOU'RE SAYING SHE'LL HAVE THE POWER TO SEE INTO THE FUTURE...?!
YES... BUT ONLY IF SAKURA-SAN WISHES IT. OTHERWISE, IT WILL NOT MANIFEST.

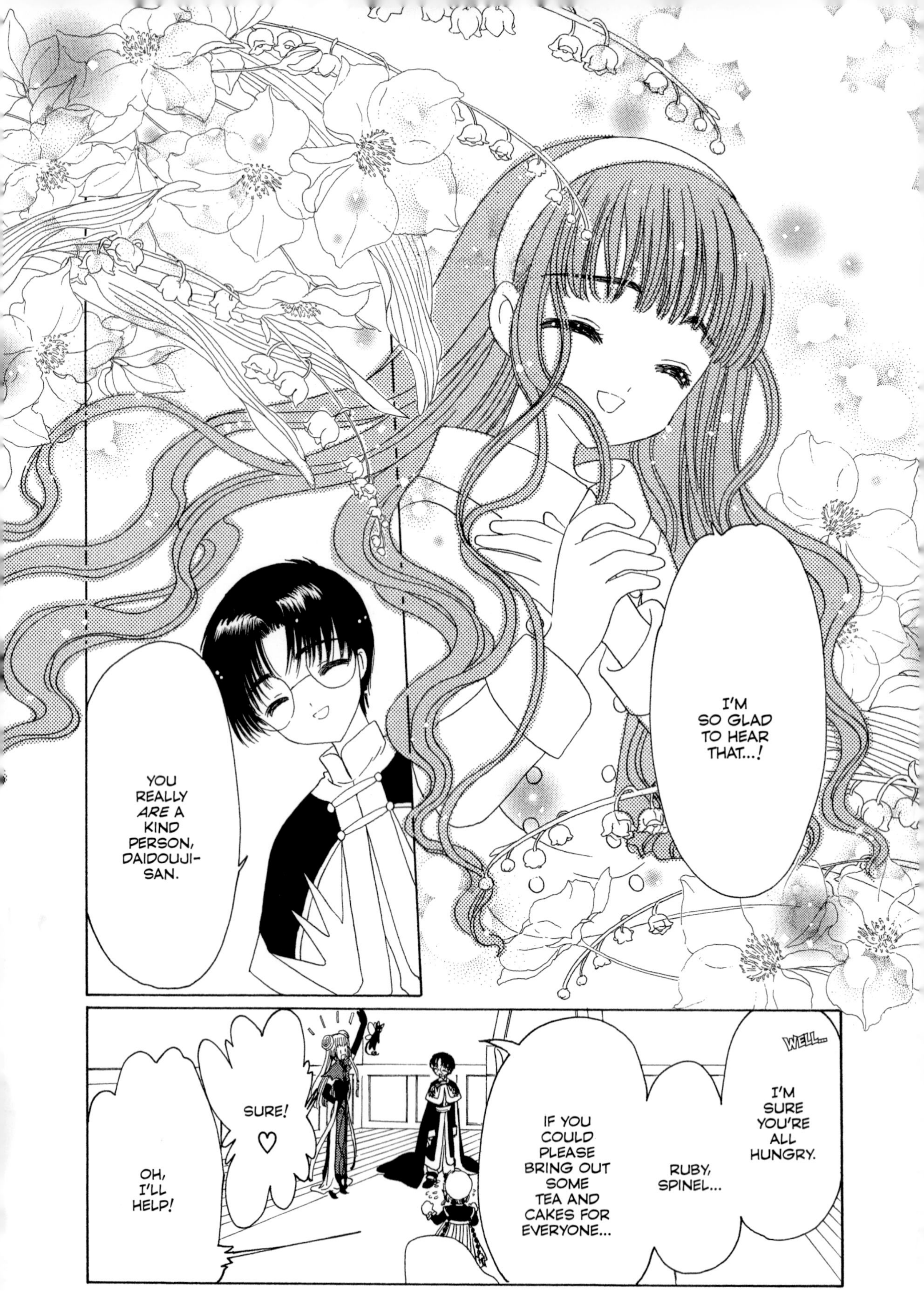

I'M SO GLAD TO HEAR THAT...!
YOU REALLY *ARE* A KIND PERSON, DAIDOUJI-SAN.
WELL...
I'M SURE YOU'RE ALL HUNGRY.
RUBY, SPINEL...
IF YOU COULD PLEASE BRING OUT SOME TEA AND CAKES FOR EVERYONE...
SURE! ♡
OH, I'LL HELP!

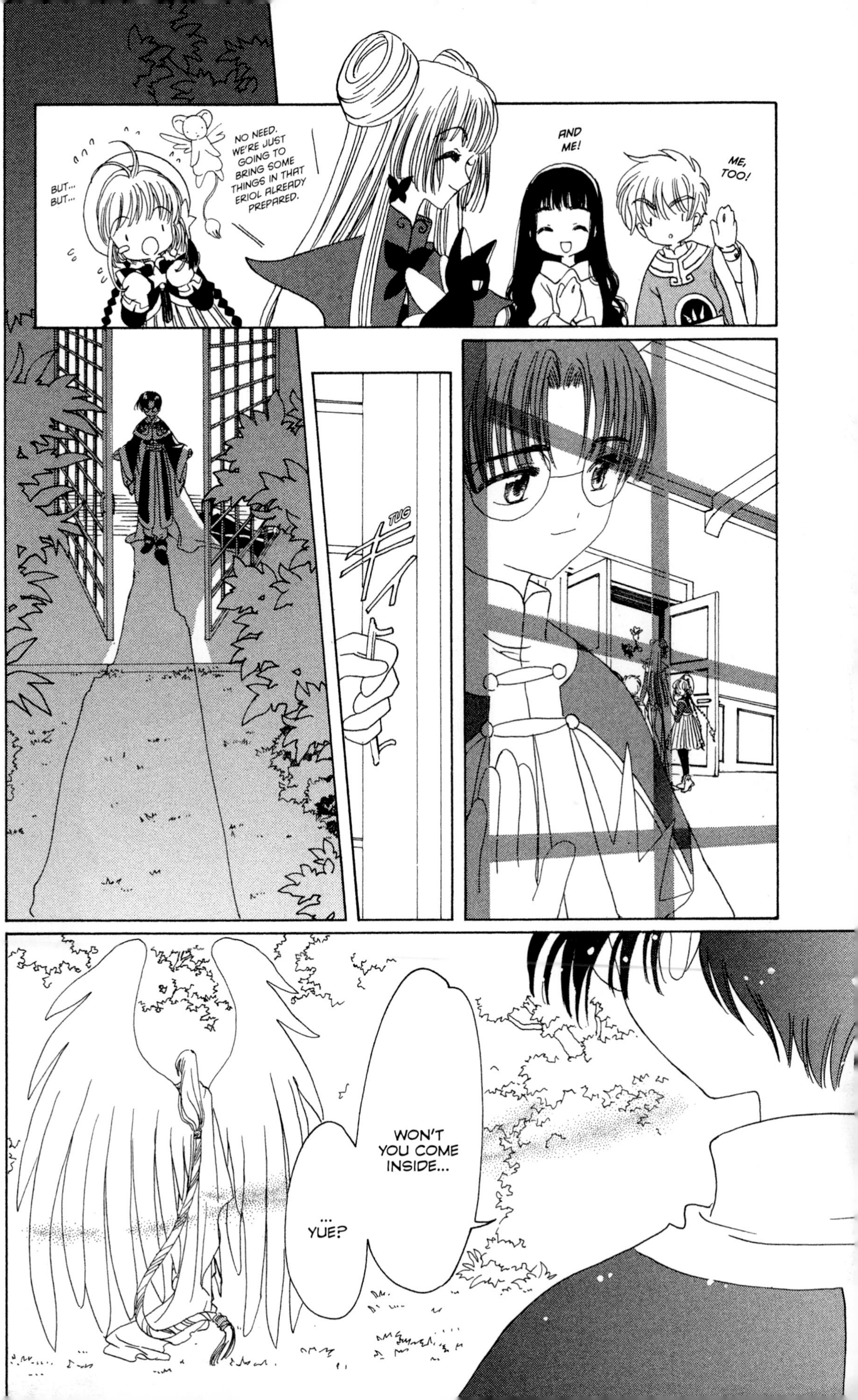
ME, TOO!
AND ME!
NO NEED. WE'RE JUST GOING TO BRING SOME THINGS IN THAT ERIOL ALREADY PREPARED.
BUT... BUT...
TUG
WON'T YOU COME INSIDE...
... YUE?

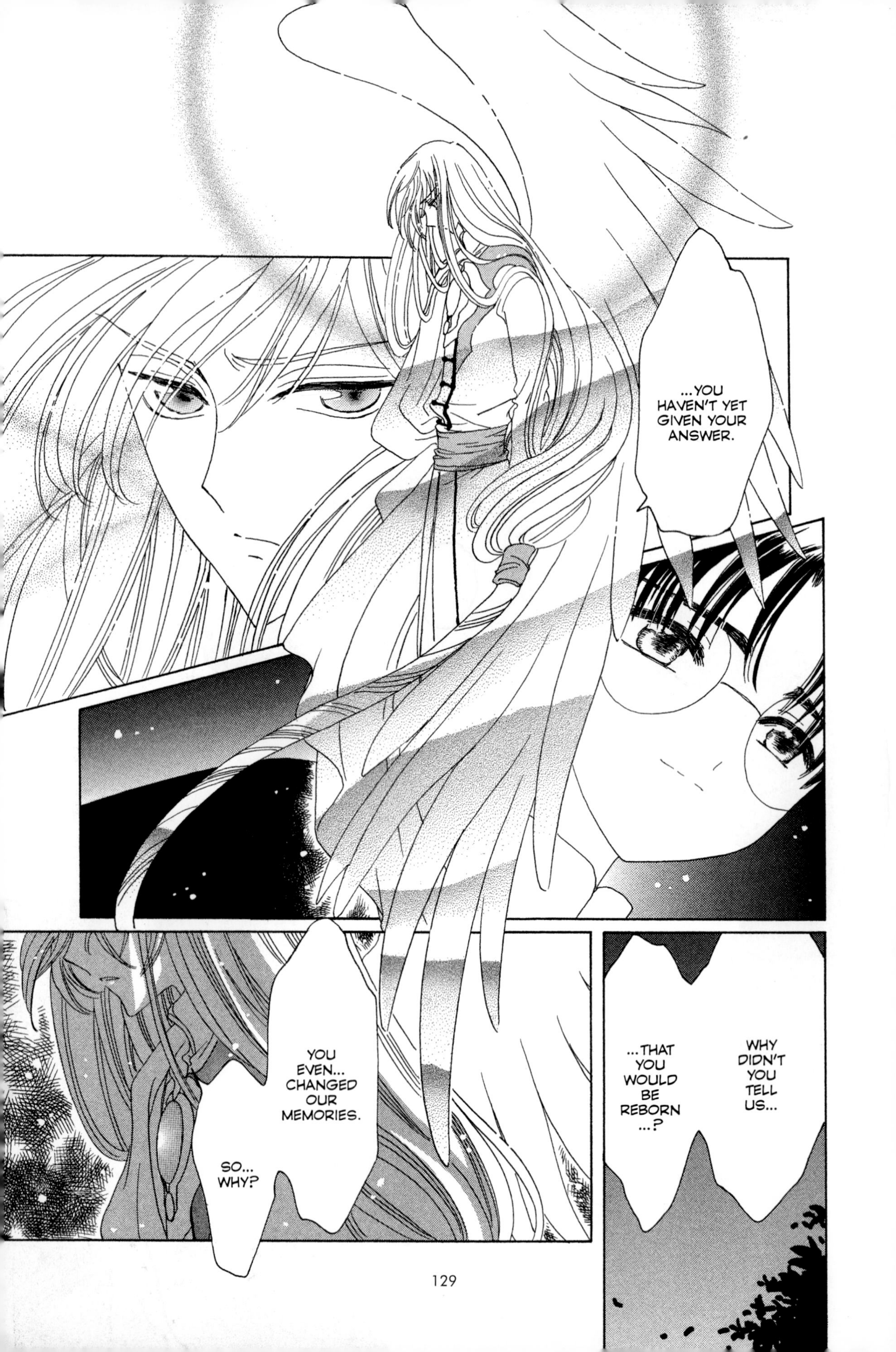
...YOU HAVEN'T YET GIVEN YOUR ANSWER.
WHY DIDN'T YOU TELL US...
...THAT YOU WOULD BE REBORN ...?
YOU EVEN... CHANGED OUR MEMORIES.
SO... WHY?

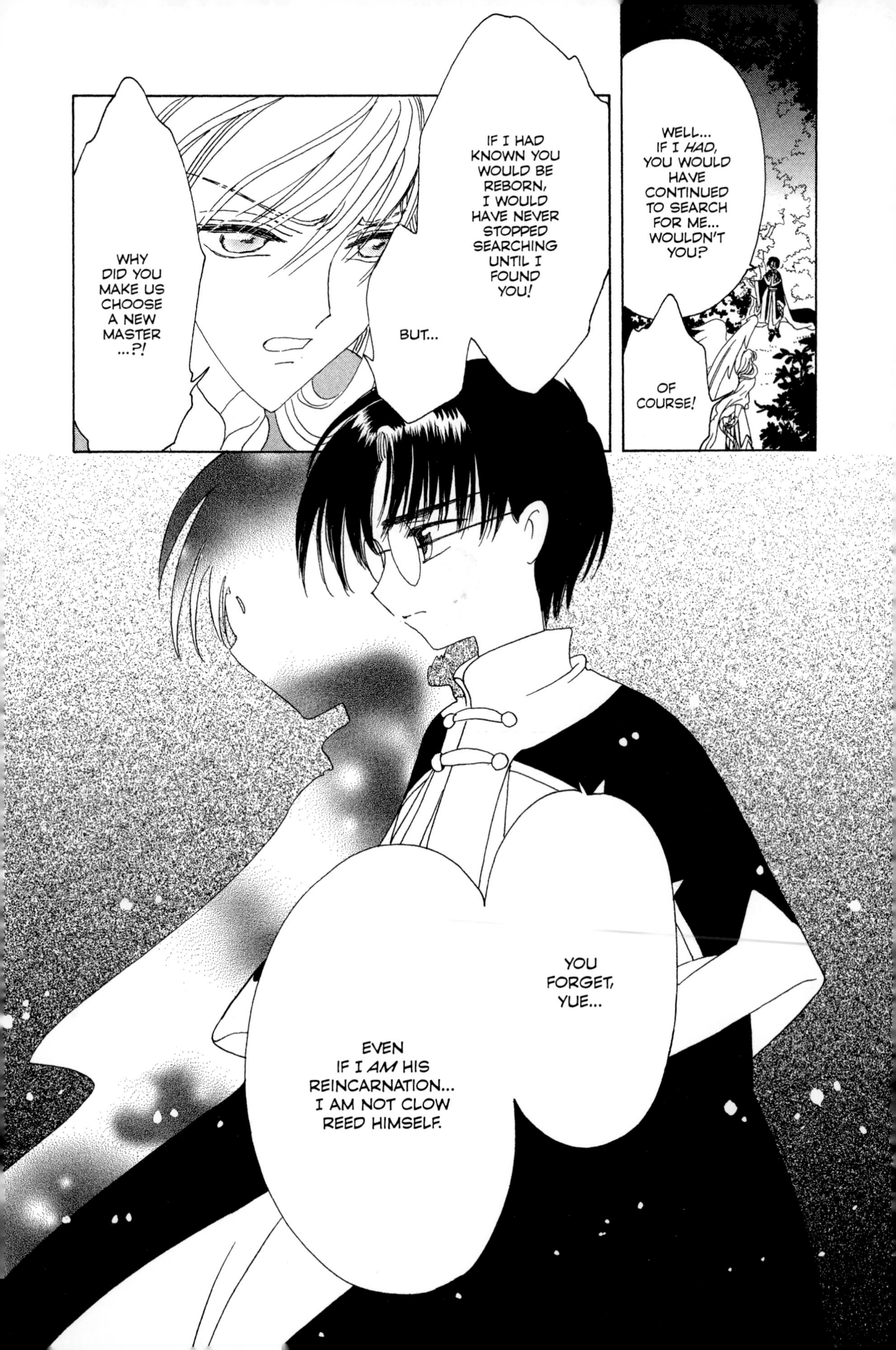
WELL... IF I *HAD*, YOU WOULD HAVE CONTINUED TO SEARCH FOR ME... WOULDN'T YOU?
OF COURSE!
IF I HAD KNOWN YOU WOULD BE REBORN, I WOULD HAVE NEVER STOPPED SEARCHING UNTIL I FOUND YOU!
BUT...
WHY DID YOU MAKE US CHOOSE A NEW MASTER ...?!
YOU FORGET, YUE...
EVEN IF I *AM* HIS REINCARNATION... I AM NOT CLOW REED HIMSELF.

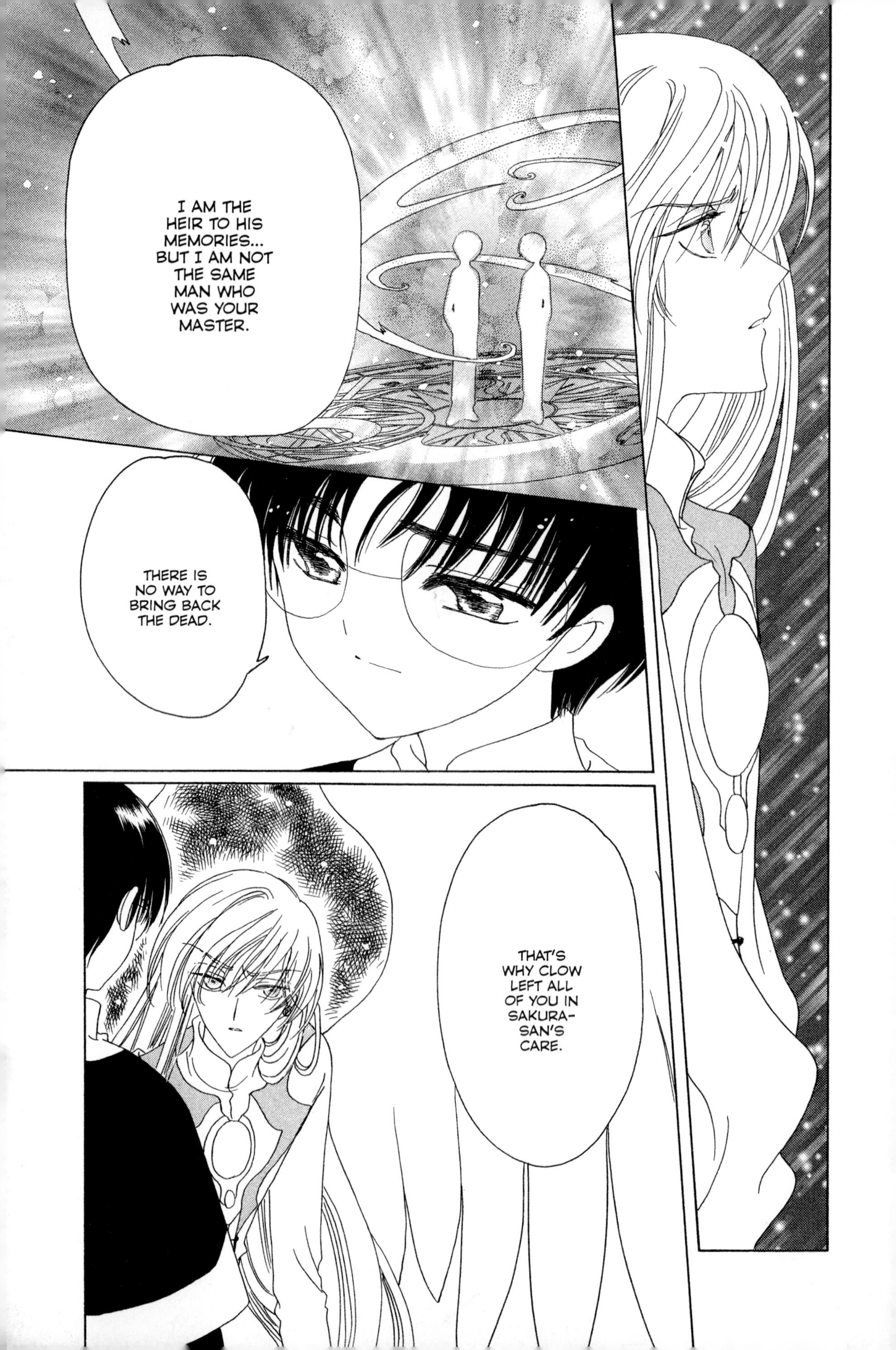
I AM THE HEIR TO HIS MEMORIES... BUT I AM NOT THE SAME MAN WHO WAS YOUR MASTER.
THERE IS NO WAY TO BRING BACK THE DEAD.
THAT'S WHY CLOW LEFT ALL OF YOU IN SAKURA-SAN'S CARE.

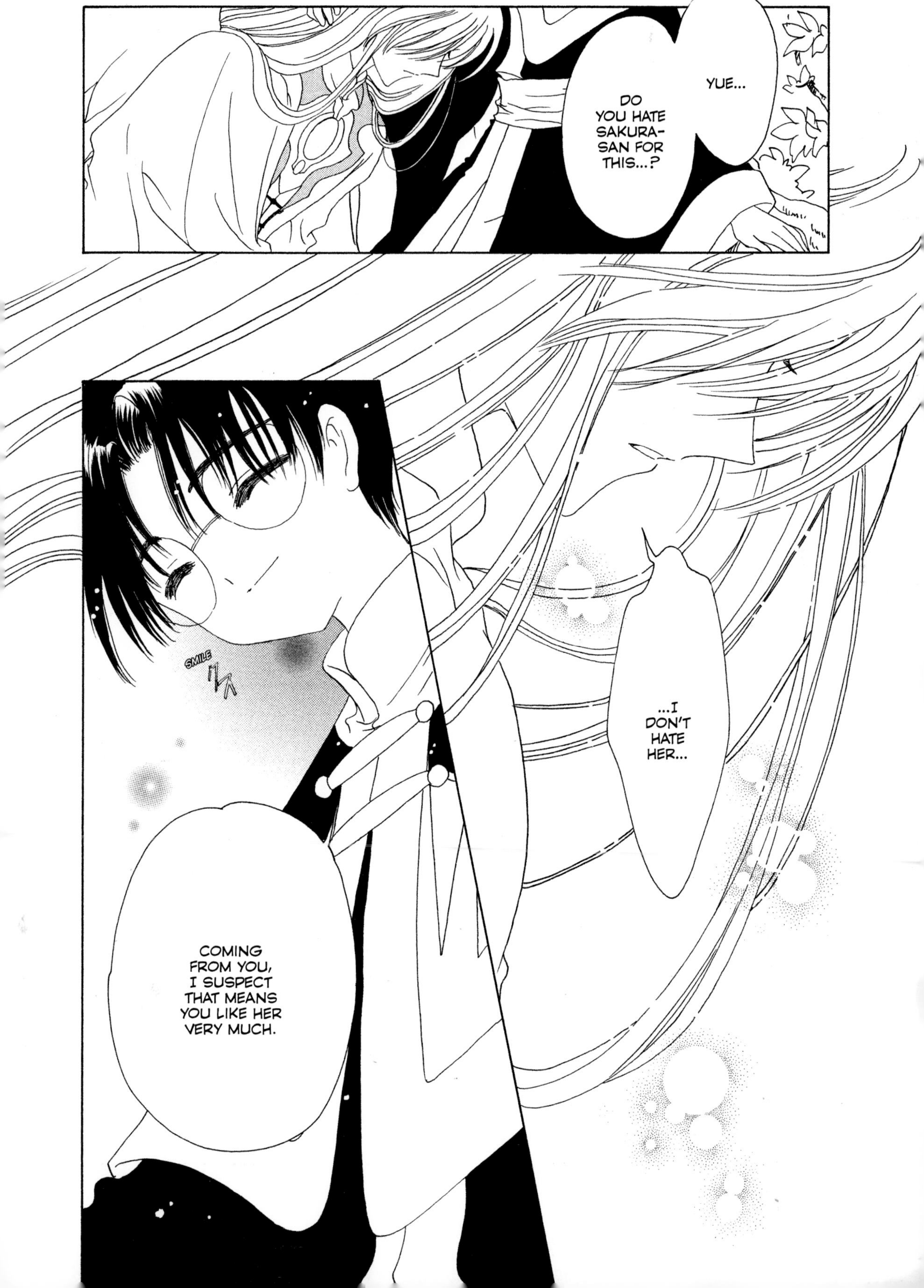
YUE...
DO YOU HATE SAKURA-SAN FOR THIS...?
...I DON'T HATE HER...
SMILE
COMING FROM YOU, I SUSPECT THAT MEANS YOU LIKE HER VERY MUCH.

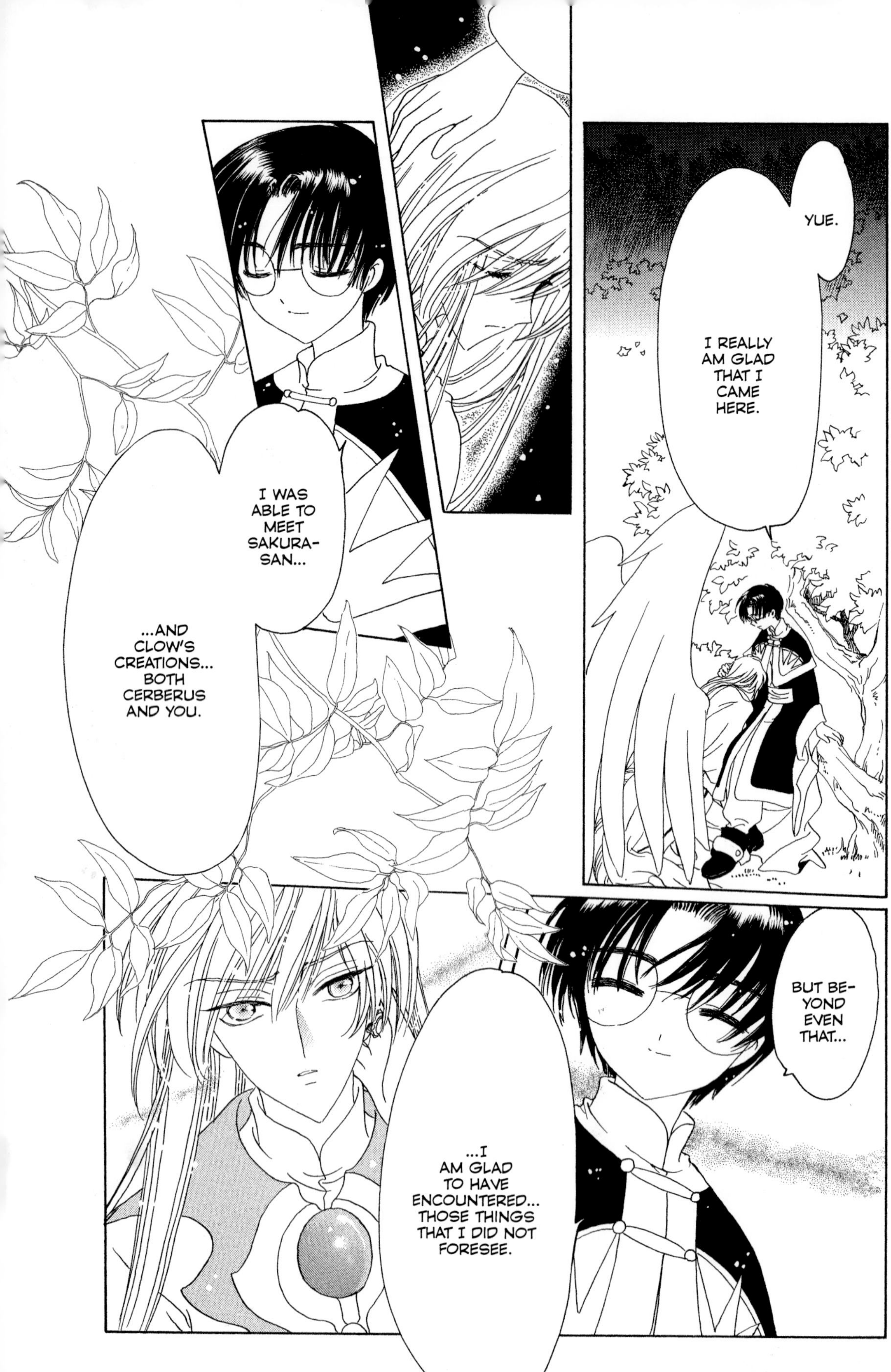
YUE.
I REALLY AM GLAD THAT I CAME HERE.
I WAS ABLE TO MEET SAKURA-SAN...
...AND CLOW'S CREATIONS... BOTH CERBERUS AND YOU.
BUT BE-YOND EVEN THAT...
...I AM GLAD TO HAVE ENCOUNTERED... THOSE THINGS THAT I DID NOT FORESEE.

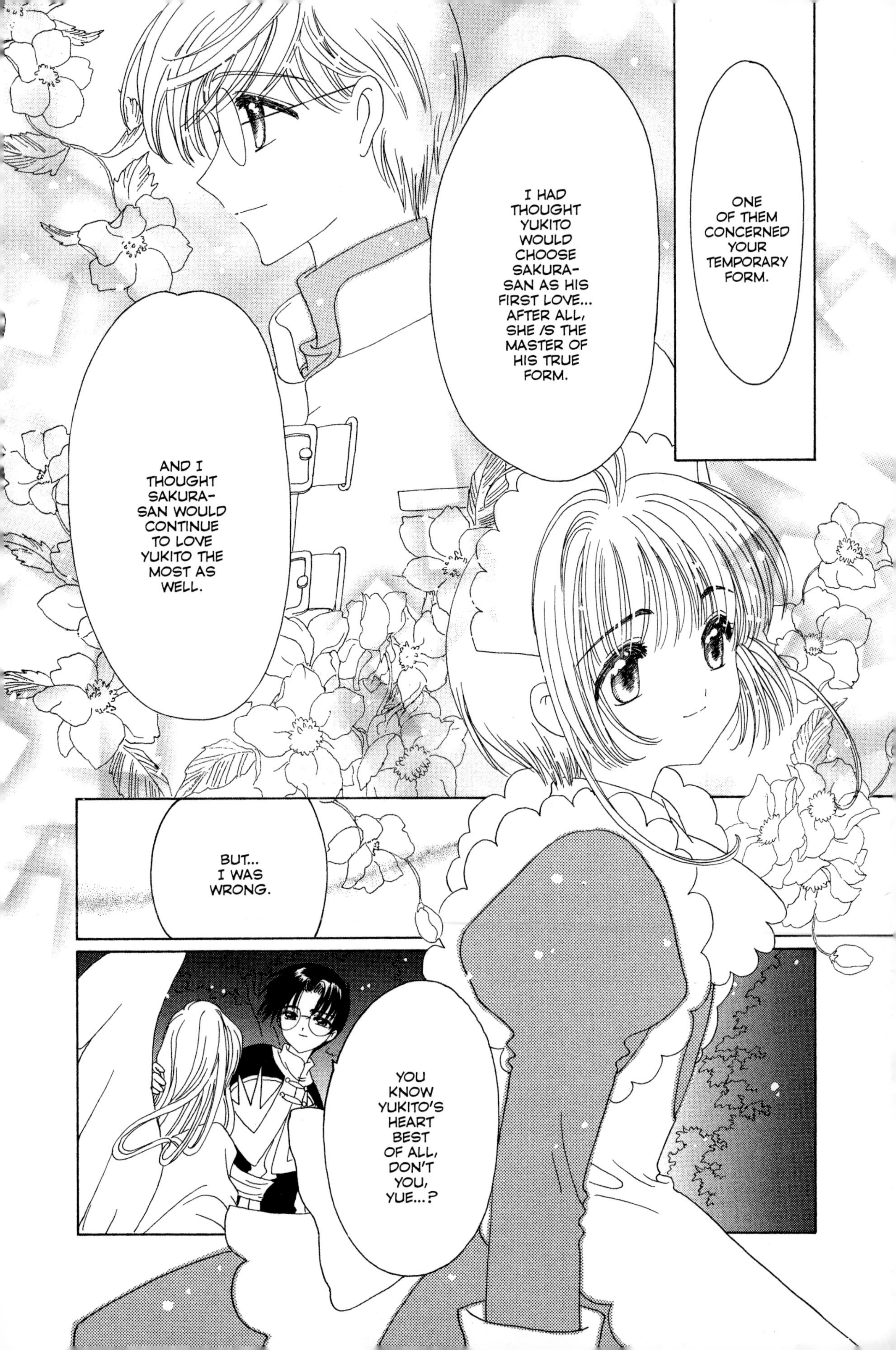
ONE OF THEM CONCERNED YOUR TEMPORARY FORM.
I HAD THOUGHT YUKITO WOULD CHOOSE SAKURA-SAN AS HIS FIRST LOVE... AFTER ALL, SHE *IS* THE MASTER OF HIS TRUE FORM.
AND I THOUGHT SAKURA-SAN WOULD CONTINUE TO LOVE YUKITO THE MOST AS WELL.
BUT... I WAS WRONG.
YOU KNOW YUKITO'S HEART BEST OF ALL, DON'T YOU, YUE...?

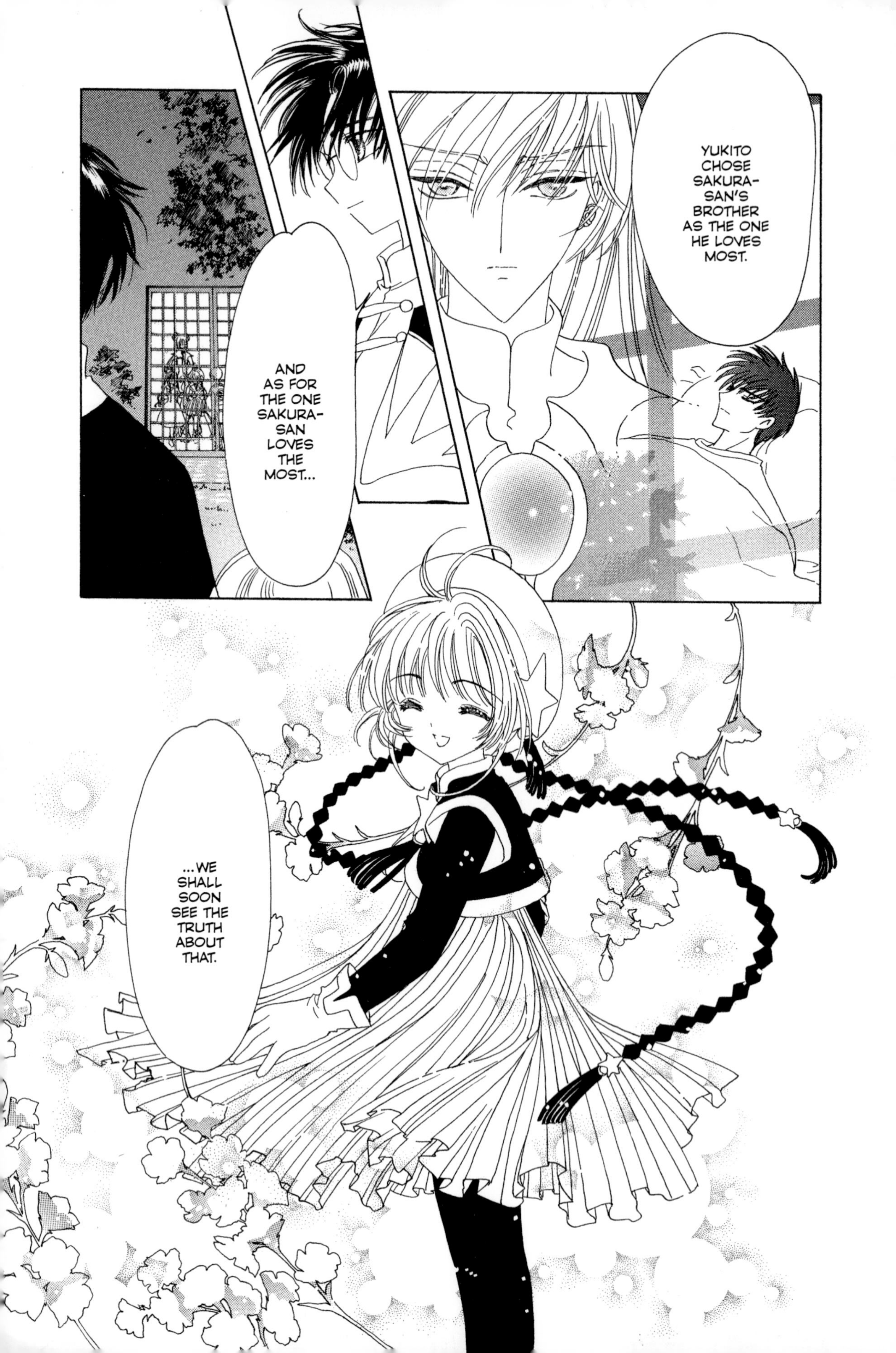
YUKITO CHOSE SAKURA-SAN'S BROTHER AS THE ONE HE LOVES MOST.
AND AS FOR THE ONE SAKURA-SAN LOVES THE MOST...
...WE SHALL SOON SEE THE TRUTH ABOUT THAT.

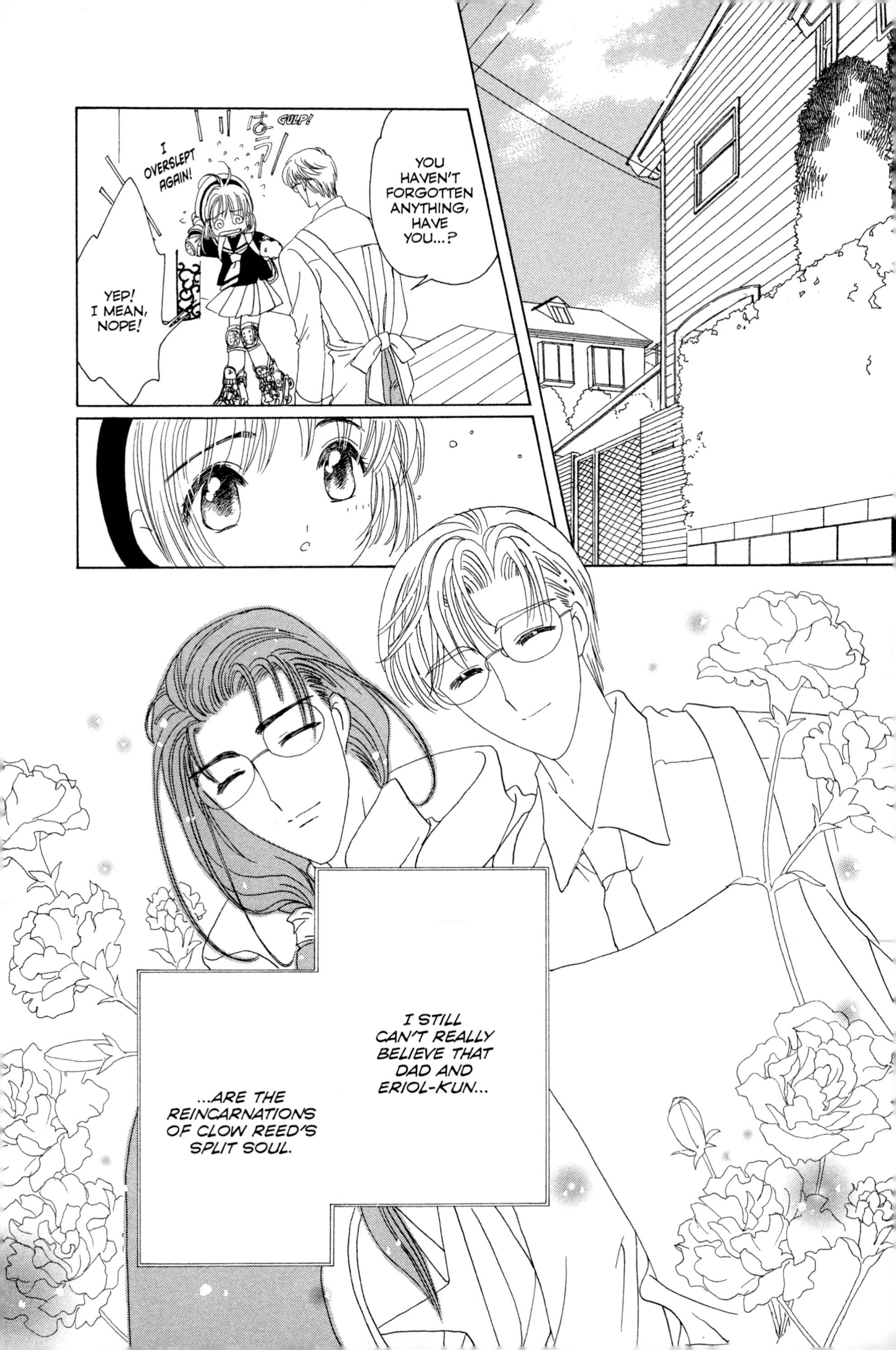
YOU HAVEN'T FORGOTTEN ANYTHING, HAVE YOU...?
GULP!
I OVERSLEPT AGAIN!
YEP! I MEAN, NOPE!
I STILL CAN'T REALLY BELIEVE THAT DAD AND ERIOL-KUN...
...ARE THE REINCARNATIONS OF CLOW REED'S SPLIT SOUL.

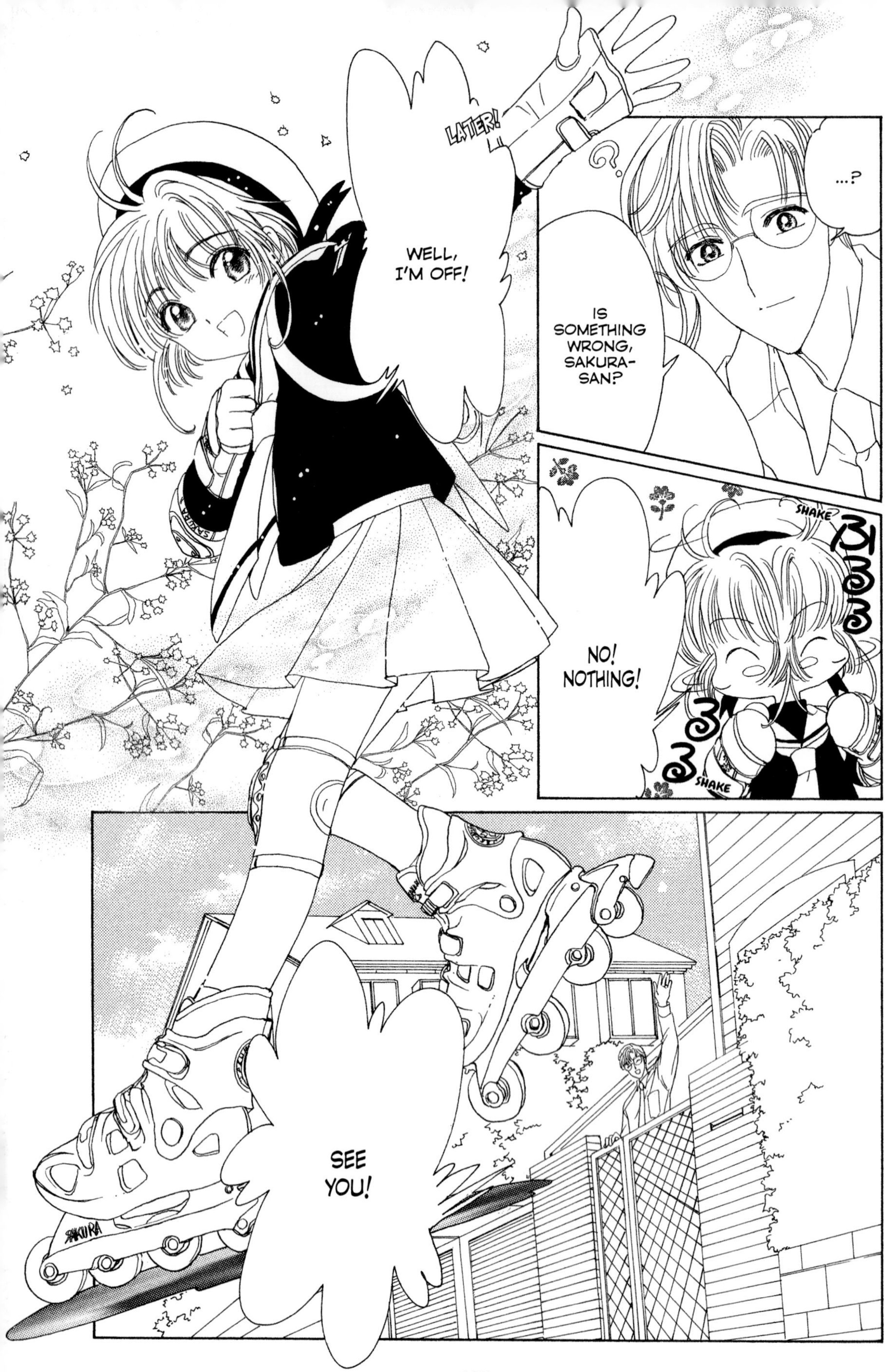
...?
IS SOMETHING WRONG, SAKURA-SAN?
SHAKE
NO! NOTHING!
SHAKE
LATER!
WELL, I'M OFF!
SEE YOU!

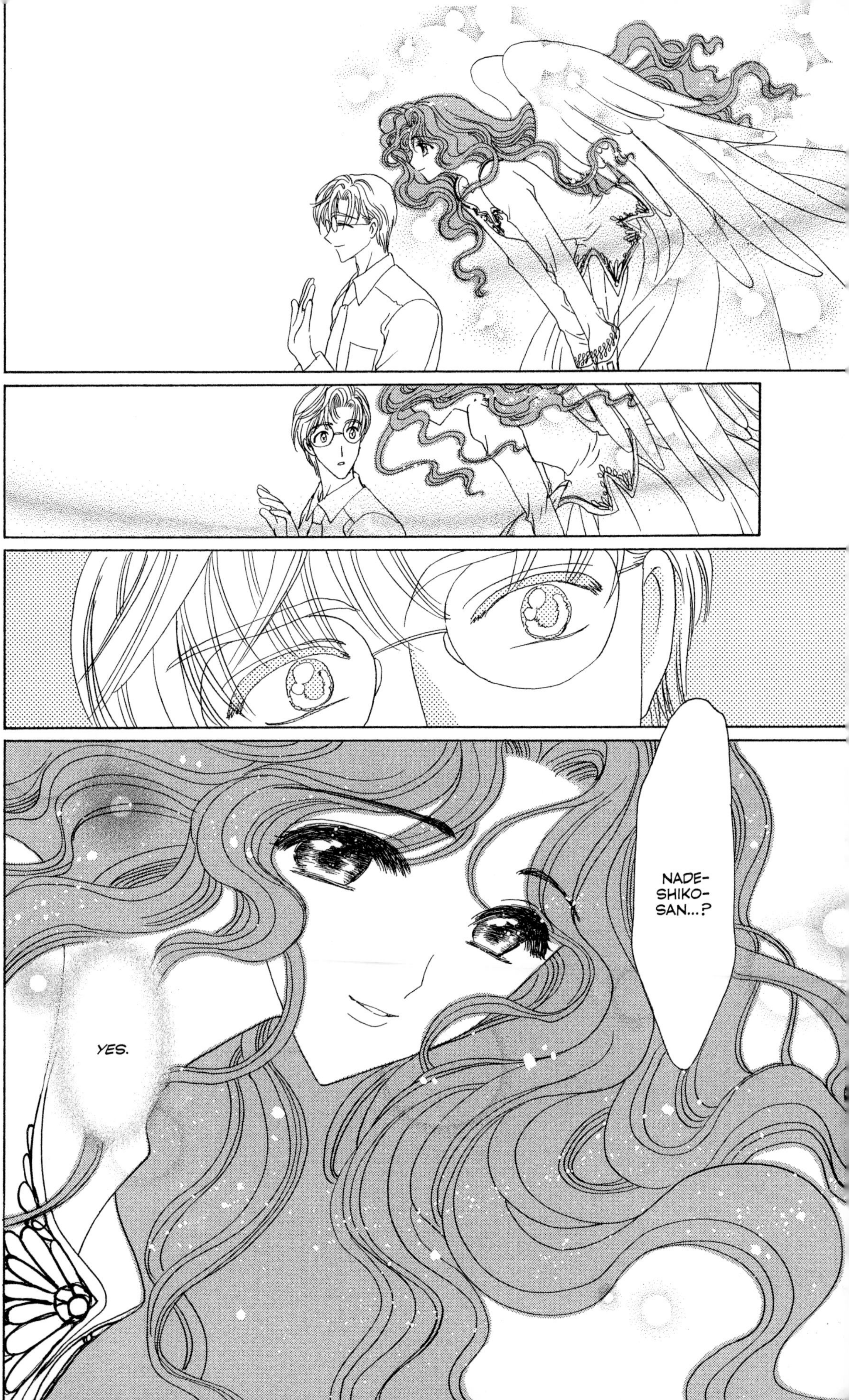
NADE-SHIKO-SAN...?
YES.

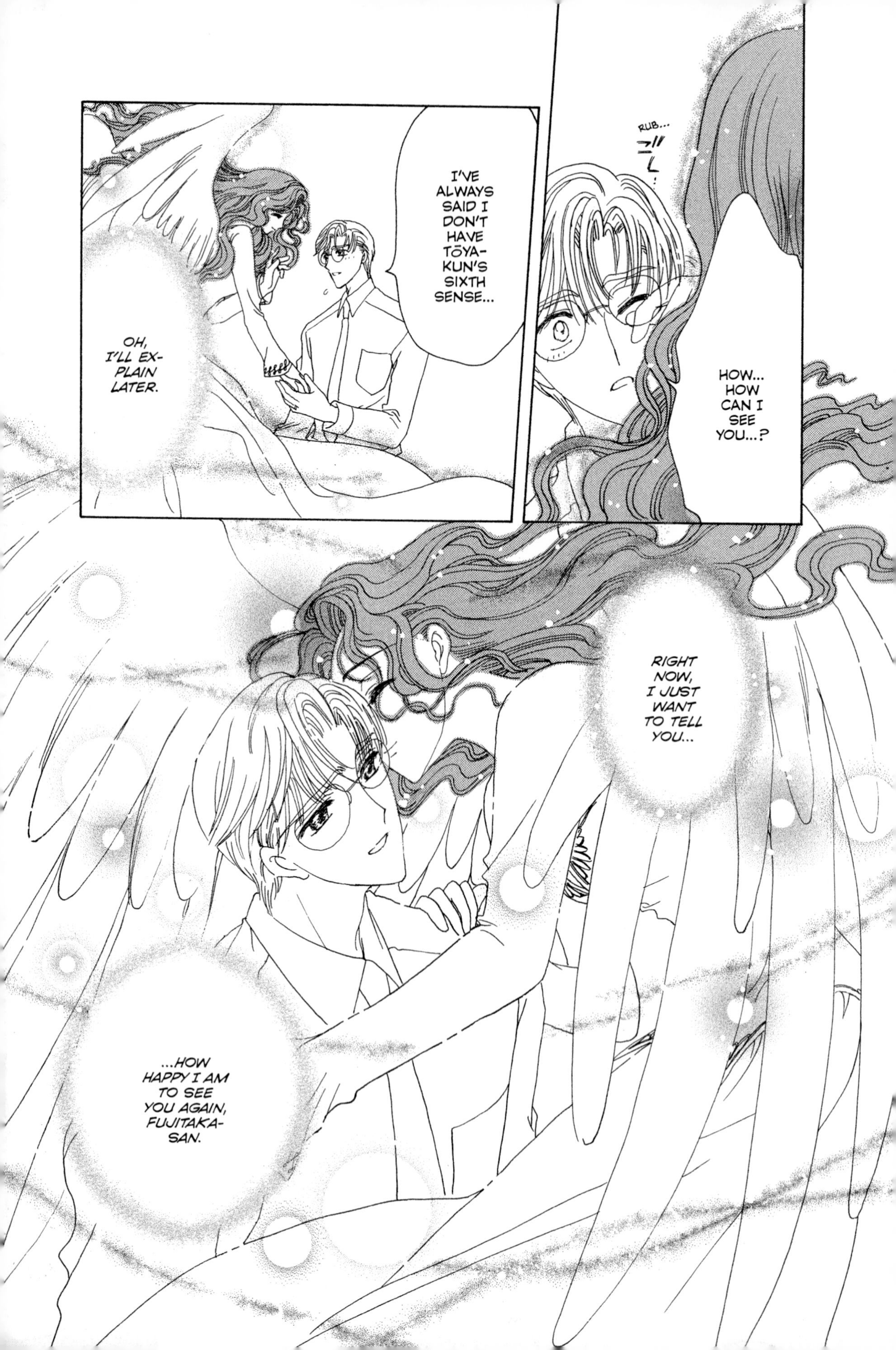
RUB...
HOW... HOW CAN I SEE YOU...?
I'VE ALWAYS SAID I DON'T HAVE TŌYA-KUN'S SIXTH SENSE...
OH, I'LL EXPLAIN LATER.
RIGHT NOW, I JUST WANT TO TELL YOU...
...HOW HAPPY I AM TO SEE YOU AGAIN, FUJITAKA-SAN.

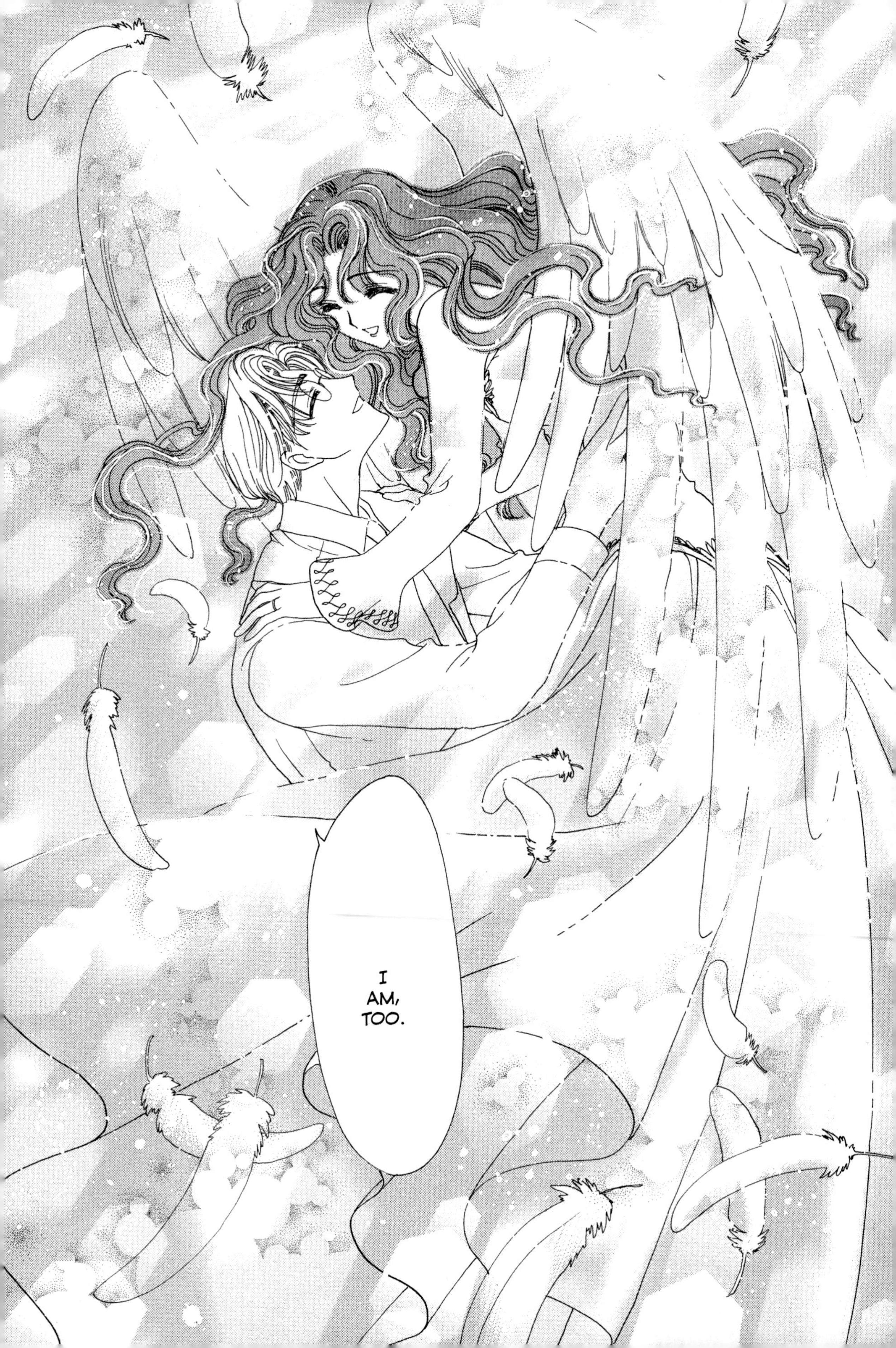
I AM, TOO.

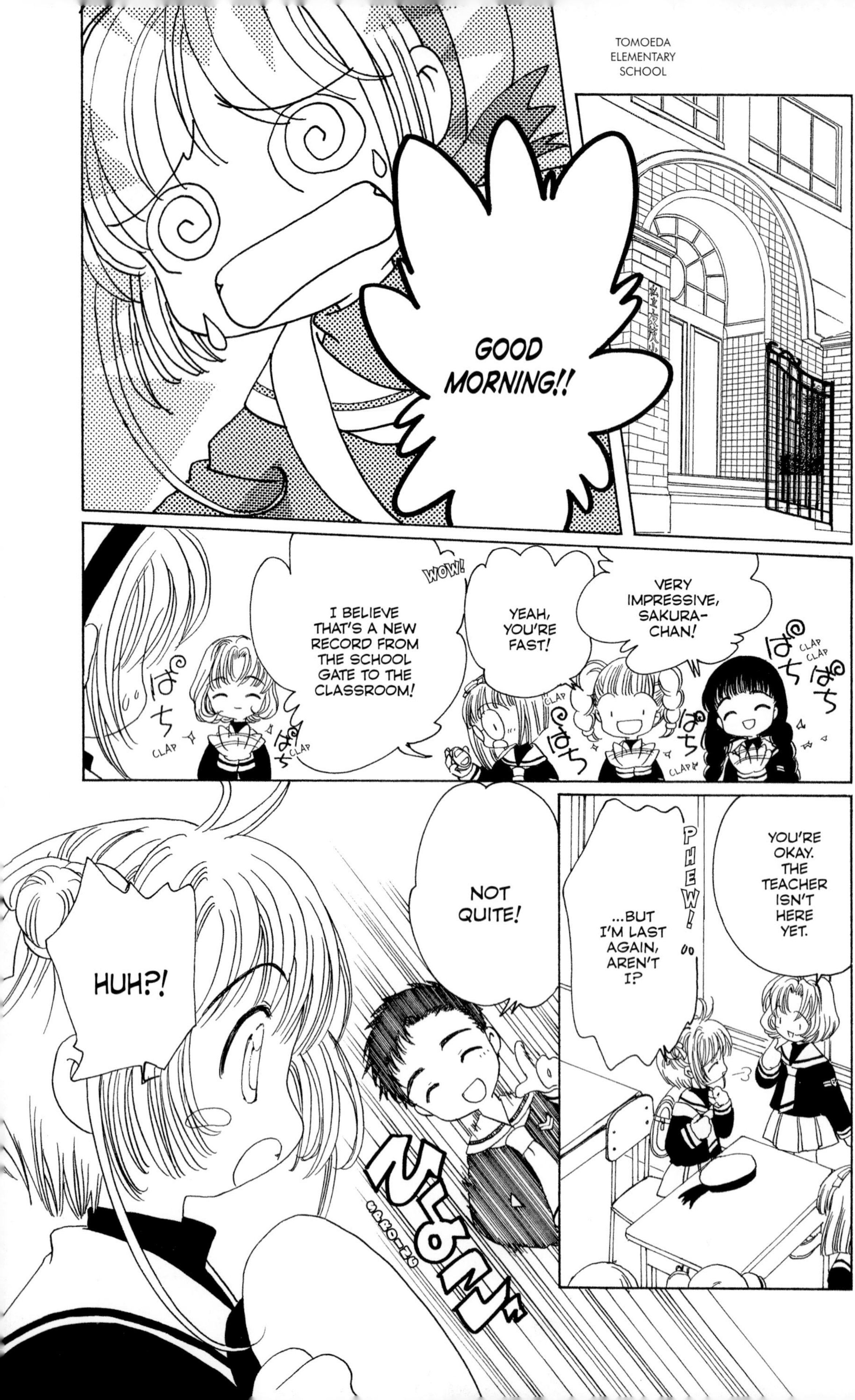
TOMOEDA ELEMENTARY SCHOOL
GOOD MORNING!!
VERY IMPRESSIVE, SAKURA-CHAN!
CLAP CLAP
YEAH, YOU'RE FAST!
WOW!
I BELIEVE THAT'S A NEW RECORD FROM THE SCHOOL GATE TO THE CLASSROOM!
CLAP
YOU'RE OKAY. THE TEACHER ISN'T HERE YET.
PHEW!
...BUT I'M LAST AGAIN, AREN'T I?
NOT QUITE!
HUH?!

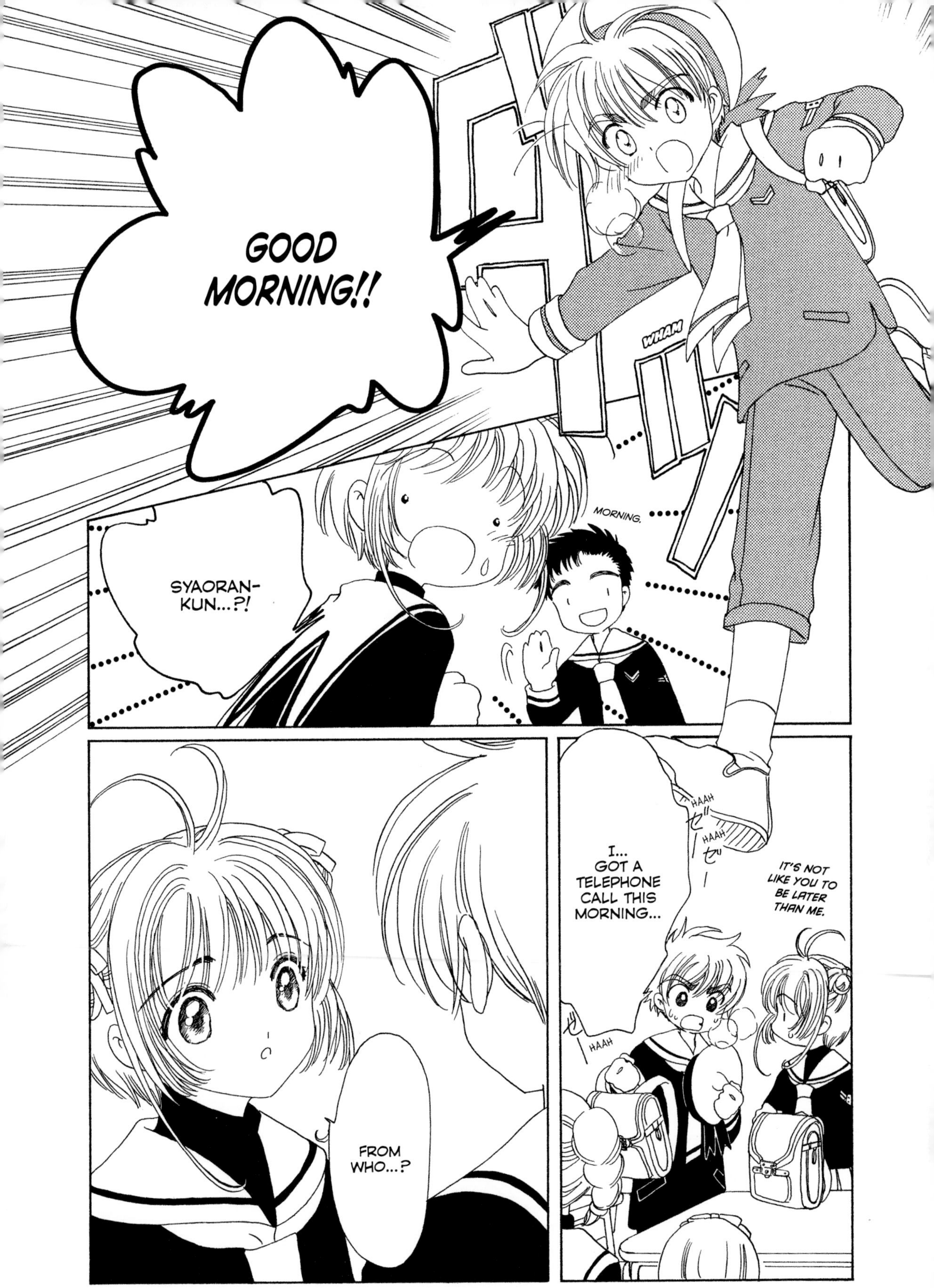
GOOD MORNING!!
WHAM
MORNING.
SYAORAN-KUN...?!
HAAH
HAAH
IT'S NOT LIKE YOU TO BE LATER THAN ME.
I... GOT A TELEPHONE CALL THIS MORNING...
HAAH
FROM WHO...?

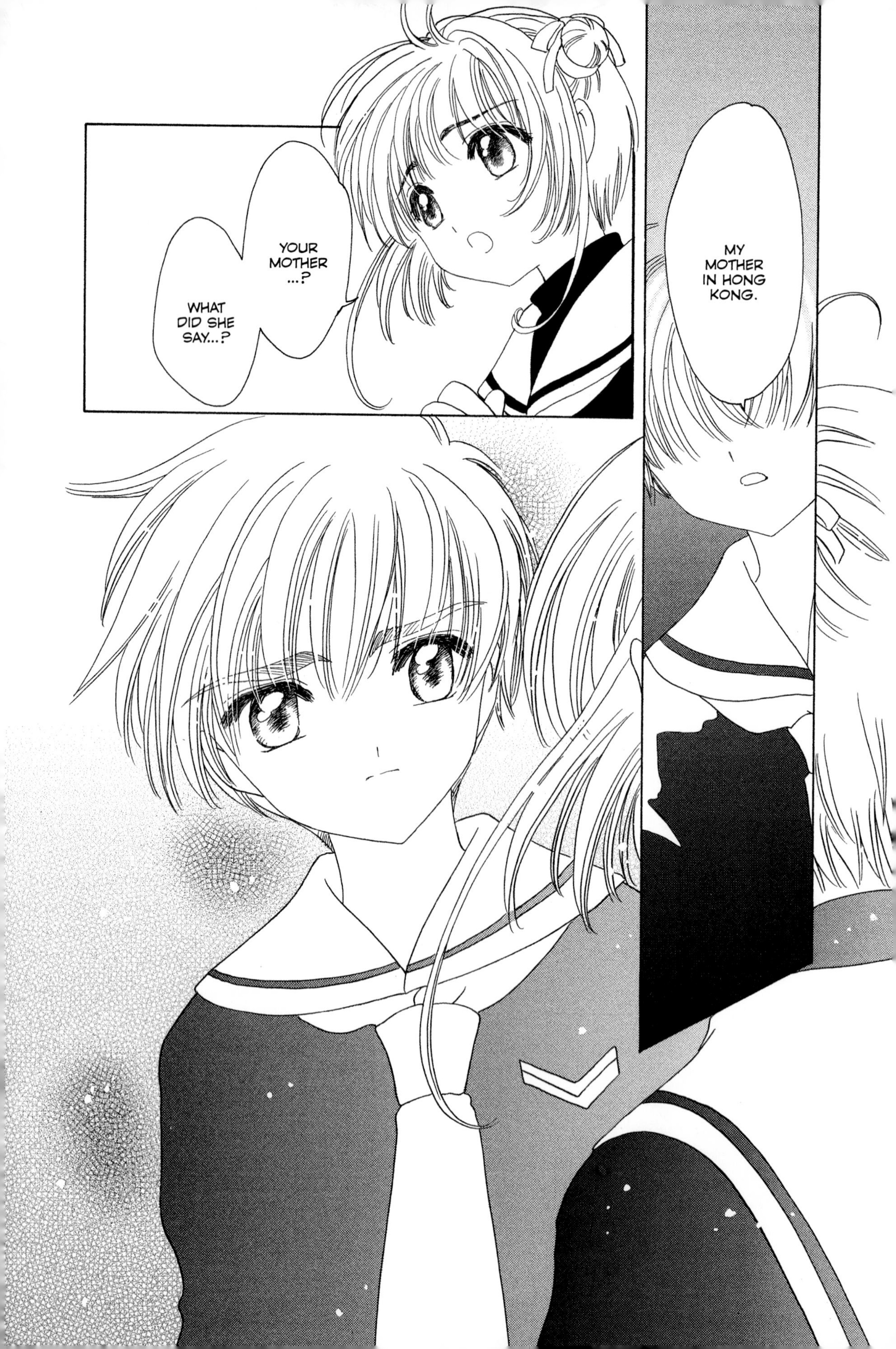
MY MOTHER IN HONG KONG.
YOUR MOTHER ...?
WHAT DID SHE SAY...?

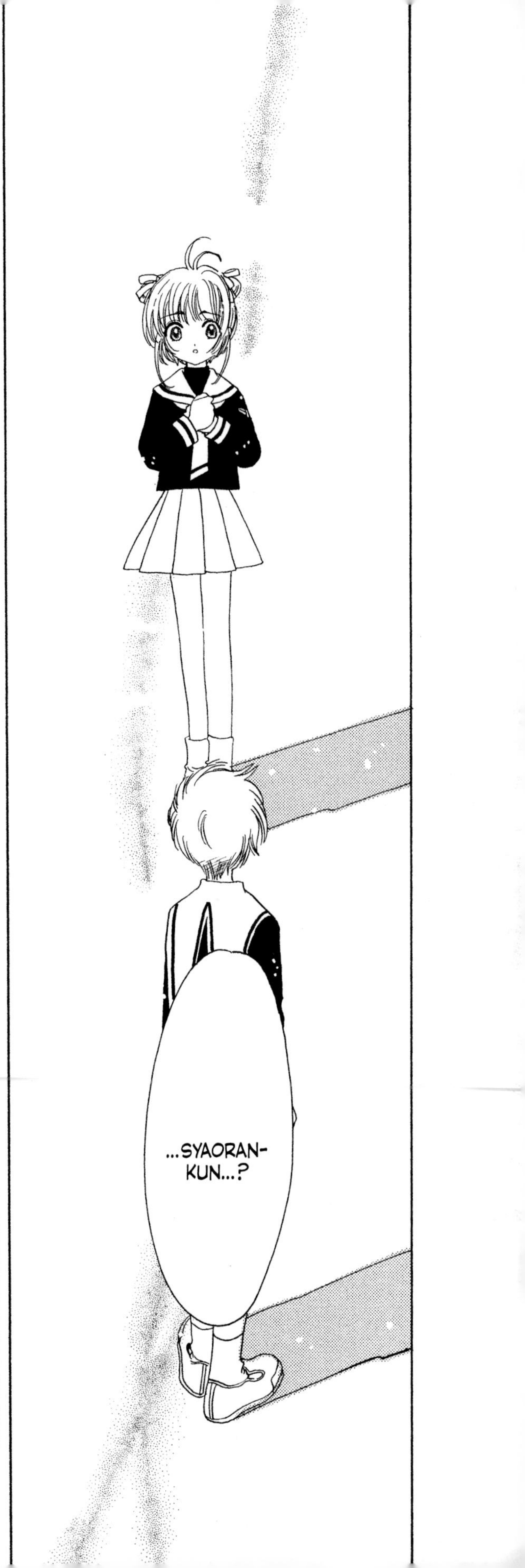
...SYAORAN-KUN...?

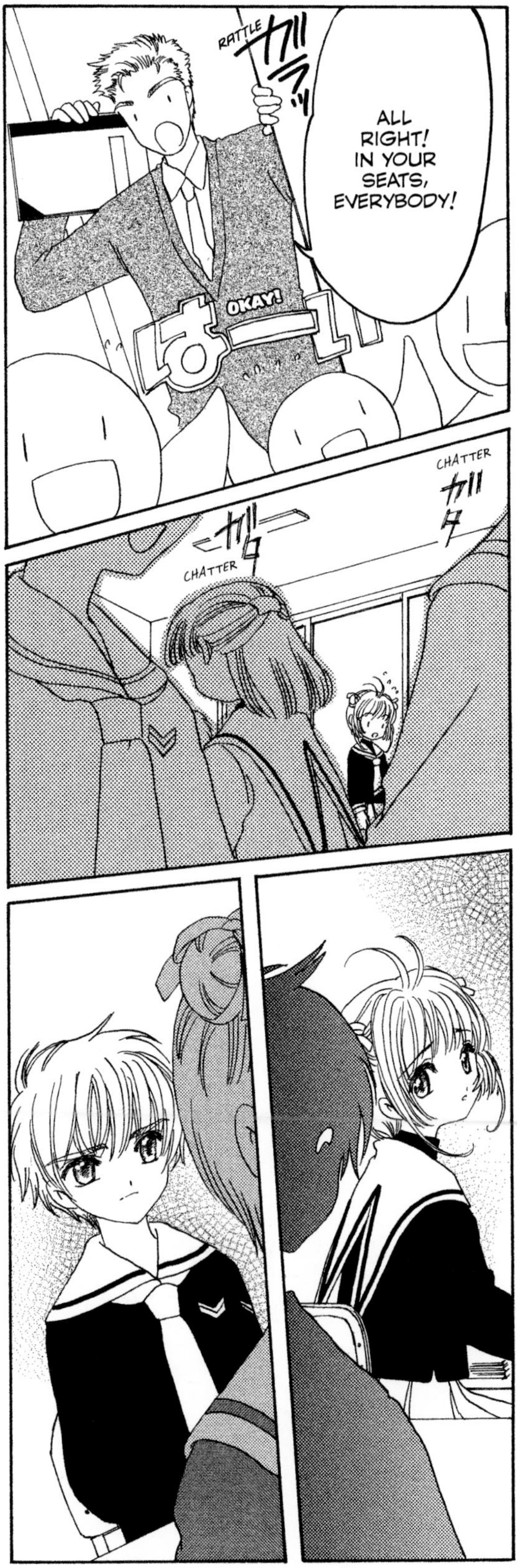
RATTLE
ALL RIGHT! IN YOUR SEATS, EVERYBODY!
OKAY!
CHATTER
CHATTER

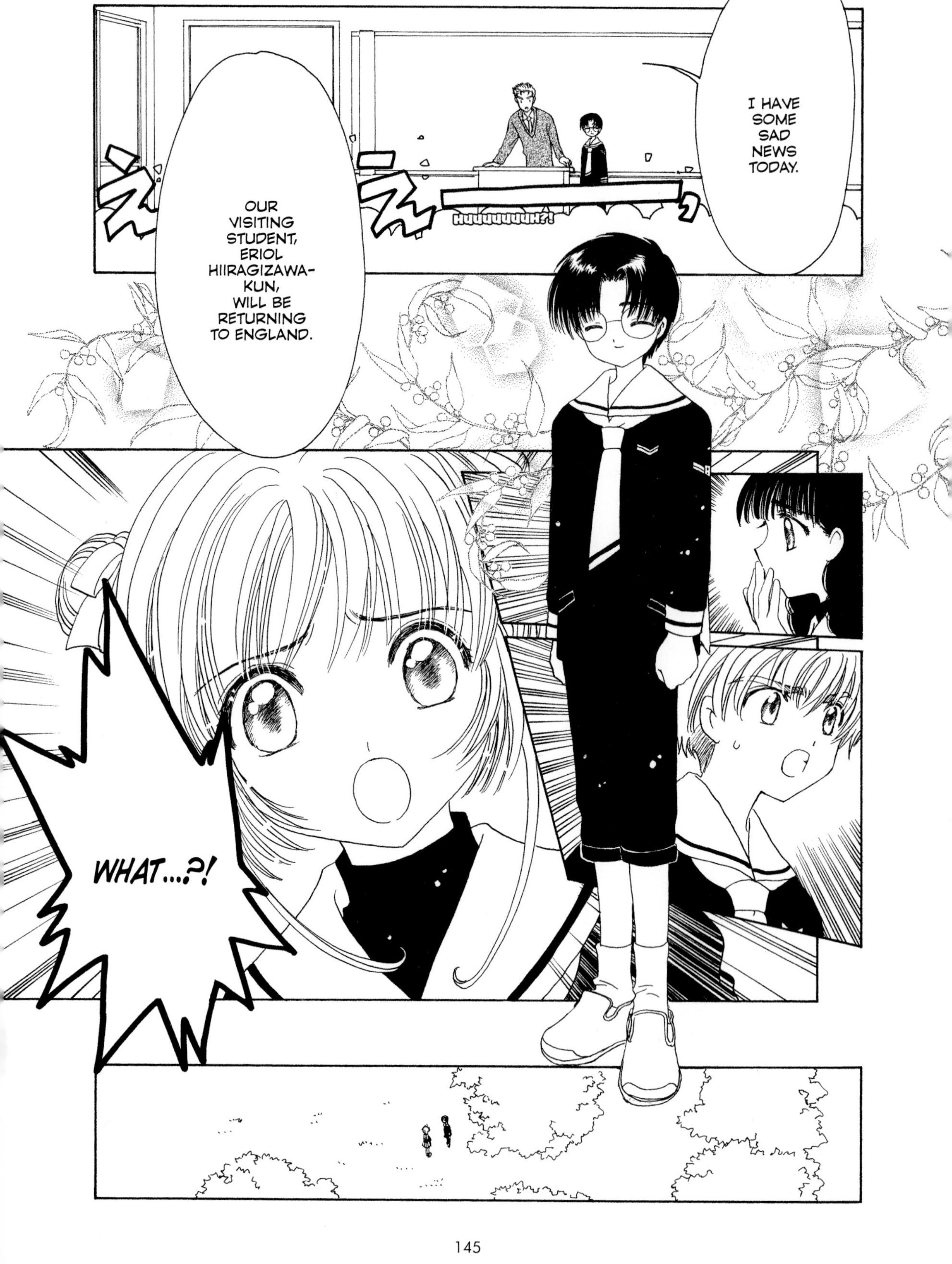
I HAVE SOME SAD NEWS TODAY.
OUR VISITING STUDENT, ERIOL HIIRAGIZAWA-KUN, WILL BE RETURNING TO ENGLAND.
HUUUUUUUUH?!
WHAT...?!

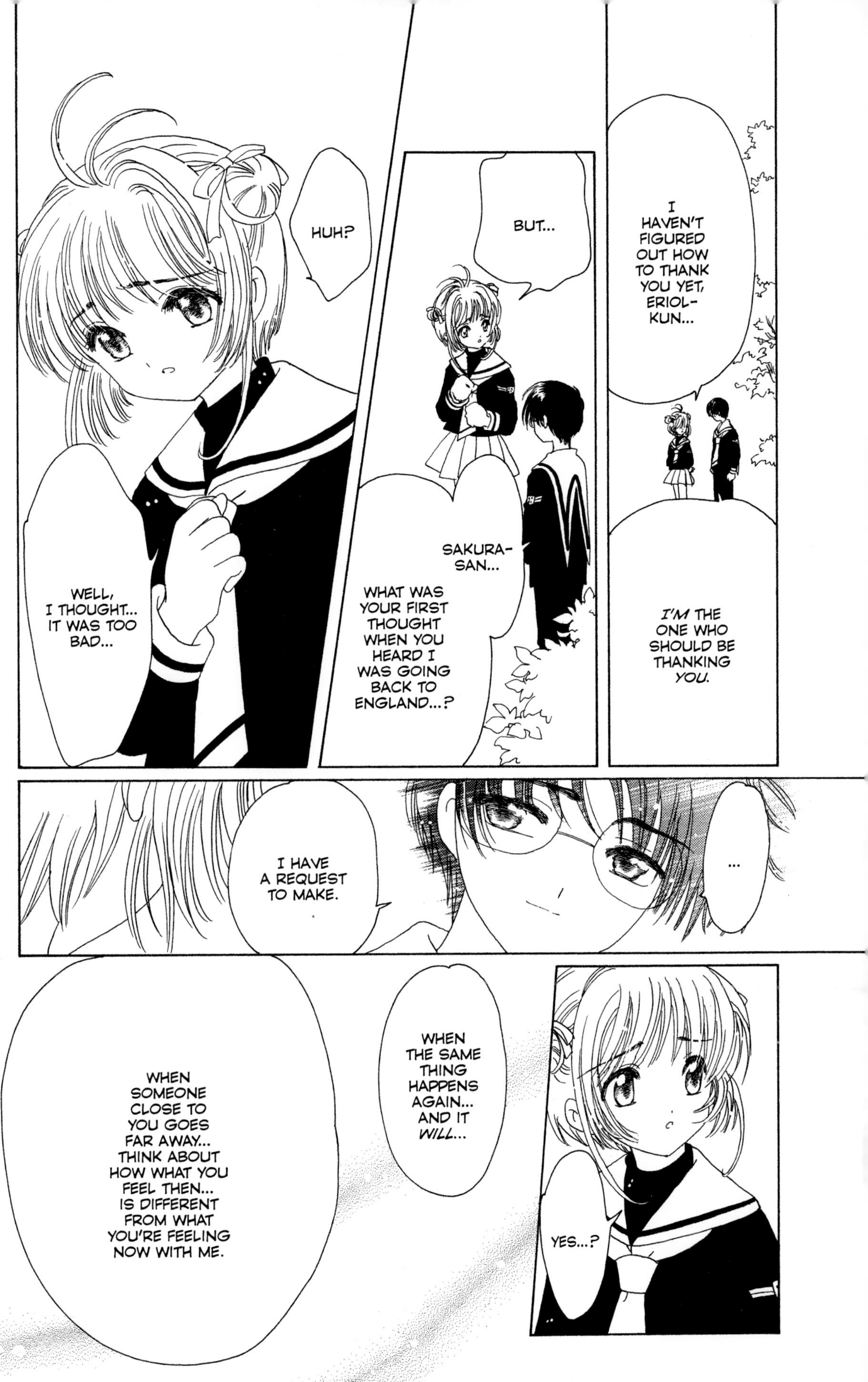

I HAVEN'T FIGURED OUT HOW TO THANK YOU YET, ERIOL-KUN...
I'M THE ONE WHO SHOULD BE THANKING *YOU*.
BUT...
SAKURA-SAN...
WHAT WAS YOUR FIRST THOUGHT WHEN YOU HEARD I WAS GOING BACK TO ENGLAND...?
HUH?
WELL, I THOUGHT... IT WAS TOO BAD...
...
I HAVE A REQUEST TO MAKE.
YES...?
WHEN THE SAME THING HAPPENS AGAIN... AND IT *WILL*...
WHEN SOMEONE CLOSE TO YOU GOES FAR AWAY... THINK ABOUT HOW WHAT YOU FEEL THEN... IS DIFFERENT FROM WHAT YOU'RE FEELING NOW WITH ME.

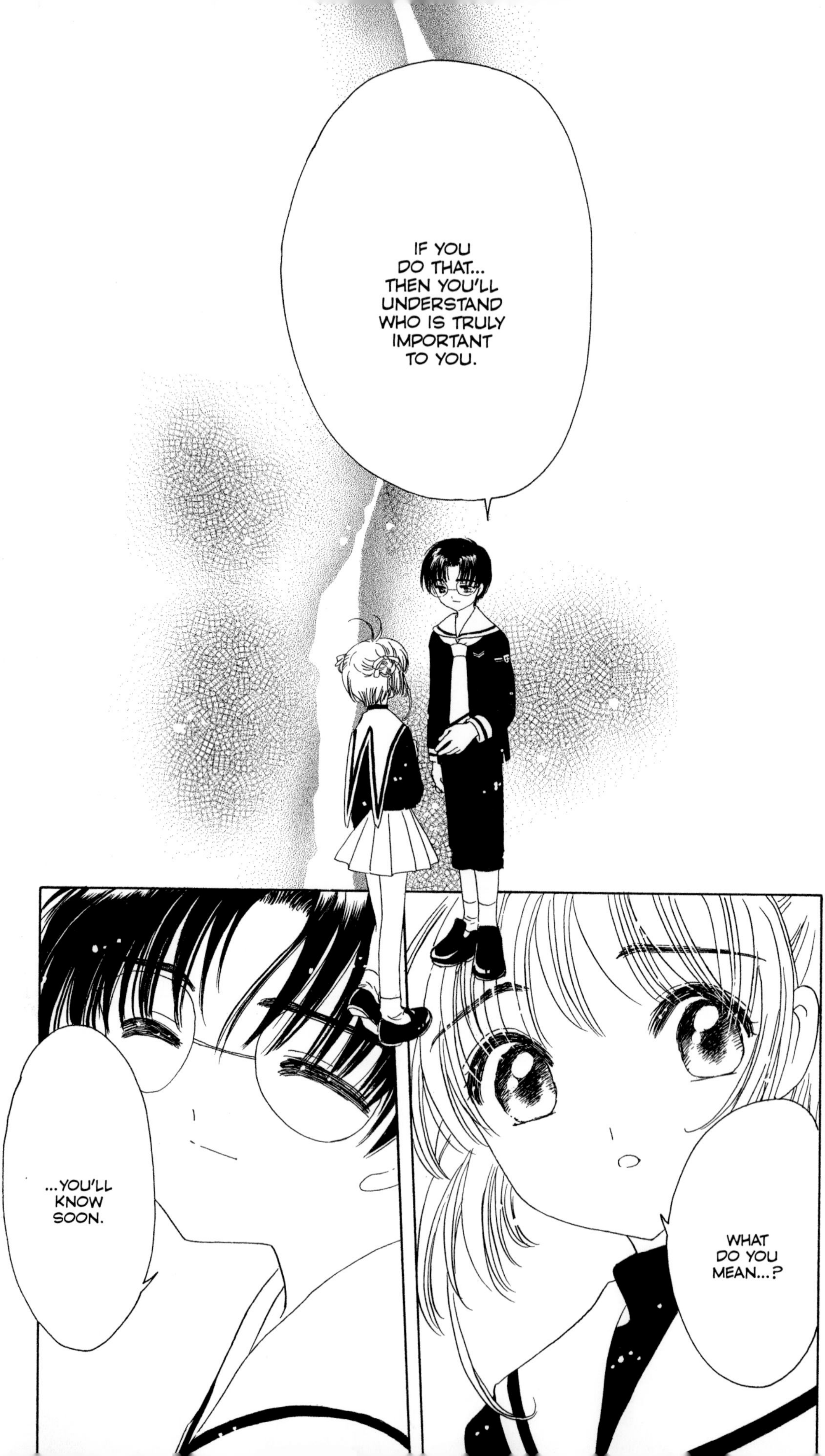
IF YOU DO THAT... THEN YOU'LL UNDERSTAND WHO IS TRULY IMPORTANT TO YOU.
WHAT DO YOU MEAN...?
...YOU'LL KNOW SOON.

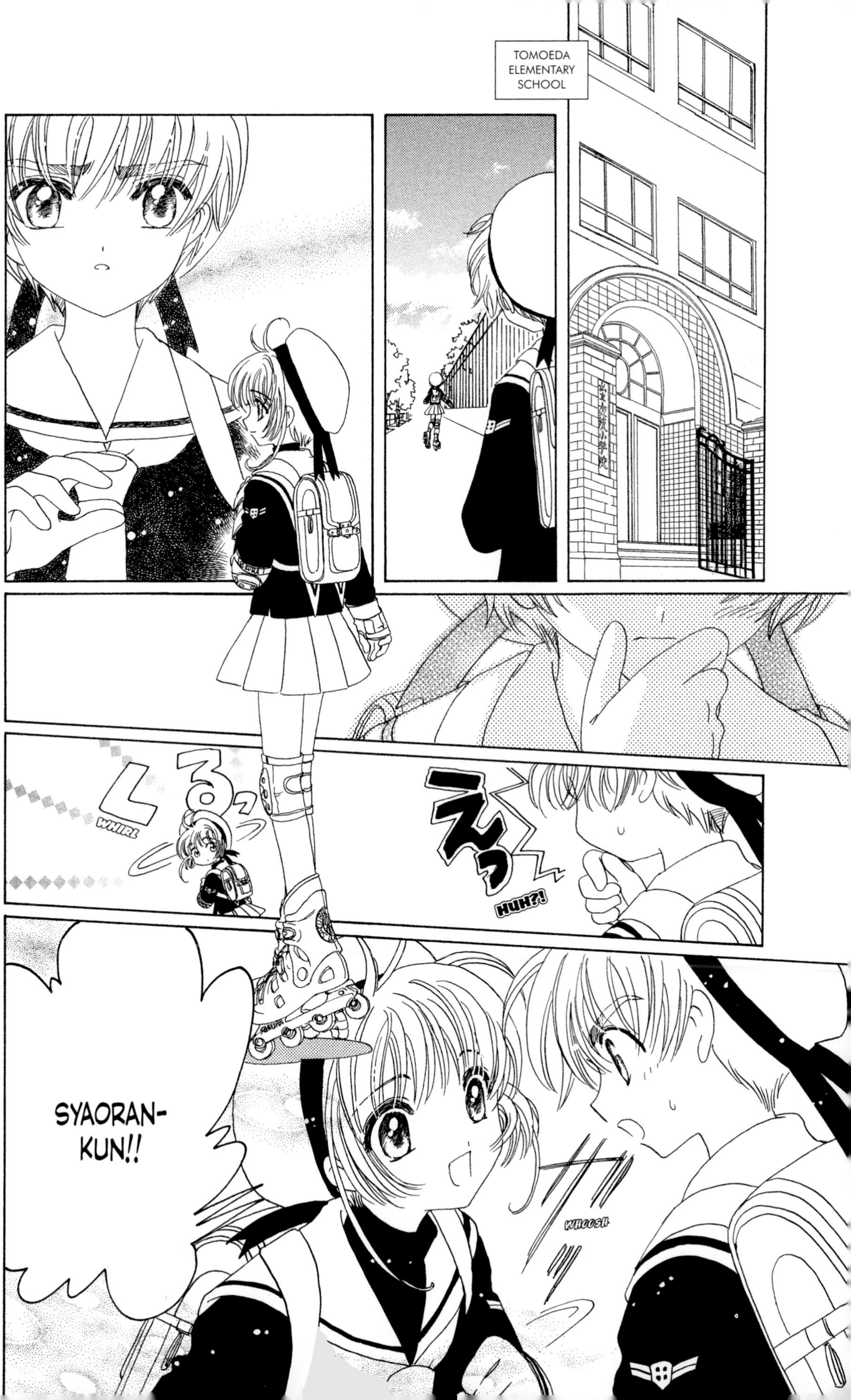
TOMOEDA
ELEMENTARY
SCHOOL
えっ
HUH?!
くるっ
WHIRL
SYAORAN-
KUN!!
WHOOSH

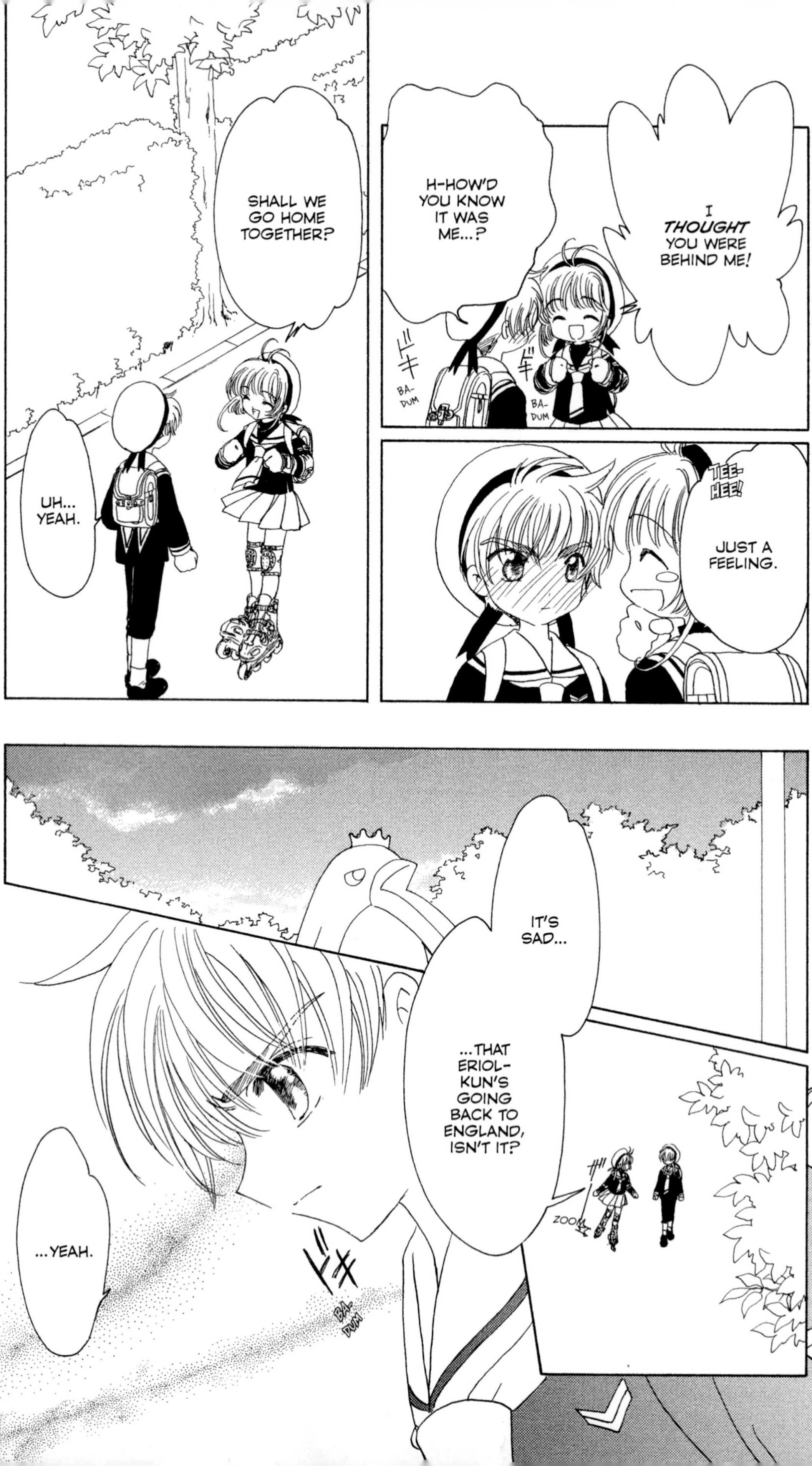

I *THOUGHT* YOU WERE BEHIND ME!
H-HOW'D YOU KNOW IT WAS ME...?
ドキ BA-DUM
ドキ BA-DUM
TEE-HEE!
JUST A FEELING.
SHALL WE GO HOME TOGETHER?
UH... YEAH.
IT'S SAD...
...THAT ERIOL-KUN'S GOING BACK TO ENGLAND, ISN'T IT?
ZOOM
...YEAH.
ドキ BA-DUM

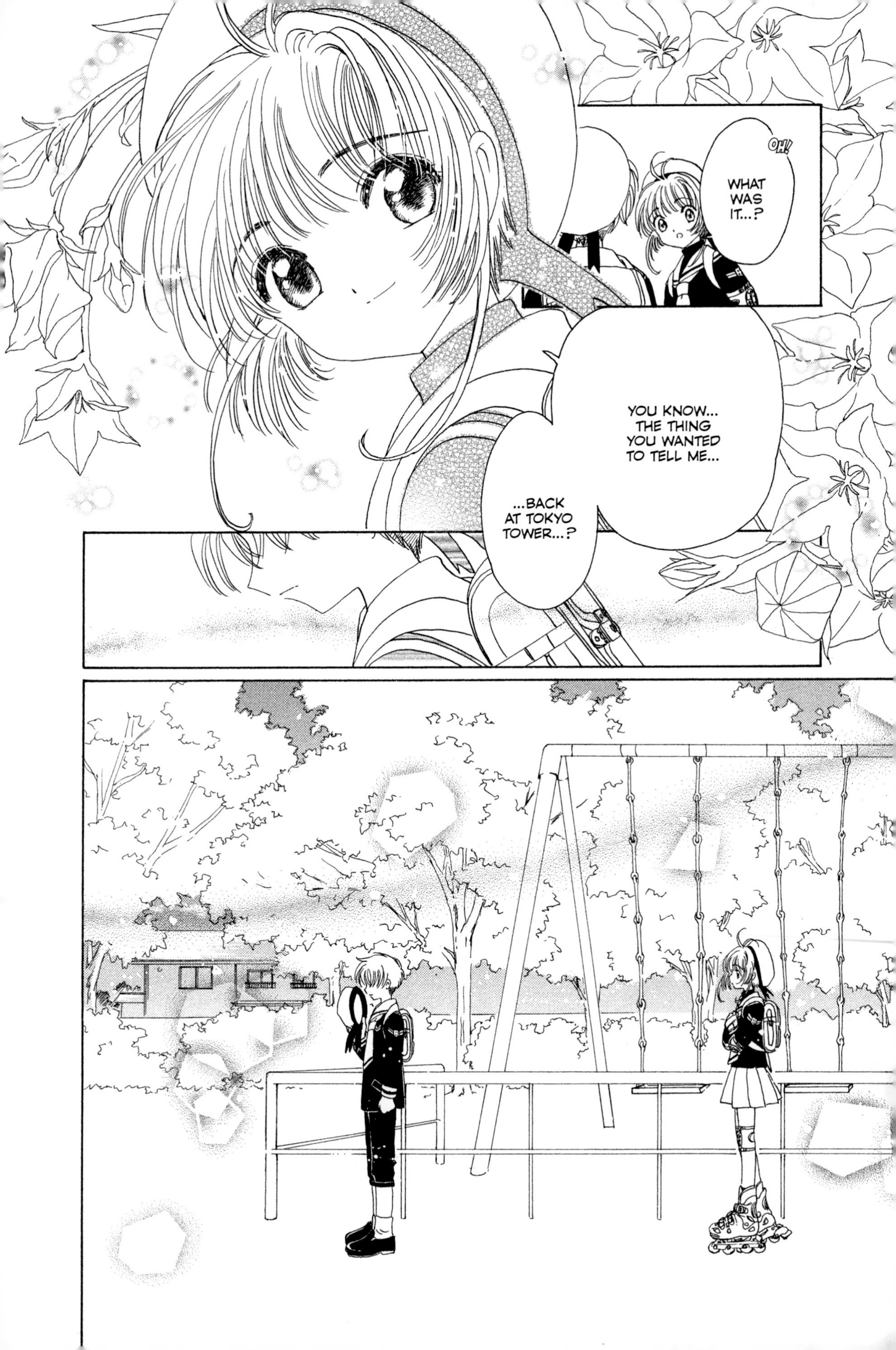
OH!
WHAT WAS IT...?
YOU KNOW... THE THING YOU WANTED TO TELL ME...
...BACK AT TOKYO TOWER...?

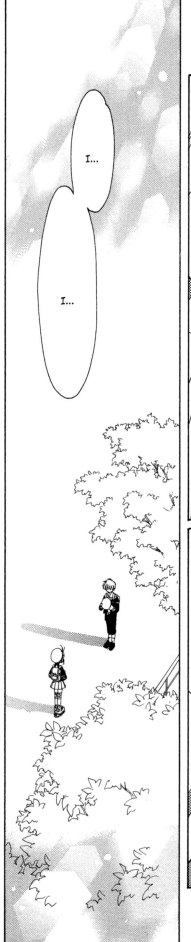

I...

I...

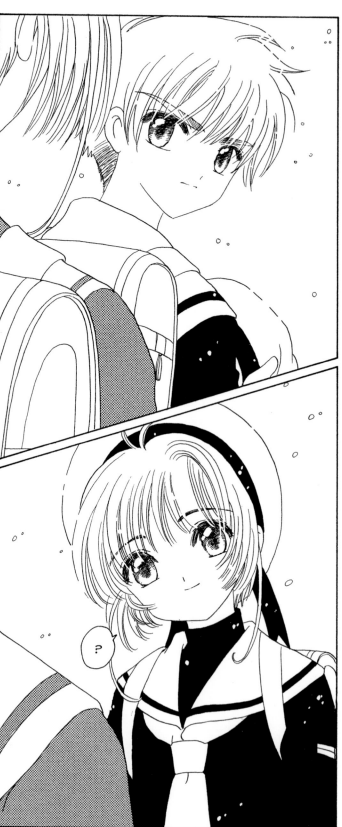

?

151

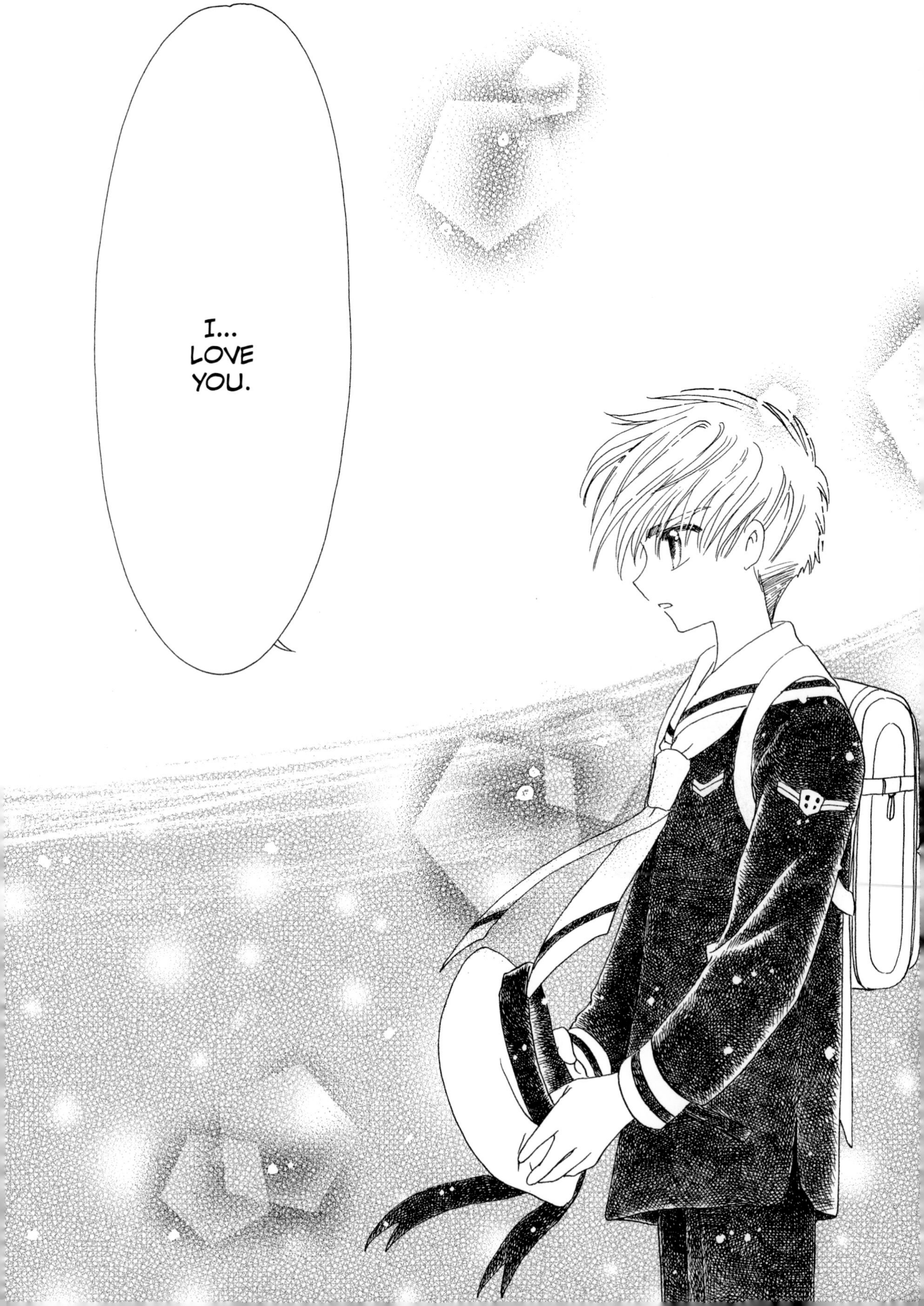
I... LOVE YOU.

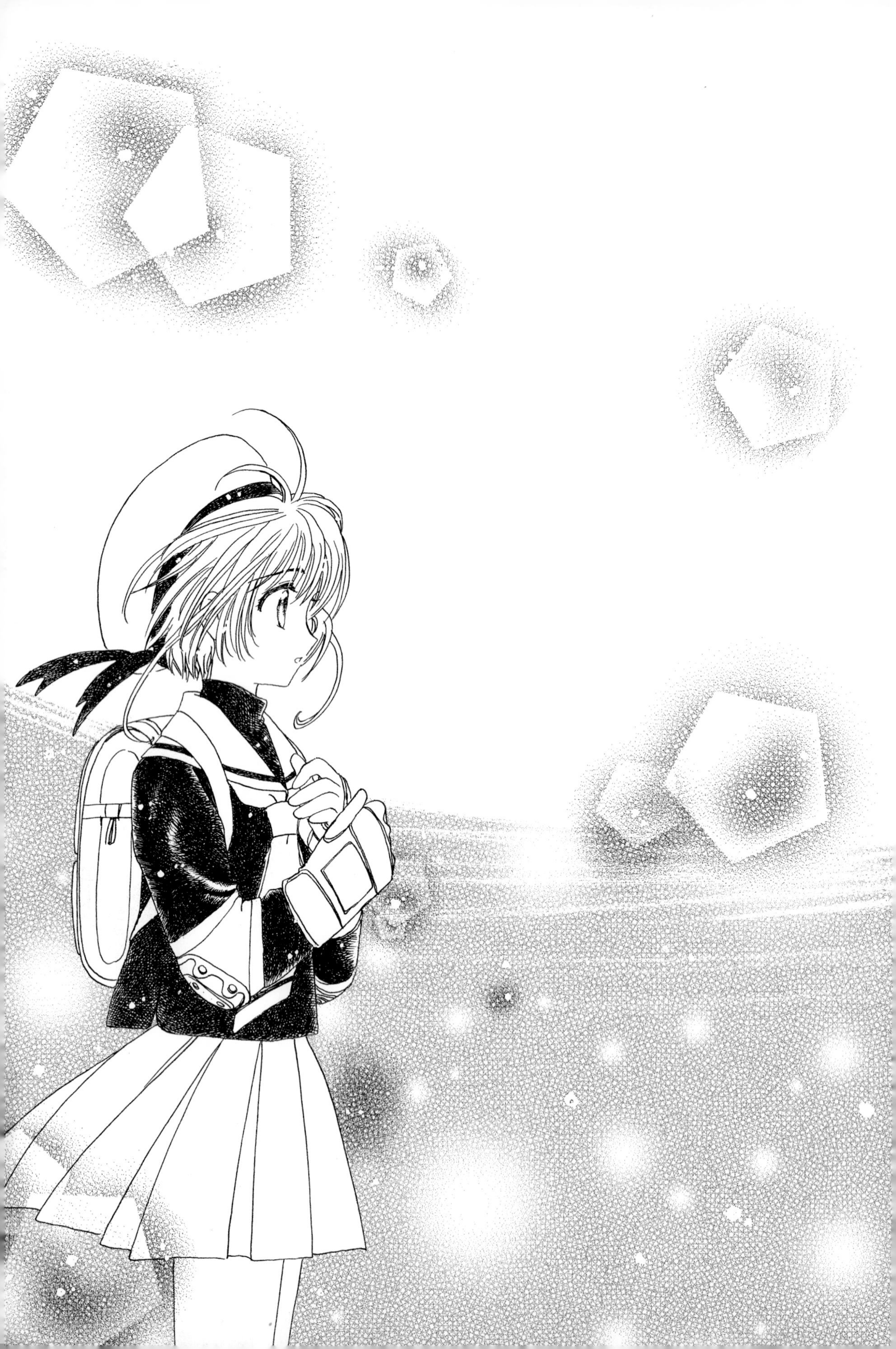

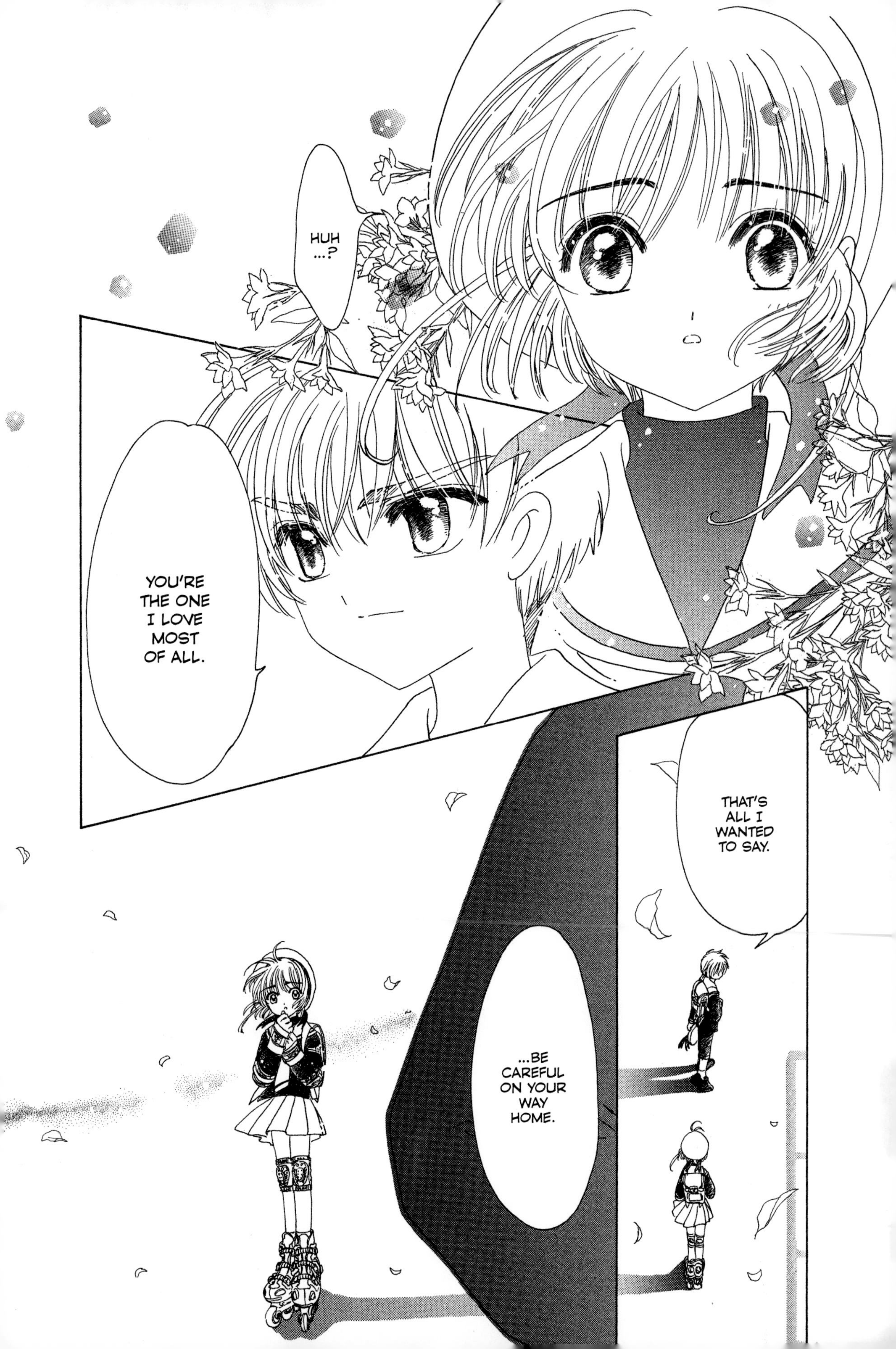
HUH ...?
YOU'RE THE ONE I LOVE MOST OF ALL.
THAT'S ALL I WANTED TO SAY.
...BE CAREFUL ON YOUR WAY HOME.

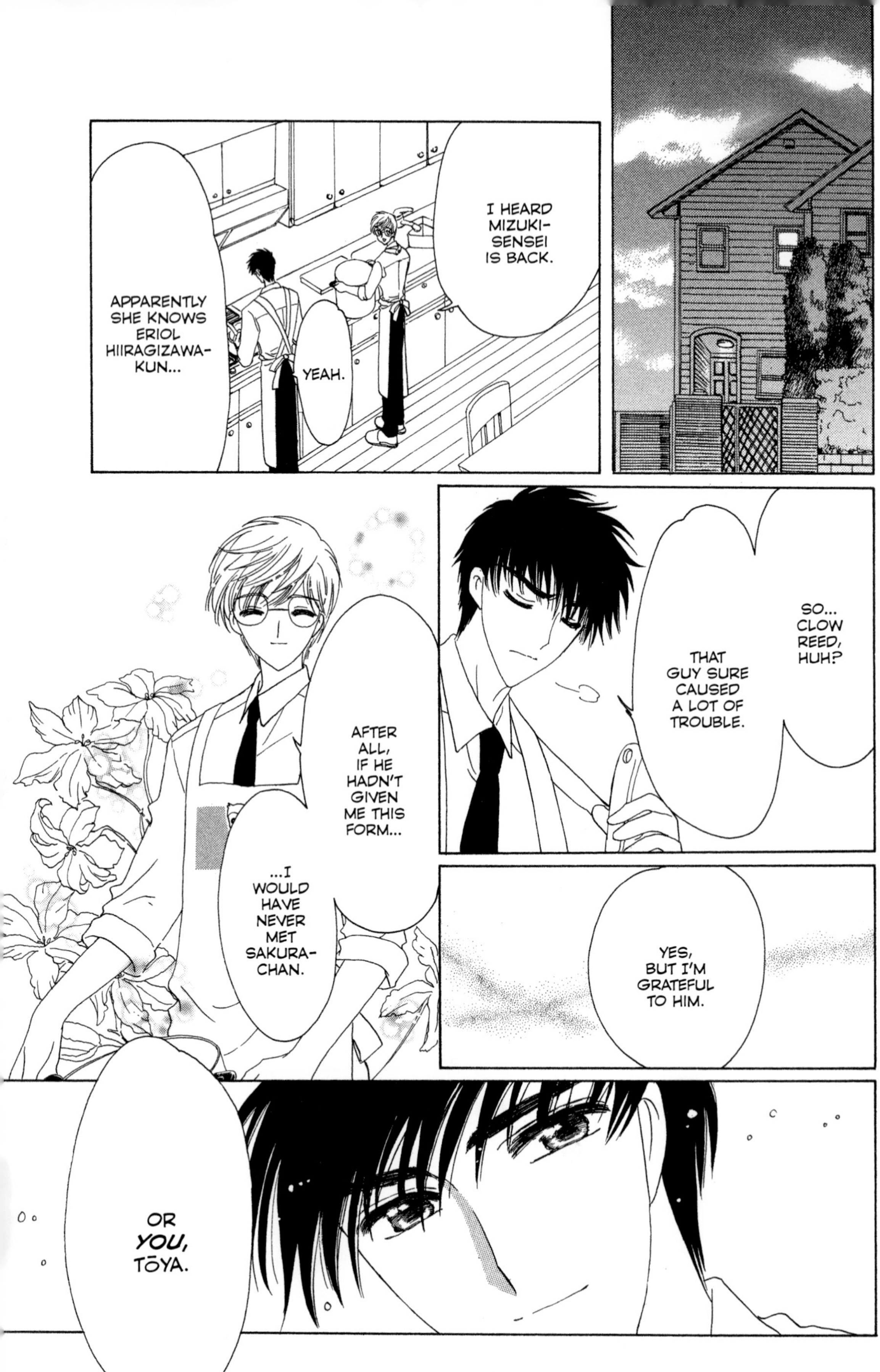
I HEARD MIZUKI-SENSEI IS BACK.
YEAH.
APPARENTLY SHE KNOWS ERIOL HIIRAGIZAWA-KUN...
SO... CLOW REED, HUH?
THAT GUY SURE CAUSED A LOT OF TROUBLE.
YES, BUT I'M GRATEFUL TO HIM.
AFTER ALL, IF HE HADN'T GIVEN ME THIS FORM...
...I WOULD HAVE NEVER MET SAKURA-CHAN.
OR *YOU*, TŌYA.

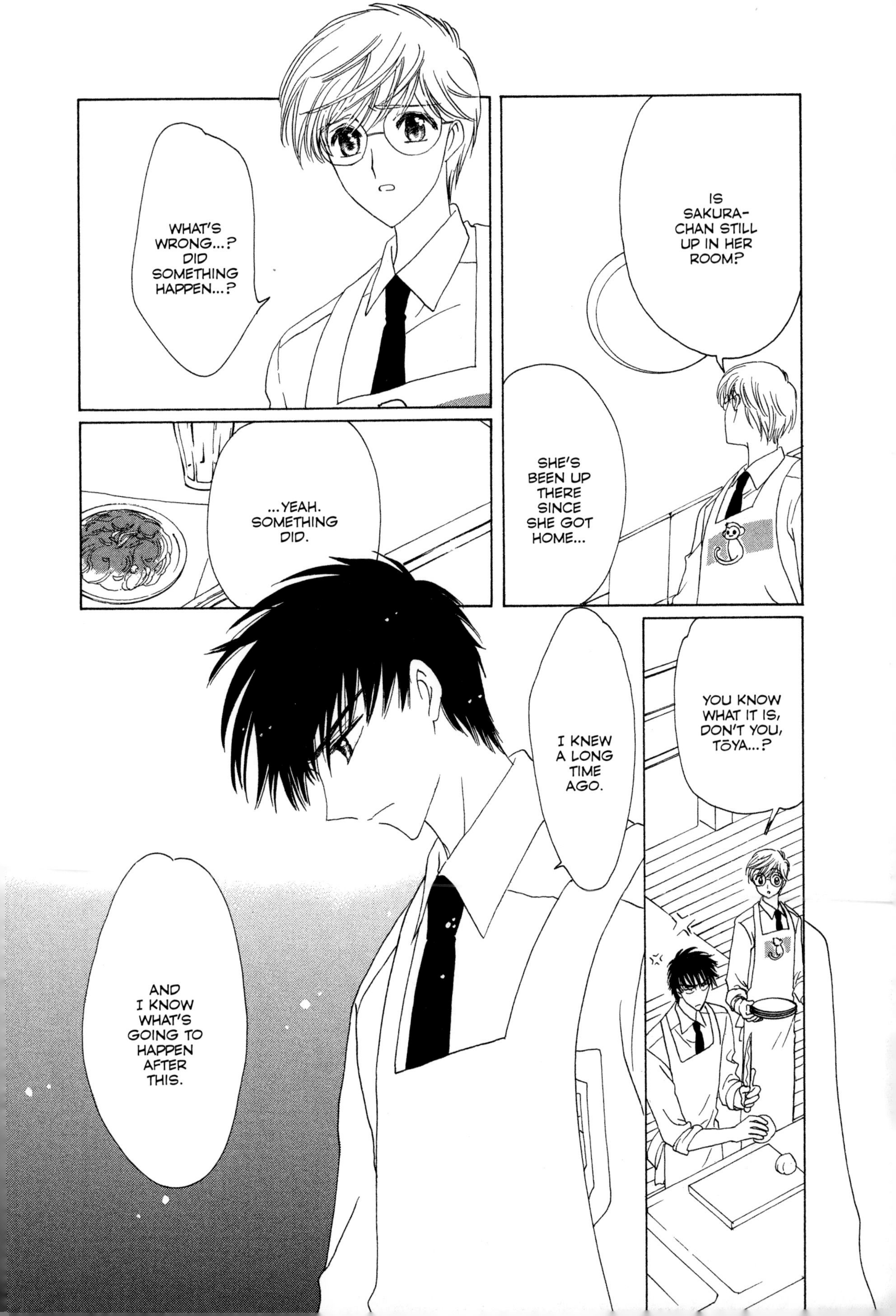
IS SAKURA-CHAN STILL UP IN HER ROOM?
SHE'S BEEN UP THERE SINCE SHE GOT HOME...
WHAT'S WRONG...? DID SOMETHING HAPPEN...?
...YEAH. SOMETHING DID.
YOU KNOW WHAT IT IS, DON'T YOU, TŌYA...?
I KNEW A LONG TIME AGO.
AND I KNOW WHAT'S GOING TO HAPPEN AFTER THIS.

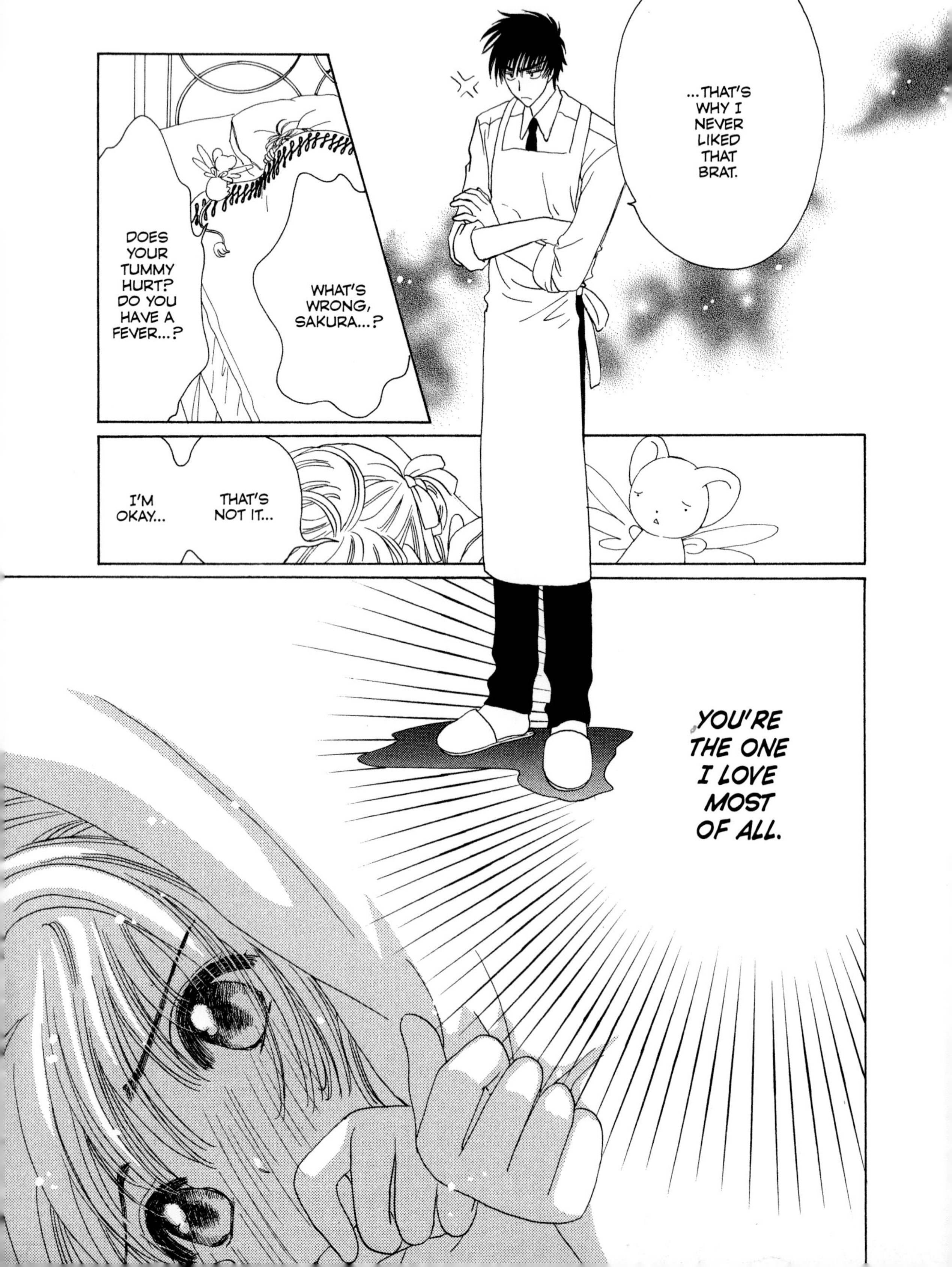
...THAT'S WHY I NEVER LIKED THAT BRAT.
WHAT'S WRONG, SAKURA...?
DOES YOUR TUMMY HURT? DO YOU HAVE A FEVER...?
THAT'S NOT IT...
I'M OKAY...
YOU'RE THE ONE I LOVE MOST OF ALL.

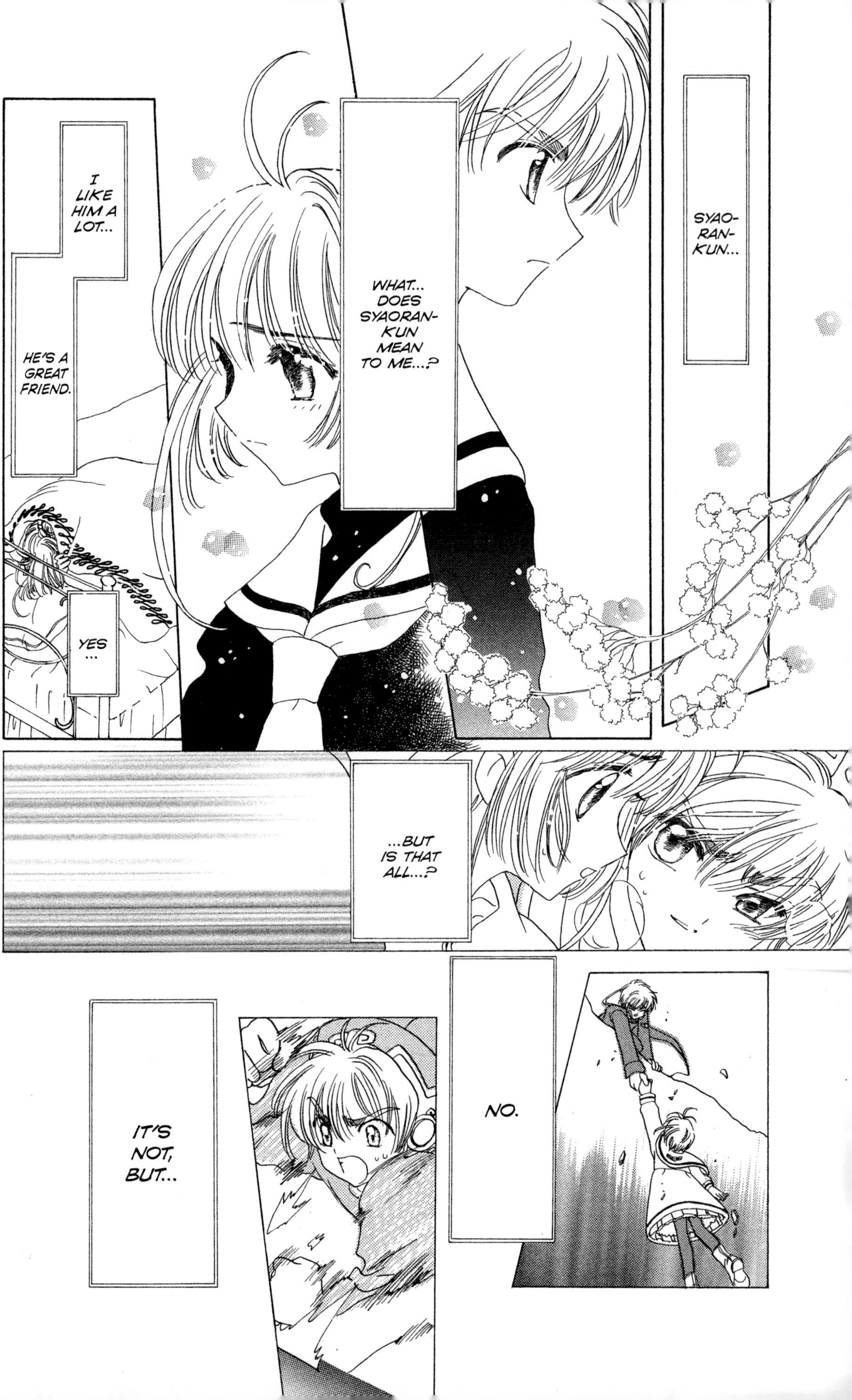
SYAO-RAN-KUN...
WHAT... DOES SYAORAN-KUN MEAN TO ME...?
I LIKE HIM A LOT...
HE'S A GREAT FRIEND.
YES ...
...BUT IS THAT ALL...?
NO.
IT'S NOT, BUT...

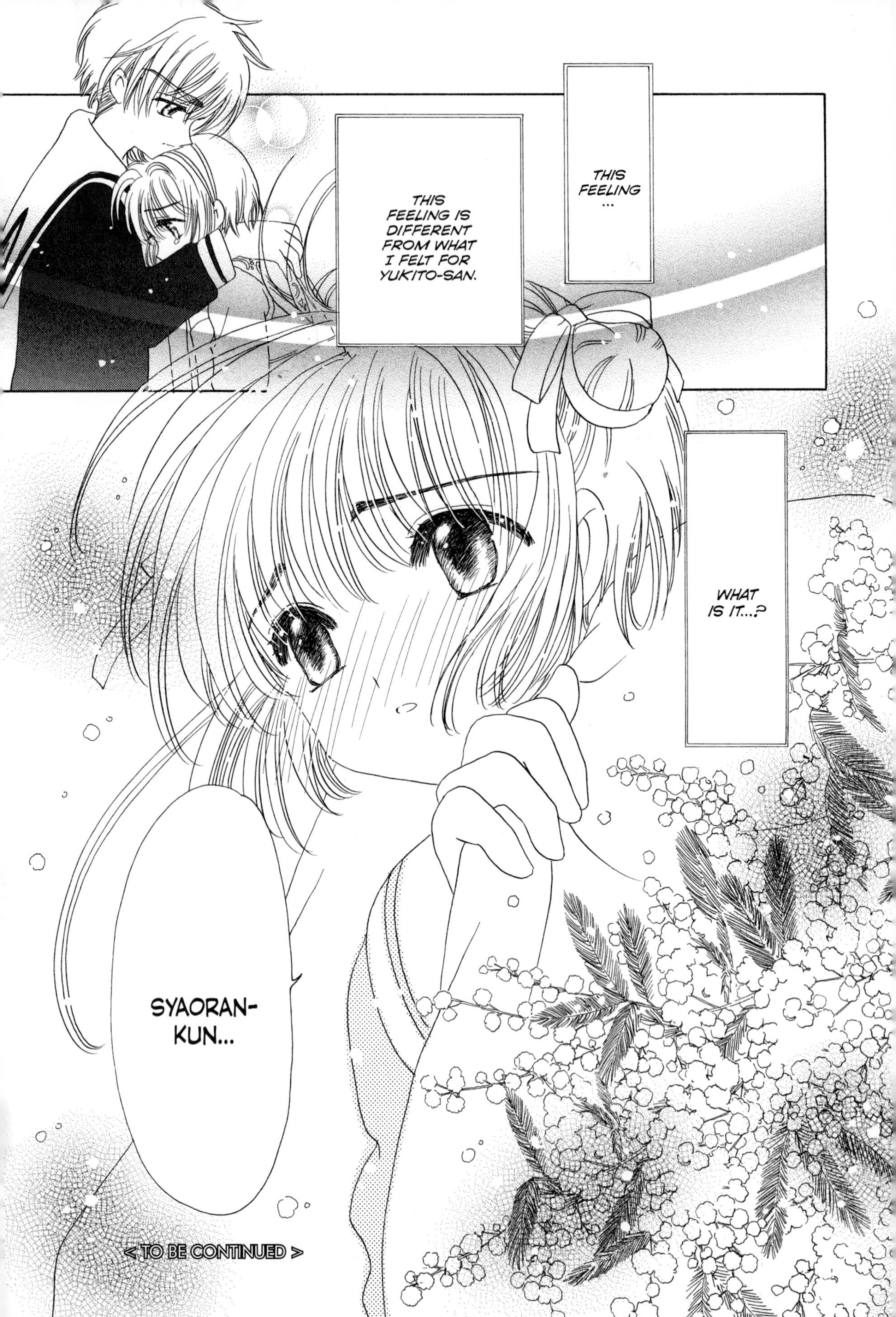
THIS FEELING ...
THIS FEELING IS DIFFERENT FROM WHAT I FELT FOR YUKITO-SAN.
WHAT IS IT...?
SYAORAN-KUN...

< TO BE CONTINUED >

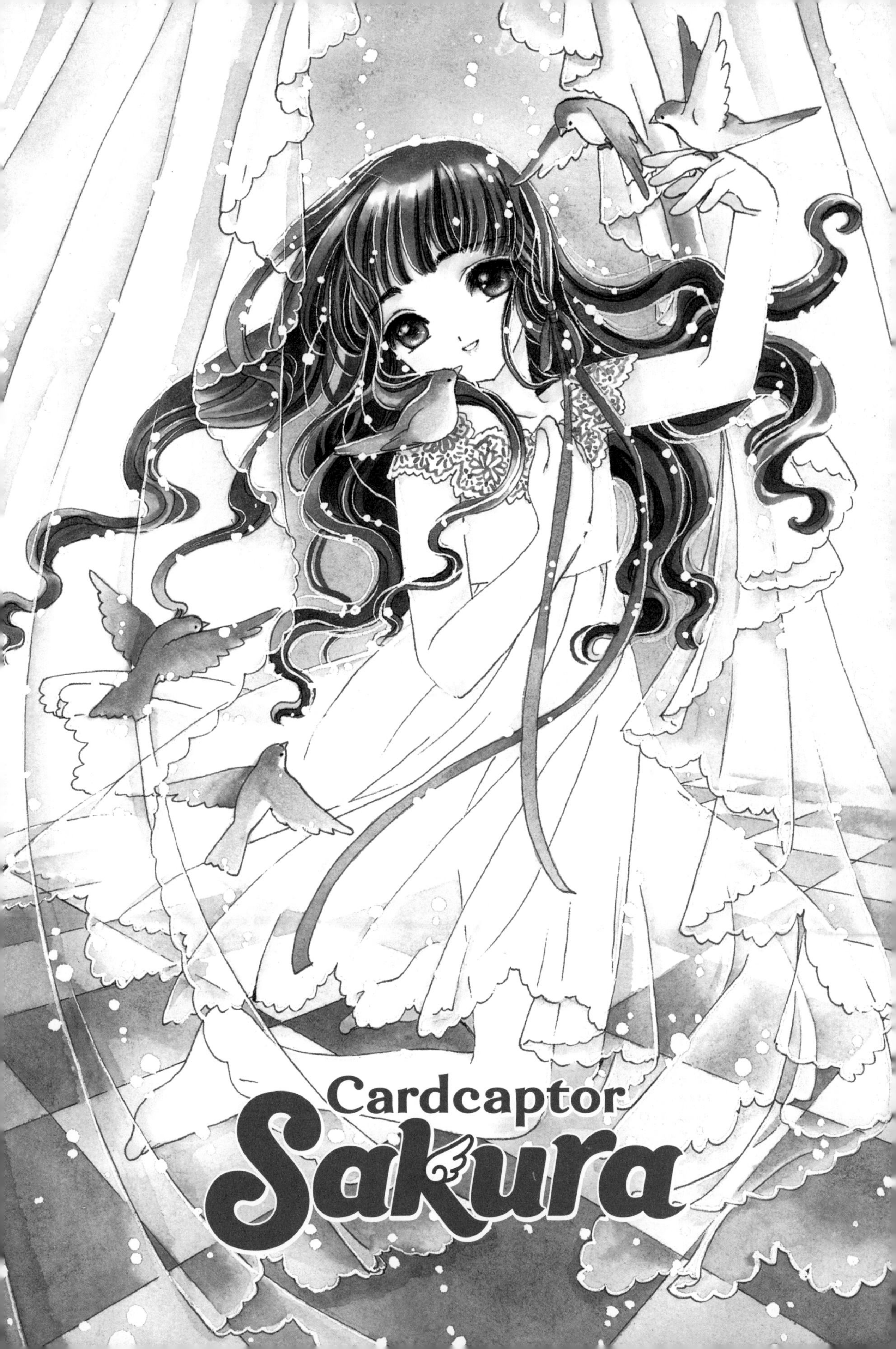
Cardcaptor
Sakura

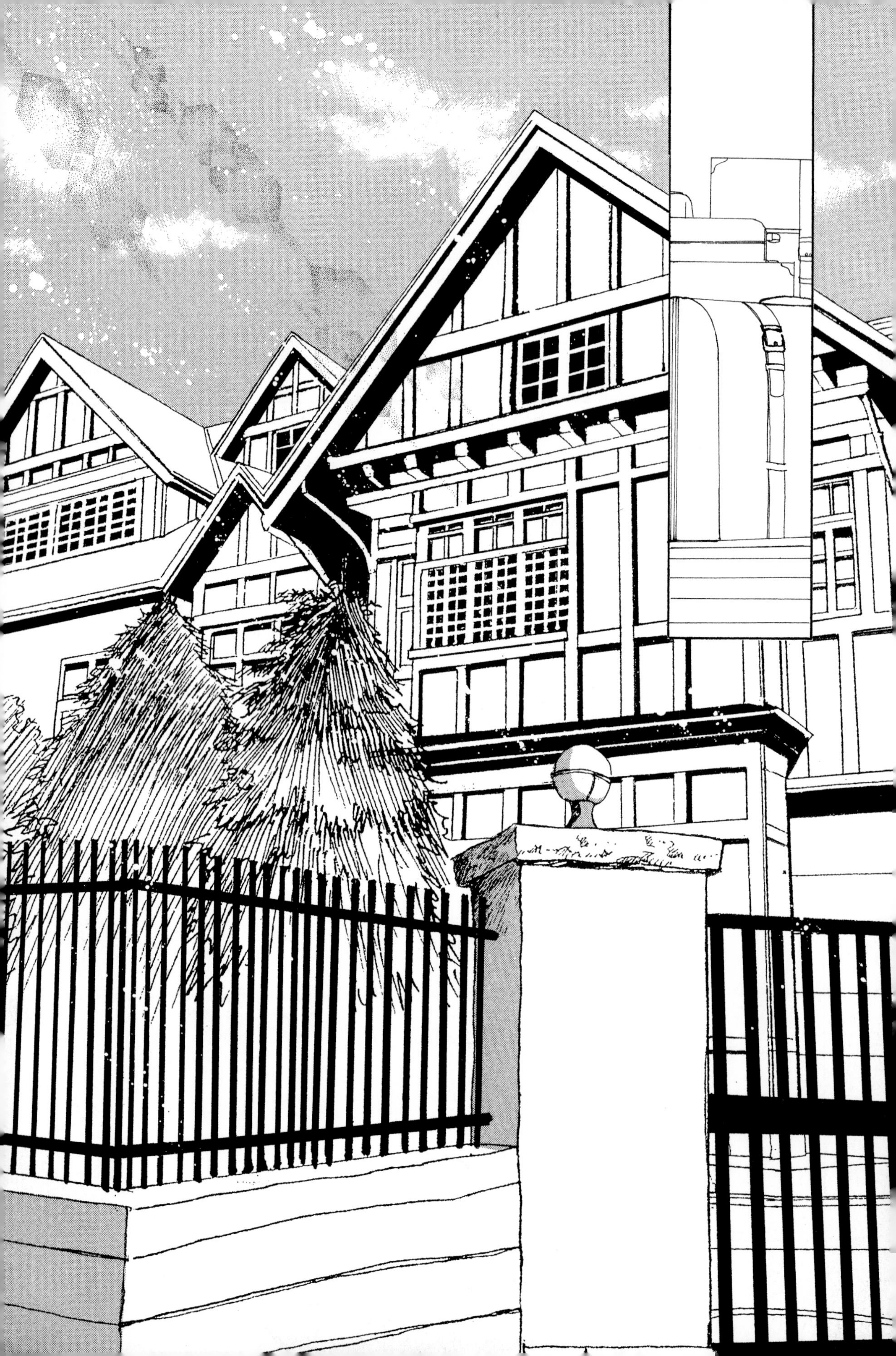

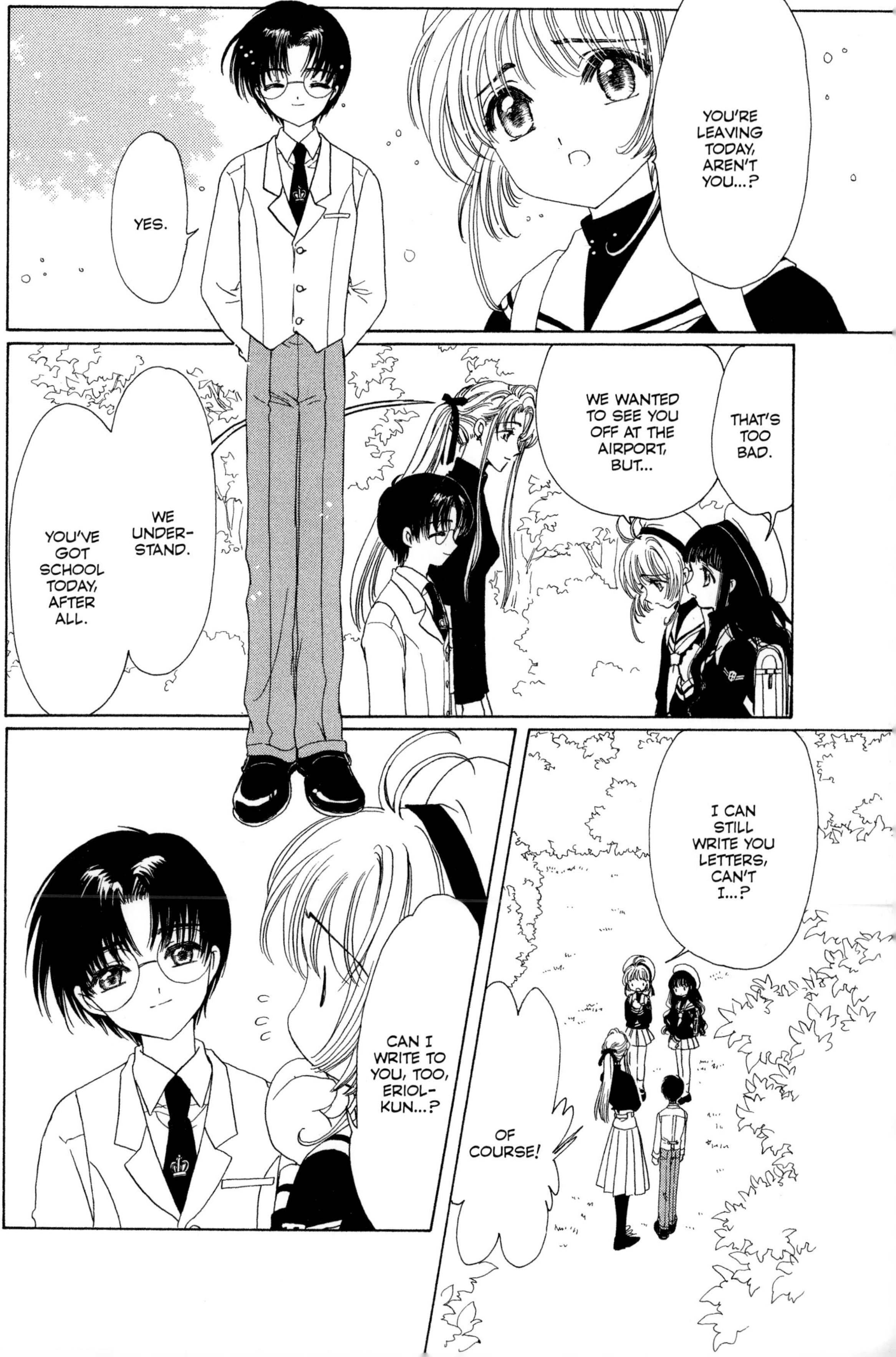
YOU'RE LEAVING TODAY, AREN'T YOU...?
YES.
THAT'S TOO BAD.
WE WANTED TO SEE YOU OFF AT THE AIRPORT, BUT...
WE UNDER-STAND.
YOU'VE GOT SCHOOL TODAY, AFTER ALL.
I CAN STILL WRITE YOU LETTERS, CAN'T I...?
OF COURSE!
CAN I WRITE TO YOU, TOO, ERIOL-KUN...?

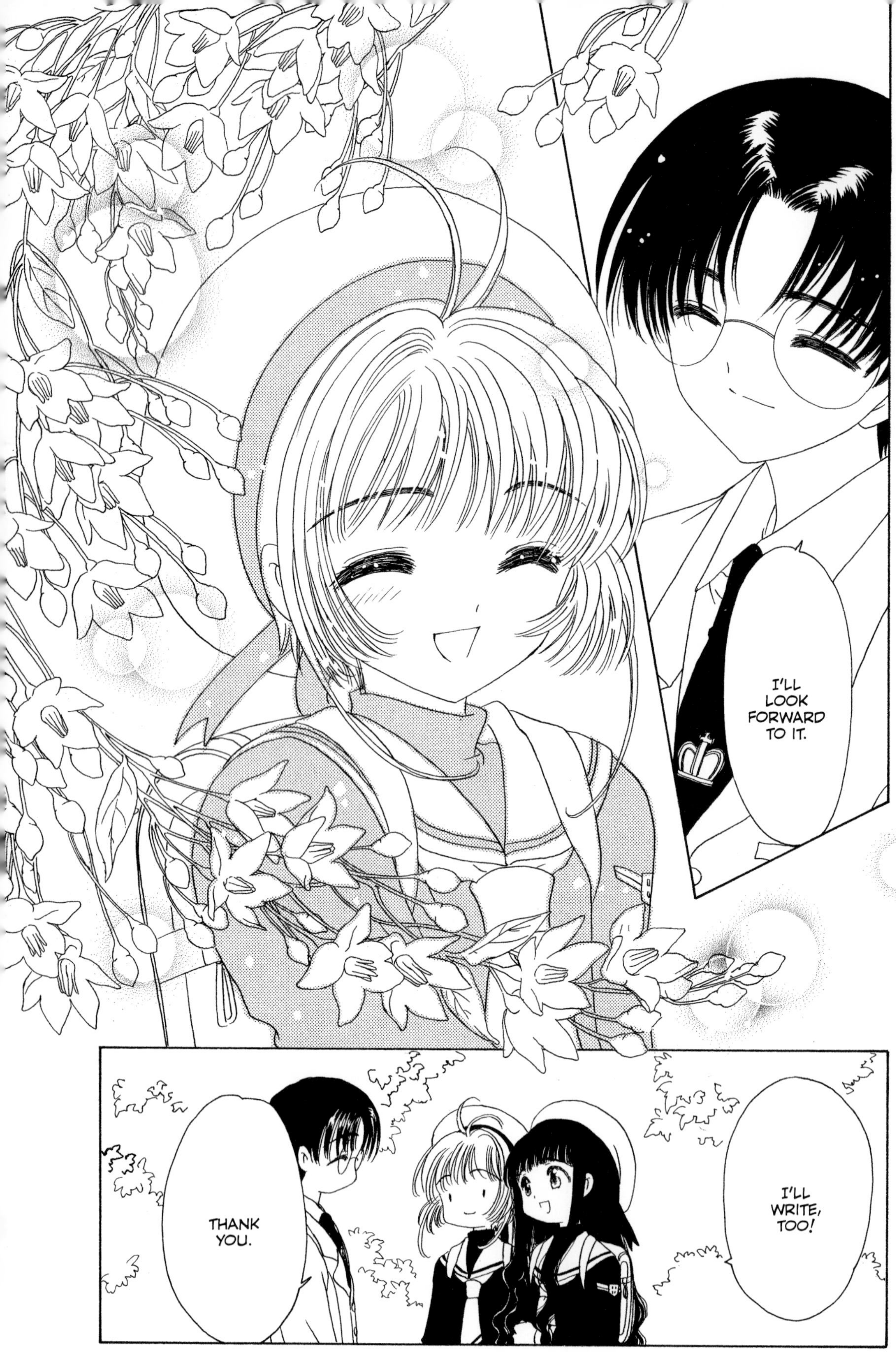
I'LL LOOK FORWARD TO IT.
I'LL WRITE, TOO!
THANK YOU.

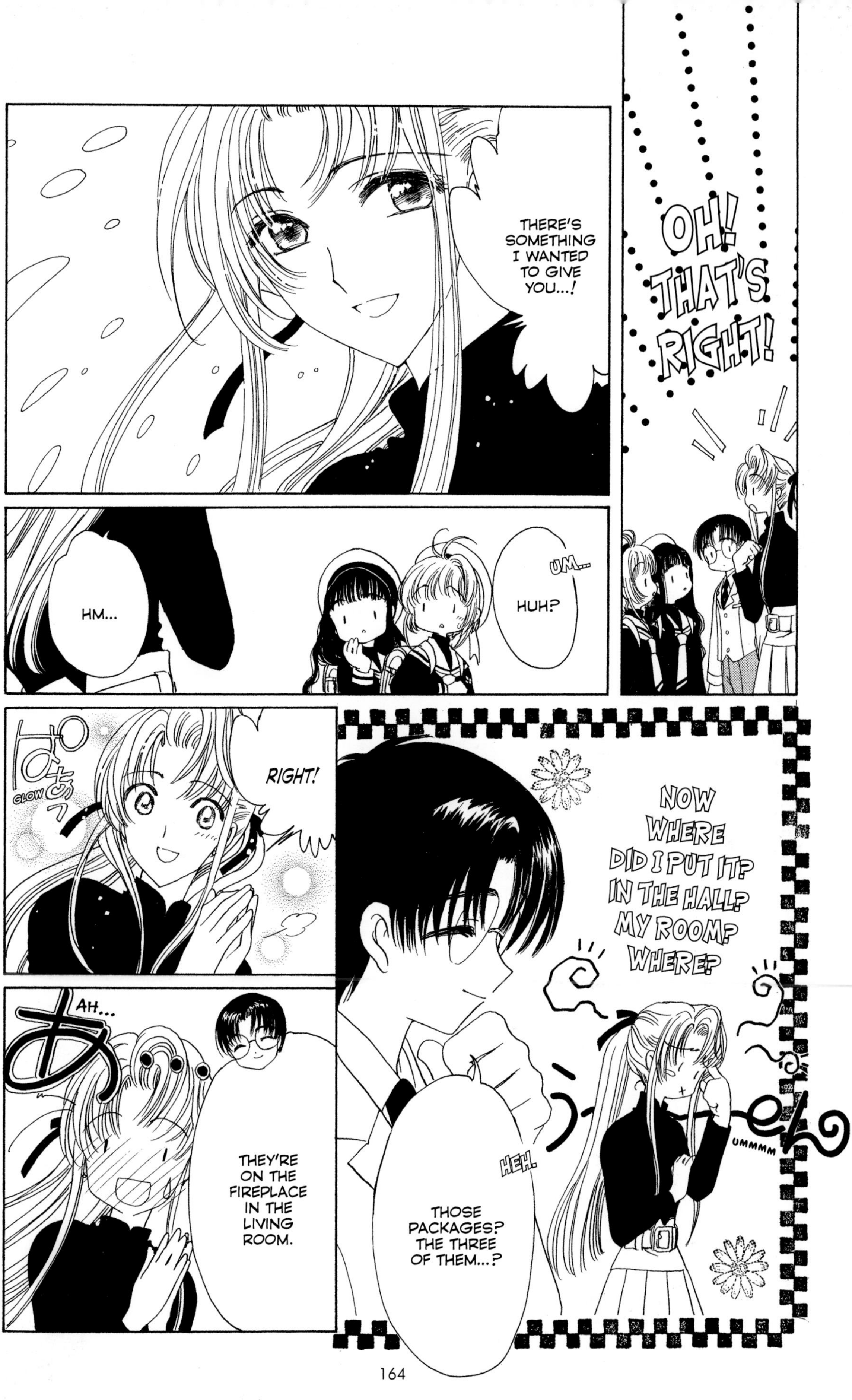
OH! THAT'S RIGHT!
THERE'S SOMETHING I WANTED TO GIVE YOU...!
UM...
HUH?
HM...
NOW WHERE DID I PUT IT? IN THE HALL? MY ROOM? WHERE?
UMMMM
HEH.
THOSE PACKAGES? THE THREE OF THEM...?
RIGHT!
GLOW
AH...
THEY'RE ON THE FIREPLACE IN THE LIVING ROOM.

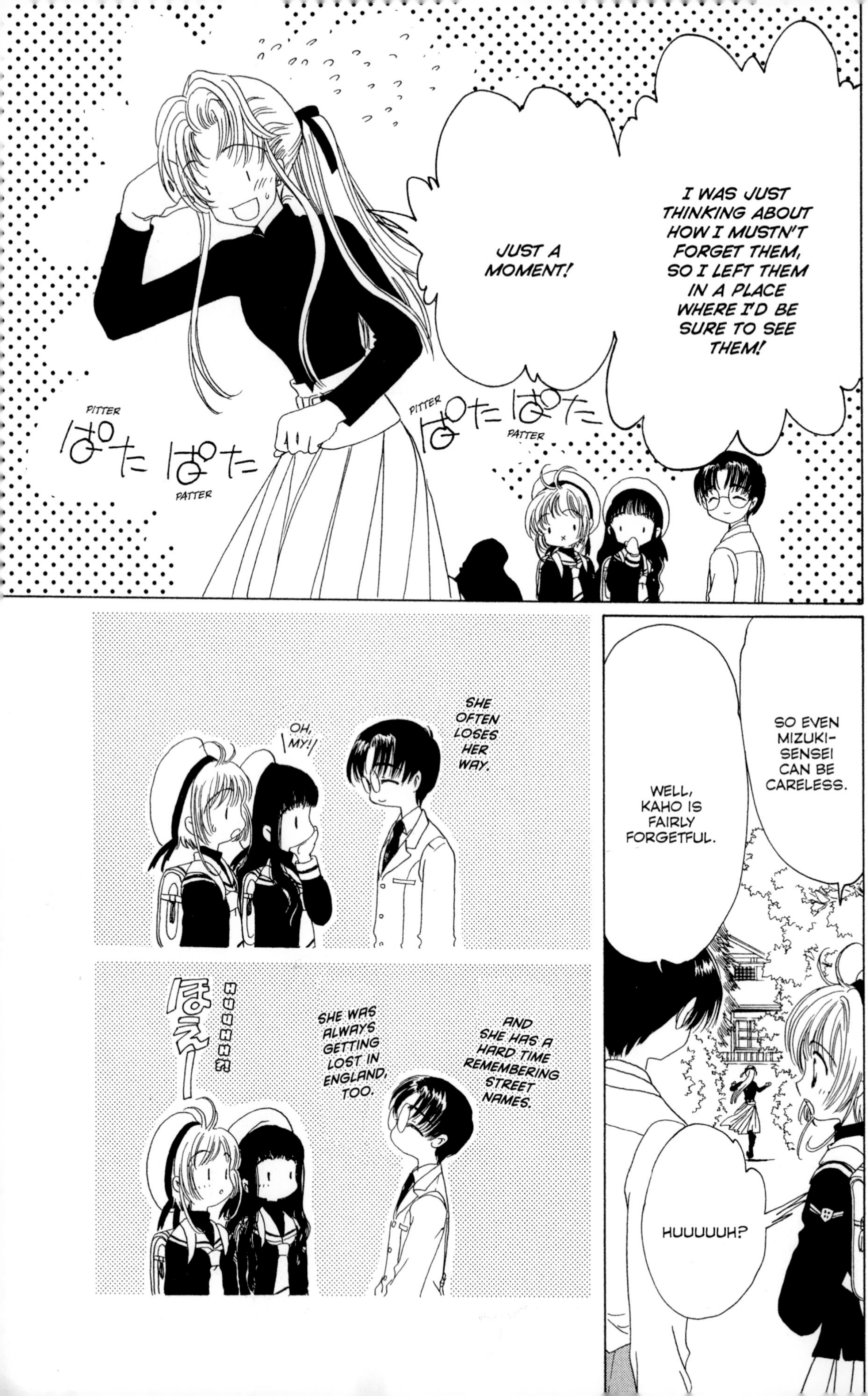
I WAS JUST THINKING ABOUT HOW I MUSTN'T FORGET THEM, SO I LEFT THEM IN A PLACE WHERE I'D BE SURE TO SEE THEM!
JUST A MOMENT!
ぱたぱた
PITTER PATTER
ぱたぱた
PITTER PATTER
SO EVEN MIZUKI-SENSEI CAN BE CARELESS.
WELL, KAHO IS FAIRLY FORGETFUL.
HUUUUUH?
SHE OFTEN LOSES HER WAY.
OH, MY!
AND SHE HAS A HARD TIME REMEMBERING STREET NAMES.
SHE WAS ALWAYS GETTING LOST IN ENGLAND, TOO.
HUUUHHH?!
ほえ～

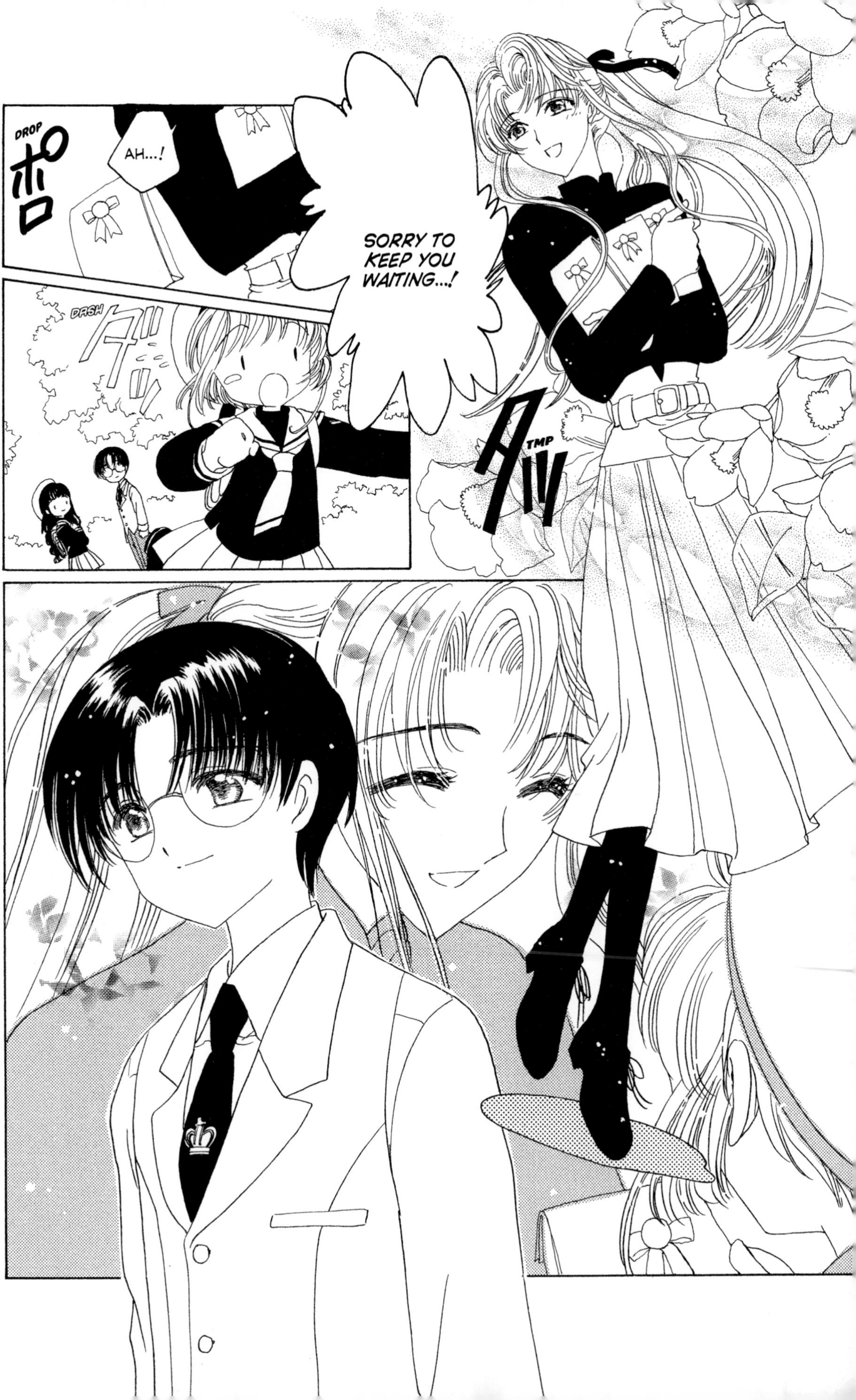
SORRY TO KEEP YOU WAITING...!
TMP
タッ
DROP
ポロ
AH...!
DASH
ダッ

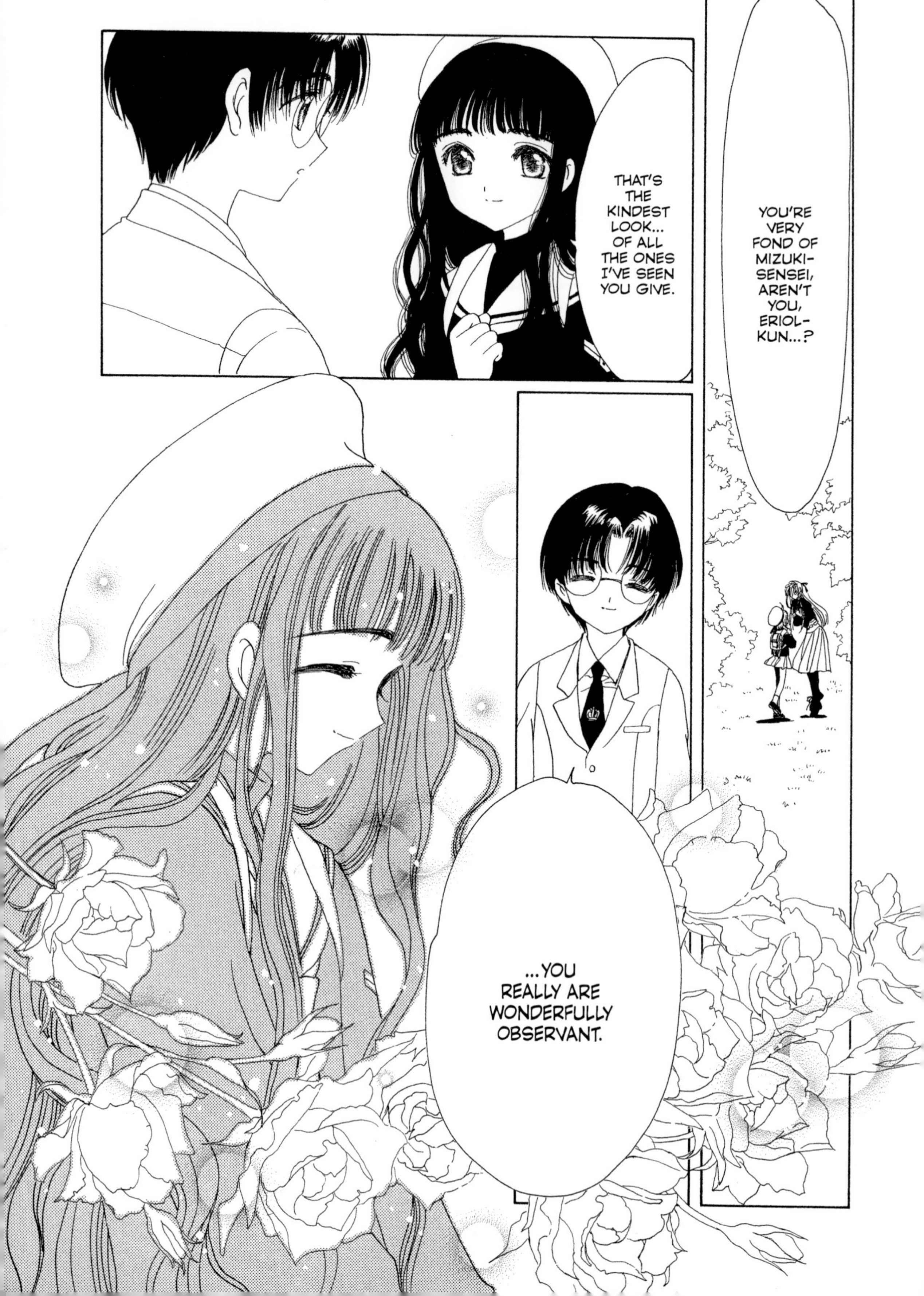
YOU'RE VERY FOND OF MIZUKI-SENSEI, AREN'T YOU, ERIOL-KUN...?
THAT'S THE KINDEST LOOK... OF ALL THE ONES I'VE SEEN YOU GIVE.
...YOU REALLY ARE WONDERFULLY OBSERVANT.

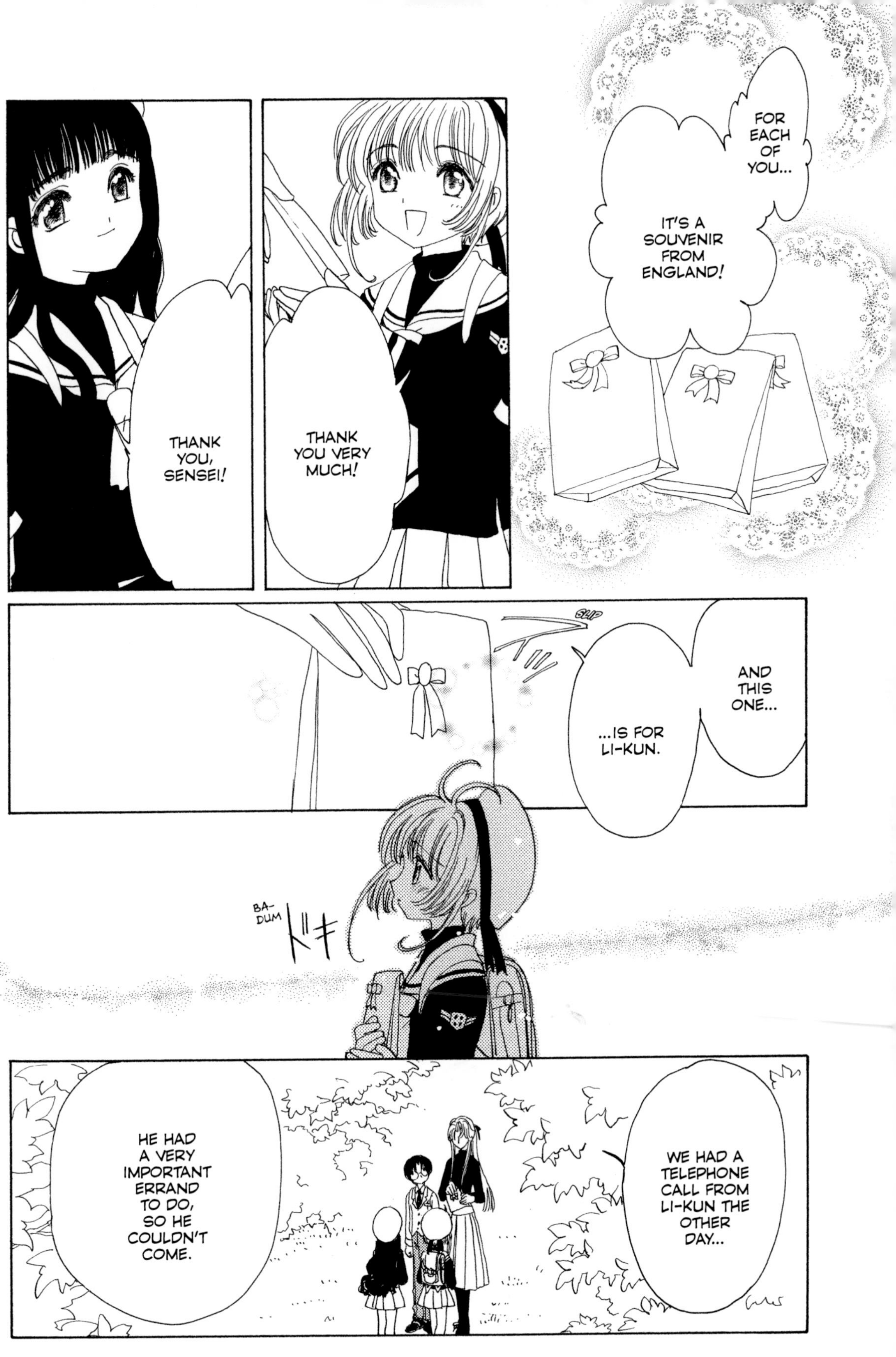
FOR EACH OF YOU...
IT'S A SOUVENIR FROM ENGLAND!
THANK YOU VERY MUCH!
THANK YOU, SENSEI!
SLIP
AND THIS ONE...
...IS FOR LI-KUN.
BA-DUM
WE HAD A TELEPHONE CALL FROM LI-KUN THE OTHER DAY...
HE HAD A VERY IMPORTANT ERRAND TO DO, SO HE COULDN'T COME.

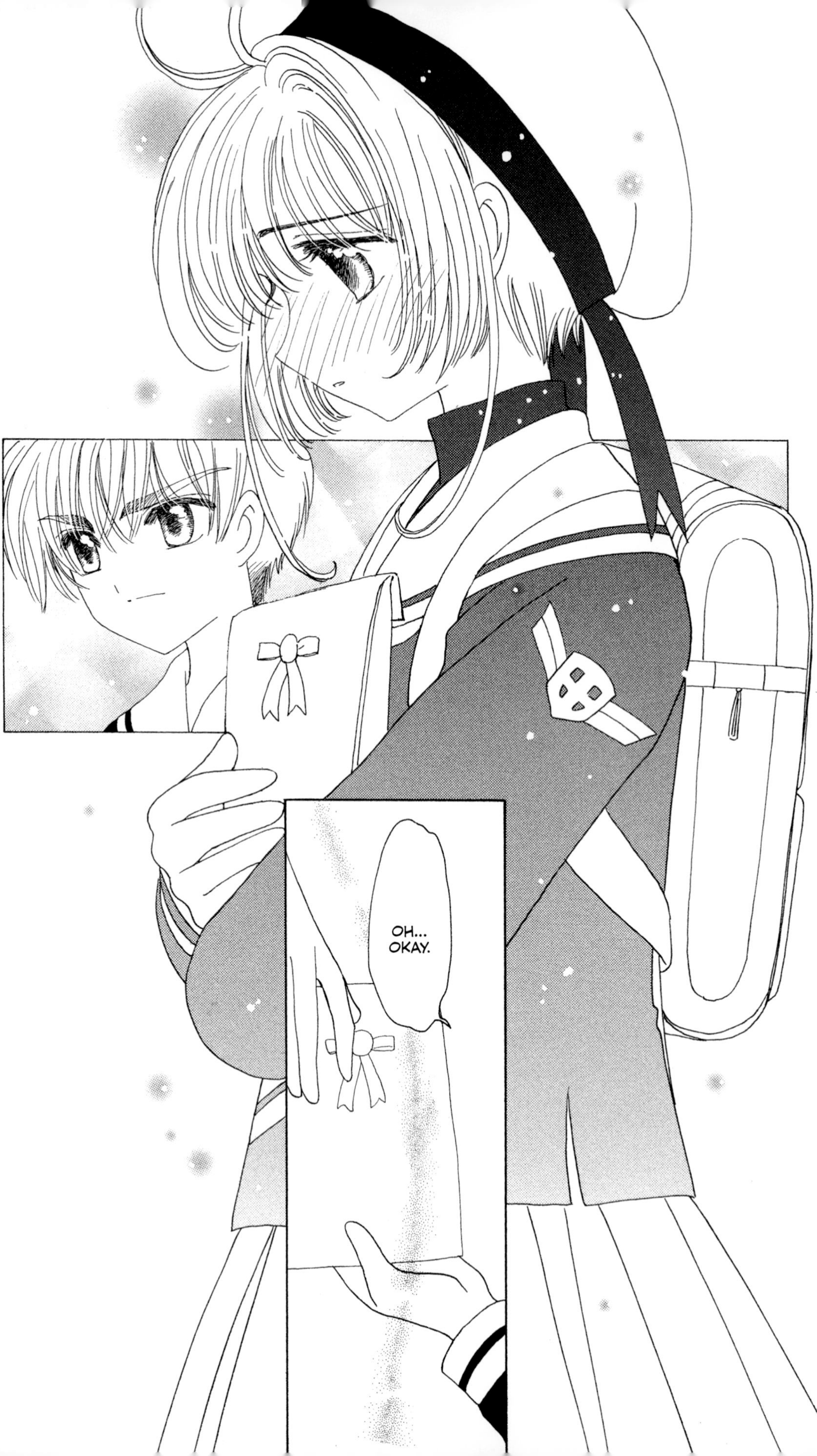
OH... OKAY.

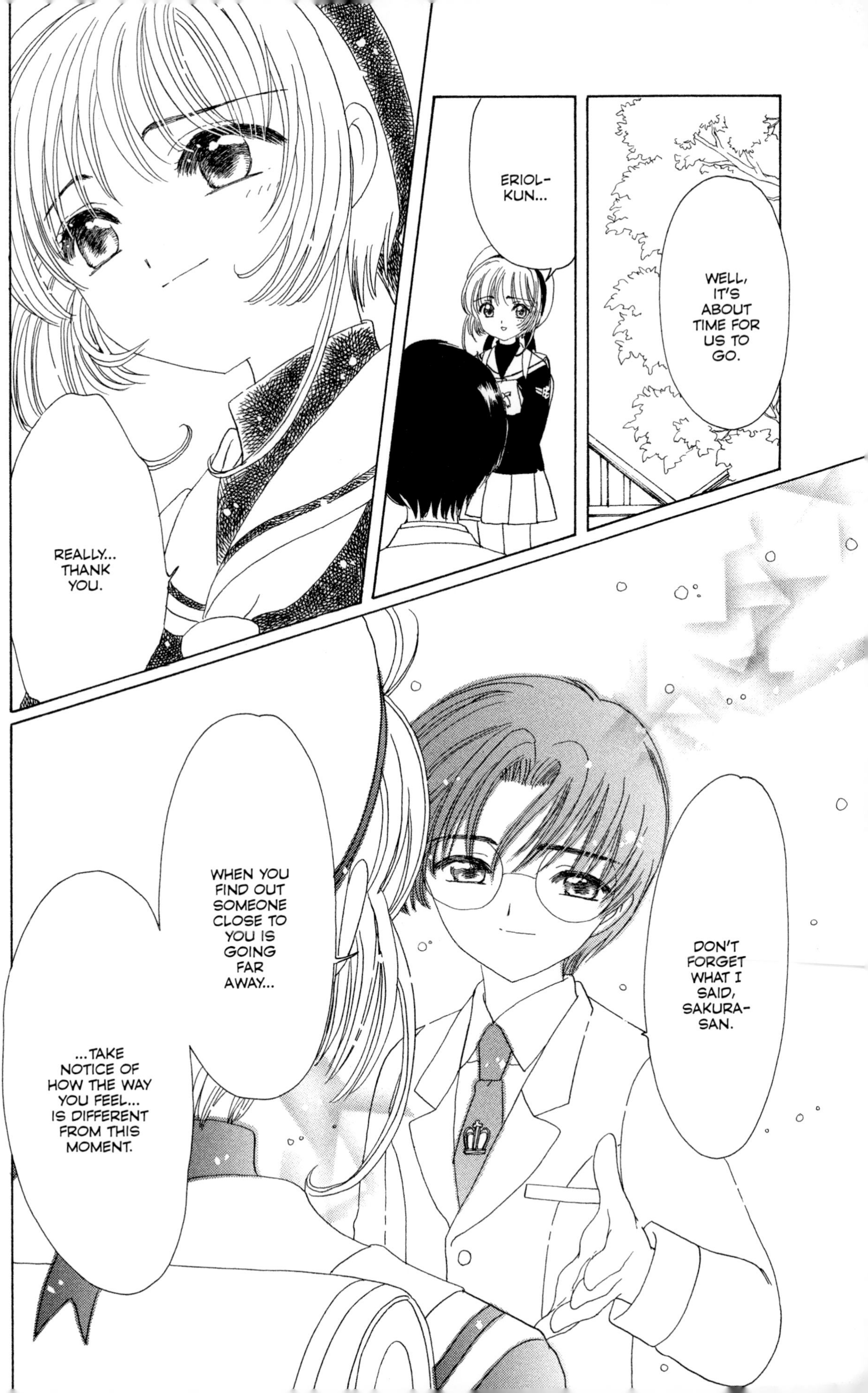
WELL, IT'S ABOUT TIME FOR US TO GO.
ERIOL-KUN...
REALLY... THANK YOU.
DON'T FORGET WHAT I SAID, SAKURA-SAN.
WHEN YOU FIND OUT SOMEONE CLOSE TO YOU IS GOING FAR AWAY...
...TAKE NOTICE OF HOW THE WAY YOU FEEL... IS DIFFERENT FROM THIS MOMENT.

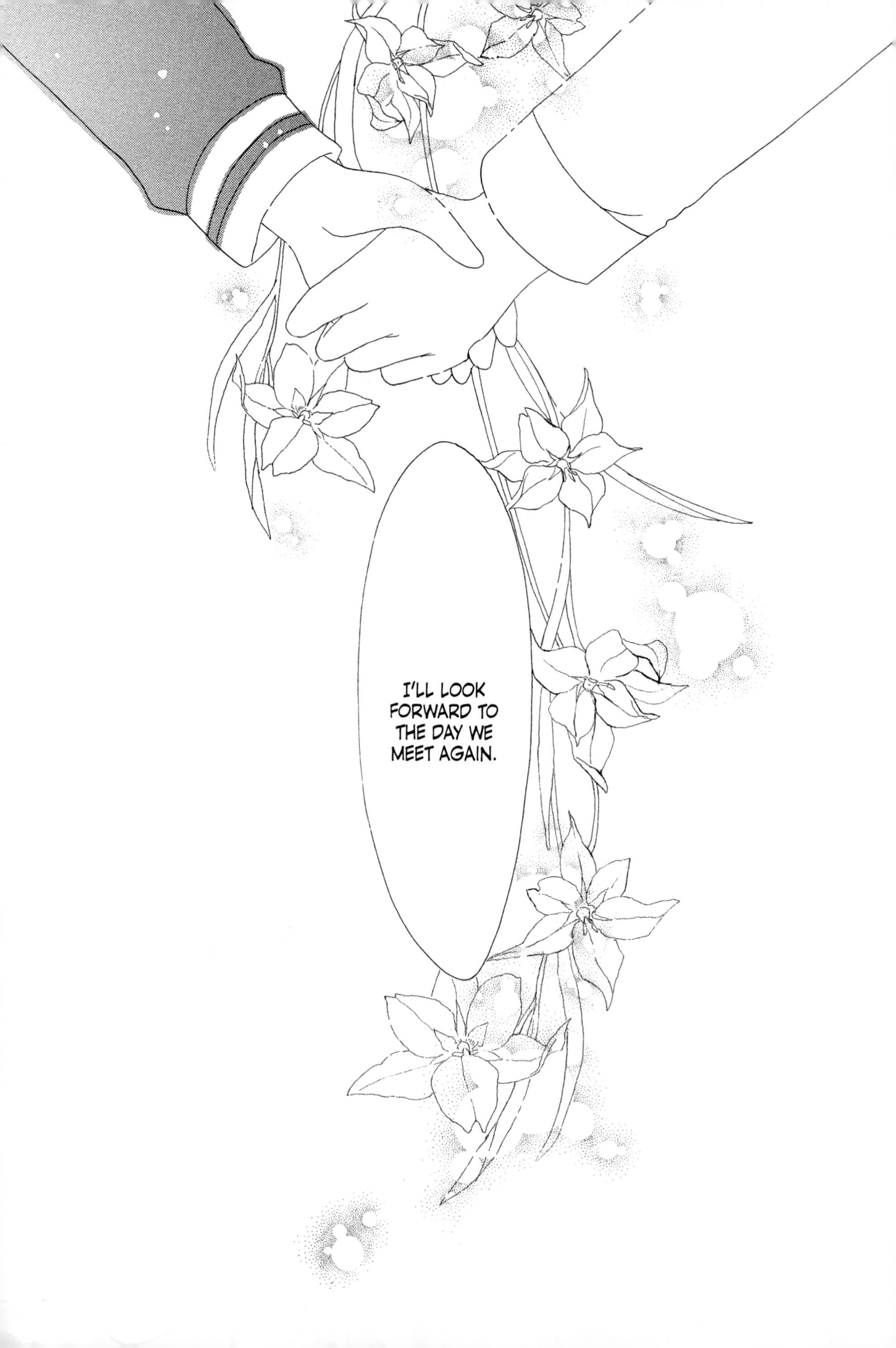
I'LL LOOK FORWARD TO THE DAY WE MEET AGAIN.

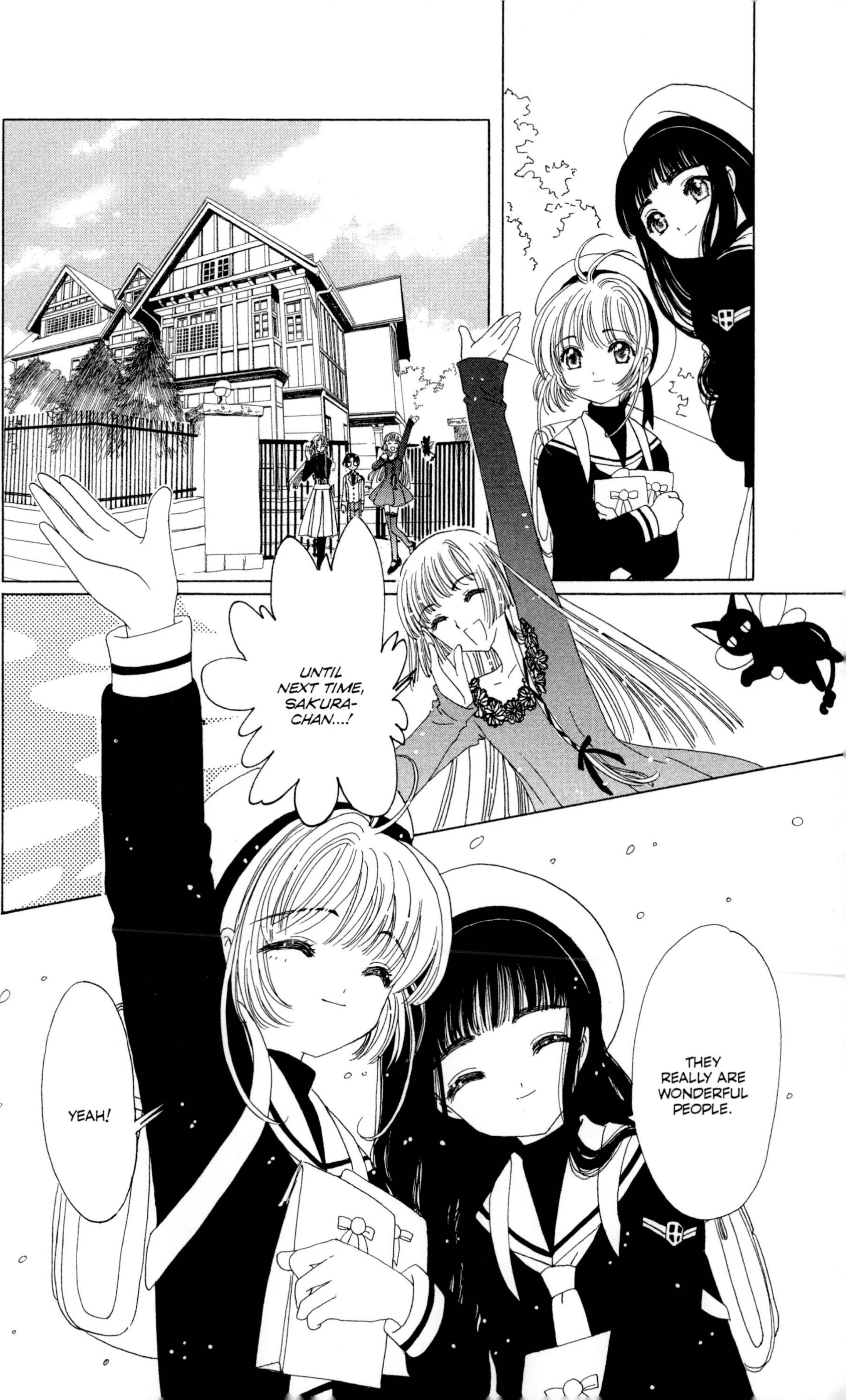
UNTIL NEXT TIME, SAKURA-CHAN...!
THEY REALLY ARE WONDERFUL PEOPLE.
YEAH!

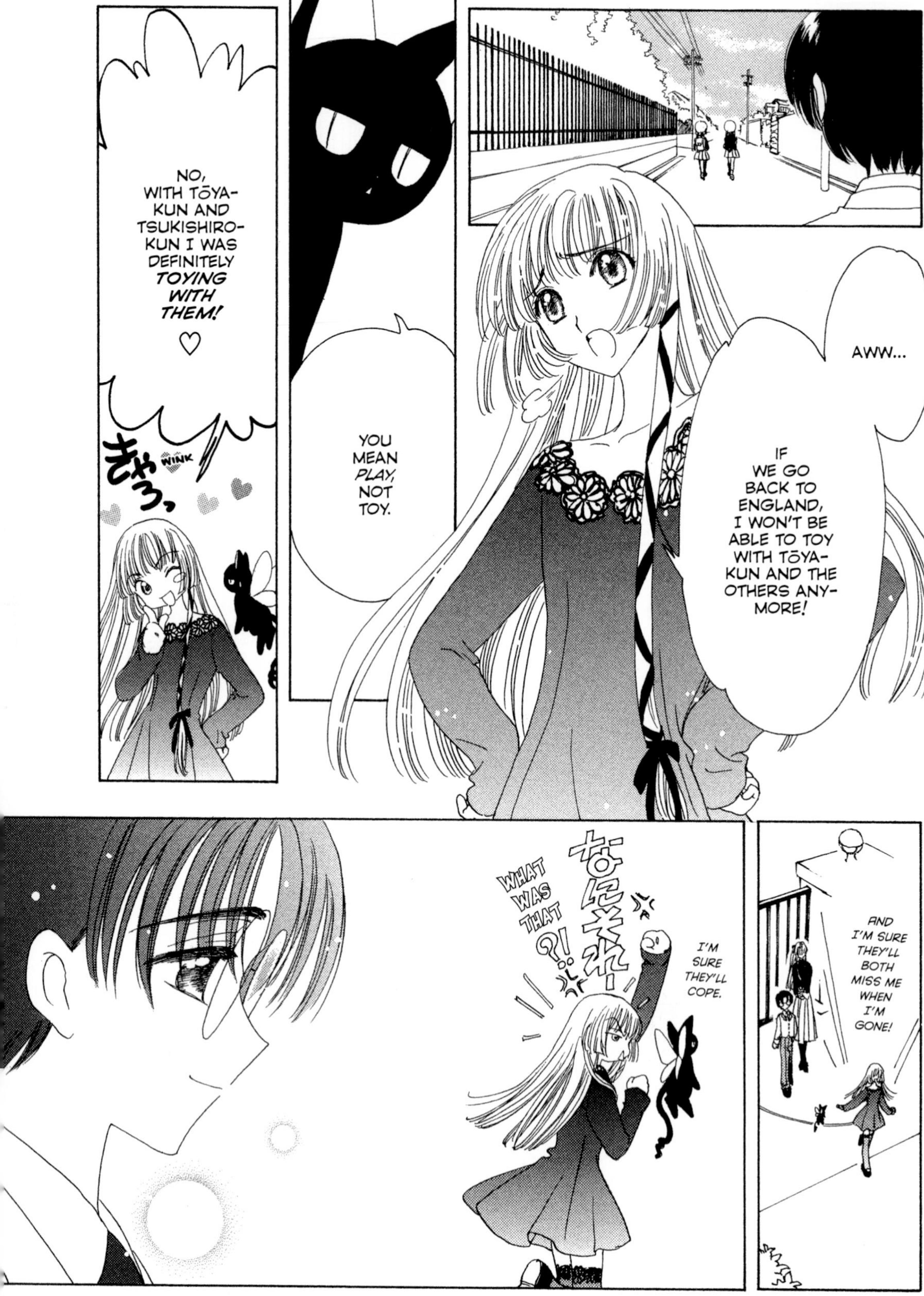
AWW...
IF WE GO BACK TO ENGLAND, I WON'T BE ABLE TO TOY WITH TŌYA-KUN AND THE OTHERS ANY-MORE!
YOU MEAN *PLAY*, NOT TOY.
NO, WITH TŌYA-KUN AND TSUKISHIRO-KUN I WAS DEFINITELY ***TOYING WITH THEM!*** ♡
きゃろっ
WINK
AND I'M SURE THEY'LL BOTH MISS ME WHEN I'M GONE!
I'M SURE THEY'LL COPE.
なにそれ！
WHAT WAS THAT?!

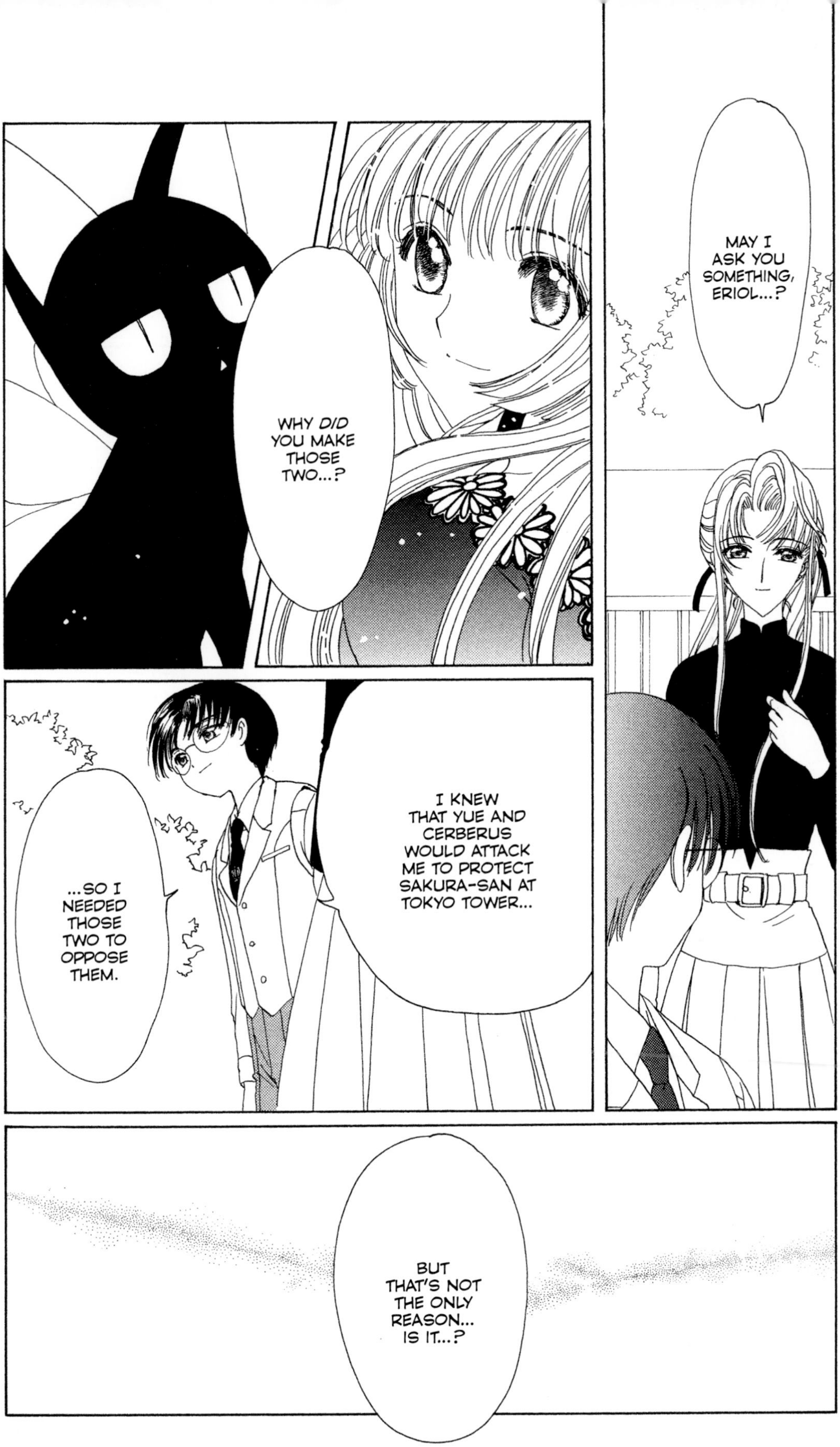
MAY I ASK YOU SOMETHING, ERIOL...?
WHY *DID* YOU MAKE THOSE TWO...?
I KNEW THAT YUE AND CERBERUS WOULD ATTACK ME TO PROTECT SAKURA-SAN AT TOKYO TOWER...
...SO I NEEDED THOSE TWO TO OPPOSE THEM.
BUT THAT'S NOT THE ONLY REASON... IS IT...?

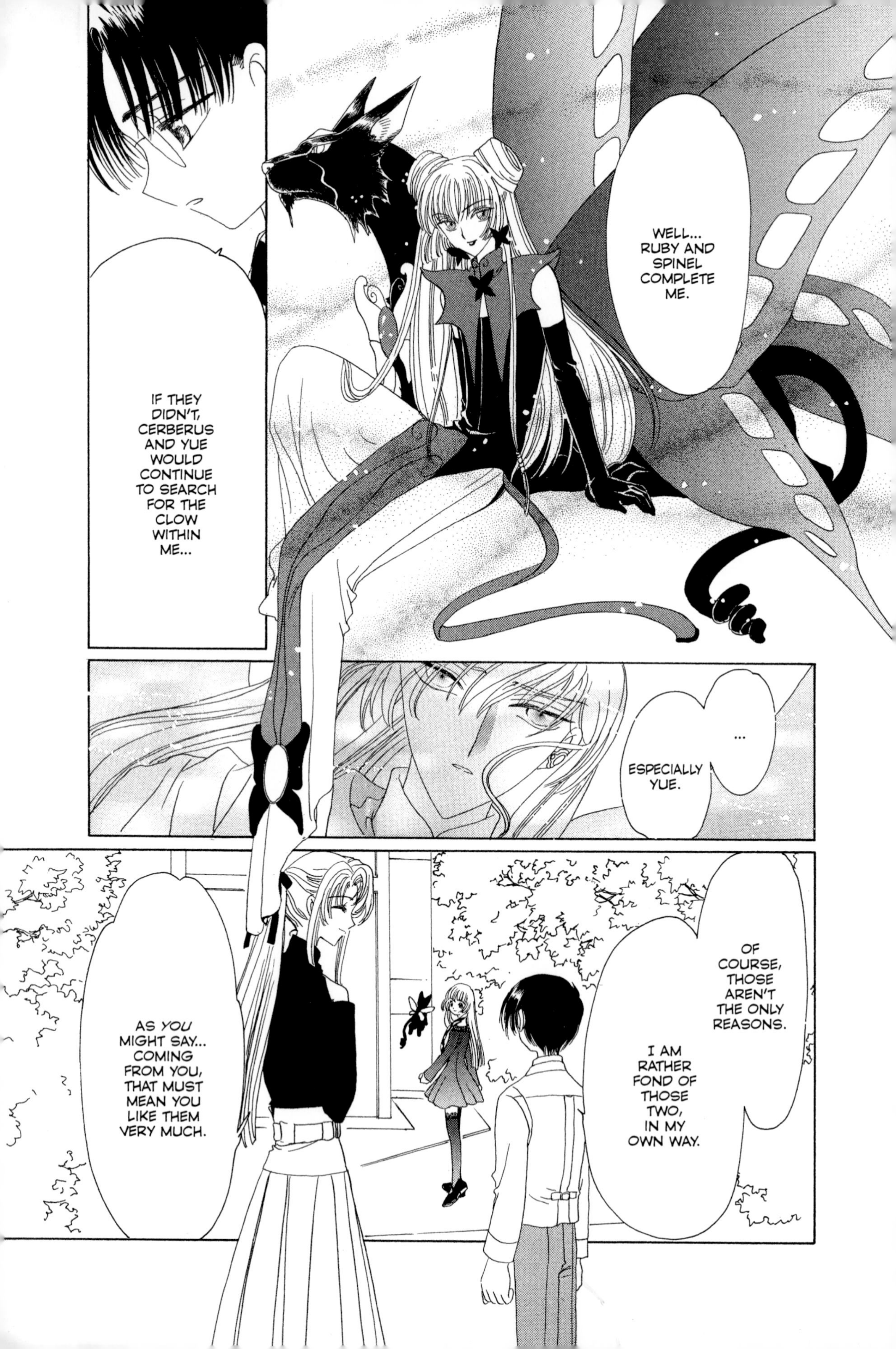
WELL... RUBY AND SPINEL COMPLETE ME.
IF THEY DIDN'T, CERBERUS AND YUE WOULD CONTINUE TO SEARCH FOR THE CLOW WITHIN ME...
...
ESPECIALLY YUE.
OF COURSE, THOSE AREN'T THE ONLY REASONS.
I AM RATHER FOND OF THOSE TWO, IN MY OWN WAY.
AS *YOU* MIGHT SAY... COMING FROM YOU, THAT MUST MEAN YOU LIKE THEM VERY MUCH.

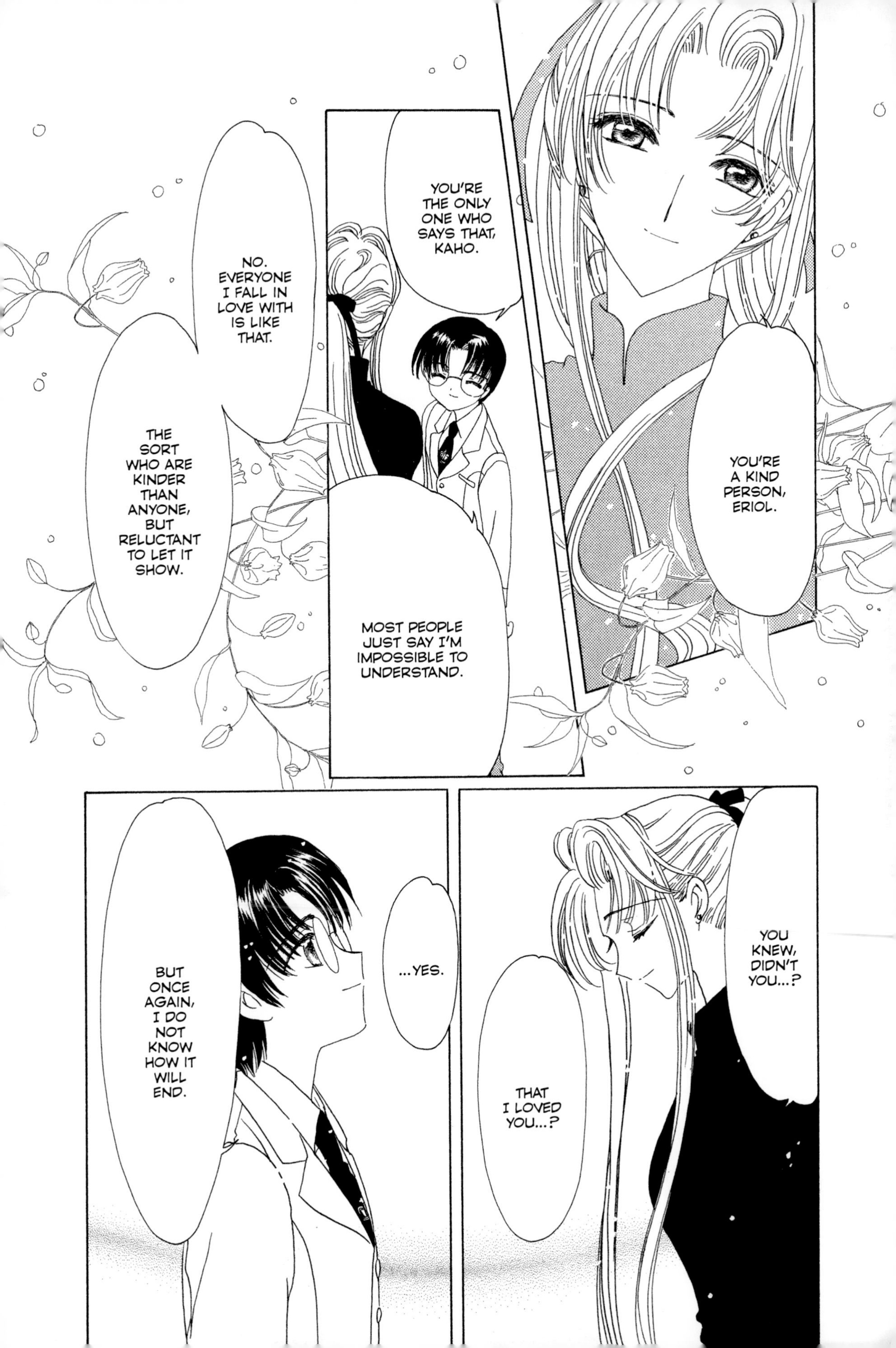
YOU'RE A KIND PERSON, ERIOL.
YOU'RE THE ONLY ONE WHO SAYS THAT, KAHO.
MOST PEOPLE JUST SAY I'M IMPOSSIBLE TO UNDERSTAND.
NO. EVERYONE I FALL IN LOVE WITH IS LIKE THAT.
THE SORT WHO ARE KINDER THAN ANYONE, BUT RELUCTANT TO LET IT SHOW.
YOU KNEW, DIDN'T YOU...?
THAT I LOVED YOU...?
...YES.
BUT ONCE AGAIN, I DO NOT KNOW HOW IT WILL END.

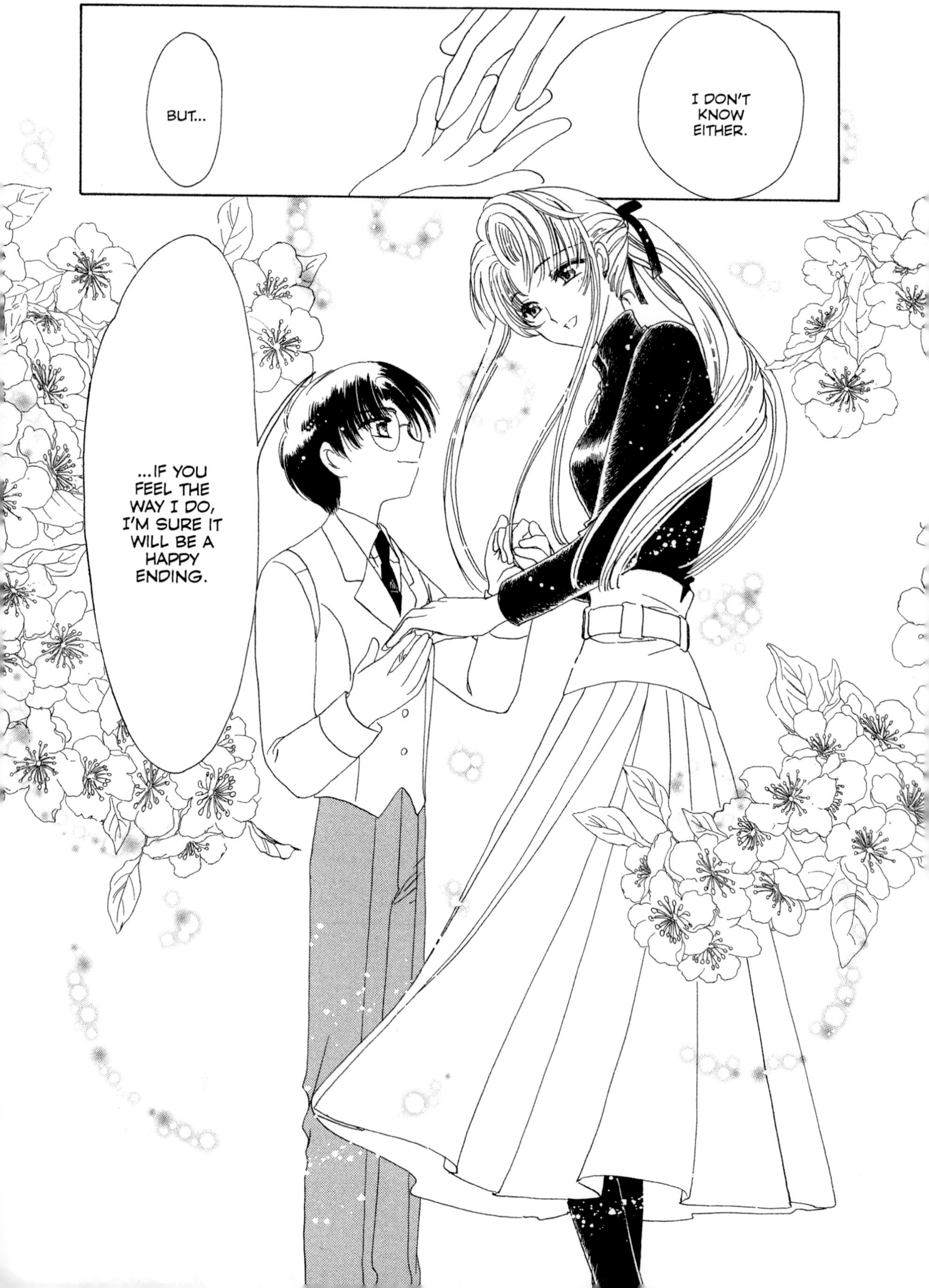
I DON'T KNOW EITHER.
BUT...
...IF YOU FEEL THE WAY I DO, I'M SURE IT WILL BE A HAPPY ENDING.

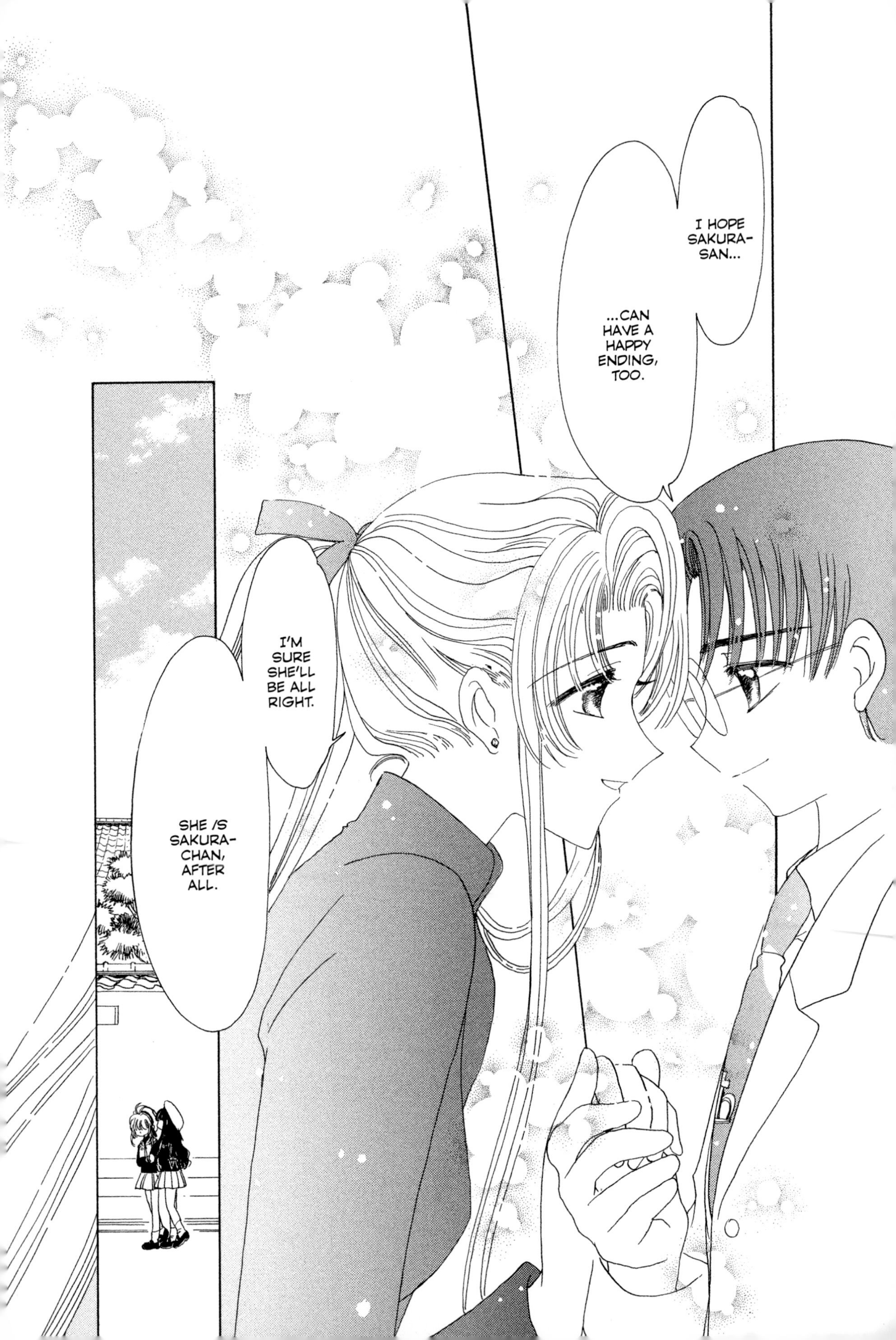
I HOPE SAKURA-SAN...
...CAN HAVE A HAPPY ENDING, TOO.
I'M SURE SHE'LL BE ALL RIGHT.
SHE IS SAKURA-CHAN, AFTER ALL.

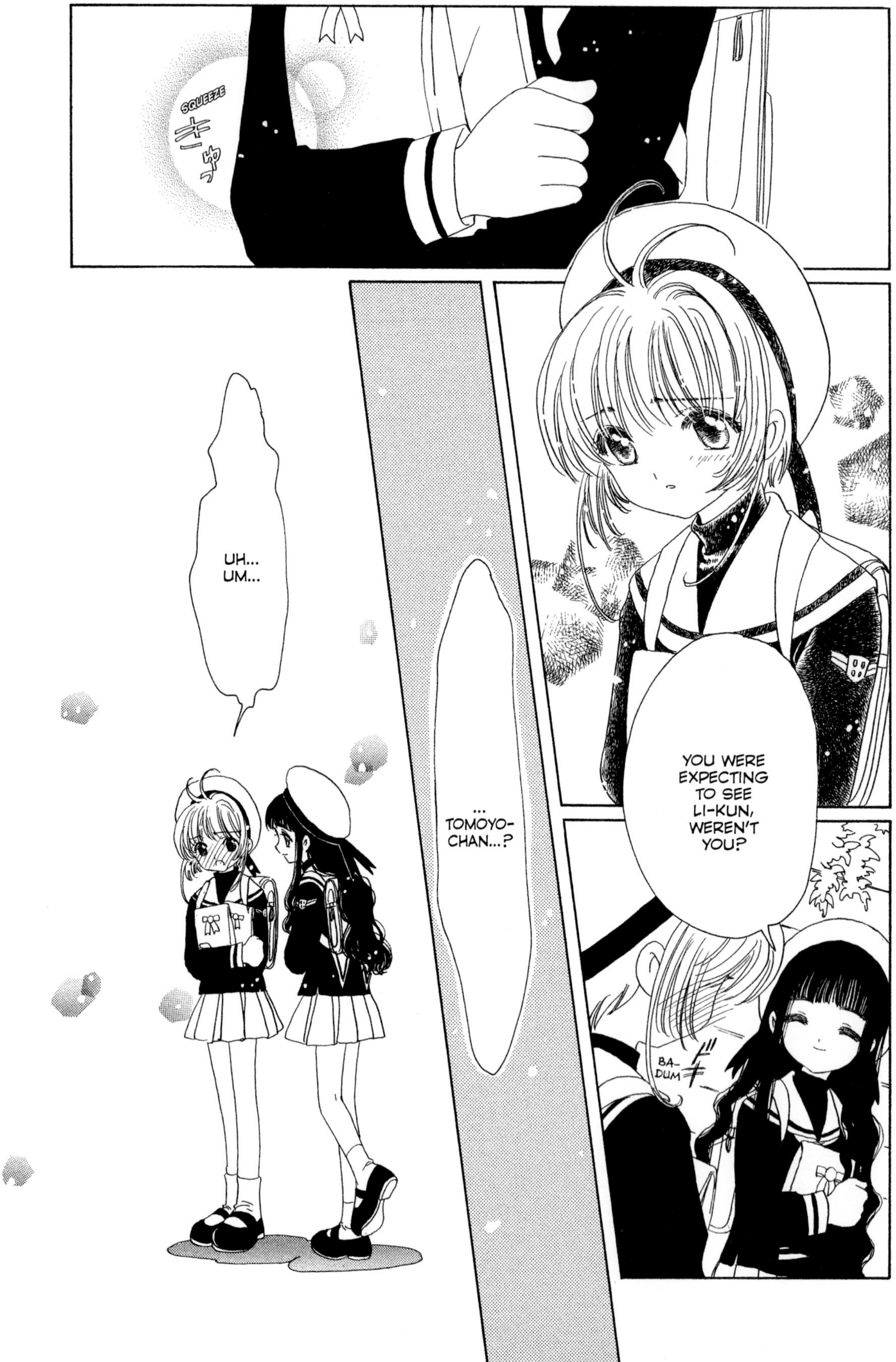
SQUEEZE
YOU WERE EXPECTING TO SEE LI-KUN, WEREN'T YOU?
BA-DUM
... TOMOYO-CHAN...?
UH... UM...

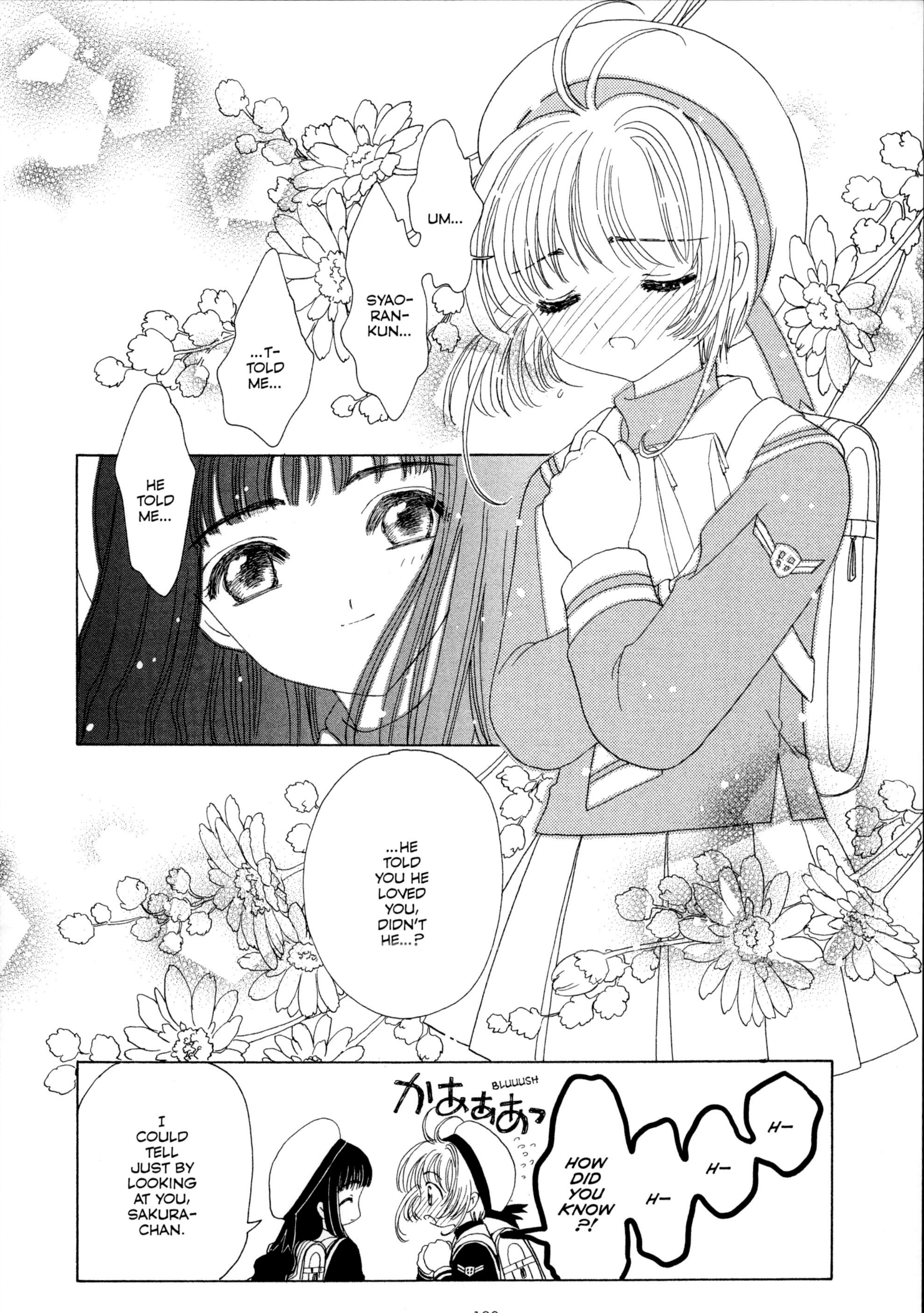
UM...
SYAO-RAN-KUN...
...T-TOLD ME...
HE TOLD ME...
...HE TOLD YOU HE LOVED YOU, DIDN'T HE...?
H- H- H- HOW DID YOU KNOW?!
かあああっ
BLUUUSH
I COULD TELL JUST BY LOOKING AT YOU, SAKURA-CHAN.

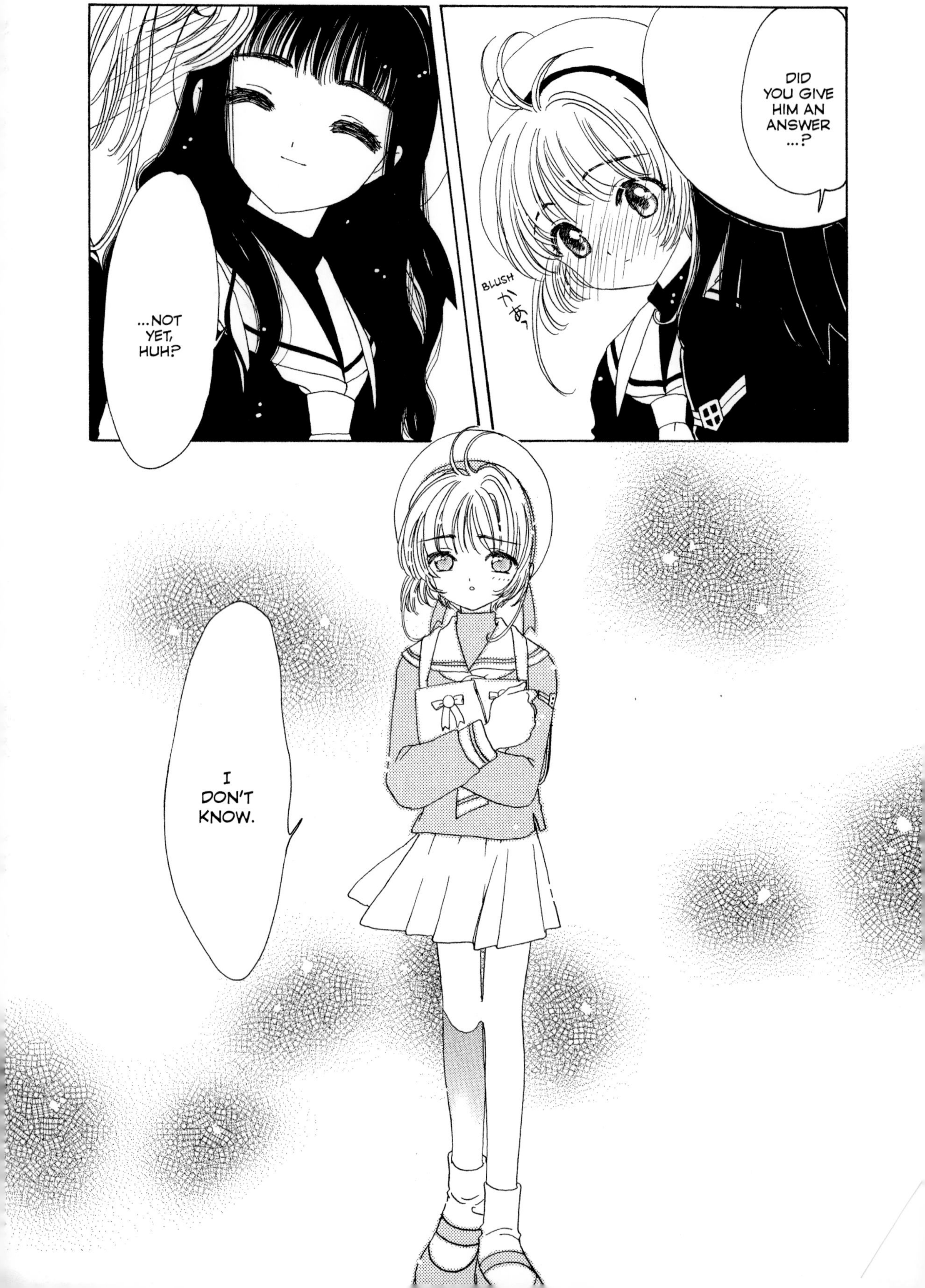
DID YOU GIVE HIM AN ANSWER ...?
BLUSH
かあ
...NOT YET, HUH?
I DON'T KNOW.

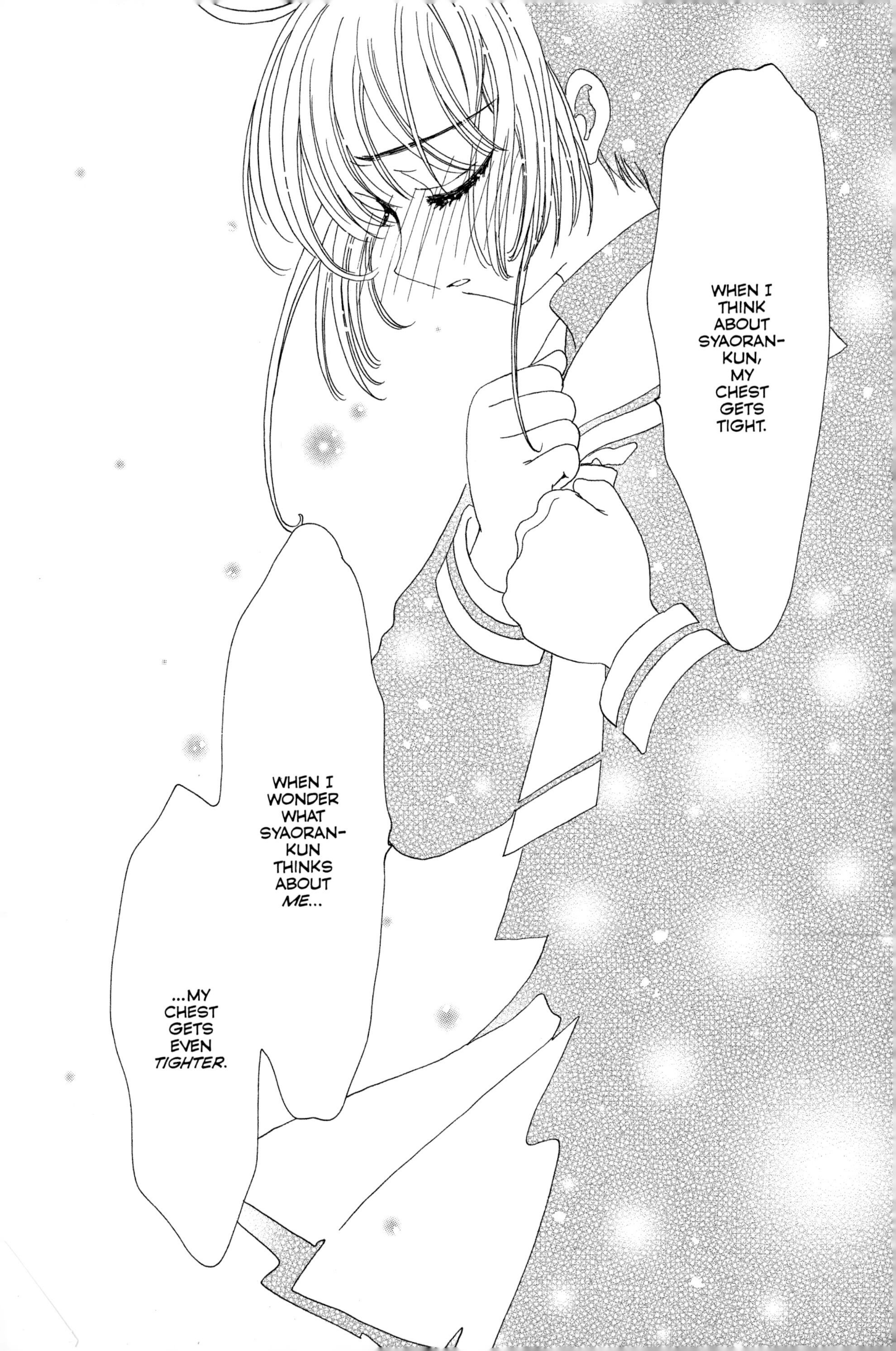
WHEN I THINK ABOUT SYAORAN-KUN, MY CHEST GETS TIGHT.
WHEN I WONDER WHAT SYAORAN-KUN THINKS ABOUT *ME*...
...MY CHEST GETS EVEN *TIGHTER*.

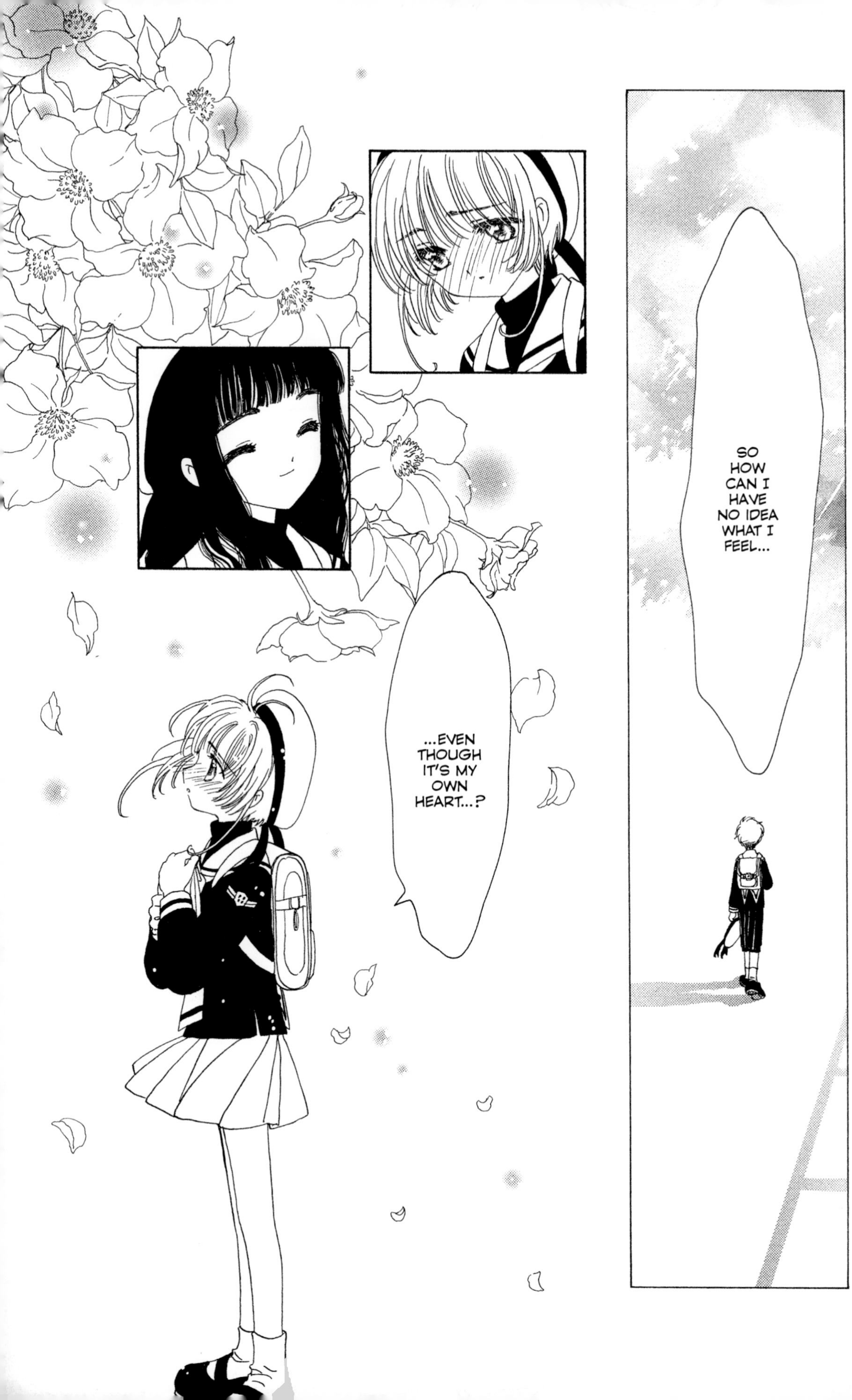
SO HOW CAN I HAVE NO IDEA WHAT I FEEL...
...EVEN THOUGH IT'S MY OWN HEART...?

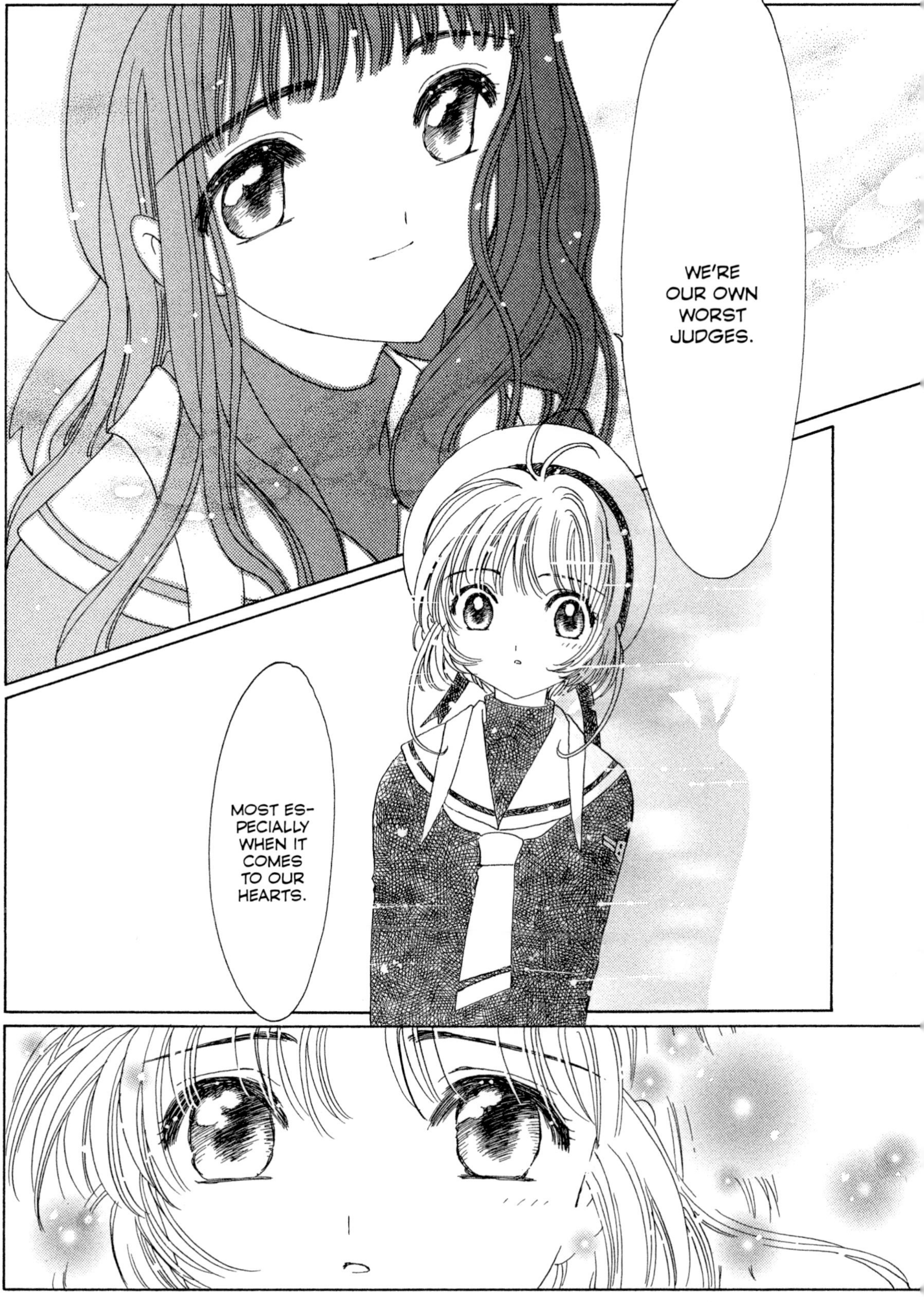
WE'RE OUR OWN WORST JUDGES.
MOST ES-PECIALLY WHEN IT COMES TO OUR HEARTS.

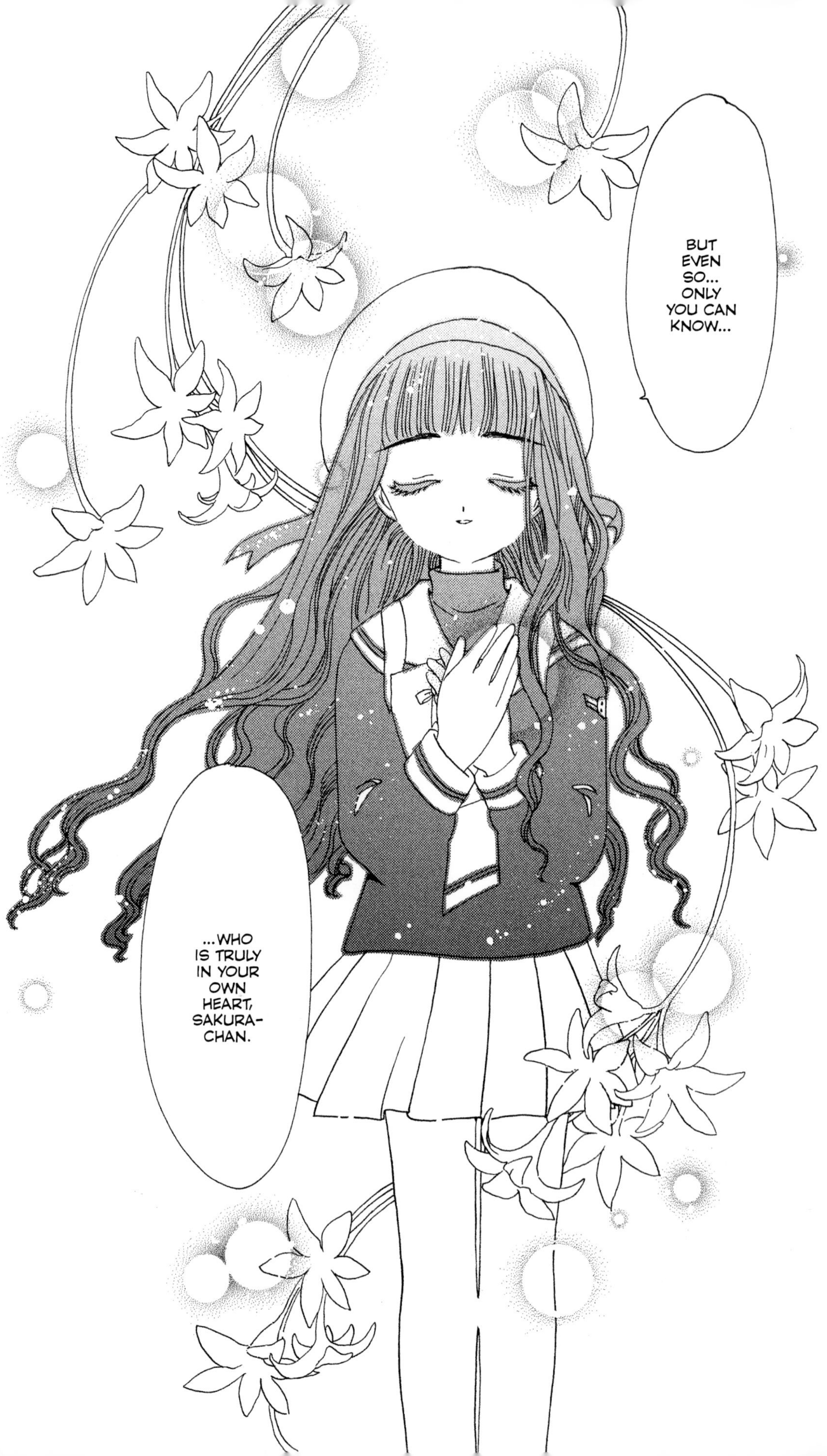
BUT EVEN SO... ONLY YOU CAN KNOW...
...WHO IS TRULY IN YOUR OWN HEART, SAKURA-CHAN.

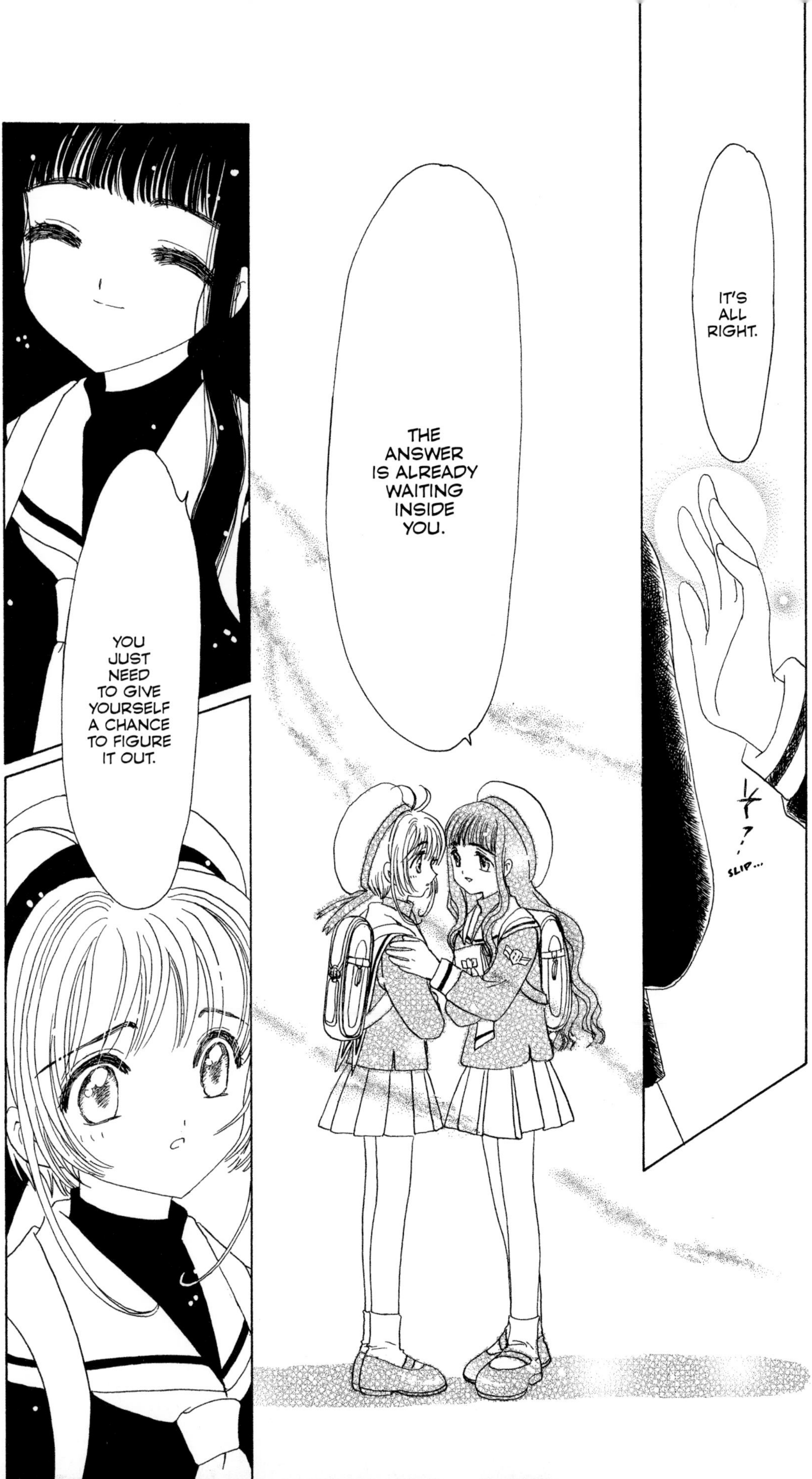
IT'S ALL RIGHT.
SLIP...
THE ANSWER IS ALREADY WAITING INSIDE YOU.
YOU JUST NEED TO GIVE YOURSELF A CHANCE TO FIGURE IT OUT.

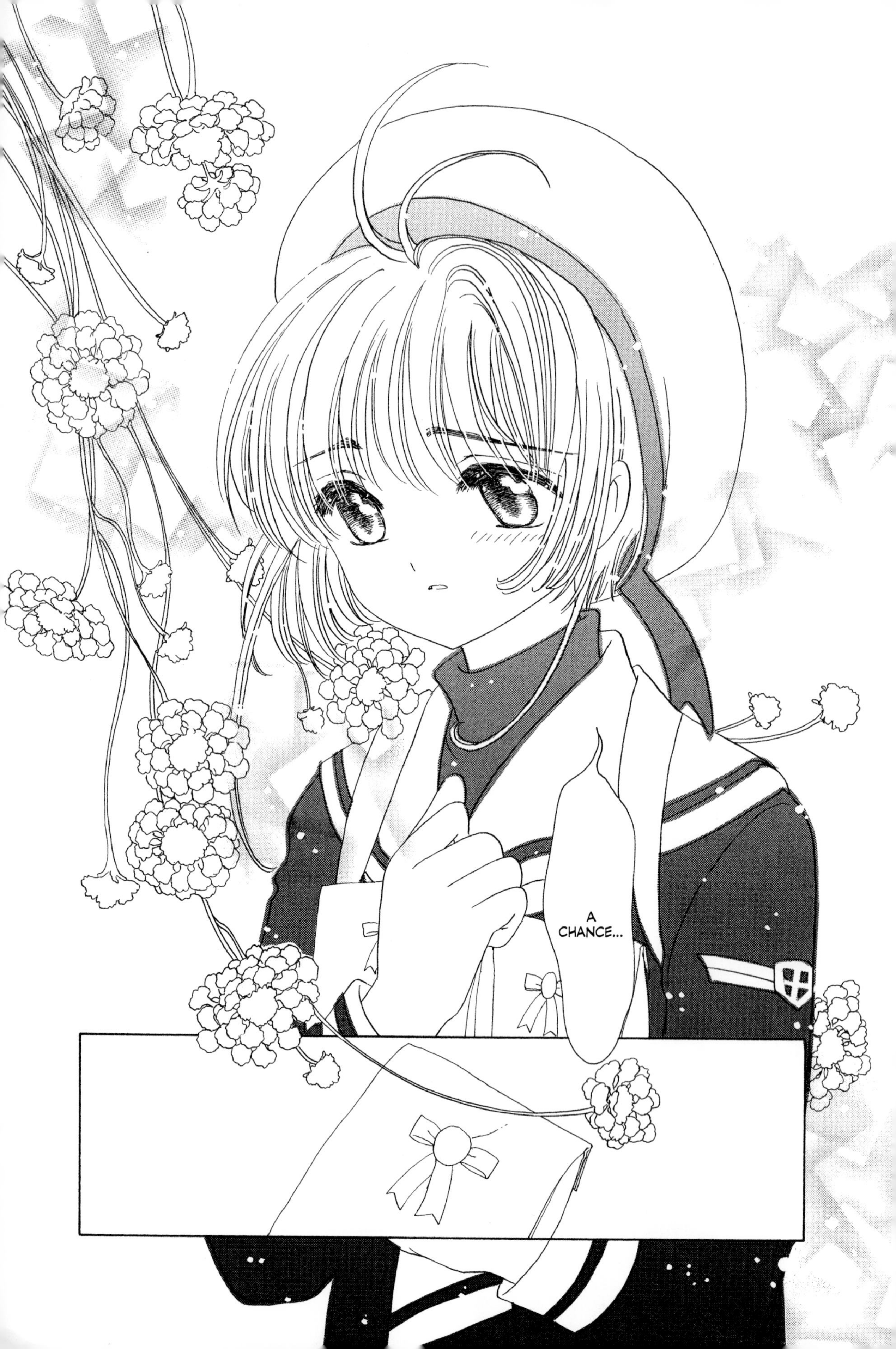
A CHANCE...

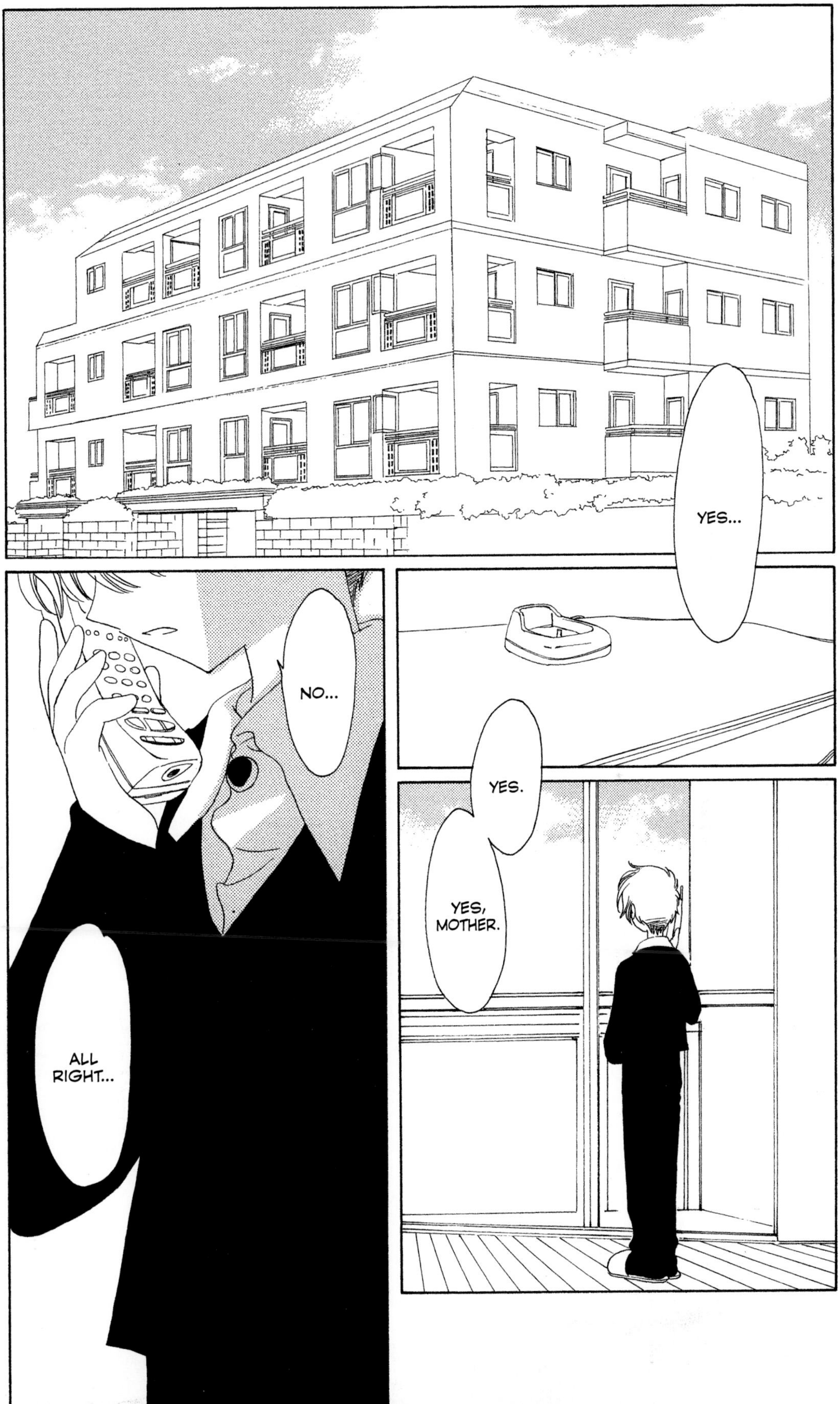
YES...
YES.
YES, MOTHER.
NO...
ALL RIGHT...

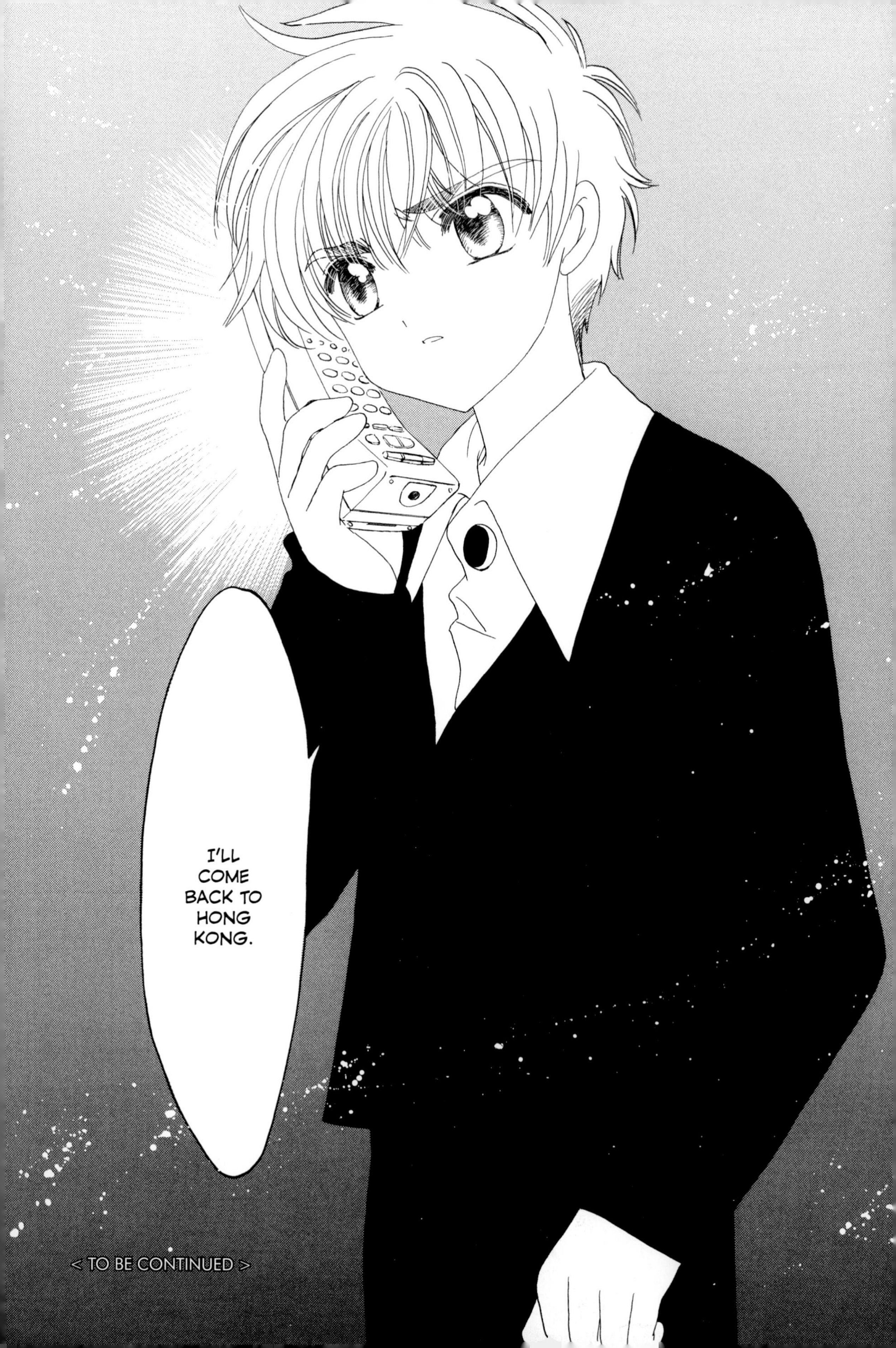
I'LL COME BACK TO HONG KONG.
< TO BE CONTINUED >

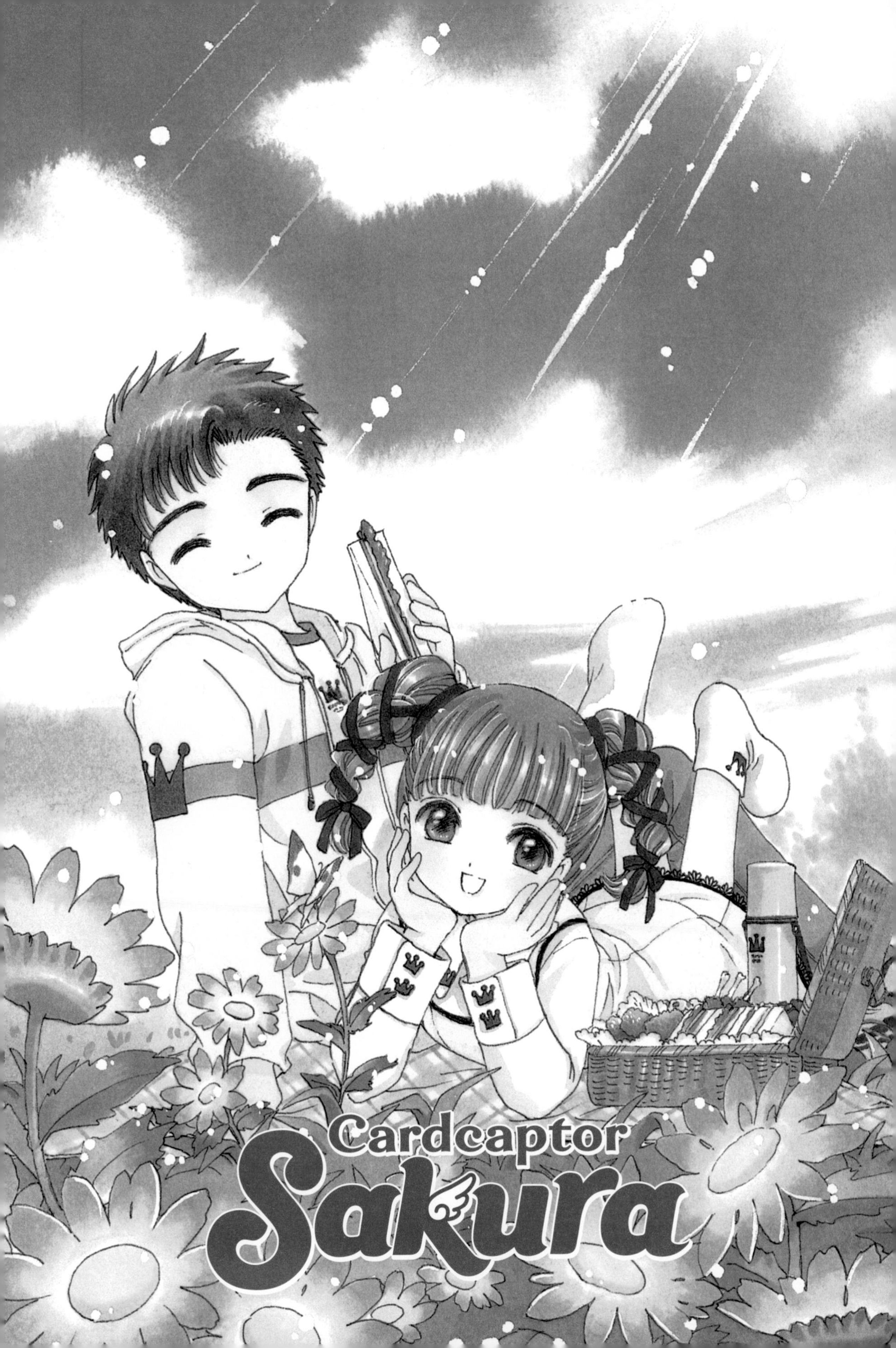
Cardcaptor
Sakura

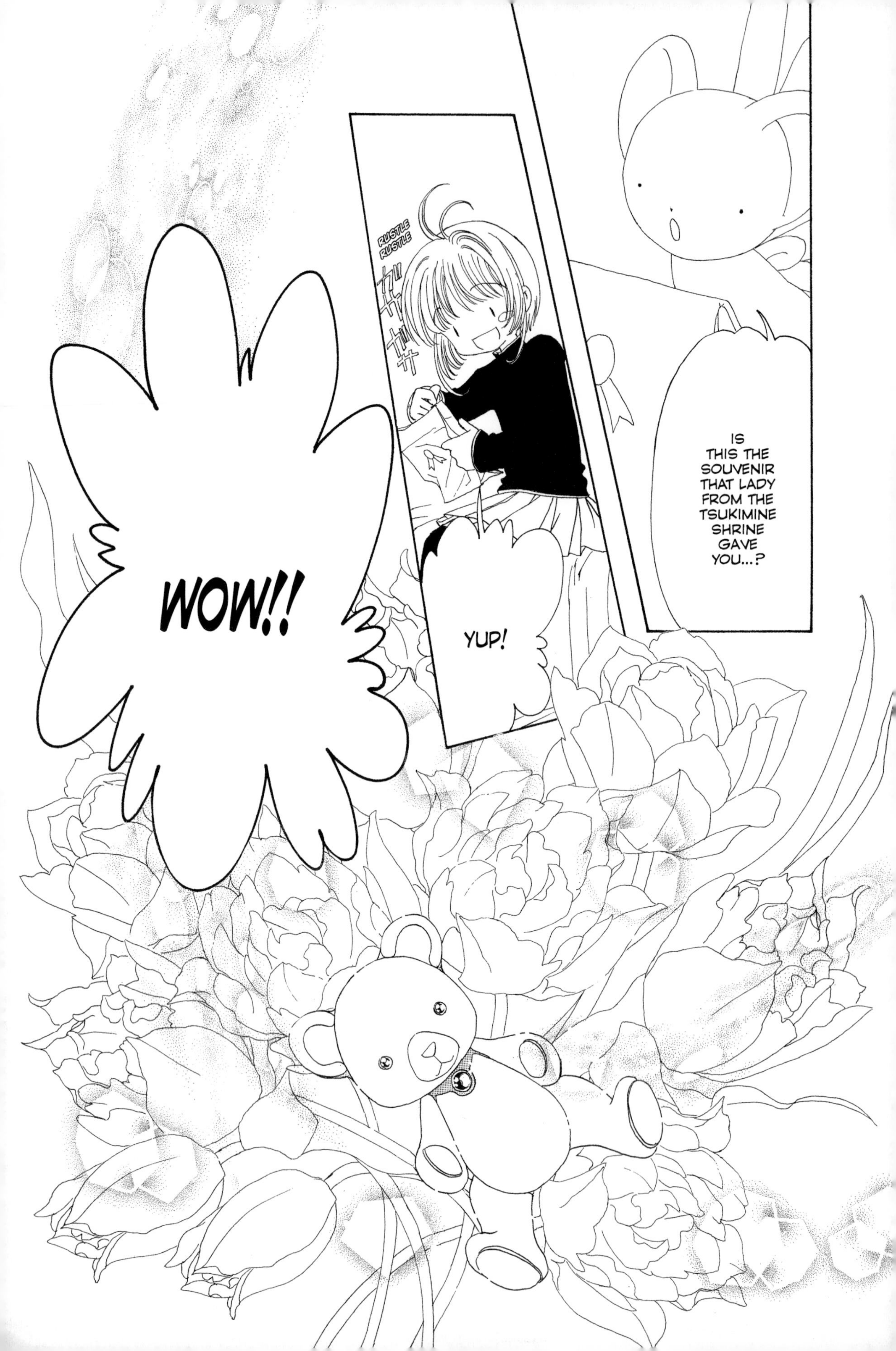
IS THIS THE SOUVENIR THAT LADY FROM THE TSUKIMINE SHRINE GAVE YOU...?
RUSTLE RUSTLE
YUP!
WOW!!

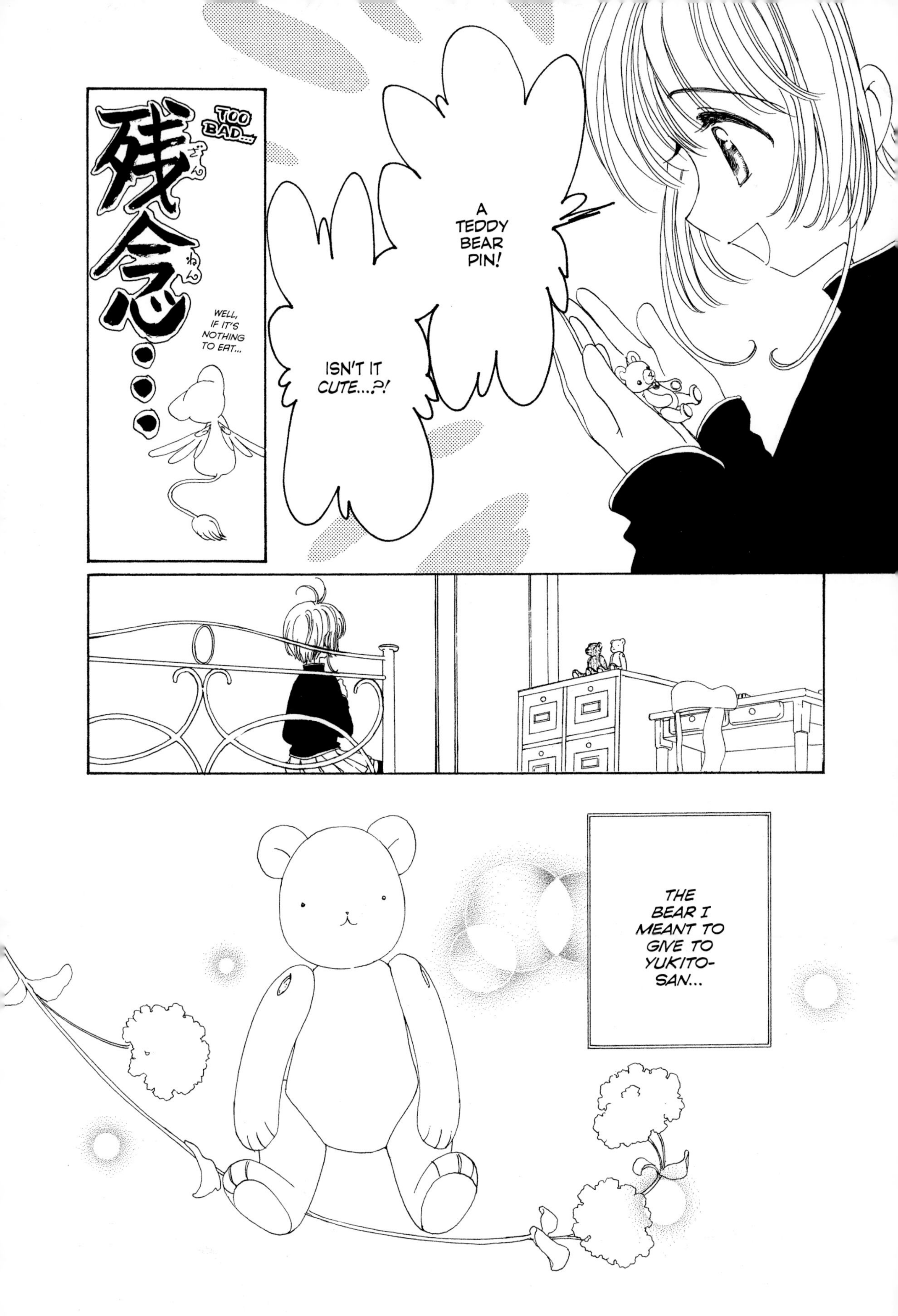
A TEDDY BEAR PIN!
ISN'T IT CUTE...?!
残念・・・
TOO BAD...
WELL, IF IT'S NOTHING TO EAT...
THE BEAR I MEANT TO GIVE TO YUKITO-SAN...

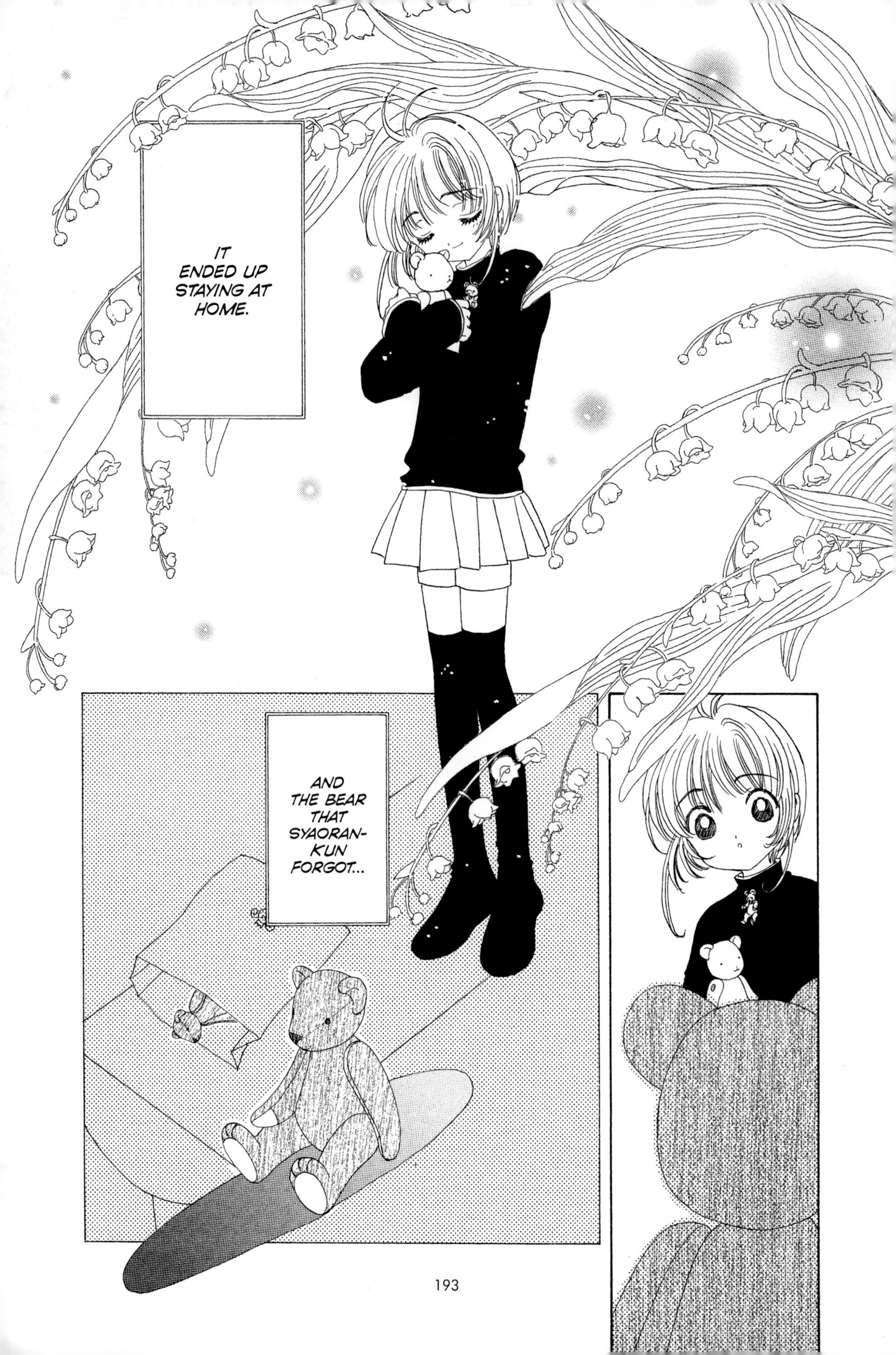
IT ENDED UP STAYING AT HOME.
AND THE BEAR THAT SYAORAN-KUN FORGOT...

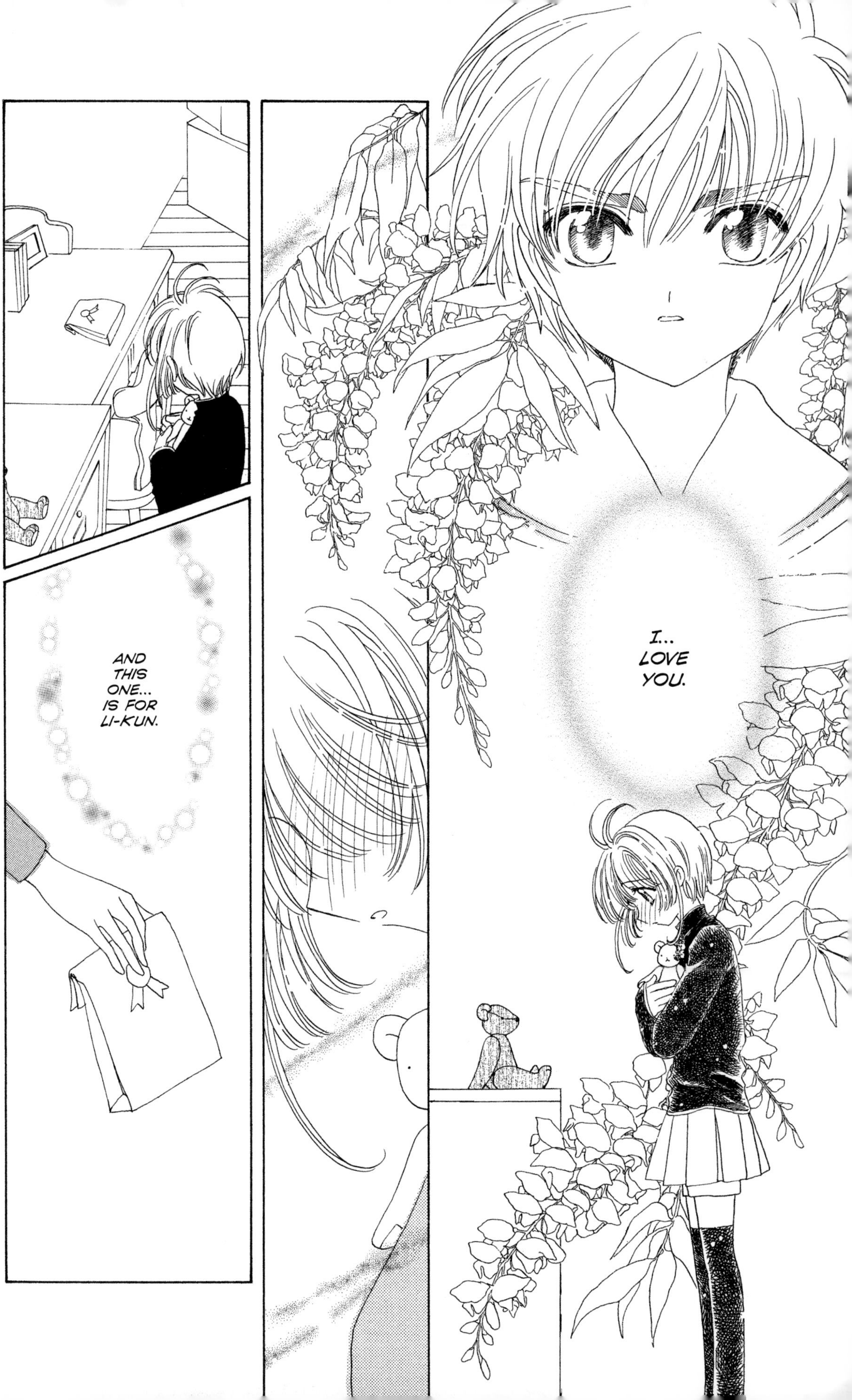
I... LOVE YOU.
AND THIS ONE... IS FOR LI-KUN.

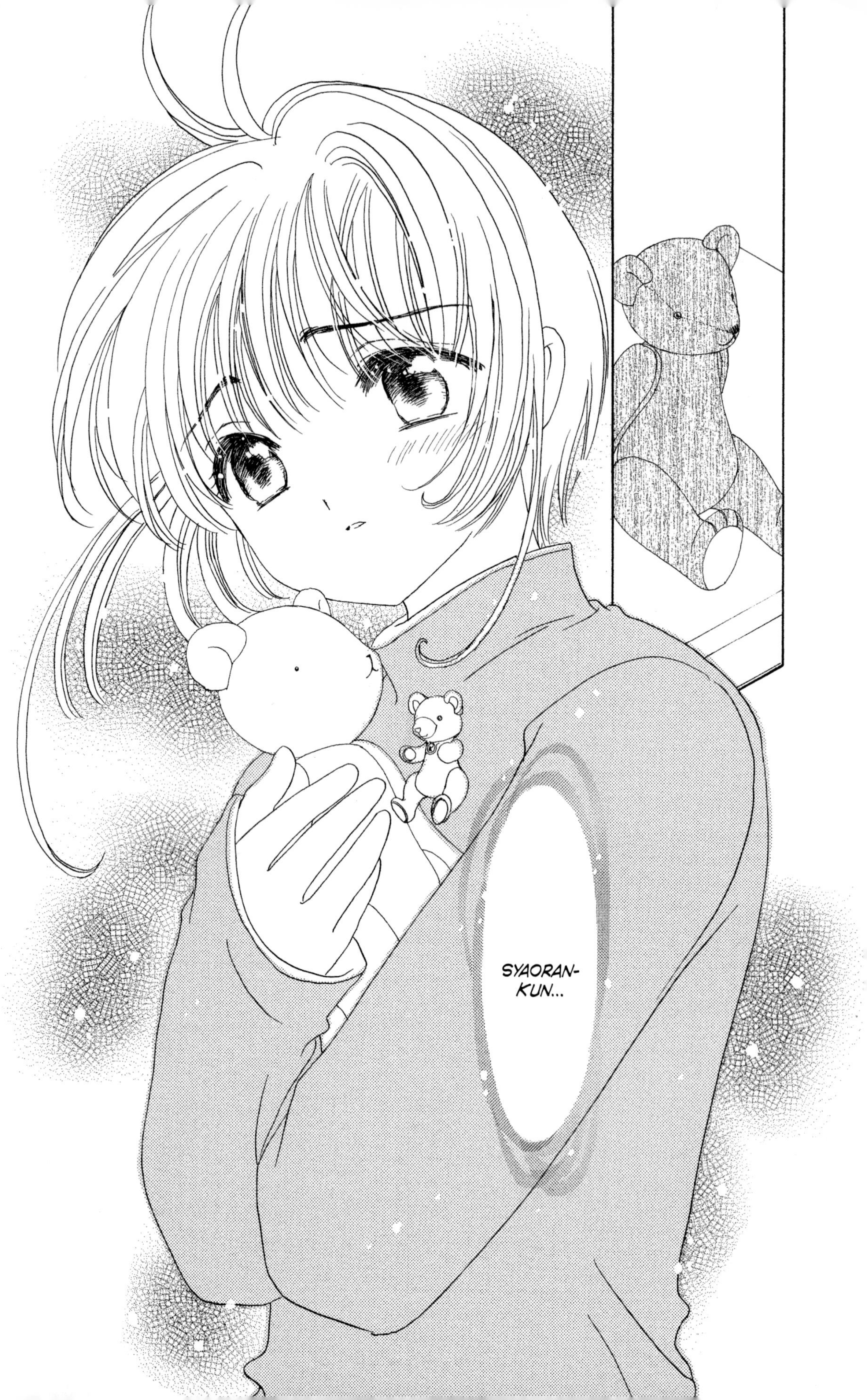
SYAORAN-KUN...

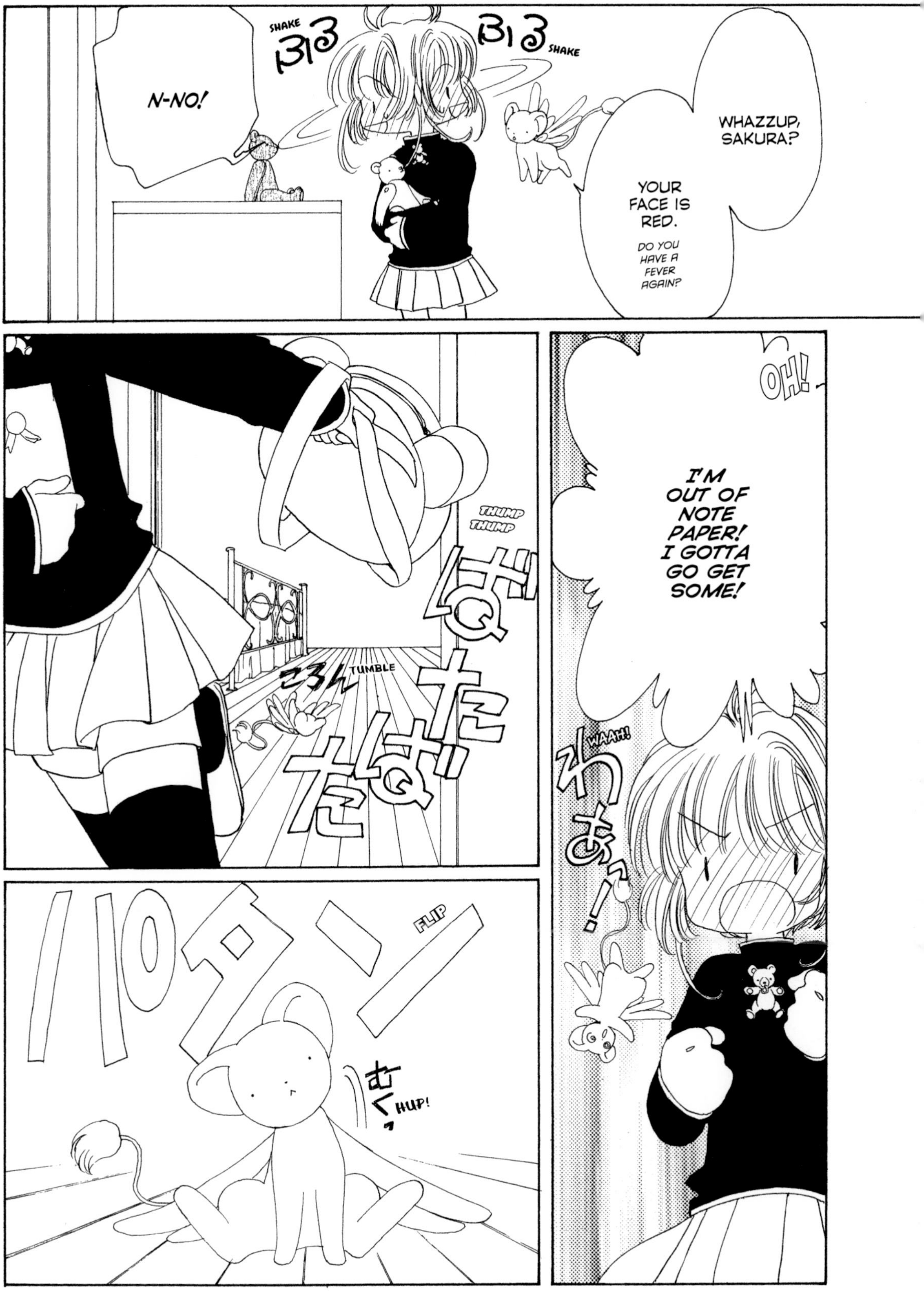
WHAZZUP, SAKURA?
YOUR FACE IS RED.
DO YOU HAVE A FEVER AGAIN?
ふる SHAKE
ふる SHAKE
N-NO!
OH!
I'M OUT OF NOTE PAPER! I GOTTA GO GET SOME!
わぁっ! WAAH!
ばたばた THUMP THUMP
ころん TUMBLE
パタン FLIP
むくっ HUP!

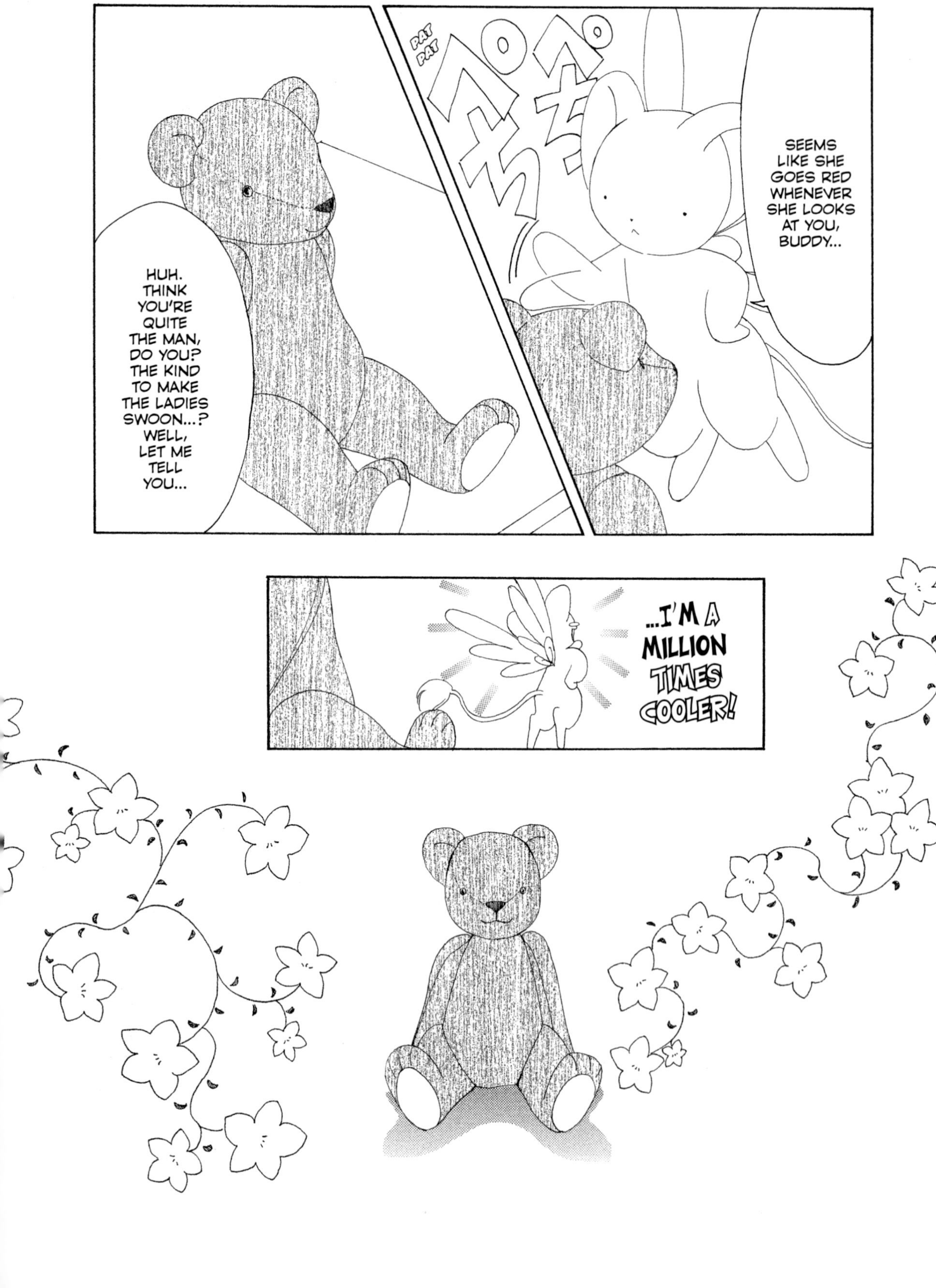
PAT PAT
SEEMS LIKE SHE GOES RED WHENEVER SHE LOOKS AT YOU, BUDDY...
HUH. THINK YOU'RE QUITE THE MAN, DO YOU? THE KIND TO MAKE THE LADIES SWOON...? WELL, LET ME TELL YOU...
...I'M A MILLION TIMES COOLER!

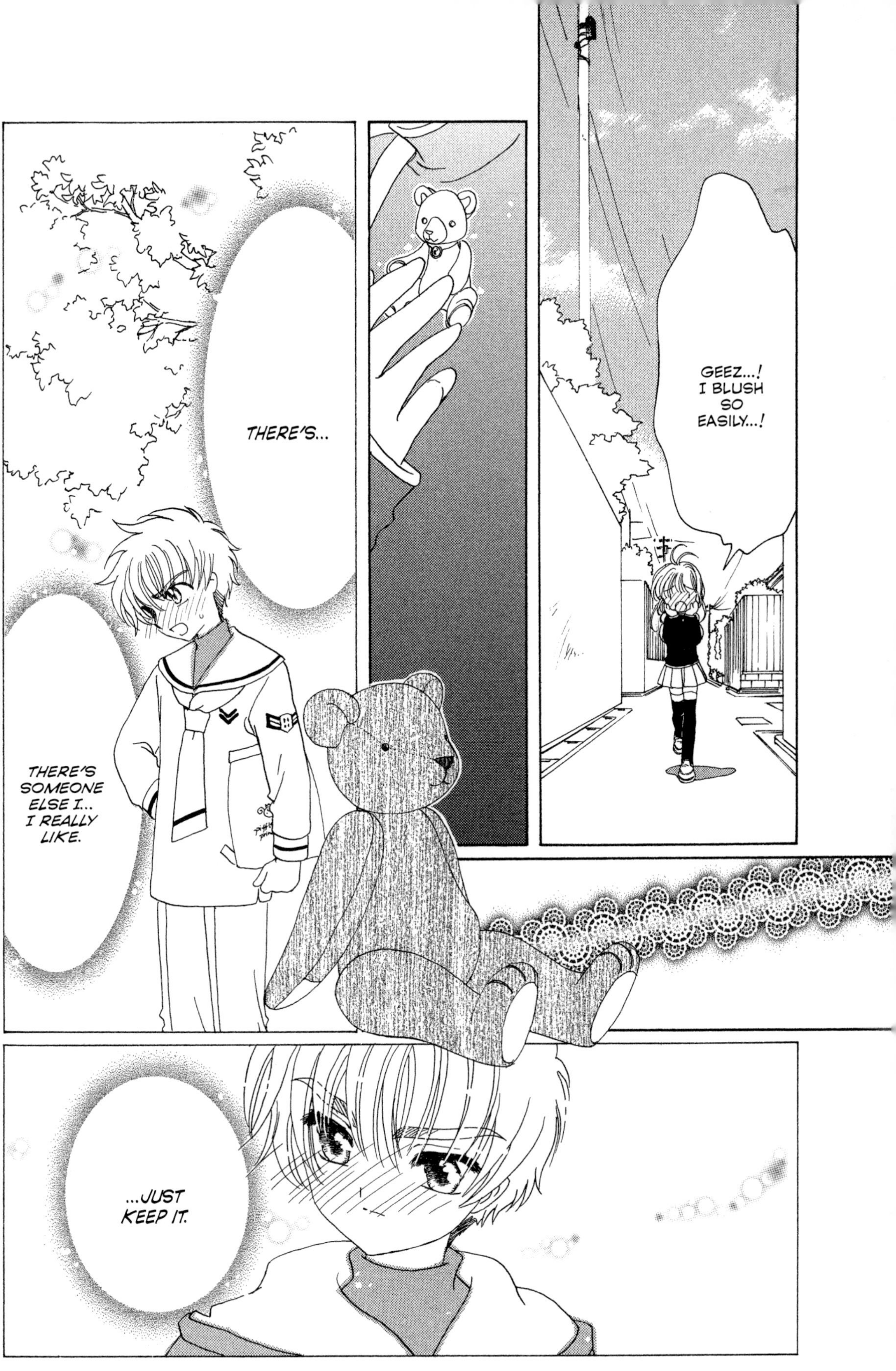
GEEZ...! I BLUSH SO EASILY...!
THERE'S...
THERE'S SOMEONE ELSE I... I REALLY LIKE.
...JUST KEEP IT.

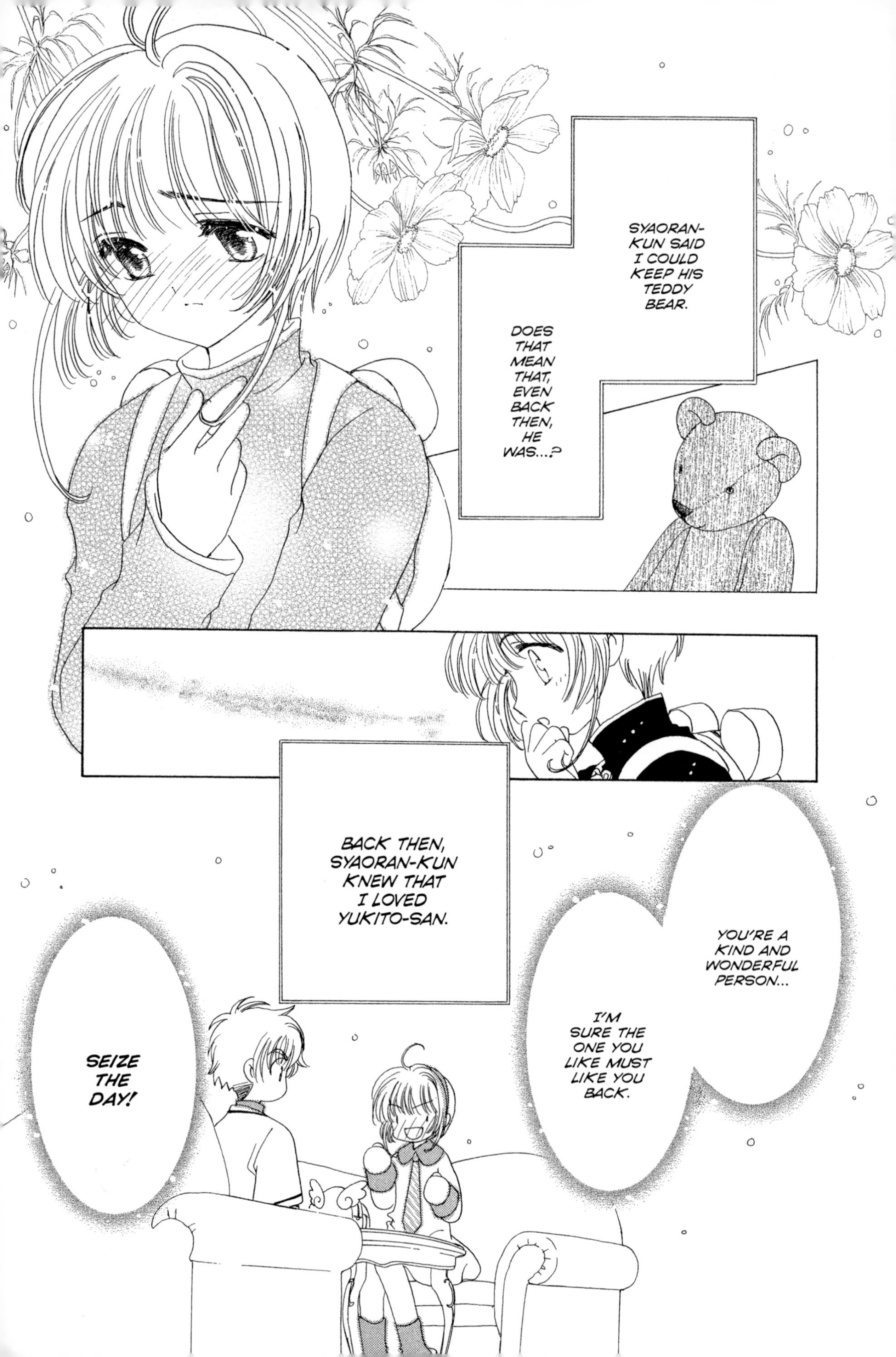
SYAORAN-KUN SAID I COULD KEEP HIS TEDDY BEAR.
DOES THAT MEAN THAT, EVEN BACK THEN, HE WAS...?
BACK THEN, SYAORAN-KUN KNEW THAT I LOVED YUKITO-SAN.
YOU'RE A KIND AND WONDERFUL PERSON...
I'M SURE THE ONE YOU LIKE MUST LIKE YOU BACK.
SEIZE THE DAY!

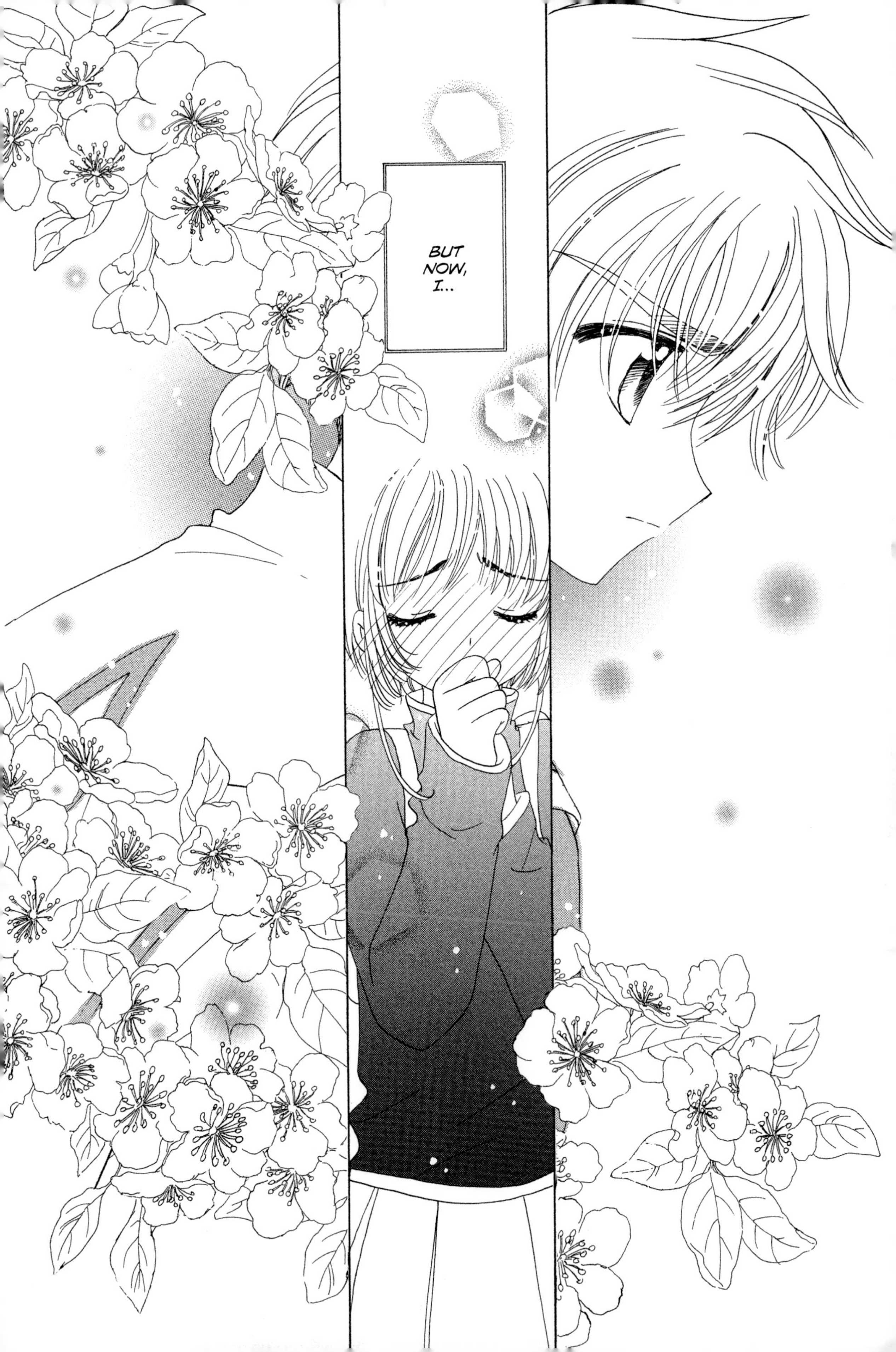
BUT NOW, I...

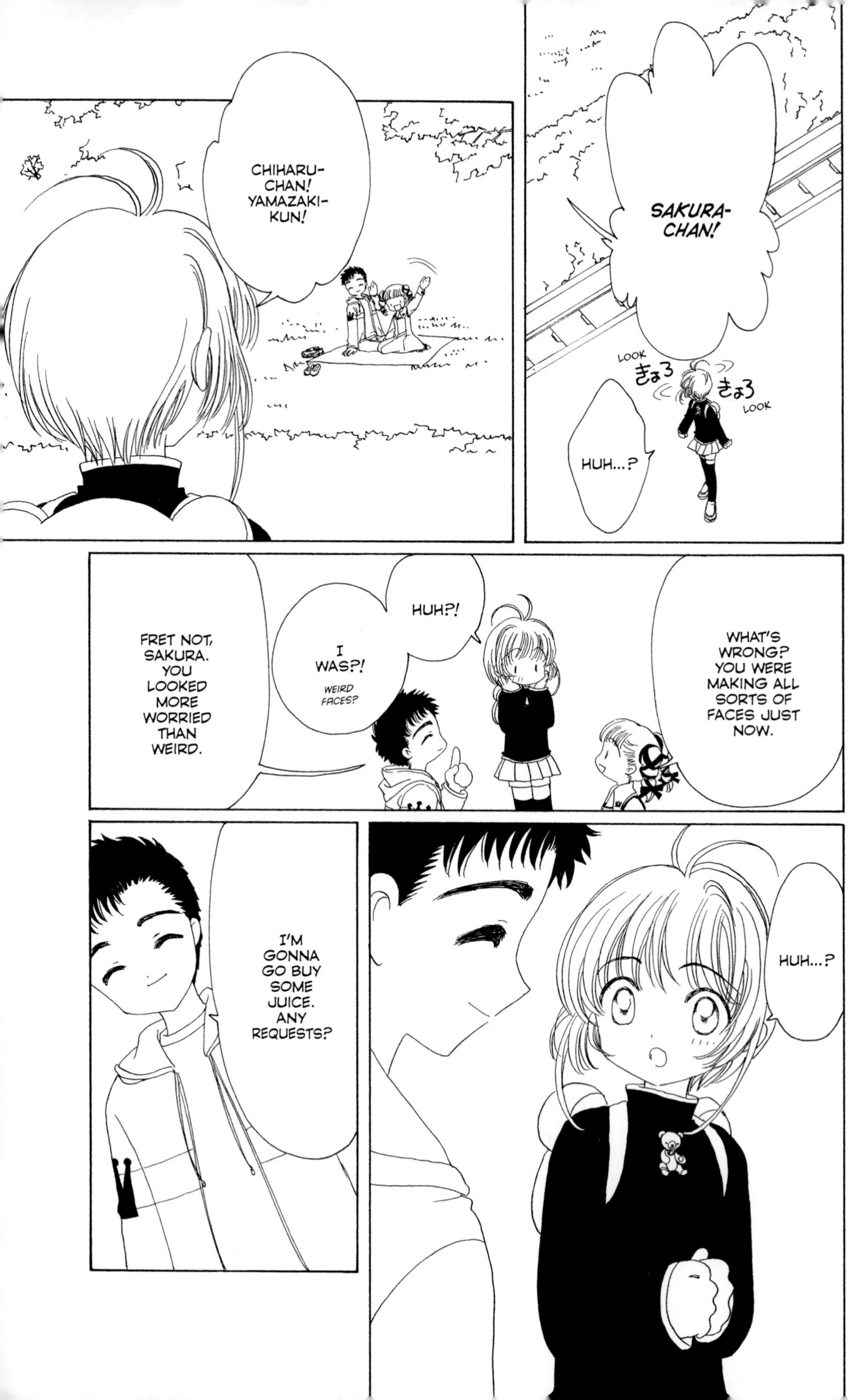
SAKURA-CHAN!
LOOK
きょろ
きょろ
LOOK
HUH...?
CHIHARU-CHAN! YAMAZAKI-KUN!
WHAT'S WRONG? YOU WERE MAKING ALL SORTS OF FACES JUST NOW.
HUH?!
I WAS?!
WEIRD FACES?
FRET NOT, SAKURA. YOU LOOKED MORE WORRIED THAN WEIRD.
HUH...?
I'M GONNA GO BUY SOME JUICE. ANY REQUESTS?

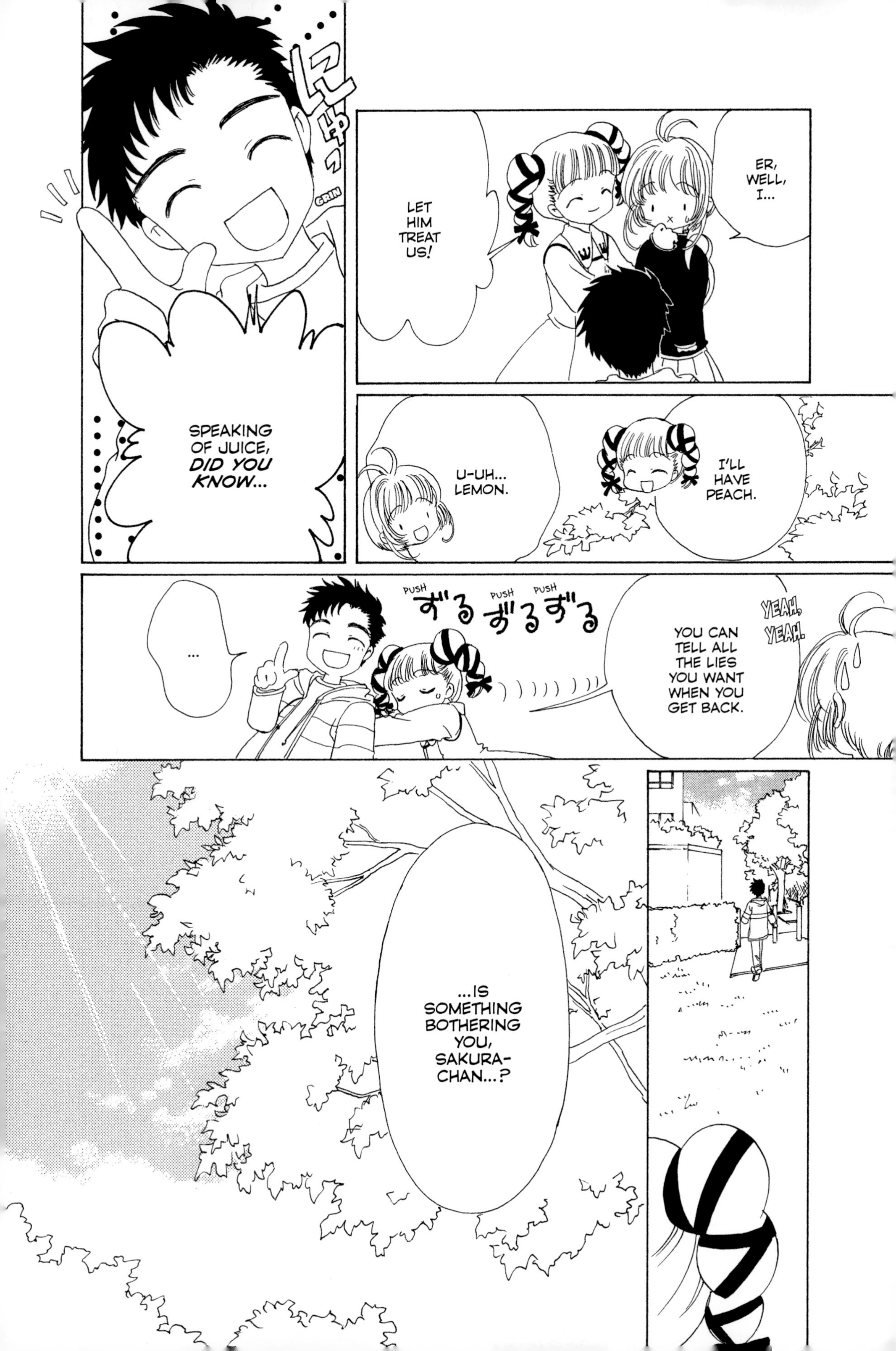
ER, WELL, I...
LET HIM TREAT US!
I'LL HAVE PEACH.
U-UH... LEMON.
GRIN
SPEAKING OF JUICE, *DID YOU KNOW...*
YEAH, YEAH.
YOU CAN TELL ALL THE LIES YOU WANT WHEN YOU GET BACK.
PUSH PUSH PUSH
ずるずるずる
...
...IS SOMETHING BOTHERING YOU, SAKURA-CHAN...?

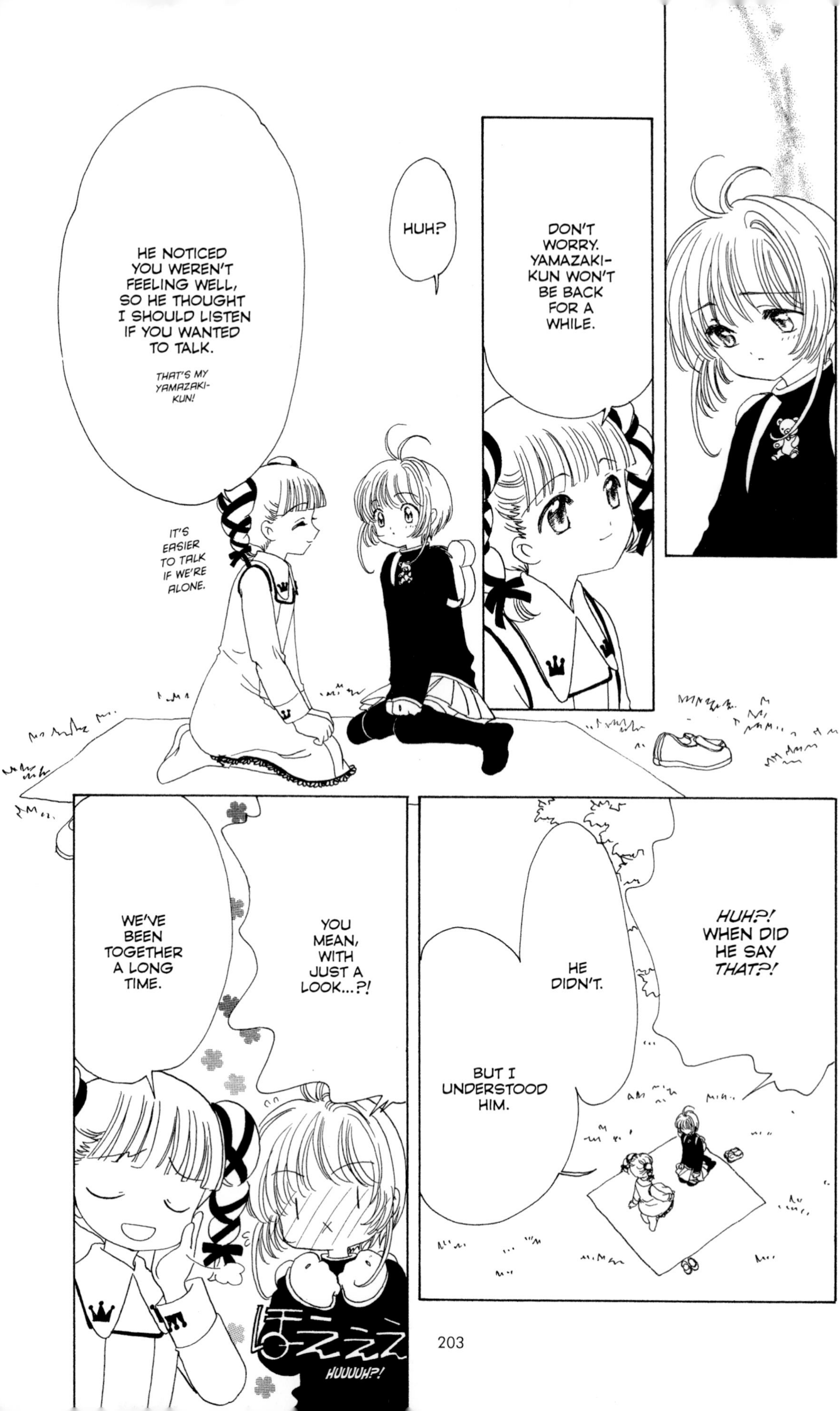
DON'T WORRY. YAMAZAKI-KUN WON'T BE BACK FOR A WHILE.
HUH?
HE NOTICED YOU WEREN'T FEELING WELL, SO HE THOUGHT I SHOULD LISTEN IF YOU WANTED TO TALK.
THAT'S MY YAMAZAKI-KUN!
IT'S EASIER TO TALK IF WE'RE ALONE.
HUH?! WHEN DID HE SAY *THAT?!*
HE DIDN'T.
BUT I UNDERSTOOD HIM.
YOU MEAN, WITH JUST A LOOK...?!
WE'VE BEEN TOGETHER A LONG TIME.
HUUUUH?!

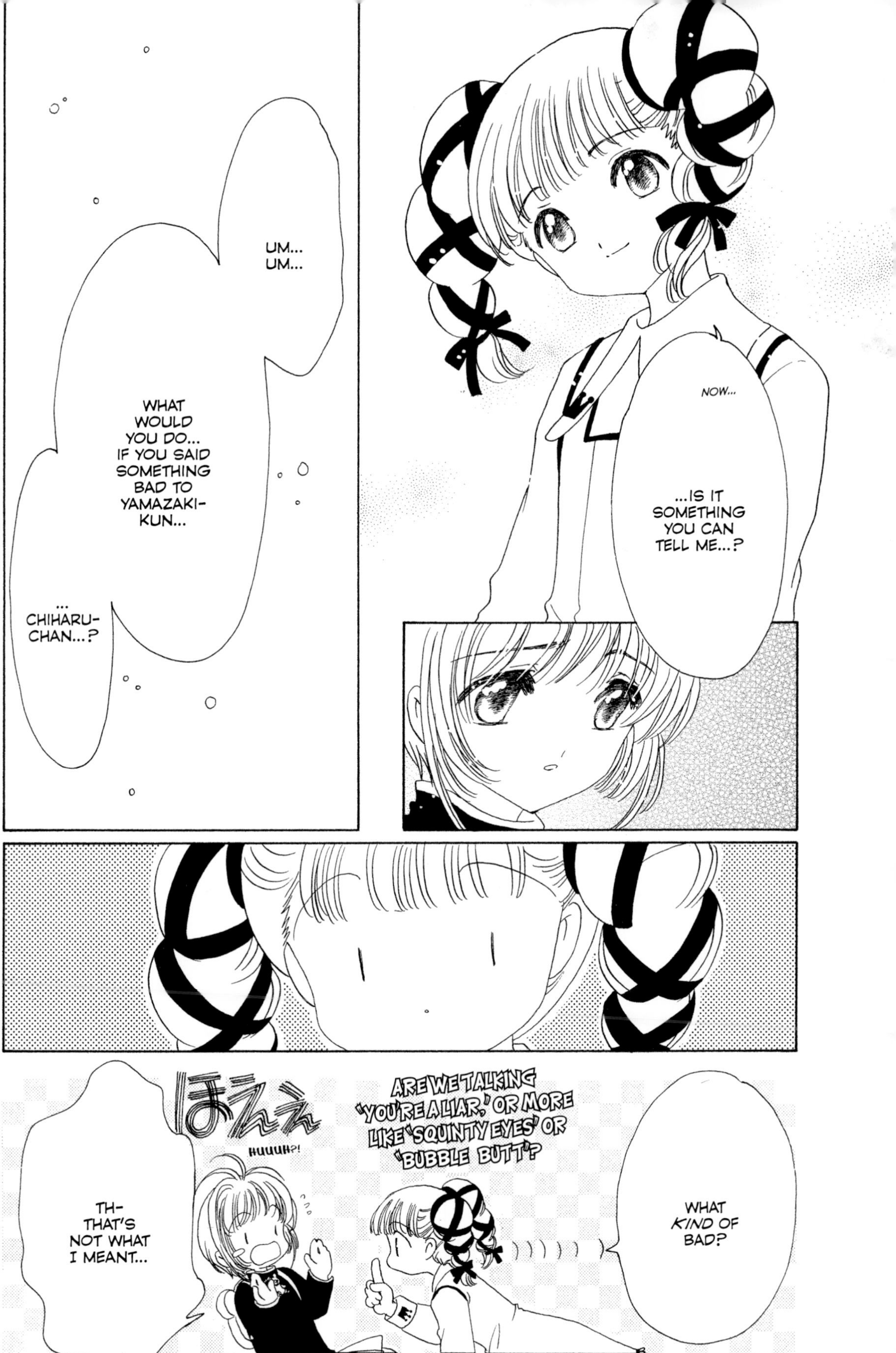
NOW...
...IS IT SOMETHING YOU CAN TELL ME...?
UM... UM...
WHAT WOULD YOU DO... IF YOU SAID SOMETHING BAD TO YAMAZAKI-KUN...
... CHIHARU-CHAN...?
WHAT KIND OF BAD?
ARE WE TALKING "YOU'RE A LIAR," OR MORE LIKE "SQUINTY EYES" OR "BUBBLE BUTT"?
ほえぇ
HUUUH?!
TH-THAT'S NOT WHAT I MEANT...

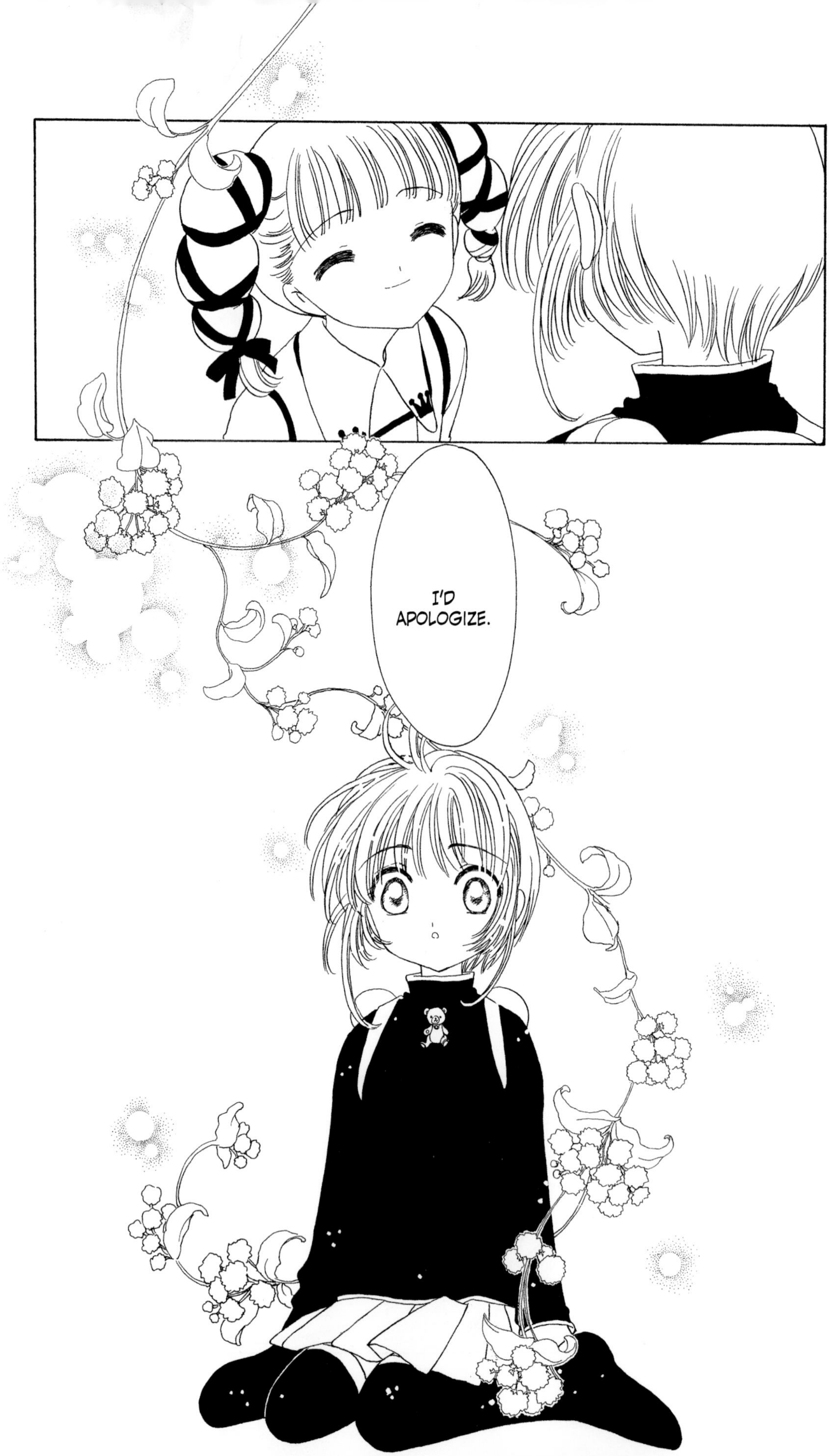
I'D APOLOGIZE.

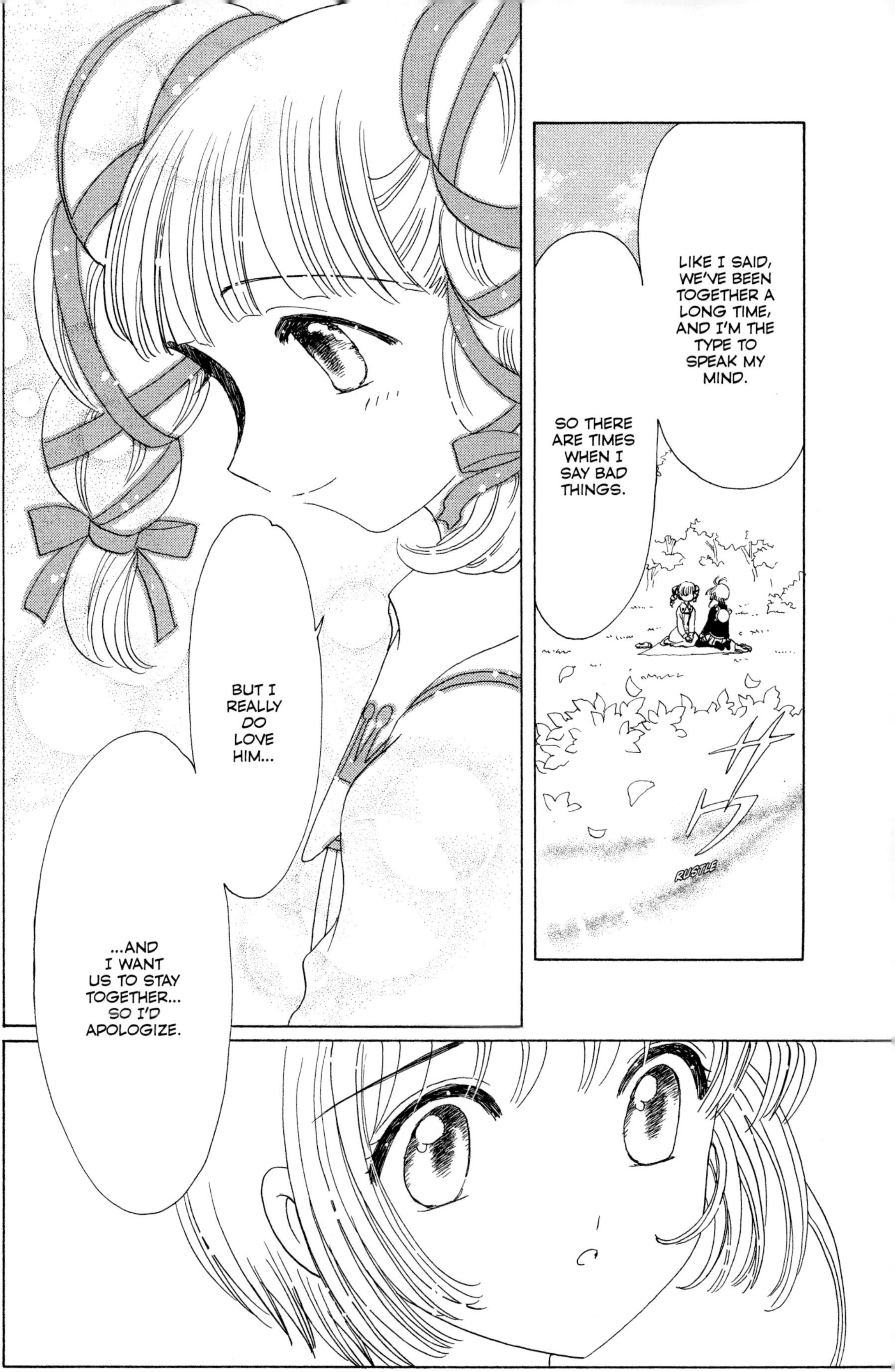
LIKE I SAID, WE'VE BEEN TOGETHER A LONG TIME, AND I'M THE TYPE TO SPEAK MY MIND.
SO THERE ARE TIMES WHEN I SAY BAD THINGS.
RUSTLE
BUT I REALLY *DO* LOVE HIM...
...AND I WANT US TO STAY TOGETHER... SO I'D APOLOGIZE.

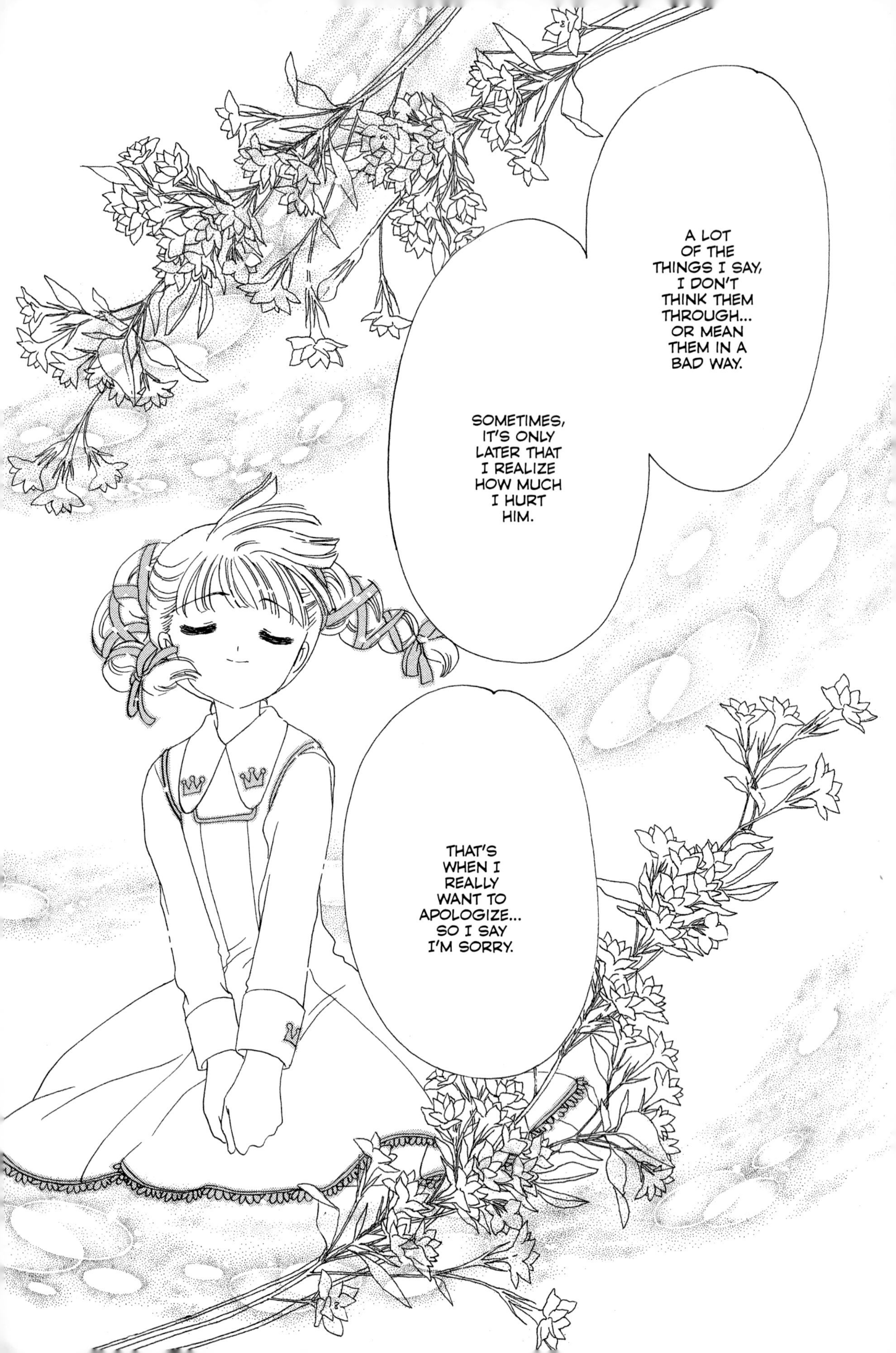
A LOT OF THE THINGS I SAY, I DON'T THINK THEM THROUGH... OR MEAN THEM IN A BAD WAY.
SOMETIMES, IT'S ONLY LATER THAT I REALIZE HOW MUCH I HURT HIM.
THAT'S WHEN I REALLY WANT TO APOLOGIZE... SO I SAY I'M SORRY.

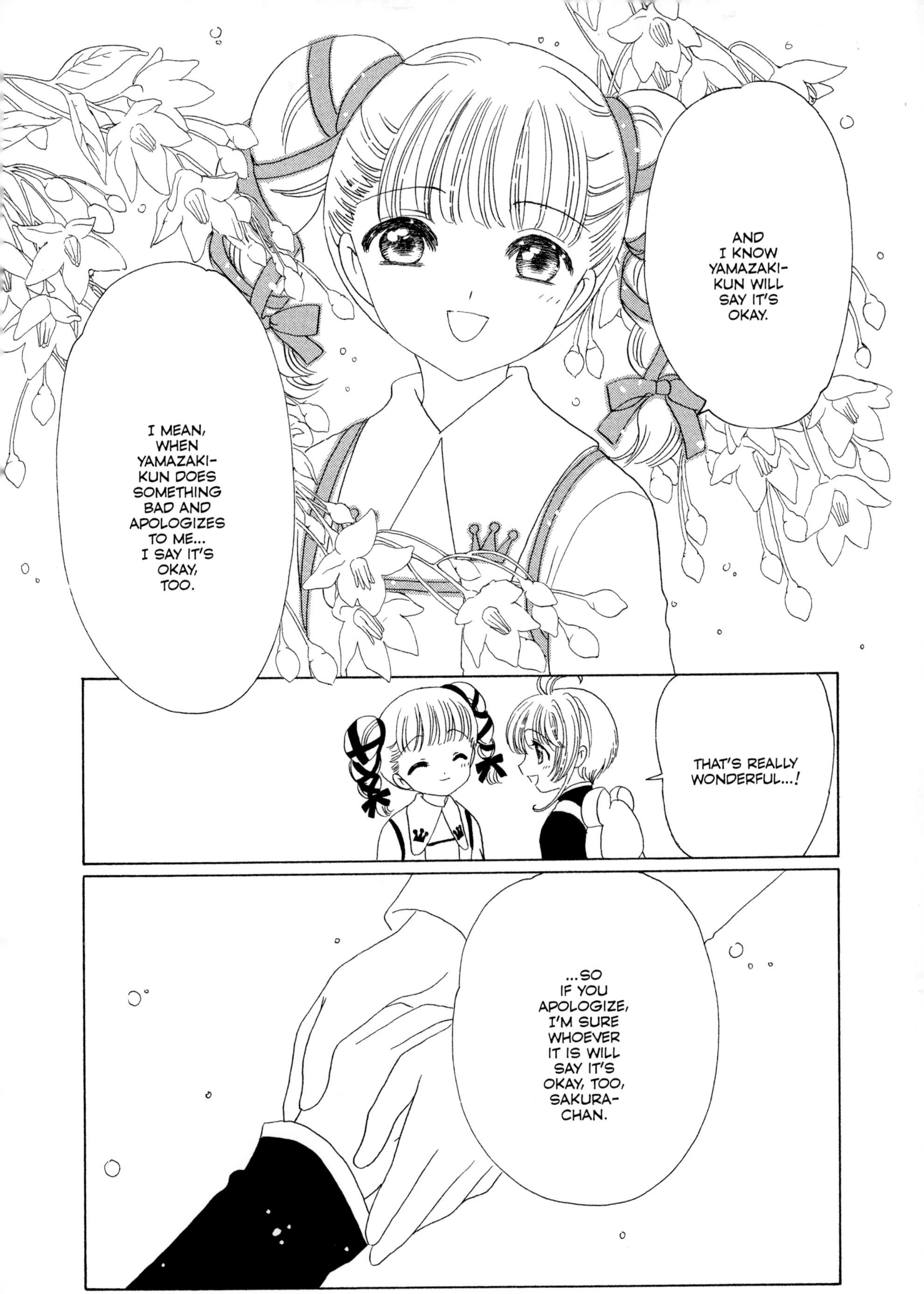
AND I KNOW YAMAZAKI-KUN WILL SAY IT'S OKAY.
I MEAN, WHEN YAMAZAKI-KUN DOES SOMETHING BAD AND APOLOGIZES TO ME... I SAY IT'S OKAY, TOO.
THAT'S REALLY WONDERFUL...!
...SO IF YOU APOLOGIZE, I'M SURE WHOEVER IT IS WILL SAY IT'S OKAY, TOO, SAKURA-CHAN.

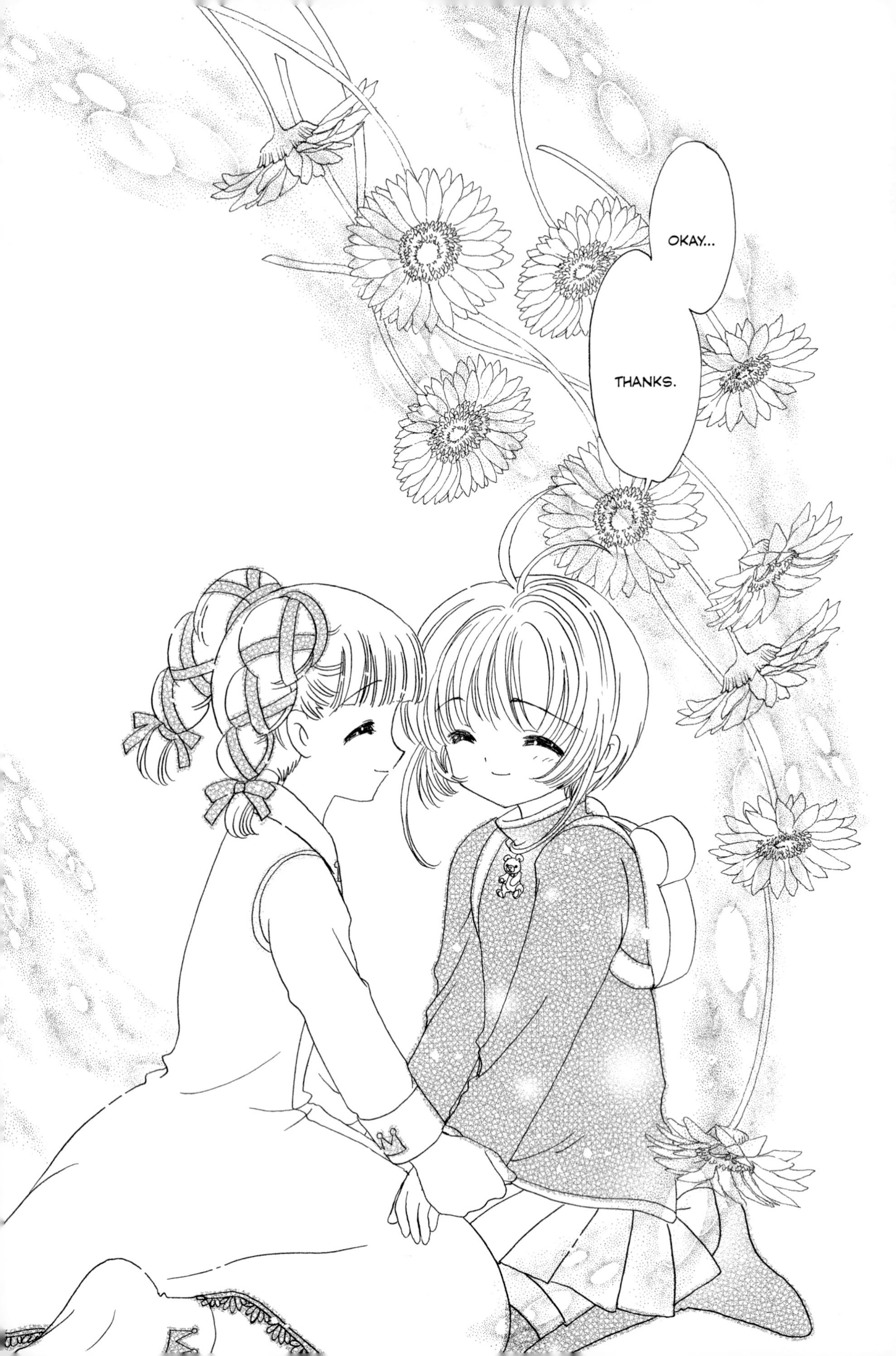
OKAY...
THANKS.

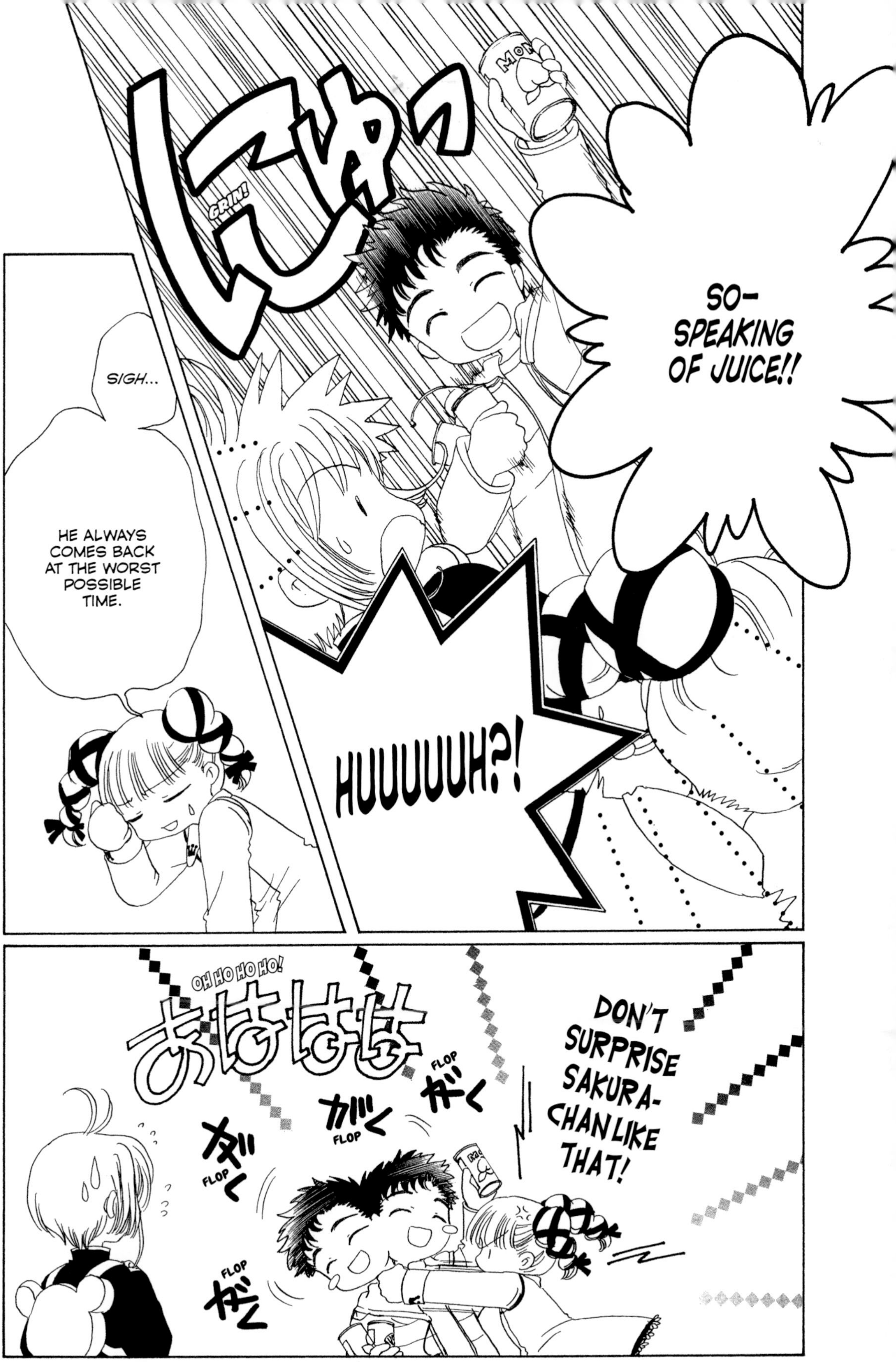
にゅっ
GRIN!
SO- SPEAKING OF JUICE!!
HUUUUUH?!
SIGH...
HE ALWAYS COMES BACK AT THE WORST POSSIBLE TIME.
DON'T SURPRISE SAKURA-CHAN LIKE THAT!
あははは
OH HO HO HO!
がく
FLOP
がく
FLOP
がく
FLOP
がく
FLOP

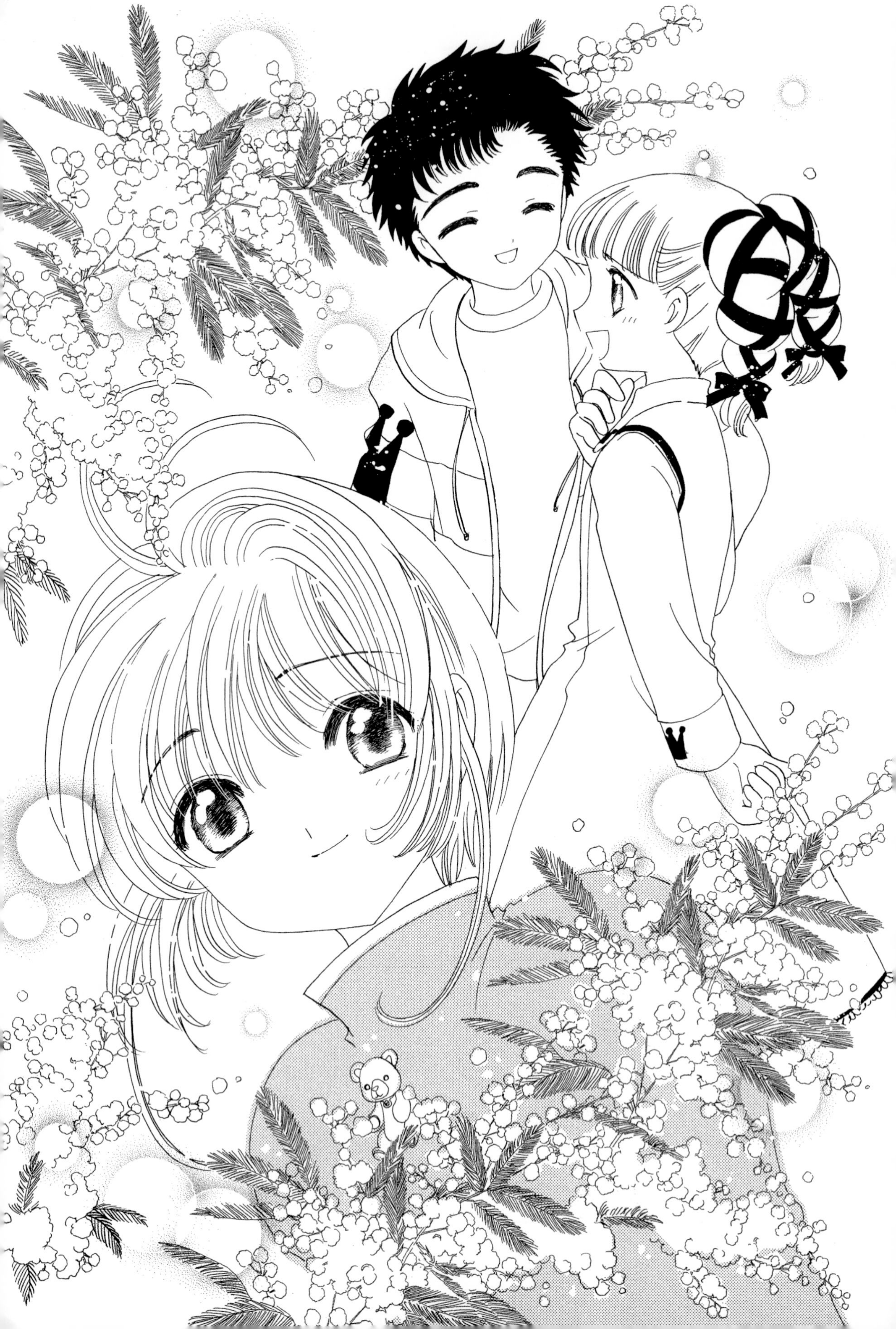

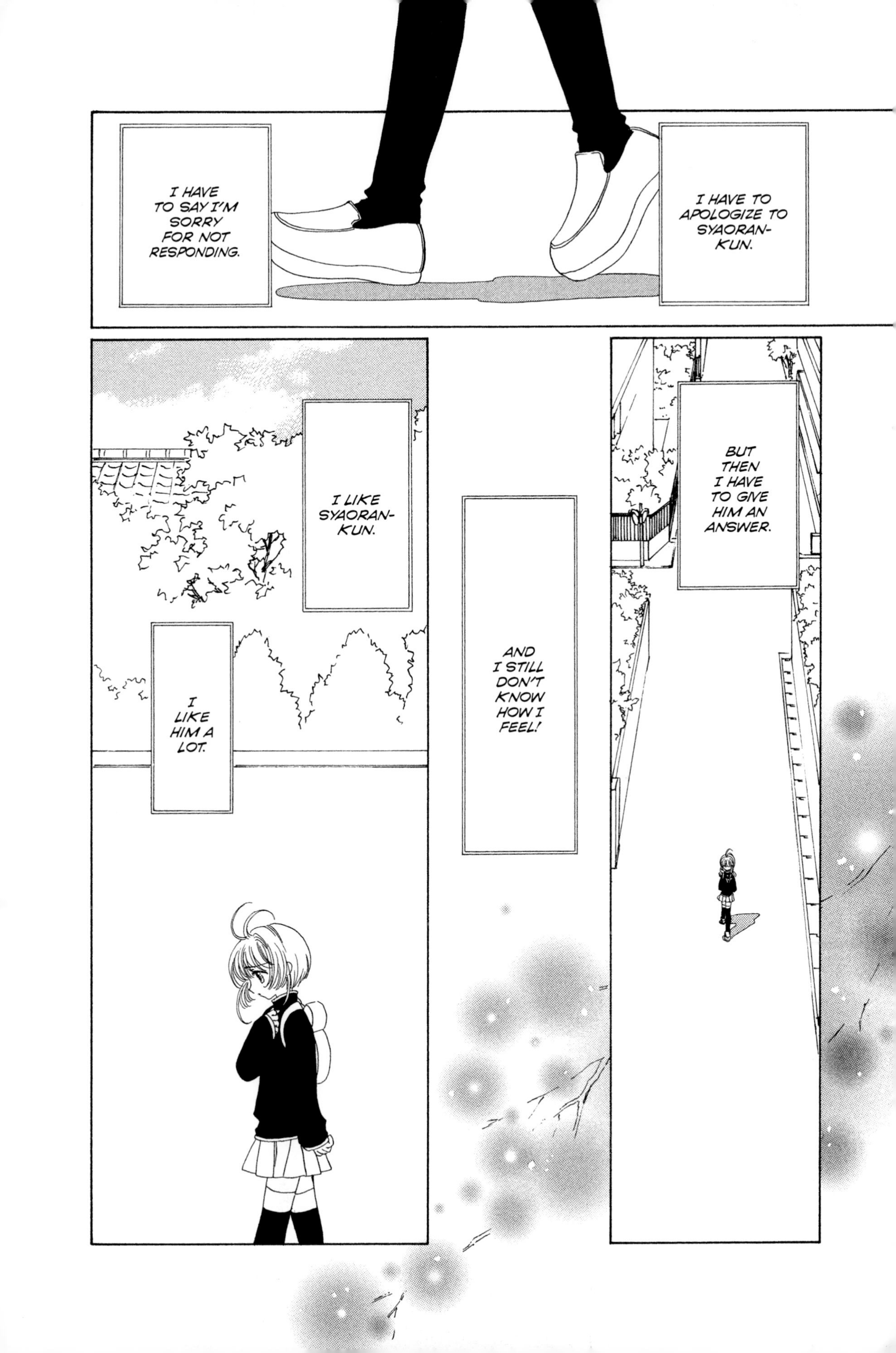
I HAVE TO APOLOGIZE TO SYAORAN-KUN.
I HAVE TO SAY I'M SORRY FOR NOT RESPONDING.
BUT THEN I HAVE TO GIVE HIM AN ANSWER.
AND I STILL DON'T KNOW HOW I FEEL!
I LIKE SYAORAN-KUN.
I LIKE HIM A LOT.

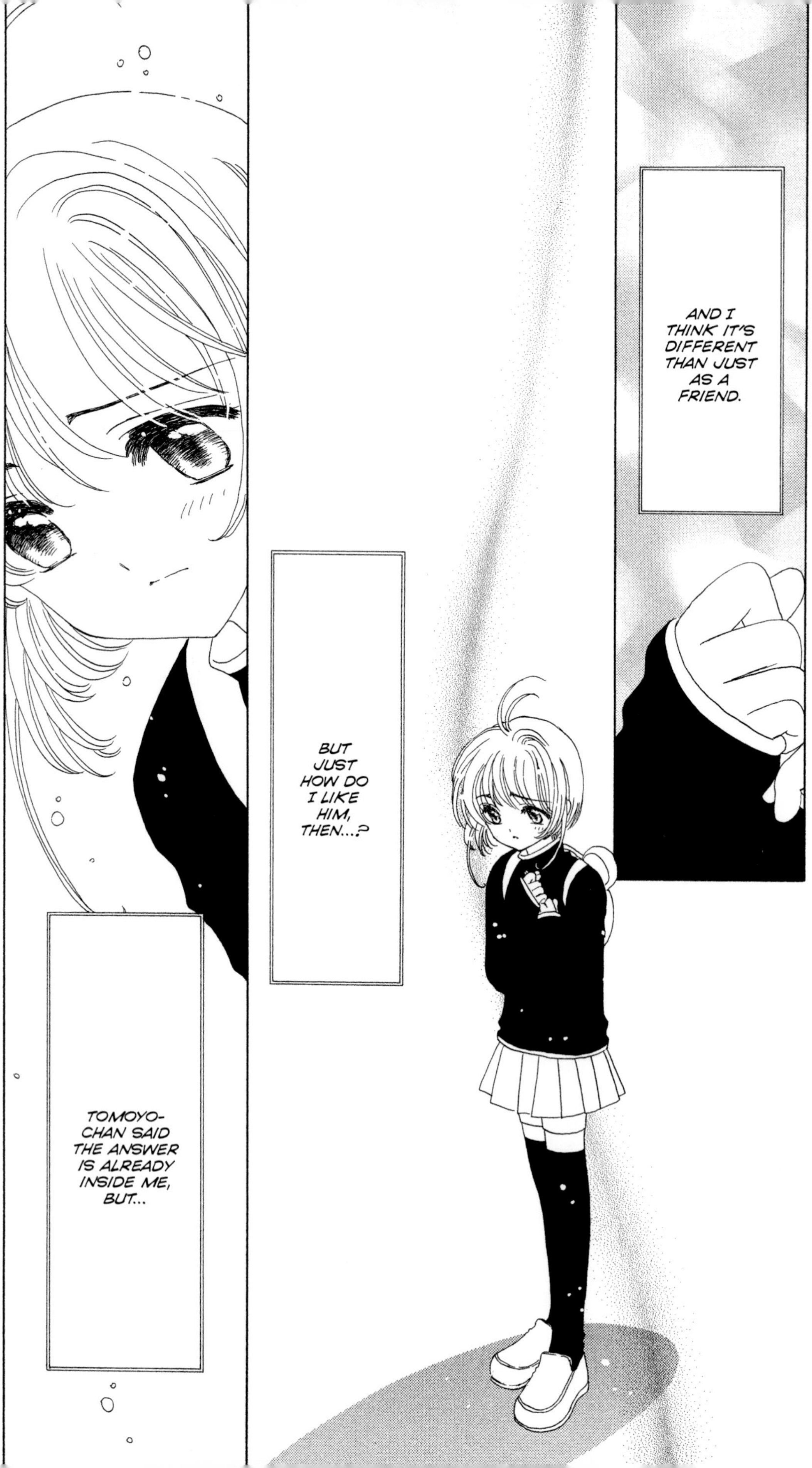
AND I THINK IT'S DIFFERENT THAN JUST AS A FRIEND.
BUT JUST HOW DO I LIKE HIM, THEN...?
TOMOYO-CHAN SAID THE ANSWER IS ALREADY INSIDE ME, BUT...

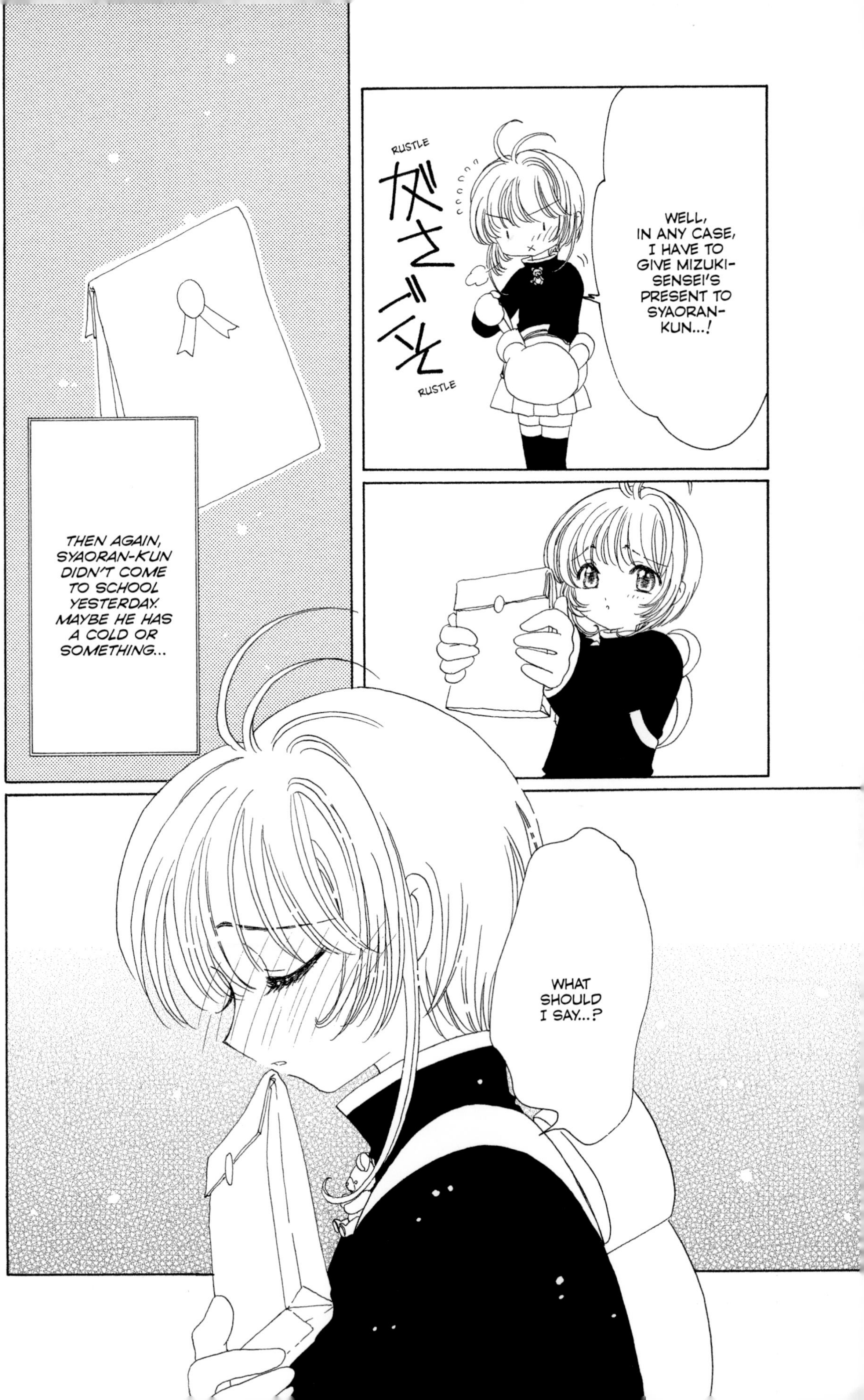
WELL, IN ANY CASE, I HAVE TO GIVE MIZUKI-SENSEI'S PRESENT TO SYAORAN-KUN...!
がさごそ
RUSTLE
RUSTLE
THEN AGAIN, SYAORAN-KUN DIDN'T COME TO SCHOOL YESTERDAY. MAYBE HE HAS A COLD OR SOMETHING...
WHAT SHOULD I SAY...?

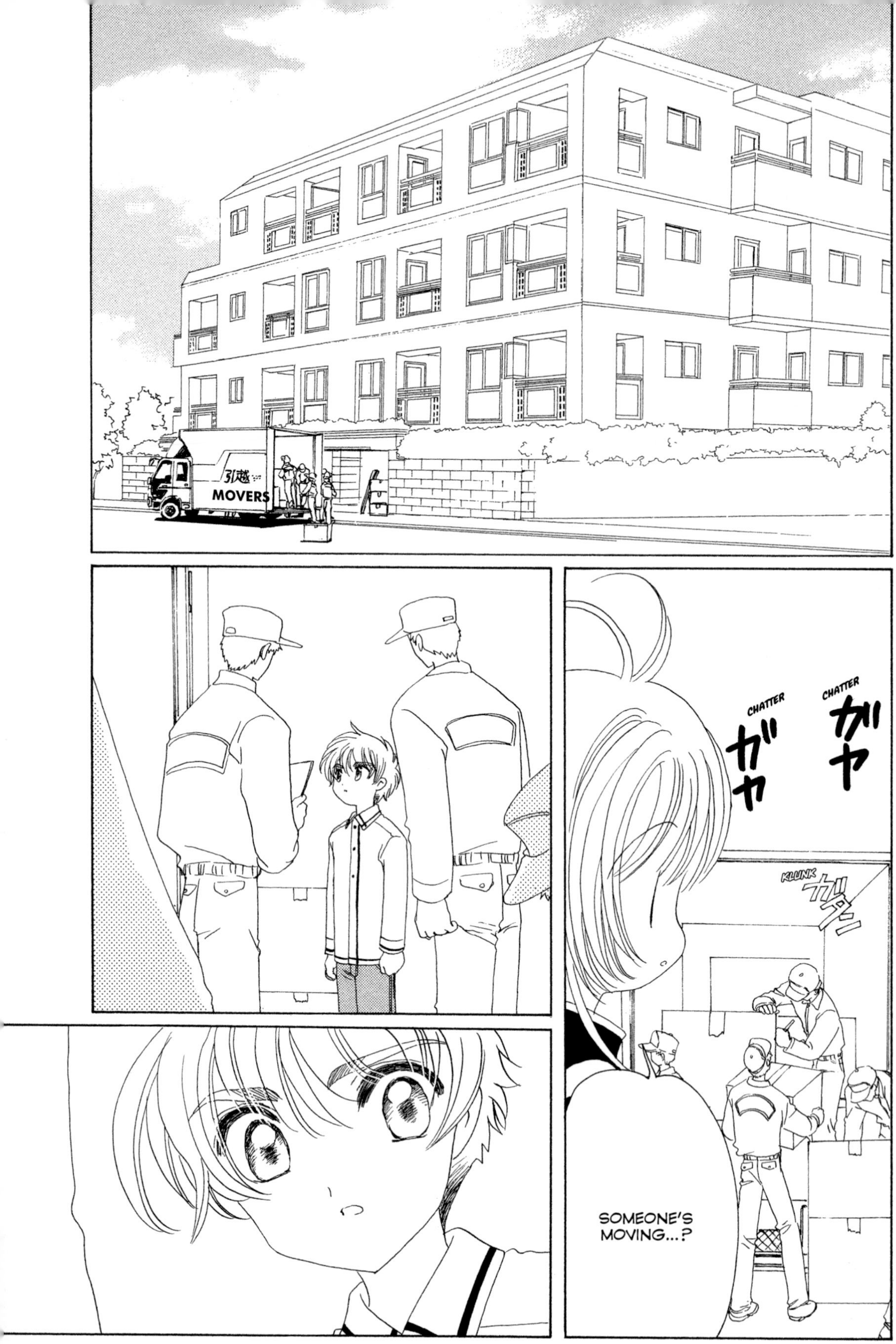

引越
MOVERS
CHATTER
ガヤ
CHATTER
ガヤ
KLUNK
ガタン
SOMEONE'S MOVING...?

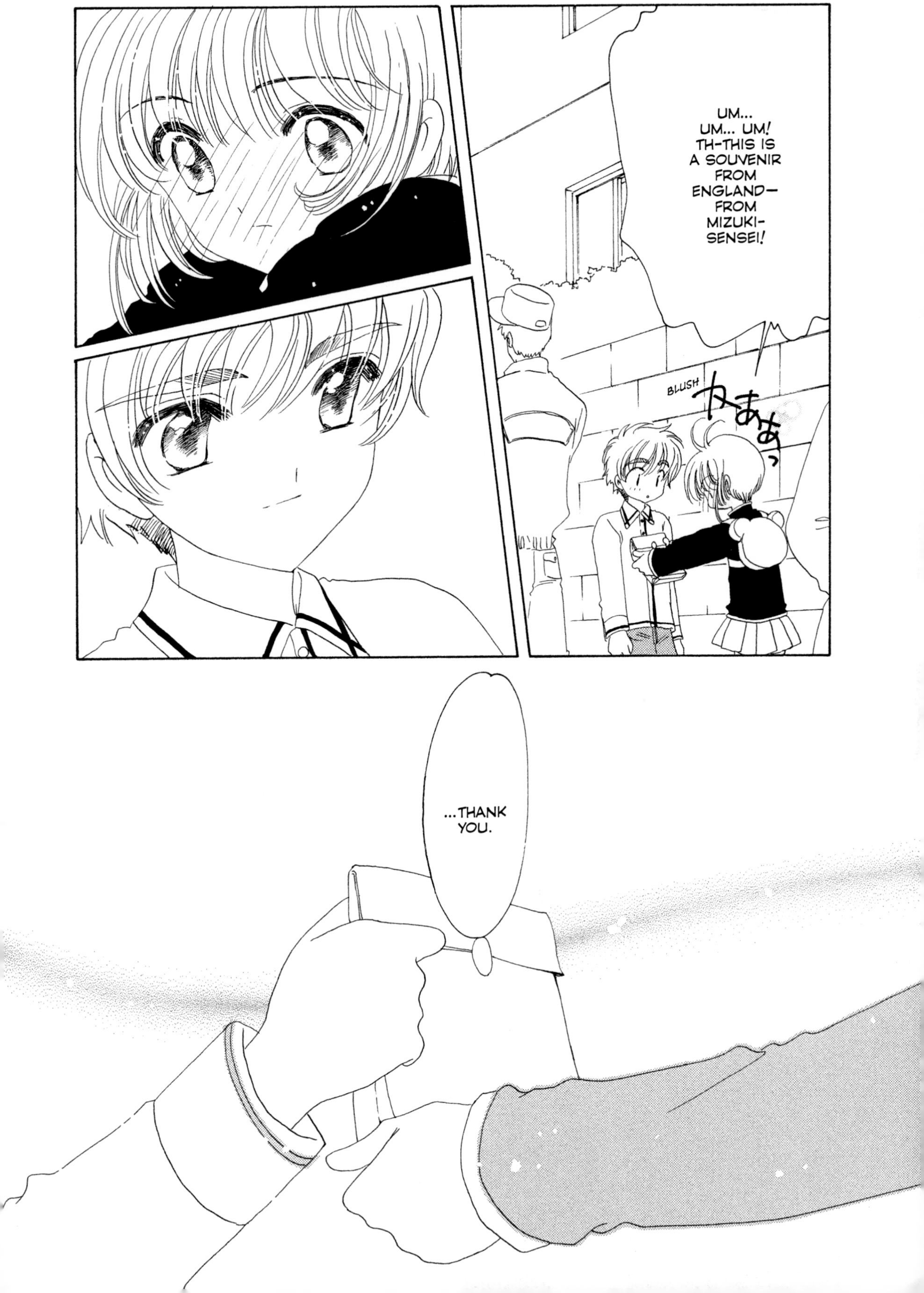
UM... UM... UM! TH-THIS IS A SOUVENIR FROM ENGLAND— FROM MIZUKI-SENSEI!
BLUSH
...THANK YOU.

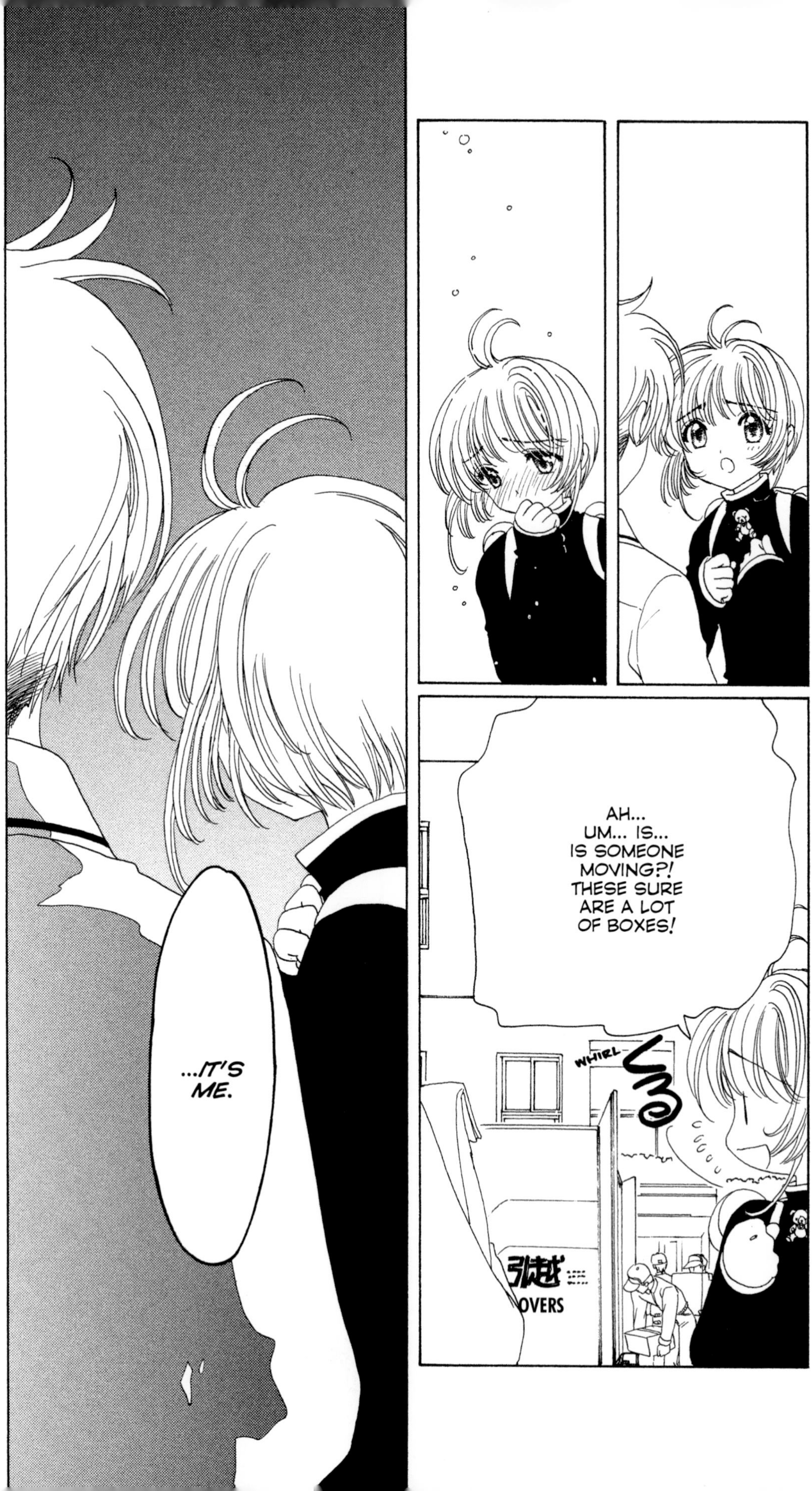
AH... UM... IS... IS SOMEONE MOVING?! THESE SURE ARE A LOT OF BOXES!
くる
WHIRL
...IT'S ME.

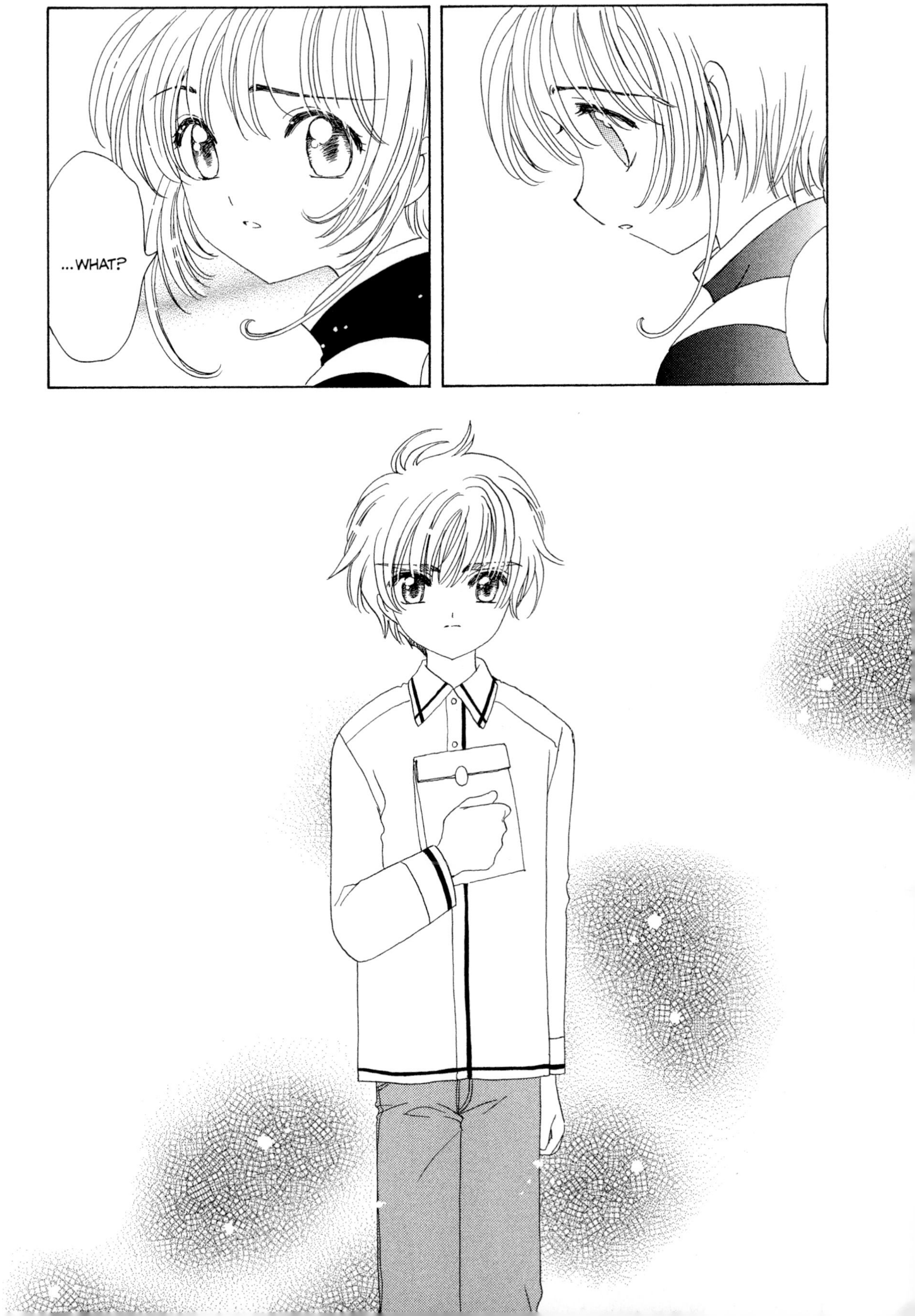
...WHAT?

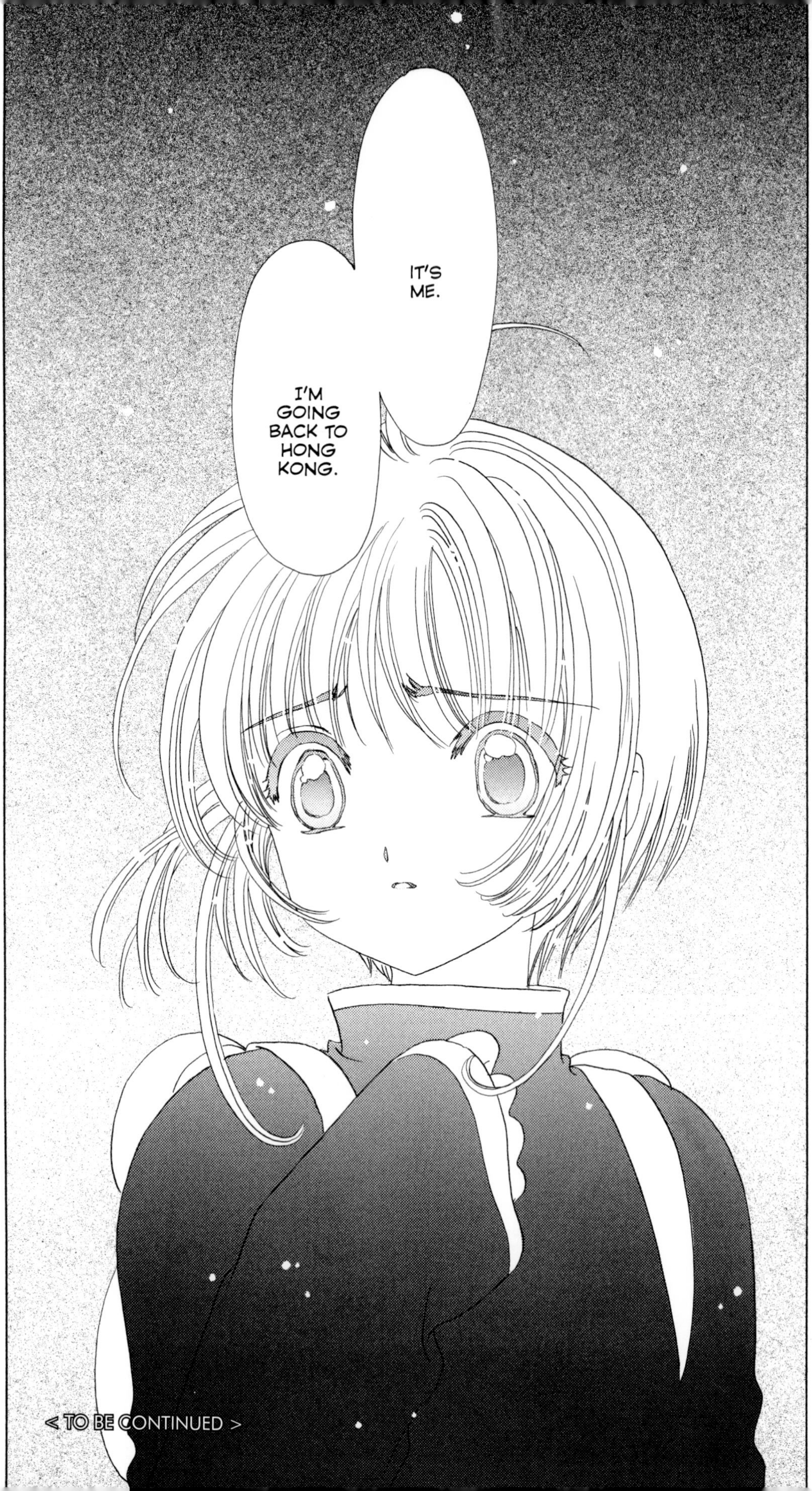
IT'S ME.
I'M GOING BACK TO HONG KONG.
< TO BE CONTINUED >

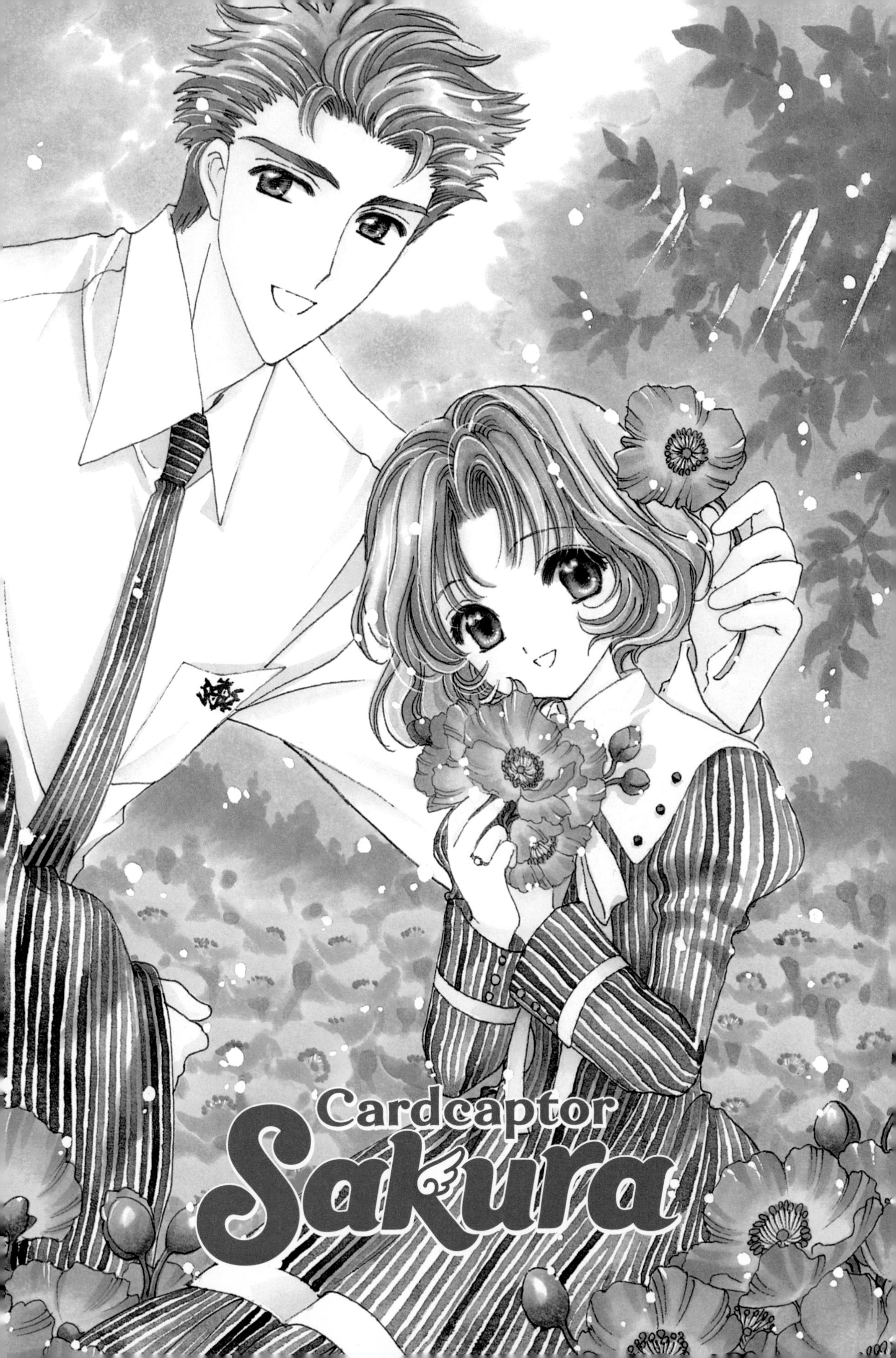
Cardcaptor
Sakura

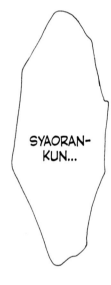

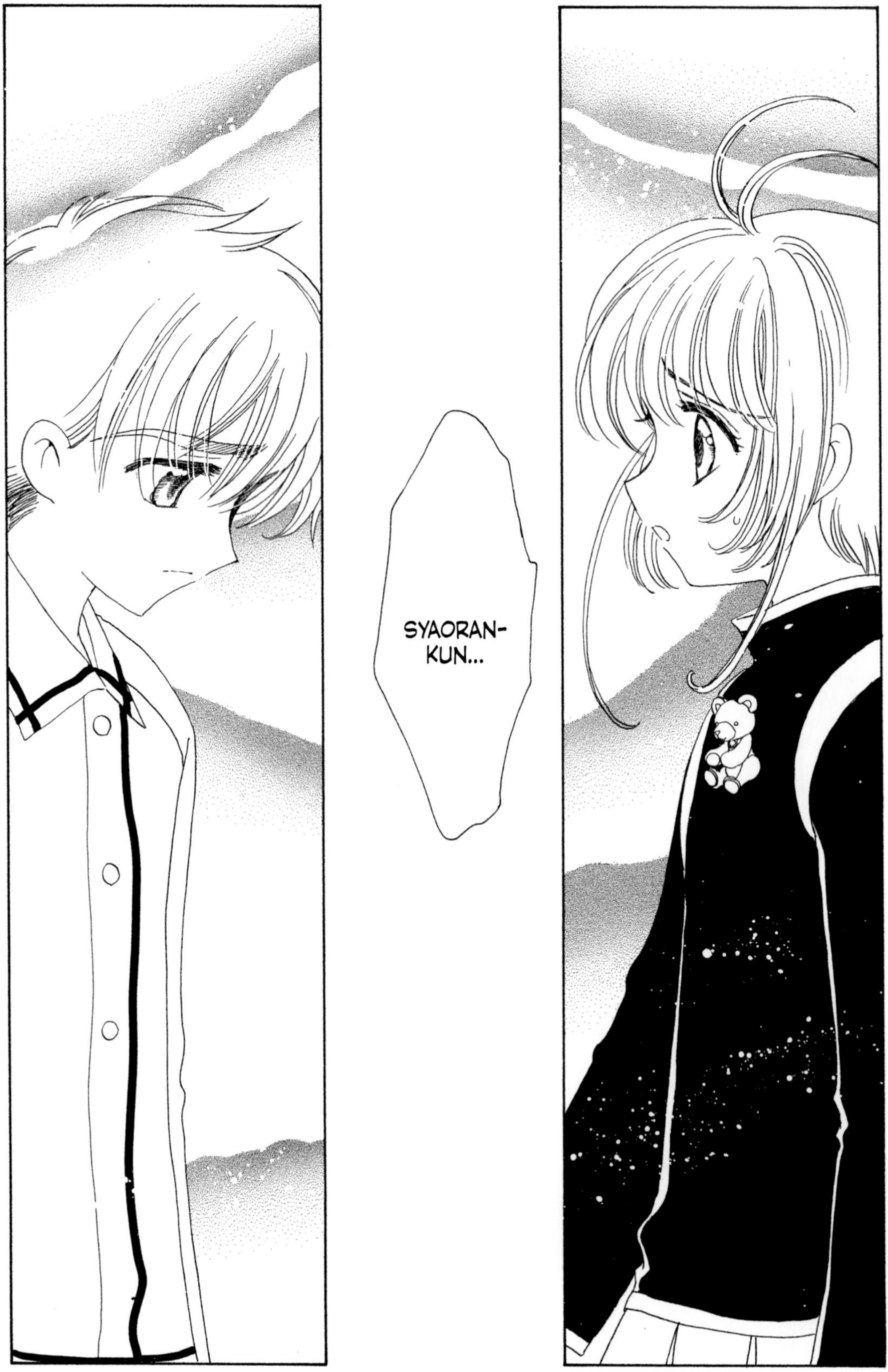
SYAORAN-KUN...

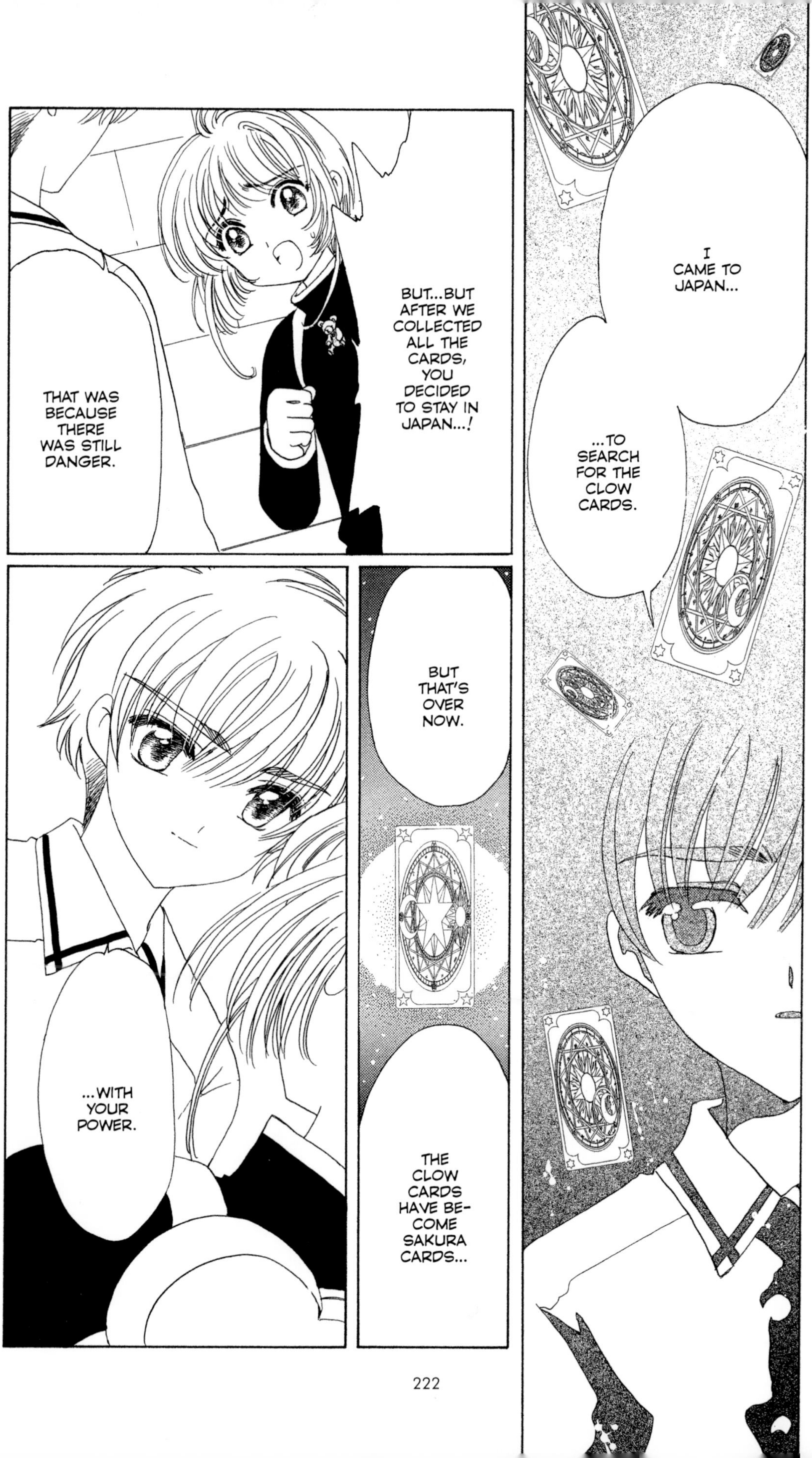
I CAME TO JAPAN...
...TO SEARCH FOR THE CLOW CARDS.
BUT...BUT AFTER WE COLLECTED ALL THE CARDS, YOU DECIDED TO STAY IN JAPAN...!
THAT WAS BECAUSE THERE WAS STILL DANGER.
BUT THAT'S OVER NOW.
THE CLOW CARDS HAVE BE-COME SAKURA CARDS...
...WITH YOUR POWER.

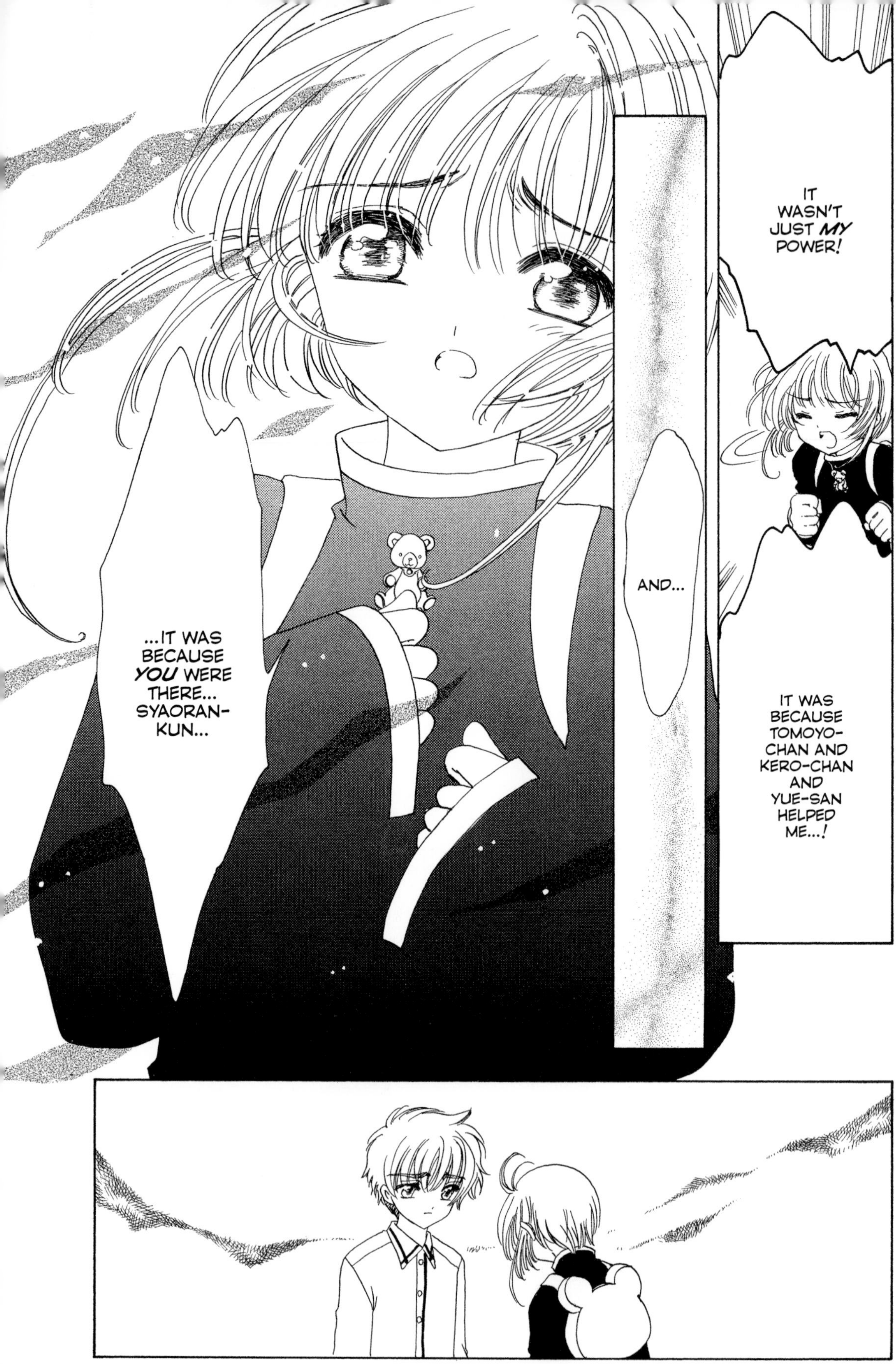
IT WASN'T JUST *MY* POWER!
IT WAS BECAUSE TOMOYO-CHAN AND KERO-CHAN AND YUE-SAN HELPED ME...!
AND...
...IT WAS BECAUSE *YOU* WERE THERE... SYAORAN-KUN...

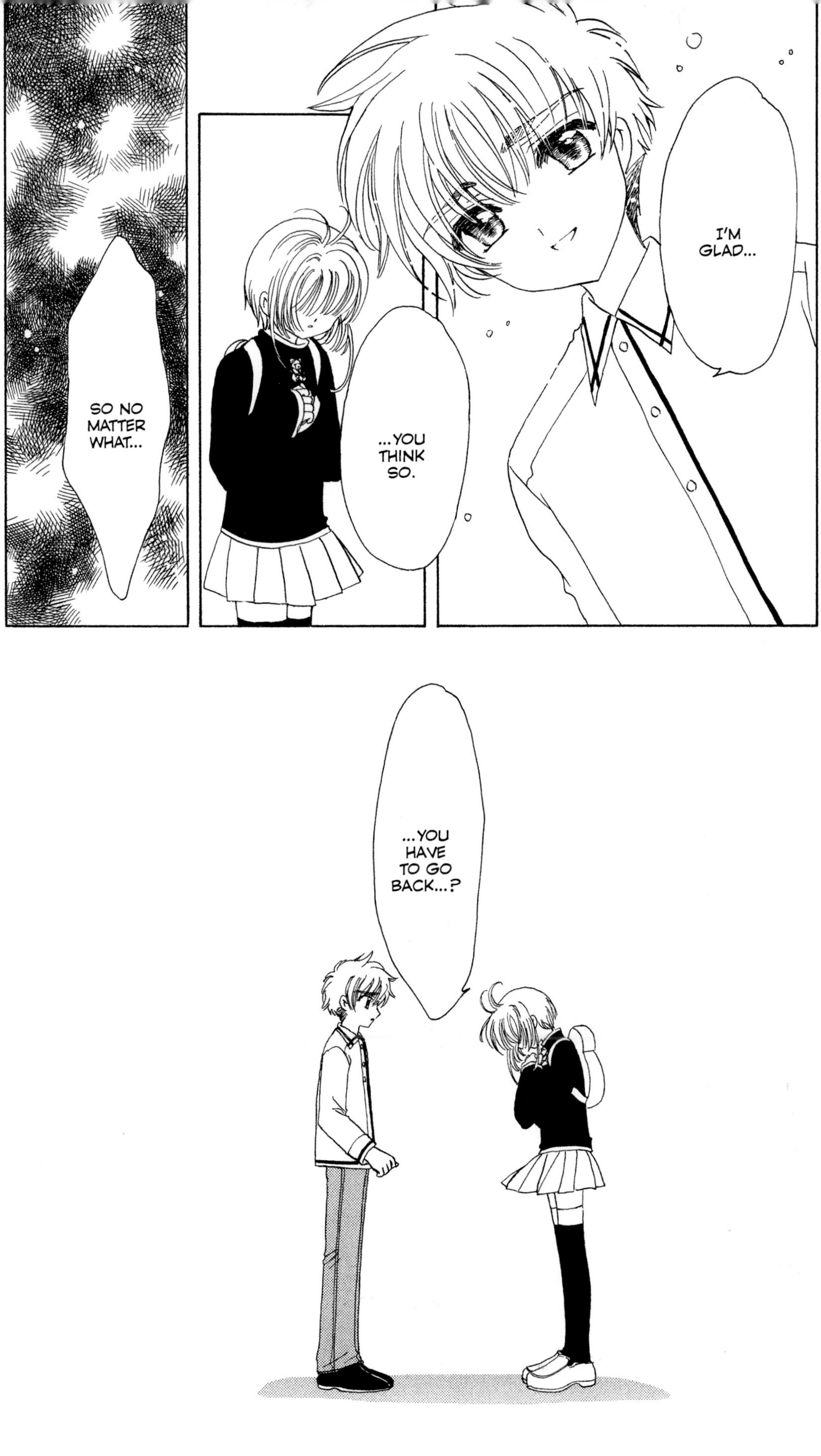
I'M GLAD...
...YOU THINK SO.
SO NO MATTER WHAT...
...YOU HAVE TO GO BACK...?

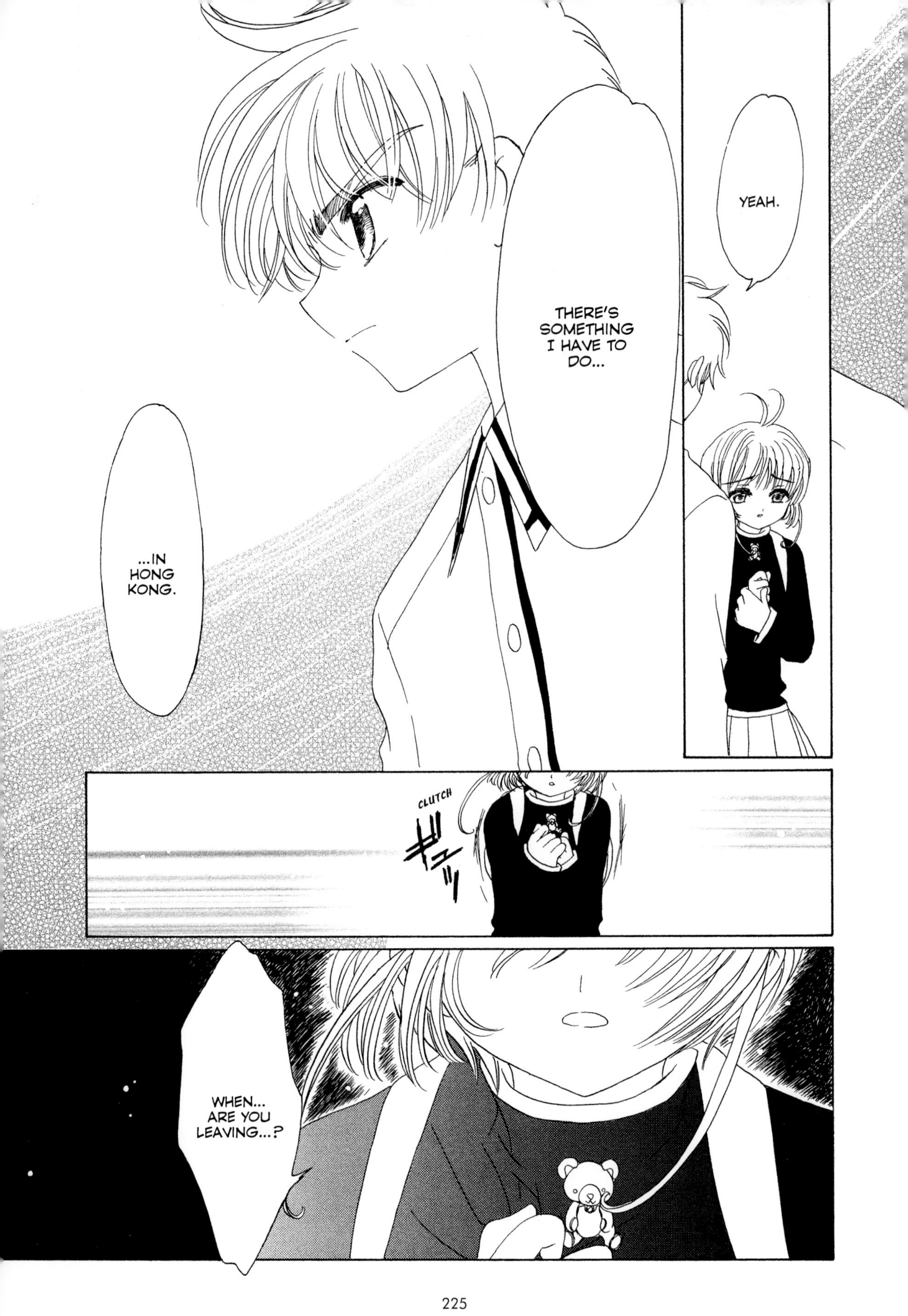
YEAH.
THERE'S SOMETHING I HAVE TO DO...
...IN HONG KONG.
CLUTCH
ギュッ
WHEN... ARE YOU LEAVING...?

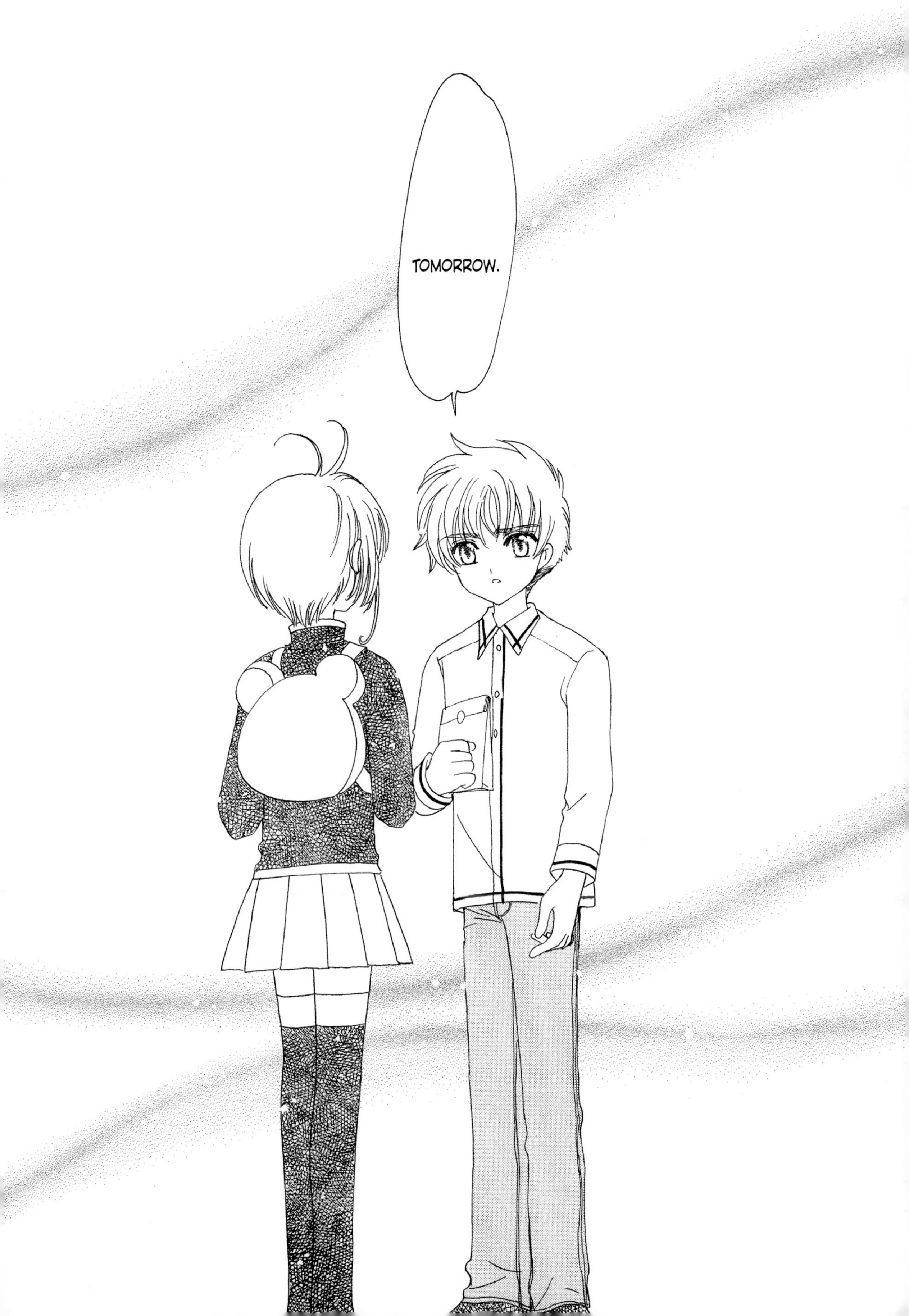
TOMORROW.

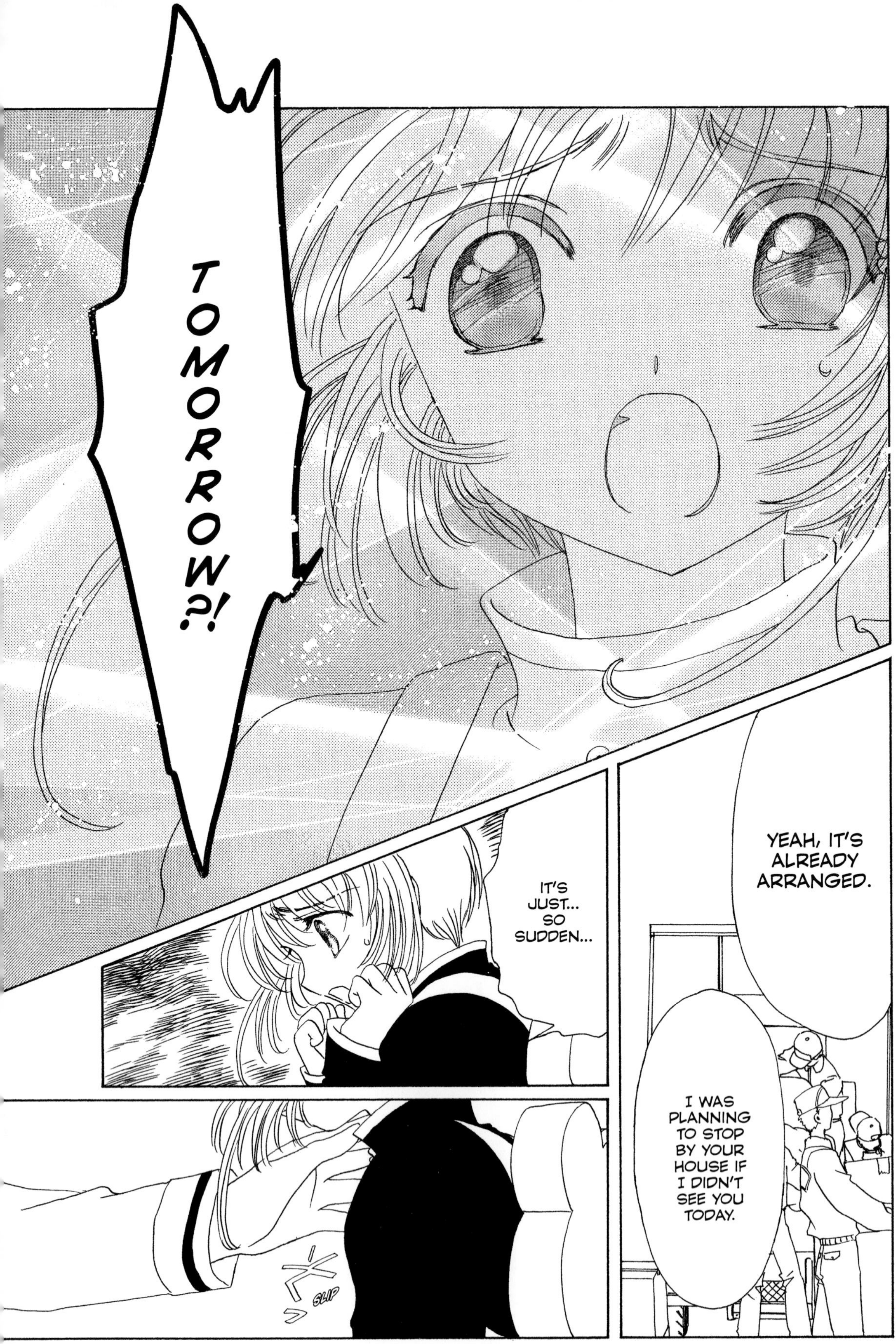
TOMORROW?!
YEAH, IT'S ALREADY ARRANGED.
I WAS PLANNING TO STOP BY YOUR HOUSE IF I DIDN'T SEE YOU TODAY.
IT'S JUST... SO SUDDEN...
SLIP

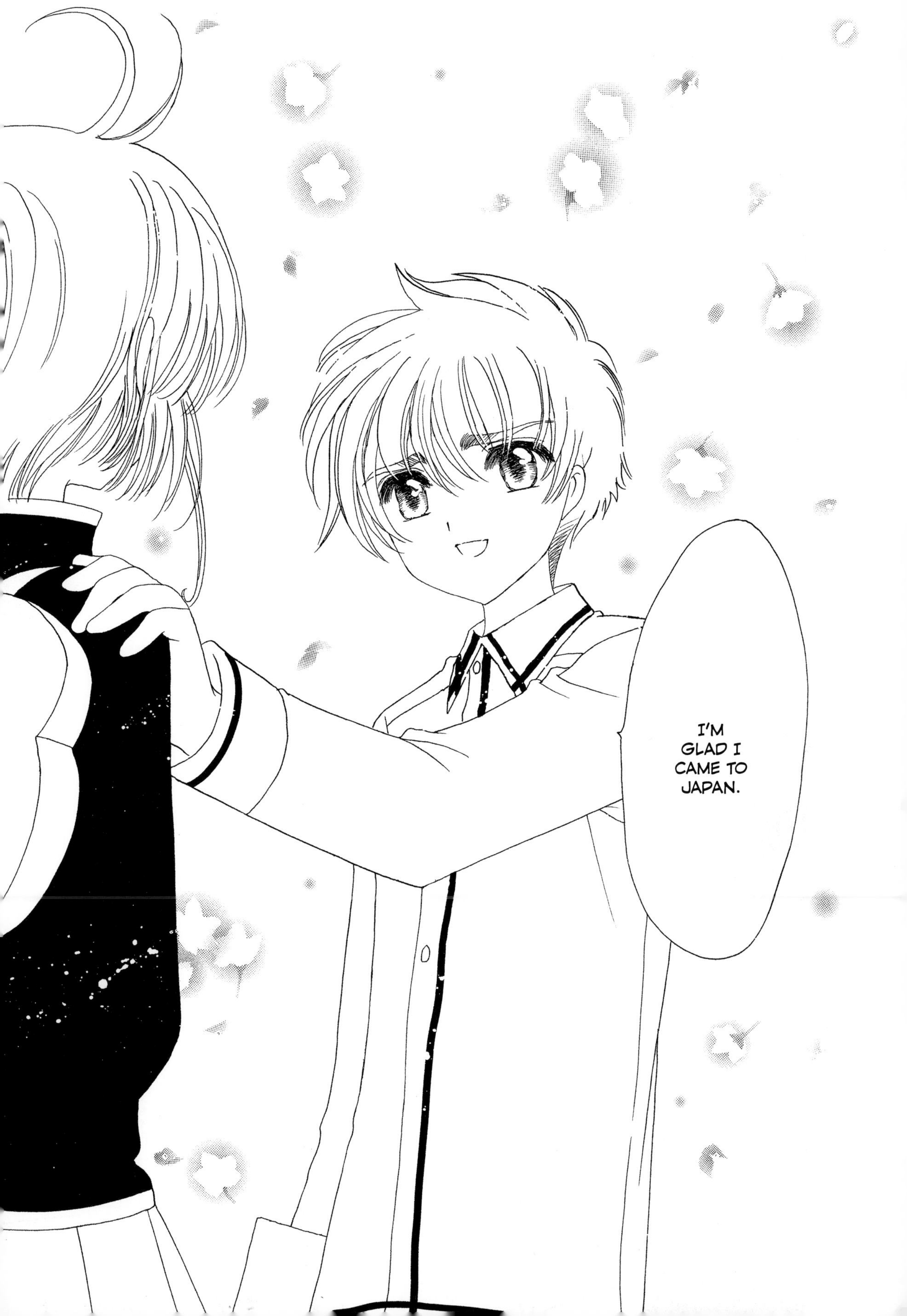
I'M GLAD I CAME TO JAPAN.

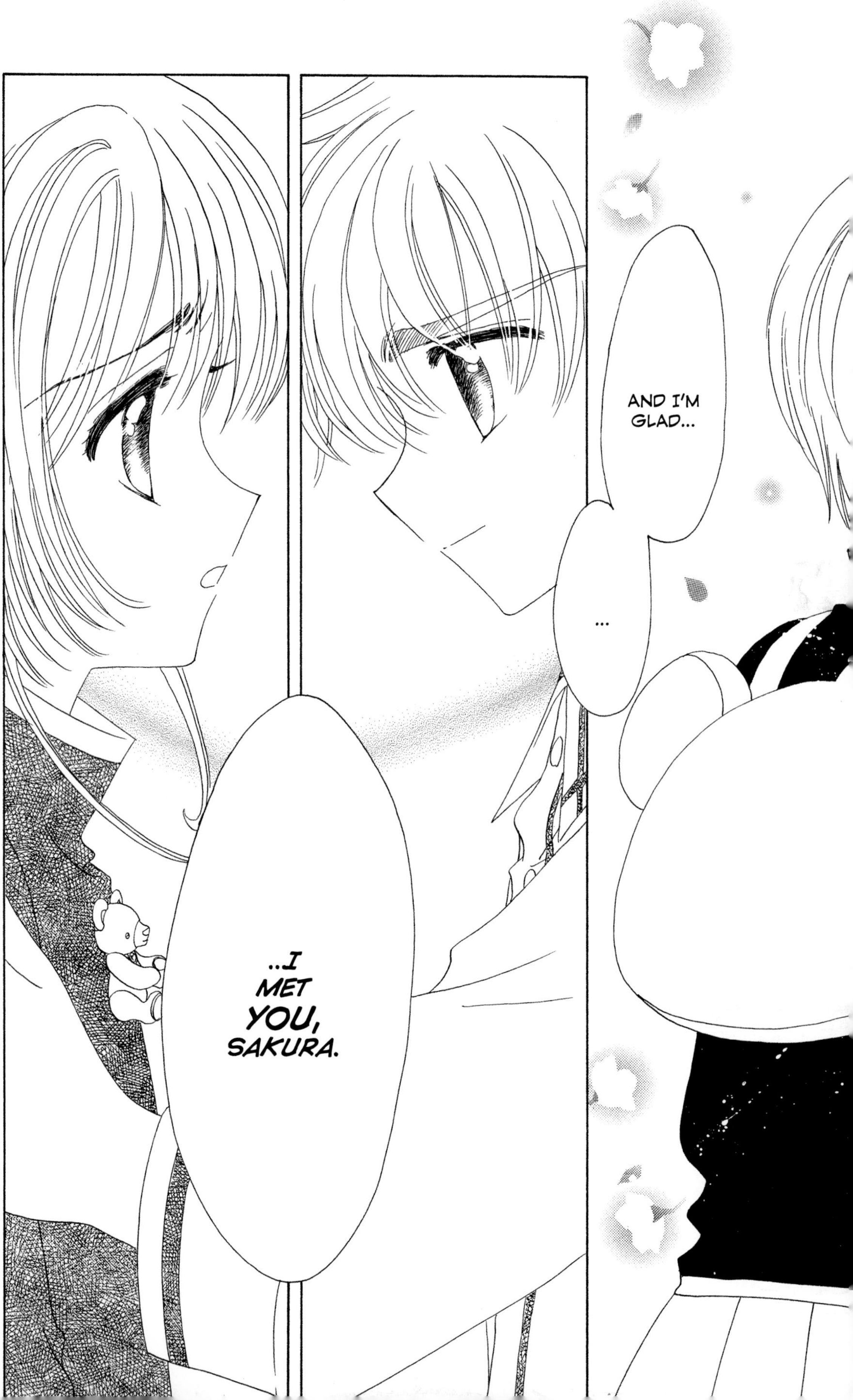
AND I'M GLAD...
...
..I MET YOU, SAKURA.

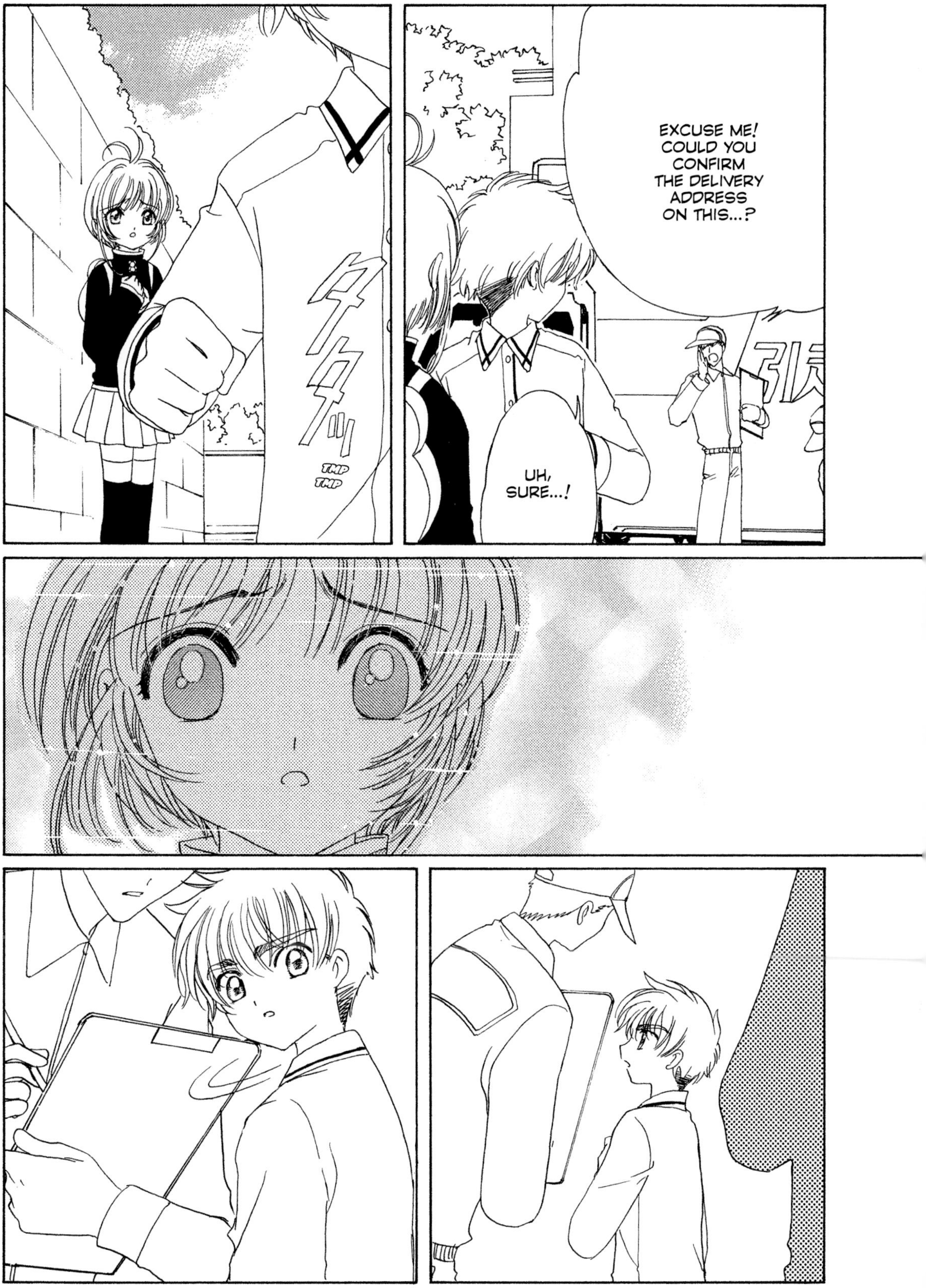
EXCUSE ME! COULD YOU CONFIRM THE DELIVERY ADDRESS ON THIS...?
UH, SURE...!
タタタッ
TMP TMP

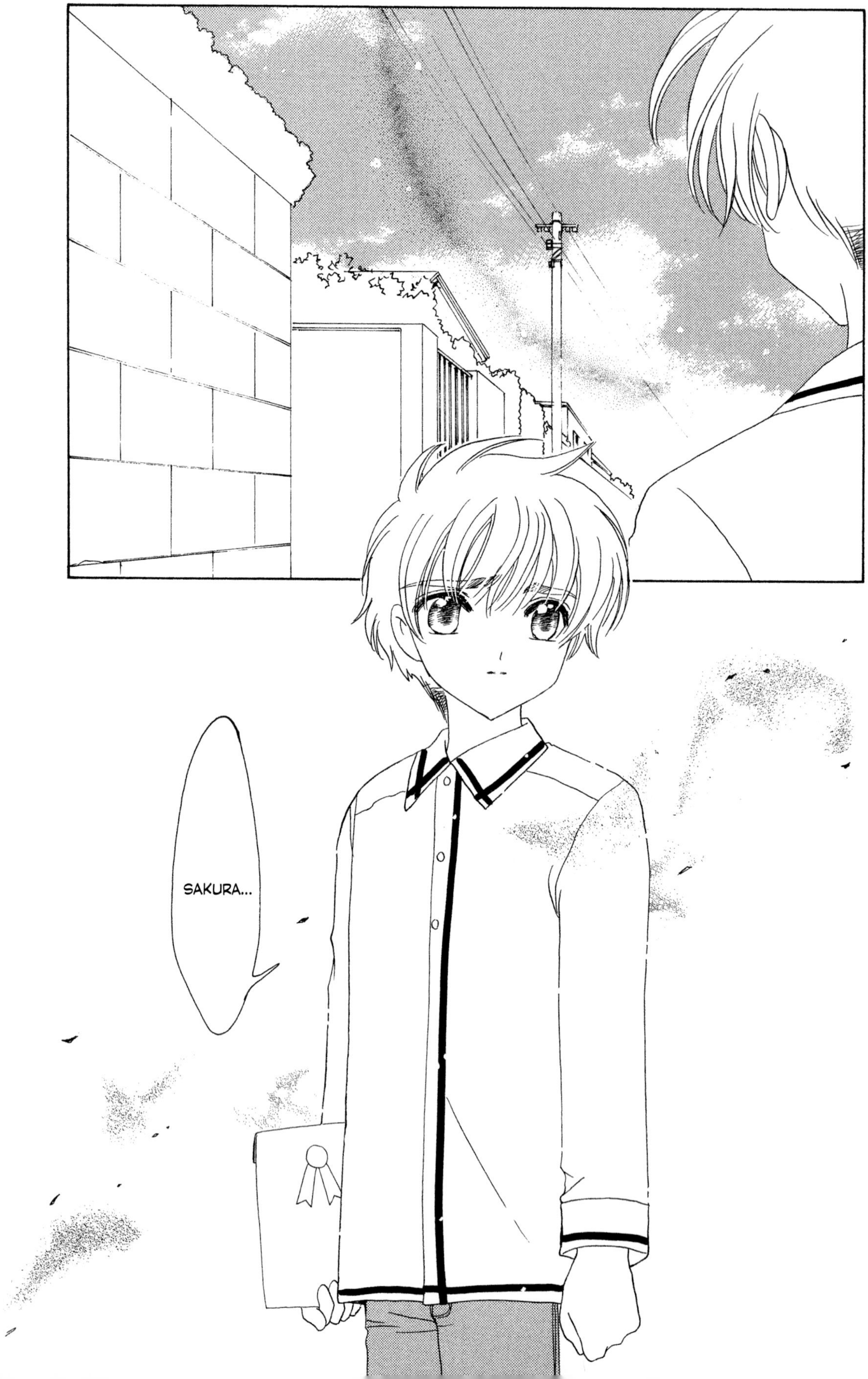
SAKURA...

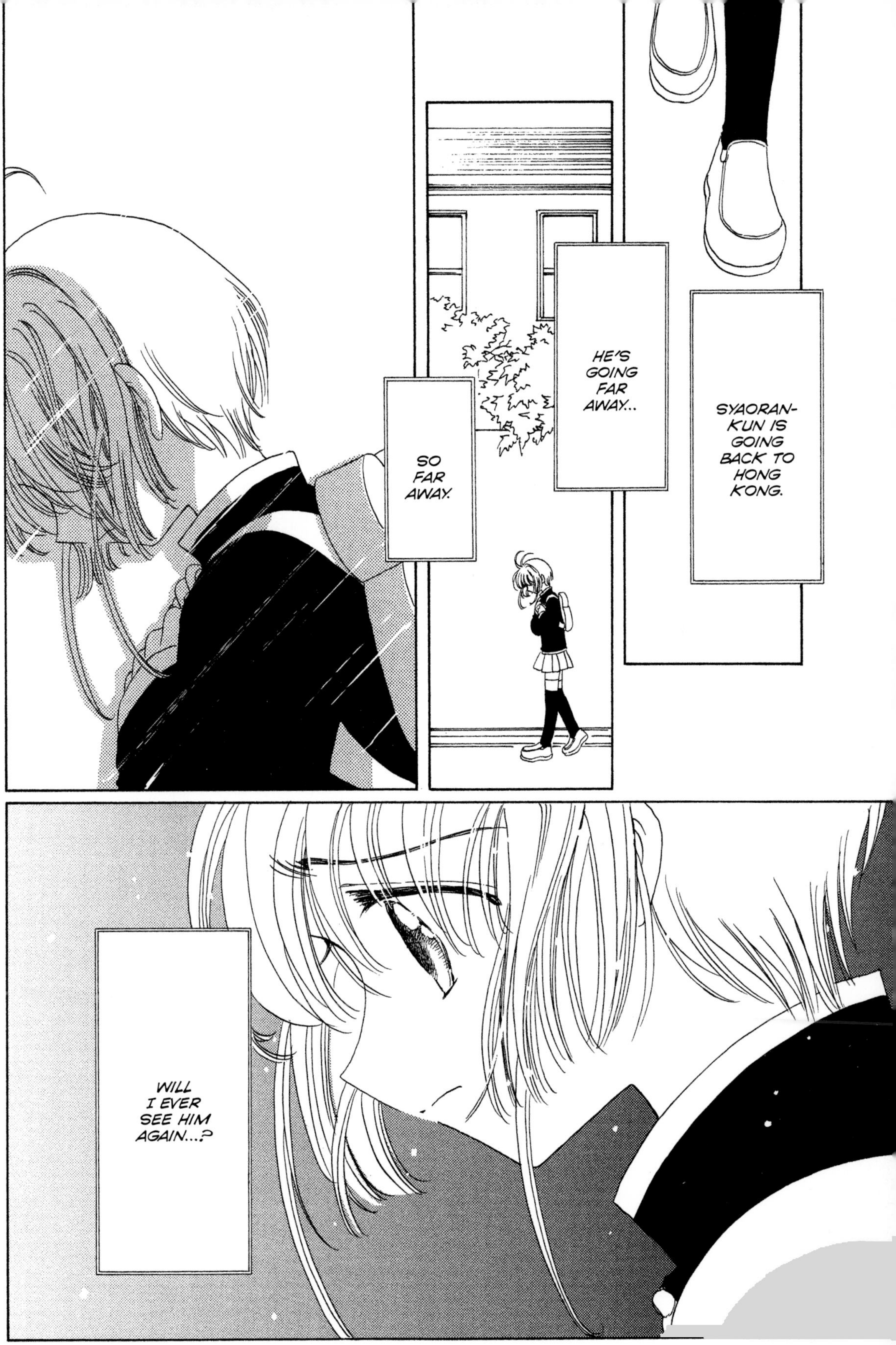
SYAORAN-KUN IS GOING BACK TO HONG KONG.
HE'S GOING FAR AWAY...
SO FAR AWAY.
WILL I EVER SEE HIM AGAIN...?

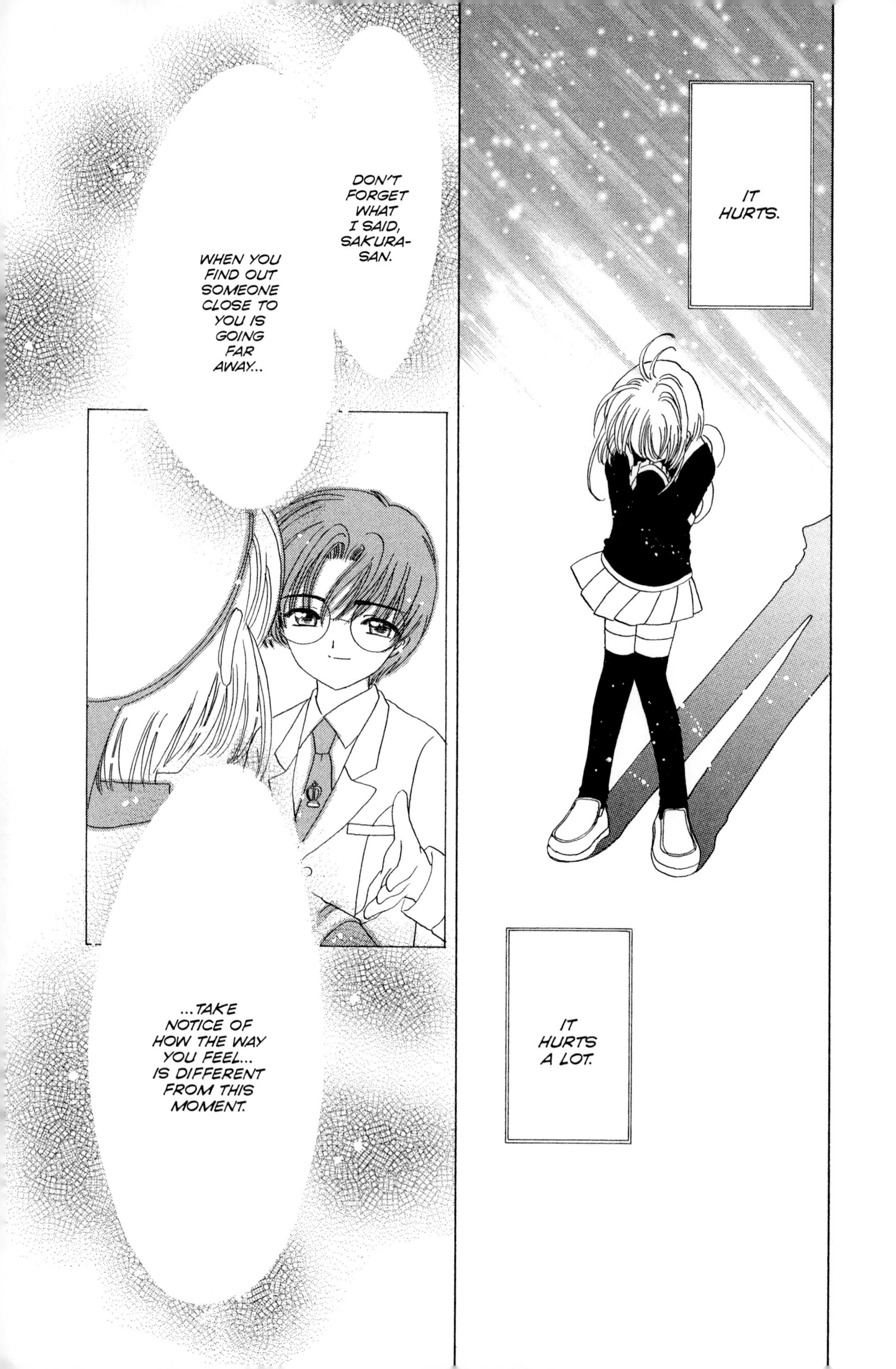
IT HURTS.
IT HURTS A LOT.
DON'T FORGET WHAT I SAID, SAKURA-SAN.
WHEN YOU FIND OUT SOMEONE CLOSE TO YOU IS GOING FAR AWAY...
...TAKE NOTICE OF HOW THE WAY YOU FEEL... IS DIFFERENT FROM THIS MOMENT.

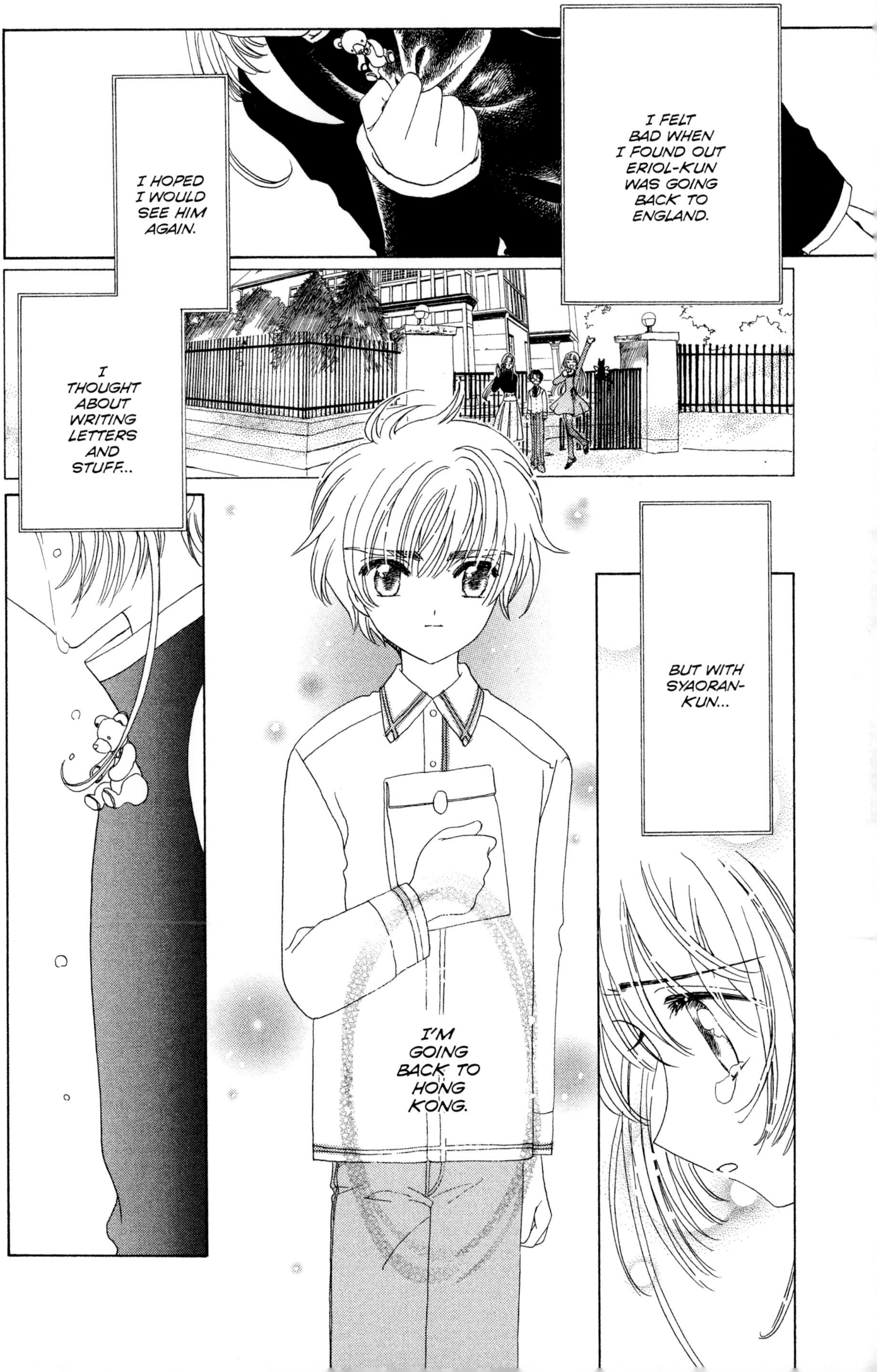
I FELT BAD WHEN I FOUND OUT ERIOL-KUN WAS GOING BACK TO ENGLAND.
I HOPED I WOULD SEE HIM AGAIN.
I THOUGHT ABOUT WRITING LETTERS AND STUFF...
BUT WITH SYAORAN-KUN...
I'M GOING BACK TO HONG KONG.

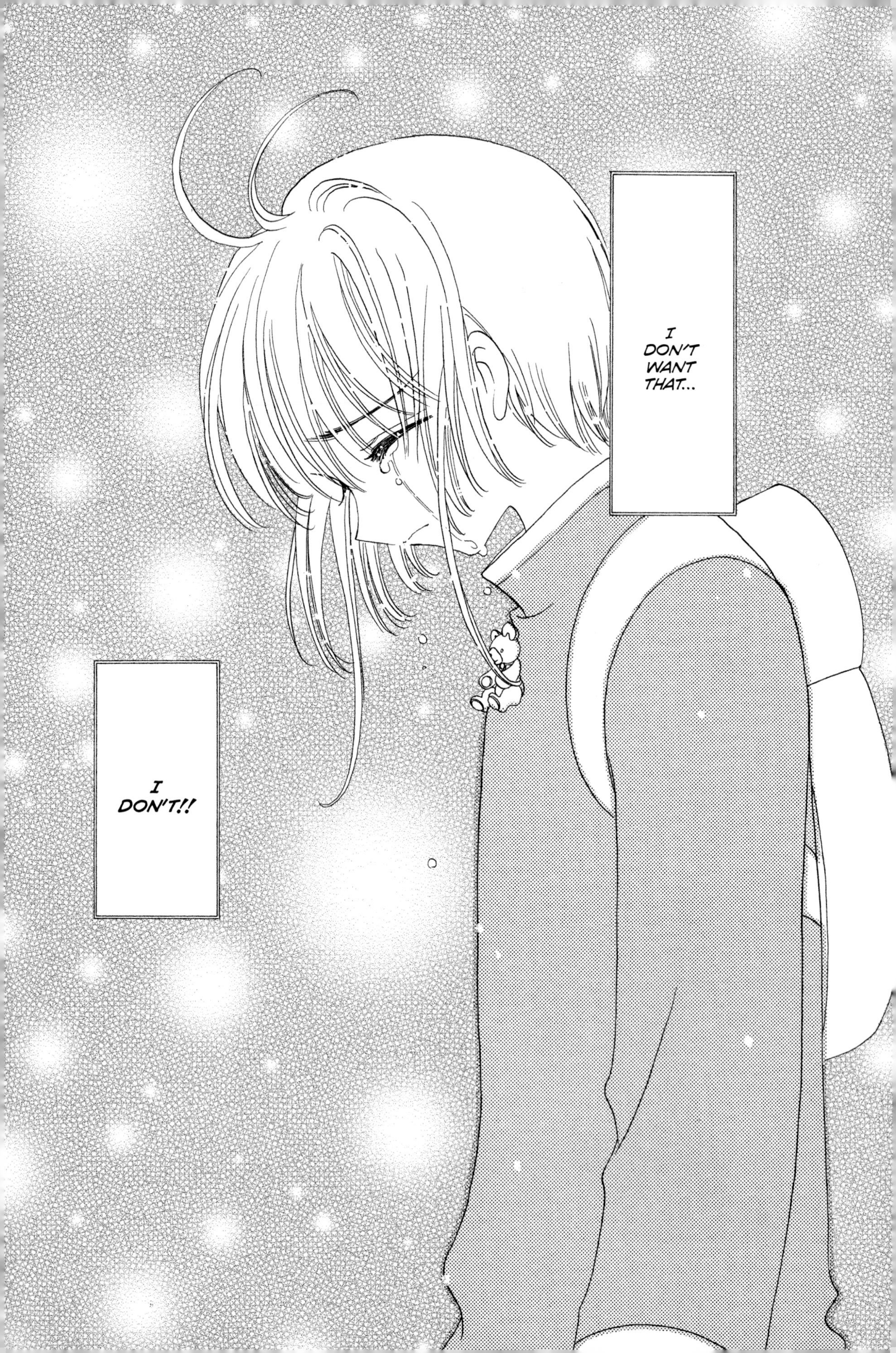
I DON'T WANT THAT...
I DON'T!!

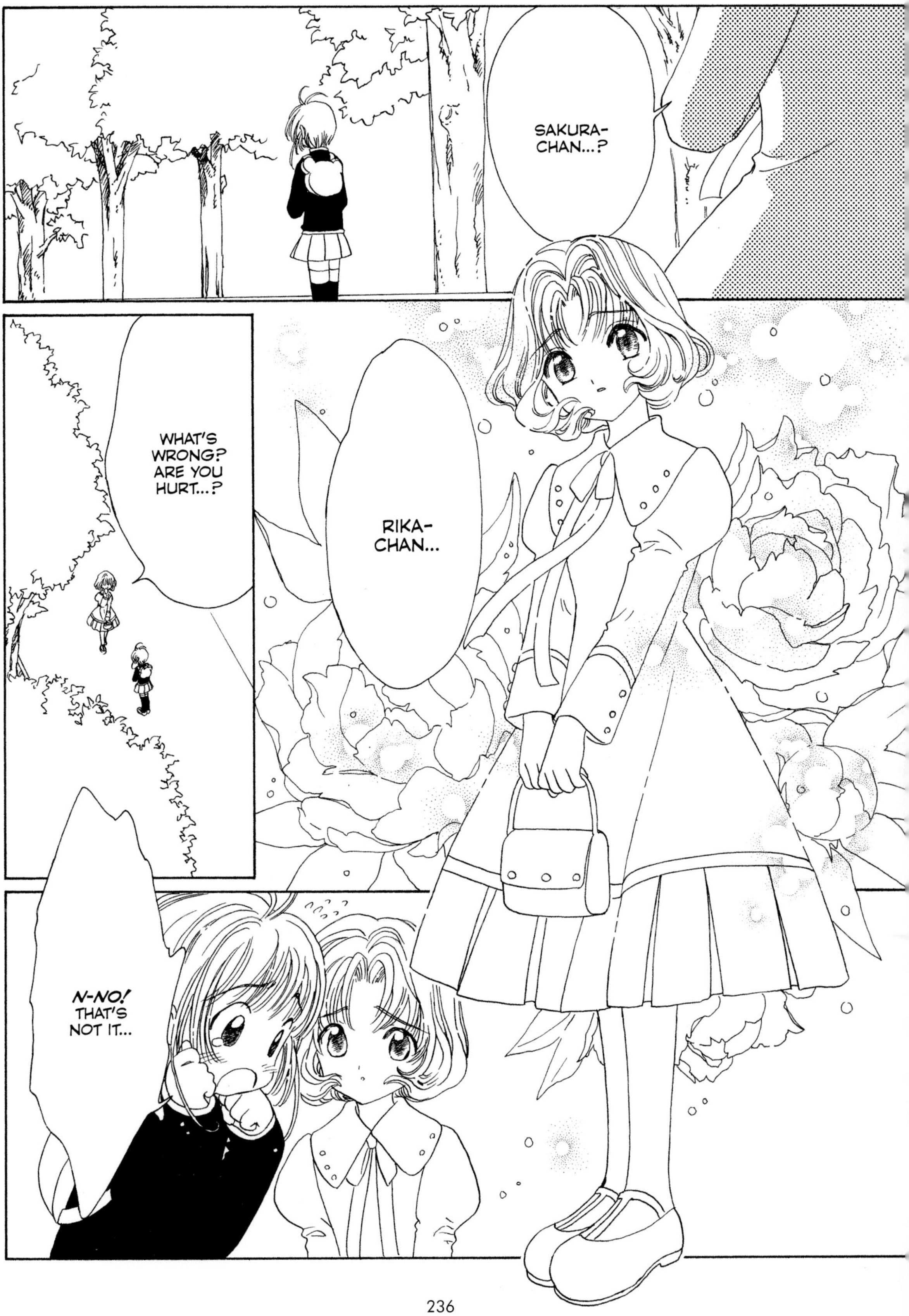
SAKURA-CHAN...?
RIKA-CHAN...
WHAT'S WRONG? ARE YOU HURT...?
N-NO! THAT'S NOT IT...

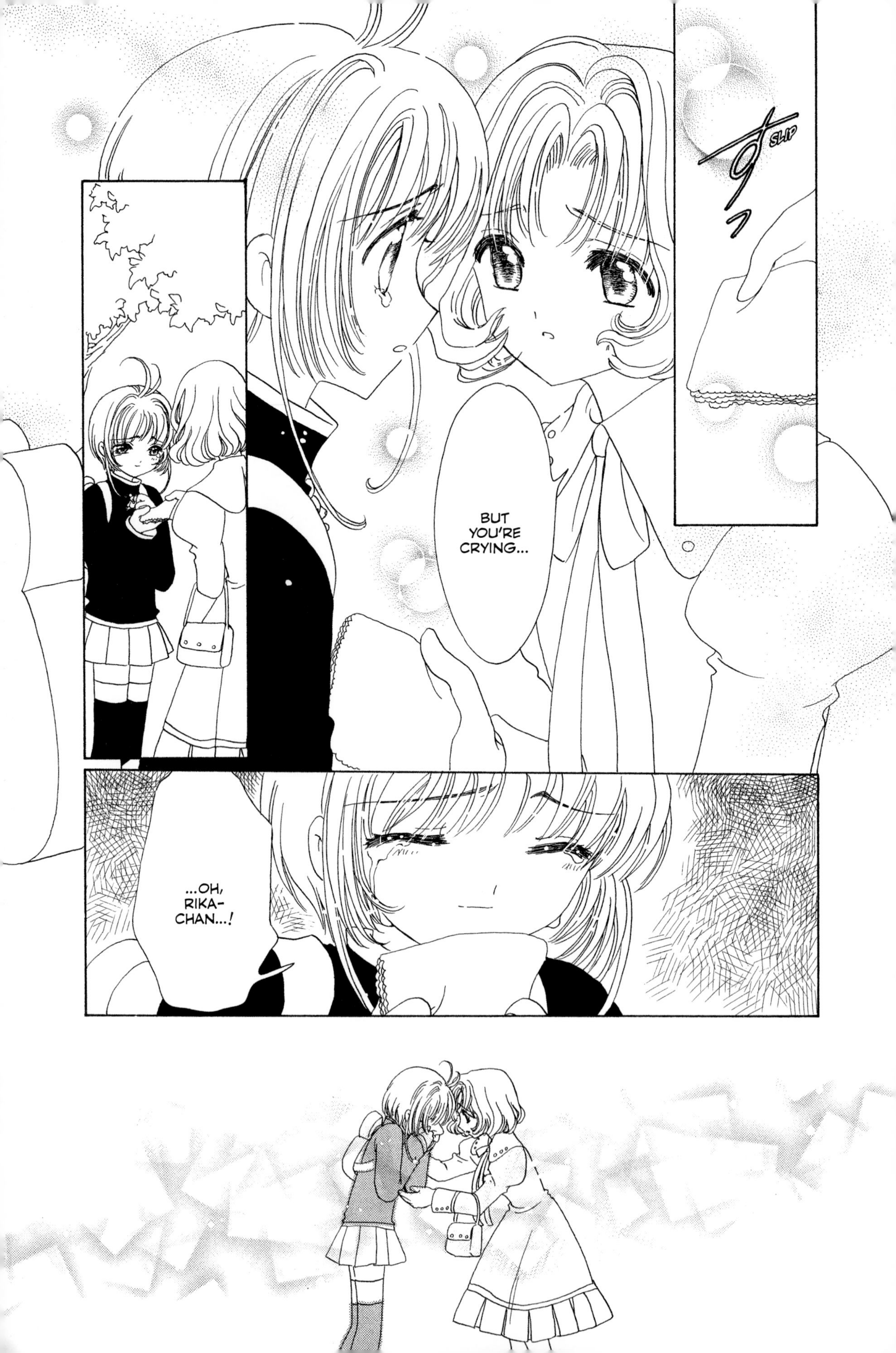
SLIP
BUT YOU'RE CRYING...
...OH, RIKA-CHAN...!

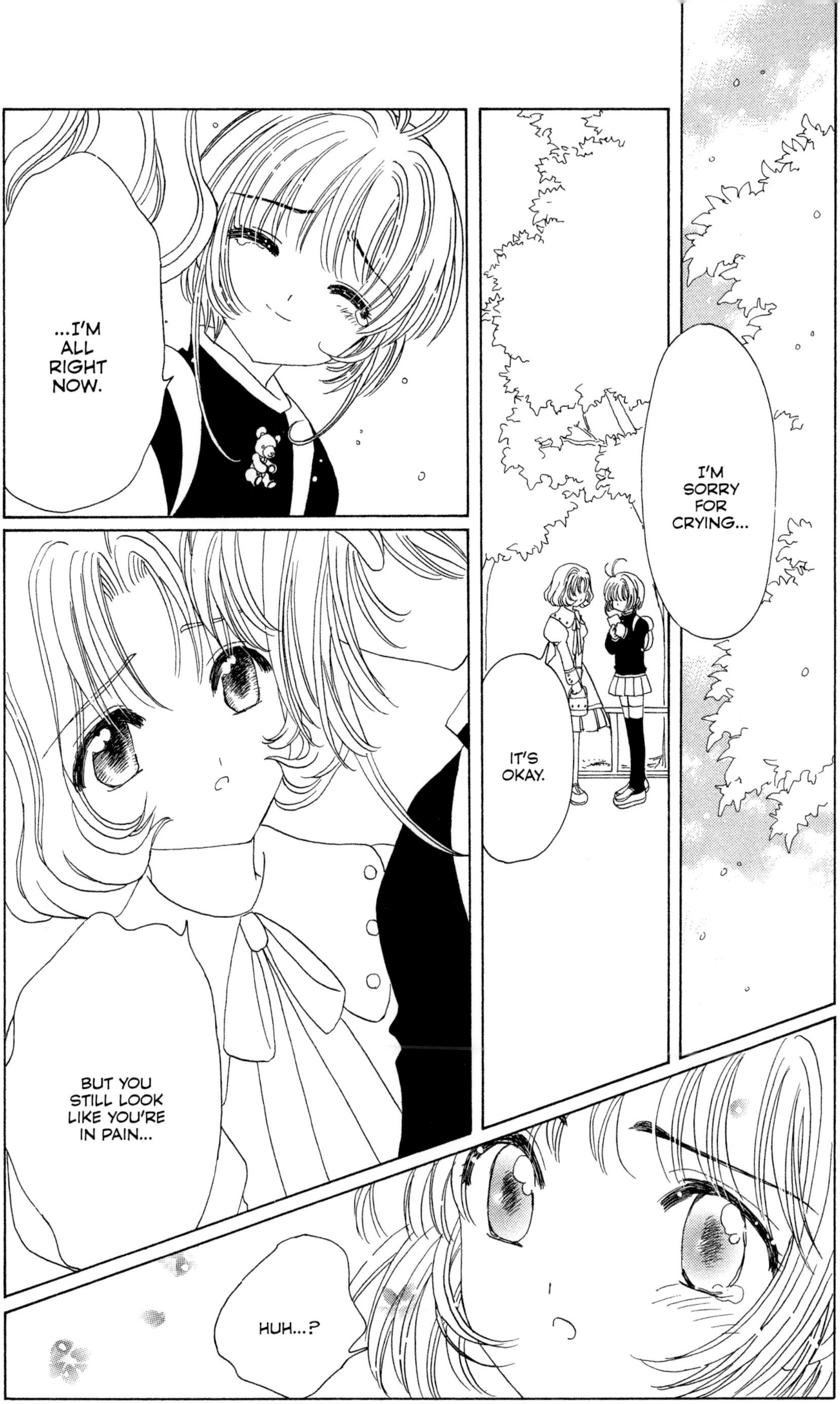
I'M SORRY FOR CRYING...
IT'S OKAY.
...I'M ALL RIGHT NOW.
BUT YOU STILL LOOK LIKE YOU'RE IN PAIN...
HUH...?

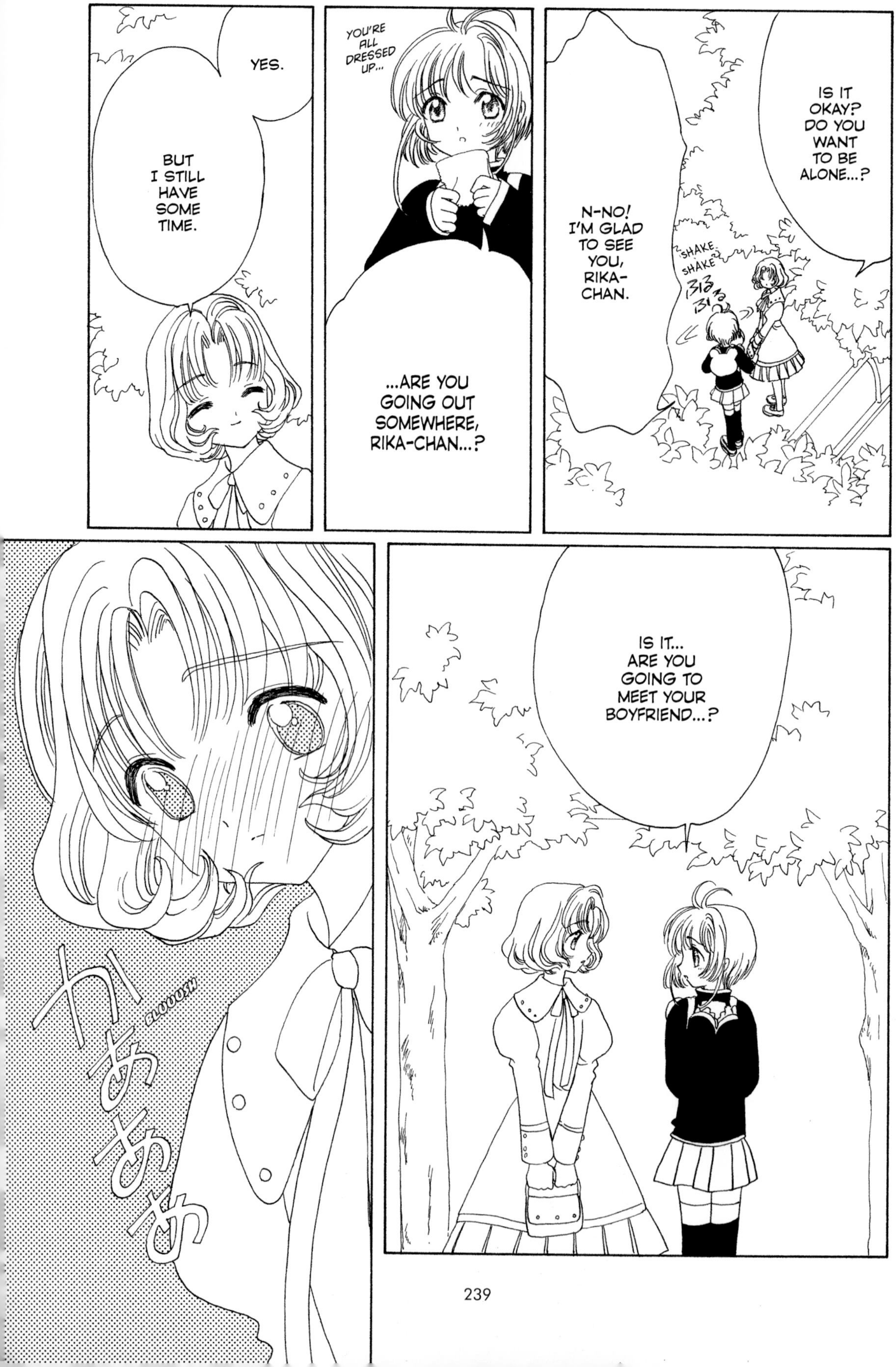
IS IT OKAY? DO YOU WANT TO BE ALONE...?
N-NO! I'M GLAD TO SEE YOU, RIKA-CHAN.
SHAKE SHAKE
ふるふる
YOU'RE ALL DRESSED UP...
...ARE YOU GOING OUT SOMEWHERE, RIKA-CHAN...?
YES.
BUT I STILL HAVE SOME TIME.
IS IT... ARE YOU GOING TO MEET YOUR BOYFRIEND...?
かあああ
BLOOOSH

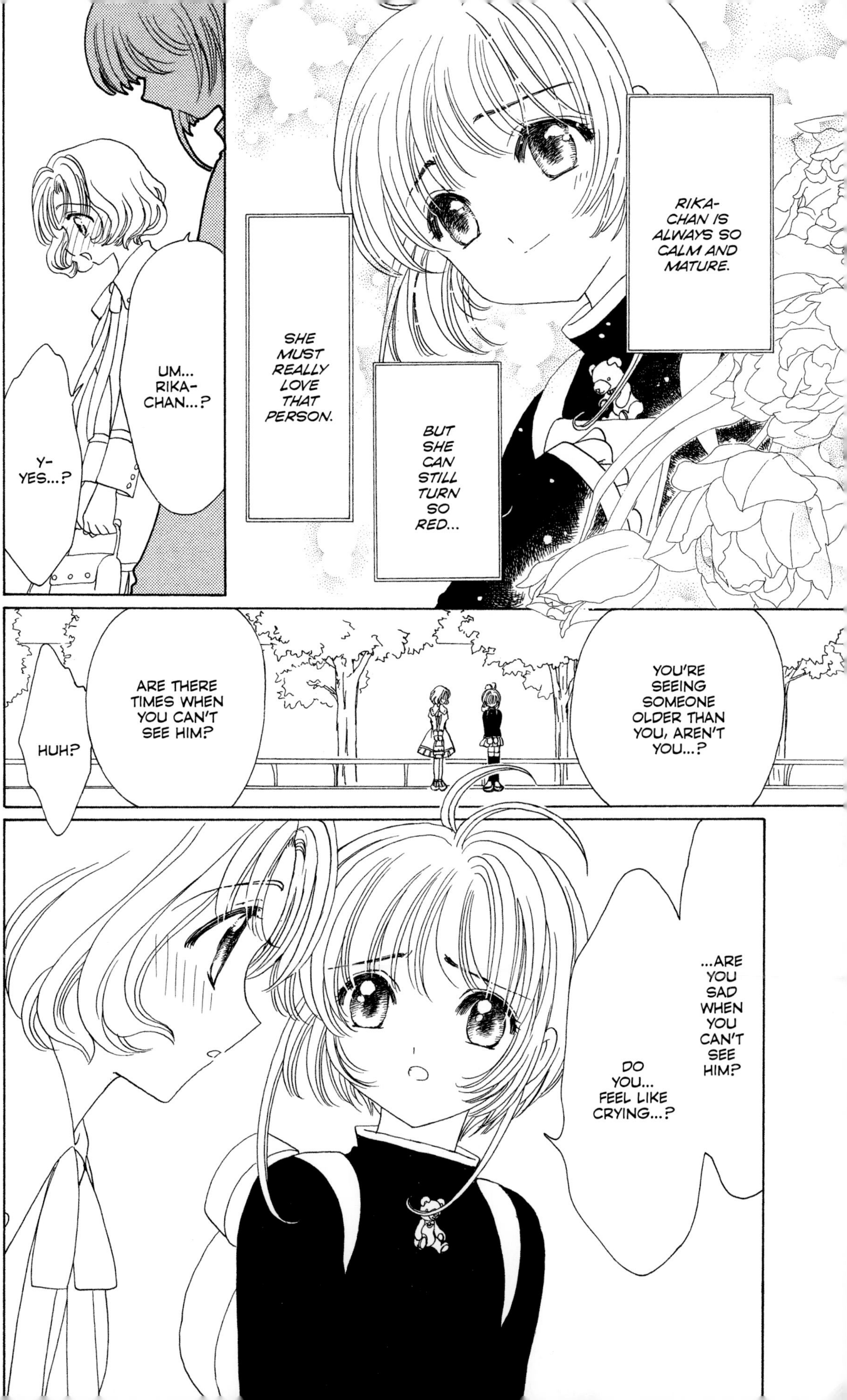
RIKA-CHAN IS ALWAYS SO CALM AND MATURE.
SHE MUST REALLY LOVE THAT PERSON.
BUT SHE CAN STILL TURN SO RED...
UM... RIKA-CHAN...?
Y-YES...?
YOU'RE SEEING SOMEONE OLDER THAN YOU, AREN'T YOU...?
ARE THERE TIMES WHEN YOU CAN'T SEE HIM?
HUH?
...ARE YOU SAD WHEN YOU CAN'T SEE HIM?
DO YOU... FEEL LIKE CRYING...?

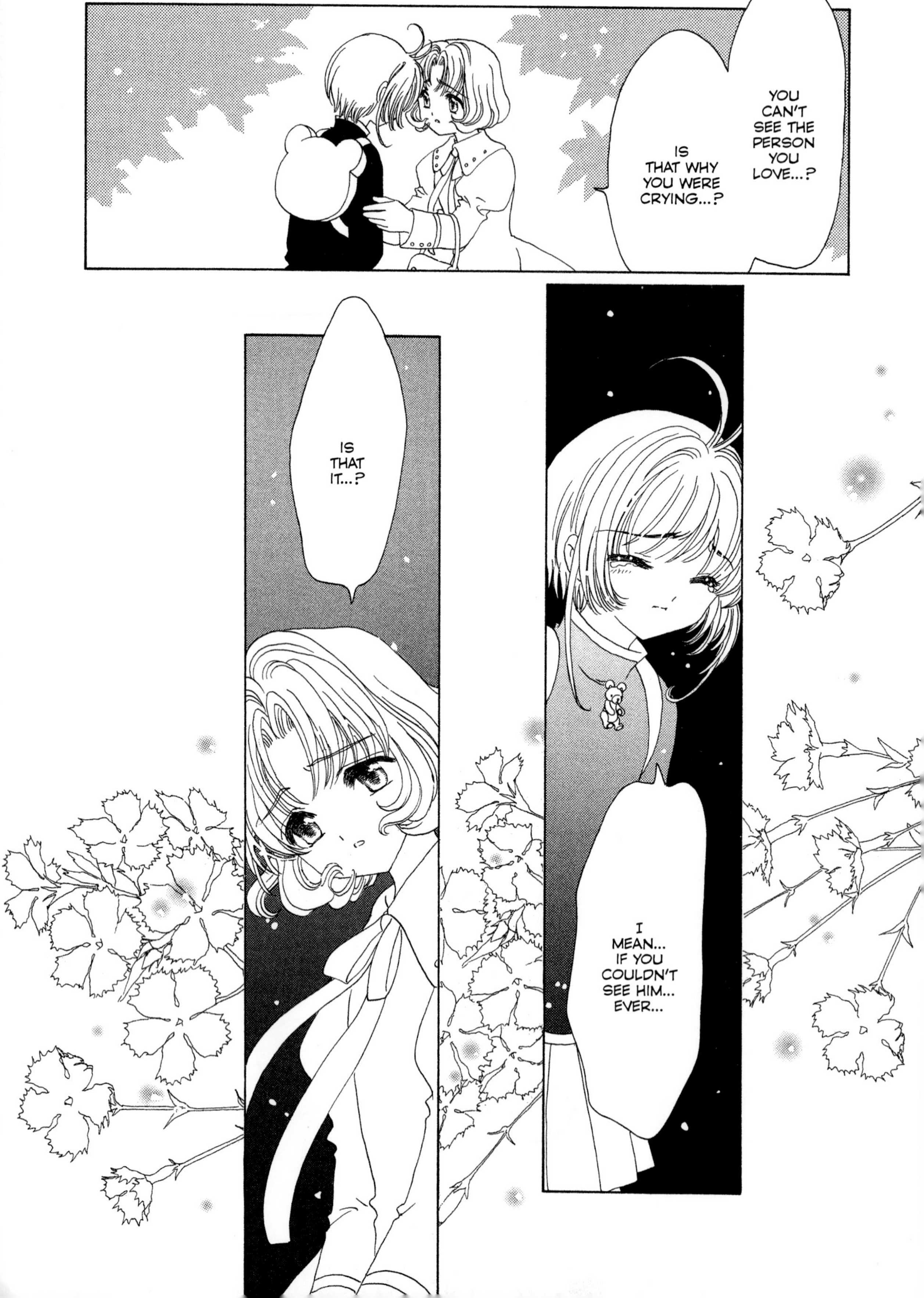
YOU CAN'T SEE THE PERSON YOU LOVE...?
IS THAT WHY YOU WERE CRYING...?
I MEAN... IF YOU COULDN'T SEE HIM... EVER...
IS THAT IT...?

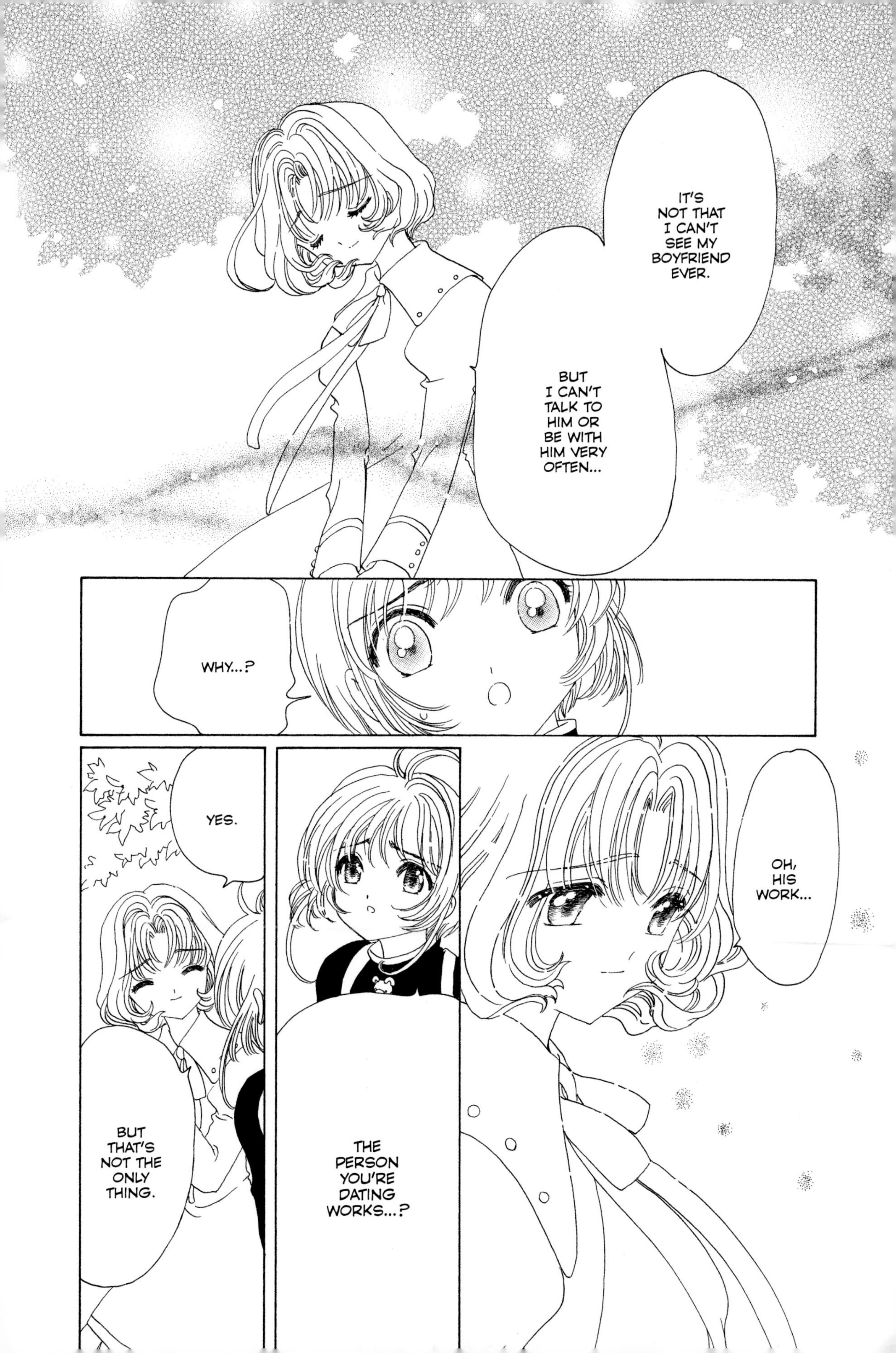
IT'S NOT THAT I CAN'T SEE MY BOYFRIEND EVER.
BUT I CAN'T TALK TO HIM OR BE WITH HIM VERY OFTEN...
WHY...?
OH, HIS WORK...
THE PERSON YOU'RE DATING WORKS...?
YES.
BUT THAT'S NOT THE ONLY THING.

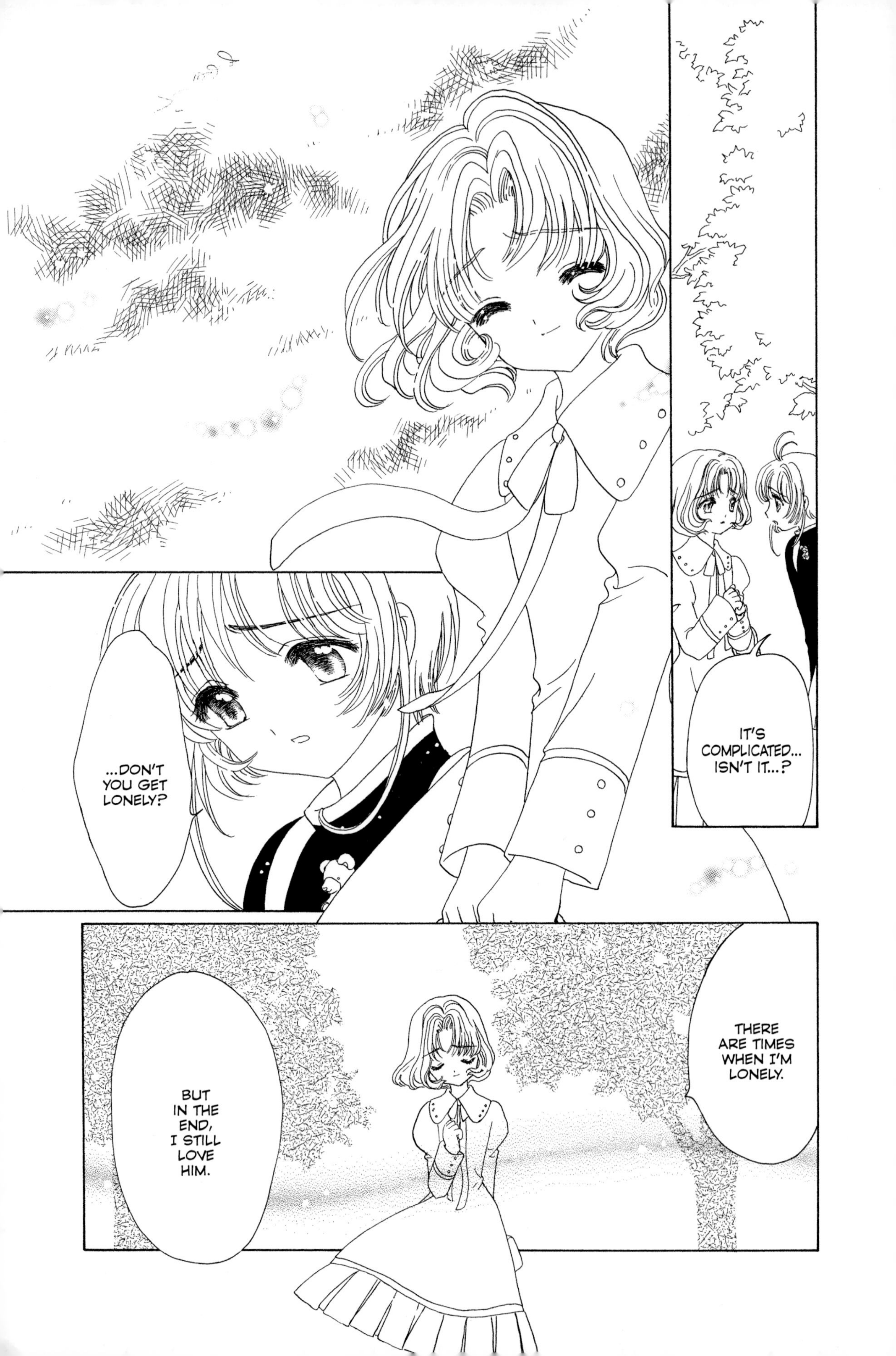
IT'S COMPLICATED... ISN'T IT...?
...DON'T YOU GET LONELY?
THERE ARE TIMES WHEN I'M LONELY.
BUT IN THE END, I STILL LOVE HIM.

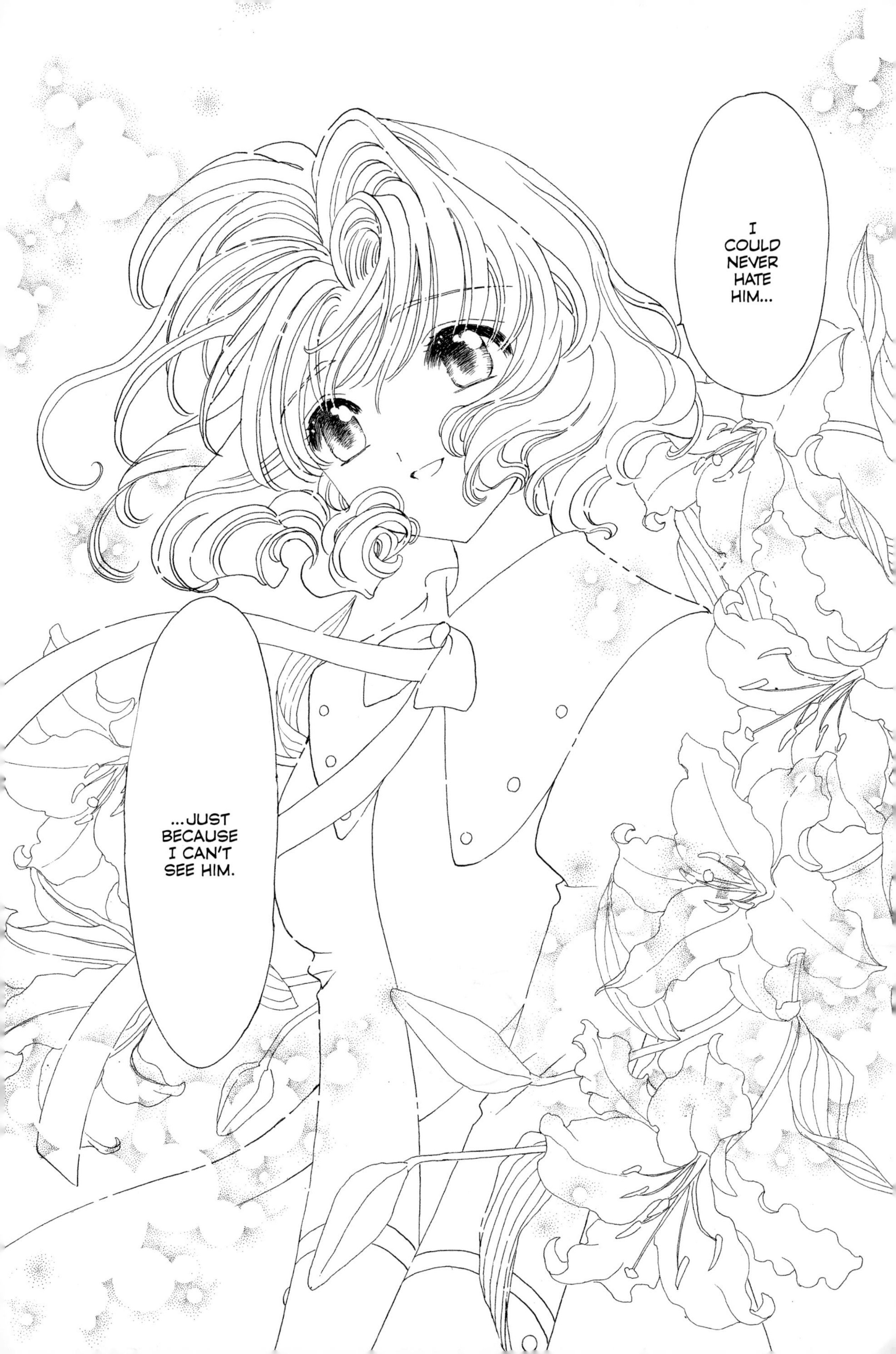
I COULD NEVER HATE HIM...
...JUST BECAUSE I CAN'T SEE HIM.

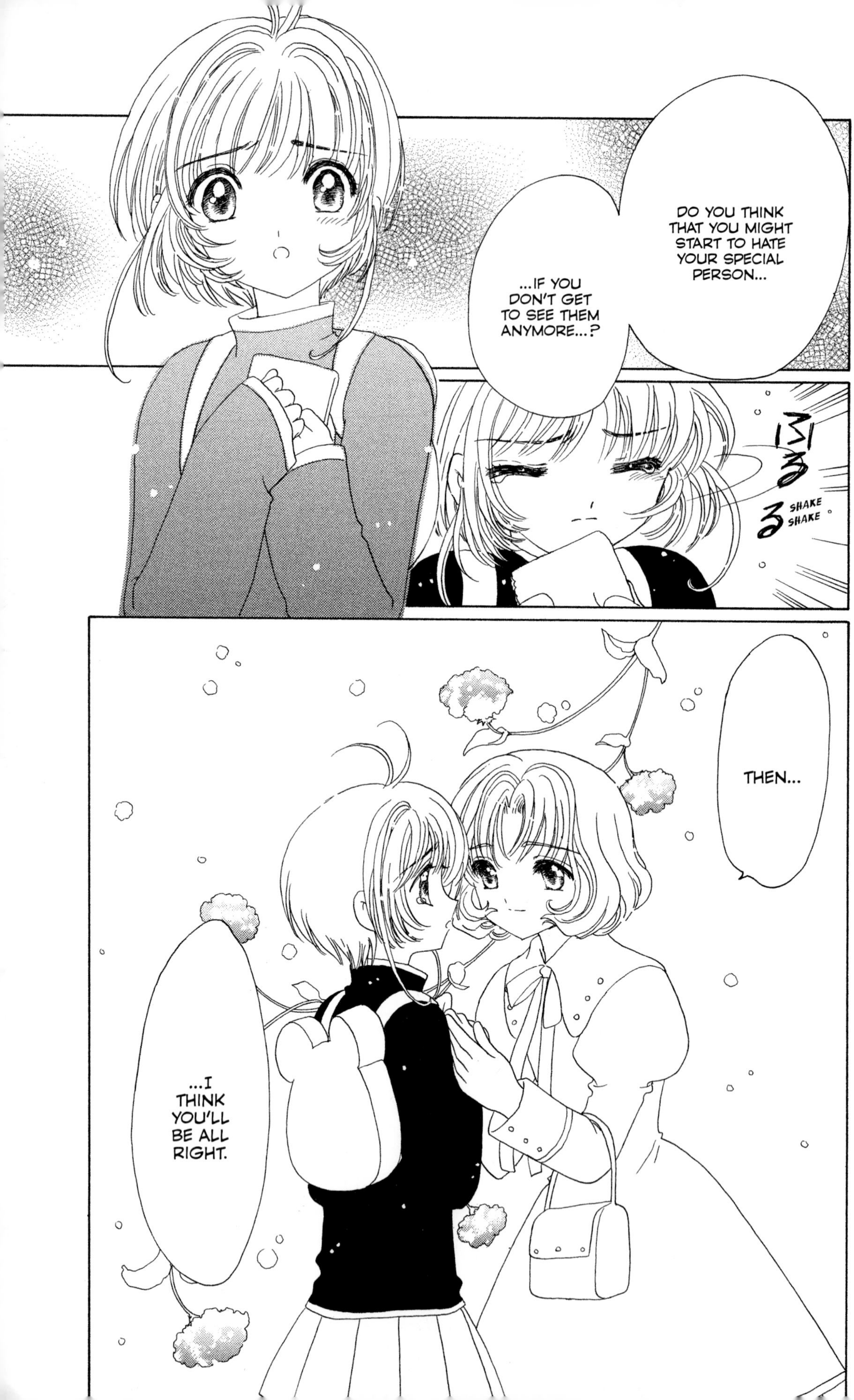
DO YOU THINK THAT YOU MIGHT START TO HATE YOUR SPECIAL PERSON...
...IF YOU DON'T GET TO SEE THEM ANYMORE...?
ふるる
SHAKE SHAKE
THEN...
...I THINK YOU'LL BE ALL RIGHT.

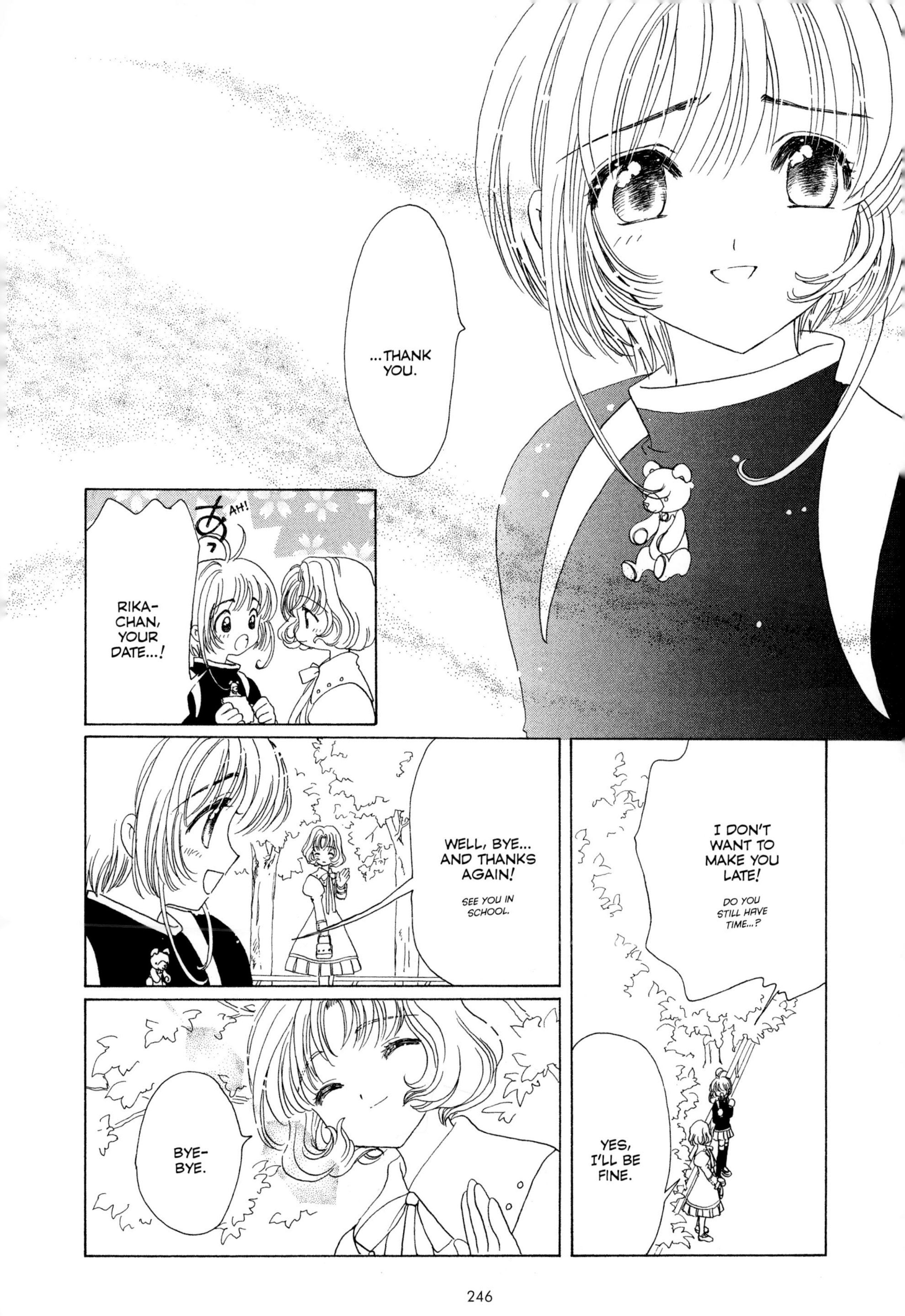
...THANK YOU.
AH!
RIKA-CHAN, YOUR DATE...!
I DON'T WANT TO MAKE YOU LATE!
DO YOU STILL HAVE TIME...?
YES, I'LL BE FINE.
WELL, BYE... AND THANKS AGAIN!
SEE YOU IN SCHOOL.
BYE-BYE.

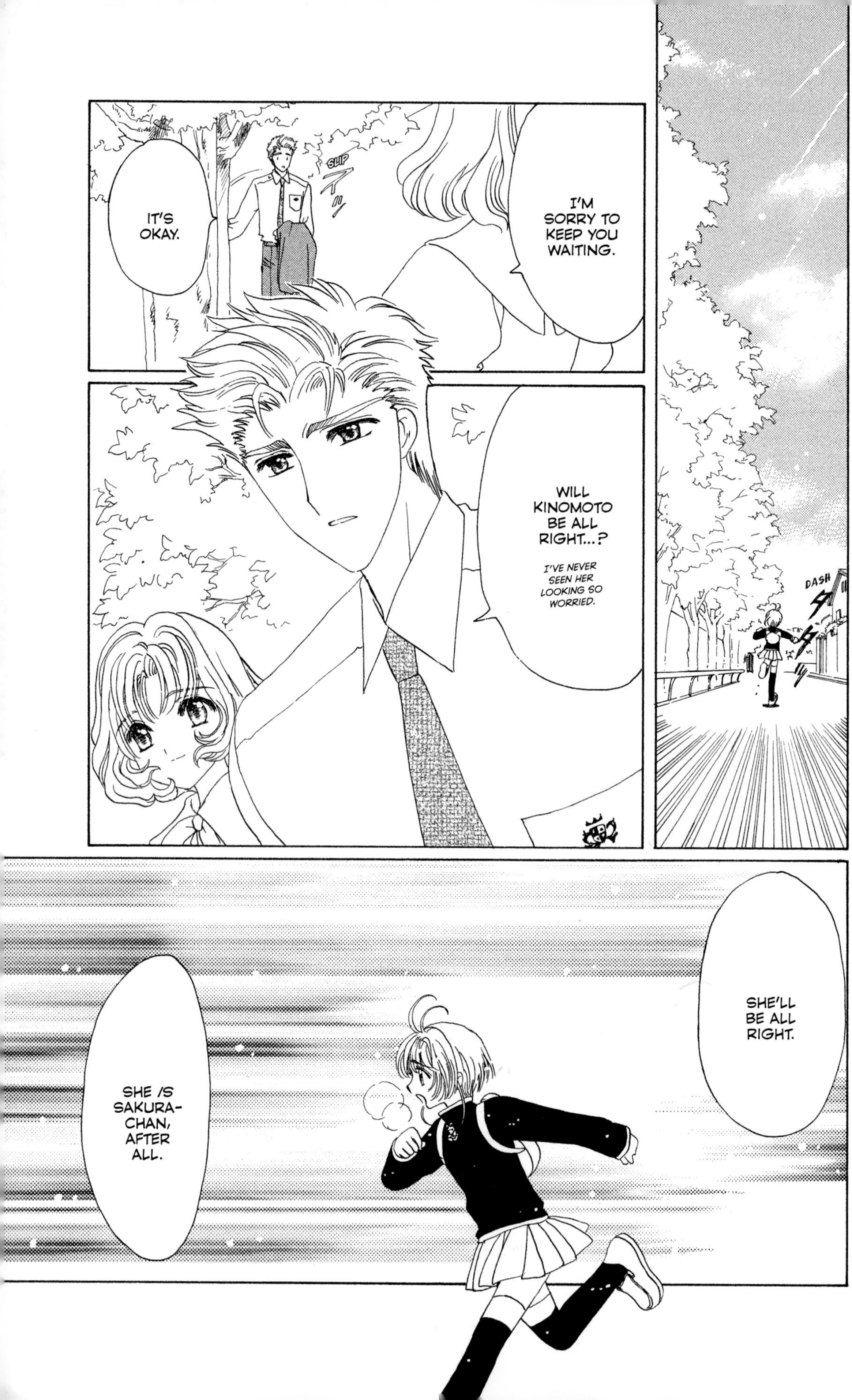
DASH
I'M SORRY TO KEEP YOU WAITING.
SLIP
IT'S OKAY.
WILL KINOMOTO BE ALL RIGHT...?
I'VE NEVER SEEN HER LOOKING SO WORRIED.
SHE'LL BE ALL RIGHT.
SHE IS SAKURA-CHAN, AFTER ALL.

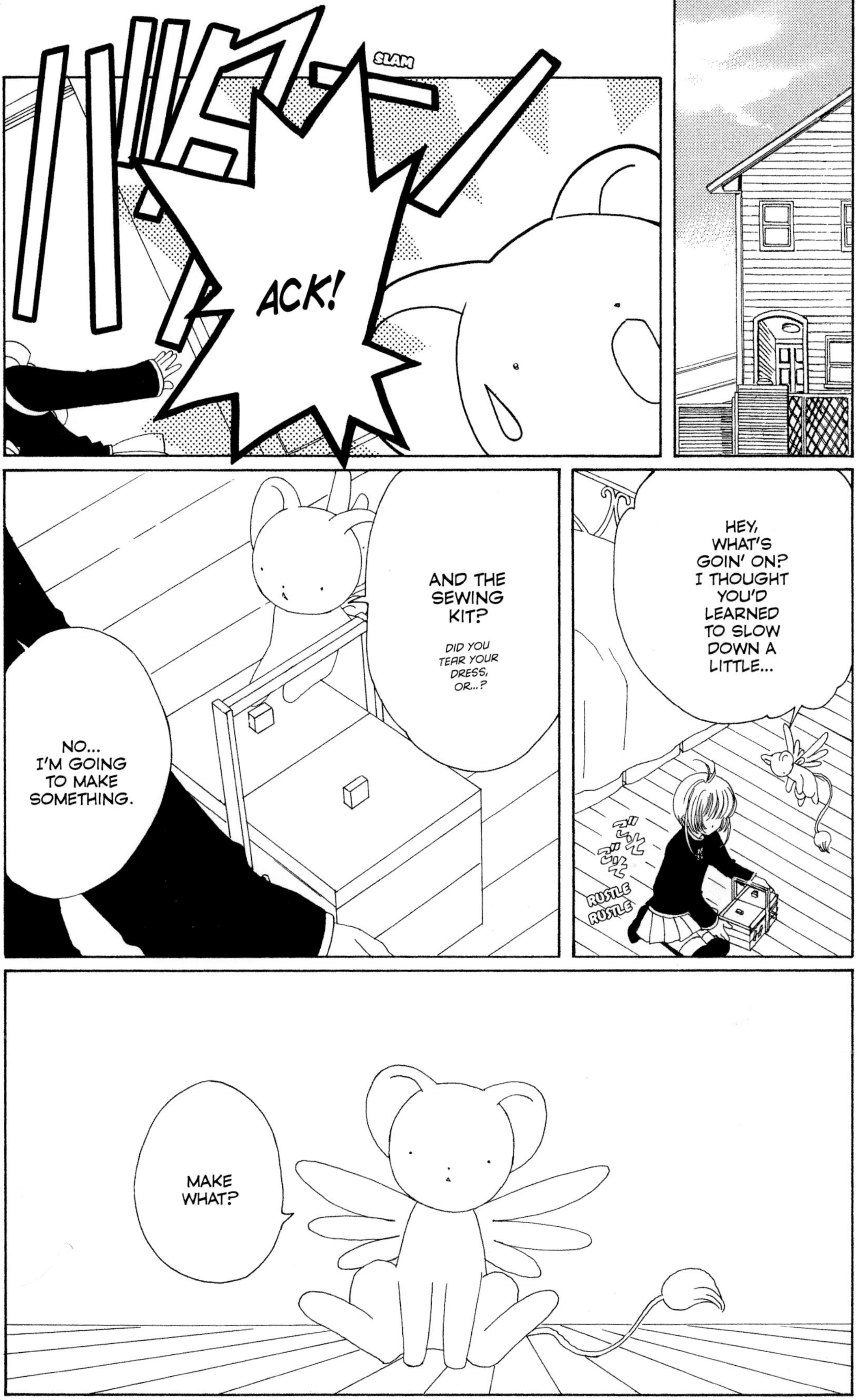
SLAM
ACK!
HEY, WHAT'S GOIN' ON? I THOUGHT YOU'D LEARNED TO SLOW DOWN A LITTLE...
RUSTLE RUSTLE
AND THE SEWING KIT?
DID YOU TEAR YOUR DRESS, OR...?
NO... I'M GOING TO MAKE SOMETHING.
MAKE WHAT?

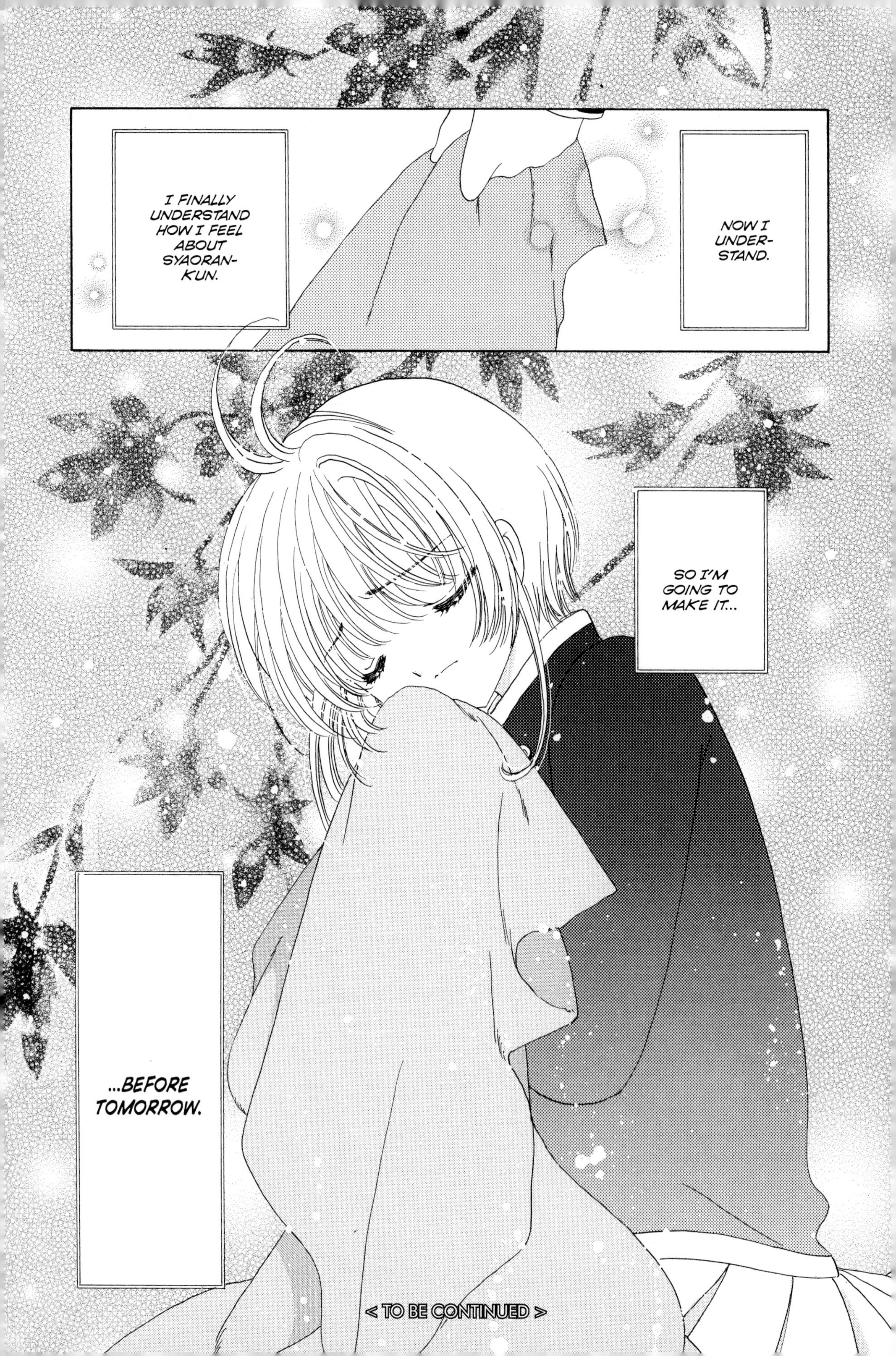
NOW I UNDERSTAND.
I FINALLY UNDERSTAND HOW I FEEL ABOUT SYAORAN-KUN.
SO I'M GOING TO MAKE IT...
...BEFORE TOMORROW.
< TO BE CONTINUED >

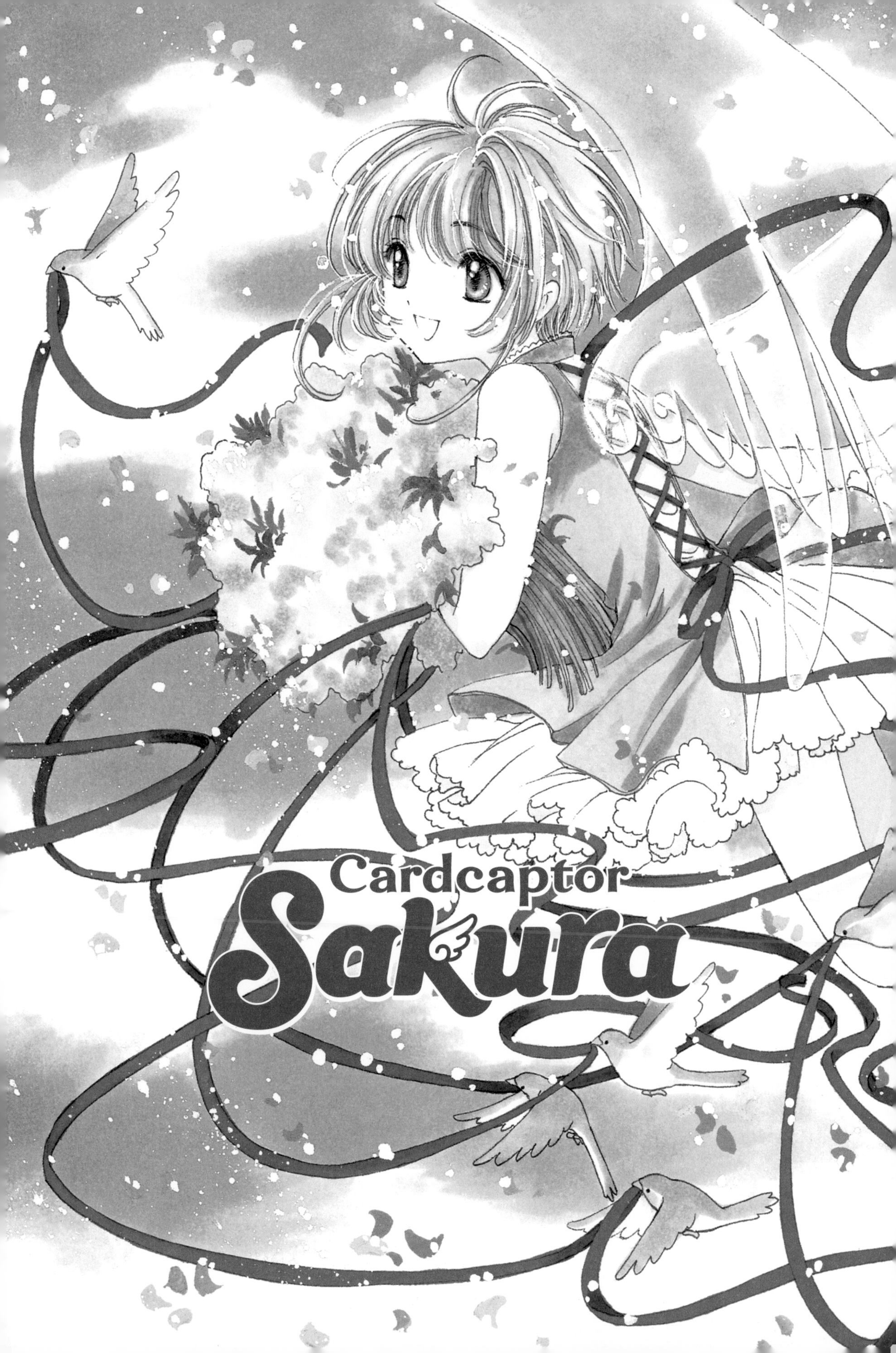
Cardcaptor
Sakura

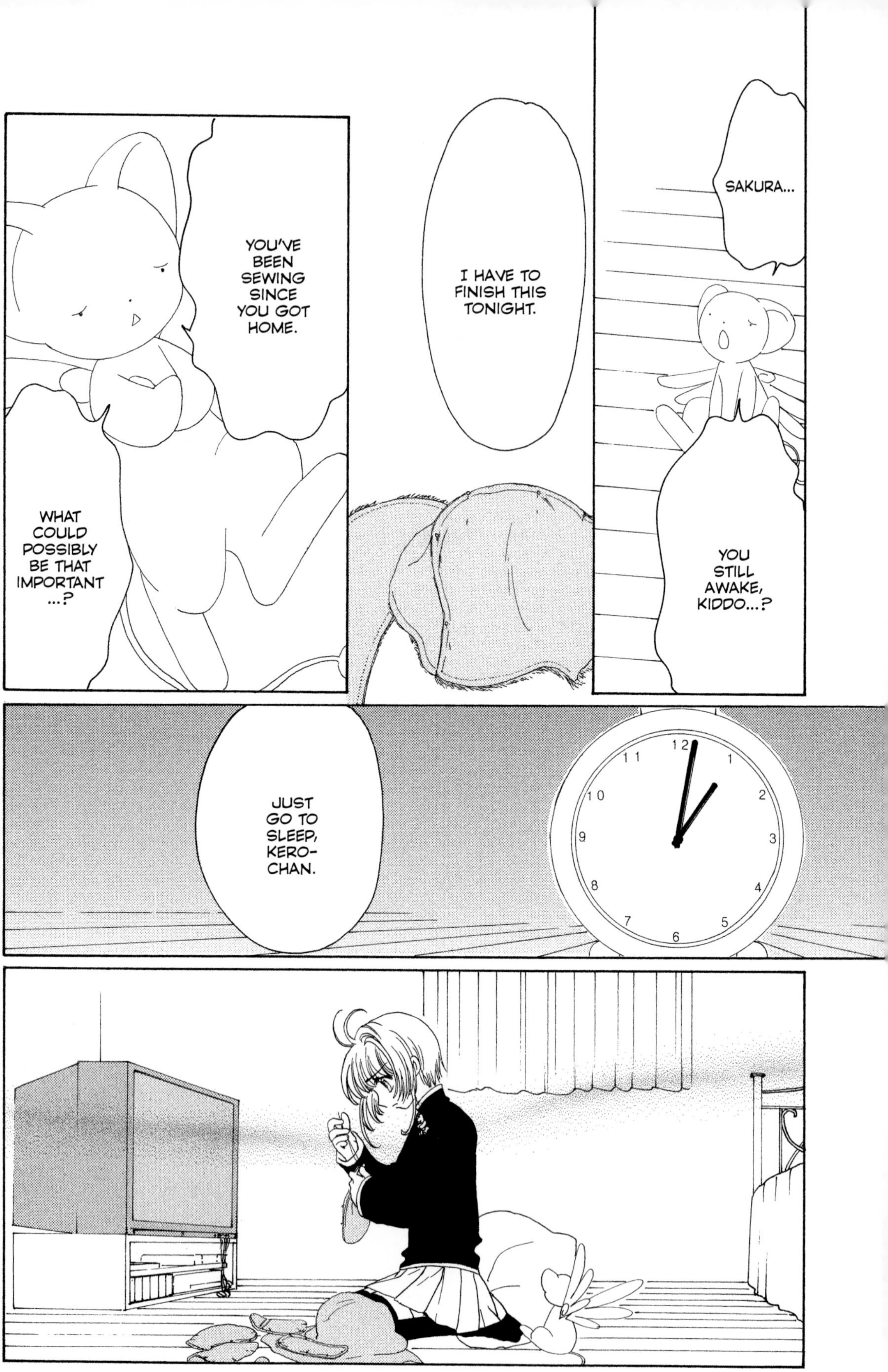
SAKURA...
YOU STILL AWAKE, KIDDO...?
I HAVE TO FINISH THIS TONIGHT.
YOU'VE BEEN SEWING SINCE YOU GOT HOME.
WHAT COULD POSSIBLY BE THAT IMPORTANT ...?
JUST GO TO SLEEP, KERO-CHAN.

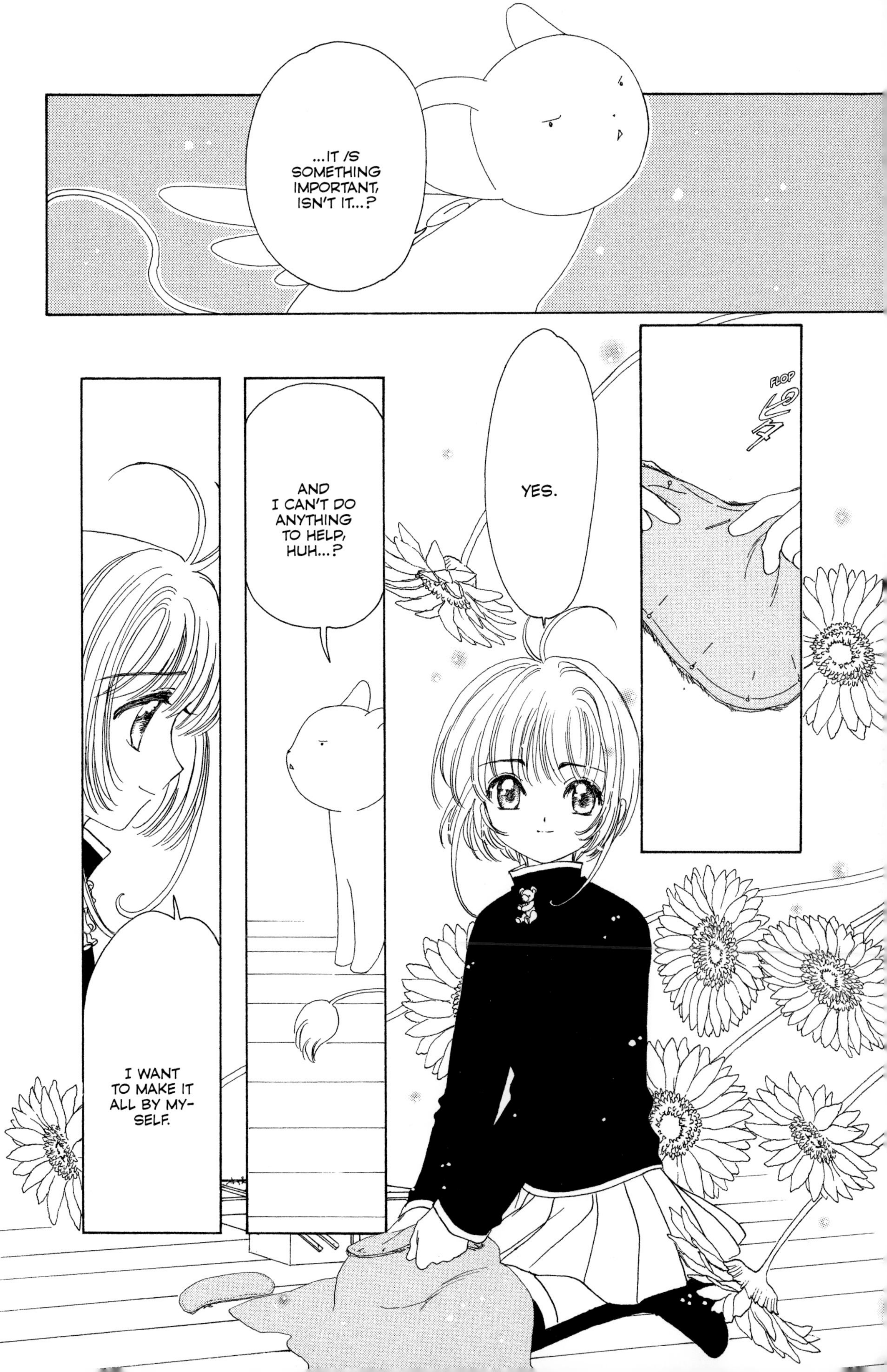
...IT IS SOMETHING IMPORTANT, ISN'T IT...?
FLOP
YES.
AND I CAN'T DO ANYTHING TO HELP, HUH...?
I WANT TO MAKE IT ALL BY MY-SELF.

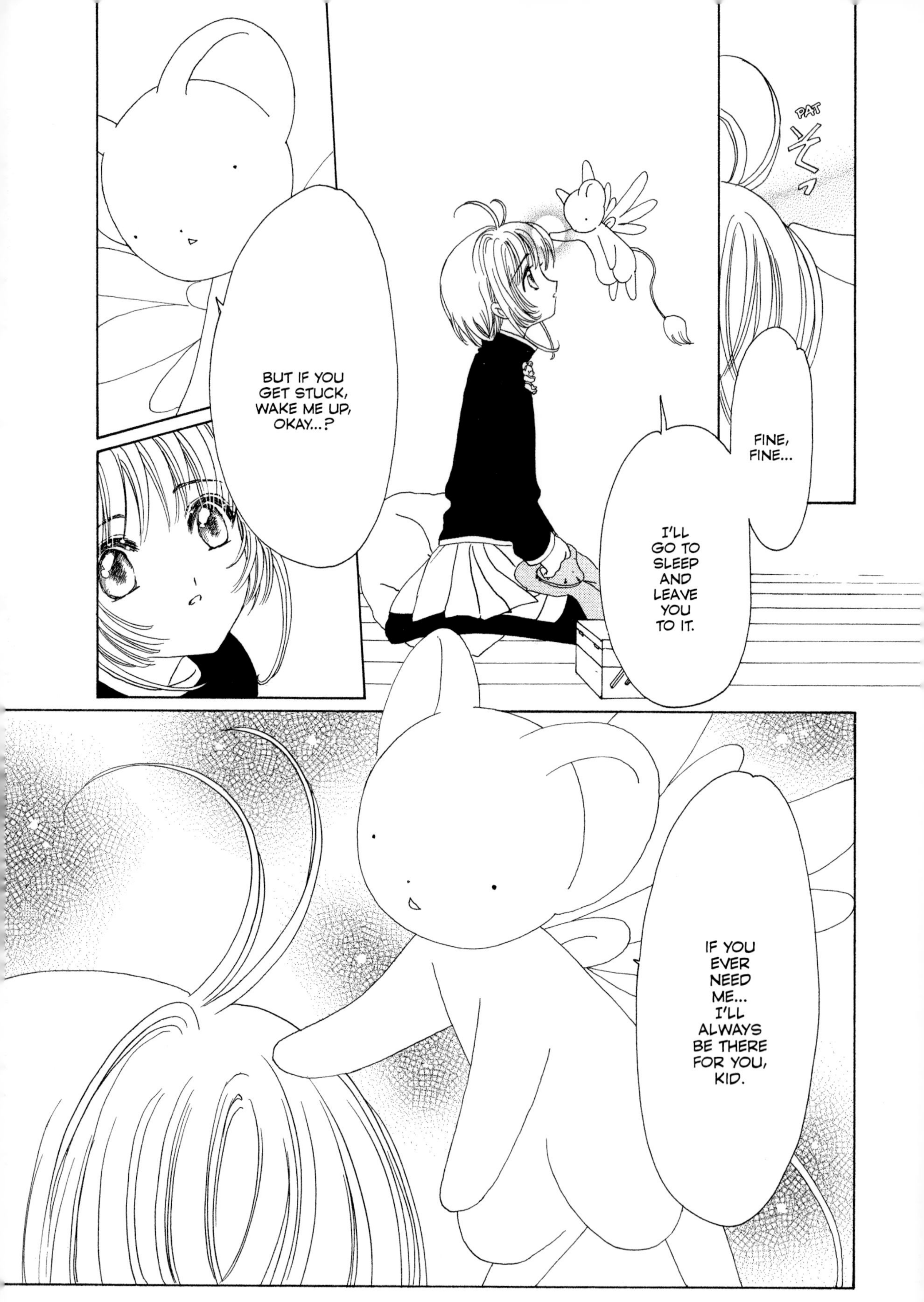
PAT
FINE, FINE...
I'LL GO TO SLEEP AND LEAVE YOU TO IT.
BUT IF YOU GET STUCK, WAKE ME UP, OKAY...?
IF YOU EVER NEED ME... I'LL ALWAYS BE THERE FOR YOU, KID.

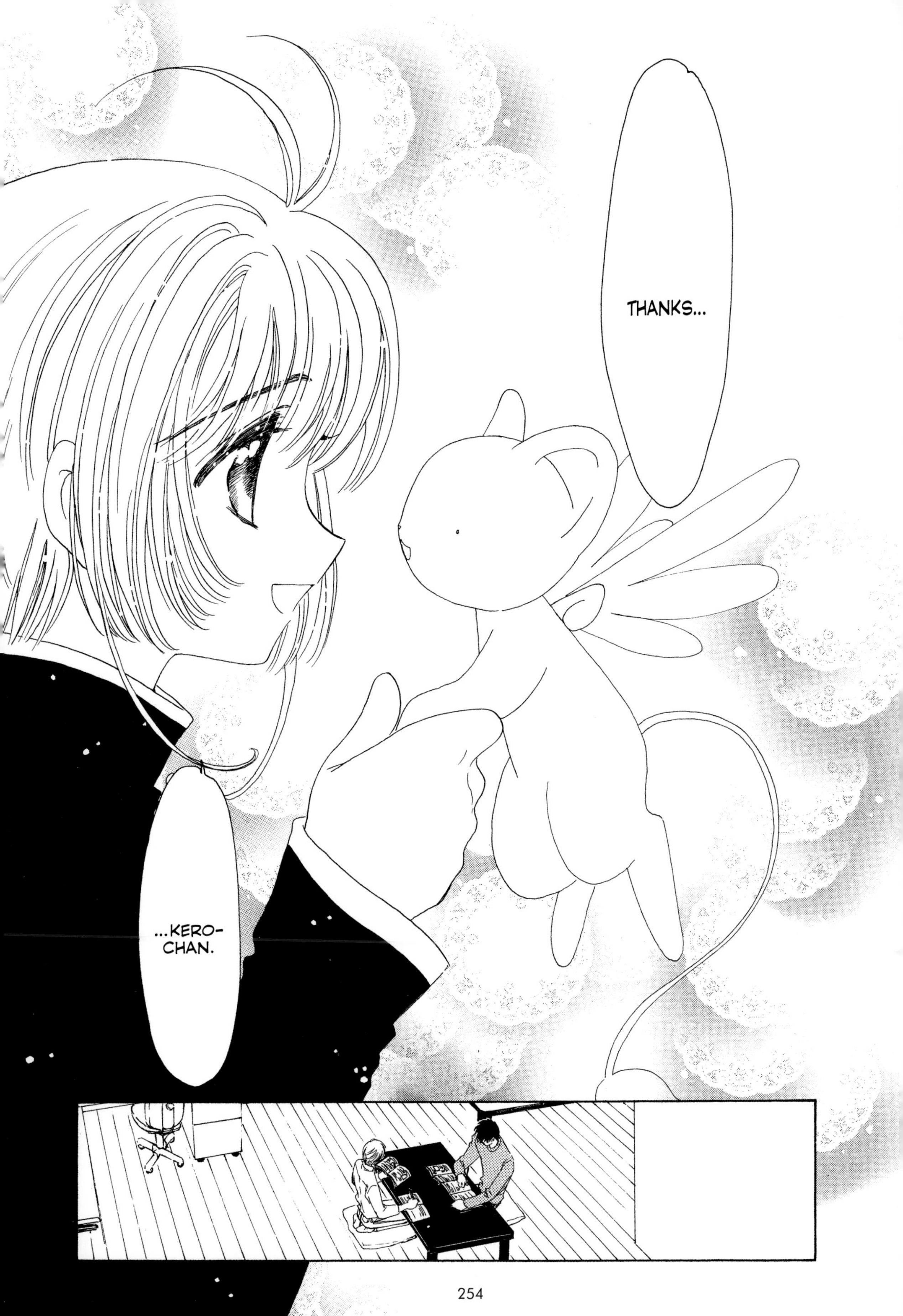
THANKS...
...KERO-CHAN.

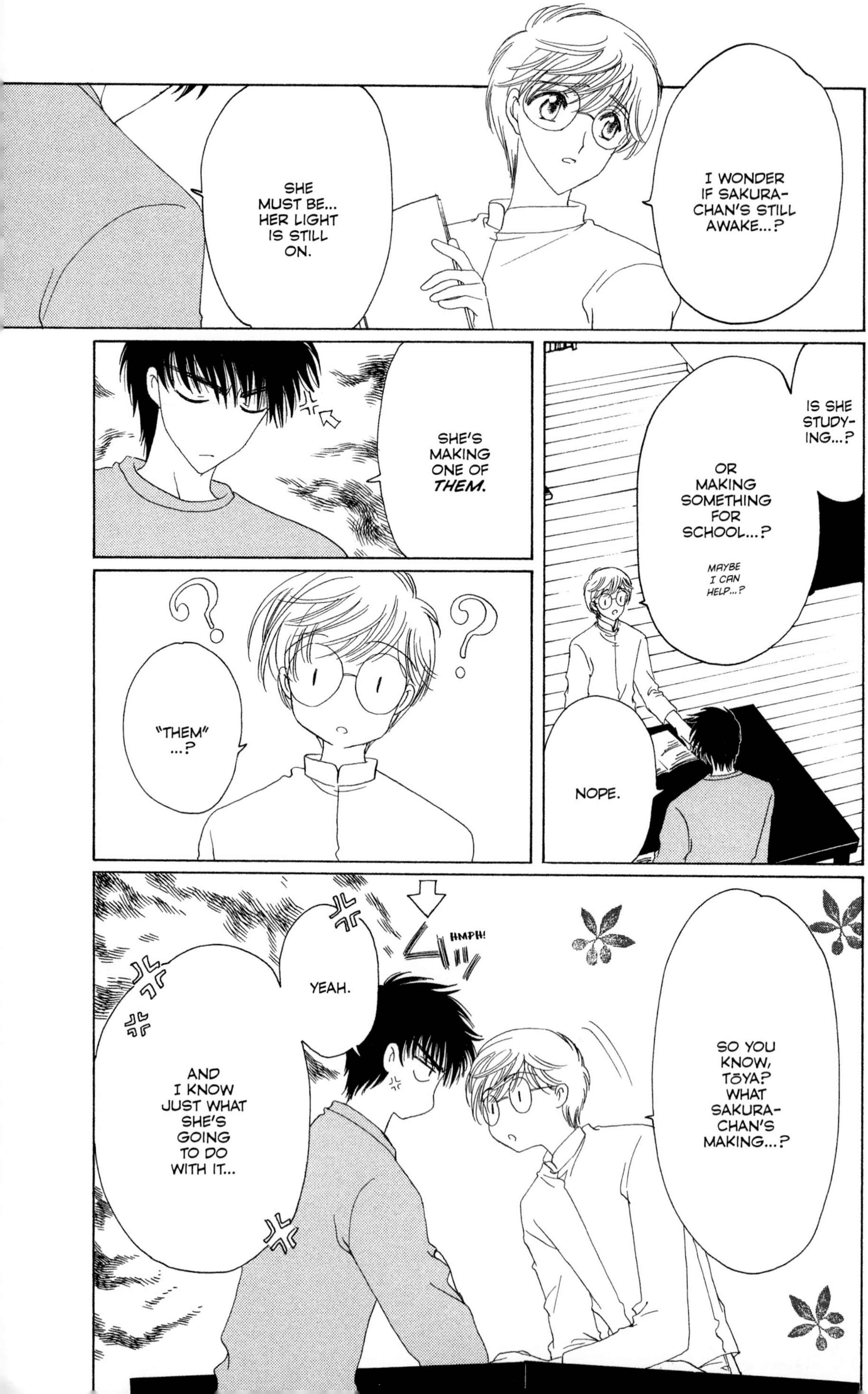

I WONDER IF SAKURA-CHAN'S STILL AWAKE...?
SHE MUST BE... HER LIGHT IS STILL ON.
IS SHE STUDYING...?
OR MAKING SOMETHING FOR SCHOOL...?
MAYBE I CAN HELP...?
NOPE.
SHE'S MAKING ONE OF *THEM.*
"THEM" ...?
SO YOU KNOW, TŌYA? WHAT SAKURA-CHAN'S MAKING...?
HMPH!
YEAH.
AND I KNOW JUST WHAT SHE'S GOING TO DO WITH IT...

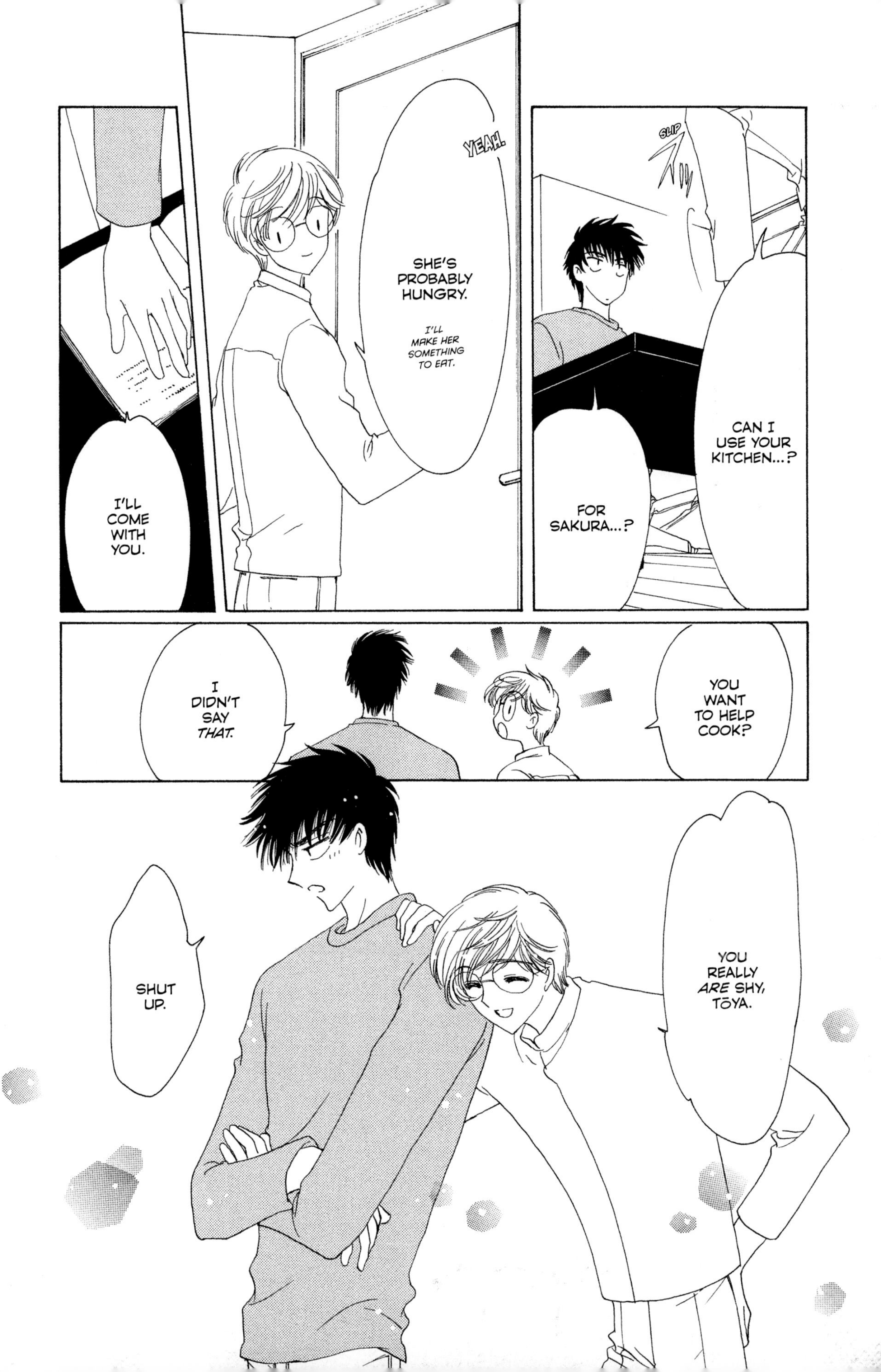
SLIP
CAN I USE YOUR KITCHEN...?
FOR SAKURA...?
YEAH.
SHE'S PROBABLY HUNGRY.
I'LL MAKE HER SOMETHING TO EAT.
I'LL COME WITH YOU.
YOU WANT TO HELP COOK?
I DIDN'T SAY *THAT.*
YOU REALLY *ARE* SHY, TŌYA.
SHUT UP.

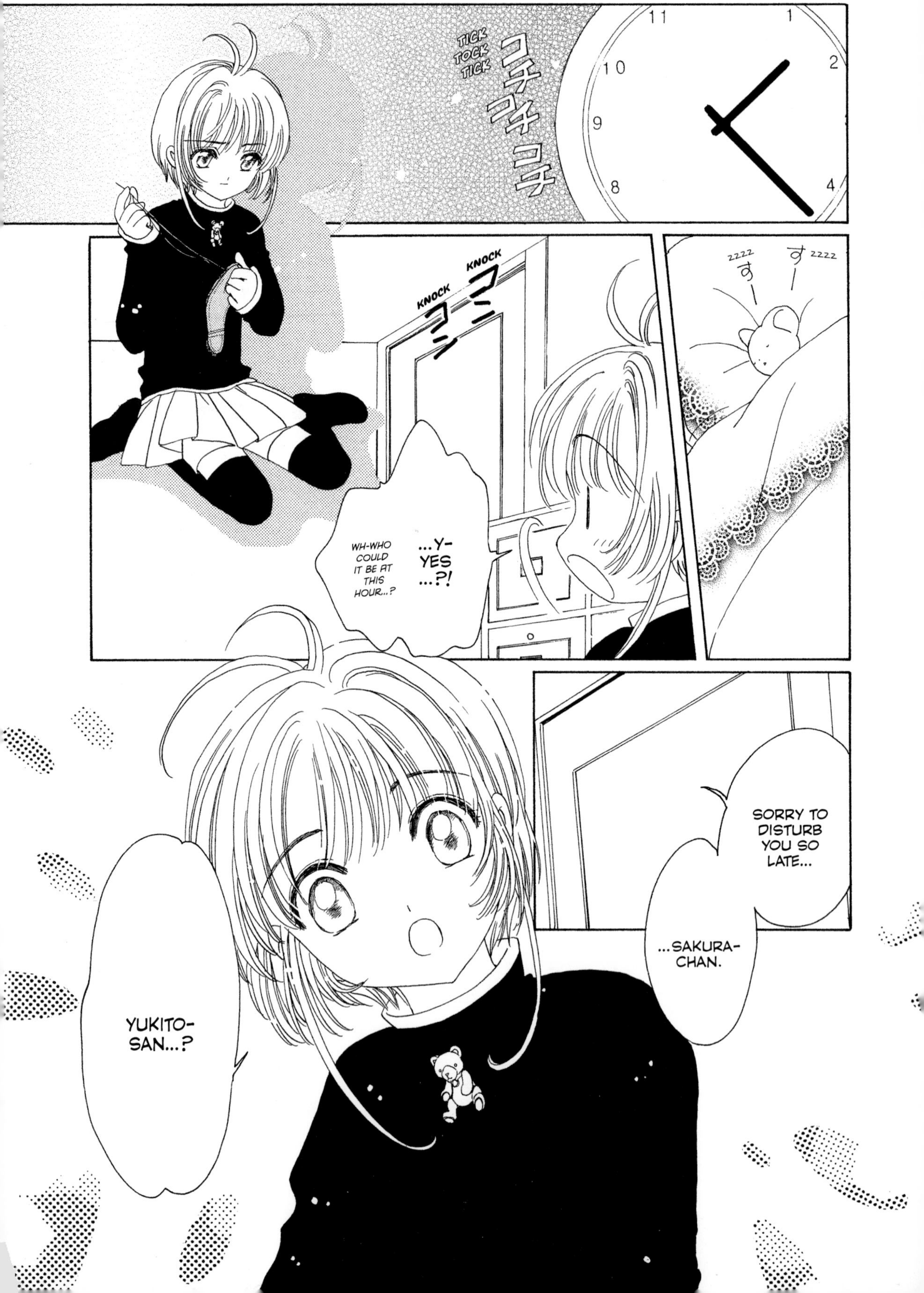
TICK
TOCK
TICK
コチコチコチ
す zzzz
zzzz す
KNOCK
KNOCK
コンコン
...Y-YES...?!
WH-WHO COULD IT BE AT THIS HOUR...?
SORRY TO DISTURB YOU SO LATE...
...SAKURA-CHAN.
YUKITO-SAN...?

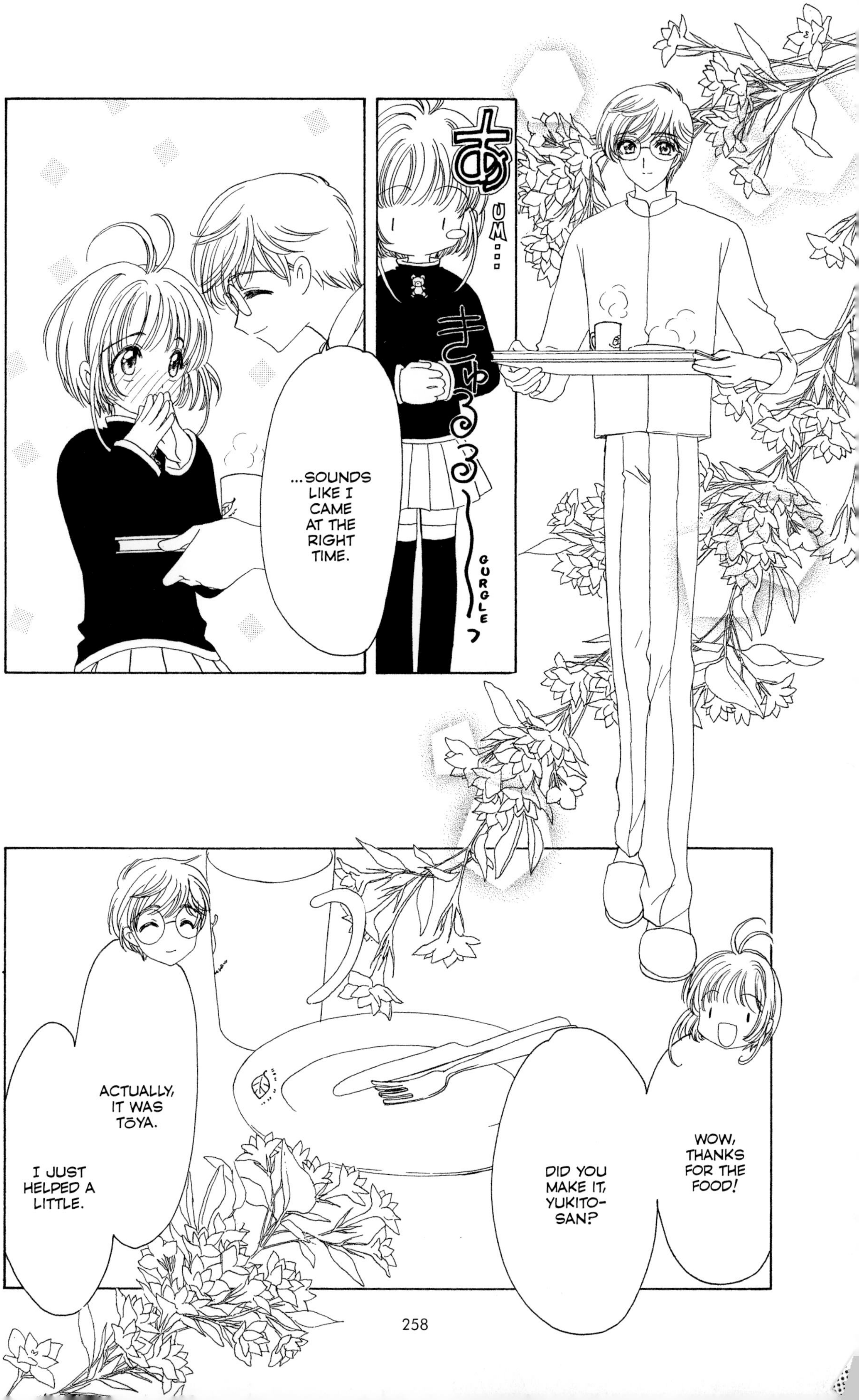

あ
UM...
きゅるるる〜
GURGLE
...SOUNDS LIKE I CAME AT THE RIGHT TIME.
WOW, THANKS FOR THE FOOD!
DID YOU MAKE IT, YUKITO-SAN?
ACTUALLY, IT WAS TŌYA.
I JUST HELPED A LITTLE.

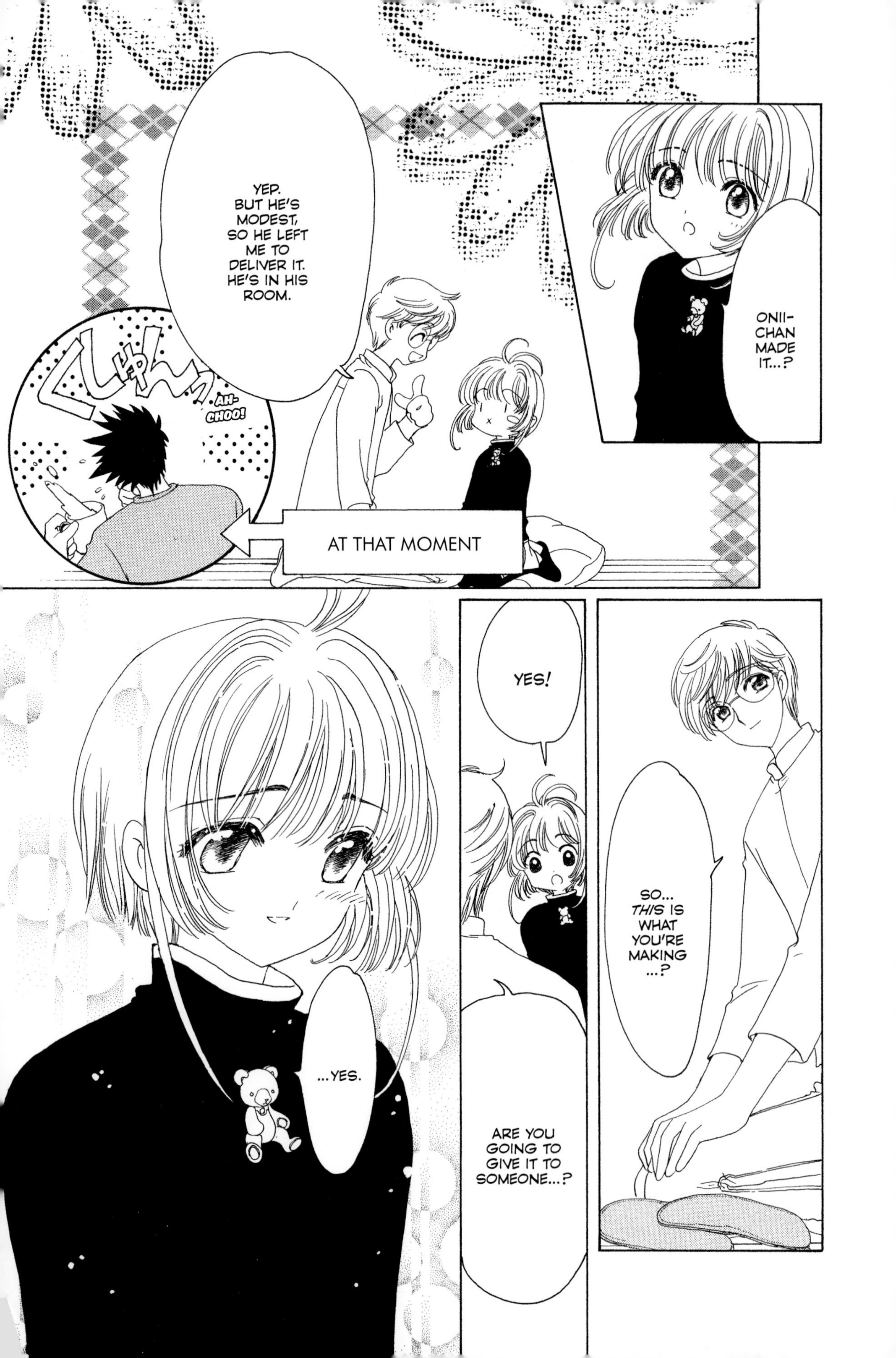
ONII-CHAN MADE IT...?
YEP. BUT HE'S MODEST, SO HE LEFT ME TO DELIVER IT. HE'S IN HIS ROOM.
AT THAT MOMENT
くしゅん
AH-CHOO!
SO... *THIS* IS WHAT YOU'RE MAKING ...?
YES!
ARE YOU GOING TO GIVE IT TO SOMEONE...?
...YES.

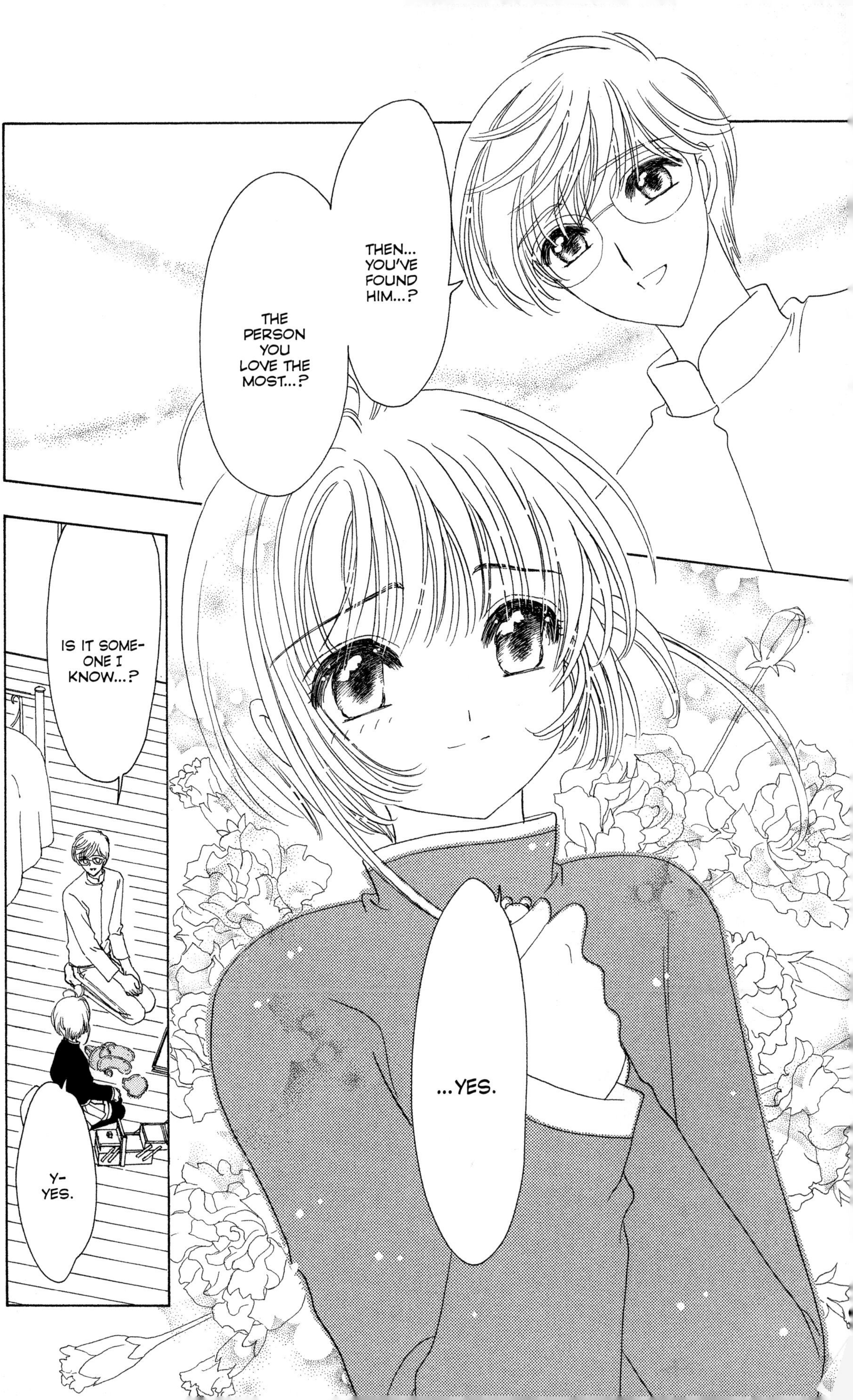
THEN... YOU'VE FOUND HIM...?
THE PERSON YOU LOVE THE MOST...?
...YES.
IS IT SOME-ONE I KNOW...?
Y-YES.

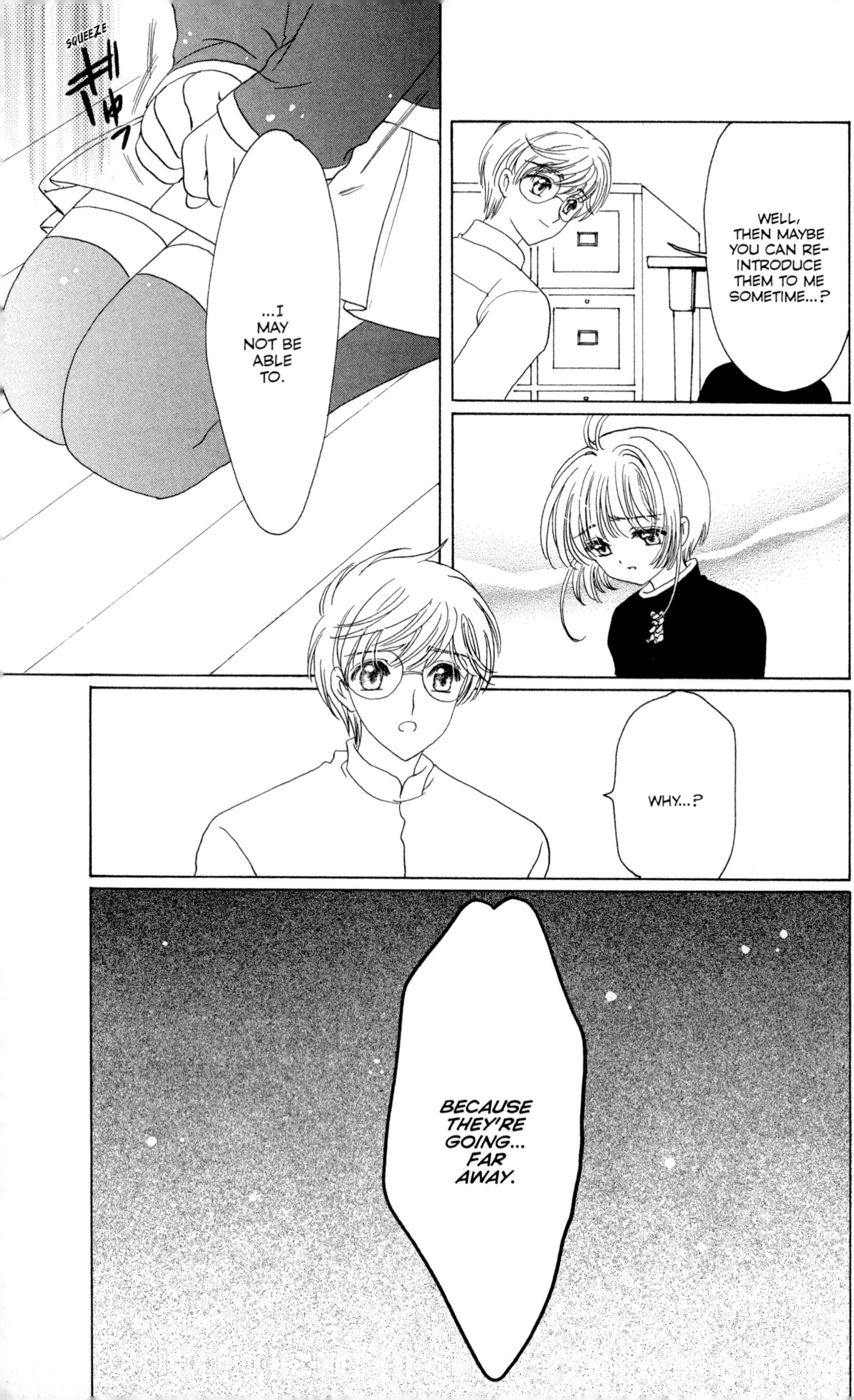
WELL, THEN MAYBE YOU CAN RE-INTRODUCE THEM TO ME SOMETIME...?
SQUEEZE
ギュッ
...I MAY NOT BE ABLE TO.
WHY...?
BECAUSE THEY'RE GOING... FAR AWAY.

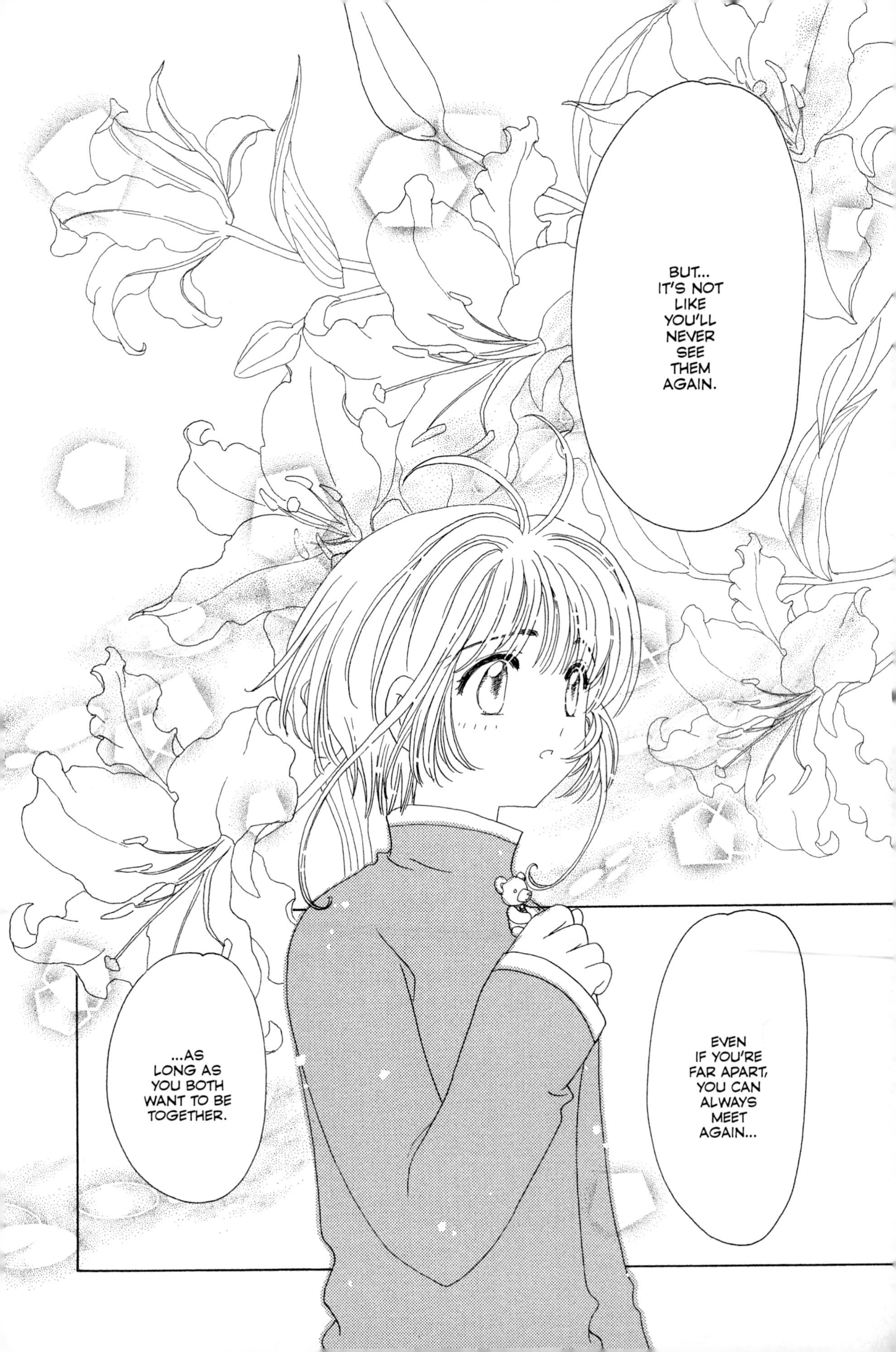
BUT... IT'S NOT LIKE YOU'LL NEVER SEE THEM AGAIN.
EVEN IF YOU'RE FAR APART, YOU CAN ALWAYS MEET AGAIN...
...AS LONG AS YOU BOTH WANT TO BE TOGETHER.

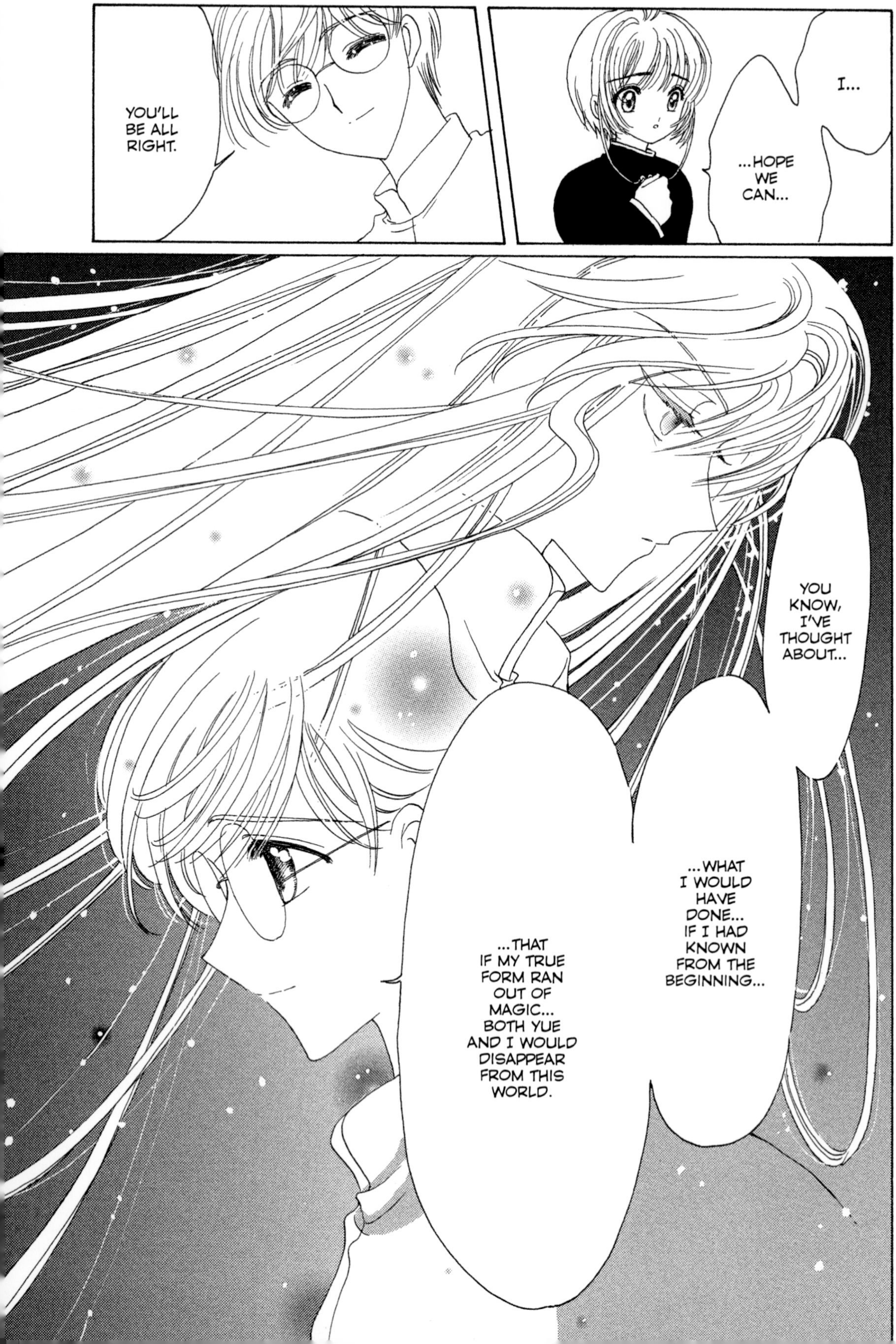
I...
...HOPE WE CAN...
YOU'LL BE ALL RIGHT.
YOU KNOW, I'VE THOUGHT ABOUT...
...WHAT I WOULD HAVE DONE... IF I HAD KNOWN FROM THE BEGINNING...
...THAT IF MY TRUE FORM RAN OUT OF MAGIC... BOTH YUE AND I WOULD DISAPPEAR FROM THIS WORLD.

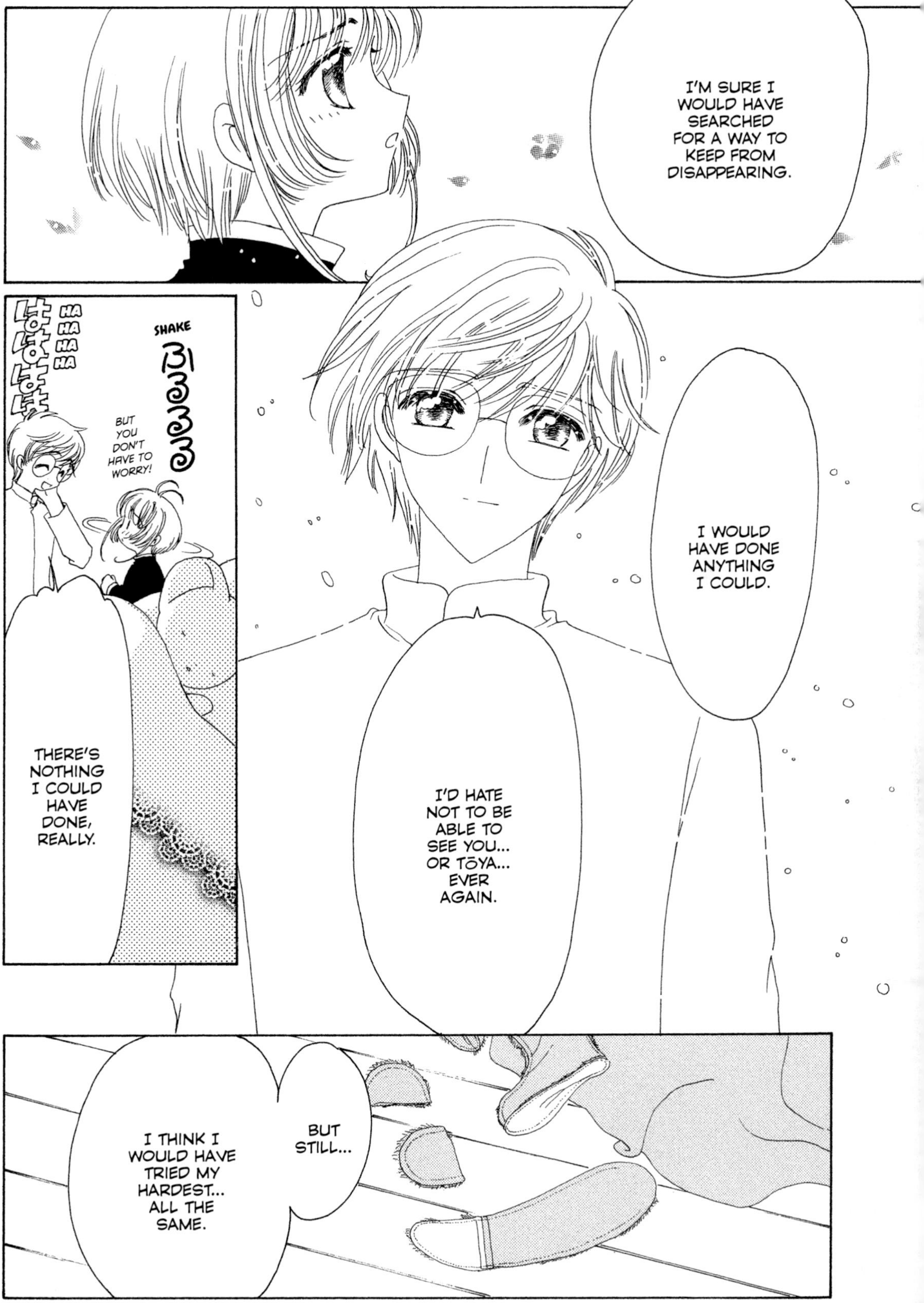
I'M SURE I WOULD HAVE SEARCHED FOR A WAY TO KEEP FROM DISAPPEARING.
I WOULD HAVE DONE ANYTHING I COULD.
I'D HATE NOT TO BE ABLE TO SEE YOU... OR TŌYA... EVER AGAIN.
HA HA HA HA
SHAKE
BUT YOU DON'T HAVE TO WORRY!
THERE'S NOTHING I COULD HAVE DONE, REALLY.
BUT STILL...
I THINK I WOULD HAVE TRIED MY HARDEST... ALL THE SAME.

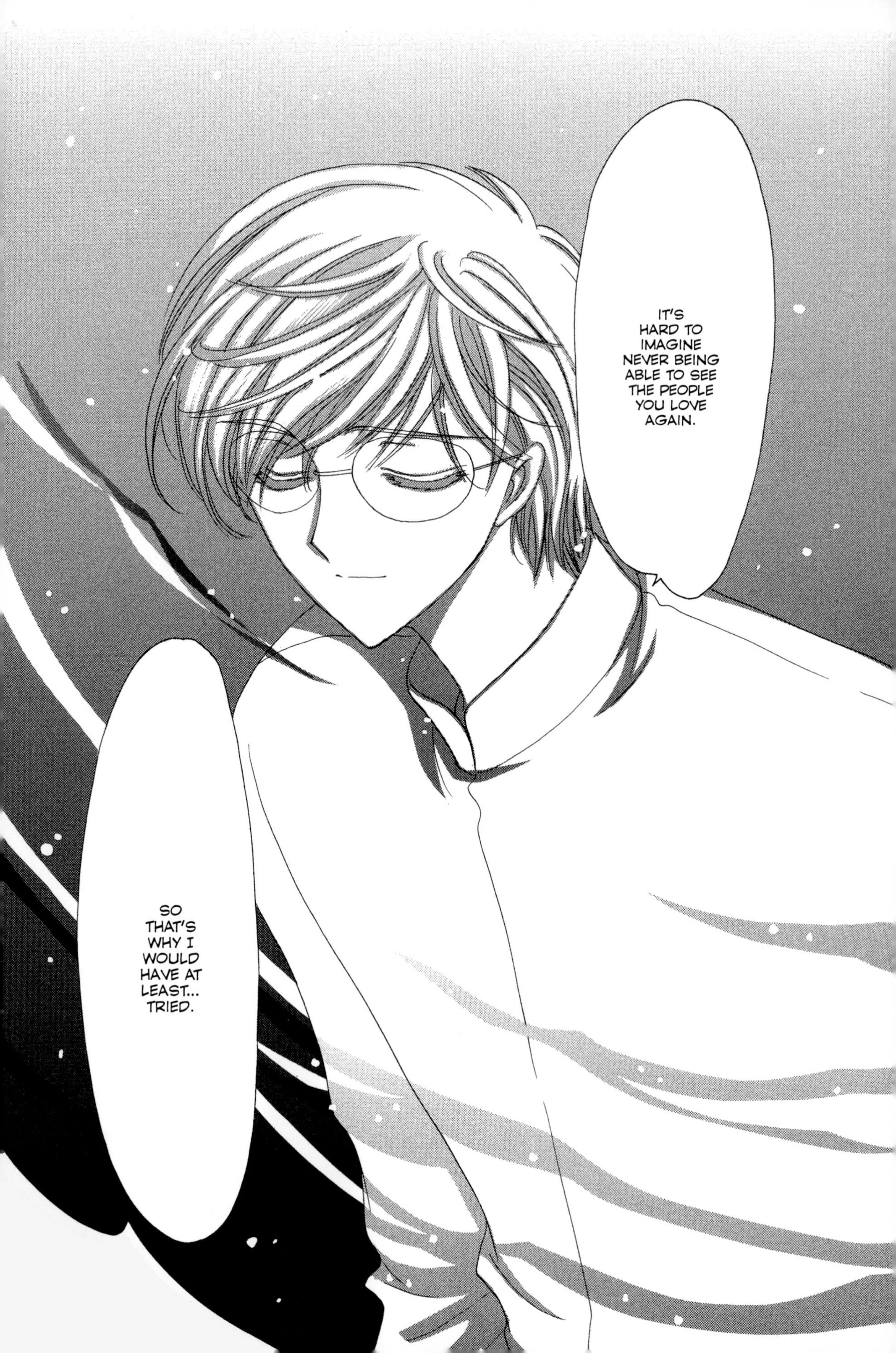
IT'S HARD TO IMAGINE NEVER BEING ABLE TO SEE THE PEOPLE YOU LOVE AGAIN.
SO THAT'S WHY I WOULD HAVE AT LEAST... TRIED.

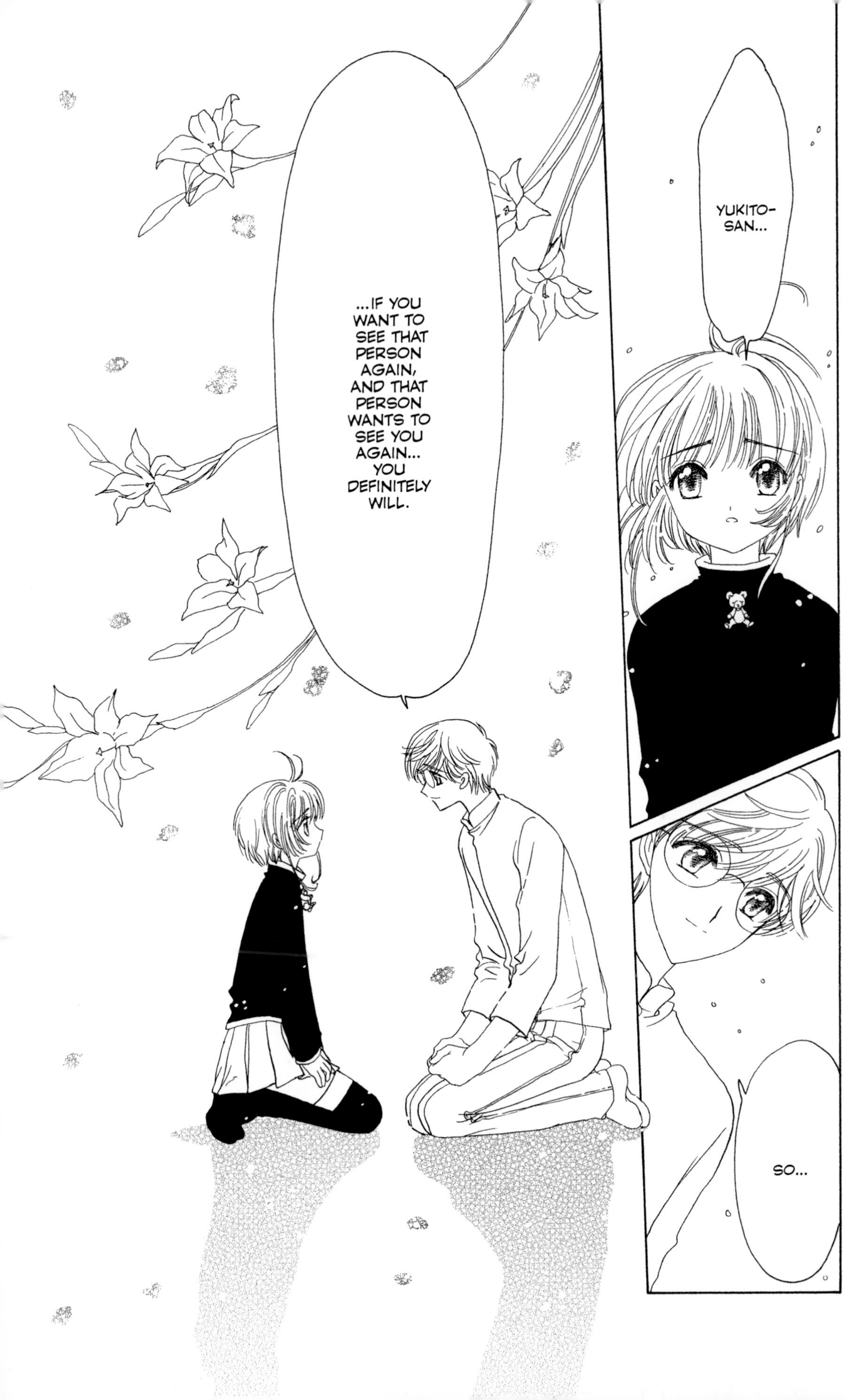
YUKITO-SAN...
SO...
...IF YOU WANT TO SEE THAT PERSON AGAIN, AND THAT PERSON WANTS TO SEE YOU AGAIN... YOU DEFINITELY WILL.

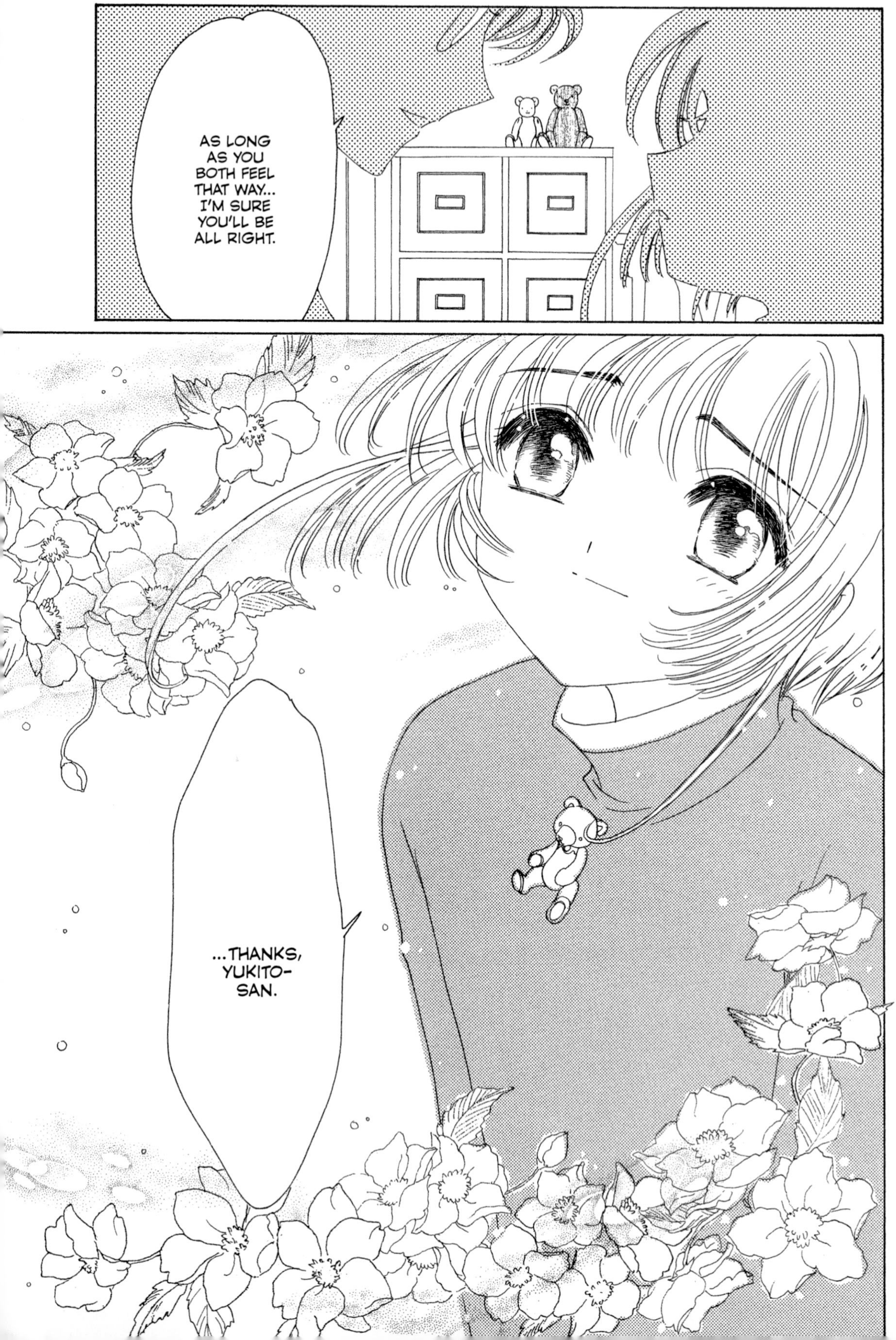
AS LONG AS YOU BOTH FEEL THAT WAY... I'M SURE YOU'LL BE ALL RIGHT.
...THANKS, YUKITO-SAN.

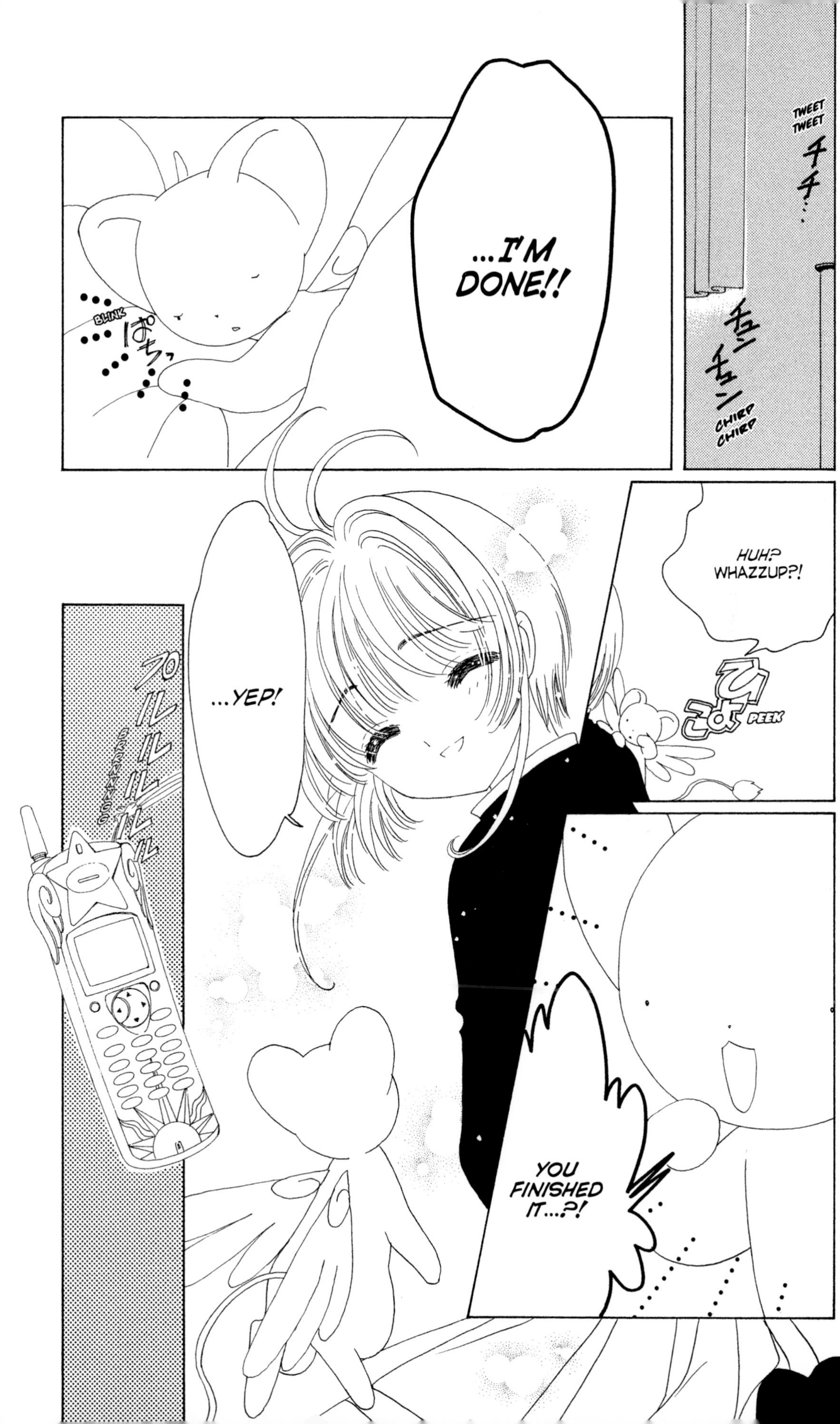
TWEET TWEET
チチ…
チュンチュン
CHIRP CHIRP
…I'M DONE!!
BLINK
ぱちっ
HUH? WHAZZUP?!
ひょこ
PEEK
YOU FINISHED IT…?!
…YEP!
プルルルルル
BRRRNNNG

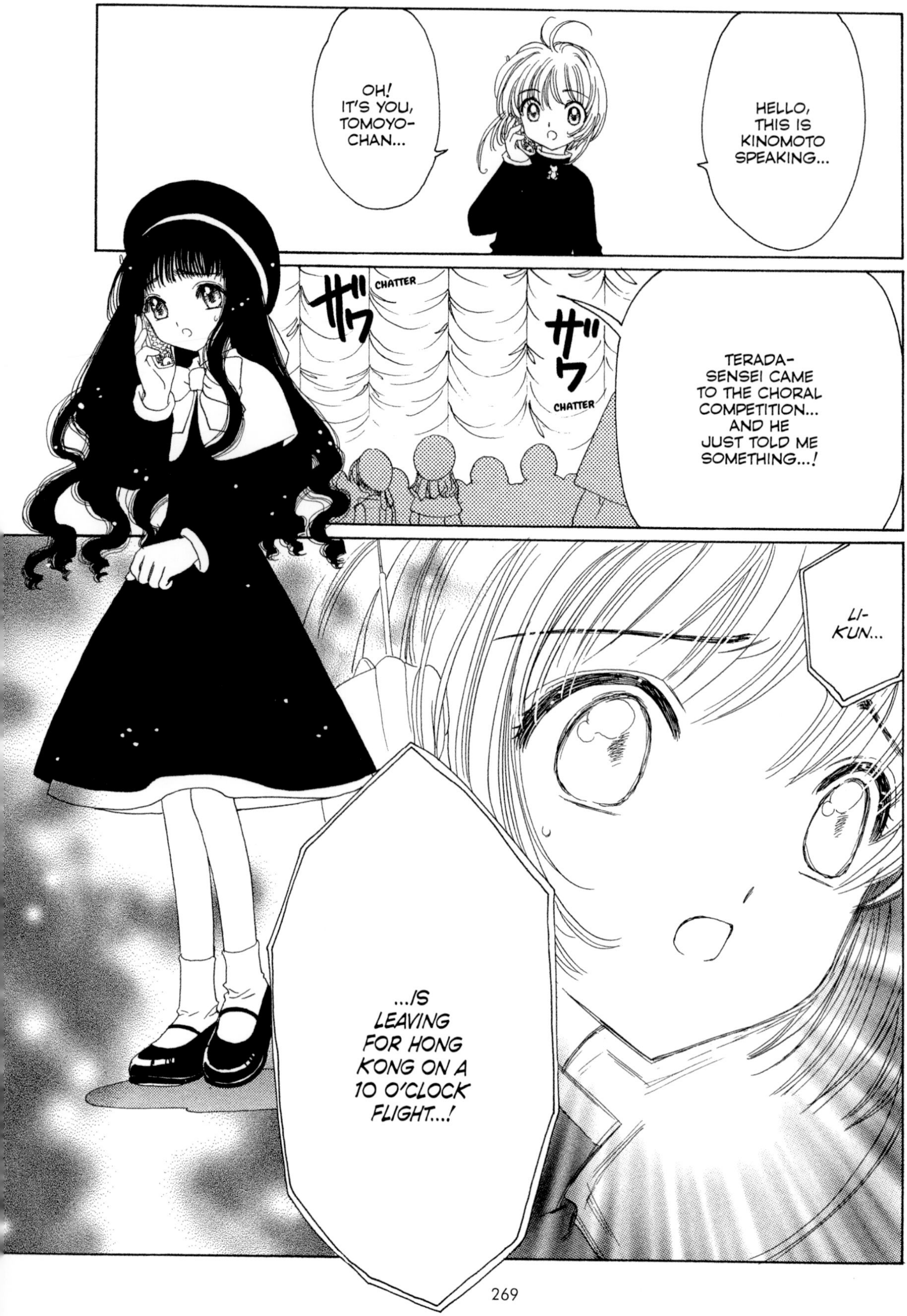
HELLO, THIS IS KINOMOTO SPEAKING...
OH! IT'S YOU, TOMOYO-CHAN...
TERADA-SENSEI CAME TO THE CHORAL COMPETITION... AND HE JUST TOLD ME SOMETHING...!
ザワ
CHATTER
ザワ
CHATTER
LI-KUN...
...IS LEAVING FOR HONG KONG ON A 10 O'CLOCK FLIGHT...!

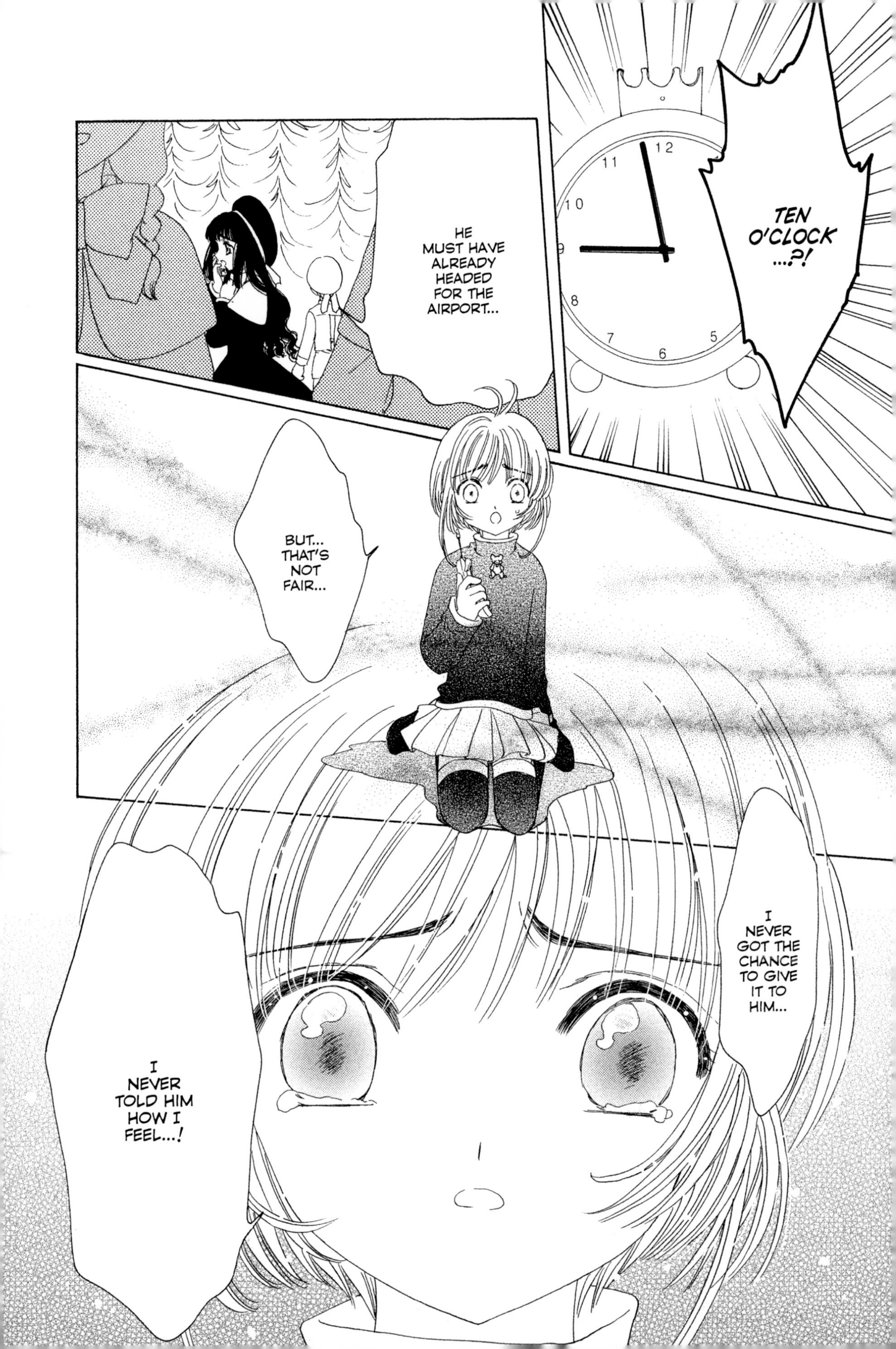
TEN O'CLOCK ...?!
HE MUST HAVE ALREADY HEADED FOR THE AIRPORT...
BUT... THAT'S NOT FAIR...
I NEVER GOT THE CHANCE TO GIVE IT TO HIM...
I NEVER TOLD HIM HOW I FEEL...!

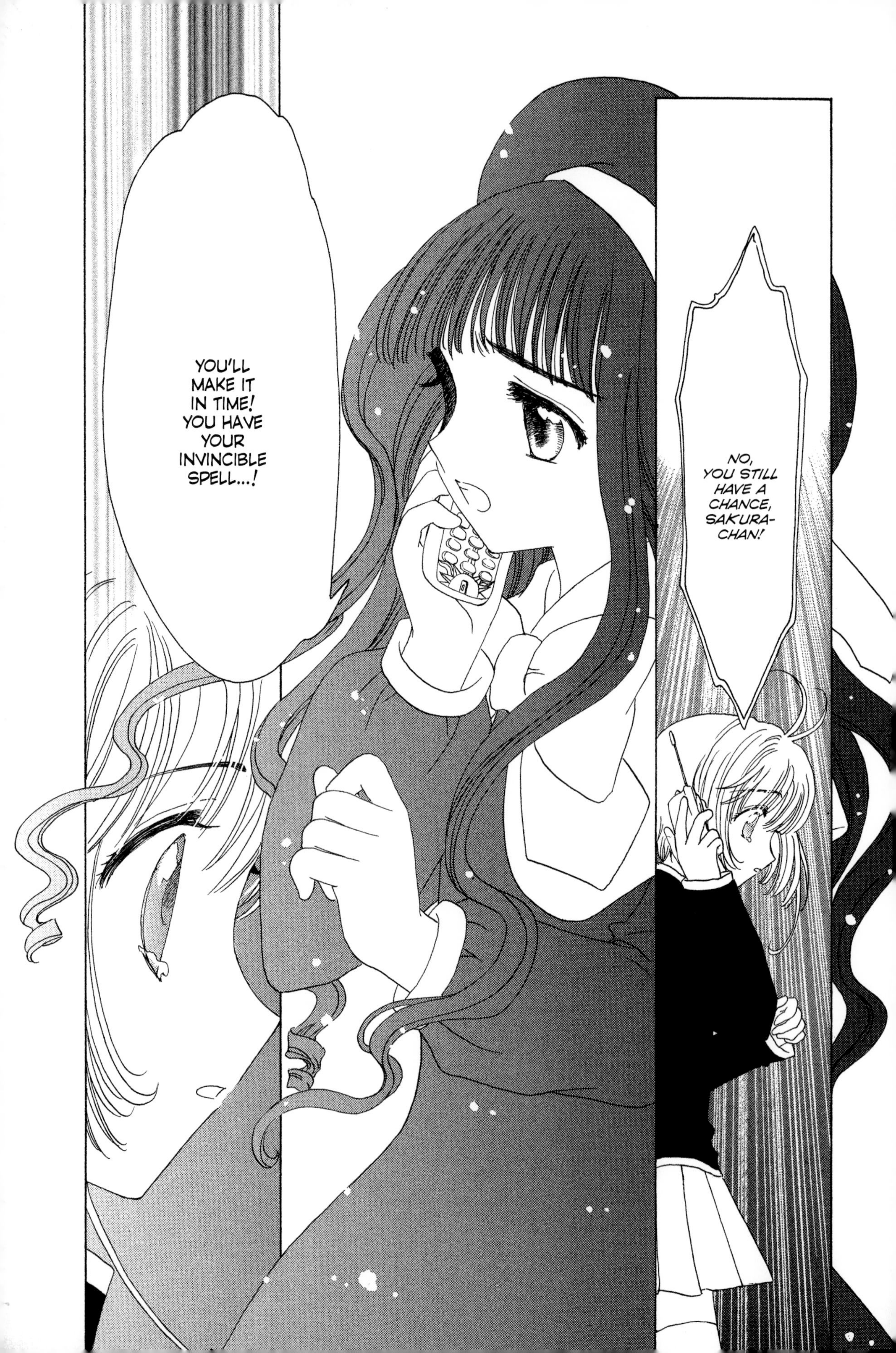
NO, YOU STILL HAVE A CHANCE, SAKURA-CHAN!
YOU'LL MAKE IT IN TIME! YOU HAVE YOUR INVINCIBLE SPELL...!

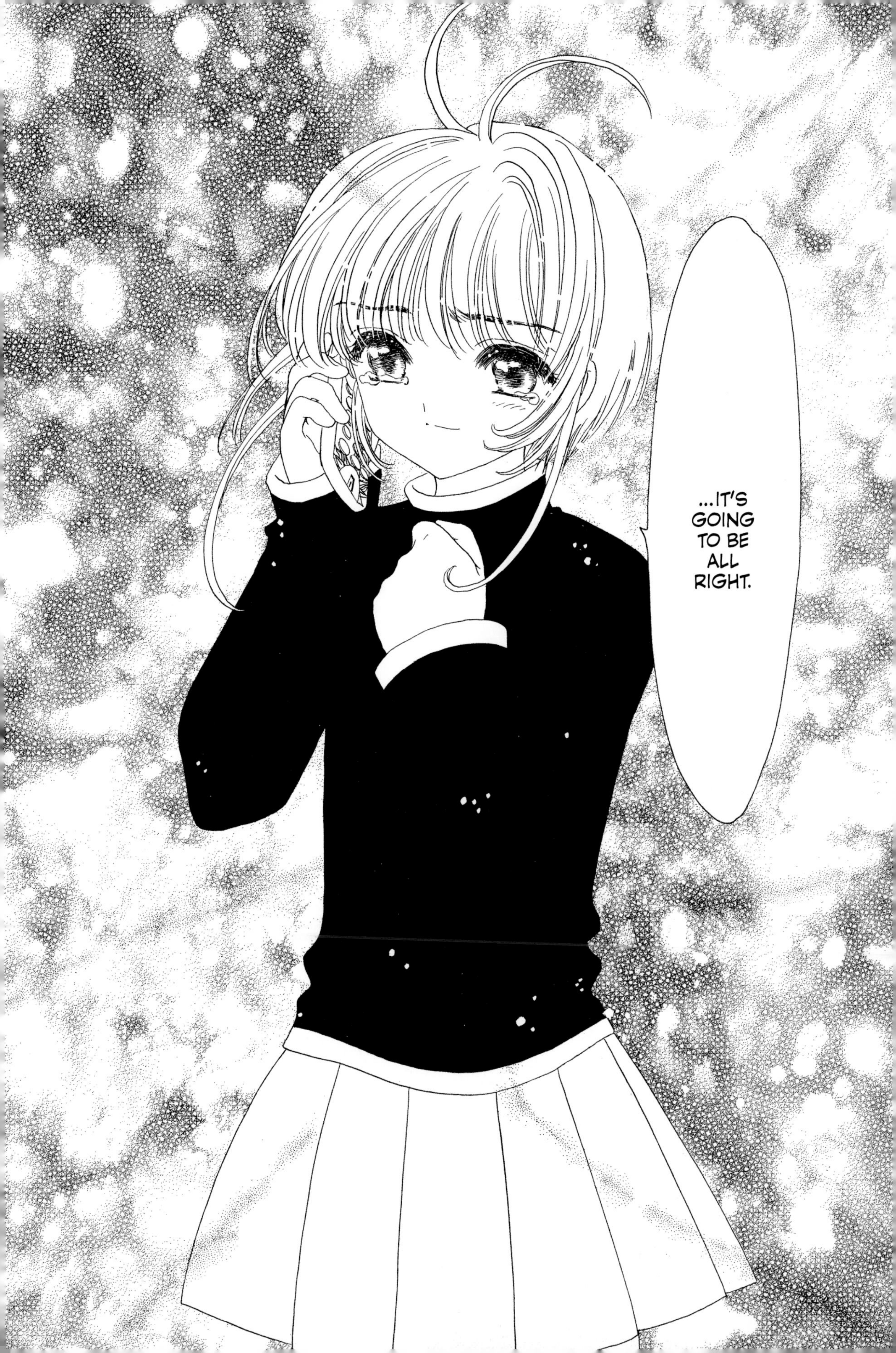
...IT'S GOING TO BE ALL RIGHT.

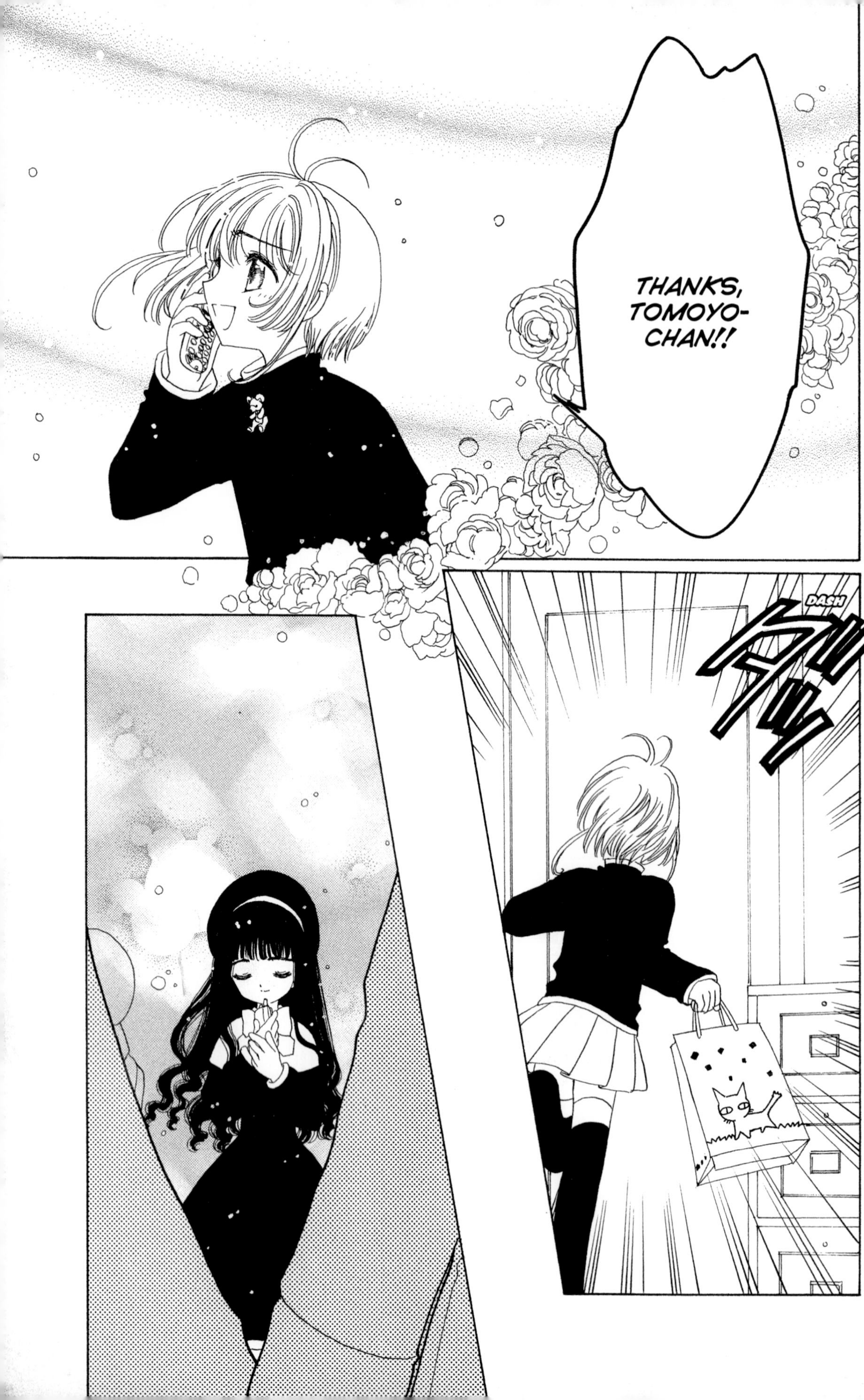
THANKS, TOMOYO-CHAN!!
DASH

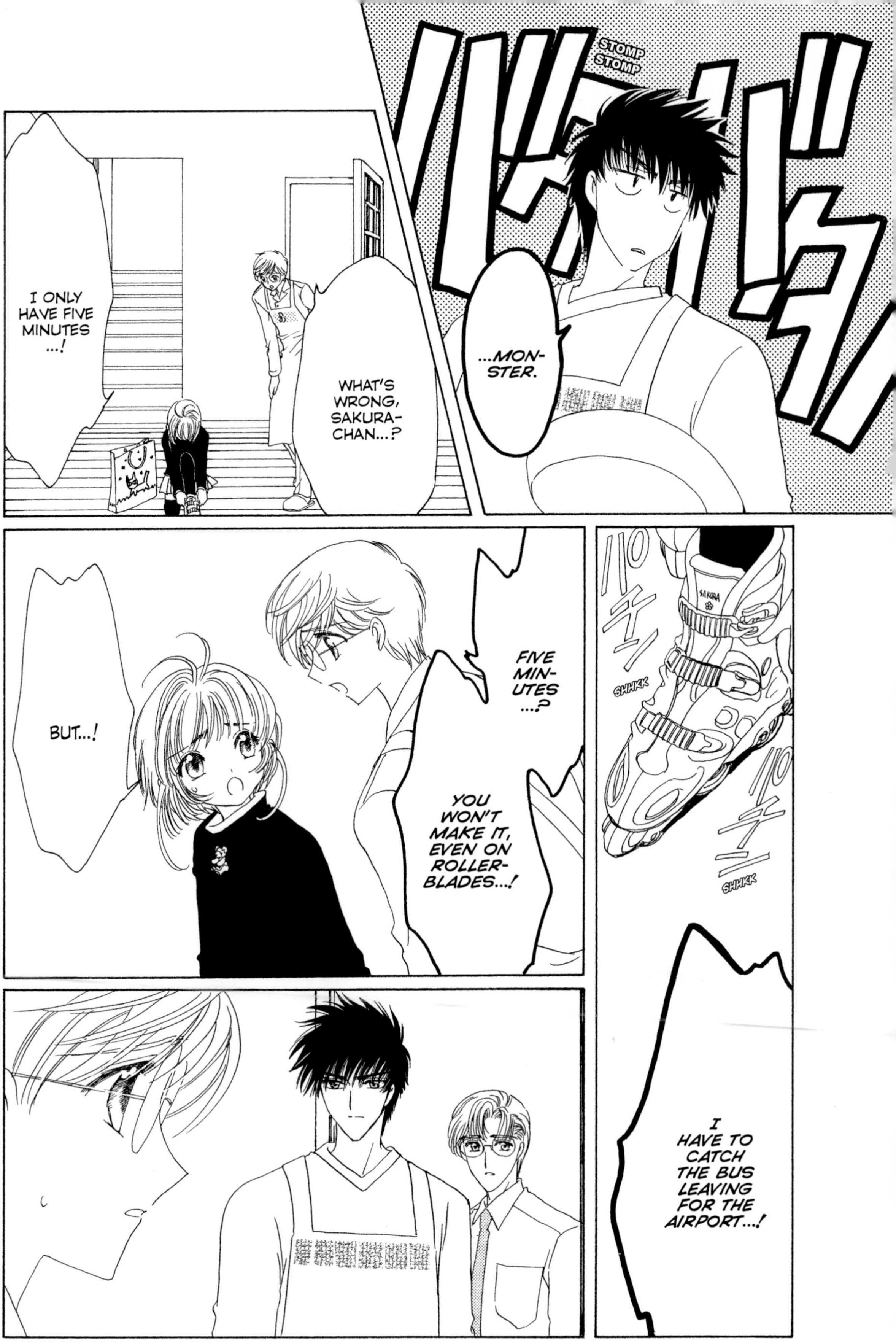
STOMP
STOMP
...MON-STER.
WHAT'S WRONG, SAKURA-CHAN...?
I ONLY HAVE FIVE MINUTES ...!
SHHKK
SHHKK
I HAVE TO CATCH THE BUS LEAVING FOR THE AIRPORT...!
FIVE MIN-UTES ...?
YOU WON'T MAKE IT, EVEN ON ROLLER-BLADES...!
BUT...!

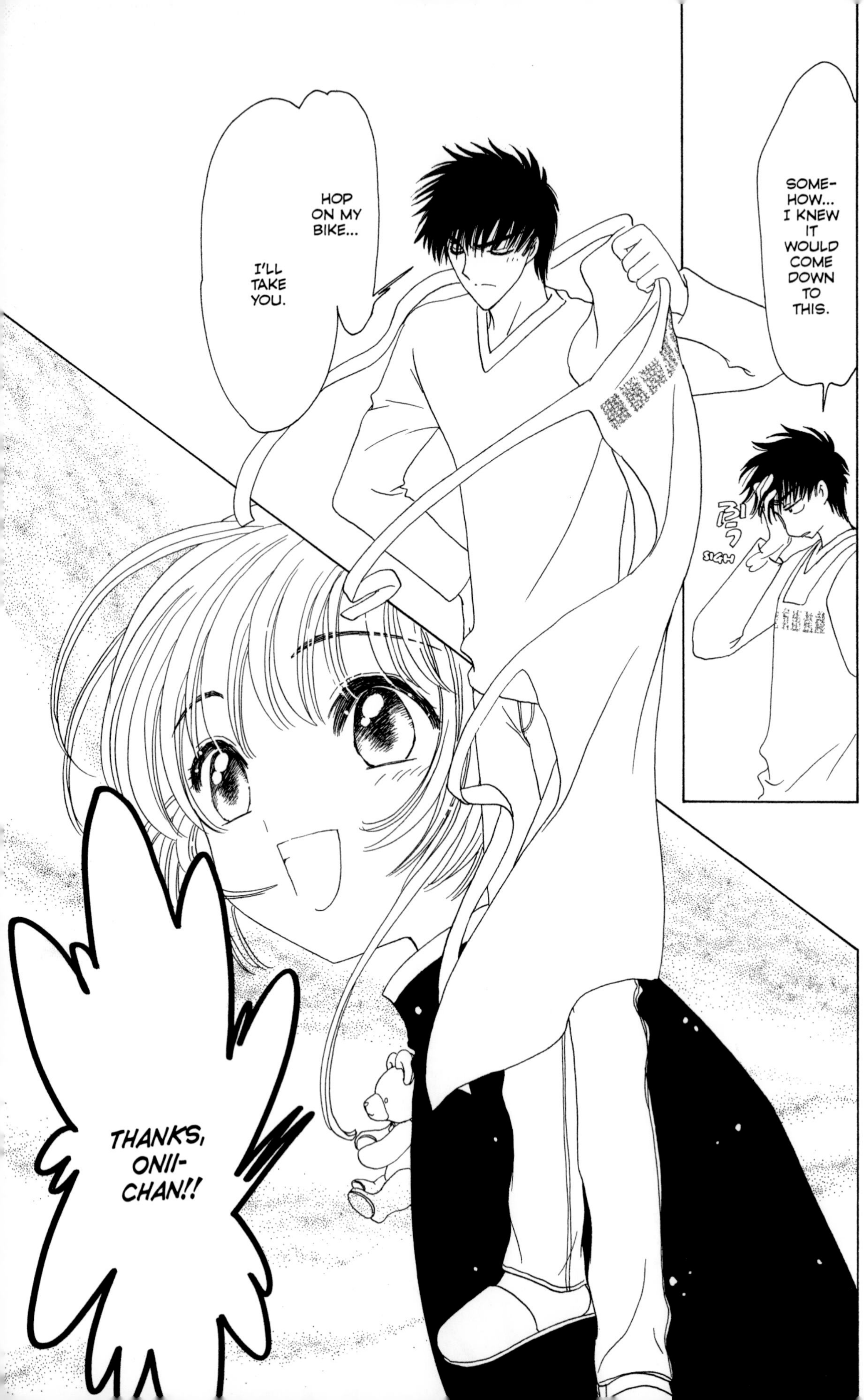
SOME-HOW... I KNEW IT WOULD COME DOWN TO THIS.
SIGH
HOP ON MY BIKE...
I'LL TAKE YOU.
THANKS, ONII-CHAN!!

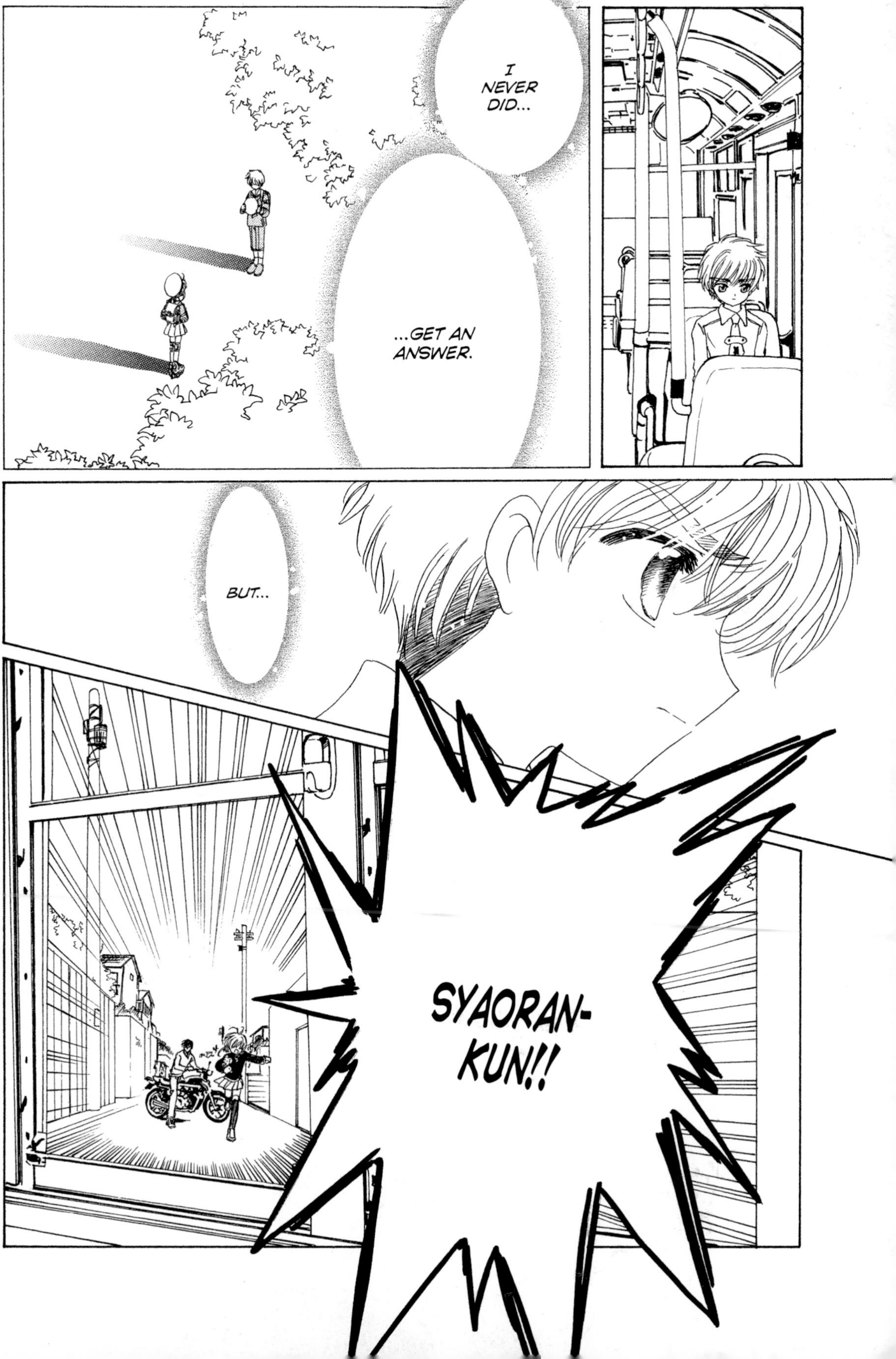
I NEVER DID...
...GET AN ANSWER.
BUT...
SYAORAN-KUN!!

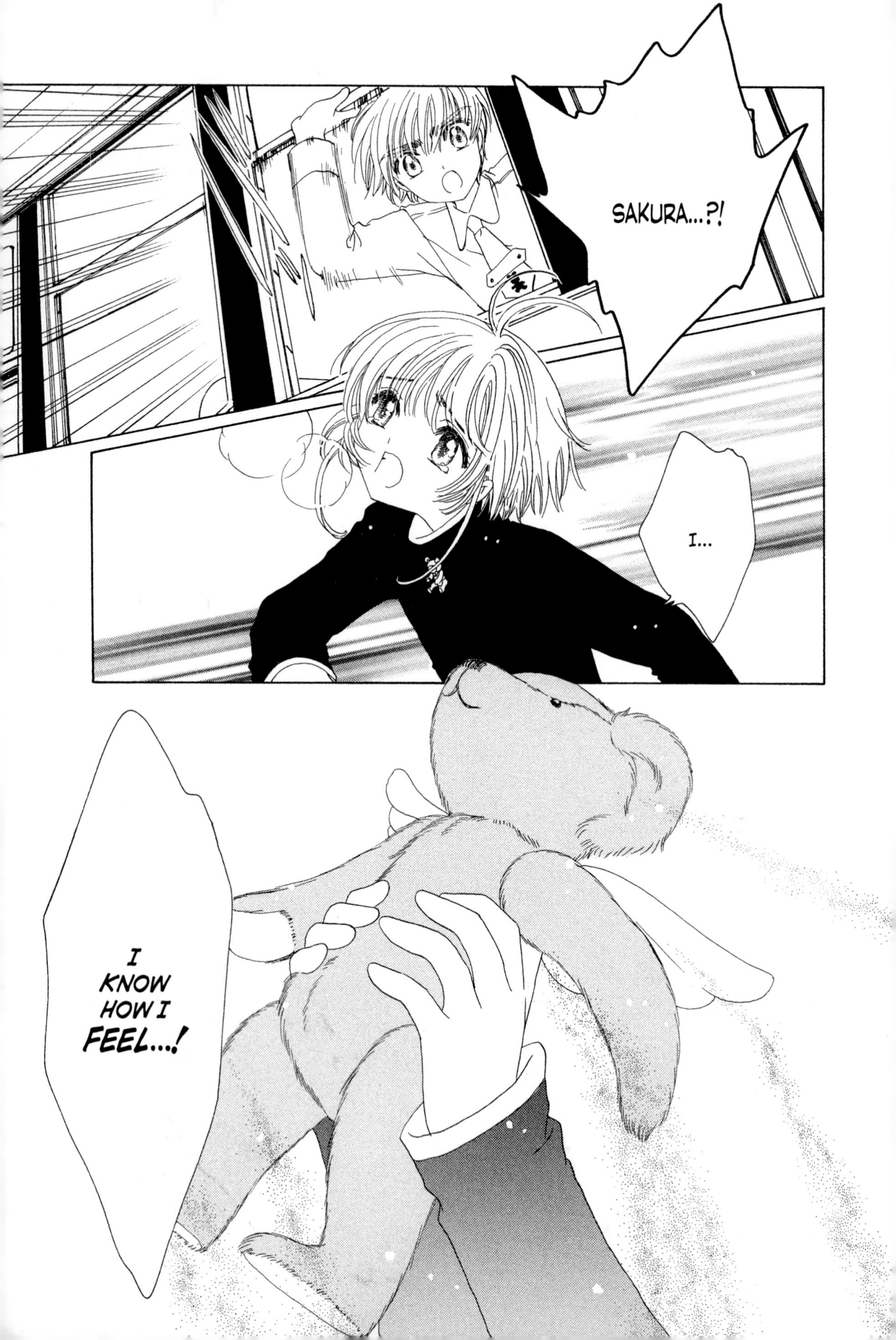
SAKURA...?!
I...
I KNOW HOW I FEEL...!

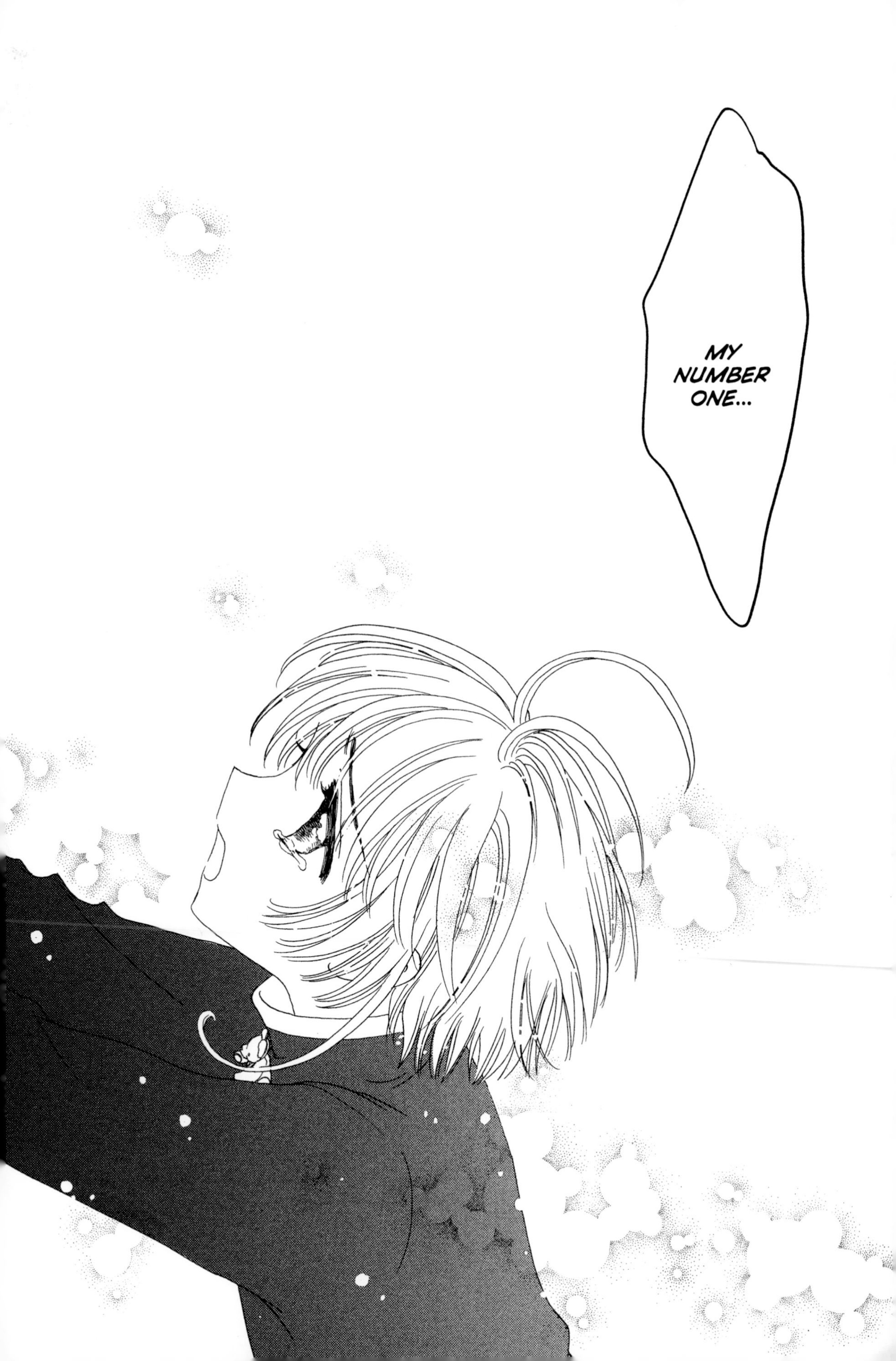
MY NUMBER ONE...

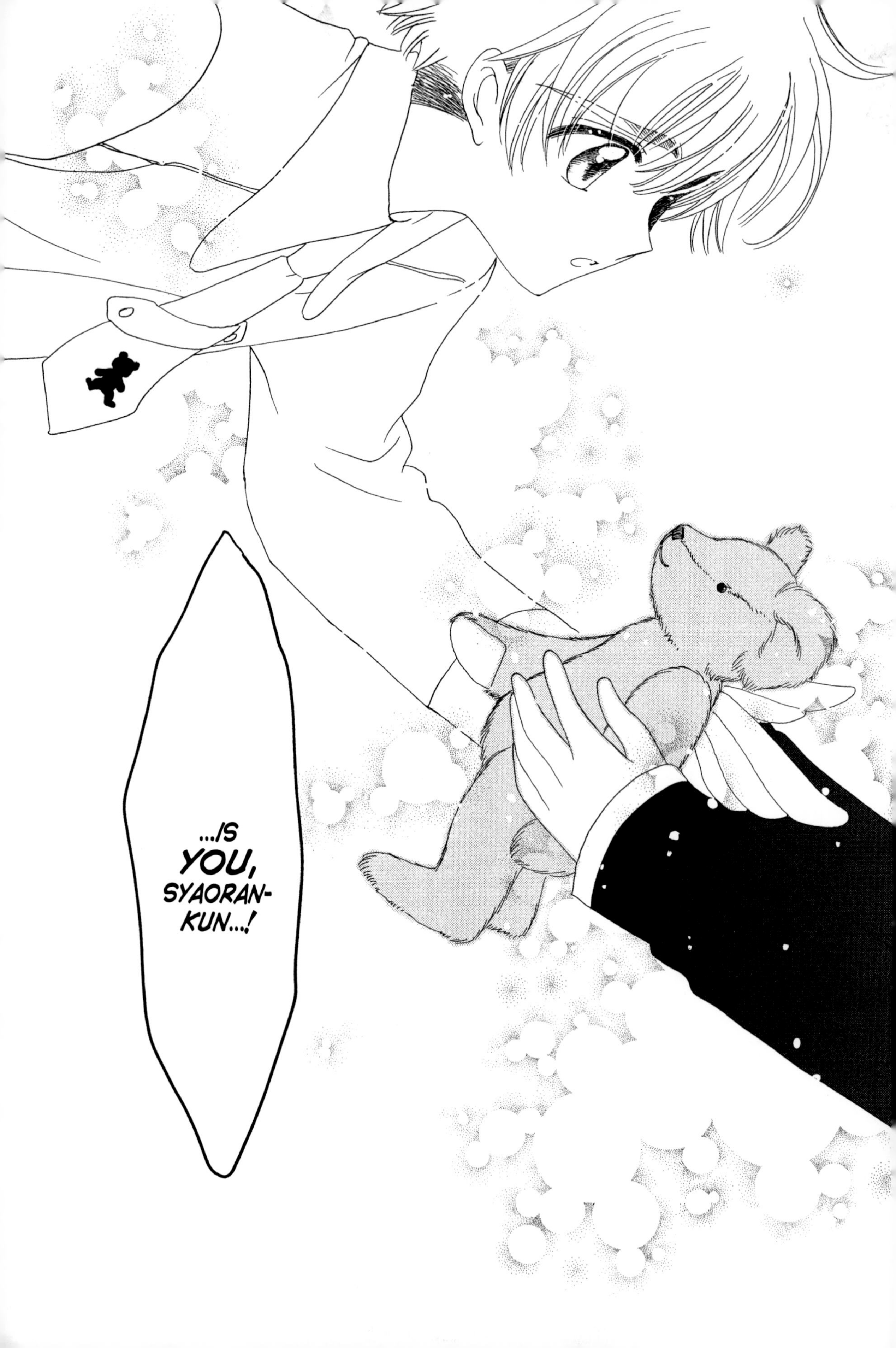
...IS YOU, SYAORAN-KUN...!

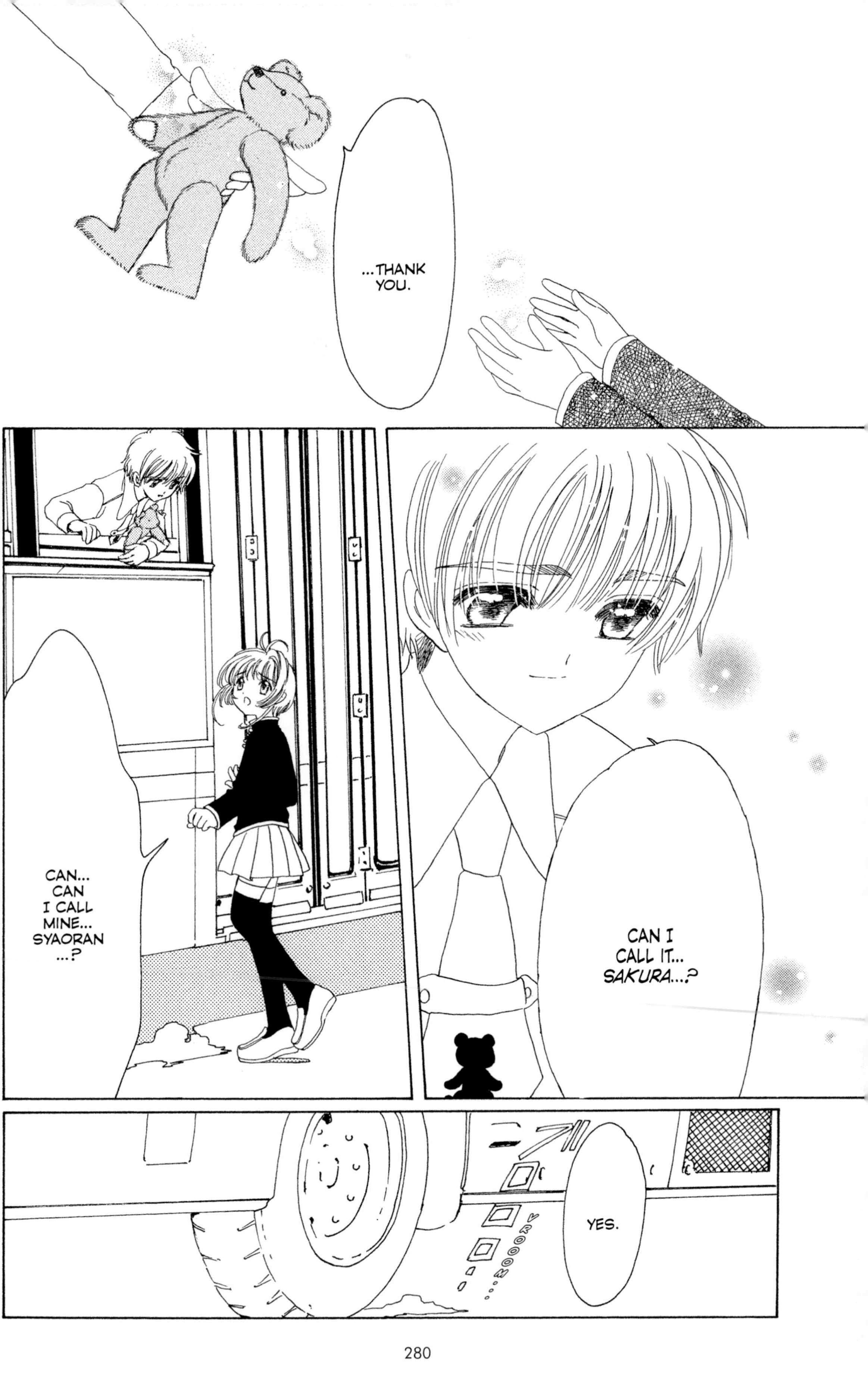
...THANK YOU.
CAN I CALL IT... SAKURA...?
CAN... CAN I CALL MINE... SYAORAN ...?
YES.
VROOOM...

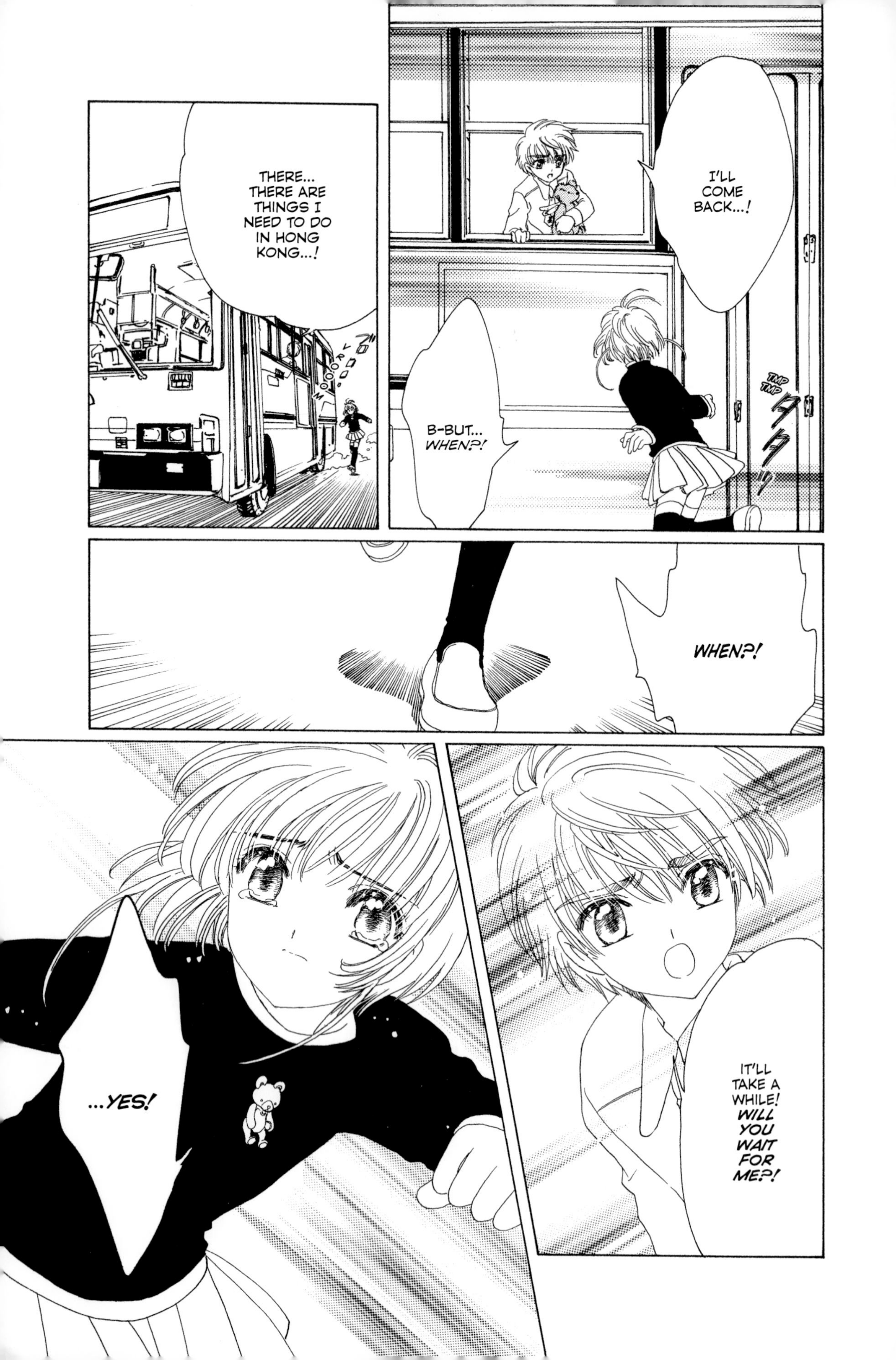
I'LL COME BACK...!
B-BUT... WHEN?!
TMP TMP
THERE... THERE ARE THINGS I NEED TO DO IN HONG KONG...!
WHEN?!
IT'LL TAKE A WHILE! WILL YOU WAIT FOR ME?!
...YES!

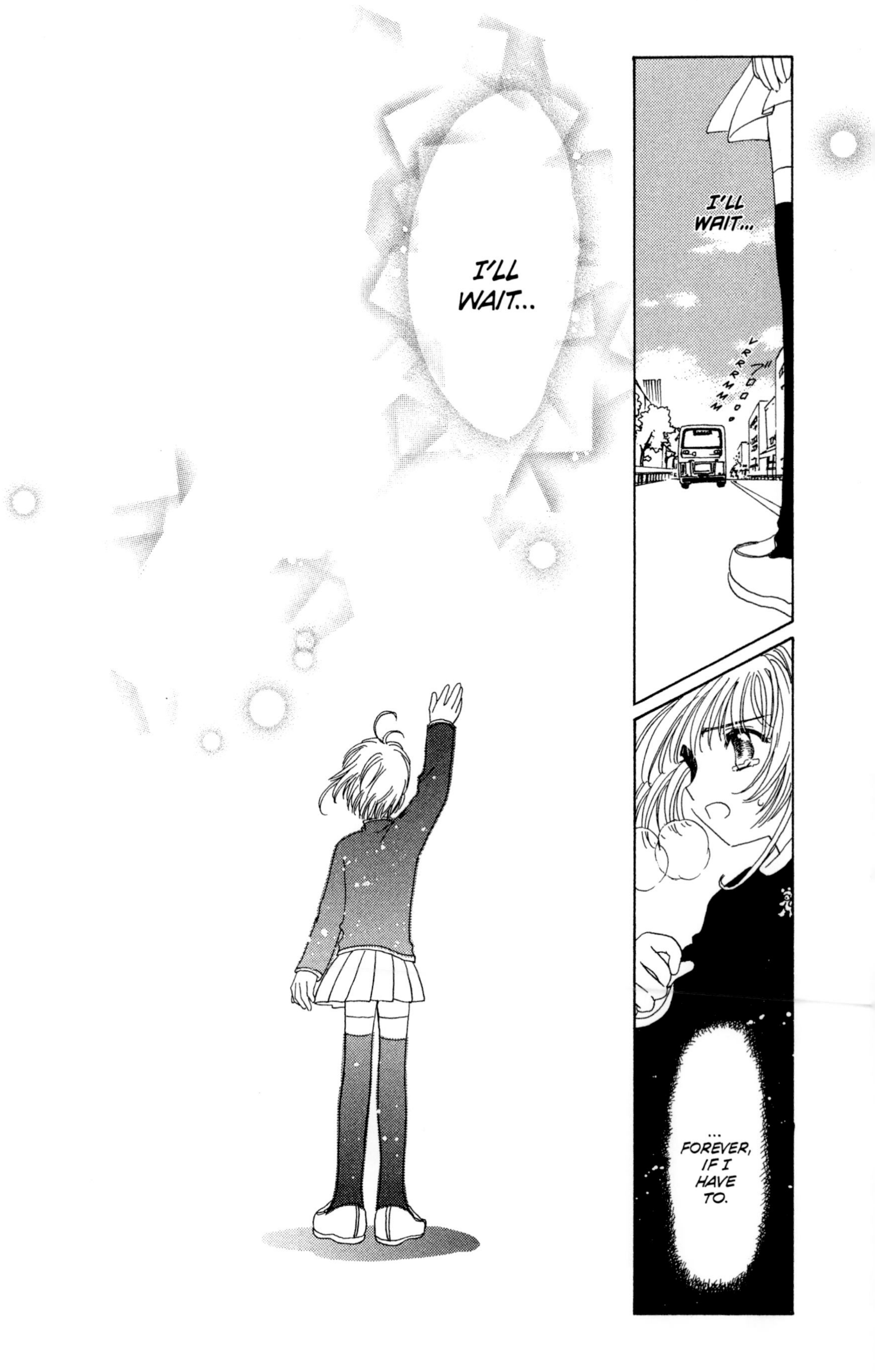
I'LL WAIT...
VRRRMMM
...FOREVER, IF I HAVE TO.
I'LL WAIT...

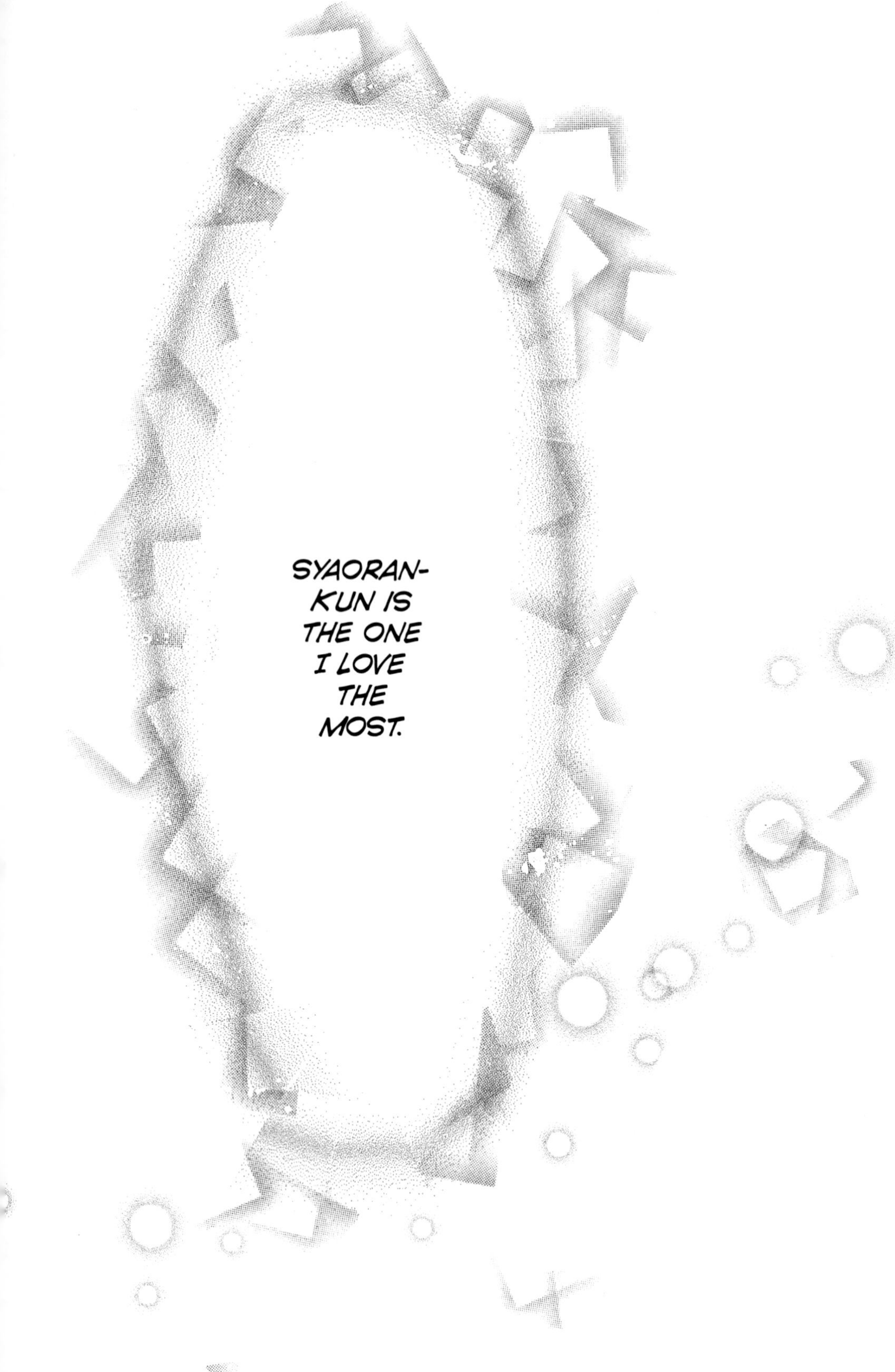
SYAORAN-KUN IS THE ONE I LOVE THE MOST.

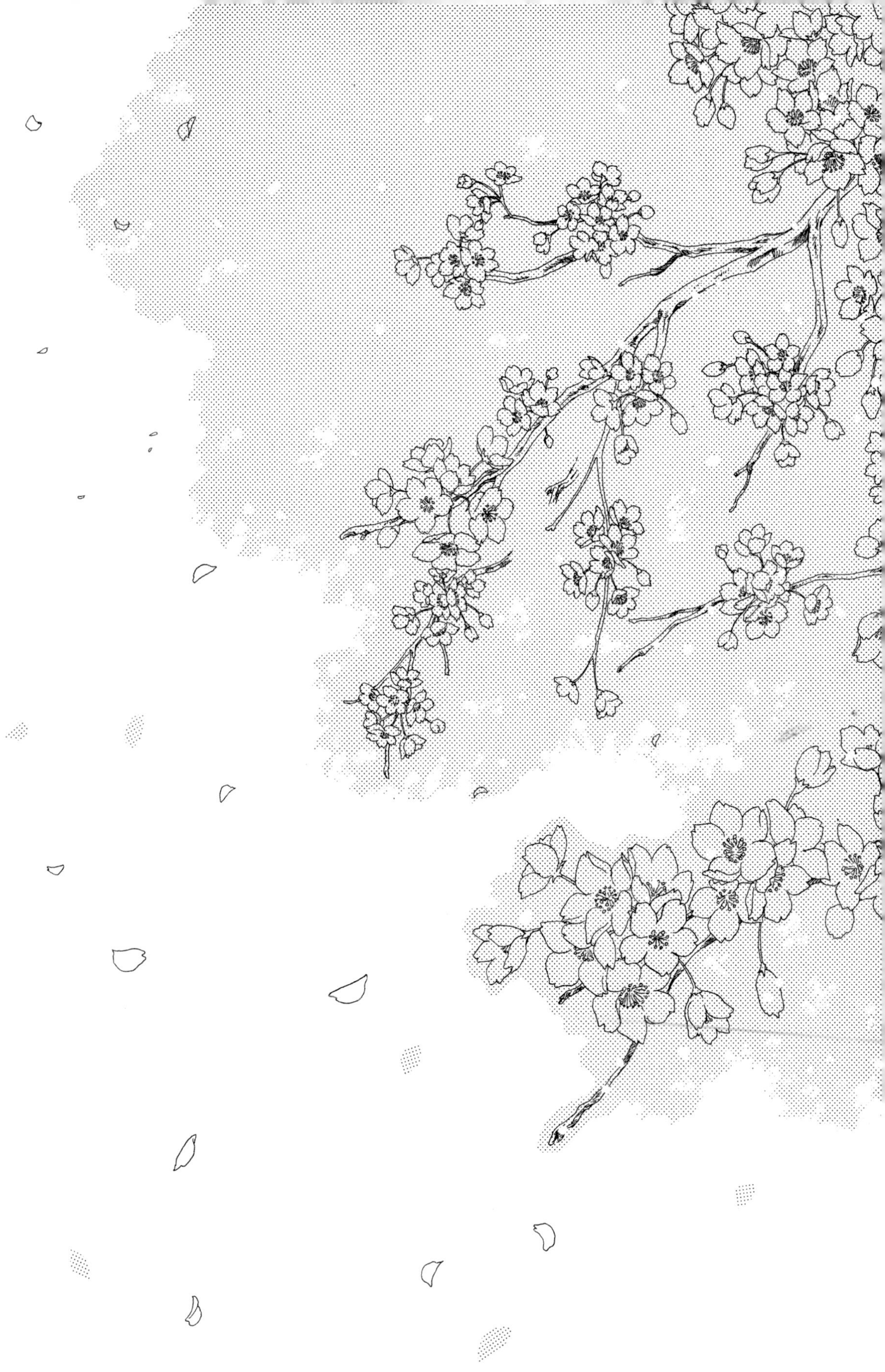

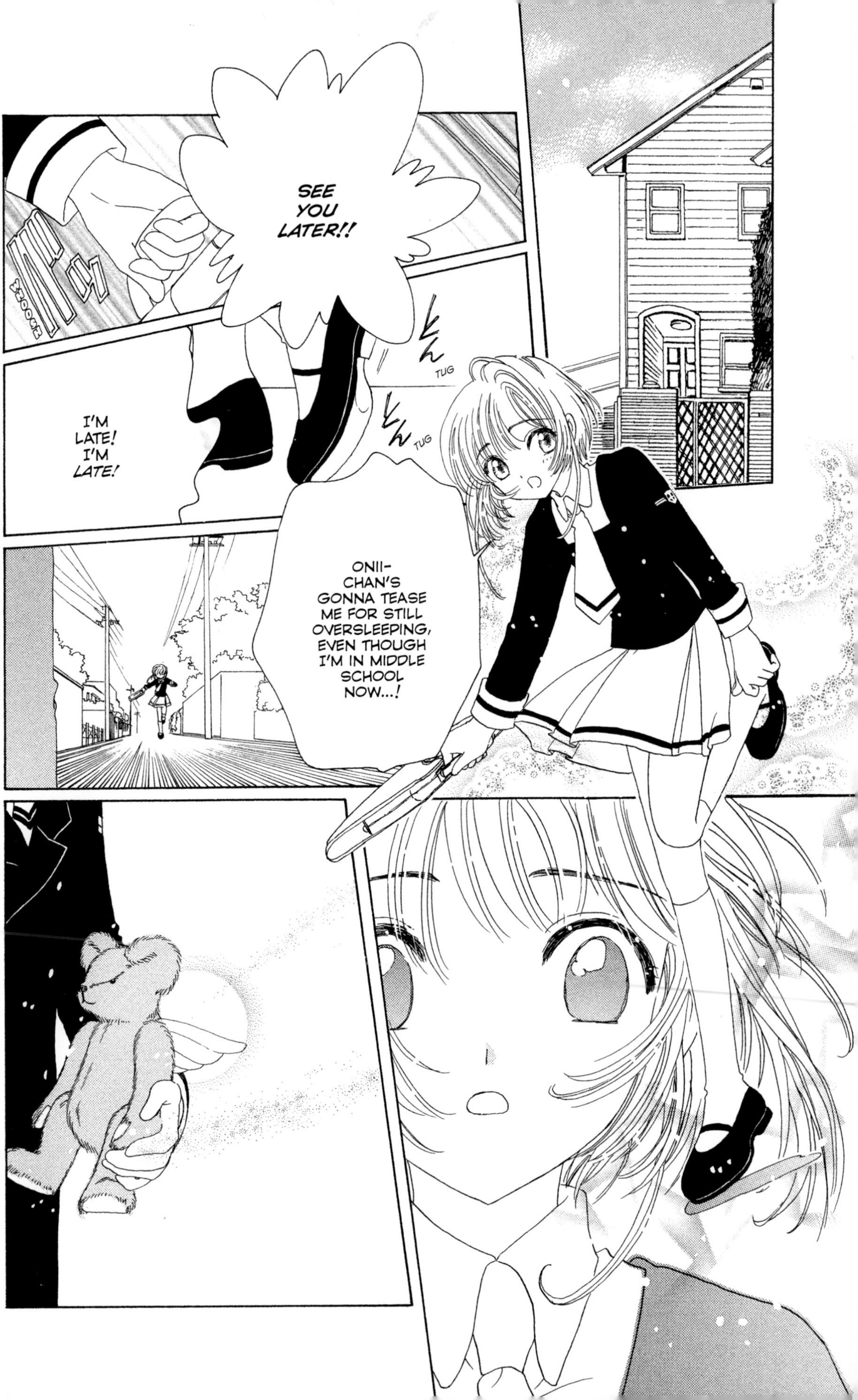
SEE YOU LATER!!
WHOOSH
TUG
TUG
I'M LATE! I'M LATE!
ONII-CHAN'S GONNA TEASE ME FOR STILL OVERSLEEPING, EVEN THOUGH I'M IN MIDDLE SCHOOL NOW...!

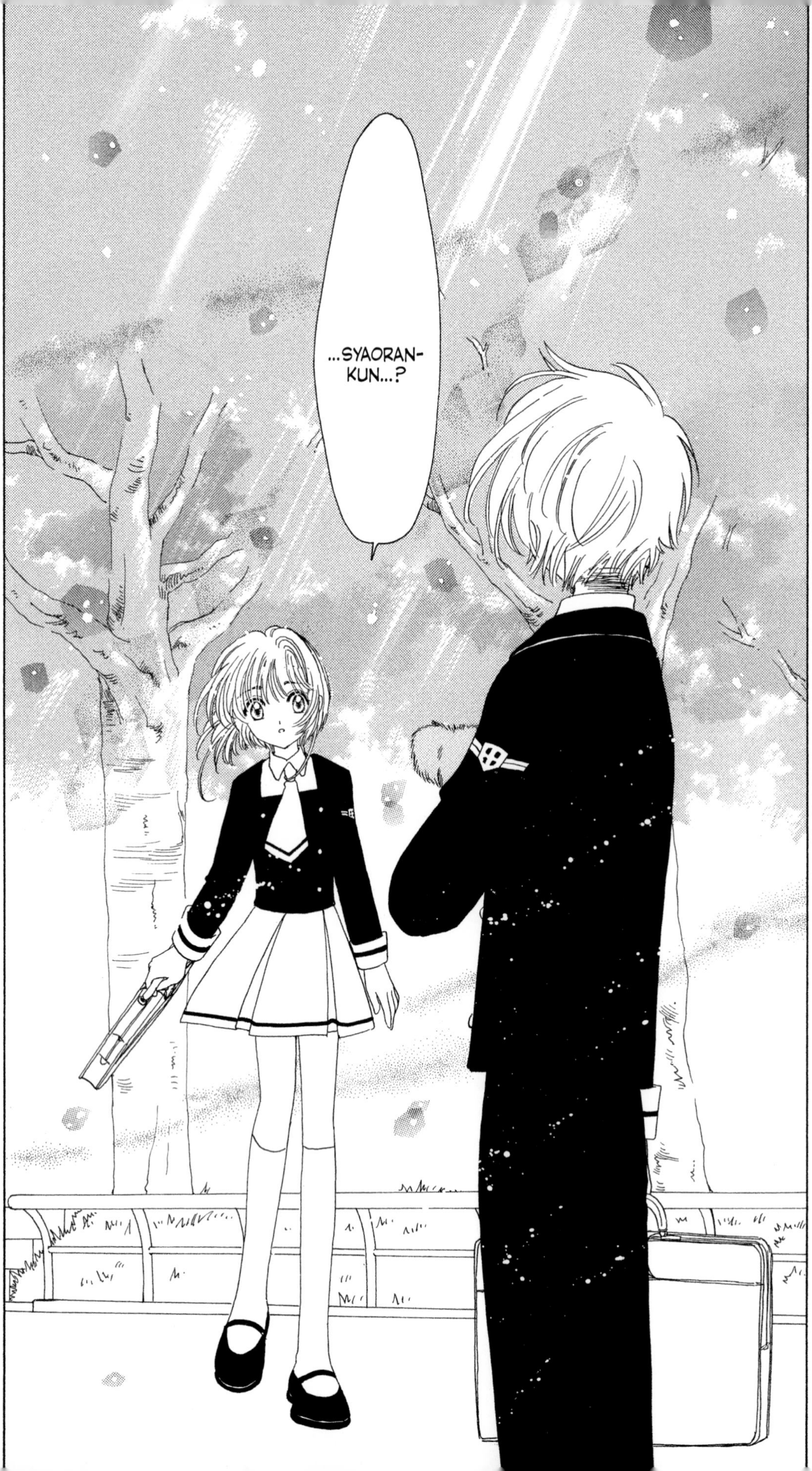
...SYAORAN-KUN...?

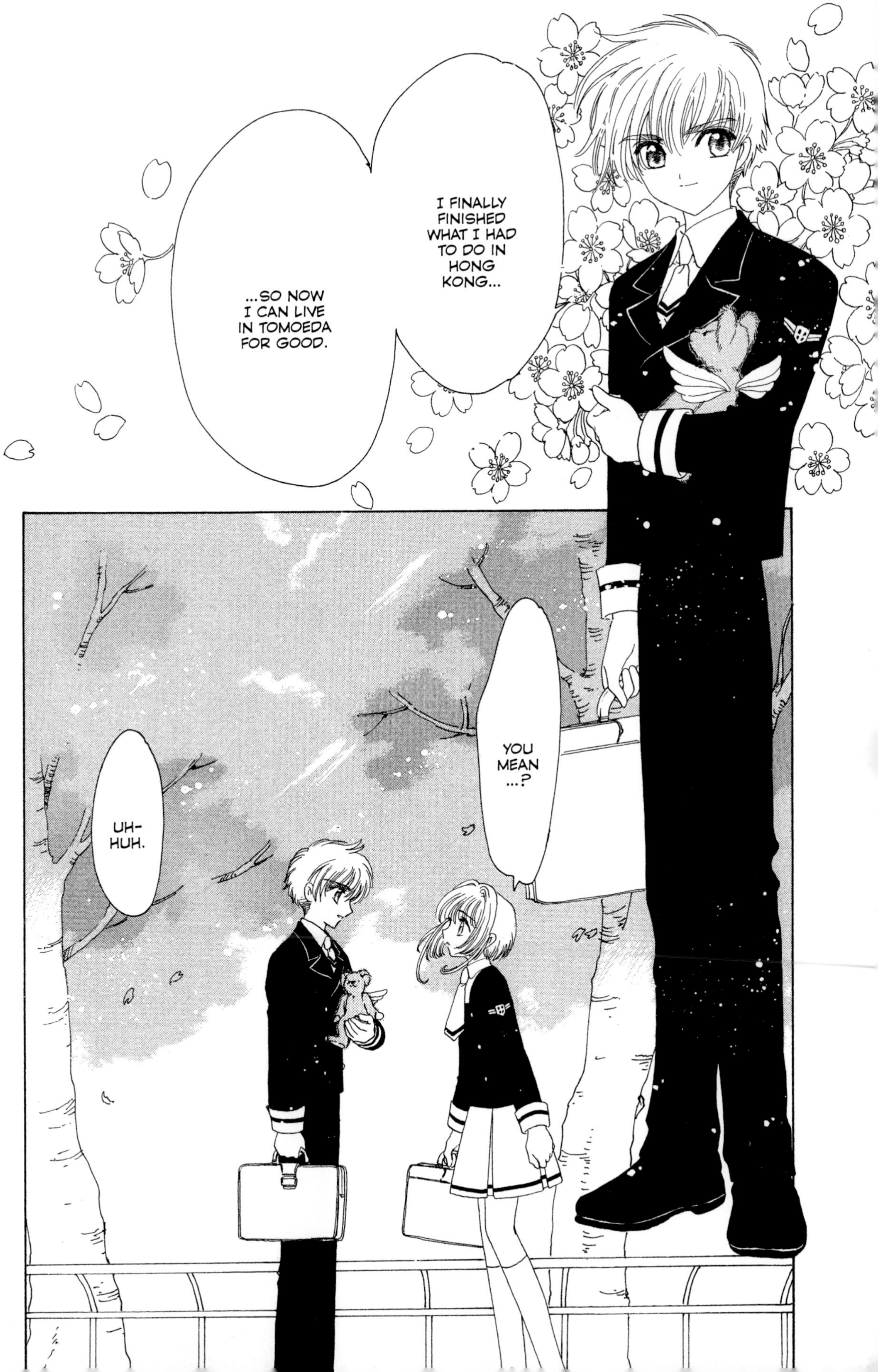
I FINALLY FINISHED WHAT I HAD TO DO IN HONG KONG...
...SO NOW I CAN LIVE IN TOMOEDA FOR GOOD.
YOU MEAN ...?
UH-HUH.

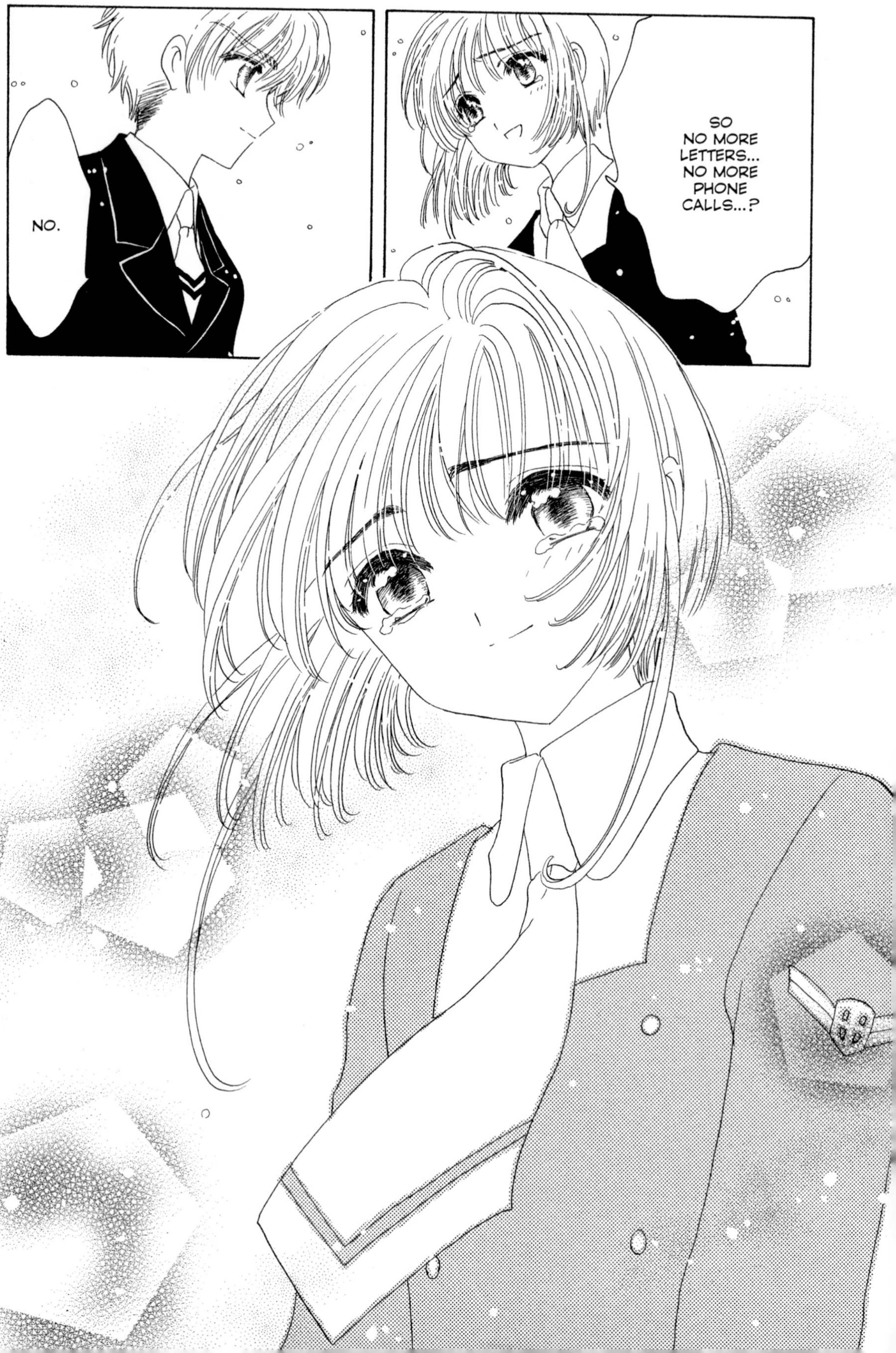
SO NO MORE LETTERS... NO MORE PHONE CALLS...?
NO.

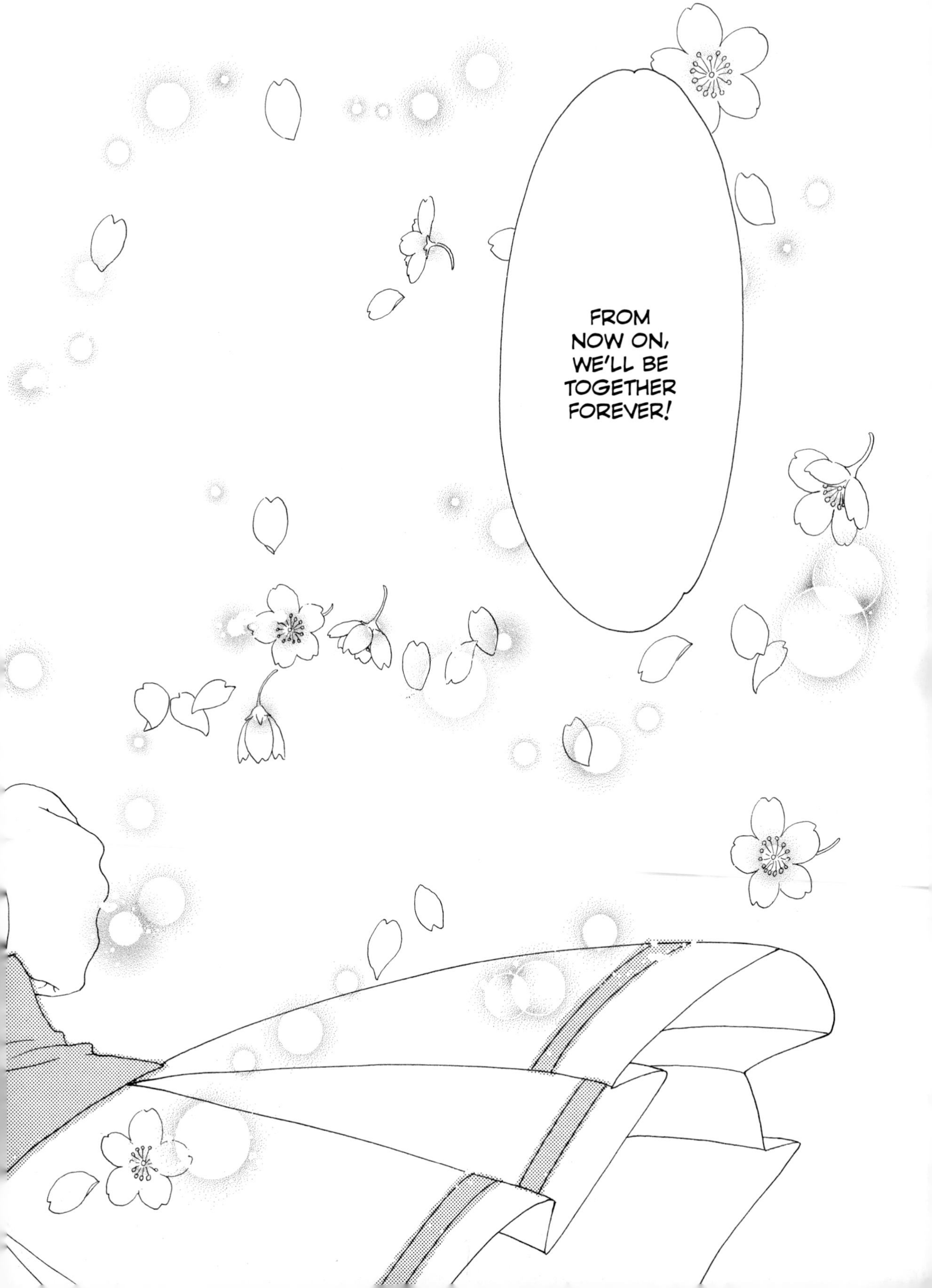
FROM NOW ON, WE'LL BE TOGETHER FOREVER!

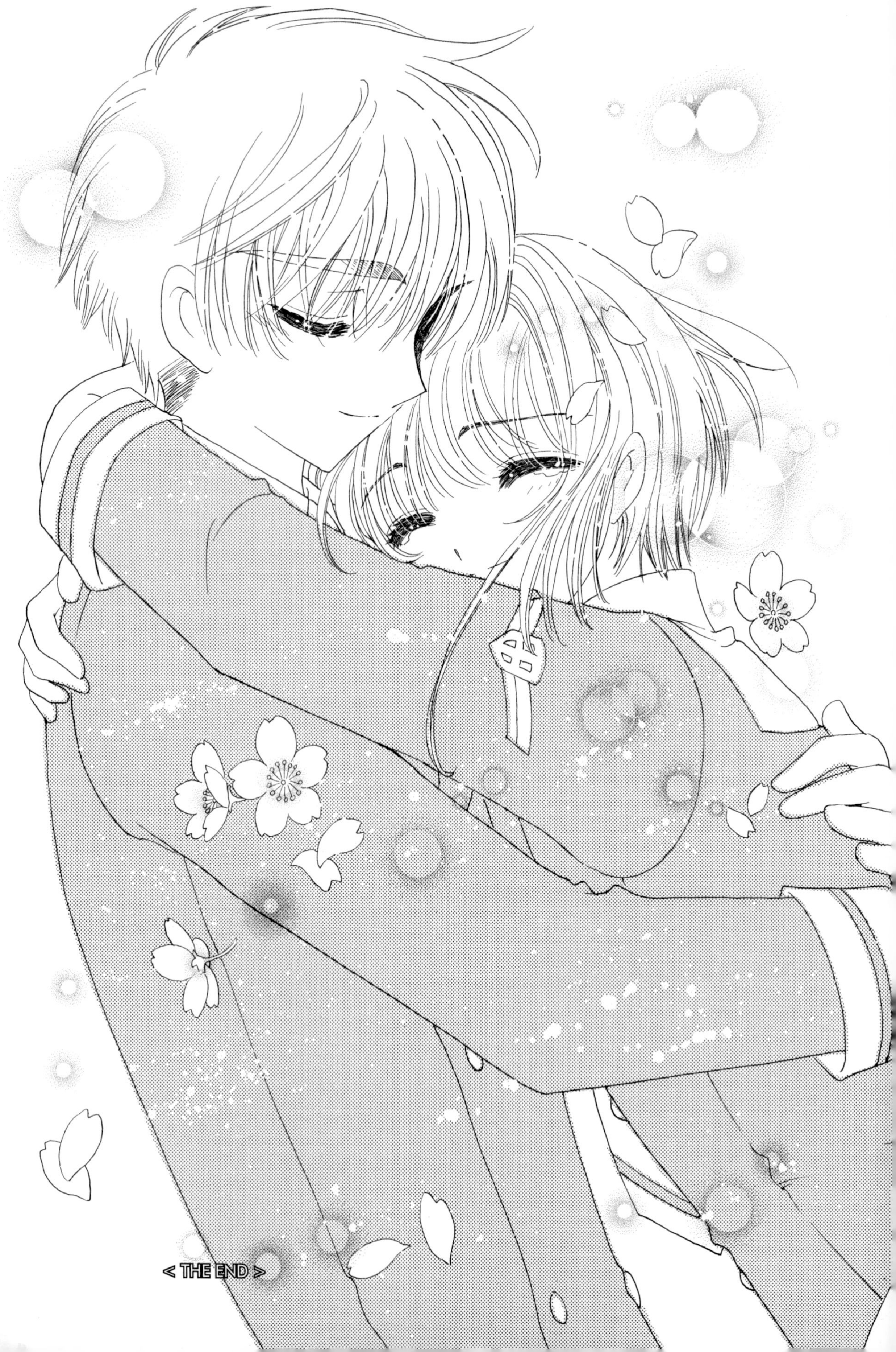
< THE END >

Cardcaptor Sakura Collector's Edition 9 copyright ©2015 CLAM
CO.,LTD. / Kodansha Ltd.
English translation copyright ©2021 CLAMP • ShigatsuTsuitachi C

All rights reserved.

Published in the United States by Kodansha Comics, ‹
Kodansha USA Publishing, LLC, New York

Publication rights for this English edition arranged
Kodansha Ltd., Tokyo.

First published in Japan in 2015 by Kodansha Lt
as *Nakayoshi 60 Shuunen Kinenban Kaadokyaputaa Sc*

ISBN 978-1-63236-881-2

Printed in China.

www.kodansha.us

9 8 7 6 5 4 3 2
Translation: Mika Onishi & Anita Sengu
Additional translation: Karen McGillicud
Lettering: Aaron Alexovich
Editing: Tiff Joshua TJ Ferentini
Kodansha Comics edition cover design by Phi

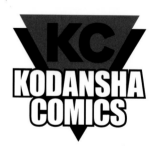

Publisher: Kiichiro Sugawara

Director of publishing services: Ben App
Associate director of operations: Stepher
Publishing services managing editor: Noell
Assistant production manager: Emi Lotto, A